'6th Beatle' Mal Evans Killed in Los Angeles

BY PATRICK SNYDER AND DOLORES ZIEBARTH

LOS ANGELES—Malcolm "Mal" Evans, 40, who was road manager and bodyguard of the Beatles from 1963 until their breakup, was shot to death by police in his rented duplex at 8122 West 4th Street the night of January 4th.

Earlier in the evening, Fran Hughes, 26, who was living ... Evans, called John ...

Mal Evans at last September's New Yo...

... Lt. Charles Higbie of the LAPD robbery and homicide division said, "Officers directed him to put down the rifle. He refused to put down the rifle." The officers then fired six shots, four of which struck Evans, killing him instantly.

Evans's manuscript, tentatively titled *Living the Beatles Legend*, was to have been delivered to Grosset and Dunlap January 12th for publication this year. Evans, who had produced part of Keith Moon's last solo album, had also contracted to produce a new group called Natural Gas, made up of Joey Molland (formerly of Badfinger), ex-Humble Pie Jerry Shirley, ex-Rare Bird David Kaffinetti and Mark Clarke (formerly of Uriah Heep). The group had not signed with any label but was scheduled to record January 5th.

Evans was described by ... both a "fantastic ...

LIVING THE
BEATLES
LEGEND

ON THE ROAD WITH THE FAB FOUR
THE MAL EVANS STORY

LIVING THE BEATLES LEGEND

KENNETH WOMACK

Pages 559–562 constitute an extension of the copyright page.

"(Let Me Be Your) Teddy Bear," composed by
Kal Mann and Bernie Lowe, courtesy of Hal Leonard.

"Family Tree," composed by Mal Evans, courtesy of
the Malcolm Frederick Evans Archives.

Mudlark
HarperCollins*Publishers*
1 London Bridge Street
London SE1 9GF

www.harpercollins.co.uk

HarperCollins*Publishers*
Macken House, 39/40 Mayor Street Upper
Dublin 1, D01 C9W8, Ireland

First published by HarperCollins*Publishers* 2023

3 5 7 9 10 8 6 4 2

Designed by Angie Boutin
Frontispiece: Mal in front of his Hillside Road home. Courtesy of the
Malcolm Frederick Evans Archives.
Case illustration of the *Abbey Road* cover shoot by Mal Evans.
Courtesy of the Malcolm Frederick Evans Archives.
Endpaper design by Richard Ljoenes and Angie Boutin
Endpaper credits: front top: (*left*) Malcolm Frederick Evans Archives;
(*right*) Tracks.co.uk; front middle: Malcolm Frederick Evans Archives;
front bottom: (*left*) Alamy; (*right*) Beatles Book Photo Library;
back top: Beatles Book Photo Library; back middle: (*left*) Bob Gruen;
(*right*) Beatles Book Photo Library; back bottom: (*left*)
Robert Whitaker; (*right*) Alamy

A catalogue record of this book is available from the British Library

ISBN 978-0-00-855121-6

Printed and bound in the UK using 100% renewable electricity at CPI Group (UK) Ltd

This book is produced from independently certified FSC™ paper to
ensure responsible forest management.

For more information visit: www.harpercollins.co.uk/green

For Lily of Allerton

Baby, let me be your lovin' teddy bear.
Put a chain around my neck and lead me anywhere.
Oh, let me be your teddy bear.

—**ELVIS PRESLEY**

I wonder what the future holds
Now that I'm fast and fancy free.
Have I destroyed my happiness
Cutting down my family tree?

—**MAL EVANS**

CONTENTS

FOREWORD

BY GARY EVANS

This book is the product of decades of toil. It would not have been possible without the initial determination of my father, Mal Evans, to capture the Beatles' story as it unfolded before him. He knew, even in his earliest days as a bouncer at the Cavern Club door, that the boys were something special. As he traveled with them across the whole of England and, eventually, the world, he recorded his memories in the pages of his diaries and filled up notebooks with his drawings and recollections, all the while taking thousands of candid photographs and saving ephemera of all shapes and sizes—a receipt here, a scrap of lyrics there.

When my dad sat down to compose his memoir for Grosset and Dunlap in 1975, he realized the difficulty inherent in taking up a pen to capture his thoughts. Fortunately, he was aided by a stenographer, who transcribed his words to the letter, and by the sage advice of Ringo Starr: "If you don't tell the truth," he told my dad, then "don't bother doing it." And so, Dad did.

On January 4, 1976, when he simply couldn't stomach the act of living another day, my father orchestrated his own demise in a Los Angeles duplex. He left behind the fruits of decades of collecting, along with a full draft of his memoir, which he planned to call *Living the Beatles' Legend: 200 Miles to Go*. He had even gone so far as to plot out the book's illustrations, with the assistance of a friend who had served as an art director, and mocked up a couple of cover ideas.

My dad's death threw all this into disarray. For a time, Grosset and Dunlap made various attempts at publishing *Living the Beatles' Legend*, but my mother, Lily, understandably distraught over her estranged husband's tragic death, simply wanted his collection to be returned to our family back in England, so that we could sort things out for ourselves. As we later learned, in the days after my father died in Los Angeles, Grosset and Dunlap transported the materials from L.A. to New York City, eventually placing them in a storage room in the basement of the New York Life Building.

And that's where they sat for more than a dozen years, to be rescued from the garbage heap only by the quick thinking of Leena Kutti, a temporary worker who discovered my dad's materials—along with the diaries, the photographs, and the memoir—recognizing she was in the presence of a most unusual archive. When her efforts to raise the alarm with the publishing house fell on deaf ears, Kutti took it upon herself to march uptown to the Dakota, where she left a note for Yoko Ono, one of the few genuine heroes in the strange progress of my father's artifacts. In short order, Yoko alerted Neil Aspinall, my dad's counterpart during the Beatles years. With the assistance of some shrewd Apple lawyering, Neil saw to it that the collection was finally delivered to our family home in 1988.

For several years, my dad's manuscripts and memorabilia were stored in our attic. I would periodically dip into them and reacquaint myself with the person whom I had lost when I was fourteen years old. Thumbing through the materials reminded me why I loved my father so dearly, in spite of the flaws that drove him away from us and led to his death at age forty. Over the years, my family has struggled with the idea of sharing Mal's story. Then, in 2004, a forger created an international sensation when he claimed to possess Dad's collection in a suitcase full of artifacts he had discovered in an Australian flea market. The news was quickly picked up and shared across the globe with much fanfare before it was proven to be a hoax.

To stem the ensuing confusion, my mum and I consented to a 2005 interview with the *Sunday Times Magazine*, even going so far as to allow the publication of a few excerpts from my dad's diaries. The tide began to change for us in July 2018, when I decided to follow in my father's, and the Beatles', footsteps and retrace the famous "Mad Day Out" photo session on its fiftieth anniversary. I was joined that day by my good friend, actor and playwright Nik Wood-Jones. Along the way, we had the remarkable good fortune to cross paths with filmmaker and Beatles aficionado Simon Weitzman, who was on a similar mission.

As my friendship with Simon developed, I confided in him about the ongoing challenge of sharing my dad's story with the world. He assured me that he knew just the guy to make it happen. Through Simon, I met Ken Womack via Zoom in 2020, during the first few months of the Covid-19 pandemic. Ken had already authored several books about the Beatles, but more important, Simon trusted him implicitly. Almost as soon as we began working together, I knew that Ken was the right collaborator to tell my dad's story with the historical integrity it required. Over the years, I have come to understand the ways in which Beatles fans the world over adore "Big Mal," and to his credit, Ken has been able to honor that connection while also mining the truth of my dad's life, warts and all.

Working with our friends at HarperCollins, we are proud to share the present book with you—a full-length biography detailing my dad's life with (and without) the Beatles. A second, even more richly illustrated book will follow in which we provide readers with highlights from my dad's collection, including the manuscripts he compiled, the contents of his diaries, numerous drawings and other ephemera, along with a vast selection of unpublished photographs from our family archives and from his Beatle years.

The present effort simply wouldn't have been possible without the saving graces of people like Leena Kutti, Yoko Ono, Neil Aspinall, Simon Weitzman, and Nik Wood-Jones. And now, thanks to Ken, readers will be able to experience my dad's story with the vividness it deserves. Ken, you kindly lent me your ears over the past three years; I got by with more than a little help from you, my friend.

My father meant the world to me. He was my hero. Before Ken joined the project, I thought I knew my dad's story. But what I knew was in monochrome; now, some three years later, it is like *The Wizard of Oz*, my dad's favorite film, when the scene shifts from black-and-white Kansas to the dazzling multicolored brilliance of Oz. Ken has added so much color, so much light to my dad's story. He has shown me that Mal Evans was the Beatles' greatest friend. Yes, Big Mal was lucky to meet the Beatles, but the Beatles possessed even more good fortune when, for the first time, all those years ago, my dad happened to walk down the Cavern Club steps. The rest is music history.

PROLOGUE

WINDSCREEN

JANUARY 23, 1963

For Mal Evans, it would be nothing short of a primal moment. For the Beatles, it would be a much-cherished memory along the unsteady road to extraordinary fame. It would exist inside their collective museum of recollections as the emblem of a more innocent time and place when everyone and everything that truly counted in their world could be measured inside the cramped interior of a van.

A Ford Thames 400E Express Bus, to be exact. Cream-colored and sporting license plate number 6834 KD, the vehicle had been the Beatles' workhorse since the summer of 1962, when manager Brian Epstein purchased it via automobile salesman Terry Doran, a Liverpool chum. With the Beatles' twenty-one-year-old assistant, Neil Aspinall, behind the wheel, the group had barnstormed through an incessant run of dance halls and ballrooms across Northern England, desperate to launch their debut single, "Love Me Do," as far up the English record charts as it could go; it reached maximum altitude at number seventeen for the week of December 27, 1962.

At twenty-seven, Mal wasn't just the new guy—he was also, quite literally, the *old* guy. He had five years on John Lennon and Ringo Starr and even more on Paul McCartney, who had turned twenty back in June, and George Harrison, still a teenager at nineteen. Mal was the odd man out in more ways than one. He held an honest-to-goodness real job, making regular money as a telecommunications engineer for the General Post Office, and he had a home and a family to boot. With his beloved wife, Lily, he had set up housekeeping in Liverpool's Allerton district, where they were raising their fifteen-month-old son, Gary.

Then there was the matter of Mal's height. At a tad over six feet, three inches, he towered over the lot of them. And he was built, too. Over the years, he had thoroughly toned his broad frame as a dedicated cyclist and swimmer. Mal was known to bike for hours—full days, even—on the rural outskirts of Liverpool. And when it came to swimming, there was scarcely a body of water he'd pass up. From the frigid Irish Sea to a serene country lake to a modest-size chlorinated motel pool, Mal lived to swim. And no mere soak would do. For him, thrashing about or playing in the shallows was for amateurs. He preferred the vigorous exertions of the breaststroke to the comparatively pedestrian aquatic splashings of ordinary folk.

It was a simple twist of fate that landed Mal behind the wheel of the Ford Thames van that January day. Aspinall, the Beatles' full-time road manager, had taken ill with the flu. He was hardly the only Briton felled during that unusually severe winter. During the last week of December, a blizzard swept across southwestern England and Wales, leaving snow drifts of up to twenty feet in its wake. The ensuing weather emergency came to be known as the Big Freeze, with dangerously low temperatures plaguing Great Britain throughout January.

Known as Nell among the Beatles' entourage, Aspinall had succumbed at an especially inopportune moment. The group's second single, "Please Please Me," had been released on January 11. When the Beatles recorded the up-tempo song back on November 26, their normally staid producer, George Martin, had gone out on an extraordinary limb. Overcome by a moment of "bravado," he announced, "Gentlemen, you've just made your first number-one record."[1] The very notion that the four Liverpudlians would release a chart-topper was so far-fetched that "the boys," as Martin and manager Brian Epstein had lovingly dubbed them, promptly broke into peals of laughter. But as January wore on—and with the Big Freeze stranding millions of Britons at home, "Please Please Me" was fulfilling the producer's daring prediction. Snowed in with radio and television as their chief sources of entertainment, record numbers of viewers watched the band's January 19th performance of the song on the popular Saturday night television program *Thank Your Lucky Stars*. That night, the Beatles held the lowest rung on a seven-act bill. But not for long.

With the single racing up the charts, Epstein had booked a fresh spate of radio and television appearances, necessitating the Beatles' journey to

London on the day after their *Thank Your Lucky Stars* appearance. But on the morning after the TV show, Neil had woken up feeling feverish. When he arrived for the band's evening gig at Liverpool's Cavern Club, he announced that he would be unable to drive them to London. The Beatles were unsympathetic, saying, "Well, you'll have to get somebody else, won't you?" In the fog of his illness, Neil "didn't have a clue who I could get. I went up the Cavern steps into Mathew Street just to get some fresh air, and Mal was standing there."

As it happened, Mal and Lily had just arrived at the Cavern that night. Having worked as a part-time bouncer at the basement club, Mal had become a familiar presence to the Beatles and their crowd of "Cave Dwellers," as deejay Bob Wooler had christened the Cavern's regulars.

"What are you doing for the next couple of days?" Neil asked Mal. "Would you like to drive the Beatles to London?"[2]

For Mal, it was a no-brainer. Being near the action was what had drawn him to the Cavern in the first place. An inveterate Elvis Presley fan, he relished the Beatles' company, swapping stories about the King and growing especially close with George, who had befriended the giant, bespectacled man. Mal enjoyed peppering the band with requests for Elvis tunes. He held a particular affection for "I Forgot to Remember to Forget," which George intentionally bungled, singing, "I'm so bloody lonely" in place of "I'm so blue and lonely." The bandmates invariably introduced their songs for Mal by playfully altering his name: "This one's for Malcontent," or "This one's for Malfunctioning," or "This one's for Malodorous."[3] Mal took it all in stride, good-naturedly playing along with his new friends.

While Mal didn't miss a beat in accepting Neil's offer, he knew he would have to take several days off from work to make the trip. And like every other Briton, he was aware of the forecast, which, in keeping with the weather patterns across that fabled month, called for heavy snow. But at this juncture, the weather was the least of the Beatles' problems. Mal knew this trip loomed large for Epstein and the band. In Brian's calculation, it was essential to consolidate their fame as swiftly as possible. And outside of a quartet of recording sessions at EMI's facility on Abbey Road—not to mention their failed January 1962 audition with Decca—the upcoming journey marked only their second visit to the capital for promotional purposes.

The first, back on October 8, in support of "Love Me Do," hadn't gone so well. After a lukewarm appearance on Radio Luxembourg's *Friday Spectacular* program, they had opted to make an impromptu stop at the offices of London's journalists. By the time they arrived at *NME* (*New Musical Express*) on Denmark Street, they had absorbed earfuls of regional prejudice. At *NME*, Liverpudlian journalist Alan Smith asked the group about their impressions of Londoners. "Not much," they told him. "If they know you come from the north, they don't want to know."[4] Determined to make the most of the upcoming trip, Brian had concocted an aggressive itinerary for the January 1963 southern jaunt, including a whirlwind press tour and no fewer than three prerecorded radio spots.

For Mal, who had never driven in Central London before, the trip would prove positively daunting. As a northerner, he was unfamiliar with the city's confusing matrix of narrow backstreets and thoroughfares, not to mention its confounding, often unpredictable traffic patterns. Yet his more immediate concern was the state of the Beatles' van. After leaving his own car in West Derby, where Neil rented a room above Mona Best's basement Casbah Coffee Club, Mal drove the Ford Thames van to his Hillside Road home in Liverpool's Mossley Hill district. The five-mile trip made for "not a very auspicious start as she was missing on one cylinder." The next morning, Mal took the van to a garage in Crosby, where a mechanic remedied the cylinder problem.[5]

By the time Mal and the Beatles began the long drive to London, around midday on Monday, January 21, the van's brakes had begun to slip. During the early leg of their journey, brakes didn't really matter. Traffic had come to a standstill outside Liverpool as they waited for the snowplows to clear the roads. By afternoon, they were barreling down the M1 without further incident—although Mal found the van's headlights somewhat ineffective in cutting through the ubiquitous fog. It was well past dusk when the fivesome arrived at EMI House in time to record the band's sophomore appearance on *Friday Spectacular*.

The cozy theater accommodated a one-hundred-person studio audience, mostly comprising young girls, autograph books in hand, ready to meet their pop idols. As the boys readied themselves backstage, Mal hastily set up their equipment, so they could lip-synch renditions of "Please

Please Me" and "Ask Me Why." Standing in what would become his familiar position at stage right, he witnessed the sudden, dramatic shift in the Beatles' fortunes in real time. As press agent Tony Barrow later wrote, "The teen audience didn't know the evening's lineup of artists and groups in advance, and before [announcer] Muriel Young brought on the Beatles, she began to read out their Christian names. She got as far as 'John . . . Paul . . .' and the rest of her introduction was buried in a mighty barrage of very genuine applause."[6]

It was well after midnight when Mal and the boys crawled into their crumbling, timeworn digs at the Hotel Cavendish, on Gower Street. But Mal didn't care. He was elated to be sharing a room with Ringo and Paul, while John bunked with George. "Everywhere we went," Mal later wrote, "the Beatles included me. It was always a case of 'meals or drinks for five,' making me feel a part of their world."[7] He simply couldn't believe his good fortune.

By the next day, January 22, things only seemed to get better. Letting the boys sleep through breakfast, Mal rose early and rounded up coffee and toast to fortify them for the day's breakneck schedule. First up was an interview on the *Pop Inn* radio program, broadcast live from the BBC's Paris Studio, on Regent Street. Mal took the opportunity to cart the Beatles' gear to their next destination, which was mistakenly listed on Brian's itinerary as "Aeolian Hall." Rather than becoming flummoxed by the hiccup, Mal began asking around, eventually learning that *Saturday Club* was being recorded at the Playhouse Theatre with Brian Matthew, Mal's "favorite compère," whom he was overjoyed to meet in the flesh.[8]

Afterward, Mal and the boys returned to Paris Studio, where the band recorded their performance, including a rousing take of "Please Please Me," for *The Talent Spot*, hosted by Gary Marshall. While the group left to meet with the *Daily Mail*'s Adrian Mitchell for an interview in Brian Epstein's suite at the posh Mayfair Hotel, Mal stayed at the Paris Studio to pack up their gear for the journey back to Liverpool. That's when he realized he didn't have the foggiest idea how to get to the Mayfair. Drawing on his natural gift of gab, he asked a member of the BBC's team to provide him with directions, which were helpfully scrawled on the back of the band's copy of the radio script. For Mal, the entire experience was a joy. "It was great meeting all the people I'd seen on TV," he admitted. "I was really star-struck." And he took pleasure in observing people as they encountered the boys' incipient fame: "I quickly realized, of course, that people were being nice, trying to get to know me, just to use me to get to the Beatles. I soon got to spot them a mile off."[9]

After a large celebratory meal at Forte's, the popular British hotel/restaurant chain, Mal and the boys set off for home, leaving London at around 10 p.m. With the exception of the fog, which seemed to have grown even more profuse, the trip was smooth sailing along the M1. Eventually, Mal pulled the van off the highway to make the rest of the journey along the regional byways leading back to Liverpool.

And that's when it happened: Sometime after midnight, as Mal drove the van along the quiet rural roads, the windscreen "cracked with a terrible bang." With the windscreen splintered into dangerous shards of glass, Paul observed as a quick-thinking Mal "put his hat backwards on his hand, punched the windscreen out completely, and drove on."[10] In the intervening years, the van's occupants would attribute the shattered windscreen to different causes, with Paul and the other Beatles citing a wayward pebble for the damage, while Mal reasoned that "the intense cold fighting the warmth of the heater inside the van [had] shattered the windscreen."[11] Either way, the Beatles were impressed with the herculean efforts of their makeshift roadie.

With the danger of the windscreen abated, Mal was left to contend with the gale-force winds now pummeling the van's interior. The bandmates leapt into action, gathering up stray caps and scarves and wrapping them about their beleaguered driver, who had pulled a paper bag over his head to battle the cold. "It was perishing," John later recalled. "Mal had this paper bag over his head with just a big split in it for his eyes. He looked like a bank robber." Meanwhile, John, Paul, George, and Ringo huddled together in the rear of the van, sharing a bottle of whiskey while stacked one atop the other to generate much-needed warmth. "And when the one on the top got so cold it was like hypothermia was setting in," Ringo recalled, "it was his turn to get on the bottom, and we'd warm each other up that way, and keep swigging the whiskey." It was, in Paul's words, "a Beatle sandwich."[12]

All the while, Mal and the boys maintained a steady banter to stave off exhaustion. As the Big Freeze raged across that long night—swirling both inside and outside the Ford van—the Beatles regularly pestered their driver about how much farther they had to go. "[Two hundred] miles to go!" Mal would good-naturedly reply, referencing the approximate distance between Liverpool and London. In this way, "it became our own private joke, and '200 miles to go, Mal' was heard whenever things were tough."[13]

By 5 a.m., Mal was back home with Lily on Hillside Road. "I was up at 7:45 but [the] lads laid in till about five that night," he recalled. "Lucky devils. They were on that night at [the] Cavern as fresh as ever, with no after effects." That evening, as Neil unloaded the band's equipment from the Ford, the fruits of Mal's labors were on full display. The van, no worse for wear, was roadworthy again and outfitted with a brand-new windscreen. "We never knew how he'd managed to get it fixed again so quickly," said Neil, "and, even if we didn't say so, it was something we remembered. Ten out of ten to Mal for not just bringing back the van and leaving it for someone else to get a new windscreen put in." Before long, Neil was joined by the Beatles themselves, who regaled him with stories of their adventures with

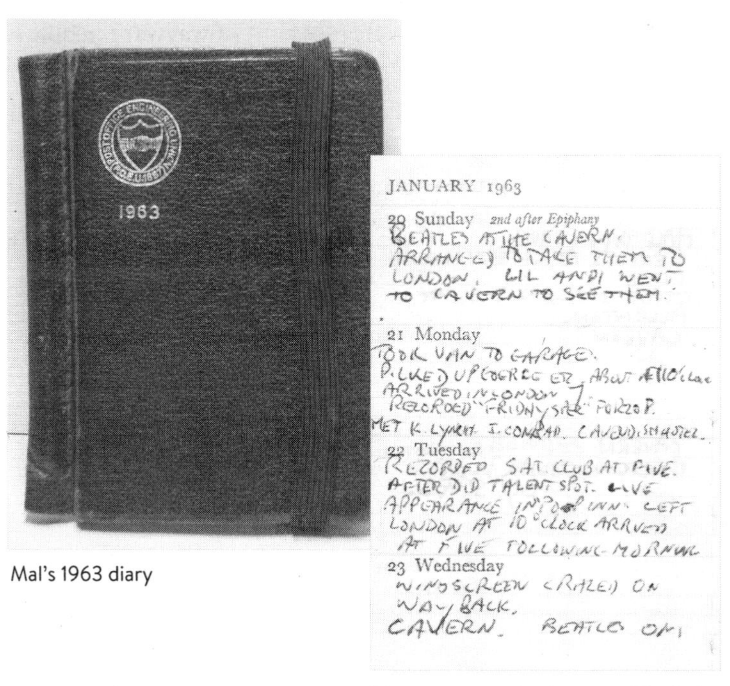

JANUARY 1963

20 Sunday *2nd after Epiphany*
BEATLES AT THE CAVERN.
ARRANGED TO TAKE THEM TO
LONDON. LIL AND I WENT
TO CAVERN TO SEE THEM.

21 Monday
TOOK VAN TO GARAGE.
PICKED UP GEORGE ETC. ABOUT AT 10 O'CLOCK
ARRIVED IN LONDON 7.
RECORDED "FRIDAY SPEC" FOR 208.
MET K. LYNCH. J. CONRAD. CAVENDISH HOTEL.

22 Tuesday
RECORDED SAT. CLUB AT FIVE.
AFTER DID TALENT SPOT. LIVE
APPEARANCE IN POP INN. LEFT
LONDON AT 10 O'CLOCK ARRIVED
AT FIVE FOLLOWING MORNING

23 Wednesday
WINDSCREEN CRACKED ON
WAY BACK.
CAVERN. BEATLES ON.

Mal's 1963 diary

Diary entry, week of January 20, 1963

Mal in the Big Freeze, two hundred miles to go, and a Beatle sandwich.[14] "This is how a band gets close," said Ringo, who was marking his sixth month as the Beatles' drummer.[15]

As for Mal, the experience had exceeded all expectations. For a start, he had earned £45 (£767 in present-day pounds) from Brian Epstein, which made for an impressive fee, all things considered. But the real reward came later that night, when he sat down at home to record his thoughts after catching the Beatles' show at the Cavern. Just three weeks earlier, he had begun keeping a journal for the first time after receiving his annual Post Office Engineering Union diary.

His original plan had been to use it to capture momentous happenings in the young life of his son, Gary. But as he jotted down the events of January 23, he began fervently chronicling his impressions of the Beatles, his experiences in London, and the people he had met along the way. At one point, he was forced to scroll to the end of the diary to gather more space for giddily recording his thoughts, which had begun spilling over onto the endpapers.

"They are all great blokes with a sense of humor and giving one the feeling they are a real team," he gushed. Even more important, he felt a growing sense of pride at having been, at such a crucial moment, a significant part of the Beatles' inner circle and no mere hanger-on. He had been right there with them—shoulder to shoulder, in the thick of *everything*. He felt an intense sense of belonging verging on pure elation. The whole experience reminded him of the first time he saw the Beatles performing live at the Cavern: "Oh, this is the greatest thing in the world!"[16]

01

A RIGHT LITTLE BASTARD

In 1975, when he began compiling his memoir at age forty, Mal Evans wrote, "I always wanted to be a cowboy."[1] The notion of traipsing from town to town as a kind of maverick—an incorrigible loner with a six-shooter by his side and no past to weigh him down—seemed to offer all the allure he could ever want in life. As an Englishman, he was hardly alone in his love affair with the Old West. Many a Briton has spoken wistfully about the lawless age most closely associated with North America, a gun-toting, rules-flouting era that never graced the history of the British Isles.

For Mal, these elements came together most profoundly in *The Gunfighter*, which he listed as his third favorite movie of all time after *Miracle on 34th Street* and *The Wizard of Oz*.[2] At age fifteen, Mal was undoubtedly drawn to the cinema by the 1950 movie's provocative tagline, which touts the gunslinger's solitary, violent existence: "His only friend was his gun. His only refuge—a woman's heart." Starring Gregory Peck as Jimmy Ringo—"the fastest gun in the West"—*The Gunfighter* ultimately depicts its hero as a casualty of his own sordid business. Even though he has grown older and wiser by the end of the film, Ringo cannot escape his bloody deeds. Not even the love of a good woman—comely Helen Wescott, as Peck's love interest—can alter his fate. As *The Gunfighter* comes to a close, Ringo dies alone, cut down in the street by a rival bent on making his own name as a gunslinger.

Years later, as he pondered the larger significance of *The Gunfighter*, Mal attributed the film's lasting impact on him to three key elements of the story—namely, the ability of a man to adapt to his surroundings, a man's unquenchable yearning for companionship, and, perhaps most important, the idea that the person a man hurts most often, and to whom he is most vulnerable, ends up being himself.[3] And if anyone could understand the notion of making his way as a maverick loner in a hard-nosed world, it was Mal's father.

Frederick William Jones Evans was born on June 24, 1905, in West Derby, Lancashire, to nineteen-year-old Elizabeth Evans. Of Welsh extraction, Elizabeth never divulged the identity of Fred's father, whom she likely met in 1904, while touring the United States as a singer and dancer on a chorus line.[4] In 1910, Elizabeth gave up her unconventional ways and married William Fitzsimons, a prosperous forty-year-old widower. A fruit buyer on the Liverpool docks, Fitzsimons treated Fred as his eldest son, even drawing him into the family business as an apprentice in the rough-and-tumble world of the fresh produce trade, which William plied at the Carriers' Dock on the River Mersey. In those days, Fred worked as his stepfather's assistant at W. David and Son, which operated a fruit market at 24 Mathew Street.

Still, for his part, Fred never truly came to terms with the circumstances of his birth, which Elizabeth and William had maintained as a carefully guarded family secret. Years later, on his seventieth birthday, in a moment of uncharacteristic violence, Fred finally spilled the beans about his origins. It all started when his stepbrother Norman, then fifty-six, greeted his elder brother by saying, "Hey, Fred, you old bastard!" Fred promptly decked the younger man, sending his birthday celebration into an uproar. "And that's when it all came out," Fred's daughter June later recalled.[5]

Not surprisingly, Fred grew to become an overachiever, desperate to prove his worth at every turn. After joining the Fitzsimons household, he spent much of his summers on the Wirral Peninsula, across the River Mersey from Liverpool. Fitzsimons owned a seaside cottage in the village of Meols, near Hoylake, and Fred taught himself to swim in the Irish Sea, while also becoming adept at sportfishing. As he grew older, he became an avid motorcyclist, competing in events sponsored by the Auto-Cycle Union across the region. By his twenties, he could be seen tooling around Liverpool on his prized blue Francis-Barnett motorcycle, complete with a vintage sidecar perfect for ferrying his dates around the city.

After leaving his stepfather's employ at W. David and Son, Fred took a job as a tally clerk for J. A. Sloan Importers, where he emerged not only as a successful tradesman in a highly competitive marketplace, but also as a natural leader who organized his dockers into a well-oiled machine capable of turning out a cargo hold in no time flat.

In the summer of 1934, Fred met his match in twenty-year-old Joan Hazel Evans (no relation). A championship swimmer from West Derby, Joan had introduced herself to Fred on a whim. At the time, he was fishing from a boat moored offshore from the Wirral. Not missing a beat, Joan took to the surf and swam out to Fred's boat. Catching sight of the strange woman approaching from the shore, he exclaimed, "Get back! You're going to be washed out to sea!"[6] But Joan wasn't deterred, and soon, she was the girl buzzing around town in Fred's sidecar.

That October, Fred and Joan were married at St. John the Evangelist's church in Knotty Ash. But their union wasn't merely the product of a whirlwind courtship. When the couple settled in their first home, at 31 Lorne Street in Liverpool's Fairfield neighborhood, Joan was already pregnant with their first child. Born at home on May 27, 1935, the strapping blond-haired, green-eyed Malcolm Frederick Evans was named in honor of British racing star Malcolm Campbell, one of Fred's personal heroes. In an early memory, Mal recalled riding in Fred's sidecar while being "held close in the warmth and security of my mother's arms."[7]

By 1939, Fred and Joan could afford to leave their modest home on Lorne Street for a semi-detached "council" house situated in Wavertree, at 75 Waldgrave Road, where they were joined by Fred's widowed mother, Elizabeth, who assisted Joan with domestic duties. Mal's early years were largely uneventful, save for a severe bout of whooping cough, which left him with an indentation in his upper chest.[8] By the end of the 1930s, Mal enjoyed a budding friendship with Ronnie Gore, who lived a few doors down. Born in November 1934, Ronnie was nearly seven months older than Mal, who resented Ronnie's unflinching obedience to his mother. As Mal later recalled, "Many times my mother was to say to me, 'Why can't you be like Ronnie? He's such a good lad for his mother.' In spite of this," Mal joked, "our friendship grew."[9]

Mal with his parents in Wales, c. 1936

Mal's sister Pamela Joan was born in August 1936, followed by Barbara Hazel in October 1938. For Mal, already obstinate to the core, Pam's birth spelled the end of his preeminence as an only child, with Barbara's arrival eroding his status further still. "This was to turn me into a right little bastard," he later wrote, "having my nose pushed out just when I was beginning to enjoy the spotlight and appreciate the attention I was getting. It was a wonder to me that this did not make me hate all women for the rest of my life." While he may have resented the shifting nature of his family circle, Mal was very much beloved by Fred and Joan, who had nicknamed him their little "Mackie."[10]

Meanwhile, Great Britain began to recognize the ominous signs of a looming world war. As if overnight, the gardens of Waldgrave Road were pocked with Anderson air-raid shelters, half-buried corrugated-steel sheds covered with sandbags. As with many of their countrymen, the Evanses were somewhat contemptuous of the shelters during the so-called Phoney War, when, for the first eight months of conflict, little actual combat took place.

When Great Britain declared war on Germany on September 3, 1939, Fred and his young family were on holiday. When they returned to Liverpool, they were issued gas masks, with Mal and Pam receiving kid-friendly respirators emblazoned with the image of Mickey Mouse. But their time back at Waldgrave Road was to be short-lived. Fred had already made arrangements for his family to live in Dyserth, Wales, in a seaside cottage called Bronallt.[11]

Even at age thirty-four, Fred knew that it was only a matter of time before he would be called up to join the armed forces. And indeed, by the time the Blitz began in earnest in September 1940, he was serving as a private attached to the Royal Air Force's Signals Corps. While he was in basic training and his family was safely ensconced in Wales, Liverpool began to reel from successive German air raids in which thousands of homes were destroyed during relentless bombing. With shelter becoming increasingly desperate, the fruit cellars on Mathew Street were deployed as makeshift air-raid bunkers. By the end of the war, the port city would suffer the loss of more than four thousand lives, second only to the death and destruction in London.

Given his skills as a motorcyclist, Fred began his tour of duty as a dispatch rider. To his family's good fortune, he was stationed at the RAF base in Prestatyn, only a few miles north of Dyserth. But his military contributions would prove relatively brief, at least at first. That December, while teaching the art of motorcycling to a group of young recruits at the base, he suffered a grievous injury. Joan would never forget the day a certain Corporal Kettle came to Bronallt to deliver the awful news. "I'm sorry, Mrs. Evans," he reported, "your husband's just had an accident. He was supposed to be demonstrating how to put the motorbike down without breaking it, but he broke his ankle instead." During his posting in Prestatyn, Fred earned a promotion to lance corporal, along with the nickname "Fishy Fred," because he would lay fishing lines on the beach every night to stock the officers' mess with a fresh catch.[12]

For Mal and his sisters, life in Dyserth was idyllic. Joan taught them how to swim from the beaches at Prestatyn, and the siblings attended a three-room schoolhouse together. Mal and Pamela enjoyed playing on the rock formations outside Dyserth or renting bicycles for sixpence apiece and riding along the promenade in Rhyl, with little Barbara in tow. The Evans kids' fondest memories were of hiking down to the Red Lion pub, where Fred, home on leave, would hold court, singing songs with the local folk, knocking back pints, and passing rounds of lemonade through an open window to Mal and his sisters.[13] Years later, Mal would wax nostalgic about his family's Welsh respite during the war, describing the period as "five of the happiest years of my life, living in the country and enjoying the Winter snow drifts and the hot golden Summers."[14]

Growing taller by the day and stocky to boot, Mal invariably stood out among his peer group. On the one hand, he desperately wanted to avoid calling attention to himself, to fit in with the other schoolchildren, yet, on the other, he longed to be known for being extraordinary—a quandary that would impinge upon the whole rest of his life. Years later, he would reflect upon the profundity of his experiences in Wales, tenderly recalling the emotional pain of being caught "hiding behind a girl's skirt on the church porch when an older boy wanted to bash me," or, even more poignantly, "being a coward and made to face and fight the school bully by an older friend," only to cultivate a much cherished friend out of his aggressor. Even as a child, he came to realize that fighting was a dead-end proposition, especially given his large size. "If I was to fight a smaller boy and win," he reasoned, "I'd be a bully. If I was to lose to a smaller boy, I'd look daft, and who the hell is going to pick on a bigger guy?"[15]

Every now and again, Mal and his family would be reminded of the terrible battles raging beyond Dyserth. Periodically, North Wales would be treated to fearsome airshows as RAF fighter planes intercepted Luftwaffe bombers conducting night raids over Liverpool. But not all the danger occurred in midair. "On one occasion," Mal lamented, his family watched in horror as "a British dispatch rider failed to negotiate a sharp corner on the steep hill on which we lived and killed himself on our doorstep."[16] As the war raged on, Fred was stationed in London, where he saw the ravages of war up close in the bombed-out city. Working in the Signals Corps, he was tasked with patrolling for V-1 flying "doodlebug" bombs, the Luftwaffe's final effort to bring Great Britain to its knees. Launched from the French and Dutch coastlines, the deadly contraptions produced a telltale buzzing sound that would characteristically go silent moments before impact.[17]

The family's Welsh hiatus would end in the spring months of 1945, when the Evanses resumed their Liverpool lives on Waldgrave Road. Before they left their beloved cottage, though, they celebrated VE (Victory in Europe) Day on May 8 in Dyserth. Barbara would vividly recall the night they joined the other villagers atop a local outcropping to mark the august occasion with singing and dancing before a blazing bonfire. Back in Liverpool, Mal and his family were relieved to discover that their neighborhood had largely been spared from the destruction wrought by the German air raids, which had left rubble-strewn remains of bombed-out buildings across much of the rest of the city.[18] "We were lucky," Mal later observed, "for at the end of the war, our family still had a father. And I myself was luckier than most in that I spent the war years with my family, for a lot of children were evacuated to the countryside and placed in the care of foster parents for the duration."[19]

Mal easily fell back into his prewar routine with Ronnie, his closest Liverpudlian mate. But outside of Ronnie and another Wavertree lad, Spud Murphy, he largely kept to himself, as did his sister Barbara. While they had reveled in the free rein they enjoyed back in Dyserth, they seemed content to be tethered close to home in Liverpool. As neighborhood chum Eunice Hayes later recalled, the Evans children "never ventured down the road toward us other kids. We had a feeling that his mum made them all stay in their garden, because that's where they always were." Eunice fondly remembered Mal's kindhearted attitude. "He was the nicest, politest, friendliest kid you'd ever meet," and he "always had a smile on his face."[20]

By this juncture, Fred's mother, Elizabeth, was no longer sharing a roof with the Evans family, having married fellow Liverpudlian Tommy Flynn in 1944. But for the Evanses, there were far more sweeping changes afoot. Mal would remember coming home one day from school in June 1946 and being surprised by the appearance of a newborn baby sister, named June. In contrast with the prewar births of Pam and Barbara, Mal took baby June's arrival in stride, resigning himself to the shifting natural order of things. "I just accepted it all," he wrote, "still believing that babies were found under rhubarb leaves!"[21]

At first, the family continued their regular jaunts to their beloved Dyserth to enjoy the tranquil seaside life. Years later, Mal's sister Barbara would wistfully recall the image of Fred piloting his Francis-Barnett motorcycle with her brother huddled behind him on the pillion. Meanwhile, Joan, Pam, and Barbara would nestle together in the sidecar with baby June resting in her mother's lap. Before long, Mal had grown so tall and broad-shouldered that he was no longer able to join his family on their motorcycling trips to Wales.[22]

During his preteen and early teen years, Mal's physical awkwardness proved to be the great bane of his existence, forcing him to retreat inward into shyness. As with his experiences in Wales, he desperately wanted to be accepted by a peer group—*any* peer group. At the time, he flirted with joining the ranks of an unsavory gang of neighborhood kids. But in the end, he couldn't bring himself to do it. "I had a horror of stealing, or maybe it was a horror of being caught," he later wrote. "When the gang roamed the stores at Christmas time, stealing all their Christmas presents, I found I couldn't join."[23]

But on another occasion, Mal found he simply couldn't resist his thieving impulses when it came to guns, the weaponry of choice for his beloved Western heroes. One afternoon, while he was on the way home from school, "some posh kid showed me his beautiful new shiny toy revolver." In a moment of pique, Mal hid the gun in a nearby bush while his schoolmate searched in vain for the toy. "Going back later and retrieving it, sneaking it home and holding it in the sanctuary that was my bedroom," Mal later recalled, "lives with me to this very day." For him, pulling off such a childish caper, possessing the toy for himself, had left him with a secret, unmistakable thrill.[24]

02

FUNFAIR

Despite the boy's occasional ethical lapses and stubborn demeanor growing up, Mal's parents doted on their only son. Fred and Joan were especially proud when he was accepted into Northway Primary School, which made him the first member of their family to pursue a formal education.

Located just across Waldgrave Road from the Evanses' housing estate, Northway left an indelible mark on Mal, whose schoolmates there nicknamed him Hippo. The name would follow him well into his high school years. Although it clearly had its origins in the world of playground ridicule, Mal preferred to see things differently. "I didn't mind being called 'Hippo,'"

Pam, Mal, and Barbara on the Rhyl promenade

he reasoned to himself, "because it always seemed to be a fairly amiable, vegetarian type of animal, not doing anybody any harm."[1]

What really bothered Mal was the growing affection he felt for one of his female classmates, a schoolboy crush he kept to himself, save for the "anonymous, threatening letters" he sent to another pupil who was paying an inordinate amount of attention to the girl. Not long afterward, Mal attended a Christmas party with the other Northway students. Desperate for attention, he "ate everybody's orange peel in the place just to impress this young lady," he recalled, "who I'm sure must have thought I was dumb, for we never did get together. It's a wonder I can still eat and enjoy oranges."[2] Mal's earliest pangs of desire turned out to be forbidden fruit for the fruit buyer's son. And so began a lifelong pattern wherein he would develop intense personal emotions he would have great difficulty expressing to others.

Fortunately, drawing proved a fulfilling outlet for self-expression. Over the years, Mal had become enamored with comic book series and took to filling sketchbooks of his own with crude drawings of Disney characters and, his favorite, cowboys. As he took greater and greater notice of the opposite sex, his sketches began to shift precipitously from carefree childhood images to pinups.

Now that he was devouring comic books on a regular basis, Mal started a newspaper route to earn extra money. But true to form, he quickly grew bored with the whole enterprise. "I used to get very fed up following the same old route," he recalled, "and so often, just for the hell of it, I would start at the end and work backwards, which caused consternation to the people getting their papers an hour late and there would be many irate phone calls to the newspaper shop." With his earnings, he purchased several comic books and a pair of classic novels: Robert Louis Stevenson's *Treasure Island* and Jonathan Swift's *Gulliver's Travels.* At first, Mal distinguished himself near the top of his class at Northway, which he attributed to the personalized education he had received in the Dyserth schoolhouse. "Mind you, this didn't last too long," he recalled, "and I usually hovered from there on in around the bottom three."[3] In 1946, having reached age eleven, he wrote his "eleven-plus" exams and earned entrance into grammar school at Holt High.

Situated just a mile away from Waldgrave Road on the Queens Drive thoroughfare, Holt High School found Mal at a familiar teenage crossroads, craving attention from the opposite sex, yet painfully shy and lacking the confidence to engage the world in any meaningful way. At this juncture, even his teachers took to mocking him. "We had a certain German teacher who spent most of his time telling us dirty jokes," Mal wrote, "and whenever he used to go around the class translating passages, he'd come to me and say, 'Ahh, well, never mind,' and go on to the next party."[4]

Mal overcompensated for his awkward demeanor by resorting to wisecracks and tomfoolery, positioning himself at school as the class clown. Try as he might to play the funnyman at home, though, he couldn't quite bridge the generation gap with his father. To win Fred's affections, Mal even attempted to develop a liking for sea fishing, the sport his father had enjoyed since boyhood. At one point, he "tried to get into it to the extent of travelling around the North Wales coastline [with Fred] on the back of an old lorry in the middle of Winter." While he still didn't cotton to sportfishing, their father-son trips revealed a key difference in their personalities—one exemplified by his father's good-natured, friendly outlook in contrast with Mal's paralyzing shyness. "My father's lovable character would be exposed in a strange pub," Mal recalled, "where he would immediately

1949 Holt High School photo with Mal on the far left

endear himself to the locals by getting up and singing in Welsh, Japanese, or Chinese, which was strange, because he was certainly no linguist, but very convincing!"[5] Fred's easy, outgoing nature was one his son desperately hoped to adopt one day.

In May 1951, when Mal turned sixteen, he considered leaving Holt High School on the strong advice of his father, who reasoned that the teen was ready to take on a career in the civil service rather than pursue an academic route. For Fred, the calculus was simple: though his only son had been the first member of their family to receive a primary school education and earn a scholarship to high school, the real goal was to land "a job with security and a real future."[6] Mal's liberation arrived in the form of acceptance into the Youth in Training Program, the General Post Office's apprenticeship scheme. A series of technical courses, along with subsequent internship opportunities, the two-year program acted as an expressway to a full-time position with the GPO.[7] To Fred's great delight, his son was accepted into the program's incoming class, which was set to begin at Lancaster House in early 1952.

At the same time, Mal began his first romantic relationship, having fallen head over heels in love with a Liverpudlian named Audrey. During the first phase of his training program, he balanced his technical course load with his budding romance. He had become so smitten with the voluptuous young woman that he began violating his curfew by sneaking out of his room after his parents had turned in for the night. "We were courting for quite a while, never getting beyond the heavy petting stage," Mal recalled, "but it's amazing how satisfying a kiss can be from someone you think a lot of."[8]

Things came to a head when Audrey went on a two-week holiday at a seaside resort in Blackpool. Lovesick Mal couldn't stomach the idea of being away from her for an entire fortnight, even if it meant making the trip out to Blackpool, which, in his view, was the poor man's Monte Carlo. After a week, he couldn't take it anymore and made the two-hour train trip up north for a surprise visit. But by this point, Audrey had already taken up with a new guy. Mal's shocking discovery left him understandably heartbroken. He would never forget spending "a lonely, gray day amongst the happy, sun-kissed crowd of holiday makers." The awful experience "left a scar that time never did really erase."[9]

Mal soothed his aching teenage heart in music, in particular the country-and-western stylings of Hank Snow, the Canadian musician whose songs celebrated the liberating possibilities of life on the open road. For Snow, moving along the highways and byways of the United States afforded a sense of freedom, a much-needed escape from society's constraints, that surely appealed to Mal. Upon later reflection, Mal would admire Snow not only for turning him onto country-and-western music, but also for the musician's signature guitar, with its inlaid mother-of-pearl design.[10]

During this same period, Mal determined to become physically fit for the first time in his life, transforming his typically stocky frame into a more lithe physique. And he achieved this feat via one of Fred's favorite pastimes. "I guess I channeled my sexual energies into cycling. I used to ride most every Sunday, rain or shine, 200 or 250 miles," he boasted, "and got a perverse pleasure at arriving home, soaked to the skin, muscles aching and so tired, but with the feeling that I personally had accomplished something."[11] Not surprisingly, Mal's increasing physical exertions led to a spate of injuries—most notably, an ingrown toenail that had to be removed surgically. It was an injury that would have later consequences.[12]

Given his newfound yen for fitness, along with his ongoing studies with the Youth in Training Program, Mal's appetite increased exponentially. The lunch vouchers provided by his apprenticeship would no longer do. As his sister June recalled, "He was tall and thin, very thin at the time when he started going to work. My mother used to take a loaf of sliced bread and make his sandwiches. He had a whole loaf made into sandwiches to take with him to work. And on Sunday tea, when my mother would make apple pies, she would make a plate-size pie just for Malcolm."[13]

At the same time, he found himself at a mental crossroads with his father. As Mal recalled, "I was feeling cocky with my newfound stature as a working man. For a long time, I'd wanted to own a pair of jeans, and so, with one of my first paychecks, [I] went out and bought a pair."[14] All hell broke loose that evening when he returned from his apprenticeship wearing his brand-new jeans, which infuriated Fred to no end. As a lifelong employee on the Liverpool waterfront, Mal's father associated denim jeans with a certain sort of dockhand. "A lot of lazy, drunken layabouts," in Fred's words, donned jeans as their uniform. Fred had spent most of his working life dealing with the dockers and their shenanigans, and seeing Mal in denim was too much to bear.[15]

As the situation with his father became increasingly heated, Mal countered Fred's anger by pointing out that he was old enough to make his own decisions. But Fred wasn't having it. "At this point," Mal wrote, as they were "standing up glaring at each other, my father struck out and punched me on the jaw, me going one way, my spectacles going the other." Mal was stunned by this sudden turn of events, to be sure, but he was even more shocked when Fred retired to the kitchen and summarily "cried his eyes out."[16] As Mal would later discover, Fred's pique of anger and disappointment may have been an aberration, but it would not be his last.

In May 1953, Mal turned eighteen. While having technically come into his majority as an adult, he still lived under his parents' roof and depended upon them for room and board. And by his own admission, he still had a long way to go in terms of achieving emotional maturity. Not long after coming of age, he would be dealt a personal blow that would reverberate in his psyche for years.

For the formerly branded "Hippo," the very idea of not being chosen—essentially for anything—was fraught with peril. The National Service Act that had ushered Fred Evans into the Second World War was still very much the law of the land, having been extended by Parliament in 1948. With mandatory conscription in the offing, Mal and his childhood mates Ronnie and Spud followed in the footsteps of their forebears and made the ritualistic visit to the local Medical Board to begin the intake process.

The results proved devastating. Ronnie and Spud were duly accepted into the army, while Mal was turned down. That August, he received his formal rejection in the form of his national service card, which listed him as Grade IV. While the first three grades permitted entrance into the armed services, albeit in different capacities, Grade IV signified as "unsuitable" and dismissed from service "those who suffer from progressive organic disease or are for other reasons permanently incapable of the kind or degree of exertion required."[17]

Mal's Grade IV classification was nothing short of "a terrible disappointment," especially given his vigorous personal fitness program over the

Mal (center) at the GPO with his future best man Gordon Gaskell (right) and boyhood chum Ronnie Gore (left)

past few years.[18] Worse yet, after a lifetime of being singled out for his size, it was his body—his most salient trait in the world's eyes—that had let him down. The medical examination board had cited his missing toenail as the primary reason for his rejection, suggesting that he would be unable to withstand the physical exertions of marching and other military practices.[19]

For a great many recruits during this era, not being selected on medical grounds might have been a welcome result. After all, World War II had been concluded for nearly a decade, and young men were understandably eager to get on with their lives. Mal was certainly not "swinging the lead," as the practice was known back in those days, in which potential recruits feigned illness or deformity in order to be excused from national service.[20] Well known among Mal's Liverpool contemporaries, the expression had its origins in the nautical world, referring to the deployment of weighted lines used to measure water depth. Lazy sailors were said to be "swinging the lead" when they called out fake measurements instead of bothering to carry out the actual work.

Shamed by his rejection at the hands of the Medical Board, Mal trudged forward with the GPO's Youth in Training Program. And he also continued his ineffectual and, at times, comical pursuit of the opposite sex. At this juncture, his virginity was "a fact which I kept carefully concealed from all the other guys I worked with." He had recently begun dating a telephone operator whom he had met through the program. At "the ripe old age" of twenty-one, she made Mal feel like "a man about town, escorting this elegant young lady who dressed so fashionably." He had typecast her as "a rather prim and proper looking lady, [an impression] heightened by the fact that she always wore her hair tied in a bun."[21]

By this point, Mal's lack of sexual experience served as a source of continual irritation for him and exposed an overarching fear of physical intimacy. "After one particular evening out," he recalled, "I ran to save my virginity as she tried to rape me on her living room sofa. What happened was that she expected my advances, obviously, to follow through, and in my innocence, and thinking the man should be the aggressor, [I] was shocked to the core when she started tearing her clothes off, and not only that, tried to get my pants down!"[22]

As Mal's awkward attempts at sexual awakening continued unabated, he learned through the Youth in Training Program grapevine that certain telephone numbers could be counted on to engage in obscene conversations. Determined to overcome his debilitating shyness, he made a point of "accidentally" eavesdropping on one of these sexual tête-à-têtes. To Mal's surprise, the seductive voice at the other end of the line proceeded to invite him over to her residence. He went. "After several attempts of knocking on the door and being told to go away—obviously, she was playing hard to get—I was admitted to the house and plied with drink," he recalled. At this point, Mal undressed, "overjoyed with the thought of at last losing my virginity." He was certain that he "was about to be deflowered by this rather gross, 250-pound female, when suddenly, she smacked me right on the mouth, screaming obscenities at me. I immediately got dressed, and once again, left in a hurry."[23]

That summer, Mal joined the ranks of the GPO as a full-time telecommunications engineer, earning a £15 weekly wage (£333 in present-day pounds). As June proudly recalled, the GPO promised "a nice, safe, respectable job with a pension."[24] In August 1954, Mal signed his name in the appointment book. Assigned employee identification number 61192, he was officially a member of the British post office's technical arm. Billy Maher, a three-year GPO veteran, recalled working alongside Mal at Lancaster House. The two hit it off almost immediately, bonding over a shared love of music, especially rock 'n' roll. Billy played guitar in the Kingfisher Four, a local skiffle group.[25] With its jazz and blues origins, skiffle was sweeping the British Isles at the time. In addition to conventional instruments such as Billy's acoustic guitar, the folksy genre often incorporated improvised instruments such as washboards and homemade tea-chest basses. Having already achieved the rank of technical officer, Billy enjoyed walking around the city center with Mal, "who was a giant of a man, and I am the opposite. I can see us now walking down Old Hall Street together—his hands were level with my ears!"[26]

As a newly minted telecommunications engineer, Mal spent most of his time away from Lancaster House, carting his GPO engineer's bag around the region as he installed automatic telephone and telex exchanges in governmental and commercial buildings. In contrast with the organization's veritable legion of postal workers, with their standard-issue double-breasted jackets and gleaming badges, telecommunications engineers adhered to a lax dress code, save for a requisite shirt sporting the GPO's insignia and a khaki dustcoat for inclement weather.

As luck would have it, Mal's first supervisor was Gordon Gaskell, a six-year veteran of the GPO. At twenty-seven, Gordon proved to be the mentor Mal sorely needed and, to Mal's delight, he "began taking me under his wing, teaching me how to be a good engineer, and, by example, a responsible member of society." More important, Gordon's tutelage buoyed Mal's self-esteem. "I felt I was a competent engineer," Mal recalled, "getting pleasure doing a job well, and certainly getting satisfaction when any praise came my way."[27]

Shortly before he settled into his new position with the GPO, Mal joined a friend for a Saturday night in New Brighton. Located across the Mersey on the Wirral Peninsula, the seaside town was home to the summer-long "funfair" and the nationally famous Brighton Wheel, the Ferris wheel dominating the fairgrounds. That evening, Mal's friend spotted a girl standing alongside the carousel-like Waltzer. Seizing the opportunity, and "acting daft as boys often are when they are out together," Mal "went down on my knees to this unknown young lady, who was wearing heart-shaped earrings, saying, 'Come on, darling, give me your heart!'"[28]

The young lady turned out to be eighteen-year-old Lily White, who had grown up a few miles away, in suburban Allerton. That evening, Mal and his pal joined Lily and her friend for a relaxing stroll among the fairgrounds. At one point, Lily complained of feeling ill and decided to return home to Liverpool. Assuming the role of gentleman, Mal escorted her on the ferry ride across the Mersey before depositing her at the tram shed bound for Allerton. "As the bus drew away with her on board," he recalled, "something inside made me risk life and limb in leaping onto the first moving bus to join her."[29]

03

A CELLARFUL OF NOISE

Mal in front of his Hillside Road home

After years of ineffectual, often humiliating efforts at cultivating a genuine romance, Mal had finally landed an honest-to-goodness girlfriend in Lily. In many ways, she and Mal had very little in common in terms of life experiences or interests, save for having grown up in suburban Liverpool.

Lily White was born on June 16, 1936, at 75 Wendell Street, in Liverpool's Toxteth district, to William and Lillian White. Her father worked as a clerk at Barker and Dobson's sweets factory, a sprawling complex located on Liverpool's Whitefield Road. For her parents, who were in their mid-thirties by that juncture, Lily had arrived as a surprise, a late-in-life child. She was the youngest of five siblings, which included sister Vera, the eldest, whose male twin had died in childbirth, and brothers Leslie, Bill, and Fred. At five feet tall, and wearing a diminutive size-four shoe to boot, Lily stood in stark contrast to Mal's looming physical presence. And unlike Mal, she possessed a vivacious, outgoing personality, along with an inner confidence and love of adventure to match her social dexterity.[1]

When she first met Mal, Lily was working as a secretary for a shipping firm in the Cunard Building, one of the so-called Three Graces (along with the Royal Liver and Port of Liverpool buildings) that tower over the Pier Head beside the Mersey waterfront. Each day, she would dress to the nines, even donning immaculate patent-leather gloves, and ride the tram into the city from Allerton, where her family had relocated during the postwar years. Her father bred Airedale and Alsatian dogs at their home, where Lily had perfected the art of cooking ratatouille and tended to an elaborate backyard garden that fueled her culinary interests. She particularly enjoyed sunbathing, although, unlike her new boyfriend, she didn't enjoy swimming in the slightest, and cycling was out of the question. On one traumatic occasion during childhood, she fell off her bike and was accosted by a rat, an incident that had turned her away from cycling for good.[2] While Mal had spent his early teen years at Holt High, Lily had studied across town, at Morrison Secondary Modern School; this was followed by a two-year program at Anfield Secretarial College.[3]

For Mal's sisters, Lily's regular presence at Waldgrave Road proved to be a great boon. Like many people, they were fascinated by their brother's and his new girlfriend's contrasting proportions. "I remember when she first came to our house," Barbara recalled. "She was so tiny. She barely fitted under Mal's arm, actually."[4] As for June, Lily's arrival at Waldgrave Road spelled an opportunity to haze Mal's new girlfriend with childish pranks. "My mother used to have brass taps in the bathroom upstairs," June recalled, "and I was a bit of a cow, because I used to take them and hide them." When Lily first came over to the Evans home for tea, she retired to the bathroom to wash her hands, only to discover that there weren't any taps in evidence to operate the plumbing. "So, I was kind of a pain in the ass, really," June recalled.[5] To her credit, Lily took June's tomfoolery in stride, and Mal's sister grew to love her. As Mal and Lily's relationship progressed, they often joined the family for day trips to the beach at New Brighton. "He and Lil would get the beach gear together, and they'd come and have a picnic with us," said Barbara. "We'd play rounders on the beach. It was good fun."[6]

Meanwhile, Mal quickly ingratiated himself with Lily's family, who marveled at his outsize appearance and his good-natured demeanor. And while he may have suffered from inveterate shyness over the years, particularly with women, he had no such qualms when it came to his new girlfriend's family, including the coterie of younger relatives. He was especially fond of Lily's five-year-old niece, Shirley Ann White, whose uncle Ken had nicknamed her "Shan" because of her penchant for drinking the dregs out of his glasses of Shandygaff beer; in later years, Shirley reasoned that the nickname was apt, sounding like an elision of "Shirley Ann."

In Shan's memory, Mal "adored children—*loved* children, being a sort of big child himself." On one unforgettable occasion, Shan and her older brother Paul watched, thunderstruck, as huge, cumbersome Mal attempted a handstand in the Whites' rear garden in Woolton and broke his arm. But it was hardly the last time he left Woolton in a cast. "Looking back," said Shan, "it's incredible how many times he injured himself at our house."[7] Meanwhile, Mal could always be counted on to show off the *Argo*, his three-foot model schooner, at the Sefton Park Boating Lake.[8]

During the early years of their courtship, Mal and Lily spent every possible minute together, often taking their lunch breaks at the Pier Head, where they shared sandwiches alongside the River Mersey. During the evenings, they could be found at the cinema, always a favorite outing for Mal; or dancing, at which Lily excelled. By 1956 and the advent of Elvis Presley, the pulsating sounds of rock 'n' roll began, slowly but surely, to permeate the Liverpool dance halls. Lily would never forget the excitement of Big Mal hoisting her above the dance floor—"scooping her to the left, scooping her to the right," in time with the music.[9] And Mal would fondly recall the thrill of discovering Elvis for the first time. As it happened, his previous idol, Hank Snow, had been instrumental in introducing the Tupelo, Mississippi, phenom to "Colonel" Tom Parker, the manager who would act as the architect of Presley's coming success. In March 1956, Mal heard Elvis singing "Heartbreak Hotel" and never looked back. He began collecting the King's U.K. releases—"Blue Suede Shoes," "I Want You, I Need You, I Love You," "Hound Dog"—as Elvis conquered the English charts. That October, Mal purchased Elvis's first LP in the British Isles, entitled *Elvis Presley Rock 'n' Roll.*

Now twenty-one years old, Mal felt a deep connection with Presley, who was just four months his senior. His unbridled enthusiasm for the King was evident at the GPO, where the other engineering techs began mocking Mal's devotion to the American rock 'n' roll star. "I'd go out and buy records, and listen to his music—we'd all be working late at night, and they'd all take the mickey out of me, saying, 'Who the hell is that singing that rubbish on the radio?'"[10]

One of those GPO techs was Roy Armstrong, who joined the technical unit that October. Roy remembered Mal as a "top bloke" and an active member in the Merseyside Elvis fan club.[11] Another one of Mal's GPO colleagues was none other than his childhood friend Ronnie Gore, who had completed his stint in the army and taken a position in Mal's unit. With their friendship having been rekindled, Mal served as Ronnie's best man at his June 1956 wedding to the former Patricia McInnes.[12]

Naturally, Mal's affinity for Elvis didn't stop with the music. In January 1957, he took to the cinema, with Lily on his arm, to view Elvis's star turn in *Love Me Tender* at the Forum; this was followed that October by *Loving You* during the film's one-week run at the Gaumont. When it came to Elvis, Mal's zeal for learning every last nugget about the King's life had no limits. In February 1960, when thirty-four-year-old mega-fan Albert Hand began publishing *Elvis Monthly* out of Derbyshire, Mal became a charter subscriber.

Whenever he was away in Staffordshire on GPO business, Mal kept in close touch with his parents. And thanks to Lily's influence, he had grown particularly close to his sisters, whom he still enjoyed taunting with pranks. As Barbara later recalled, "He never really grew up. That's the thing with Malcolm. He was always going to the joke shop to buy things like plastic spiders or dog poo."[13] On the surface, Fred and Joan couldn't have been prouder of their son. Formally educated and employed in a plum position with the GPO, Mal was poised to add "husband" to his portfolio after becoming engaged to Lily.

Even so, his parents—Joan, in particular—were concerned about Mal's fitness for marriage. Joan saw in him limited romantic experience and, worse, a glaring level of immaturity, and she announced to Mal that perhaps "Lil deserves better than you."[14] Joan's unease over his character was truly troubling for him. Playing to form, Mal was determined to prove his worthiness when it came to Lily and defy his mother's expectations. On September 28, 1957, he married Lily at St. Agnes and St. Pancras Church in Toxteth Park. With Gordon Gaskell as his best man, Mal recited his vows in the ornate late-Victorian church's stone-inlaid interior. Afterward, he tenderly lifted up his bride and carried her to the limousine as a gentle rain pierced the sunshine.[15] Perhaps he would prove his mother's misgivings wrong and rise to the gravity of adulthood and marriage after all.

For Mal and Lily, two virgins on their wedding day, their three-year courtship had been a blur of family, friends, and relations. Their honeymoon involved a sightseeing tour of Northwest England, including a lengthy stay in Carlisle, the erstwhile Roman settlement and onetime prison for Mary, Queen of Scots. In a letter of October 2, 1957, Mal commented on the joys of being married to the love of his life, reporting that the two were contented to gaze upon each other and bask in the glow of finally being "Mr. and Mrs. Evans."

As the couple settled into their first home in Wavertree, a tiny row house at 12 Kenmare Road that they shared with Lily's mother, Mal and

Mal and Lily's wedding day

Lily made a pact that Mal would always leave home smiling and that they would never allow the seeds of marital discord, no matter how small, to fester. That Christmas, an adoring Lily presented her new husband with an acoustic guitar. Over the years, he had been known to play the banjo, but to Mal, the guitar was the epitome of rock 'n' roll, of Elvis Presley and America.

Inspired by his newfound confidence, Mal later tried his hand at learning guitar and, perhaps even more daringly, performing in public. A childhood friend now living in London, Eunice Hayes, recalled attending a party during this period at which Mal showed off his banjo skills. "Our families often got together for sing-alongs," Eunice said. "I do remember vividly him sitting cross-legged alongside his sister Pam on the carpet belting out 'Last Train to San Fernando,' and we'd all sing our heads off. He had a good voice, too!"[16] While Mal enjoyed the low-stress opportunity to play music at parties with family and friends, his efforts at learning to play the guitar were not idle ones. In fact, they betrayed a more serious, long-held secret ambition. As he later confessed, "All my life, since I was a kid, I wanted to be an entertainer."[17]

In January 1958, Mal and Lily purchased a home at 28 Hillside Road, in Mossley Hill. Located just a few blocks from the Penny Lane bus roundabout, the house had ready access to Menlove Avenue, a major Liverpool

Mal and Lily's wedding departure

thoroughfare. To his parents' great pride, he was the first member of the family to take out a mortgage and begin the journey of homeownership. At slightly over a thousand square feet, the home had three cozy bedrooms—perfect for an aspiring family. By the spring of 1961, Lily learned that she was pregnant with their first child. Not long afterward, Mal notched yet another milestone in his belt when he became the first person in his family to own a car, having bought a used 1959 Humber Hawk, an estate car decked out in dark silvery-green trim.[18]

It was during this era, with rock 'n' roll in his heart, that Mal first descended the steps of a dank basement club on Mathew Street. Located a brisk ten-minute walk from the GPO's Lancaster House offices, the Cavern had originally made its name as a jazz club under the management of Alan Sytner, who had refashioned the former fruit warehouse in the image of Paris's Le Caveau de la Huchette. After Ray McFall bought the Cavern in 1959, he began rebranding the club as the go-to hangout for blues bands and Beat groups. In May 1960, McFall began hawking a series of nightly Beat sessions, the first of which featured local skiffle artists Rory Storm and the Hurricanes, including their flashy drummer, nineteen-year-old Ringo Starr, born Richard Starkey.

As he ambled around the city center on his lunch break, Mal found himself drawn to the raucous sounds emanating from the Cavern. As he later recalled, "I used to go out window shopping on my lunch hour. And I went down Mathew Street—it was a small, dingy street with warehouses down the side." As he walked along the narrow street, "the most incredible music I'd ever heard was coming from beneath my feet. So I paid my shilling and went in."[19] What Mal discovered inside the distinctive setting below the streetscape would be utterly transformative, not merely because of the music, but also because of the club's atmosphere.

Debbie Greenberg (née Geoghegan), a dedicated Cave Dweller, was at the Cavern that day. She would always remember the anticipation she experienced as she walked along Mathew Street on her way to a lunchtime gig. "You couldn't wait to get down those eighteen stone steps because you could hear the thrill of the music before you even got in," she recalled, "and once you got past the pay desk, you knew that the heat was going to send your senses reeling, because it was so hot, and it didn't matter whether it was winter or summer or whatever. It was the same temperature all the time." In those days, the Cavern "was a concoction of many things, including the perspiration from the kids huddled in front of the stage, the condensation dripping down the walls, and the cigarette smoke that hung in the air." Then there was the odor. The Cavern's regulars were relentlessly assaulted by a peculiar brew of smells that included the stale aroma of the soup and hot dogs on sale for lunch intermingled with a bracing whiff of toilet disinfectant, the residual stench from the rotting fruit in the warehouse across the street, and all manner of human effluvia.[20]

At twenty-six, Mal was much older than the usual lunchtime crowd, which skewed toward the teenage set. But for him, the age difference, much less any unpleasant odors, didn't matter in the slightest. The main attraction was the music. And the act onstage that day was the Beatles, the remnants of a onetime skiffle band having just returned from a rough-and-tumble residency in postwar West Germany, where they had played the clubs on Hamburg's notorious Reeperbahn.

Decked out in their leathers, the group comprised rhythm guitarist John Lennon, bassist Paul McCartney, lead guitarist George Harrison, and drummer Pete Best. "The place was smoky," Mal recalled, "and these guys were doing a very good set of rock, a little bit like Elvis music." He was so captivated that "I could sit there for three hours and think maybe 10 minutes had gone by." Mal took special note of the three vocalists—John, Paul, and George: "They were very high-pitched and there was harmony." By the time he made his way back up to the street, he was hooked. "I fell in love with them,"[21] he later said.

As he reflected on the Beatles' performance that day, Mal felt invigorated by the band that had "got my Elvis groove going." But it was more than that. There was something special about these four local boys. Mal couldn't have known this, but they were a far cry from the crude group of players who had left Liverpool for Hamburg the previous August. By the early months of 1961, when he first encountered them, they were tight, confident, and professional. "When they took to the stage," Debbie recalled, "they just blew us away. They were dynamic, they were vibrant, they were energetic. The music was incredible, it was loud, and they were humorous, and it was exciting."[22]

Over the next several months, Mal made regular forays into the basement club to see the Beatles, befriending eighteen-year-old Roberta "Bobby" Brown in the process. The local Beatles Fan Club secretary, Bobby acted as Mal's first guide into the Beatles' cloistered world below the street. In addition to asking the imposing, bespectacled telecommunications engineer to save her a seat near the stage, she introduced him to the band. "Mal was a really, really nice person, and because he was often saying how much he loved the Beatles and wanted to meet them, I introduced him to Paul."[23] The bass guitarist took an instant liking to Mal, recalling that "he was a lovely, big, huggable bear of a man."[24] From his place behind the drum kit, Pete also took notice of Mal's hulking presence. "He would stand there, just watching us play," Pete recalled. "He was first and foremost a fan."[25]

Whether he was sitting in the front row with Bobby or standing alongside the stage, Mal simply couldn't get enough of the Beatles, who had begun to recognize the towering figure among the throng of regular Cave Dwellers. Before long, he had begun making "rather extended" lunchtime visits to the Cavern, eventually stopping by after work to take in the Beatles' evening shows as well. Mal became particularly close with George Harrison during this period. One night that summer, he brought George home to meet Lily in Mossley Hill, where the trio shared a meal before spinning records and talking about rock 'n' roll into the wee hours of the morning.[26]

By the early fall, the frequency of Mal's Cavern visits had begun to ebb considerably as Lily's pregnancy progressed. Back in May, she had given up her position at the Cunard Building, and, in the intervening months, her pregnancy had become fraught with complications. As Mal later recalled, "In the last stages of carrying our baby, Lil developed severe blood poisoning, and it was a case of having to take the baby, or maybe losing both." By late September, Lily was admitted to the Women's Hospital on Catharine Street in Liverpool. Mal was understandably overjoyed when their son, Gary Malcolm Evans—named after Gary Cooper, one of Mal's father's favorite Western silver screen heroes—was born on October 11, 1961. "Death tried to steal this precious gift," Mal wrote, "and I nearly lost my wife and son."

As it turned out, they weren't out of the woods quite yet. "Gary was a six-week premature caesarean birth, spending the first few weeks of life in an incubator, weighing only three pounds, 12 ounces," Mal recalled. "I spent hours just standing, praying, staring into the incubator, wondering what life would hold for him."[27]

Lily struggled mightily during her lengthy hospital stay with her newborn, and before long, her husband's incessant presence, no matter how well meaning, became a source of irritation. Her family realized not only that Lily needed a break from Mal, but that Mal's state of mind during the couple's medical ordeal had become concerning. As it happened, they were organizing a coach trip—a *sharra*, in Liverpudlian, short for *sharrabang*, an Anglicization of the French *char à banc* (meaning "horse-drawn wagon")—to see the Blackpool Illuminations, the seaside town's annual autumn festival of lights. "When you go on a sharra, you hire a coach and go somewhere with your family and friends," Shan recalled.[28] Northerners adored these sorts of impromptu outings. While the Blackpool festival featured a specific destination, sharra trips were often billed as mystery tours, wherein the attendees would pack some beer and a well-stocked picnic basket and simply go for a ride. Sharrabang trips enjoyed a long history in Great Britain, dating back to the days of horse-drawn carriages. In recent decades, they had come back into vogue and now involved single-decker bus day trips as an inexpensive means for a getaway during the lean postwar years.[29]

While he realized the kindness and goodwill inherent in his in-laws' invitation, Mal initially declined the offer, contending that his place during this arduous time was with Lily and Gary. Besides, he didn't really cotton to Blackpool's touristy nature. But Shan's grandmother simply wasn't having it. "You're going to come out and have a break with us," she announced. "You've been worried sick—we've all been worried—but we're going to Blackpool to enjoy ourselves." But for Mal, the sharra trip was a nonstarter, and he told his in-laws, "I can't leave Lil and Gary in hospital when they're doing so poorly"—which is why everyone was surprised, a few days later, when he joined them aboard the motor coach, where he was promptly greeted by a round of cheers. Settling into his seat beside eleven-year-old Shan, Mal joked that "you're my wife for the night!" For Shan, the October 1961 sharra trip would be one of her most cherished memories of her uncle. "We spent the whole of the time together, walking around the illuminations, eating toffee apples, and wearing 'kiss-me-quick hats.' It was a smashing night. I had a lovely time, and I had him all to meself!"[30]

The doting parents had scarcely brought little Gary home from the hospital when they were dealt a tragic blow. Within a matter of weeks, Lily's sixty-one-year-old mother was felled by a brain tumor. The sad tidings were tempered only by the baby's healthy progress. By the dawn of 1962, Mal and Lily finally felt that their new family was out of danger. "A bad start in life didn't hold him back any," Mal reflected on his son, "and Gary Malcolm developed into a beautiful, strong, healthy boy."[31] Having regained her strength, Lily occasionally joined Mal for his regular jaunts to Mathew Street to take in the Beatles' set and service his ongoing addiction to rock 'n' roll. "I went to the Cavern and saw the walls wet with condensation," she later recalled, "but not very often, because I was at home with the baby."[32]

By this point, the Beatles had begun to take special notice of the outsize regular frequenting their shows. "He'd sit there among all the other people and request Elvis songs," George recalled. "After a while, we caught on that here was this guy who always wanted Elvis songs, so we'd say, 'Well, now we'd like to do a request for Mal.'"[33] Paul recognized that Mal "first and foremost was a Presley freak. He took *Elvis Monthly* all the time."[34] Indeed, Mal could always be counted on when it came to the latest issue of the newsletter, which the Beatles devoured right along with him. One evening, George invited Mal over to his family's home in Speke, a suburb of Liverpool, where they hung out, had dinner, and listened to records. That's when George hatched the idea of Mal working as a bouncer: "Look, you're big and ugly enough, why don't you be a bouncer on the door? You get paid for it, you get in the band room, and you meet the bands."[35]

The notion of working as a part-time bouncer in the evening was a no-brainer for Mal. With a new baby at home, he and Lily could use the extra money. Besides, as George had pointed out, the idea of being close to the action and consorting with the music makers themselves was simply too enticing for a devoted fan like him to ignore. And as far as he was concerned, the Beatles were an outfit worth following.

While Mal had been tending to Lily and Gary that autumn, the Beatles had enjoyed the good fortune of landing a manager in twenty-seven-year-old Brian Epstein, the scion of a prominent Liverpool family who operated NEMS (North End Music Stores), the most successful record retail outlet in the North. Although he may have been a novice, Epstein was a born entrepreneur, bristling with vision for the band's future. Having glimpsed them for the first time, like Mal, in the Cavern's free-wheeling, high-octane environment, Epstein would boast, without a trace of irony in his voice, that the Beatles would be "bigger than Elvis," a prediction that even the Beatles themselves found absurd.[36]

When it came to working as a bouncer, Mal not only had the requisite physique, but also the mind-set for carrying out such a precarious position—the kind of job that can go from the mundane to the serious, and even deadly, in the blink of an eye. "Mal was exactly what the Cavern's Ray McFall was looking for," George recalled. "Someone big and strong, not necessarily menacing, but looking like he meant business." To his credit, Mal self-consciously understood his aptness for the role. "I was a middle-class bouncer, most of them coming from a much harder school than the one I was brought up in," he wrote. "My idea was to talk people out of trouble before it started. Being an ardent coward helped a lot—getting punched in the mouth not being my idea of fun."[37]

Fortunately, Mal would rarely be called upon to work alone at his post outside the club. McFall employed a rotating cast of bouncers—including Paddy Delaney, hired back in 1959, and future Olympian Wallace Booth.[38] A prizewinning wrestler who would later win a silver medal at the Commonwealth Games in Jamaica, Booth enjoyed working the door. While he liked the club's "fabulous rock 'n' roll atmosphere," he preferred standing at his post at the top of the steps. "The Cavern was made up of bricks and arches, and you never ever wore good clothes downstairs because the sweat was running down the walls. And if you leaned against them, you were in for a mess."[39]

John Quinn, a Liverpudlian metalworker, was there the night Mal made his debut at the top of the Cavern steps. "I sometimes took my wife to town and ended up at the Cavern for one hour before going home," he recalled. The club was "not so full then, just workers coming in to listen to the bands." That night, Quinn was particularly struck by Mal's imposing height and quiet demeanor.[40] John Fanning, who managed Ted "Kingsize" Taylor and the Dominoes, a popular Merseyside rock combo, remembered observing Mal as he "worked the door along with two other large chaps, just making sure all the boys that came in were going to behave themselves."

When things got tight, Fanning recalled, Mal was always "very helpful with the guys in the groups that struggled to get their equipment down the stairs into the hot and sweaty Cavern."[41]

During the earliest days of his career as a bouncer, Mal had become keenly aware of the comings and goings of other acts, along with the road managers, or "roadies," who lugged bands' gear, prepped their stages, and ensured their timely transit from place to place. Road managers had been key players on the popular music scene since as early as the 1920s. The term was first seen in print in a 1944 feature story in *The New Yorker* about jazz orchestra leader Duke Ellington, whose "steps are usually dogged by his road manager, Jack Boyd, a hard, brisk, red-faced little white man from Texas." Boyd worked tirelessly on Sir Duke's behalf, acting as a jack-of-all-trades and organizing nearly every aspect of his famed client's life, from booking hotel rooms and train journeys to working as a human wake-up call to ensure that Ellington arrived on time for his much-ballyhooed orchestral spots. The word "roadie" wouldn't formally enter the lexicon until 1969, when it featured in Jenny Fabian and Johnny Byrne's novel, *Groupie*, but in practical usage, it had been around for years, reflecting the more blue-collar aspects of road-managing a rock 'n' roll band, with its array of instruments and heavy equipment.[42]

It was a world that Mal, as bouncer, would come to know very well. On one unforgettable occasion, he was drafted by fellow Liverpudlian Mal Jefferson to transport Paul's new QUAD, or "Quality Unit Amplifier Domestic," into the depths of the Cavern. A musician in his own right, Jefferson had been working with Adrian Barber, the amp's designer and the lead guitarist for the popular Liverpool quartet Cass and the Cassanovas, and his own father, a retired ship's captain and self-taught engineer, to build the amp's cabinetry. With its immense fifteen-inch, thirty-watt speaker, Jefferson proclaimed it "the loudest amp in Liverpool." And at more than five feet tall, it was also the heaviest. Painted a distinctive black, the amp became known as "the Coffin."

When Barber completed work on the Coffin, Paul was understandably eager to try out the powerful amp in conjunction with his Höfner violin bass. Jefferson would later remember looking on in amazement as Mal single-handedly lifted the massive speaker cabinet, carted it across Mathew

Street, and deposited it onto the Cavern's stage.[43] During performances, the Coffin's pounding sound was so relentless that it succeeded in loosening the calcium deposits inside the club's brickwork, which the Beatles christened "Liverpool dandruff" as it rained down on audience members' heads.[44]

To Mal's great satisfaction, George had been spot-on about the value he would glean from working as a bouncer. Mal remembered his time at the door as "fabulous, giving you the chance to get to know all the musicians because we often helped them hump their gear in and out of bandwagons."[45] And it was in precisely this capacity, as he was standing guard atop the Cavern steps, that Mal first met twenty-year-old Neil Aspinall. An accounting trainee who had left his job the previous July to work as the Beatles' full-time roadie, Neil was a hard-nosed, no-nonsense Liverpudlian. But even he couldn't help responding in kind to the friendly new face—the "gentle giant" who was now manning the Cavern door.[46]

04

ROADIE?

Mal's turn as a professional bouncer wasn't entirely trouble-free. The Cavern took on an edgy quality at night, when the kids, clerks, and secretaries of lunchtime gave way to the blue-collar set. One evening in the summer months of 1962, Mal was accosted by a drunk outside the Cavern. The old sot landed a solid punch to his jaw, dislodging a tooth. And while Mal, self-described "ardent coward" that he was, opted not to respond in kind, the drunkard held little hope of making his way past the imposing bouncer and into the basement club. Mal stood his ground.

As the year went on, Mal's bouncing opportunities grew beyond the Cavern's clammy confines, largely thanks to Brian Epstein, who was devoting all his energy to making the Beatles a success. There had been stumbling blocks, to be sure—most notably, the band's rejection by Decca Records earlier in the year. But such setbacks only steeled Brian's determination more, and he booked the band into as many gigs as they could possibly perform. On several occasions, they would climb into Neil's gray-and-maroon Commer van and drive from one club or dance hall to another, doing sometimes as many as three gigs in a single evening. Back in April, Brian had even succeeded in adding a mighty dose of class to the Beatles' act when he convinced them to trade in their leathers for suits. In May, he scored a bona fide record deal with EMI's Parlophone label, and the band's debut recording session was slated for June 6, with thirty-six-year-old A&R (Artists and Repertoire) man George Martin.

With so much effort being accorded to the Beatles, Brian had begun assembling his team at a steady pace. He invited Mal to serve as head bouncer for NEMS Enterprises, the business that Epstein had orchestrated to oversee the band's interests. That July, seventeen-year-old Freda Kelly, a Cavern regular, joined secretary Beryl Adams to handle NEMS's growing workload. Meanwhile, Brian hired sixteen-year-old Tony Bramwell to serve as his assistant.

For Mal, acting as head bouncer meant working as the Beatles' bodyguard. As with his part-time job at the Cavern, not to mention his continued employment at the GPO, he enjoyed dressing to the nines and assuming his role as a quiet, even dignified professional. Working for NEMS allowed Mal to further supplement his young family's income, but the implications of his increasing duties were not lost on Lily, who was disappointed by her husband's absence from home both day and night. Still, Mal would occasionally enjoy a rare and much welcomed day off.

That July, he and his family attended the celebration of the "Wavertree Mystery," an annual event held to commemorate the anonymous donation of a beloved local playground back in 1895. Mal later recalled that "Lil and I were proudly pushing Gary in his pram when she turned to me and said, 'There's a weird guy over there—keeps staring at us. Now he looks like a real Cavernite to me.' On turning, I was to see Paul standing there, unshaven, with a denim jacket thrown over his shoulder and chewing on a toffee apple." After engaging in the niceties of introducing his wife to the scruffy musician, Mal took Paul for a jaunt. "We spent the rest of the day together," Mal wrote, "Paul and I daring each other to go on things like the parachute drop and other displays that took nerve, neither of us accepting the challenge." At one point, they stopped in front of an automobile exhibition. Paul announced to Mal that "'one of these days I'm going to own one of those cars,' pointing to one very humble saloon [sedan] type car."[1]

Mal made it up to Lily a few weeks later, when they attended the "Riverboat Shuffle," a package tour that Cavern owner Ray McFall had booked aboard the MV *Royal Iris*. A three-hour voyage along the Mersey River, the show was headlined by Johnny Kidd and the Pirates, with the Beatles playing second on the bill, followed by a Manchester act, Pete MacLaine and the Dakotas. Known as the "fish and chip boat" for its greasy cuisine, the ferry was not for the squeamish. Bramwell would never forget "those hot summer nights when we hit the choppy cross-currents of the Irish Sea. Everybody would be dancing away in a frenzy, the band would be playing—looking green—and the first passengers would be off to throw up in the gullies. A few minutes later, they'd be lurching about almost upright again, grinning at their heroism, swigging beer, and ready to heave again."[2]

That night before the Beatles' riverboat performance, George invited Mal to "come down and see us in the dressing room."[3] After the show, Mal took the guitarist up on his offer and introduced Lily to the rest of the band, whom, save for Paul, she was meeting for the first time. "On this occasion," Mal later recalled, "Lil and I bought the fish and chips for the group and ourselves, as they could only muster enough money between them to pay for the teas."[4] Although she had her misgivings about Mal's part-time bouncing efforts, Lily enjoyed getting to know the bandmates. "After gigs," she later recalled, "George would come back to our house for bacon and eggs. He sometimes came back before Mal to keep me company. I'd be washing baby clothes and nappies or ironing. I liked him the best." Lily fondly remembered the time she pushed the bangs from Harrison's face, saying, "Let's see what it looks like with your hair back. I like that better." But George wasn't having it. He combed his hair forward, telling her, "That's the way I have to wear it; it's the Beatle cut."[5]

By this juncture, Mal moved easily inside the Beatles' orbit, a seemingly tight-knit circle that included the Beatles themselves—John, Paul, George, and Pete—Brian, and, of course, Neil, who had been working with the boys since February 1961. In truth, Neil had known them, at least individually, much longer.

As with Mal's family, the Aspinalls had fled the Liverpool air raids for safer pastures in North Wales. Neil was born in October 1941 in Prestatyn, "Fishy Fred" Evans's former fishing grounds, while his father was at sea with the Royal Navy. In 1950s Liverpool, twelve-year-old Neil attended English and art classes with Paul at the Liverpool Institute. During this same period, he met George behind the institute's air-raid shelters, where they shared cigarettes. Not long afterward, Neil came into John's orbit while the older boy was attending the Liverpool College of Art. After scuttling his career in accountancy, Neil had begun ferrying the Beatles around in his old Commer van, license number 208 UFM, charging them five shillings per gig. And while he was tall and lank in comparison to Mal's even taller, sturdier build, Neil was no slouch. As a student of martial arts, he could hold his own with the best of them.

With Mal working in his part-time capacity as the band's bodyguard, Neil had not only gained a "good friend," but also a fellow traveler to negotiate the daily goings-on in the Beatles' increasingly complex lives as novice rock 'n' rollers. For example, "if we had any special friends we wanted to get into the Cavern when the Beatles were on, we'd just tell them to ask for Mal on the door, and he'd fix them up," Neil recalled.[6] As for Neil, he had already proven himself an invaluable asset for the band members. Back in those days, "Neil had to do everything," George later remarked. "It was hard, organizing all the equipment; although there wasn't much—just a drum-kit and three amplifiers. But there was still quite a lot to get in and out. Packing up, Neil would have to get the equipment, carry some out, open the van, put it in the van and then lock the van so it wouldn't get stolen; and then go back in, get the next bit and come back out, open the van, put it in, lock it again."[7]

As Mal and Neil were shortly to discover, the onerousness of their duties—standing guard as head bouncer and managing the band's equipment, respectively—was the least of their concerns. On August 16, Pete Best was dismissed from the band after two years of service and subsequently replaced by veteran Liverpool drummer Ringo Starr, formerly of Rory Storm and the Hurricanes. Pete simply hadn't seen it coming, nor had Mal and Neil. For the Beatles' roadie, the dismissal amounted to a personal body blow. Pete was Neil's best mate, for one thing. Also, only a few weeks earlier, Pete's mother, Mona, had given birth to Neil's son, Roag, whom the two had conceived in the Bests' West Derby home above the Casbah Coffee Club.

Given Neil's close, albeit scandalous, ties with Pete's family, Brian and the Beatles were understandably concerned about their roadie's loyalties. But in truth, their worries were for naught. As Neil later recalled, "When Pete was sacked, he wanted to drink with me all through the afternoon, but I said, 'No, I have to drive the van tonight.' He said, 'But I've just been sacked!' and I said, 'You've been sacked, Pete, I haven't been sacked. I've still got a job to do.'" A professional to the core, Neil had no intention of shirking his duties. The Beatles promptly rewarded him with a raise, increasing his weekly wage to £10.[8]

As with the other Cave Dwellers, Mal was uncertain of the reasons behind Pete's dismissal, relying on the rumor mill to satisfy his curiosity.

Bobby Brown attributed Pete's sacking to his dour demeanor, pointing out that in contrast with Ringo, "Pete never smiled."[9] To Mal, Pete's moodiness made for a flimsy pretense for his firing, and he would soon learn that he had been correct in his doubts. The seeds of Pete's demise had been sown back in June, when George Martin expressed displeasure to Brian over the drummer's musical abilities. With an honest-to-goodness EMI contract in hand, the other Beatles simply couldn't risk their future on a middling drummer whom, truth be told, they didn't much like anyway.

Mal would never forget the night Ringo made his Cavern debut. It was Sunday, August 19, 1962, and he was working double duty manning the door and serving as the Beatles' bodyguard, although he fell considerably short in the latter capacity. From the outset, the evening was fraught. "I was on duty in the Cavern the first night Ringo drummed as a Beatle," he later recalled. "Feelings ran high, and the many Pete Best supporters took exception to the change." Cave Dwellers would remember the sight of girls sobbing in Mathew Street over Pete's dismissal, while others chanted, "Pete forever, Ringo never!" Afterward, George—as one of Ringo's strongest supporters—received a bloody nose during a scrape that occurred outside Mal's sphere of protection.[10]

Mal wasn't on hand a few days later, when George suffered yet another injury. Dave Dover, a loyal Cavernite, witnessed the mayhem that continued to unfold over Pete's sacking during a Granada Television shoot at the basement club. "Ringo was looking sheepish," he recalled, "and McCartney was doing his usual, hands in the air, sorry, but trying to be diplomatic. Lennon couldn't care less, but George Harrison was being sarcastic, so he got thumped as he came out for the break by Mickey Flynn," receiving a black eye to go along with the guitarist's wounded nose.[11]

In retrospect, Mal recognized the wisdom inherent in Ringo's addition to the band. He had heard Pete's lapses with his own ears, especially the former drummer's penchant for losing tempo at times. To Mal's mind, Ringo represented a certain quality that the Beatles had hitherto lacked: "He was the final ingredient to the cake," Mal later wrote.[12] And the proof was in the pudding: that fall, the Beatles' debut single, "Love Me Do," notched a Top 20 showing on the U.K. charts, a clear sign of better things to come.

Mal's opportunities to work with the Beatles in his capacity as head bouncer were naturally limited by the constraints of his GPO obligations. For the most part, he could travel with Neil and the boys only on weekends, often pitching in to help Neil out with the gear. On Saturday, September 29, he joined them for an evening gig at Manchester's Oasis Club, riding over in the Ford Thames van, which he had loaded with their equipment. Things came to a head that night when Neil prepared to set up their gear, suddenly realizing that Mal, in his haste, had left the Beatles' microphones back in Liverpool. With no time to spare, Mal called Barratts, a local music store, getting in touch with Brian Higham.

By this point, Mal was in a full-blown panic, not wanting to disappoint Neil and the band. In short order, Higham carted three late-model Reslo directional microphones, along with a trio of Valan mic stands, over to the Oasis. "As soon as I arrived outside the club," Higham recalled, "waiting for me was a very relieved Mal Evans." After Higham set up the mics, he watched as "Paul pushed his and George's mics together like as if they were one. I looked at Mal; he looked at me and said that that was the way they like it, and so it was. With Ringo perched on his drum kit, they did a bit of 'Some Other Guy,' 'I Saw Her Standing There,' and one or two others I can't remember."[13]

Mal's tenure as head bouncer would simultaneously reach its zenith and its nadir on October 12, 1962, when he met Little Richard, who was headlining a twelve-act show at the New Brighton Tower Ballroom, across the Wirral. "Being head bouncer had its own privileges," he later recalled, "and the uniform of black Dickey bow [bowtie] and dark suit gave me access to all the dressing rooms." With the Beatles performing in a supporting role, Mal enjoyed the chance to meet the American star, who was supported in the five-thousand-seat venue by a full band, including sixteen-year-old organist Billy Preston. Mal got the requisite autograph and later recalled that "Little Richard was a real delight, fervently shaking my hand, wishing me much love and happiness."[14]

And that's when things started to get dicey. As he left Little Richard's dressing room, the New Brighton Tower Ballroom's security team informed Mal that a fight was imminent. "So, striding manfully into the crowded ballroom," he wrote, "I stepped in between two young lads squaring up at each other, glaring and threatening to kill each other." As he sized up the situation, Mal noticed that some three-dozen friends of the combatants had arrayed behind them.

Adopting a "placating" tone, Mal said, "Look lads, we don't want any trouble, do we?"

Suddenly, things became even more heated. "The 20 friends standing behind the guy on my right joined with the 20-odd friends behind the guy on my left in muttering threats against my person," Mal later wrote. Realizing that there wasn't another "Dickey bow in sight," he adopted his "ardent coward" persona and beat a hasty retreat.[15] A few months later, after witnessing a beer-fueled skirmish outside the Cavern, Mal registered his ever-growing doubts about his fitness for the role Brian had assigned him: "Am I forceful enough for a bouncer?"[16]

On a personal level, Mal couldn't imagine being happier—his family life was exceeding expectations, and in stark contrast with the latter half of 1962, his work-life balance had begun to improve precipitously. On January 1, 1963, he put pen to paper, writing in his new Post Office Engineering Union diary that 1962 had been "a wonderful year." After all, he had been blessed with a "beautiful wife" in Lily and a beloved son in Gary, along with a house and a car to boot. They had even added a puppy to the family ménage. Rescued by Lily from a medical lab, "Lady" was a beagle cross who, like her adult owners, adored Gary, having taken to sleeping beside him in his pram. Yes, Mal was elated, all right. "Guess I was born with a silver canteen of cutlery in my mouth," he scrawled in his diary. "Wanted a part-time job for a long time—now bouncing—not too often in 1963, I hope."[17] As events would come to show, Mal would be correct on one account: he certainly wouldn't be working as a bouncer as much in 1963.

Mal had begun compiling his diary as a means of tracing fifteen-month-old Gary's growth and development. As his firstborn child, Gary had emerged as an endless source of fascination for Mal, who had taken to referring to him as "Boss," for the manner in which the baby lorded over Mal's and Lily's lives. Mal, in particular, was besotted with him, narrating his every milestone—from early January, when the toddler was "crawling everywhere," to April 6, when he could not only walk unaided, but also march up and down the stairs, which he did seven times in a row. There were harrowing moments, too—such as the time, on April 2, when Gary managed to lock Lily out of their Mossley Hill house, requiring Mal to dash home to the rescue.[18]

As the New Year progressed, Mal spent plenty of time at the Cavern, just as often to take in a show with Lily as to stand guard at the door. In January, he even managed to carve out time to see Elvis's latest flick, *Kid Galahad*, at the Odeon. He simply could not get enough of the King. His and Lily's niece Shan recalled sitting in the front parlor with her uncle and spinning Elvis records, especially "Angel," her favorite Elvis tune, which she would beg him to play over and over again.[19] During this period, and with his newfound optimism in full bloom, Mal fulfilled a long-held ambition and enlisted in the Royal Army Emergency Reserve, more commonly known, in those days, as the Territorial Army. Still smarting over his rejection by the Medical Review Board back in 1953, Mal had been determined to correct what he perceived as an affront to his character, if not his manhood. With Lily's indefatigable support, he looked forward to undertaking a two-year stint with the army reserve, especially buoyed by the notion of proudly donning a military uniform in service to his country.

On the weekend of April 6, 1963—as the Beatles played a show at Buxton's Pavilion Gardens Ballroom—Mal made the long drive from Liverpool down to Bournemouth, on the southern coast of England, where he joined the other new recruits. Basic training was everything he hoped for and more. On that very first weekend alone, he learned mouth-to-mouth resuscitation while relishing lectures on first aid and, his favorite, map reading. He spent the evening getting to know the other recruits, who, like him, were well lubricated at the local pub. The next day, Palm Sunday, Mal started weapons training, fulfilling his every childhood gunslinging fantasy. The day was highlighted by the opportunity to fire a World War II–era Sterling submachine gun. For Mal, the whole weekend was a dream come true, and he happily accepted his army pay, which amounted to slightly more than two pounds.[20] Sure, it wasn't much, but he was grateful for everything he had.

And he was ecstatic about the Beatles' recent spate of successes. His efforts at road-managing the band during the weekend of the windscreen incident in late January had paid off handsomely. On February 22, "Please Please Me" topped the charts. It was a truly incredible moment: A band from the North had seemingly done the impossible. A regional act had beaten the odds and become a national sensation. Neil must have been beside himself, shuffling like a madman from one ballroom to another and then squeezing in a day trip to London to boot. Mal had worked dozens of Cavern gigs in the interim. He'd even driven the van up to Sunderland, so the Beatles could take a break from their first national tour (headlined by sixteen-year-old pop phenom Helen Shapiro) to record their debut album in London—all in the space of a single day, no less—with George Martin at the helm.

Mal knew full well that he had played a small yet meaningful role in the Beatles' good fortune. The windscreen incident had made for a bonding moment, to be sure. On a personal note, their breakneck London trip had already paid dividends. Thanks to the incident with the Ford van, Mal knew a handy auto shop for windscreen replacement. On March 19, he saw a repeat of the events of January 23—save for the nightmarish winter conditions—when a stone grazed the windscreen of the family car, setting him back six pounds. And while he deployed his outsize physique as the Beatles' bodyguard—in those days, mostly in Liverpool, that is—he was always careful to make his exit before any actual scrapes commenced. That spring, he had even skirted the GPO's stringent regulations when one of the Beatles' amps failed during a lunchtime gig at the Cavern. Not missing a beat, Mal rushed the malfunctioning amp over to Lancaster House, where he and a tech colleague repaired it "on GPO property, with GPO equipment, and on GPO time!"[21] Years later, Ringo would comment on the spectacle of seeing Mal single-handedly picking up the Coffin for the first time. "He was pretty strong," the drummer recalled. "He could lift the bass amp on his own, which was a miracle. He should have been in the circus."[22]

As the weeks wore on, and the music business took the Beatles farther and farther afield from Liverpool, Mal acted as bodyguard for other bands in Epstein's growing stable of acts, including the Merseybeats and Gerry and the Pacemakers. Founded by Gerry Marsden back in 1956, the Pacemakers were hot on the Beatles' tail during this period, with a new single, the Mitch Murray–penned "How Do You Do It," soaring to the top of the charts. Mal was excited by their success, and by the increasingly raucous crowds they were attracting at the Cavern. Fortunately for him, Gerry and the Pacemakers' fan base was largely well behaved.

On April 9, Mal enjoyed an evening at home with Lily and the baby, watching excitedly as little Gary danced to the Beatles' latest single, "From Me to You," which debuted on the children's television program *Tuesday Rendezvous*.[23] Not long afterward, Mal passed an unforgettable Sunday of target practice at Liverpool's Altcar Training Camp.

Located in Hightown, on the far northern end of Merseyside, the 620-acre military installation was a regular outpost for Emergency Reserve recruits as they conducted basic training. For Mal, the shooting range was a dream come true. Firing an L1A1 Self-Loading Rifle under "wet and windy" conditions, he notched eighteen out of twenty bull's-eyes with five-round magazines, followed by twenty-eight out of forty bull's-eyes with the more arduous ten-round magazines. As with his first stint with the Territorials, Mal enjoyed the fellowship almost as much as the military training. Afterward, he knocked back several convivial pints with the Altcar staff before making the drive back to Mossley Hill.[24]

On May 4, working at the Cavern paid off yet again for Mal. That weekend, ABC-TV filmed two different television specials at the club, which had quickly become one of the country's hottest venues thanks to the recent chart-toppers by the Beatles and Gerry and the Pacemakers. That Saturday, Mal observed the proceedings as the network prerecorded the next installment of *Rave Wave*, with appearances by the Silhouettes, the American R&B group that, in 1958, had topped the hit parade with "Get a Job," and Johnny Sandon and the Remo Four, the latest Merseyside sensation. The next afternoon, the Cavern served as the setting for ABC's *Sunday Break*, a religious-oriented program with a vast and varied roster of performers that included the Epstein-managed Merseybeats and Tommy Quickly and the Challengers.[25]

In his diary, Mal excitedly reported that his image would appear on *Rave Wave* no fewer than three times—and on national television, no less. By contrast, while noting that the *Sunday Break* live broadcast had been nothing short of "terrific," especially the performance by the Dennisons, a local Beat group, he lamented the fact that he didn't appear in any of the footage. "I was not on" *Sunday Break*, he tersely added, but "could have been!"[26]

Mal's weekend under television's bright lights was a revelation, underscoring an aspect of himself he had discovered after his snow-addled trek to London with the boys back in January. For him, the most "incredible" facet of his life in the Beatles' orbit—a life that allowed him to enjoy a "taste of show business" from a front-row seat—confirmed "all the secret longings I'd had."[27] From his earliest years through the present, though he struggled at times with a debilitating shyness and social awkwardness, Mal, in his private thoughts, clearly yearned to be a star in his own right. But if he couldn't make it happen on his own, he'd be content to do it by proxy—just as he did on May 19, when he met American rocker Gene Vincent at the Cavern Club. For Mal, the show was "nothing spectacular"; meeting the musician was his primary ambition. He had even purchased a new autograph book for the occasion.[28]

That same month, he and Lily began plotting their inaugural family vacation with Gary. By virtue of his position with the GPO, Mal was allotted an annual two-week leave, which the Evanses planned to spend, perhaps ill-advisedly from a financial perspective, in the Cornish seaside town of St. Ives. Despite holding down a full-time job and working, on average, three nights a week at the Cavern, Mal was "down in the dumps" over his lingering money problems.[29] Even so, he and Lil had plenty of time, despite their economic issues, to go to the local cinema, where they saw Elvis's movie musicals *Girls! Girls! Girls!* and *It Happened at the World's Fair*, as well as the religious epic *Barabbas* in a revival at the Gaumont.

As Mal toiled to make ends meet, Neil became single-handedly responsible for loading and unloading the Beatles' equipment. Then things went from bad to worse, when Johnny Clapson, the tour manager, informed Neil that he'd have to look after the lights, too. By the end of their third national tour, a late spring/early summer jaunt with Roy Orbison as the headliner, with the Beatles and Gerry and the Pacemakers in supporting roles, Neil was beginning to feel the effects of his breakneck job in profound, and potentially dangerous, ways. "My weight went down to about eight stone [about 112 pounds]," he joked, "and I told Brian I needed somebody to help."[30]

During the Orbison tour, the Beatles' popularity had soared, and by early June, when the tour concluded, they had replaced the American star as the headlining act. As far as Neil was concerned, something had to give.

Later that summer, when the Beatles shared a residency with Gerry and the Pacemakers at Weston-super-Mare's Odeon Cinema, Neil simply couldn't take it anymore. He pointed out that Gerry and the Pacemakers had two roadies—"One to look after the boys themselves and another to look after the gear. When am I going to get someone else?" he demanded.[31]

As it turned out, Brian had already been working the problem—and likely as early as the first week of July. In the intervening years, a folklore has emerged over Epstein's selection of Neil's counterpart in the Beatles' entourage. Epstein's assistant, Tony Bramwell, then seventeen, would later suggest that *he* was originally considered for the role, but was overlooked for the simple reason that he didn't hold a driver's license. That summer, Tony had joined Neil in the van on several occasions, often taking responsibility for setting up the instruments while Neil tackled his mounting roster of duties.[32]

Wallace Booth, the part-time Cavern bouncer and future Olympian, would claim that he had been tapped by Brian to assume the role, but in Neil's memory, Mal was the natural candidate all along.[33] On July 4, Brian requested that Mal join him at his Whitechapel offices, where he offered him the job. Mal chalked up the opportunity before him to the fact that he had "delivered the van back to Neil with a new windscreen after our eventful journey to London." Likely motivated by his recent financial woes, he asked for £25 per week, a tidy sum in comparison to his current £15 wage from the GPO.[34] His new wage would net him an annual salary of £1,300 (£22,152 in present-day pounds), in comparison with the average Briton's 1963 take-home pay of £824 per annum.[35] While Brian may have bristled at the sum—it would necessitate raising Neil's wages to maintain parity among his road team—he must not have argued too vehemently. The next day, Mal went to Lancaster House, where he approached the GPO's Gordon Gaskell about the possibility of taking a leave of absence.[36]

While Gaskell had become a much-beloved friend for Mal—and the feeling had been mutual—he likely gave the idea a chilly reception. Indeed, Mal soon discovered that the GPO's administration harbored serious concerns about the quality of his work performance. It surely hadn't been lost on Mal's supervisors that he had been taking increasingly longer lunches at the Cavern, often putting in only a few hours of work afterward before calling it quits for the day.

Mal also sought advice from Billy Maher, who recognized that "it was a big deal to give up a steady daytime job." But for Billy, the decision was simple: "Mal never had the qualifications to move up a grade, so my feelings were that he should join [the Beatles]." Besides, working with the band might afford Mal "an exciting life of music, laughter and adventure."[37]

Although Mal had made up his mind the instant Brian asked him to serve as the Beatles' full-time roadie, he must have recognized the inherent challenge of convincing Lily, not to mention his parents and sisters, of the wisdom of joining the entourage of a Beat band that would, in all likelihood, be yesterday's news by Christmas. Flipping open his diary to the "Notes" section, he began compiling a crude list of pros and cons, as if the choice could be made merely by weight of enumeration: "Job for future. Pay. Holidays. Pension. Time away from home. Army for two years."[38] It was a daunting list, to be sure, and one that seemed not to promise any upside.

In Lily's memory, Brian's job offer was an agonizing prospect for her husband. "He had a lot of sleepless nights, wondering if he should go on with them," she recalled. "I didn't want him to. I told him, 'You're a person in your own right—you don't need to follow others.' But he was starstruck."[39] When her arguments didn't make so much as a dent in Mal's state of mind, Lily changed tack, already resigned to the outcome: "It's right for you," she told him, "but it isn't right for me. I am going to be left alone a lot."[40]

On July 13, Mal and Lily left Liverpool to begin their seaside holiday with Gary in St. Ives. Mal would recall the two-week vacation with great joy, remembering the simple pleasure of watching Gary eat his first ice-cream

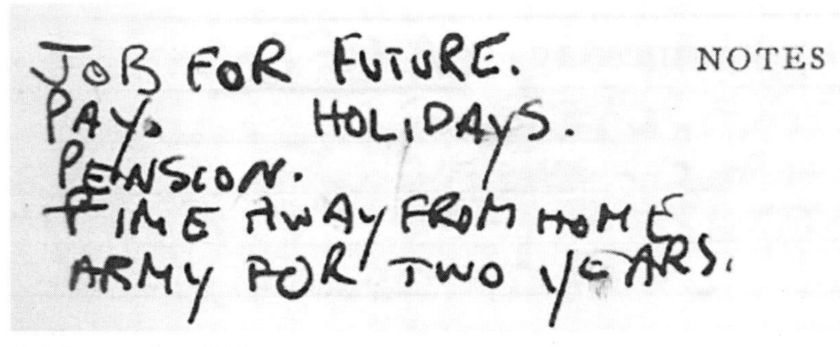

Mal's "pros and cons" list

cone, soaking up the sun on Chapel Porth Beach, and shopping with Lil in Falmouth. Even so, his decision must have weighed heavily on their minds, particularly the prospect of informing Fred and Joan when they returned to Liverpool. When the moment finally came, Lily stood quietly by her husband. Years later, Fred would write that "we were rather dismayed at first when he packed everything up for them."[41]

According to Mal's sister June, Fred's recollection was an understatement of the highest order. In truth, everything went "apeshit" when Mal told Fred and Joan the news.[42] For Joan, the notion that her son was considering such a momentous, even reckless decision must have confirmed her worst suspicions about his level of maturity. As with their parents, Mal's sisters were gobsmacked by the idea that their brother would so easily give up the security of a respectable job and a pension.

But Mal just stood there, quietly taking the blows. Buoyed by Lily's unwavering support, he was resolute in the decision that would change all their lives.

05

A FREE MAN

And so it was that on Wednesday, July 31, 1963, twenty-eight-year-old Mal Evans informed the GPO that he was calling it quits. A few days later, he made it irrevocable when he signed the "Official Secrets Act Declaration," affirming, under threat of prosecution, that when it came to any sensitive information or material he had encountered during his employment, he would maintain his discretion in perpetuity. There was no going back now.

On Sunday, August 11, Mal made the forty-minute drive from Mossley Hill to Manchester Airport, where the Beatles were set to arrive after fulfill-

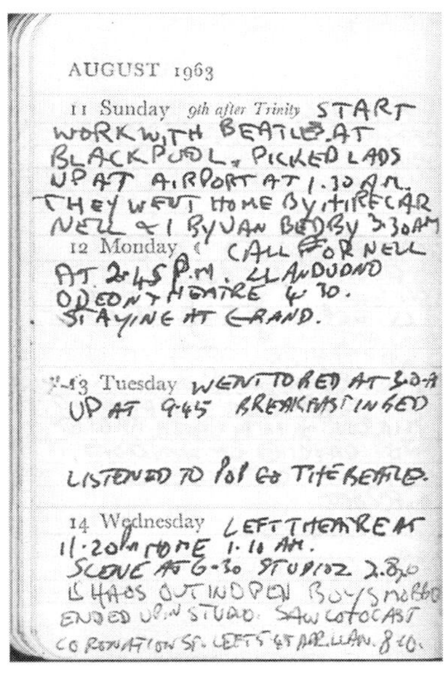

AUGUST 1963

11 Sunday *9th after Trinity* START WORK WITH BEATLES AT BLACKPOOL. PICKED LADS UP AT AIRPORT AT 1.30 A.M. THEY WENT HOME BY HIRE CAR NELL & I BY VAN BED BY 3.30 AM

12 Monday CALL FOR NELL AT 2.45 P.M. LLANDUDNO ODEON THEATRE 4.30. STAYING AT GRAND.

13 Tuesday WENT TO BED AT 3.0 A UP AT 9.45 BREAKFAST IN BED

LISTENED TO [illegible] THE BEATLES.

14 Wednesday LEFT THEATRE AT 11.20 HOME 1.10 AM. SCENE AT 6.30 STUDIO 2 [illegible] CHAOS OUT IN OPEN BOYS MOBBED ENDED UP IN STUDIO. SAW CO[illegible] CAST CORONATION ST. LEFT [illegible] 8.40.

Mal's diary entry from his first day with the Beatles

ing a quartet of gigs on Jersey, in the Channel Islands. He was determined not only to excel in this new role, but to honor Lily, who, despite her misgivings, "never once stood in my way, knowing that I always had been yearning to be in show business, to be an entertainer, and road manager for the Beatles was, for me, the next best thing." He later recalled being awash in nerves as he awaited his new employers' arrival. Then, suddenly, there they were—John, Paul, George, and Ringo—and "all my fears were dispelled when the four of them greeted me with smiles, saying, 'nice to have you with us.'"[1] Not long afterwards, Pete Best learned the news that Mal had joined the band's entourage on a full-time basis. While he was still smarting over his dismissal from the Beatles' ranks, he felt nothing but elation over Mal's good fortune. "I was happy for him when he hooked up with the boys and started traveling with them," said Pete. "Couldn't have happened to a nicer guy."[2]

To a man, all the Beatles understood implicitly the gravity of the decision Mal had just made. Each of them had been chastened, if not outright chastised, by all manner of friends and relations, parents, girlfriends, and the like, about the madness of taking a risk on a rock 'n' roll group. But for Mal, given his status as a family man, the decision had come with even greater risk, with much higher stakes, and with Lily and Gary's well-being hanging in the balance. Only Brian Epstein's gamble had come closest to Mal's.

Epstein's parents, Harry and Queenie, held deep concerns about their son throwing in his lot with a group of Liverpool ruffians, on the one hand, and neglecting his duties on behalf of the family's music stores, on the other. While his father had been "infuriated" by Brian's ambitions for the Beatles, his parents knew that Brian was driven by a desire to be the best, that he would not accept a second-place showing to anyone for his clients.[3] It was not any different from his insisting that the Beatles and the other acts in his stable wear suits. For Brian, it came down to managing the quality of his organization's reputation by dint of public perception.

During his first gig as road manager, an evening show at Blackpool's ABC Theatre, Mal wore a suit at Brian's direction, with the expense deducted from his wages. From that very first day, he realized that part-time bouncing and serving as the Beatles' full-time roadie were two vastly different experiences. For one thing, the Cavern was already in the band's rearview mirror. A week earlier, on August 3, they had played their 292nd and final show on the club's basement stage, which they had outgrown in more ways than one. As compère Bob Wooler later recalled, "We all felt it was their swan song and that we would never have them at the Cavern again."[4] Mal was there, too, acting as the band's protector, staving off the encroaching fans while suffering under an ungodly heat, both from the weather and the intense pressure of the crowd.

After joining Neil and the Beatles in Manchester, Mal routinely didn't get to bed until 3:30 a.m., only to be awakened by a 9:45 a.m. call. Years later, he reflected on his first few weeks in the Beatles' employ—like Neil, he was truly in *their* express employment, never working for NEMS or under the jurisdiction of any record company. In those days, his overriding concern was being cut loose for sheer incompetence. Being on call both day and night was one of the band's unstated requirements. "I was still green at the job of roadie, and the Beatles had been very tolerant with the mistakes I made while settling in and learning my new trade," Mal wrote. "Mind you, in the first week I worked with them, I was to be fired about seven times, as first one thing then the other went wrong."[5]

First, there was the matter of setting up Ringo's drum set, which Mal had never seen up close before. "Neil helped me the first couple of days, but the first time I was on my own was terrible," he wrote. In desperation, he asked another band's drummer to help out, only to belatedly "realize each drummer likes his cymbals at a special height."[6] On one occasion, during this initial spate of shows, Ringo's cymbals slid down to the stage, while during another, his bass drum simply toppled over mid-performance. In such moments, Mal stood in the wings as the mishaps mounted up, wondering if he'd just put in his last night as the Beatles' roadie. At one point, Paul asked him what he would do if they actually fired him. "I'd cry, Paul. I'd just cry," he replied.[7]

Mal finally learned how to properly set up and dismantle Ringo's drum kit courtesy of twenty-three-year-old Derek Hughes, the roadie for Billy J. Kramer and the Dakotas, who were also on the bill when the Beatles played Llandudno, a town in Wales. "He hadn't the vaguest idea how to go about setting up the drum kit," Hughes recalled. "I spent the next two days building the drum kit up and stripping it down, building it up and stripping it down, and showing him how to do it."[8]

The band's brief residency in Wales was a pressure cooker for Mal, given that their *Twist and Shout* EP had earned a Silver Disc Award for notching sales of more than 250,000 copies, and the cinema was packed to the gills. Neil was simply relieved that the Beatles' operation was finally catching up with that for Gerry and the Pacemakers and that there was finally a proper distribution of duties: "Mal started driving the van and looking after all the equipment and the stage-clothes," Aspinall recalled, "while I tended to look after the Beatles and the press and other people in our lives."[9]

Cynthia Lennon remembered things slightly differently. Married to John since August 1962, she recalled that the plan was for Mal to handle "all the transporting of their equipment, the setting up and dismantling at concerts, while Neil looked after their personal needs for transport, food and so on. At least, that was the theory, but in practice," she added, "they both did anything and everything that needed doing, from getting the Beatles safely onto a plane to finding sandwiches when they felt peckish."[10]

The vagaries of life on the road with the Beatles were complicated by the fact that the boys simply didn't like to be handled, an aspect of their jobs that forced Mal and Neil to walk a fine line. "The Beatles aren't boys who are used to servants," Neil pointed out. "They hang up their clothes, do their personal packing, shine their own shoes, and such. Frankly they'd much rather do it themselves than have someone hovering all about them, waiting on them."[11] And then there was Neil himself, who expected Mal not only to drive the van, but also to maintain a steady pace. A preternaturally deliberate, even plodding sort, Mal was typically content to drive within the posted speed limit. During their very next trip, which entailed a weeklong residency in Bournemouth, Neil took issue with the new roadie's driving, saying, "Come on, Mal, put your foot down, we've got a show to get to."[12] Mal took Neil's advice to heart. By late August, he had earned a warning for a busted taillight, and on August 29, he received his first speeding ticket in the Beatles' employ.

While Mal's peccadilloes as a new roadie hardly ended with his difficulties with Ringo's drum kit or the occasional driving infraction, Neil and the boys were unfailingly impressed with his ability to lift the heavy amps—especially Paul's notorious "Coffin"—all by his lonesome. And as it turned out, he was able to put his unusual strength to good use in other ways. With Billy J. Kramer and the Dakotas sharing the bill with the Beatles in Bournemouth, Derek Hughes was on hand to see Mal save the day after John's cleverness nearly got the better of him. As it happened, the band's quarters in the seaside town were in the Palace Court Hotel, which, fortunately for the Beatles, was part of the same city block as the Gaumont Cinema. To reach the venue while avoiding fans, they need only climb the hotel's fire escape, walk across the roof, and then take another fire escape down into the Gaumont. "John got a bit fed up with doing this," Hughes recalled, "so he decides he's gonna get a disguise and go out through the front of the hotel and walk to the theater. He managed to get as far as the door to the Gaumont when somebody spotted him." To Hughes's amazement, "Mal just picked John up, threw him over his shoulder, and made a quick dash for the back of the stage. It was quite comical."[13]

During their stay in Bournemouth, Mal, Ringo, and a few of the Dakotas were invited to attend a party in town. Hughes later recalled making the drive into Bournemouth with Mal behind the wheel of the Ford. At the party, the group encountered "a load of Hooray Henrys, well-to-do young people—you know, educated and financially well off. And we're all public school boys." Hughes soon came to realize that "all they wanted us there for was to try and belittle us." Not surprisingly, a ruckus ensued, with Mal tossing one of the mouthy youths through a window.[14]

Mal's capacity for exuding grace under pressure would continue to serve him well. But as he soon discovered, he couldn't fake things with Lily. During his first fortnight on the road, he had failed to call or telephone home. By the time he returned to Mossley Hill on August 25, Lily was understandably furious. After supporting him in his decision to join the Beatles' team, she and Gary had been rewarded with neglect. When Mal crossed the threshold that day, Lily gathered up Gary and went to stay at the home of Mal's sister Barbara and her husband, Eric Hoyle. For nearly the entirety of his stay in Liverpool, with the Beatles in residency in nearby Southport, Lily kept her distance. She finally returned on August 30, having made a truce with her husband, on the condition that from that point forward, he write or call home every day.[15]

The next evening, Lily made a point of attending the Beatles' closing show at the Odeon Cinema. Writing in his diary, Mal reflected on his relief that the cold war at Mossley Hill had thawed. But Lily had made herself resoundingly clear about her expectations. To his credit, Mal redoubled his efforts, more often than not penning letters to his wife and, as his new life with the Beatles unfolded, regularly sending postcards to his parents from places near and wide.

While Mal had belatedly recognized the error of his ways, he also knew the source of his absentmindedness: he adored the freedom that his new life offered. He especially enjoyed the times when Neil and the boys traveled separately and he was alone in the van, transporting the Beatles' equipment on the open road. In short, having the balance of his time to do with as he chose allowed him to feel like "a free man."[16]

The Southport residency marked the final shows in which Neil assisted Mal in setting up the equipment. As with his first week in the Beatles' employ, Mal's most significant issues involved Ringo's drums. "I well remember the first night I was to be left on my own, with all of what seemed a million parts spread around the theatre stage," he observed. "Neil had let people help him, but I wouldn't. I wanted to do it all myself for several reasons. One being I knew exactly where I was up to at any time, the other because I was possessive of the Beatles, and didn't want to share them with anyone." But it was more than that. On one "disastrous" occasion, Mal had learned his lesson about working alone after accepting assistance from a local stagehand. By this point, Mal could strip down and pack up the drum kit in two minutes flat. Not wanting to reject the stagehand's kind offer, he asked the man to disassemble Ringo's drums for transport. Unfortunately, the stagehand took Mal's instructions far too precisely. "I turned around to be greeted with a pile of individual nuts and bolts and pieces of drum kit stacked all over the stage," Mal recalled. "The guy had literally taken it apart. After that, I really was on my own."[17]

With Neil tending directly to the Beatles' needs and assuming a more administrative role—just as he and Brian had originally planned—Mal developed a steady routine for handling the equipment responsibilities. On a typical show day, he would unload the gear at 3 p.m., which gave him plenty of time to set up and test out the guitars, amps, and drums. Later, the Beatles themselves would arrive, and Mal would join them for tea and sandwiches. "The last half hour before the show was taken up with getting stage suits ready, polishing boots," he wrote, "for one thing was for sure, I was very proud of my boys and wanted them to look their best, so no job was too menial to further this aim. In between shows, Neil and I would arrange for meals to be brought in, or I would go out and collect them. During this period, hanging shirts in boiler rooms to dry, for the Beatles always put their hearts and souls into a show and came off stage soaked with perspiration."[18]

During that last night in Southport, Lily was treated to one of the earliest live performances of "She Loves You," a new song in the Beatles' repertoire. Released as a single on August 23, the record had racked up a phenomenal five hundred thousand advance orders. Something was brewing in Mal's and the Beatles' world, something clearly of a different caliber than their earlier experiences on the hit parade with "Please Please Me" and "From Me to You." Back in Llandudno, Mal caught wind of fans checking into the Beatles' hotel on the off chance they might get to meet their idols. But this was only a taste of things to come. By the time the Beatles and their entourage made their way to Southport, Mal found himself walking the gauntlet of the growing and increasingly hysterical hordes of fans who congregated prior to each show. For this reason, managing the Beatles' shows was becoming ever more difficult for local police forces as summer transitioned into fall.

As Mal soon discovered, the most pressing problems typically developed *after* the Beatles' performances, when the police often abandoned their posts after Neil had secreted the bandmates inside their lodgings. "But because the Beatles dropped their guitars and were on the road before the last chords had reached the balcony," Mal observed, "the audience would not believe they had left the building, hanging around for hours afterwards making the loading of the van extremely hazardous at times."[19]

Mal soon developed a system for bringing a gig to a close under such dire conditions: "I would carry one piece out, unlock the van, stow [it] in, lock the van, and it would take quite a long period of time. During this, I would be pushed and pulled, having the feeling that I was defending [the band's] equipment with my very life, ending up with my clothes covered in lipstick, for the fans had lovingly scrawled, 'I love you Paul, George, John, and Ringo' all over the van."[20] George later pointed out that the Ford van had increasingly become a liability: it was "the center of attention every time it pulled up. It was brush-painted in red and grey, and from head to foot was covered in graffiti." The van also presented an ongoing security problem, because "if anything was going to get nicked, it was obvious where it was kept."[21]

That September, the monthly fanzine *The Beatles Book* published an official welcome message for Mal, capturing both the necessity of his new role and the scope of the Beatles' fame at this juncture: "The Beatles have a permanent new roadie to complement the overworked but still cheerful Neil Aspinall. He's Mal Evans, who had taken over much of the responsibility for getting the Beatles and their instruments to the right place at the right time. Despite a run of number one singles, the boys are still a long way from Rolls-Royces and chauffeur-driven limousines!"[22]

06

THE BIG CLUBBO!

After barnstorming their way down to London, Mal and the Beatles arrived at 3 Abbey Road, the home of EMI Recording Studios. Fronted by a white-painted Georgian-era town house in tony St. John's Wood, the complex had opened in November 1931 and consisted of three studios constructed behind the original estate, which served as administrative quarters. The largest facility, Studio 1, could accommodate a full orchestra and chorus, with Studios 2 and 3 providing progressively smaller creative spaces.

Mal made his first visit to EMI Studios on Wednesday, September 11. Working with producer George Martin, the Beatles were in town to put the finishing touches on their second LP, *With the Beatles*. The band hadn't been to the studio since July 30, shortly after Mal and Lily returned from their holiday teetering on the precipice of a life-changing decision. Now, scarcely more than a month later, Mal was sitting in Studio 2—as a small mouse crept out of the shadows and gingerly played about his shoes—observing the Beatles record five new songs.[1]

The next day, Mal listened in as the Beatles recorded messages for Australian deejays in advance of a planned 1964 Oceanic tour. Brian had struck the deal with Australian promoters back in July, and Mal was positively chuffed. He had recently applied for and received his first passport—which listed his occupation as "road manager"—just in time for the Beatles' upcoming October 1963 Swedish tour. Mal had long fantasized about Scandinavian beauties and a progressive "free love" movement that was rumored to be launching Northern Europe into an uninhibited sexual frenzy. He simply couldn't wait. In the meantime, he was expected back in Bournemouth for the next installment of his military training.

As it turned out, he missed the morning train out of Liverpool, having arrived only a few hours earlier after ferrying the Beatles in the Ford van on their return trip from London. With Mal behind the wheel, they made the drive in just under five hours, including a stopover for a quick meal at the Blue Boar Inn, one of Mal's favorite haunts on the M5. Having caught a later train, he finally joined the other first-year Territorials in Bournemouth.

Yet, gone was Mal's overriding excitement for the soldiering life. The zeal for redemption he had nursed since being rejected by the Medical Board in 1953 had utterly dissipated. As the ensuing months mounted up, Mal ignored the Emergency Reserve's recurring reminders about his service commitment. Eventually, he was quietly discharged by the Territorials, having completed a grand total of three training sessions.

The next day, Mal left the Reserve back in Bournemouth, catching the first train to London, where, that night, the Beatles were headlining the Great Pop Prom, a benefit event for the Printers' Pension Corporation, held at the Royal Albert Hall. The boys, supported by up-and-comers the Rolling Stones, rocked the house to its foundations. Mal wouldn't have missed it for the world.

Although his life with the Beatles had been moving at a breakneck pace, he had managed to build in regular visits with Lily and Gary, and he showered his adoring wife with love letters when he couldn't be in Liverpool in person. Incredibly, the Beatles' tidal wave of fame was about to crest to even greater heights. On September 12, "She Loves You" vaulted to the top of the U.K. charts, setting a spate of sales records in the process and creating the conditions for one of the most remarkable moments in the history of the British Isles. And Mal Evans would be caught up in the center of the whirlwind.

As with the events that brought Mal and the Beatles to London during the Big Freeze, television would serve as ground zero for the momentous happenings of October 1963. With "She Loves You" burning up the charts, and the Great Pop Prom having added to their luster, the Beatles were slated to appear on the October 13 installment of Val Parnell's popular variety show, *Sunday Night at the London Palladium*. For the Beatles, the implications couldn't be clearer. Parnell's program was a national sensation, and the boys had been selected to play their set during the coveted second half

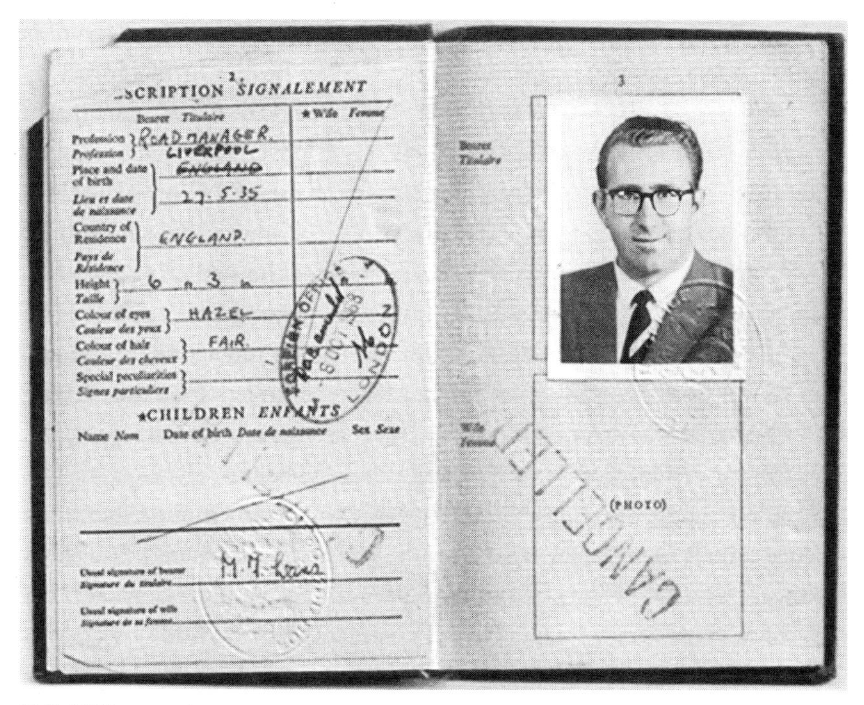
2
SCRIPTION SIGNALEMENT
Bearer Titulaire
Wife Femme
Profession Profession ROAD MANAGER.
Place and date of birth Lieu et date de naissance LIVERPOOL ~~ENGLAND~~ 27.5.35
Country of Residence Pays de Résidence ENGLAND.
Height Taille 6 ft 3 in
Colour of eyes Couleur des yeux HAZEL
Colour of hair Couleur des cheveux FAIR.
Special peculiarities Signes particuliers
CHILDREN ENFANTS
Name Nom Date of birth Date de naissance Sex Sexe
Usual signature of bearer Signature du titulaire M. M. Evans
Usual signature of wife Signature de sa femme
3
Bearer Titulaire
Wife Femme
(PHOTO)
CANCELLED

Mal's 1963 passport

of the show. As Mal later recalled, the Beatles "rehearsed and rehearsed" at the Donmar Theatre in advance of the program, determined to take full advantage of the opportunity that lay before them. For his part, Mal checked and rechecked the equipment before the evening's broadcast, while the "staff at the London Palladium bent over backwards to give me all the help I needed."[2]

At one point, Mal and Neil took a break to pick up sodas and hot dogs for the Beatles and their entourage from a Carnaby Street café. At the beginning of the day, a few hundred fans had begun to gather outside the Palladium. By the time Mal and Neil returned to the theater with the food, the crowd had swelled considerably. With fans mistaking the roadies for the Beatles themselves, the preshow excitement reached a fever pitch. "This is usually a problem," recalled Neil. "You see, I'm recognized by the fans as being with the Beatles. Before, I could go out unnoticed and get the car, and the boys would just troop in. Now I have to keep in the background, and the new road manager, Mal Evans, goes out for the car. It all has to be planned like a military operation."[3]

After the show, while Mal and the Beatles celebrated with friends and relations at the Grosvenor House Hotel, a mêlée erupted outside the Palladium as the crowd, numbering in the thousands, spilled into the streets. "Screaming girls launched themselves against the police—sending helmets flying and constables reeling," the *Daily Herald* reported.[4] As they would soon discover, the adulation was real. A national television audience of fifteen million viewers had seen the Beatles that night. The next morning, the band dominated the London headlines, with the *Daily Mirror* trumpeting "BEATLEMANIA!" on newsstands across the country. In retrospect, Mal considered the Palladium his "first big engagement with the Beatles." His efforts in support of the boys' four-song set had come off without a hitch. Even so, the Palladium show was merely "a taste of the hysteria that was to follow the Beatles in the coming years."[5]

A few days later, Mal left Great Britain for the very first time, notching his inaugural plane ride in the bargain. Back in September, while he transported the band's equipment in the Ford down to London for an episode of BBC Radio's *Pop Go the Beatles*, the boys had made the journey by plane. It turned out to be a harrowing experience for them, as engine trouble forced the pilots to scrub the first flight, and George was confronted by a malfunctioning window on the second flight, before the third flight was able to safely make the trip to the capital. Ironically, Mal succeeded in beating the lads down to London, pulling into the city in four and a half hours.

By the time the group flew to Sweden, George was an admittedly nervous flier, and Mal feared he would follow suit. Although his first flight came off without a hitch, white knuckles aside, his adolescent fantasies about Northern European women would come up bust. In his imagination, there existed an idyllic, bohemian netherworld where women openly engaged in all manner of sexual exploits. "My first taste of foreign parts was a trip to Sweden," he recalled, "and for me, a myth was to be exploded. The much talked about free love one expected in Sweden was impossible to find." Apparently, the Scandinavian beauties of which Mal dreamt had no time for him. Even so, he took special note of the ways in which young women had

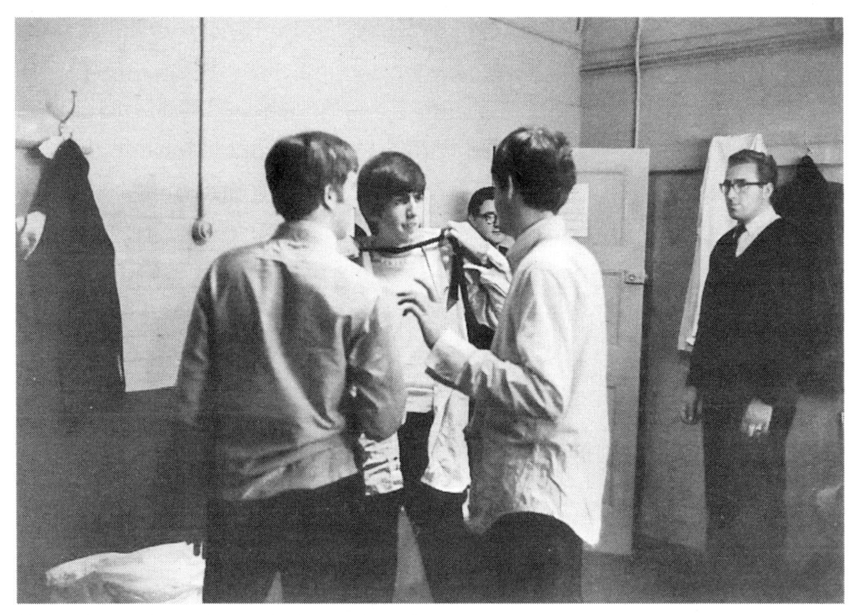

Mal backstage during his early days with the Beatles

begun throwing themselves at the Beatles. Perhaps free love existed after all—at least, for some parties.[6]

By the end of October, Mal and the Beatles had returned to the United Kingdom, where, on November 1, after a lightning-fast turnaround, the band began an autumn tour that would take them through the holidays and to year's end, as Brian had booked them for a series of Christmas shows at the Finsbury Park Astoria. As usual, they were working at a blistering pace, which they managed on a steady diet of Preludin, or "Prellys" (generic name: phenmetrazine), the uppers they had been supping on since their Hamburg days. Mal kept a steady supply of the pills on hand, often procuring them through the local black market. On November 4, the Beatles took a break from the tour to play a quartet of songs for the Royal Command Performance held at the Prince of Wales Theatre, with the Queen Mother and Princess Margaret in attendance. Before concluding their set with "Twist and Shout," John cheekily remarked to the venue's regal audience, "For our last number, I'd like to ask your help. The people in the cheaper seats, clap your hands, and the rest of you, if you'd just rattle your jewelry."[7]

Mal remembered that "excitement was running high, and nerves were stretched a little" that night, especially with John having threatened, during the Beatles' rehearsals, to ask the audience to "rattle your *fucking* jewelry," a remark that left Brian paralyzed with fear. "You could almost hear him exhale," publicist Tony Barrow later recalled, after Lennon delivered the line without using the expletive.[8]

Mal's yen for meeting the rich and famous was also quenched when he met Marlene Dietrich, the German-born star of film and stage. He recalled that she "came high kicking out of her dressing room. My amazement at her exposing, accidentally, her 'pubes,' was only overcome by my feeling of awe at being in the presence of such a wonderful and well-known personality. She looked fantastic and was bigger than any boy's image could have created over the years. And I can well understand how even British soldiers during the war could fall in love with her."[9]

Any residual exhilaration Mal felt after meeting the German diva dissipated not long afterward when Brian confronted him about his conduct. "It was during this period that Brian Epstein took me to one side for a little chat," Mal wrote, "to my amazement telling me, 'Mal, I don't like your attitude, and you're looking scruffy.'" Apparently, Brian was chagrined over Mal's fashion choices, to say nothing of his general disposition. In recent weeks, the roadie had stowed away his suit in favor of more casual threads, going tieless with a dress shirt and pants, khaki trousers, or denim jeans, mostly. It was a replay of the incident with his father back in the early 1950s, when Fred Evans accused him of looking like a lowly Liverpool dockworker. Mal was hurt by Brian's disparagement, particularly as he was working for very little pay. "I guess the attitude that bugged him was a permanent smile," Mal reasoned. "I also got the feeling he was jealous because I was popular with everybody, enjoying the stresses and strains and doing a good job." Whatever the cause, Mal wouldn't so easily forget his treatment by the Beatles' manager, concluding that "Brian should have known better."[10]

A few nights later, with Brian away in the States negotiating terms for the Beatles' upcoming American debut, Mal found himself assuming the unfamiliar role of spokesman. On November 7, the Beatles made their Irish debut, performing a pair of shows at Dublin's Adelphi Cinema. As the first set concluded, the Adelphi took on the look and feel of the street outside the Palladium back in October. The 2,300-member strong audience was clamoring for encores; at the same time, several thousand concertgoers were gathering outside for the evening performance. As the intensity of the fans mounted, the clash of humanity became riotous, overturning cars, breaking windows, and setting fires.

The next morning, as the band prepared to leave Dublin for Belfast, Mal was forced to overcome his preternatural shyness and face the horde of journalists. "It was a wonderful reception," he announced to the press corps, "but the boys feel bad for the people that got hurt. Although it was a hectic night outside the theatre, the boys had a much quieter time. It was only when they left by the rear door in a van and reached O'Connell Street that they really got a look at what had been happening while the show went on. This was our first show in Ireland and naturally we were a bit worried about what sort of a reception we would get. The boys were extremely pleased with it—they enjoy the enthusiasm and all that."[11]

Given the growing challenges of ferrying the Beatles from place to place, Mal and Neil had devised a solution for making a hasty escape from the boys' increasingly rabid fan base. The equipment van had simply become too recognizable, as had the tour buses that were the hallmark means of transportation for package tours. Working with Liverpool chum Terry Doran, Mal and Neil devised a new exit strategy for the group that involved placing a limousine near the stage door for easy egress at the end of each performance. Newly minted NEMS general manager Alistair Taylor was on hand in East Ham, where he witnessed the escape plan in its infancy. To Taylor's surprise, Neil pulled up in a glimmering black Austin Princess, rather than the top-of-the-line limo he had expected for stars of the Beatles' ilk. But selecting the Austin Princess had been no accident, Mal explained. Working with Neil and the boys, they had tested several makes and models before concluding that the Princess featured doors that opened wide enough to allow the Beatles to dive into the vehicle.[12]

Before the concert that night, George Martin arrived bearing the incredible news that the band's latest single, "I Want to Hold Your Hand," still three weeks away from its U.K. release, had already amassed more than one million advance orders. After witnessing the boys' whoops of delight,

Alistair Taylor watched the performance with Mal from backstage. As the Beatles finished up their set with "Twist and Shout," Mal told Taylor to begin making his way to the limo. "In a minute, Mal. I'm enjoying this," Taylor replied. At this point, the roadie—determined to protect life and limb for the band and their entourage—"whispered something very uncomplimentary in Alistair's left ear, which left him in no doubt that he had no choice in the matter."[13] And sure enough, Taylor settled into the passenger seat just in time to see the Beatles hurl themselves, one after the other, into the waiting limousine. With local police acting as their escort, the Austin Princess disappeared into the night, eluding the Beatles' more zealous fans in the nick of time.

When they weren't taking their lives into their own hands evading the eager clutches of their fans, the Beatles were suffering an onslaught of jelly babies, the soft, sugary sweets made of gelatin. In an unguarded moment, George had admitted to reporters that "I can't leave jelly babies alone. If there are any in sight, I just have to eat them."[14] After his words wafted across the pages of the music rags, the Beatles began to be regularly pelted by the candies during their concerts. Mal later recalled that when he wasn't battling incessant flashbulbs, he was enduring a fusillade of gelatin as he made his way about the stage. "If one only had foresight and invested money in flashbulbs and jelly babies," he opined, "we could have made a fortune!"[15]

As with the Palladium show, the fan frenzies in Dublin and East Ham underscored the shift of the Beatles' fame into unknown territory, a peculiar brand of adulation markedly different from the fervor associated with Frank Sinatra's "bobby-soxers" or, more recently, with Elvis's 1950s-era hip-gyrating explosion in the States. Newspaper reports regularly depicted young girls growing faint at the sight of the Beatles, while crowds became increasingly daring, willing to risk anything for the opportunity to glimpse the band. Later that year, Mal's sister Barbara attended the Beatles' performance at Liverpool's Empire Theatre, where she sat in the second row. That night, the audience's attendant roar proved absolutely deafening. "The screaming was so loud," Barbara recalled, that the Beatles "might just as well have been miming."[16]

By the time the tour made its way through Birmingham, where the

Beatles played the Hippodrome on November 10, Tony Bramwell began to perceive an unusual zeal among Beatles fans, one unbounded by the conventional social behaviors of the day. "As if attacked by a virus that changed their moral standards, teenage girls wanted sex with the Beatles and they didn't care how they got it," he wrote. "When they tried to grab a live one, crawl through windows or hide in wardrobes, they were sorted out by Mal and Neil Aspinall like M&Ms, to be sampled and tasted first. Brian—who was puritanical where his protégés were concerned—would have had a fit had he only known, but he was kept totally in the dark."[17]

For Mal, the sudden availability of sex, seemingly free from consequences—the "free love" he had been seeking in Northern Europe—represented an irresistible bonanza. After a lifetime of self-doubt over body issues and inveterate shyness, he simply couldn't control himself. "Big Mal was a demon for sex," Tony wrote. "His stamina would have been remarkable in a harem. In the flat, sooty back streets of Birmingham or Manchester, he was a stud straight from the Kama Sutra. Like sacrificial virgins, a lot of the girls willingly accepted that they would have to do it with Mal to get to John, Paul, George, or Ringo, and Mal knew it."[18]

And there was another thing that really got Tony's goat. "Brian and Neil and I had developed this policy that we wouldn't pose in photographs with the Beatles," he recalled. "Fans wanted to take pictures of the band, and they didn't want us hanging around beside the boys." But Mal had clearly developed a yen, early on, for being as near as possible to the Beatles' vortex of fame. The flashbulbs and the band's celebrity were simply too much for him to resist. Consequently, said Tony, "Mal was always in the fucking photographs."[19]

After the Beatles played a pair of shows at the Coventry Theatre on Sunday, November 17, Mal and the bandmates were set to enjoy a rare day off that Monday before resuming the tour in Wolverhampton, only a few hours south of Liverpool. Excited by the opportunity to spend the day with Lily and Gary, Mal packed up the gear in the lipstick-covered Ford. The large post-show crowds hindered his efforts, and by the time he left, "adoring souvenir-hunting fans" had pilfered the van's windscreen wipers and outside mirrors. When he reached the outskirts of the city, he was caught in a deluge. "At that particular time of year in England," he recalled, "we often get storms that sweep the coasts, and this year was no exception. Promenades were being battered by huge waves, and the countryside generally was beset with high winds and heavy rains."[20]

After catching a few hours of shuteye in a roadside rest stop, Mal continued on, eager to resume his homeward trek. When he awoke, the rain had slowed considerably. Back on the road, he struggled to pilot the Ford through gale-force winds. As he attempted to regain control of the van, the Ford careened into a thirty-foot-tall lamppost, which demolished its passenger side. The van that had served the Beatles since 1962 was finished, lying on its side on the roadway in a heap of twisted metal. Incredibly, the Beatles' gear suffered very little in the way of damage, but Mal himself wouldn't be so lucky. "I was thrown clear and landed on my head," he wrote, "coming to at one point to find the headlights of a huge lorry standing over me, the driver only just stopping in time."[21]

Fortunate to be alive, Mal was hospitalized for nearly a week at the Stafford General Infirmary in Cannock, where he received twenty stitches. Beatles fans quickly caught on to his predicament and began haunting the hospital halls in the hope of meeting a Beatle. But their efforts would go unrewarded. Neil and the band had already traveled to the next series of gigs, leaving Mal to recuperate in Cannock. During his convalescence, he was moved by a letter he received from Paul. Referring to Mal as a "Big Clubbo," Paul advised him to leave the nurses alone and get some rest.[22]

For the space of a few days, Mal took Paul's advice to heart, relaxing in Mossley Hill with Lily and Gary as the Beatles continued their journey across the North. As the hours mounted, though, he grew eager to rejoin the tour as it wound its way through the Midlands, making a beeline for London, where the Beatles would close out that incredible year. His anxiety soon got the better of him, and ignoring Lily's well-meaning objections, he left Hillside Road in a huff, slamming the door behind him in mid-argument and storming out on his wife in the bargain. For the first time, he later reflected, "I broke the pact which Lily and I had made, and that was always to leave home smiling."[23]

Naturally, Mal resolved never to behave in such an odious manner again, just as he had promised back in August to maintain the vital threads of communication that sustain a marriage across distance and time. But the simple truth of the matter was that Mal, for reasons both good and ill, simply couldn't wait to get back on the road.

Though he and Lily would make up soon enough, she was crestfallen by their new state of affairs. "He'd been such a considerate husband," she lamented. "Now it was worse than him having another woman. It was like him having four mistresses: John, Paul, George, and Ringo."[24]

07

MAL, CRIPPLES!

Mal and the Beatles mercifully closed the book on the autumn tour in mid-December—just in time for the Christmas shows Brian had booked, including the shows at Finsbury Park's Astoria. That same week, "She Loves You" ended its reign at the top of the charts, having been bumped out of the number one spot by "I Want to Hold Your Hand." With the nation abuzz with Beatlemania, Mal prepped the Beatles' equipment for opening night at the Astoria. "Everything had been set up and tested beforehand," he recalled, "the sketches and the rest of the acts had all finished, and it was time for the Beatles to end the show."

Mal could feel his opening-night jitters beginning to subside when, suddenly, just a few bars into "Roll Over Beethoven," the power onstage failed completely.[1] In his distress, Mal bounded out of the wings, determined to fix everything as swiftly as possible. "I would like to introduce our road manager, Bill Haley," Paul quipped as Mal lumbered onto the stage. The roadie managed to correct the problem with a few quick adjustments, chalking it up to the Beatles' regular equipment upgrades from Vox.

The constant parade of new gear from Vox had kept Mal busy adjusting shifting wattages, changing power supply configurations, and patching into house-specific public-address systems. And sometimes, the road-weary roadie simply made mistakes. In one instance, "I switched an amp on before connecting it to the speaker. This was very naughty of me—for when I did plug it in, the speaker blew. It was just one more item I had to remember."[2]

Mal later recalled the complex nature of the stage setup at Finsbury Park, which involved a pair of rostrums that held the gauze-encased amplifiers in place during the show. To feed the cables to the amps simultaneously, the roadies took turns sitting inside the rostrums to ensure that the cables remained in place throughout each group's set. Not surprisingly, said Derek Hughes—with Billy J. Kramer and the Dakotas on the bill, Hughes was also at the Astoria Theatre that Christmas—"It's quite loud when you've got two amplifiers about six inches away from your head going full blast in order to try and be heard above all the screaming."[3]

But the Finsbury Park residency wasn't all frustration for the Beatles' newest addition. During the last show of the series, Hughes decided to pull a prank. "So I made a little white flag," he recalled, "and when it got to the last number, I shoved this flag up through a hole in the rostrum and started waving it about in surrender. But Mal wasn't content with that," the roadie added, "and he ripped the gauze off the front of the rostrum and jumped out and ran offstage, yelling at the top of his voice, 'Free at last! I've just spent three bloody weeks in there.'" For a moment, Hughes felt upstaged. Mal "got a bit of a good laugh from the crowd and from the group, George and Paul especially, but luckily it was the last number, so it didn't matter too much." In Hughes's memory, Mal was "a hell of a nice bloke, and he'd do anything to help anybody, but he sure did like to get into the limelight."[4]

Following the Christmas break, in which Mal had the pleasure of returning to Lily and Gary for a brief spell, 1964 got off to an unfortunate start when John's guitar went missing. A 1962 Gibson J-160E "Jumbo" acoustic-electric, the guitar already enjoyed a storied past. John had played it on such early Beatles classics as "Love Me Do," "She Loves You," and "I Want to Hold Your Hand." The nearest Mal could figure was that the Jumbo had disappeared after one of the Astoria Theatre shows that January.[5]

Mal received a severe tongue-lashing from John, especially after it had been suggested that perhaps the roadie had misplaced the guitar and simply didn't want to admit it to his employer. "I fairly got it that day," said Mal, who later described the loss of the guitar as one of the lowest moments of his Beatles career.[6] For years, John needled him about the missing Jumbo, saying, "Mal, you can have your job back as soon as you find my guitar."[7]

The loss of any Beatles' gear shouldn't have been a surprise. By this point, with the band's fame on a spectacular upward trajectory, the backstage area at their concerts made for an increasingly chaotic scene. There was the usual coterie of fans hoping to mingle with the Beatles, of course, not to mention all manner of press and local bigwigs eager to meet the boys. At times, the Beatles' backstage throng would include physically challenged visitors schlepped in by well-meaning friends and relations who had come to believe the bandmates possessed otherworldly healing powers.

As Mal knew full well, when it came to the disabled, the Beatles—and John, in particular—had an ignoble track record. In his teen years, John often contorted his face in the presence of the mentally and physically handicapped and disfigured war veterans, cruelly mimicking them, "hunching his back and dragging a leg like Quasimodo." In postwar Hamburg, John incorporated "cripping" into the Beatles' stage act, a practice he had continued to the present day. Brian had succeeded in curbing some of the band's unprofessional proclivities—swearing and eating onstage, for example—but John was loath to give up this odious behavior.[8]

In a strange form of karma, John and the other Beatles found themselves increasingly face-to-face with disabled fans who had been deposited backstage for a quasi-religious laying on of hands. As Ringo later recalled, "People would bring in these terrible cases and leave them in our dressing room. They'd go off for tea or whatever and they would leave them behind. If it got very heavy, we would shout 'Mal, cripples!' and that became a saying—even when there were no handicapped people present. If there were any people around we didn't like, we'd shout, 'Mal, cripples!' and they'd be escorted out."[9]

When Mal wasn't negotiating his way backstage among the handicapped and the headstrong, he was devising innovative workarounds to avoid past calamities and satisfy his bosses' every professional, and often personal, whim. As George recalled, "He had a bag that he developed over the years, because it would always be 'Mal, have you got an Elastoplast? Mal, have you got a screwdriver? Mal, have you got a bottle of this? Have you got that?' And he always had everything. If he didn't have it, he'd get it very quickly. He was one of those people who loved what he was doing and didn't have any problem about service."[10] Indeed, there seemed to be no upper limit to Mal's capacity for meeting the Beatles' needs. He and Neil had even begun signing the bandmates' autographs to keep up with their fans' insatiable demand, slowly perfecting, as best they could, the idiosyncrasies of John's, Paul's, George's, and Ringo's signatures.

For that January, Brian had booked the Beatles for an eighteen-day residency at Paris's Olympia Theatre, where they headlined a nine-act bill, often performing multiple sets per day, joined by such stars as French singer Sylvie Vartan and American Trini Lopez. The Paris residency presented a rare opportunity for Lily and Gary to enjoy an extended visit with their absent paterfamilias. "When the Beatles played in Paris," Lily recalled. "Mal was told that he could take me and the baby with him. It was very nice, but we were repaying Epstein the cost of our fares and hotel for months."[11]

On January 14, the boys took the brief flight from London to Paris. After a one-off performance at Versailles, Mal accompanied the band's gear by train to the Olympia. With little Gary in tow, he and Lily stayed at the elegant Hôtel George V during the Beatles' residency. With the hotel only a few minutes' walk from the Champs-Élysées, Lily relished the chance to do some sightseeing.

Prior to beginning the Paris run, Mal prepped the band's equipment, readying the backstage area for the Beatles' arrival. By this point, he fashioned himself as a kind of emissary, working on the band's behalf to ensure a wholly professional experience at the venue. "One of the beauties of being road manager is that you are always there first at any show," he recalled. "Everybody in the place knew me—police, security guards, and the management personnel. This enabled me to travel in and out of the theatres at will." Even so, Mal remained wary of Brian, hoping to avoid any further conflicts with him. "When Brian Epstein first arrived at the Olympia to see the show," he later wrote, "no one would believe that he was the Beatles' manager, thinking that if you are going to come up with a tall story, that's one of the best. Eventually, he managed to get word to me. I came to the stage door and vouched for him. He was fuming, and I know that really got him uptight."[12]

The Paris residency began in unforgettable style for Mal and Neil, who found themselves embroiled in a full-on backstage riot on the very first night at the Olympia. Fortunately for the Beatles' roadies, hulking 250-pound chauffeur Bill Corbett had accompanied them on the trip. As Mal later recalled, "He had impressed us with the fact that, one, he could speak fluent French, and two, he had been a courier on the continent for several years, knowing the streets of Paris like the back of his hand."[13]

And on the afternoon of January 16, Corbett was on the scene when all hell broke loose. It all started when the band's press officer, Brian Sommerville, neglected to arrange for a preshow press conference. Known as "Pinkle Bone" among the entourage, Sommerville had unwittingly raised the ire of the local press, with reporters and photographers having waited for more than two hours to press the flesh with Vartan, in particular. To make matters worse, Sommerville tried to lay the blame for the ruckus at George Harrison's feet.

At first, the French journalists had been in a festive mood as they arrived at the Olympia. Having just returned from reporting on the Pope's visit to the Holy Land, they amused themselves by wearing novelty Beatles wigs. But then they grew restive,[14] and as Mal looked on in horror, the French press corps forced their way backstage, determined to make their deadlines. "The Beatles beat a hasty retreat to the curtained off part of the dressing room," he recalled, "and were to be heard shouting from behind the safety of the curtains, 'Go get 'em, Mal—throw them out!'"

Hearing his cue, Mal lifted the wayward journalists and hurled them through the dressing room door. With Corbett acting as his eager second, Mal emptied the dressing room, cold-cocking one of the photographers during the mêlée. Meanwhile, George threw a glass of orange juice at Pinkle Bone, furious over the press officer's shortsightedness in managing the journalists. "Eventually, calm was restored to the backstage area," Mal wrote, "and this was the only fight I got involved in on behalf of the Beatles."[15]

The Beatles' residency at the Olympia wouldn't be just a chaotic representation of a band's meteoric rise. The Olympia Theatre concerts would also form some of the emotional baseline of Gary Evans's pleasant earliest memories. He remembered, as a toddler, watching one of the concerts from the wings with his mother. "I used to get very animated when they sang 'From Me to You,'" Gary recalled. "I can remember being at the side of the stage, looking at the band, and trying to wrestle my way out of my mum's arms and run towards them."[16]

As it turned out, Gary's exhilaration was only a taste of things to come. On the night of January 17, as Mal and the Beatles returned from their latest Olympia gig, Brian Epstein rushed into the band's suite clutching a telegram from Capitol Records and announced that "I Want to Hold Your Hand" was poised to top the American charts.

Caught up in the thrill of celebration, the bandmates took turns climbing onto Mal's back, with the big man parading them around the room. "They went mad!" Mal recalled. "They always act this way when anything big happens—just a bunch of kids, jumping up and down with sheer delight. Paul climbed on my back demanding a piggyback. They felt that this was the biggest thing that could have happened. Gradually, they quieted down, ordered some more drinks and sat down to appreciate fully what had happened. It was a wonderful, marvelous night for them. I was knocked out."[17]

To Mal's delight, Brian threw an unforgettable celebration that night at the George V, with George Martin and his girlfriend, Judy Lockhart Smith, on hand for the occasion. The Beatles' producer was in town to supervise the band's German-language recordings of "She Loves You" and "I Want to Hold Your Hand" at EMI's Pathé Marconi Studios. The festivities that evening included dinner at the gourmet restaurant Au Mouton de Panurge, where Brian playfully wore a chamber pot on his head as the Beatles and

George riding piggyback on Mal

their entourage toasted their good fortune. The celebration continued back at the George V, with Brian throwing a party with the Beatles, George and Judy in tow, while, in the next room, "a couple of newspaper friends put on a private show involving several prostitutes for our entertainment, one of them being very pregnant." As Mal recalled, "It was a little unnerving to have these ladies performing before our eyes with each other in one room, with Brian, George Martin and Judy, and the rather more staid members of the press in the adjoining living room. I guess celebration caters to everybody's different tastes."[18] The party raged on until five o'clock the next morning. That day, Mal saw Lily and Gary off at the airport for their return flight.

Meanwhile, the Beatles had several more gigs at the Olympia, including a February 1 show where Paul nearly missed his cue, having become enchanted with a woman backstage. With the curtain about to go up, Neil nervously strapped on Paul's Höfner bass and took his place onstage. At the last moment, Paul leapt into action. But Neil had been ready to make a go of it, and he later scrawled in Mal's diary that he had been "quite prepared to fake it."[19]

The Paris residency concluded on February 4. As if to convey his relief that he had been spared any Olympia-related glitches that day, Mal wrote, "Last show—nothing happened."[20] Plenty was on the verge of happening, of course, thanks to "I Want to Hold Your Hand" lording it atop the American charts. By the time Mal returned to London with the equipment on February 5, the Beatles were scheduled to perform yet another hasty turnaround. That Friday, February 7, they were booked to make their maiden voyage to America.

Back in November, Brian had arranged for the Beatles to perform on CBS Television's *Ed Sullivan Show* on consecutive weekends. As with Val Parnell's *Sunday Night at the London Palladium*, the American variety show afforded the four Liverpudlians the opportunity to play in front of a massive TV audience. When Brian originally struck the deal, the Beatles were relative unknowns Stateside. But now, with a slew of Beatles songs making their way up the charts, the magnitude of their upcoming American visit was beginning to take on unforeseen proportions.

08

MY FAVORITE ANIMAL

In preparation for the Beatles' maiden voyage to the States, Mal spent Thursday, February 6, 1964, roaming the London music stores. As with such Liverpool stalwarts as Hessy's, he had already become acquainted with several vendors in the capital. In the early 1960s, Ivor Arbiter had opened a pair of music stores that catered to the burgeoning pop music trade, including Drum City, on Shaftesbury Avenue, and Sound City, which specialized in guitars and amps, on Rupert Street. As the exclusive U.K. dealer in Ludwig equipment, Drum City was ground zero for Mal's pre-USA efforts, which largely concerned Ringo's kit, among other sundry items. "I was kept busy getting drums and cymbal cases, covers for the amplifiers and speakers," Mal later wrote, "generally getting all my spare equipment together, such as plectrums, spare guitar leads, drumsticks, as well as the Hacks cough drops and the jars of honey that [the band] used to ease their sore throats after long nights of singing on the road."[1] Drum City loomed large in Ringo's legend. Back in April 1963, Arbiter, at Brian's request, had designed the Beatles' drop-*T* logo, with its exaggerated capital *B*, for the front skin of Ringo's Ludwig bass drum.[2]

Mal would never forget the chartered Pan Am flight to New York City—the longest such journey of his life thus far. He and Neil sat in coach, flush with anticipation, nervous about what might await them on the ground at John F. Kennedy International Airport, recently rechristened in honor of the fallen president. Fittingly, Ray McFall was there, too, given the Cavern's significant role in helping the Beatles become a Liverpool mainstay.

Then—arrival. The passengers, one and all, were thunderstruck: three thousand fans had gathered to greet the band at JFK. American Beatlemania had truly been born.

Mal's wildest dreams of hobnobbing with luxury and fame would never be surpassed by his experience in New York City that weekend. "We were staying at the Plaza Hotel," he later wrote, "and I'm sure the Palm Court has never witnessed such hysteria, being absolutely besieged by fans, with the whole New York police force guarding us."[3]

The next day, the Beatles rehearsed in advance of their first appearance on *The Ed Sullivan Show.* With George having been felled by the flu, Neil stood in his place on the CBS stage. On Sunday, February 9, the day of the broadcast, the band received a congratulatory telegram from Elvis and Colonel Tom Parker. Paul couldn't help ribbing Mal, saying, "You're his biggest fan, Mal, how come you didn't get a good luck telegram?" As the roadie looked on, "the whole episode ended up with the boys fighting about who was going to keep it as a souvenir."[4]

Fortunately, George recovered in time for the broadcast, but as showtime approached, Mal realized that Brian's carefully choreographed image of the Beatles was in jeopardy. "This particular incident took place after

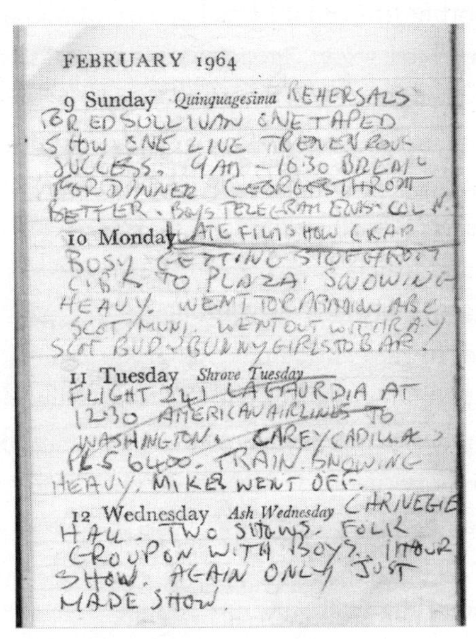

FEBRUARY 1964

9 Sunday *Quinquagesima* REHERSALS FOR ED SULLIVAN ONE TAPED SHOW ONE LIVE TREMENDOUS SUCCESS. 9AM – 10.30 BREAK FOR DINNER GEORGES THROAT BETTER. BOYS TELEGRAM ELVIS COL. N.

10 Monday LATE FILM SHOW CRAP BOSY GETTING [illegible] C.B.S. TO PLAZA. SNOWING HEAVY. WENT TO [illegible] SCOT/MUNI. WENT OUT WITH RAY SCOT BUD & BUNNY GIRLS TO BAR.

11 Tuesday *Shrove Tuesday* FLIGHT 241 LAGAURDIA AT 1230 AMERICAN AIRLINES TO WASHINGTON. CAREY CADILLACS PL5 6400. TRAIN. SNOWING HEAVY. MIKE R WENT OFF.

12 Wednesday *Ash Wednesday* CARNEGIE HALL. TWO SHOWS. FOLK GROUP ON WITH BOYS. 1 HOUR SHOW. AGAIN ONLY JUST MADE SHOW.

Mal's *Ed Sullivan Show* diary entry

rehearsing all day, and about a half hour before the show was due to go on the air live," Mal recalled. To his horror, Ringo's drumhead, with the group's signature logo, was nowhere in evidence. "When a group records, it's normal for the front skin on the bass drum to be removed to facilitate the entry of a microphone to get a better sound," Mal wrote. "With only minutes to go before the group was to be seen for the first time live in America, the whole front of the bass drum loomed large and empty as a railway tunnel. I had forgotten to replace the drum skin with their name on it. I stood rooted to the spot, [having] wet myself with fright. But with minutes to spare, I managed to restore that famous name for the waiting millions of fans to see."[5]

That night, 73 million viewers watched the Beatles' performance on *The Ed Sullivan Show*, fully eclipsing the hysteria at the Palladium the previous October. It was a watershed moment, to be sure, ushering in a British Invasion that would swiftly reshape the pop music landscape. Then, on Tuesday, February 11, they made their American concert debut at Washington, DC's, Coliseum. For Mal, it would be one of the strangest gigs in the group's history, an instance where things went wrong on a grand scale.

At first, it was a small matter involving the band's microphones, which he remedied in short order. And there was the usual onslaught of jelly babies, of course—rendered even more dangerous by the Stateside presence of jelly *beans*, the candy's American cousin. A much more durable confection, with a hard, less forgiving exterior, the jelly beans whizzing onto the Beatles' stage in a near-constant onslaught pelted Mal and the Beatles with considerably more sting than their British counterparts had.

To accommodate their performance, the stage had been set up "in the round," which allowed the band to play while facing different quadrants of the venue. In the center of it all was Ringo's drum kit, which had been secured to a revolving electrical rostrum. The contraption had worked perfectly during rehearsals, "but wouldn't you know it," Mal later wrote, "when it came to the actual show, the thing refused to move, and I ended up jumping on stage every couple of numbers and manhandling it to its new position."[6]

After the show at the Coliseum, the Beatles attended a reception at the British embassy, an event that was to have far-reaching implications in Mal

Mal setting up Ringo's drum kit at the Washington Coliseum

and the group's story. That night, some three hundred elite guests had congregated for a benefit supporting the National Society for the Prevention of Cruelty to Children, the favorite British charity of Lady Ormsby-Gore. The Beatles' entourage was joined by photographer Harry Benson, who recalled the mortification the bandmates experienced as the upper-class guests turned up their noses at the Liverpudlians. Things went from uncomfortable to dicey when a British debutante slipped behind Ringo and cut off a lock of his hair as a souvenir. With that, the Beatles demanded to leave, and Benson recalled the group's humiliation as they rode away from the embassy that night. "They were very sad. They looked as if they wanted to cry, John, in particular."[7] As a result of the British embassy fiasco, the Beatles sternly rebuked Epstein for accepting the invitation in the first place and insisted that they never again be made to submit themselves to such degradation.

As they made their way back to New York City for a pair of concerts at

Carnegie Hall, Mal's zeal for the Old West was rewarded in fine style when the American truckers who had assisted him in transporting the group's equipment gifted him with a white Stetson cowboy hat. After the Carnegie Hall concerts, the boys and their entourage flew to Miami, where the band was slated to perform again on *The Ed Sullivan Show*, which would be broadcast from the Deauville Beach Resort on Sunday, February 16. As with their first *Sullivan* show, in New York City, Mal found himself on tenterhooks moments before airtime. With the previous act having concluded their slot, Sullivan stepped in front of the curtain to chat with the audience as CBS ran the usual series of television advertisements. "As the seconds ticked away," Mal recalled, there was "no sign of the Beatles."

An irate Ed Sullivan stuck his head through the curtain, saying, "Mal, where the fuck are they? Where are the Beatles?" The roadie later learned that Neil and the band had been waylaid by fans in the crowded hotel. "Ed Sullivan was at the point of putting a standby act on when the Beatles appeared and were on stage with seconds to spare," Mal wrote, "in fact, as the last advert was running out. With hardly time to tune up, the curtain opened and the show was on. It's at moments like these that Fate must sit in the wings with a devilish grin on her face watching the antics of us poor humans."[8]

By Monday evening, Mal would be on a plane ferrying the Beatles' equipment back to London, while the boys stayed behind for a much-needed rest. That Tuesday, Mal missed the opportunity to join them as they pretended to spar with twenty-two-year-old Cassius Clay (soon to be known as Muhammad Ali), the heavyweight boxer who was training in preparation for his upcoming title bout against Sonny Liston. Still, the American journey was a dream come true for the roadie. "I was to find myself at the center of attention on many occasions, and I must admit, I enjoyed every bit of it," he wrote. "Standing on the beach with a crowd of blue-haired old ladies, clamoring for my autograph, was the show business I wanted to be a part of."[9]

At the same time, he was appalled by the cultural differences he encountered. "The American attitude was also foreign to our nature," he observed, "and they were to laugh at our 'pleases,' 'thank-you's,' and 'excuse-me's,' which we were used to saying. We found Americans to be rude from our point of view when they would demand things, not only from us, but from each other, without saying 'please,' but feel that America is our sister country [in] that we speak the same language and share the same differences."[10]

Back in London, Mal watched a screening of *The Running Jumping & Standing Still Film*, a 1959 sketch comedy short starring Peter Sellers and directed by Richard Lester, who had been tapped to direct the Beatles' big-screen debut. And then it was back to Liverpool on Friday, where he was reunited, if only briefly, with Lily and Gary. After writing in his diary that it was "wonderful to be home," Mal was back in London with the Beatles by Sunday night, where he was gobsmacked to meet *Avengers* stars Patrick Macnee and Diana Rigg during the taping of the band's appearance on the TV talk show *Big Night Out*, at Teddington Studios.[11]

While Mal enjoyed, as always, the opportunity to hobnob with the rich and famous, the next morning proved a sobering one, as he was due in court on charges stemming from his November fiasco in Cannock with the Ford van. Represented by NEMS attorney Rex Makin, he had been charged with driving without proper insurance, given that the policy attached to the car specified only John, George, Ringo, and Neil as permissible drivers. (Ironically, John wouldn't obtain a driver's license until February 1965.) The case was ultimately dismissed when NEMS's insurance carrier assured the court that it would have provided coverage for the roadie. For Mal's part, his anxiety was at a fever pitch, and he was fearful he might yet again raise Brian's ire and, potentially, lose his job.[12]

As Mal and the Beatles settled in for an extended round of recording sessions at EMI Studios for the feature film, Mal redoubled his efforts to make good on his promise to Lil to be a more considerate, and regular, correspondent. But, as it happened, he didn't manage to put pen to paper until March 3, while on the film set at Minehead Station, in Somerset, and other locations with the group and Dick Lester.

The film shoot had moved to Somerset from Marylebone Station to capture a series of scenes of the Beatles in and around a British Rail train. When the engines overheated outside Minehead, throwing a wrench into Lester's plans for that day, Mal rushed back to London, where he outfitted Madame Tussaud's wax Beatles exhibit with guitar props. "This is about the third letter to you I have written tonight," he wrote to his wife. "I used to love writing letters, found it quite easy, but I guess lack of practice is making it hard. I am certainly going to write regularly in the future, darling, for I have not been fair to you in the past." He closed the letter, still contrite: "I love this job, as you know Lil, but when I hear Gary on the phone, like tonight, it really breaks me up, and I want to be with you all the time. This won't be for always, doll, and we will be together more once again."[13]

In the feature film—which would shortly be entitled *A Hard Day's Night* after a "Ringo-ism" the drummer had uttered during an interview on March 17—Mal was played by British TV comedy star John Junkin. As "Shake," Junkin effected Mal's avuncular, boy-next-door mannerisms as a member of the on-screen Beatles' inner circle. On March 11, Mal wrote to Lily again, his mood having improved greatly because he had now contributed to the film shoot. "Here is your Loving Mally with a letter to you," he wrote. "Today, for the first time, I got involved with the film. Morning started as normal hanging around getting sore feet and doing nothing. Then they wanted equipment on the set so away I went. All afternoon it has been hectic, fixing equipment up in a guard's van for quite a funny scene in which the boys do card-playing and finish up by singing a number ['I Should Have Known Better']."[14]

The next week would prove one of the busiest for Mal during the whole

George on the set of *A Hard Day's Night*

Paul in a railway car holding a photo of Elvis

of that crazy year, beginning in exemplary fashion as he enjoyed private screenings of the American comedy *Irma la Douce* and the James Bond flick *From Russia with Love* in the Beatles' company. As usual, the boys enjoyed teasing their roadie—at one point, George placed plastic cups inside Mal's shirt pockets, which the Beatle then irreverently filled with milk. In a tenderhearted moment, John announced to Mal that "after sarnies [British slang for 'sandwiches'], you are my favorite animal." With his caustic wit, the Beatles' rhythm guitarist had long been a source of intimidation for Mal—especially after the loss of his much-cherished Gibson Jumbo. The instance was not lost on the roadie, who, in his diary, worried about his role in the Beatles' orbit, which often felt precarious.[15]

On the day after that diary entry, Mal's place in the band's ecosystem was put to the test yet again. After performing two shows—including an appearance on *Top of the Pops*—the Beatles attended a charity event at London's Dorchester Hotel. In the wee hours of March 19, Mal began lugging their equipment into the ballroom for their performance. "I was dismayed and felt rather terrible at having to set up the equipment in the middle of the floor amongst a tie and tail crowd dressed in my 'on the road' clothes, wearing a jacket with leather elbow patches," he wrote. "The audience was a mixture of high society and famous film, television, and recording personalities." Even Prime Minister Harold Wilson was on hand, posing for photos with the boys after presenting them with "Show Business Personality of 1963" awards.[16]

As usual, Mal enjoyed the event—particularly the chance to mingle with such personalities as Welsh comedian Harry Secombe, who served as master of ceremonies. But he felt exposed that night for appearing unprofessional among the glitterati, clearly still smarting from Brian's admonition back in November about his clothing and comportment. As if to make matters worse, that Friday night, he committed a faux pas during the taping for the rock/pop TV show *Ready, Steady, Go!*, when he walked in front of the camera, inadvertently upstaging presenter Keith Fordyce.

By this point, the Beatles' unprecedented brand of fame had forced them to make unusual arrangements to conduct their lives. On March 21, hoping to avoid the regular encampment of fans who followed the bandmates' every move, Neil and Mal were forced to work in the pre-dawn hours of the morning to move George and Ringo into their new digs, a flat at Whaddon House, in Knightsbridge. For their part, John and Cynthia had taken up residence in a cozy apartment in Kensington with baby Julian, while Paul moved in with his girlfriend, Jane Asher, at her family's Wimpole Street town house. Having just turned eighteen, Jane was one of the London theatrical scene's most promising young actresses.

By this point, Mal and Neil had added a new van to replace the Ford. A blue Commer, registration number 6677 ED, the vehicle was a veritable workhorse, ferrying the two all over London and beyond with the Beatles' equipment and taking them home periodically to visit with their families. For Mal, the new van had quickly become an additional burden, requiring frequent repairs as the Beatles and their entourage pushed the vehicle to its capacity.

As with George and Ringo, Mal and Neil were in need of more dependable accommodation, having spent numerous nights at London's President Hotel. "We all gradually moved to London," Neil recalled. "I think Mal Evans and I were the last ones to get a flat because we couldn't afford it. Eventually, they had to get us a flat, because staying in hotels, as we did, was even more expensive."[17] Now ensconced with Neil at 16 Montagu Mews West, Mal was grateful for the new flat, which felt vaguely like home. Even so, London was a culture shock for the Beatles' team of transplanted Liverpudlians. As Tony Bramwell pointed out, "We found Londoners hard to get along with. They saw us as Scousers and whacks and witty scallywags, speaking a strange lingo that nobody seemed to understand."[18]

By this juncture, Mal's sister June had also relocated to London, having been accepted at the Central School to begin her dramatic studies. As Mal made his trips to Liverpool and back, he would often return to London with care packages for June from Waldgrave Road. "Malcolm would bring food parcels down from Liverpool," June later recalled. "But of course, Malcolm was very busy, so I'd get the parcel a week late, and the eggs would have gone rotten." Her brother ensured June that she would be able to observe some of the band's recording sessions. "But I was a folk singer," said June, "and I was really snooty about rock 'n' roll music." By her own admission, this attitude would later backfire when she passed on an opportunity, helpfully arranged by her older brother, to sing backup for Eric Clapton, a relatively unknown guitarist at the time.[19]

Come April, the Beatles brought their work on *A Hard Day's Night*—both the film and the LP of the same name—to a close. Mal even found time between set calls and recording sessions to visit the dentist, who provided him with a new tooth to replace the one dislodged by the drunken Caverngoer back in the summer of 1962. By this juncture, his days as a bouncer must surely have felt like a lifetime ago.

It was during this period that he began catering to the Beatles' every whim, ensuring that their meals—previously acquired on the road courtesy of hotels, luncheonettes, and restaurants—were there precisely when they needed them. To this end, Mal developed a routine that accommodated their lives both as film actors and as recording artists. "Filming in the studios was always easy for me," he wrote, "as early morning breakfasts for the boys when they arrived on the set could be obtained from the studio canteen—tea and toast with jam and marmalade usually being the order for the day."[20] And for their long hours at EMI, Mal rustled up their meals from the studio's basement canteen or, for a change of pace, from all manner of St. John's Wood eateries of which, slowly but surely, he was developing a working knowledge.

By this point, Mal was clearly burning the candle at both ends. As with Neil during his pre-Mal roadie days, he had not only lost considerable weight, but had begun to suffer maladies, including an ear infection that landed him in the hospital. He was also struggling to balance his obligations to the Beatles in London with those to his family back home. "One early Saturday morning, while driving to Liverpool for a day at home with my family," he wrote, "I fell asleep at the wheel of the van, coming to with a start only yards before I would have hit a large roundabout near Liverpool." Having narrowly escaped calamity—and nearly losing the new Commer van in the process—he could only conclude that "somebody up there likes me."[21]

At the same time, he and Lily were beginning to feel the financial pinch associated with their new lives. With Mal juggling expenses in the capital and Lil trying to make ends meet on Mossley Hill, their ability to stretch a pound note—even though the wages Mal received with the Beatles were higher than those he had from the GPO—was no easy feat. Always on the lookout for additional income, Mal happened upon an idea. In recent months, he had begun to document the Beatles' meteoric rise, photographing them in performance, on Lester's film set, and on various forms of transportation from one concert venue to another. Writing to Lil on April 17, Mal told his wife that "I am taking some photos of the Beatles, and I showed them to a freelance journalist who thinks that he may be able to sell some to newspapers. Would be 'fab,' wouldn't it, if I could make some money out of it? But please don't say anything to anyone," he added, "because the least people know about things like that the better. Still, keep your fingers crossed for us."[22]

With a spring mini-tour under their belts during the last week of April, Brian had booked the Beatles for a full-fledged world tour. Slated to begin on June 4, in Copenhagen, the multinational jaunt would take them from Northern Europe to Hong Kong and then through Australia and New Zealand before they made a midsummer return to their homeland. It was an ambitious tour by any measure, one that had taken months of careful planning on behalf of Brian and his team and NEMS.

After performing a warm-up show at the Prince of Wales Theatre on May 31, the band was in top form, ready to take on the world. Mal, who had turned twenty-nine just four days earlier, spent the balance of his time ensuring that the boys' instruments were prepped for the arduous tour ahead. Prior to the Prince of Wales performance, he made another one of his regular visits to Drum City, in this instance to outfit Ringo with a new kit, a top-of-the-line Ludwig Super Classic model with oyster-black pearl trim. By now, he had developed an easy routine in which he would circle among the city's instrument vendors to maintain the Beatles' gear—Drum City for Ringo, Sound City to acquire Paul's preferred bass strings, and Selmer for John's favorite plectrums. Everything seemed to be falling into place.

Then, on the afternoon before the tour was set to begin in Denmark, disaster struck in St. John's Wood. On June 3, as the Beatles posed for a photoshoot with *The Saturday Evening Post*, Ringo collapsed in a heap. Neil rushed him to the hospital, where he was diagnosed with acute tonsillitis and pharyngitis. Meanwhile, back at EMI, Mal observed as "a feeling of gloom hung over everybody" when they contemplated the upcoming world tour without their drummer.[23] In the moment, it seemed nothing short of unthinkable.

"How," Mal wrote, "could the Beatles appear without Ringo?"[24]

09

THE DEMON

With Ringo having been admitted to University College Hospital, Mal watched the Beatles' brain trust descend into a storm of divergent viewpoints. On the one hand, George Martin sided with Brian in terms of moving forward with the tour. For the past several months, Epstein had been working with promoters a world away by arranging for venues, hotels, motorcades, security, and merchandising. There were no "out clauses" in effect, and cancellation, to Brian's mind, meant the possibility of lawsuits and, worse, a potential PR disaster that might upset the band's fame, which he was working so tirelessly to consolidate worldwide. For Martin, the old adage that the show must go on became literal.

However, George Harrison came out strongly against the idea of moving forward with the tour. "George is a very loyal person," Martin remembered. "And he said, 'If Ringo's not part of the group, it's not the Beatles. And I don't see why we should do it. I'm not going to go.'"[1] Mal wholeheartedly agreed with Harrison's perspective; Ringo was the band's drummer—end of story. John and Paul seemed considerably less horrified by the idea of making the trip to Copenhagen without Ringo. As they contemplated hiring a stand-in drummer, the notion of bringing in Pete Best briefly emerged, although John quickly dismissed the idea, pointing out that their erstwhile drummer had his own group now, the Pete Best Four. Besides, "it might have looked as if we were taking him back, which is not good for him."[2]

With momentum now in favor of Brian's position, Martin turned to his extensive Rolodex of London-area studio musicians, eventually phoning up an East End drummer named Jimmie Nicol, who had played in the Shubdubs (a band whose only claim to fame was a minor hit single called

"Humpty Dumpty") and, more recently, with Georgie Fame and the Blue Flames. Jimmie was quickly summoned to Abbey Road for an audition.

"It was very mysterious—nobody wanted to commit themselves," Nicol recalled. "So I had to go along to EMI and meet them all and just rehearsed about five numbers. And that was it."[3] As Jimmie began to take his leave, the roadie saw his cue: "My name is Mal Evans," he told the drummer. "I'm with the Beatles. Here is my card. It's got a phone number on it. Any time you need anything, at any time of the day or night, 24 hours, anything you want—call me."[4]

Within the space of twenty-four hours, Mal would be squiring the Beatles and Nicol on the band's inaugural world tour. As with the other members of the entourage, Mal felt Ringo's absence acutely. During their flight to the Continent, the Beatles resorted to humor, their favorite balm, to make light of their predicament. "The boys really had fun at the pilot's expense, as he didn't know Ringo wasn't present and kept asking for his autograph," Mal remembered. "George jumped in at one point and said to Paul, 'Go on, Ringo—give him your autograph. Don't be mean!'"[5]

The significance of Ringo's absence certainly wasn't lost on the drummer himself. "It was very strange, them going off without me," he said. "They'd taken Jimmie Nicol, and I thought they didn't love me anymore—all that stuff went through my head."[6] Mal understood Ringo's position implicitly. Indeed, he had lived and breathed it, existing in a near-constant state of anxiety over his status with the Beatles.

By the time the band—plus Nicol—got to Amsterdam on June 3, Jimmie had fallen into the natural rhythms of the Beatles' touring life. The boys enjoyed the drummer's easygoing ways, especially his penchant for saying "It's getting better" when surveyed about his experience in the Beatles' extraordinary fishbowl. Amsterdam, meanwhile, proved a great source of liberation for the Beatles and their entourage. With the Dutch police lessening their protective custody, the boys felt free to roam the city. George would never forget the afternoon they sailed along the canals in a glass-topped boat as some thirty thousand fans looked on from the shore. It was on board the boat that he got to witness the level of Mal's dedication to fulfilling the band's every need: "We were boating along the canals, waving and being fab, and we saw a bloke standing in the crowd with a groovy-looking cloak on. We sent Mal to find out where he got it from. Mal jumped off or swam off the boat and about three hours later turned up at our hotel with the cloak, which he'd bought from the guy."[7]

The degree to which Mal allowed his self-doubt to color his interactions with the Beatles was simply unwarranted. Sure, he had made plenty of foibles during his full-time efforts on their behalf, but his competence as a roadie had increased in remarkable ways. At one juncture, George fretted about the number of guitar strings he consumed during the band's live performances. "You know, Mal, they're going to break as soon as I get on stage," he lamented. "And sure enough, they did, one by one," Mal wrote. "But we always have a spare guitar on stage for him to use, and I would run on, grab the guitar, change the strings while he used the spare guitar, and have it back to him as soon as possible. It was at these moments that my mind used to go blank—I'd be on and off the stage and have it done with all systems working on automatic."[8] In a matter of months, Mal had not only mastered the intricacies of handling the band's guitar and drum works, but had done so under the high-pressure conditions of a live concert.

After the Dutch shows wrapped up for the night, Mal and the band would take advantage of the cover of darkness to carry out one of their more audacious expeditions of the Beatles' touring years—and they pointedly did so while Brian was back in England. "We managed to escape this particular night, and ended up frequenting the brothels which line one of the canals," Mal wrote. "It was dark when we arrived and we were congratulating ourselves at having gotten away with something. Imagine our dismay on leaving and finding daylight greeting us, along with several thousand Beatle fans lining the banks and shouting, 'Yay, Beatles!' So we hurriedly took our red faces back to the hotel!"[9]

Incredibly, the Beatles and their entourage managed to leave the Continent unscathed by the kinds of press reports of scandalous, even reckless behavior that might have spelled doom for another band. But it wouldn't be the last time their brazenness went unchecked. Before they left the Netherlands to begin the Far East leg of their tour, Mal made a point of demonstrating the awesome power of the Beatles' fame for their temporary drummer. "I was to take Jimmie outside in the intermission between the shows to give him some idea of the size of the Beatles' following," Mal wrote. "It was nice for him to be able to walk around and enjoy this until the moment arrived when somebody recognized him, and he really got off on being chased back to the stage door!"[10] It was only a few days into the tour, but Jimmie now understood the looking glass through which he had stepped and the changes the experience had wrought. "The day before I was a Beatle, not one girl would even look me over," he later remarked. "The day after, when I was suited up and riding in the back of a limo with John Lennon and Paul McCartney, they were dying just to get a touch of me."[11]

On June 7, the Beatles and their entourage returned to London, where they boarded the first of five scheduled flights on their way to Hong Kong, where they performed a pair of concerts at the 1,700-seat Princess Theatre. While the group stayed behind at the hotel, Mal ventured alone into the city: "I was the only one of the party to take a Rickshaw ride," he recalled, "and I got my leg pulled a lot when I recounted the story to the boys. There I was, sitting in the back of a Rickshaw, drunk as a lord, late at night, waiting to see the sights of Hong Kong. The Rickshaw bowling along in fine style when we entered a tree-lined avenue." At this point, the driver tried to tempt Mal with a carnal menu that included a woman, a young girl, and a little boy. "I got him to take me back to the hotel—mind you, I'm not adverse [*sic*] to a bit of hanky-panky, but there are limits."[12]

Apparently, Mal's appetites were not sated by a mere rickshaw ride. The "demon for sex" whom Tony Bramwell had observed the previous autumn was clearly in evidence that night in Hong Kong. Mal later ventured out to one of the city's exclusive teahouses—the kind where gentlemen sip tea while a madam parades young women for their consideration. "The idea was to take her back to your hotel," said Mal, "and on suitable reimbursement, the young lady would entertain you for the evening. After my young lady kept saying, 'You have such beautiful eyes—I've never seen such beautiful eyes,' it did my ego a lot of good when I got my money back!"[13]

Before departing Hong Kong, Mal accompanied the boys on a shopping trip, with the Beatles springing for an array of newly sewn clothing, courtesy of the city's tailoring establishments. George also purchased a Pentax camera from one of Hong Kong's vaunted dealers, an Asahi 1 model, the first of many such cameras he would buy; the Beatle later gifted it to Mal, knowing of the roadie's budding interest in photography, particularly in terms of documenting the Beatles' movements—not to mention supplementing his income.

With Hong Kong behind them, the boys and their entourage made their way to Oceania, where they prepared for a harrowing pace that thirty-two shows in eighteen days across Australia and New Zealand would demand. As it turned out, the Beatles' reception Down Under not only rivaled but also far exceeded the fanfare they had witnessed in Great Britain and the United States. They arrived in Sydney on the morning of June 11, inauspiciously greeted by a driving rainstorm. Nearly a thousand fans battled the elements to welcome them—though one group, proclaiming to be the Anti-Trash Society, protested the band's arrival, sporting a placard that announced, "Go Home, Bugs!"

Things were markedly different the next day in Adelaide, where more than two hundred thousand people lined the route from the airport to the city center. An additional thirty thousand people ensconced themselves at the city's Town Hall, where the mayor held an audience with the Beatles.

By this point, thirty-two-year-old Derek Taylor, the erudite former writer for the *Daily Express*, had taken over the press duties previously assigned to Brian Sommerville, who had acquitted himself so poorly back in Paris. As Brian Epstein's assistant, Derek had ghost-written the manager's autobiography, *A Cellarful of Noise*, which would be published later that year. After joining the tour, he was astonished by the fervor that greeted the Beatles in Australasia. "Each time we'd arrived at an airport, it was as if de Gaulle had landed, or better yet, the Messiah," Derek wrote. "The routes were lined solid, cripples threw away their sticks, sick people rushed up to the car as if a touch from one of the boys would make them well again, old women stood watching with their grandchildren, and as we'd pass by, I could see the look on their faces. It was as if some savior had arrived and all these people were happy and relieved, as if things somehow were going to be better now."[14]

Meanwhile, Mal continued his movable feast of a nightlife in Sydney on the band's very first night on the continent. In the enthusiastic company of Jimmie, he strolled into the Chequers nightclub, where, since the 1950s, American singer Frances Faye had performed a racy, highly sexualized act. Faye took an instant liking to Jimmie, whom she invited to play the drums with her band during the evening's second act. For the Beatles' stand-in, playing at Chequers proved to be one of the highlights of his fortnight on the road with the band. After performing just two more shows in Adelaide, Jimmie found his Beatles tenure come to a close. To the boys' and their entourage's great relief, Ringo returned to the fold, having received a clean bill of health back in London. Accompanied by Brian Epstein, he arrived in Melbourne on the morning of June 15, delighted to reclaim his place behind the drum kit.

For Jimmie, Ringo's return spelled the end of the road, although the substitute drummer also managed to raise Brian's ire during his final hours with the Beatles after he decided to enjoy the Melbourne nightlife one more time. Borrowing a car, he stealthily left the hotel for a few drinks at a nearby pub, violating Brian's midnight curfew in the bargain. Within half an hour, he was intercepted by Mal and Derek Taylor, who demanded that he return with them to the hotel. While Mal had had no issue hanging out with Jimmie in a bar the previous evening, Brian's return had signaled a radical shift in how he and Derek engaged the drummer.

"You can't come out here. You mustn't be out on the streets. You can't come into a bar," they told him.

Jimmie replied, "What are you talking about, I'm not a Beatle anymore."

Taylor exclaimed, "You are a Beatle until we put you on the plane."[15]

In the matter of only a few hours, Brian personally saw Jimmie off at the airport, where he gifted him with a gold watch and a £500 fee for his efforts as Ringo's much-ballyhooed stand-in.

Epstein's appearance on the scene had indeed marked a change in the tour's atmosphere—albeit not to its overarching debauchery, which was conducted in hotels under a thin veil of discretion. Years later, John would liken the Beatles tours to Fellini's *Satyricon*, suggesting that their world-beating jaunts were a fantasia of sexual decadence.[16] Lloyd Ravenscroft, the Australian tour manager, confirmed that the band members "had girls in their room, yes. That was in the hands of Mal Evans, who was very good at picking the right girls. It was very discreet and well-organized. When they were getting involved in that sort of thing, I kept right out of the way."[17]

With Ringo back in the fold, the Beatles returned to Sydney on June 18. There, Mal was reunited with Eunice Hayes, his childhood neighbor, who was now living in the city with her husband, Stan. Knowing that Mal was in Sydney, Eunice had been determined to see her old friend. After pretending to be a guest at the Beatles' hotel, she managed to make her way up to Mal's floor, with her friend Robyn in tow, where the roadie clasped her in a giant bear hug, thrilled by the unexpected reunion. Eunice later recalled that "we sat and talked, and I noticed his door was kept open. He said he *always* had to have his door open. He explained it was so that he would know if any unwanted persons tried to sneak in at any time. Even as we were speaking, the emergency door opened, and I watched as two young teenagers who had somehow got up the stairs crept through the door. Mal jumped up and said, 'Here we go!' They begged and pleaded with him to let them see the boys, but Mal kindly but firmly sent them back, saying, 'Sorry girls—can't let you in.'"[18]

As Mal and Eunice became reacquainted, they were interrupted by a loud voice announcing, "C'mon lads, it's waving time!" Eunice followed the roadie out to the balcony. "I was astounded," she recalled. "From one end of the long street to the other, as far as the eye could see, there were masses of screaming, frantic, cheering, waving people. I looked across the road, and even the Chevron-Hilton Hotel opposite had faces filling every space in every window peering out. Some kneeling, some sitting, and some standing on chairs, waving like mad!" Afterward, she learned that Sounds Incorporated, one of the opening acts on the tour, occupied the floor directly below the Beatles' suite. "Mal said to me, 'Have a look at this,' and took me down there. He opened a door, and in the semi-darkness, you could see sprawled all over the floor was this group writhing around with girls who'd been 'brought in' for them. Mal told me everything was prearranged prior to the lads' arrival in any city."[19]

When Mal wasn't arranging the boys' nocturnal pleasures—while always being sure to satisfy his own desires in the bargain—he spent much of his free time doing the sightseeing that the Beatles, trapped inside their fame, could not. When the band and their entourage made their way to Brisbane, Mal visited the Lone Pine Koala Bear Sanctuary, where he was photographed holding native koala bears and pythons. "Of course, the koala bear I picked, after being told they were the most friendly things in the world, went and bit me on the nose—maybe we should not have told it!

Mal with a koala bear in Australia

Mal with a python in Australia

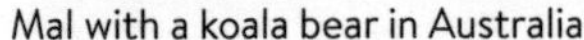

But they really are one of the most beautiful little animals I've come across, giving some answer as to why teddy bears are a universal child's toy."[20]

Things became dicey for the Beatles in New Zealand. At one point, their Cadillac became mired in the awaiting throng just thirty feet from their Auckland hotel. With no alternative, Mal, Neil, and Lloyd Ravenscroft locked the Beatles inside the car and pushed it toward the hotel's garage door, fighting off fans every inch of the way. The whole operation took twenty minutes and, despite their best efforts, some two hundred Beatles fans managed to get into the garage with them. Mal and Neil were forced to toss the fans out, one by one, while the Beatles fled to the safety of their rooms. The band encountered a similar mêlée in Dunedin, where Paul's face was scratched, and John had a large clump of hair yanked from his head. The next day, the group traveled to Christchurch, where a thirteen-year-old girl hurled herself at the Beatles' limousine. Incredibly, she came away unscathed.[21]

The same could not be said for a twenty-year-old woman in Wellington, the victim in one of the strangest episodes in the history of the Beatles' touring years. The incident took place in the early morning hours of June 23, during the group's first stop in New Zealand. And most problematic of all for Mal, whatever befell the young woman almost certainly happened in his sixth-floor hotel room at the tony St. George.

As it turned out, Mal had met the woman the previous evening, when she and her mother invited him, along with band members from Sounds Incorporated, over to their home for tea. It had already been a taxing day, thanks to a subpar public-address system at Wellington's Town Hall and to the struggle that occurred after the concert. As it happened, the city had allotted only two police officers for crowd control, forcing Mal to climb out of the Beatles' limo and clear a path for the vehicle by physically pushing fans out of the way.

So, when it came to having tea in the company of an amiable New Zealander and her Beatles-fan daughter, Mal was game. "The atmosphere at their home was congenial," he wrote, "and having been on the road for several weeks, I was quite content sitting back with my feet up, enjoying tea and conversation. Sounds Incorporated and the young lady decided to go into town and party there, but I was too comfortable and decided to enjoy the hospitality of her mother."[22]

Unbeknownst to Mal, a very different drama then played out at the St. George. At the time, the official story involved a twenty-year-old female fan who, having secreted her way into the hotel, chose to slash her wrists in Mal's room after being unable to talk her way into the Beatles' suite. Fortunately, police caught sight of the young woman through a window and broke down the locked door with a battering ram. She was subsequently taken to a local hospital and discharged that same day.

Concerned about the possibility of the Beatles becoming embroiled in an international sex scandal, Derek Taylor got in front of the story, affirming that there was absolutely no connection between the Beatles, or any of their party, and the young woman in question. He suggested that the woman had gained admission to the hotel room by masquerading as a relative of a member of the party, noting that autograph hunters had been roaming the halls in search of the Beatles throughout the tour. There was a further suggestion that it was actually Mal who had discovered the woman, after trying to gain entrance to his room. Derek underscored the fact that police filed no charges as a result of the incident—which the press trumpeted across the wire services as "Girl Tries to Die for Beatles," a headline in keeping with those for a spate of recent Australasian stories involving overzealous fans attempting to meet the band.[23]

For his part, George would recall the story somewhat differently. In his memory, someone "had a girl in his room who tried to slash her wrists whilst he was out at the pub. I remember Derek panicking as the story was immediately on the wire service all over the world, 'Suicide Attempt in Beatle Hotel.'"[24] Years later, Ravenscroft and Australian deejay Bob Rogers admitted that the cover story had been hastily fabricated to avoid any hint of scandal. In Rogers's memory, the woman was actually "in her mid-20s and looked a lot like Angela Lansbury. She had booked into the hotel in an attempt to meet the Beatles, something that was quite common in every city, but had only managed to get into bed" with someone else at the hotel. Afterward, the couple lounged around in Mal's room, drinking champagne, but when she found out he couldn't help her get to the Beatles, "she became hysterical, and when he went out to the show, she locked herself in, broke the top off of the champagne bottle, and cut her wrists. When the police were called, they showed up with an actual battering ram and smashed the door off its hinges. They'd been watching too many movies."[25]

However, Mal's narration of the events pointed to something perhaps even more sinister at play in the Beatles' entourage, an aspect of the affair he had luckily avoided by virtue of enjoying teatime away from the St. George. "On arriving back at the hotel at two in the morning," he wrote, "I was greeted by a crowd of police and detectives as the elevator doors opened at my floor. On verifying that I occupied a particular room number, they very solemnly escorted me there, where to my horror on opening the door, I found the bathroom and bedroom covered in blood. Apparently, what had happened [was] several people had gang-banged her in my bedroom. She was so distraught, she took a razor blade from my razor and slashed her wrists, but was discovered in time and recovered in hospital. Obviously I was a prime suspect, but I had the best alibi in the world—I was drinking tea with her mother."[26]

The incident at the St. George would leave a lasting impression on Mal. His "demon" persona was still alive and well, to be sure, but there would be perceptible shifts in his outlook as the group's touring days moved forward. As the band's stint in Oceania came to a close, Mal found himself reaching new levels of exhaustion. For the duration of the world tour, he had served as road manager not only for the Beatles, but for the supporting acts as well. Sounds Incorporated demonstrated their appreciation for his efforts by, at first, playing an elaborate joke on him. It all started when the members of the group woke him out of a deep sleep, shouting, "The Beatles' equipment has gone off, they need you!" Mal fell for the ruse until he realized that "the first act of the second show had just started and it was not the Beatles at all." At this point, the Sounds Incorporated band members "ganged up on me, shoving me roughly into a corner of their dressing room, and threatening gestures and angry shouts, such as 'we've got ya now, you're gonna get it,' 'we're gonna give it to you, Mal,' 'we've put up with you long enough.'"

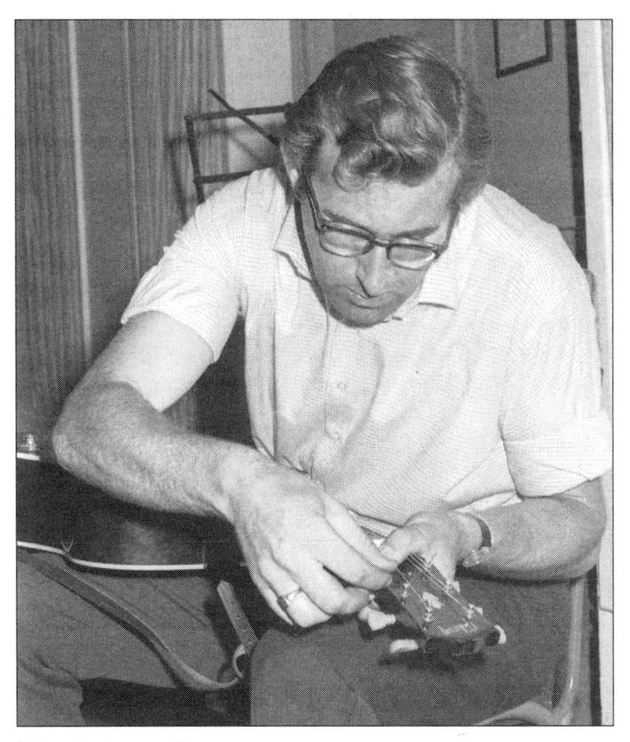

Mal stringing a guitar

At first he was crestfallen, but then "they proceeded to present me with a solid-gold link bracelet as a token of their affection and thanks, inscribed on one side 'Mal,' and on the other, 'Thanks, Sounds.'"[27]

On June 30, the Beatles and their entourage made the long flight home, arriving back in London on July 1. It had been an unforgettable, eye-opening tour for Mal. He had seen the awesome power of Beatlemania in full flower, as hundreds of thousands of fans were drawn together simply to catch a glimpse of their idols. But at the same time, he observed darker aspects of the Beatles phenomenon beginning to take flight—one in the form of the Anti-Trash Society, whose membership, however small in number, marked the end of the Beatles' visit by hurling eggs at them during the final show Down Under in Brisbane. "What particular axe they had to grind, I never did find out, being too annoyed at having to get the egg stains off the suits," he wrote.[28]

But Mal was buoyed nonetheless, especially by his ability to keep the Beatles' show in forward motion, both as an equipment manager and as bodyguard. "It was pretty hectic over there," he later reflected, "and we had a lot of trouble, but I managed to deal with everything, and towards the end of our Down Under visit, John turned round to me and thanked me for keeping them going on stage." It was a powerful realization for the roadie, who knew full well that the band members "don't make friends easily, and I don't think I was completely accepted by them until we went on the Australian tour."[29]

10

MR. NICE GUY

July 1964 would mark one of the busiest eras in the history of the Beatles. The world premiere of *A Hard Day's Night* was slated for July 6, followed by a gala event in support of the feature film on July 10. On that same day, the accompanying LP and "A Hard Day's Night" single would also see release.

On July 5, Mal finally put pen to paper, writing a letter to Lily, which he mailed to their Mossley Hill address. Only, Lily wasn't there. She and Gary were in the midst of a six-week stay in Norway, where one of Lil's pen pals lived, and they would be there for at least another week. In his letter to Lily, Mal apologized for his lapse in correspondence. In his haste to begin the world tour—complicated, no doubt, by Ringo's hospitalization and the brief ascendance of Jimmie Nicol—he had left her Norwegian address, along with his diary, in the Commer van.[1]

Planning to return to London for the film's world premiere, Mal and Neil drove home to Liverpool for a quick respite after the lengthy tour. With only a few miles to go, the van began leaking clutch fluid, necessitating repairs that would force Mal to stay in Liverpool, with Neil taking the train back to the capital in time for the screening. For the first time in months, Mal was alone. "The house is just a house at the moment without you and Gary," he wrote to Lil. "With no laughter or warmth in it at all, and I feel very miserable and sorry for myself as you can imagine. I miss you both so. Every pretty girl I see brings your face to my mind, and while I was away, there were so many little boys who looked like Gary waving to me from the crowd."[2]

As it turned out, two-and-a-half-year-old Gary would cause a minor ruckus when he returned from Norway. Having overheard his mother's pen pal using the Norwegian word *skit*, which translates—and, indeed, sounds like—*shit* in English, he went around Liverpool for several days saying "shit" at every opportunity, before being corrected by Lily.[3] Lily and Gary would return to England by ship on July 12, having missed the chance to attend the gala Liverpool debut of *A Hard Day's Night* just two days earlier. The event afforded Mal a sense of much-needed validation, even pride, in his professional life with the Beatles. As a bonus, he appears in the movie as an extra in the press party scene.[4]

"The film premiere in Liverpool was very exciting for all of us at being honored in our own town," Mal later wrote. "Not that the shouting and cheering of the thousands that lined the route from the airport to the Town Hall were for me, but I was very proud of my association with the Beatles." And with so many events associated with the band, Mal found himself at the center of the action. "The Town Hall was absolutely packed with local civic dignitaries, and in the ensuing scuffle for autographs," he wrote, "I was to lose my wristwatch. I was talking to George afterwards and complaining that they were worse than most of the fans and bemoaning the loss of my watch. George, at the soonest opportunity, went out himself and bought me a new one."[5]

Gary with Lady the dog

The day proved to be a mixed bag for Paul, his "hometown hero" status notwithstanding. In recent months, he had become cognizant of a growing feeling in Liverpool that the Beatles had forsaken the city for London, that they were no longer proud to celebrate their roots. "We weren't *really* apprehensive about going back to Liverpool for the other première," he commented. "We'd heard one or two little rumors that people felt we'd betrayed them by leaving, and shouldn't have gone to live in London. But there were always those detractors."[6]

That same week, Paul was the subject of a leaflet campaign that had been timed to coincide with the feature film's hometown debut. Since 1963, nineteen-year-old Anita Cochrane had been claiming Paul's paternity for her baby. When the issue came to NEMS's attention, Brian provided the young Liverpudlian woman with a £5,000 cash settlement. Misrepresenting himself as Anita's irate uncle, her mother's boyfriend wasn't satisfied with Epstein's effort, and he pasted leaflets up and down the city streets claiming that Paul was a cad and a delinquent parent. As word of the leaflets spread, Mal was quietly dispatched to quell the girl's "uncle," while gathering up and disposing of the embarrassing leaflets.[7] A paternity test would later reveal that Paul was not the baby's father.[8]

In many ways, Mal's role in the Beatles' universe had been expanding for some time. While his duties had, from the beginning, consisted of acting as equipment manager and bodyguard, he could sense that his work had grown more porous, that he had transformed into an all-around fixer and unspecified jack-of-all-trades.

On July 12, while Lily and Gary were making their passage from Norway back to Liverpool, the Beatles undertook a mini British tour that would take them to mid-August, when they were set to begin their first full-fledged North American tour. Prior to making the trip, Mal visited a Liverpool tailor. With Gary in tow, he upgraded his wardrobe in advance of the tour, a lengthy jaunt that would place him in close quarters with Brian's disapproving eyes. Later, when they picked up Mal's new wardrobe, the roadie was right chuffed with the tailor's work. As for Gary, he "was not awfully impressed," Mal recorded in his diary.[9]

The next day, Mal returned to London, where he made the rounds of the city's instrument vendors. With Alistair Taylor by his side, he went to

Sound City, where they filled the Commer with new guitar stands, guitar leads, and drumsticks, among other sundry items. Mal also dropped off Paul's massive bass amp for repairs in advance of the tour, picking it up the next day, now "mended," in Dartford.[10] A few days later, prior to the band's show at Scarborough's Futurist Theatre, he took delivery of two new hundred-watt Vox amps from Dick Denney, the inventor behind the pioneering portable speakers.[11]

The day after the band's final tune-up performance at the Blackpool Opera House on August 16, Mal and Derek left for North America. By the time Neil and the Beatles joined them in San Francisco, the stage was set for the group's inaugural show at the Cow Palace, a 17,000-seat arena in Daly City, California.

As in Australia, Mal and Neil, with considerable input from Derek, were tasked with managing the Beatles' every move. For this reason, it was vital for them to liaise with local law enforcement. While the Beatles deplaned in San Francisco on August 19, Mal and Derek strategized with San Mateo County Sheriff's Office and San Francisco County lawmen about providing security as the band and their entourage traveled from the airport to the Cow Palace. As they stood on the tarmac, the officers lectured them, often vituperatively, about following safety regulations.

To his credit, Derek spoke up, hoping to impress upon the lawmen the need to be prepared for the coming hordes. "There will be a great many people waiting here for them," he said as calmly and diplomatically as possible, "and if we don't do something, there *will* be trouble."

That's when the deputy barked his response: "*Don't* tell *me* what my job is or there *will* be *trouble*!"

Derek and Mal could only exchange blank looks. The deputy was simply clueless. And the very same scene would happen time and time again that year, as local authorities continued to vastly underestimate the thrall the Beatles held over their massive and growing fan base.[12]

As it happened, the Beatles were greeted at the airport by more than 9,000 fans. The San Mateo authorities cordoned off a twenty-five-foot zone, nicknamed "Beatlesville," that served as a meet-and-greet area prior to the group's trip to the Cow Palace, where Mal was making last-minute preparations for the gig. The San Mateo sheriff's office—more than 180 strong—could barely hold the fans at bay, with many scaling the barriers in the process.

Meanwhile, at the Cow Palace, Mal was holding court. "I was always a bit of a bastard the first night of any tour, on the assumption that the Beatles were the reason for everybody being there," he recalled. "They were top of the bill and, of course, came first in my eyes. So I would usually give the other road managers a hard time, establishing my position on the stage, the rest of the acts having to fit in around the Beatles. For me, it was the only way to act, because the following night, having established that routine, I could then back off and be Mr. Nice Guy, helping the other road managers with their equipment, ensuring smooth changeovers between acts, and thereby giving some professional polish to the whole show. Maybe it wasn't the right attitude, but for me at that time, it really worked, and I got on well with all the other roadies."[13]

Incredibly, the Beatles—the world's most popular act by a wide margin—were once again entering the fray with a minuscule entourage. "The first time in America had been absolutely marvelous," Ringo recalled. "Our personal road crew then was Neil, Mal, and Brian, with Derek to look after the press. Brian was the manager, but he didn't actually do anything. Neil would get us a cup of tea, and Mal would fix the instruments. There were four people with us."[14]

Consisting of thirty-two shows in twenty-four cities and spanning just thirty-three days, the whirlwind North American tour was managed by Bob Bonis, who had recently completed a stint with the Rolling Stones. The whole shebang began, as before, with a telegram from Elvis and Colonel Tom Parker. As on previous tours, the Beatles' dressing rooms were fairly porous, with all manner of celebrities, politicians, and the like making their presence known.

Mal took careful note of the glitterati. Indeed, his autograph book, which at that point was filled with the signatures mostly of musicians whom he had encountered at the Cavern and during the Beatles' 1963 Christmas shows, was about to get a serious workout. He was especially taken with Jackie DeShannon, "a lovely singer and an exceptional songwriter, and I was just one of many who came under her spell—and had a crush on her." In Las Vegas, "two very welcome backstage visitors were Liberace, and Pat

Boone and family. The latter bringing with him his own photograph of the Beatles for them to sign."[15]

But by this juncture, as Neil pointed out, Mal had emerged as a celebrity in his own right, thanks to publications such as *The Beatles Book*, which fans gobbled up month in and month out. "It was okay for him," Neil recalled, "going out in front getting the instruments ready. Dead popular he was. As they cheered and shouted at him he talked to them and made jokes. He didn't have to physically fight them off, once it started."[16]

The Beatles were supported on the North American tour by (in order of appearance) Bill Black's Combo, the Exciters, the Righteous Brothers, and DeShannon. That night at the Cow Palace, the Beatles took the stage at 9:20 p.m. Wearing freshly pressed dark suits, they performed some twenty-nine minutes, with the gig interrupted twice due to the usual fusillade of jelly beans. Afterward, they dropped their instruments onstage and ran for the exit, where they hurled themselves into a waiting ambulance—Neil was stranded in the limo, which had become overrun by fans. As Mal ran the usual gauntlet to secure the instruments, amps, and other gear, the local authorities assessed the casualties, which included one boy with a dislocated shoulder, two fans who were arrested, nineteen girls treated with first aid during the concert itself, and another fifty fans who sustained minor injuries. Beatlemania had returned to America's shores.

Back at the hotel, Mal met twenty-six-year-old Ivor Davis, a British journalist who served as the West Coast correspondent for the *Daily Express*, a London-based newspaper that boasted circulation of four million daily copies. Davis later recalled the moment he arrived at the Beatles' San Francisco lodgings: "I shook hands with Mal Evans, a burly six-footer sporting heavy, dark-framed glasses, and Neil Aspinall, a thinner, boyish-looking young man who looked as though he might be a relative of the Fab Four. They could have been Laurel and Hardy, but they were the Beatles' longtime road managers."[17]

Davis was embedded with the entourage for the duration of the tour, as was Larry Kane, a twenty-one-year-old correspondent with WFUN Radio in Miami and the only broadcast journalist to provide the Beatles with coast-to-coast coverage during their first two North American tours. As with Davis, Kane's initiation into the world of Beatlemania came courtesy of Mal and Neil, whom he spotted pacing up and down the hotel corridors, always on the lookout for interlopers.[18] Kane took an immediate liking to Mal, whom he revered for maintaining a pleasant demeanor—even when the chips were down. "When it came time to bite the bullet, he would become serious in an instant, but you knew he was faking," Kane wrote. "This was a man whose smile and cheerful demeanor were contagious."[19]

On August 20, the Beatles' entourage set up camp for the show at Las Vegas's Convention Hall, where the whole rigamarole reinvented itself all over again—only, this time, the band would skirt even closer to the sort of sex scandal that had seemed to waft in the ether around their tours since Australia, if not longer. Recognizing the restricted nature of the band's touring experience, the Sahara Hotel arranged for slot machines to be installed in their suite. As he observed the proceedings, Ivor Davis came to realize that the mothers of Beatles fans were just as determined, if not more so, than their daughters in their quest to meet them. "Sexual activity was rarely, if ever, performed by the girls," he recalled, "but it was being performed by mothers as a passport for their daughters."[20]

Prior to the first show that day, Kane interviewed Paul about American racial segregation practices, noting that the band would be playing in Florida during the tour's final stretch. Paul was firm about the Beatles' belief that "you can't treat other human beings like animals," adding that "I wouldn't mind 'em sitting next to me. It's the way we all feel."[21] While the matinee passed without incident, the problems began with the Beatles' second Vegas show, which was briefly delayed by a bomb threat, perhaps from the American equivalent of the Anti-Trash Society.

For his part, Mal was impressed by the Las Vegas police, who had formed themselves into a human blockade in front of the stage. But the real action occurred that night at the Sahara, after the band returned to the hotel inside the safety of a Brinks armored truck. As Mal and Neil took up their usual posts, patrolling the hallways and acting as traffic wardens for the bandmates' guests, fifteen-year-old Georgiana Steele and her friend Arlene joined in the post-show party. Georgiana's mother was at the Sahara to play the role of chaperone, periodically seeking reassurance that the girls' purity was still intact. And it was, for the most part—aside from Georgiana's. She made out with George and was chased around the suite by John, who was clad only in a pair of red-and-white polka-dot boxer shorts. Eventually, Georgiana fell asleep from the effects of alcohol, which had been flowing liberally throughout the night.[22]

The real trouble still lay ahead. At 5 a.m., Mal rapped on Larry Kane's door, ordering the reporter to get dressed and "put on a jacket and tie."

Groggy from sleep, Kane asked, "Why me?"

In a moment laden with irony, Mal replied, "Larry, you're a reporter. You look more trustworthy."[23]

With Kane in tow, Mal attended to an irate mother, whose twin fourteen-year-old daughters had also joined the party that night. The girls' mother—possibly inebriated after a night of gambling in the casino downstairs—demanded access to the Beatles' suite. She had already gone so far as to telephone the Clark County Sheriff's Office, reporting that her daughters were being held captive. Two detectives arrived on the scene, which now included Neil and Derek, and began taking statements from John and Brian. Meanwhile, Derek attempted to run interference, explaining that the girls' mother had given permission for her daughters to attend the party. Kane glanced at Mal and Neil, looking for signs of sincerity, for affirmation that, indeed, nothing untoward had occurred. "Where are the girls?" Kane asked. In response, "Malcolm grinned," while "Neil said nothing."[24]

And that's when the elevator door opened and the woman's twin daughters, accompanied by a police officer, casually strolled into the corridor, smiling and seemingly no worse for wear. They claimed that they had been in the Beatles' suite with John, who had been a perfect gentleman all night. Satisfied that no laws had been broken, the detectives took their leave. For his part, Brian provided the woman with a fistful of cash for her trouble. John shrugged off the whole affair, apparently blind to the fact that they had narrowly avoided a full-blown scandal and possibly even statutory rape charges courtesy of the Vegas police.[25]

With dawn ushering in a new day, Mal broke up the party, such as it was. With any luck, Mr. Nice Guy could grab a few winks before breaking camp at the Sahara. After all, they had to be on a plane to Seattle in only a few short hours.

11

SEVEN LEVELS

By the time the tour reached Los Angeles on August 23, Mal was suffering from exhaustion. The previous evening, he had been forced to get physical after the band's show at Vancouver's Empire Stadium. "In our harrowing escape," Kane recalled, Mal had "shielded John Lennon from onrushing fans, at one point stiff-arming a boy who tried to get to the Beatles' car. That move would have made an NFL running back proud. On the plane later, I laughingly complimented him on his prowess. He replied, 'Just wait for me next act.'"[1]

For the duration of their visit to Los Angeles, where the Beatles played at the famed Hollywood Bowl, the band and their entourage stayed at the rented Bel Air home of British actor Reginald Owen. To Mal's barely contained glee, Colonel Tom Parker visited them several times, bringing greetings, and gifts, from the King of Rock 'n' Roll, who had already left the city for his Graceland estate, in Memphis. To Mal's great chagrin, "Neil and the boys received albums and a pioneer covered wagon table lamp, and I was very hurt at being left out. One of the boys quietly mentioned this to Colonel Tom, and he made a special return trip with a whole collection of albums and presented me with a very special Wells Fargo stagecoach lamp from him and Elvis." Back in Liverpool, Mal would proudly display the lamp. Later, Lily was fond of saying that "if there was a fire at home, Mal would save the stagecoach and Elvis records and come back for me."[2]

Several days later, Mal enjoyed the thrill of his life, at first vicariously, when Chris Hutchins, editor of *NME*, arranged for Paul to speak on the phone with Elvis. Mal later wrote that "to my delight, after speaking to Elvis for about 10 minutes, Paul said, 'Elvis, I'd like you to say hello to one of your biggest fans. He works for us, he's our road manager, Malcolm Evans.'" Mal was tongue-tied. "The first words Elvis said to me were, 'It's a pleasure to talk to you, sir.' After that, I went blank as I burbled thank-you's [*sic*] to him, telling him what pleasure he had given me over the years. I was so knocked out that he would take the time to talk, and amazed how polite he was to me, a mere fan."[3]

During their stay in Los Angeles, Mal enjoyed plenty of opportunities to mingle with the stars of the day. At a garden party held on behalf of the Hemophilia Society, he hobnobbed with the likes of Frank Sinatra, Jane Fonda, Kirk Douglas, and Dean Martin, among a cavalcade of others. For the occasion, which the Beatles headlined as a courtesy to Capitol Records president Alan Livingston, Mal donned one of his new tailored suits. Model Peggy Lipton was there, too, having crashed the event on the off chance that she might meet the Beatles. At seventeen, the future star of TV's *Mod Squad* joined the entourage back in Bel Air.

By this point, the rented manse had become a focal point for the rich and famous. That week, Mal penned a long-overdue letter to Lil, regaling her with stories of his epic stargazing experiences. On one unforgettable evening, the band and their entourage had joined Burt Lancaster at his home, where the actor screened *A Shot in the Dark*, the new Peter Sellers film. Mal was thunderstruck by Lancaster's luxurious digs: "He has a wide screen fitted in his living room," he wrote to Lily, "a truly fabulous home which cost about a million dollars. He has a gymnasium fitted in, sunken bath, and a gorgeous swimming pool that is warm and even steaming. George, Ringo, and myself went in for a swim, and Burt lent me his own personal swimming trunks. You can imagine how thrilled I feel about it all."[4]

The Beatles were on the verge of enjoying a life-changing thrill of their own. On August 28, as the boys and their entourage rolled into New York City for a pair of concerts at the Forest Hills Stadium in Queens, they checked into the Delmonico Hotel. The first show was a difficult one—not for Mal or the Beatles, but for the Righteous Brothers. "Things came to a head when in the middle of their act, the Beatles dropped behind the stage onto the tennis courts at Forest Hills by helicopter," Mal recalled. "[The Righteous Brothers] just couldn't be heard above the roaring crowd chanting, 'Beatles.' Everyone stood up, pointing to the helicopter and completely

Mal and the Beatles at Forest Hills

ignoring the wonderful artists on stage. Preceding the Beatles must surely be the hardest gig in the world."[5]

About an hour after the concert, as Mal and the Beatles settled into their suite at the Delmonico, folk musician Bob Dylan dropped by the hotel as they were sitting down for a late-night meal with Brian and Neil. *New York Post* columnist Al Aronowitz was there, too, having set up the meeting of rock's reigning voices. Not long after Dylan's arrival, the Beatles offered their guest a sample from their motley collection of pills—Drinamyls and Preludin (both uppers), mostly. But Dylan wasn't having it, instead suggesting "something a little more organic." At first, Brian demurred, sensing the Beatles' apprehension.

That's when Dylan said, "But what about your song—the one about getting high?" At that, he began singing the middle eight from "I Want to Hold Your Hand": "And when I touch you, I get high, I get high."

John quickly interjected: "Those aren't the words. It's 'I can't hide, I can't hide.'"[6]

Ringo tried the marijuana first. A few puffs from Dylan's joint left him smiling and suddenly marveling at the way the ceiling seemed to float down onto him. Soon, they were all stoned. George recalled that "we were just legless, aching from laughter." And for Paul especially, the Beatles' first brush with the devil weed seemed not only mind-blowing, but a moment of great import. To him, it felt exactly like the kind of experience that should be captured for posterity. Having dutifully provided his roadie with a pencil and paper, Paul ordered him to "get it down, Mal, get it down!" Despite being quite stoned in his own right, Mal managed to record the Beatle's most insightful thoughts. The next morning, Mal retrieved the musings, which boiled down to a single sentence: "There are seven levels," his notes read.[7] Roadie? Bodyguard? Fixer? Now Mal could add "amanuensis" to his evolving portfolio.

Having duly expanded their minds with Dylan, the Beatles took a much-needed respite in Atlantic City after performing there on August 30. With sixteen cities still ahead of them, the North American tour hadn't even reached its halfway point, and the band and their entourage were already fatigued. Tempers were running high, and when things got heated, Mal and Neil inevitably felt the brunt of their employers' ire. Mal later recalled that "my ideas about the fellows soon changed. Up to then, they'd been four beautiful people. I'd looked upon them as gods. I soon found out they were just ordinary blokes, not made of platinum. I got some bellyaching and I couldn't answer back. I just had to put up with it."[8]

John held no illusions about the Beatles' behavior, later admitting that "we were bastards. You can't be anything else in such a pressurized situation, and we took it out on Neil, Derek, and Mal. They took a lot of shit from us because we were in such a shitty position. It was hard work and somebody had to take it. Those things are left out, about what bastards we were. Fucking big bastards, that's what the Beatles were. You have to be a bastard to make it, and that's a fact. And the Beatles were the biggest bastards on earth. We were the Caesars. Who's going to knock us when there's a million pounds to be made, all the handouts, the bribery, the police, and the hype?"[9]

And the Caesars were demanding overlords, indeed. As the Beatles' entourage moved into the final three weeks of the tour, they had clearly become cannier in the ways to conduct the boys' post-show activities. There was still a reckless element to their thinking, to be sure. This was the United States in 1964, after all, where a conservative morality still reigned. At this point, Kane observed, "the few teenagers who showed up late at night were fan-club leaders delivering gifts and mail, and they were given soda and a chance to take pictures with the band, nothing more." But then there was the issue of the Beatles' other late-night female guests, which was no small matter and which they had no interest in forgoing, in spite of the attendant risks. "The system was simple," Kane recalled. "Getting women into the hotels required somebody with the power to do so. The Beatles couldn't just wait in the lobby for someone to show up! So Mal Evans and Neil Aspinall would arrange for access and transit. For the most part, Neil or Mal would select the women who would have access to the band, with some obvious benefits attached."[10]

When it came to identifying female companionship for the boys, Mal had become "a suave and smooth procurer," in Kane's words, "able to spot a target with incredible intuition. It was as though he could pick up on the scent of women who were willing. Only rarely did I see him alone in a hotel corridor. At least his flair for recruiting included an understanding of the difficulties the Beatles could face if any female companion was underage or wronged in any way. If one could get an Oscar for safely procuring women, Mal Evans would have received the lifetime achievement award."[11]

In a particularly chilling moment prior to the Chicago gig on September 5, Mal was called upon to reprise his bodyguard role. As the boys and their entourage exited the Sahara O'Hare Hotel, he spotted a woman in the crowd making a beeline for Paul with a pair of handcuffs. "The fans were very inventive," he recalled. "What she had done was attach one end of the handcuff onto her wrist, and she was going to attach the other end onto Paul's wrist. It was a great idea, but she just didn't make it."[12] After taking another detour through Canada for shows in Toronto and Montreal, the tour was briefly diverted in Key West, where the Beatles rode out Hurricane Dora. On September 11, they played Jacksonville's Gator Bowl, where the band triumphed over the stadium's primary tenants, who favored racial segregation despite the passage of the Civil Rights Act in July 1964, and performed before an integrated audience.

During the flight to Massachusetts for the September 12 show at the Boston Garden, Mal's long-standing feelings of intimidation around John came to a head. Sitting next to Kane in the rear of the plane, he broke down in tears, telling the reporter that "John got kind of cross with me—just said I should go fuck off. No reason, ya' know. But I love the man. John is a powerful force. Sometimes he's rough, if you know what I mean, man. But there's no greater person that I know." In many ways, it was as if Mal's lack of self-confidence, a key aspect of his persona for the balance of his life, had returned with a vengeance. Before Kane could ascertain what had happened between the two men, he caught sight of John approaching Mal and embracing him.[13]

For Mal, the mid-September show at Cleveland's Public Auditorium would be memorable in more ways than one. As he later recalled, "I arrived, as always, in the afternoon to set up all the equipment, and upon looking for the main [electrical] supply for equipment, found there wasn't any. I immediately collared the promoter, and on asking what about electricity for the stage, he turned to me and said quizzically, 'They play guitars, don't they?' He really thought they all played acoustic guitars and didn't need it. There then followed a frantic hour of tying cable together to supply the stage with power."[14]

The real problems occurred during the gig itself, when the boys found themselves in near-riot conditions. "The tour was one mad kaleidoscope of sights, sounds, and the inevitable hot dogs, all the shows, except one, completed," Mal wrote. "This was in Cleveland, when the police insisted upon stopping the Beatles halfway through their act as the thousands of kids rushed on stage. One girl explained to me later it was because they couldn't see from their seats, which were behind pillars."[15] A few days later, the Beatles and their entourage made an unplanned stop in Kansas City, Missouri, after promoter Charlie Finley offered the unheard-of sum of $150,000 for the band to perform at Municipal Stadium, home of Major League Baseball's Kansas City Athletics.

In terms of lax security, things really came to a head the next day, in Dallas, where the city's police department requisitioned only two policemen on motorcycles to combat the thousands of fans awaiting the Beatles at the airport. "As we touched down," Mal recalled, the police officers "disappeared beneath the stampeding fans, who gave us the fright of our lives as they climbed on the wings of the plane as we taxied in. How somebody wasn't killed is beyond me."[16] The lack of effective crowd control continued after the show at the Cabana Hotel, where a girl was pushed through a plate-glass door.

With a charity concert slated for New York City, where they would close out the tour on September 20, the Beatles traveled to a remote ranch in the Ozarks to enjoy a few days off. By this juncture, Mal needed a break—not only from the tour, but from the Beatles themselves. "As much as I love them," he later wrote, joining them at the ranch meant that "I would still be working."

Setting up digs with the supporting acts at the Riviera Idlewild Hotel in Jamaica, Queens, Mal befriended one of the policemen assigned to the tour's security detail. Together, the two bonded over one of Mal's favorite pastimes: "I have always been a Western fan, fascinated by guns, for they are not available in England." To his delight, the officer "took me around all the gun shops, where I bought a Western holster. I had great fun walking around the hotel with [the] holster on, cowboy hat, and packing a replica six-shooter."[17] The pistol would be the first entry in the roadie's gun collection, which he proudly displayed in his family's Mossley Hill home.

By September 21, the boys and their entourage were winging their way back to England, the Beatles' having grossed $1.2 million, an incredible sum at the time for a rock 'n' roll tour. Looking back on the American jaunt,

Mal posing with gun and holster

Mal noted that "each of us lost one and half stone [about 21 pounds] in sweat."[18] They had drifted dangerously close to the shoals of scandal, only to emerge unscathed and possibly wiser.

For Mal and Neil, the boundary lines were slowly being redrawn in some instances, while remaining as loose and porous as ever in others. Derek Taylor later recalled a minor scrape between Brian and the boys over their in-flight seating arrangements. Mal, Neil, and Derek typically flew economy, while Brian and the Beatles sat in first class. Derek remembered one instance during the tour when the bandmates sent Brian to economy to fetch their support crew. "He came through to economy to get Mal and Neil and me out into first class," said Derek. "He was sent through by the Beatles actually. 'What are they doing back there? We made a fucking fortune on the tour. Get them up here. You go and get them.'"[19]

In truth, traveling first class afforded Mal and Neil little reward, given the services they were expected to provide the band. By this point, the Beatles had long been cognizant of the importance of the roadies to their

Mal with Neil and George

success story, and Mal and Neil's job-related duties seemed to expand by the moment—yet this didn't necessarily translate into more dollars and cents. George Harrison later recalled the weekly wages the Beatles enterprise grossed at the onset of Beatlemania—prior to the band's 1964 tours, no less—sums that highlighted the staggering differences in their respective compensation: "From the starting figure of £72,000," he said, "we made about £4,000 each. Brian Epstein took £2,025 a week, and Neil and Mal got £25 each."[20]

By the time the band and their entourage arrived back in England on September 21, the Beatles' inner circle had been reduced by one person—and a vital one, at that. Derek Taylor had resigned after an incident with Brian Epstein at the Riviera Idlewild Hotel. In many ways, it came down to a frequent conundrum in the Beatles' circle involving interpersonal jealousy—especially regarding face time with John, Paul, George, and Ringo. Tensions had been running high between Brian and Derek for some time, but things came to a head after the press officer usurped Brian's authority—and, indeed, the manager's personal limousine—and rode with the boys back to the hotel. Brian responded by screaming at Derek, who promptly quit. "I'm not taking any more of this man's shit," Taylor said at the time. "I love the Beatles, but I'm not hanging around to be fired another hundred times. I'm off."[21] He was replaced by twenty-eight-year-old Tony Barrow, who ran the PR division for NEMS. Tony was a known quantity among Mal and the Beatles, the brainchild behind the band's Christmas fan club releases, and the writer responsible for coining the popular nickname "the Fab Four."

After her brother returned from the States, June recalled that "Malcolm came home knackered, absolutely shattered from that tour." In addition to registering his considerable weight loss, she discovered that he had begun compartmentalizing his life. "I think Malcolm kept things quite separate, kept his home life and his work life in distinct spaces," she said. Her brother and the Beatles were living in a "totally unreal world—an extraordinary, horrendous, wonderful, terrible place that they were all existing in during that period. And they were all damaged by it. They suddenly could have anything they wanted."[22]

12

CHANNEL SWIMMER

Mal's work with the Beatles would receive a great boon on October 1, when thirty-five-year-old Alf Bicknell joined the payroll as the band's chauffeur, having driven movie stars around London for the BBC. Alf's weekly wage was £30 (£496 in present-day pounds), necessitating a well-deserved pay raise for Mal and Neil in order to maintain parity among the boys' inner circle.

From the beginning, Alf understood his role implicitly. Part driver, part bodyguard, he recalled, "I took a lot of the pressure off Neil and off Mal," who "was always busy with the musical instruments."[1] Taking up the wheel of the Austin Princess, Alf was a timely addition to the Beatles' team, especially after Mal earned yet another ticket, his third moving violation, and briefly saw his driver's license suspended.[2]

With only a matter of weeks before the Beatles were set to begin an autumn tour of the United Kingdom, George Martin hustled them back into the studio to record their next album. Mal was on hand for the session at EMI Studios on October 18, when Martin produced "I Feel Fine," the group's latest single. Martin was eager to continue "the Roll," his term for the band's run of consecutive number one singles in their homeland. From "Please Please Me" through "A Hard Day's Night," the Roll currently stood at six. The high-octane "I Feel Fine" seemed like a surefire bet to grow that number further still.[3] For much of the session, Mal sat in a corner, by turns replacing guitar strings and reading a detective novel. "This is when you get proud of them," he said, referring to the Beatles' achievements in the studio. "They can be difficult, but when you see how good they are, you forgive them everything."[4]

To this end, Mal recognized the essential work he was carrying out on the band's behalf, especially when it came to keeping them fed, which allowed them to work increasingly longer hours in the studio. During a recent session, John had said, "We need some tea," only to look up and see Mal ambling into Studio 2 with a beverage service. "You get to be a mind-reader in this business," the roadie quipped.[5]

In spite of the additions of Barrow and Bicknell to the team, Mal's job duties were about to expand yet again: the Beatles' all-around fixer was poised to add marijuana procurer to his responsibilities. In the intervening months since meeting Dylan back in August, the bandmates had developed a keen appetite for weed. Mal and Neil became quite adept not only at rolling the cigarettes, but also at maintaining a ready supply of the stuff for their employers. In the United Kingdom, cannabis had been rendered illegal in 1928, as an addendum to the Dangerous Drugs Act of 1920, and growing the plant had been outlawed in 1964, which put the Beatles' roadies in jeopardy should they ever be caught trafficking in the stuff.

From the outset, George Martin knew the band was up to something. At EMI Studios, "They always used to disappear and have a little puff," he said, "but they never did it in front of me. They always used to go to the canteen, and Mal Evans used to guard it."[6] As the Beatles' marijuana use grew more frequent, Mal would discreetly roll joints behind Ringo's drum screen in Studio 2, in order to maintain a ready supply. Even as early as October 1964, marijuana had become so prevalent in their lives that it had infiltrated their music. Paul managed to slip a sly reference to it into "She's a Woman," recorded that same month as the B-side for "I Feel Fine." John later recalled that "we were so excited to say, 'turn me on'—you know, about marijuana and all that, using it as an expression."[7]

But Mal had more important things on his mind that fall—namely, the organization of the U.K. roadies into a more cohesive, cooperative unit. It may have been a fool's errand at the time, but he was determined to get his colleagues into a bona fide union. The impetus for the initiative emerged from his disgust over the amount of work it took to tear down a stage show, not to mention how angry it made him when other roadies went out of their way *not* to cooperate. John Fanning, former manager of Ted "Kingsize" Taylor and the Dominoes and now the road manager for Sounds Incorporated—and one of Mal's closest friends—recalled "an occasion when we had just finished setting up, and of course the Beatles were topping the bill. One of the London groups with a couple of flash roadies started to set up across the front of us and pushed some of our amps out of the way. I told them that if it was me, I wouldn't do that." As the other roadies watched in a kind of stunned silence, "Mal quietly walked over, looked at what they had done, and picked up one of their amps at arm's length, like it was a piece of tissue paper. Then he walked to the edge of the stage, held the amp out, and then let it go, dropping it about fifteen feet, where it broke into several pieces. They got the message."[8]

With an eye toward staving off such conflicts in the future, Mal hatched an idea: "I had in mind to form an association of road managers, the aims of which were basically to place the groups on stage, fully equipped and on time so they could perform their job, which was to entertain the public," he wrote. "Things like breakdowns of group vans, equipment, and the problems of having equipment stolen and road managers going sick could be rectified easily and quickly with the aid of such an association." He made inquiries with petrol companies to see about issuing credit cards for members of the association, while also looking into providing a nationwide twenty-four-hour replacement and maintenance service for vehicles and gear. "Unfortunately, the response from most road managers was purely selfish," he discovered. "All they were interested in was shorter working hours, more money with paid holidays, which was not the point of the RMA [Road Manager's Association] at all. A road manager's lot is not an easy one, and there's not too many who work just for the money involved. It's one of those strange occupations that you have to dedicate yourself to, for you spend many hours travelling, not only handling all the equipment, but devoting yourself to the group generally."[9]

By October, the Beatles and their entourage were back on the road for an autumn tour that would, as in the previous year, transition into a series of Christmas shows, this time to be held at the Hammersmith Odeon. It was in Glasgow, on October 21, that Mal found himself once again at loggerheads with Brian Epstein. On this particular evening, Mal had been forced by the local police to park a significant distance away from the venue. He and Neil devised what they believed to be a reasonable plan, where Neil would keep an eye on the gear while Mal went to get the van. Mal arrived backstage as the Beatles were making their exit with an escort that included hundreds of police officers. As he walked into the dressing room, Brian "really let blast at me, saying that I had deserted his boys and put them in danger by not being there. At one point raising his hand to strike me, his face red with anger. I'm afraid that I stood there and nearly laughed, not at his sincerity, but at the thought of him hitting me."[10]

Mal began to visualize the headlines that would have been concocted had he become embroiled in a punch-up with the group's manager. "The difference in size between Brian and I [*sic*] would not have done him any good at all," Mal wrote, "but it did please me no end that even with all the police protection the Beatles had, Brian still wanted me at hand to look after them. I have an extremely high tolerance level, and it takes a lot for me to get angry." To their credit, the Beatles were keenly aware of the tensions Mal experienced on their behalf, often joking, "We've never pushed you to your limit, have we Mal?"[11] For his part, the roadie wasn't entirely sure what marked the outer limits of his temper. Would there—*could there*—be an instance when he would throw up his arms in disgust and exit their lives forever?

During the residency at the Hammersmith Odeon, Mal found himself embroiled in yet another conflict with Epstein. "After a couple of weeks," Mal wrote, "the show tended to get very free and easy, with a lot of ad-libbing in the sketches, and usually by the end of the season, the sketch didn't bear much resemblance to the original written script. One night, during their act on stage, they talked me into sitting on the stage with them, drinking cups of tea and reading a newspaper. It was a funny idea at the time, but after the show, Brian gave me a right roast."[12] While Mal was chagrined by Epstein's short temper, he understood its fount. One afternoon, during a break in the Christmas shows, George Martin stopped by to share his season's greetings. Martin "admitted to me that when I first joined the group, he was a little antagonistic at somebody else getting close to the Beatles. I understood exactly what he meant, for I have the same feeling for them. One not only gets very protective, but a little selfish and jealous of anybody who gets close to them."[13] Their conversation underscored the ways in which members of the entourage often felt a sense of ownership over the boys, becoming envious of others who happened to share their orbit.

As if the fracas with Brian weren't trouble enough, Mal found himself at odds with the Yardbirds, one of the Beatles' supporting acts during the Christmas residency and during their upcoming tour on the Continent. "They preceded the Beatles," Mal wrote, "and unfortunately, the drummer [Jim McCarty] had broken his snare drum skin. Now the snare drum to a drummer is his pride and joy. It seems to take years of playing to break in the skin to get it sounding exactly as he likes it. This particular night, having broken his, [McCarty] just took Ringo's snare drum from the side of the stage and proceeded to put his stick through that one, then didn't have the grace to tell me about it. It was only until the Beatles were due to go on stage that I discovered this, then it was panic for a few minutes. But as I always carried spares for everything, it was soon replaced. You can borrow anything except the snare drum—to a drummer, that is sacred."[14]

And then there were the usual issues with jelly babies, which continued to greet the Beatles in a hailstorm as soon as the curtain opened. After the shows, Fanning recalled working with Mal to swab up the candy's awful residue: "Night after night, we would have to clean all the guitar leads and mic cables of squashed sticky jelly babies. A huge pain in the ass."[15]

That Christmas, Mal and Neil handled the shopping duties for the Beatles, purchasing big-ticket items such as televisions and other electronic gadgetry for their friends and relations. By this point, the roadies were responsible for carrying large amounts of petty cash in order to handle the bandmates' expenses, from picking up bar tabs to much loftier purchases at their discretion. Mal was unable to make it home to Liverpool for the holidays that year, but Fanning good-naturedly offered to ferry Christmas gifts to Mossley Hill for Lil and Gary on his behalf.

On Christmas Eve, Fanning recalled that both Mal and Neil received tiny packages from the boys. For his part, Neil was flabbergasted when he opened his present, which contained the keys to a lightly used, 2.4-liter Jaguar sports car. Mal's gift was more practical but equally welcome: he received the keys to a Humber Super Snipe estate car—perfect for a family man, not to mention a person of his stature.[16]

With the Christmas residency completed, the Beatles enjoyed some much-needed rest before regrouping with Mal at EMI Studios on February 15, 1965. As usual in Beatle World, things were moving at lightning speed. For one thing, Ringo had tied the knot with the former Maureen Cox. And now, just as suddenly, the band was back in the studio to begin compiling new music for their second feature film, tentatively titled *Eight Arms to Hold You*, a zany, James Bond–era farce for which principal photography was set to begin in the Bahamas only eight days later. Ray Coleman, a reporter from *Melody Maker*, was on hand at the February 18 recording session, where he took note of the boys' special relationship with Mal. With Paul working the electric piano on "Tell Me What You See," John exclaimed that "I like electric pianos, Mal. Buy me one tomorrow." As Ringo climbed up on Mal's back for a ride, the music writer couldn't help appreciating the group's obvious affection for their roadie.[17] For their part, Neil and Alf whiled away most of the session playing chess.

As Mal devoted more and more of his working hours to the Beatles' efforts in the studio, he became increasingly fluent in their instruments of choice, along with each musician's preferred string gauges, guitar leads, drumsticks, and plectrums. On February 16, Mal made the rounds of the London music vendors with an eye toward purchasing a pair of Fender Stratocasters for George and John. "It was funny," George later recalled, "because all these American bands kept coming over to England, saying, 'How did you get that guitar sound?' And the more I listened to it, the more I decided I didn't like the guitar sound I had. It was crap. A Gretsch guitar and a Vox amp, and I didn't like it. But those were early days, and we were lucky to have anything when we started out. But anyway, I decided I'd get a Strat, and John decided he'd get one too. So we sent out our roadie, Mal Evans, said 'go and get us two Strats.' And he came back with two of them, pale blue ones. Straight away we used them on the album we were making at the time."[18] George played his Sonic Blue Strat on "Ticket to Ride," the rollicking tune that emerged as the Beatles' next single. Mal had rounded up the 1961 Strats, which retailed for approximately £180 apiece (£2,843 in present-day pounds), while trolling the London music vendors.

By the time they left for the Bahamas to begin the film shoot in late February, the Beatles' weed habit was in full bloom. American actor Brandon de Wilde was along for the ride, bringing with him a healthy supply of pot for the trip to the islands. George recalled that "de Wilde was an actor, a James Dean type. He liked the Beatles' music, and he heard we were going to film in the Bahamas, so he came over from the States with a big bag of reefer. We smoked on the plane, all the way to the Bahamas. It was a charter flight, with all the film people—the actors and the crew—and we thought, 'No, nobody will notice.' We had Mal smoking cigars to drown out the smell."[19]

As the Beatles' jack-of-all-trades, Mal prided himself on being prepared for nearly any contingency. During his years with the band, he had discovered that the best way to avoid being ribbed by the boys was to be ready for virtually anything. To this end, he continued to supplement his ever-growing doctor's bag to meet the Beatles' every possible whim. It was now swollen with musical instrument paraphernalia—plectrums, guitar strings, and the like—along with household items such as aspirin, chewing gum, a flashlight, potato chips, cookies, tissues, and cigarettes, of course.[20] He kept a ready supply of Senior Service, his favorite brand—"Tobacco at

Paul and John on the *Help!* set

its finest," according to the advertising copy of the day. In recent months, he had taken to carrying around yet another piece of luggage, which he lovingly called his "dope bag." A brown suede bag with an om sign prominently displayed, the carrier served as a miniature head shop, complete with freshly rolled joints and other sundry items.

After arriving in the Bahamas, the Beatles and their entourage settled into a series of beachside bungalows at the Balmoral Club. In Nassau, Mal was reunited with Larry Kane, with whom he made plans for the band's summer North American tour, especially their five-day respite in Hollywood. Kane quickly ascertained that Mal and the Beatles were high. As with Paul's revelation back in August that "there are seven levels," John was repeating his own new revelation by that time: "Everything is wide open, anything can happen."[21]

After admonishing Kane to refrain from reporting on the Beatles' pot use, Mal joined his American friend for a night on the town. "The evening out with Evans and [fellow reporter] Long John Wade allowed me to observe the depths of Evans' newfound love of marijuana combined with drink," Kane recalled, "a love that sent us off to several nightclubs and climaxed with Long John and me dragging Malcolm by his arms back to my hotel room."[22] When Kane asked him to name his favorite member of the band, Mal replied, "Wanna get me sacked? [I] do love George, you know—there is a soul inside that skinny face. Paul is a sweetheart. Yeah, I'm an errand boy, fixer, handy mate, ya know, but I would do anything for them. Paul is easier to like than John, but John's a mad genius—and Ringo, just a sweet man."[23]

The next morning over coffee, Mal seemed remarkably refreshed, even cheerful. As it happened, he was due on set that morning—not as the Beatles' roadie but as an actor. Along with the band members, he spent hours on the Nassau beach working with director Richard Lester and his crew. For this film, he was to play "Channel Swimmer," a wayward aquanaut searching in vain for the White Cliffs of Dover.

But during the shoot, he experienced a moment of sheer, unexpected terror: "As the scene is finalizing on the beach," he wrote, "I had to swim out to sea for one-half mile and tread water until the scene is ready to be shot. The film crew are situated higher up on the beach and suddenly, Dick Lester is shouting at me saying, 'Come in, Mal. Come back, Mal!' And so, just thinking they weren't ready for the scene, I swam leisurely to shore, not knowing at the time there was a huge stingray chasing me!"[24] Standing safely with the crew back on the beach, Mal finally spotted the giant fish, which was more than fifteen feet long.[25]

During another evening in Nassau, Mal and Neil hit the bars with thirty-three-year-old Louise Harrison Caldwell, George's older sister. While chatting over drinks, they overheard two patrons, sailors, disparaging the Beatles. Louise recalled that "one remarked, 'I knew them in Liverpool when they all had dirty necks, and never took a bath.'" In nearly the same instant, she and Neil observed Mal standing up. "Towering over them," Louise recalled, "he told [the sailors] quite vehemently to apologize or they could choose to 'Drop Dead.'" The sailors made a hasty exit, leaving their drinks behind and muttering under their breaths. "Well, they found out at that moment," said Louise, that "you do not make derogatory remarks about the Beatles."[26]

As Mal noted in a February letter to Lily, he was enjoying his time in the Bahamas, but he had become increasingly annoyed by "all the Americans who are like a plague here, for every bush seems to hide one with his cine camera, and they really are very rude and bad-mannered." His favorite moments during the Bahamas shoot inevitably came when he was with the Beatles, whether it was tooling around the island with them in rented sports cars or wearing the straw hats he had bought for the boys and himself. Having just received his driver's license, John couldn't wait to get behind the wheel, insisting on going for a drive with Mal at the end of each day's shoot. "Only John could treat a famous race circuit with such contempt!" Mal wrote. The Beatle's "method of driving was to push the accelerator to the floor from the word 'go' and leave it there! And believe me, a 10-minute drive with John hurtling around hairpin bends must have taken a year off my life!"[27]

On March 13, Richard Lester's production changed locations—continents, even—and the cast and crew flew to Austria. The band and their entourage stayed at the Edelweiss Hotel, with easy access to the ski slopes in Obertauern, a winter sports resort. Four days later, Mal reprised his role as the Channel Swimmer. As in the Bahamas, what should have been a simple cameo appearance turned into something more harrowing. Tony Barrow would never forget the sight of Mal standing in the bitter cold. "Poor Mal must have been absolutely frozen," Barrow wrote. "All he was wearing was an old-fashioned swimming costume with cap and goggles and a very thick layer of grease to protect him from the cold. Everyone was a bit concerned that he would freeze to death before the scene was over."[28]

With snow-covered mountains as a backdrop, the scene called for the Beatles to be engaged in a good-natured curling match when one of the film's villains substitutes a bomb for a curling stone. It explodes, blowing a hole in the ice and allowing the Channel Swimmer to surface. "This scene had to be shot three times," Mal recalled, because "I was so cold, I just couldn't speak! Going down again and coming up, I spoke my lines, but on submerging again, [I] could not stay down and kept popping to the surface." That's when "somebody had the bright idea of putting a large weight in the bottom of the hole for me to hang onto, with the instructions from director Dick Lester, 'Stay down as long as you can, Mal, so we can finish the shot.' Being a real trooper, after I said my lines I submerged, took hold of the weight and stayed down holding my breath."[29]

Unbeknownst to Mal, Lester had been shouting—with increasing desperation—"You can come up now. Mal, come up now!" Meanwhile,

Mal portraying the Channel Swimmer in *Help!*

the roadie was nestled below the surface, pushing his lung capacity to the limit in order to land the scene. "Finally, self-preservation brought me up for air," he wrote. "Wrapped in a towel, I walked in my bare feet about four-hundred yards . . . while the whole crew stood up and cheered. I spent two hours in the hottest bath with a bottle of rum, thawing out. It was pins and needles from head to toe, but the cheers and the clapping made it all worthwhile."[30]

From Austria, Dick Lester's production relocated to London, where they would return to Twickenham Film Studios to shoot the film's interior scenes. It was there, on April 5, that the Beatles shot a scene in an Indian restaurant, complete with a group of Indian musicians performing an Eastern-tinged instrumental version of "A Hard Day's Night." During a break, George picked up one of the musician's sitars—a moment that marked the birth of Harrison's love affair with Indian classical music. That same month, the film was retitled *Help!*, prompting John to compose the title track that same night.

With the film in postproduction, the boys ensconced themselves with George Martin at EMI Studios to complete work on the *Help!* LP, a groundbreaking effort that included classically trained studio musicians performing on such Lennon-McCartney compositions as "Yesterday" and "You've Got to Hide Your Love Away." On May 27, Mal celebrated his thirtieth birthday with a rare day off in Liverpool with Lily, Gary, and the rest of the Evans clan. Brian marked the occasion with a telegram wishing the roadie many happy returns. But aside from the manager's warmhearted intrusion, Mal and his family were experiencing a rare moment outside the swells of Beatlemania.

For Lily in particular, the global phenomenon of the Beatles had occurred largely outside her purview. She was well aware of their music, which dominated the airwaves—"Ticket to Ride" and "Help!" would continue the Beatles' unbroken "Roll" at the top of the U.K. charts. But to her mind, Beatlemania was synonymous with loneliness. Outside regular visits from her fifteen-year-old niece, Shan, Lil spent the majority of her time in the company of a three-year-old. Other than Mal's growing collection of band mementos, the Beatles held little sway in her home.

Indeed, Mal had been gone so often, and for such extended periods, that the bandmates themselves left only a fleeting impression on Lily. There was the time, while she was visiting her husband in London, for example, when Paul debuted an early version of "Yesterday" while they shared a sofa. And there were the pleasant memories sharing tea and conversation with George in Liverpool, while the Beatle and her husband smoked cigarettes. But mostly, "I always felt we came in second," she said. "It was very hurtful," especially when she was forced to cover for her husband with Gary, inevitably telling him that "Daddy has to be away for work."[31]

Mal on the *Help!* set in the Alps

Mal on the *Help!* set in the Bahamas

13

GREEK GOD

In June 1965, the Beatles and their entourage traveled to Europe, fueled by a soothing bounty of weed, courtesy of Mal and Neil. Judging by the events back in the Bahamas, Mal was now a bona fide pot smoker himself. And to ensure that the group had a ready supply of joints on tour, he and Neil developed a system whereby they bought twenty cartons of cigarettes at a time, removed the tobacco from each ciggie, and replaced it with pot.

For Brian Epstein, the Beatles' Italian visit became a source of great irritation when an unscrupulous promoter claimed that the band was losing its luster and was no longer able to sell out concert venues. As Mal later wrote, "After Brian had arranged everything many months before, the promoter had gone ahead and doubled the admission price, also booking the Beatles into halls that were twice as big as originally planned. Now the general population in Italy couldn't afford the higher prices, so the halls were never completely packed as we had come to expect on previous shows. The press were quick to pick up on this, for I guess bad news makes good news, from their point of view."[1]

For the Beatles themselves, the highlight of their European sojourn was the Italians' wide-eyed wonder at the image of colossal Mal lugging their equipment from place to place. "I've been called many things in my life, but it was on the Italian trip that the people backstage called me 'Mammut.' I kept thinking it was an Italian version of my name, until I found out it meant mammoth! The language barrier causing both hilarity and misunderstanding. Everyone I met seemed to be small of stature, and I would see three of them struggling with a heavy piece of equipment, and strolling over, [I would] take it off them, hoist it on my own shoulders and walk away with it, so gaining my own little admiration society. They thought I was one of the strongest men in the world. And for quite a while after, I got called Mammoth, instead of Mal, by the Beatles."[2]

As with their counterparts across the globe, the Italian authorities had great difficulty controlling the crowds. In Genoa, police were clueless when it came to dealing with Beatles-induced hysteria. Writing in *16 Magazine*, Mal recalled that "the show that night was crazy. The Italian police had never had to deal with anything like the Beatles before, and they just didn't have the first idea as to what to do. The fans went so wild that the police seemed to panic and kept turning all the lights—stage ones included—*off!* The Beatles sang most of their last number, 'Long Tall Sally,' in a complete blackout!"[3]

By the time that they reached Nice on June 30, a different vibe had wafted over the Beatles' entourage. On the one hand, there seemed to be a heightened sense of danger—earlier, in Lyon, fans had tossed firecrackers onstage, briefly throwing Mal and the group into a panic. On the other hand, the band members seemed to be becoming more cavalier with their safety, daring to venture outside the bounds of their fame. Perhaps because of the claustrophobia and sense of being isolated in hotel rooms, the boys began venturing out to see the sights.

Meanwhile, the Beatles' penchant for raucous, late-night merrymaking seemingly came to an end during the European tour, with the boys sometimes retiring for the night as early as eight o'clock on their off days, often ignoring their usual scrum of adoring female fans. The languor-inducing pot may have been one cause for this. But Mal's "demon," as always, was fully present. After the Nice show, "Paul for some reason went straight to bed," Mal recalled, but "yours truly stayed up entertaining all those beautiful young ladies, getting slightly drunk out of his head, going to bed around 7:00 in the morning."[4]

An hour later, Paul woke up Mal, persuading him to undertake a driving tour that brought them to the gates of Princess Grace's palace in Monaco, where they debated whether to knock on the gate and ask for the former Hollywood star. After scrapping the idea, Mal and Paul visited an aquarium in the South of France instead. As they wandered around the attraction, Mal observed the "usual crowd of spectators" gathering, "more interested in Paul than the local sea life."

That evening, the Beatles were invited to try their hand at go-carting in Nice. "Alf, our chauffeur, and being a chauffeur, was determined not to be outdone by any of the Beatles," Mal wrote, "trying so hard to win that he crashed his go-cart and broke his leg!"[5]

The tour concluded in Spain, and by July 4, almost as quickly as they had set off, the boys and their entourage had returned to England. Eager to see his family, Mal drove the Commer van to Liverpool, with Ringo hitching a ride to see his wife, Maureen, back in their hometown. Driving up the M1, Mal and Ringo stopped at a roadside café for lunch. "We were sitting at the counter," Mal recalled, "and the chap next to me had obviously been trying to make up his mind whether it really was Ringo with me. Suddenly, he turned to me and said, 'I don't care if it is him or not.' Ringo nearly choked with laughter as I teased the fellow, saying, 'No, it's not him. But it gets terribly embarrassing taking him anywhere because everybody mistakes him for Ringo!'"[6]

On July 29, Mal and Lily attended the *Help!* premiere at the London Pavilion. It was a star-studded affair, complete with a dinner celebration afterward. Lily vividly recalled John asking her and Mal to join him at his table, reasoning that "unlike the other Beatles, [Lennon] didn't have much family," save for Cynthia and Julian.[7] Earlier that same month, Ringo and Maureen purchased Sunny Heights, a lavish home in Weybridge, Surrey, not far from John's Kenwood estate—a matter of great convenience for Mal, who often ferried the Beatles back and forth among their residences. George, now engaged to model Pattie Boyd, had lived at Kinfauns in Esher, also in Surrey, since mid-1964.

The day after the *Help!* premiere, Mal and the Beatles gathered at the Saville Theatre, operated by NEMS Enterprises, to begin rehearsing for their upcoming North American tour, a sixteen-day, twenty-show sweep beginning at New York City's Shea Stadium and concluding with a return engagement at San Francisco's Cow Palace. Working with General Artists Corporation (GAC), the tour promoter, Brian had enacted several key changes to ensure the band's safety and their fans' enjoyment during the American jaunt. In addition to Epstein's standard proviso that the boys not be required to perform before a segregated audience, the group's rider specified a "hi-fidelity" sound system—an effort, likely futile, to drown out the roar of the Beatles' fans—and a "one-ton enclosed truck" to be available at each venue to transport the boys between the venue and their hotel accommodation. Perhaps most significantly, the rider called for "not less than 150 uniformed officers" to be provided, along with a "strong fence or barrier to prevent any of the audience from climbing over."[8]

On August 13, with the tour looming, the boys and their entourage landed at JFK in preparation for the Beatles' fourth and final appearance on *The Ed Sullivan Show*. At the airport, the band felt a pang of anxiety when they were greeted by "only a handful of kids instead of the thousands we normally expected." Mal later discovered that "the New York cops had done their job too well. With their walkie-talkies and good organization, they had succeeded in barring all the kids from the airport precincts, and only a few had managed to get past the barriers."[9]

The next day, the boys were scheduled to rehearse for their *Sullivan Show* appearance, which would be prerecorded for broadcast on September 12 for the program's fall television premiere. For Mal, the trouble began after he brought the Beatles to CBS Studio 50 to begin the three-hour rehearsal. Larry Kane was there, too, embedded with the band in advance of the Shea Stadium concert. The reporter later recalled seeing the roadie for the first time since the Bahamas, where he had been in top spirits. But now Mal "looked dour and almost depressed," said Kane. "His eyes squinted through his signature plain glass-frame glasses, and a cigarette dangled between two shaking fingers. Concern was written all over his face as he trailed the Beatles into the compact dressing rooms." A few minutes later, Kane got the scoop. According to Mal, John was "sweating, shaking, looks like too many pills and shit." As the rehearsal continued, so did Mal's sense of alarm, especially after John verbally attacked one of the show's technical staff. When the group finally taped their performance, Kane took special note, wondering how Lennon would fare under the lights. "Just before curtain time, John led the Beatles toward the stage," Kane wrote. "Sweat was soaking through the top of his shirt. He glanced over and suddenly his eyebrows arched upward, the visual sign that things were okay. Mal Evans and Neil Aspinall looked nervous, then somewhat relieved."[10]

But they weren't out of the woods just yet. After the taping, Mal whispered to Kane, "Now we'll keep our fingers crossed for tomorrow night. To me, it's only another show, but it's really big for them."[11] The Beatles' Shea Stadium concert, set for Sunday, August 15, 1965, promised to be the largest event in rock 'n' roll history, with a sold-out audience of more than 55,000 people expected to attend. On the eve of the record-breaking event, the Beatles held a blowout party at the Warwick Hotel, "a happy, hippy swinging affair," in Mal's words. By midnight, the gathering had proven to be a rollicking party by the Beatles' standards, but it was shortly to be transformed into something even more raucous still. The arrival of Mick Jagger and Keith Richards propelled the party into a higher gear. And the two Stones weren't alone, having been joined by "a couple of the Supremes, the Tamla-Motown chicks that the Beatles really dig." The bandmates were especially taken with the Rolling Stones guitarist's coat—"a sports jacket that was a straight lift from a rainbow. Immediately, the Beatles wanted one each." In addition to Bob Dylan, who brought along an acetate of his new album, "Del Shannon and the Ronettes were other guests at the party," Mal wrote, "which went on until well into the early hours. But despite the noise, the smoke, and the pretty girls, plus all the excited chatter, I was well-whacked and fell asleep in an armchair in the corner of the room."[12]

As Mal had predicted, the Beatles were curiously nervous that Sunday. Shea Stadium marked arguably the biggest show of their careers. "The boys were unusually quiet," he wrote. "They get as highly-strung and nervous as any other top performer. Once on that stage, making music, they are relaxed and confident; beforehand, they tend to worry about how things will go, have doubts about the equipment sending out their correct sound and that sort of thing."[13] Setting up the gear was ineluctably simple at Shea: to afford fans a fighting chance of hearing the band that day, Mal had to place the microphones directly in front of the Vox amps and Ringo's drum kit and turn up the guitar amps to maximum volume. In order to avoid the high, squelching sound of feedback, the mic'd speakers near the sides of the stage had to be turned to a lower level. Simply put: this meant that the Beatles could hear their guitars when standing in front of the amps, but very little, if any, of their own vocals.[14]

As Mal prepared for the show that day, it was clear that the band's souped-up hundred-watt Vox amps would be no match for the massive

George and Mal with a Vox amp

crowd and their attendant noise. In order to gain a few extra decibels, the instruments' audio was wired into the stadium's public-address system. But his efforts were in vain. Shea's PA system—little more than a series of small speakers hanging throughout the stadium on steel support girders—had been designed, of course, to deliver announcements during sporting events, a far cry from the raucous, amped music of a rock concert.[15]

To ensure their safe and timely arrival at Shea, the Beatles were transported by helicopter from Manhattan to the Port Authority heliport. From there, they traveled by Wells Fargo armored car into the packed stadium, where the 55,600-strong crowd was shaking the place to the rafters. Appropriately, Ed Sullivan made the introductions, exclaiming, "Now, ladies and gentlemen, honored by their country, decorated by their Queen, loved here in America, here are the Beatles!"

After the Beatles took the stage, Mal could only gaze around the stadium in wonder. The band's audience had finally crossed the Rubicon and managed to drown out every possible bit of sound, leaving nothing but the whirring tumult of white noise in their wake. "I have never heard such an ear-splitting din as those kids kicked up when the Beatles made their entrance that night," he wrote. "The whole place went absolutely crazy. There could not have been one person in the audience who wasn't yelling at the top of his or her voice. It was just incredible. Overhead, a blimp floated into view with a neon sign blazing the words 'Welcome Beatles' and several hundred flashguns from the mass of photographers packed around the stage went off to make the scene like Guy Fawkes' fireworks night back home."[16] In retrospect, it was clear the venue's PA system hadn't made a whit of difference. "You couldn't hear what the boys were doing unless you happened to be sitting right next to one of the big amplifiers."[17]

That same weekend, a group of Indianapolis girls were holding a slumber party when they learned that the Beatles were staying at the Warwick Hotel in New York City. "We were giggling and screaming, listening to the radio," sixteen-year-old Georgeanna Lewis recalled, "and one of the girls dared me to make a phone call" to the Beatles' hotel. Though wary of accruing long-distance charges, Georgeanna placed the call anyway. When the hotel operator answered, she said, "Can I speak with Paul McCartney?" Amazingly, the operator put the call through. Georgeanna recalled that "the phone was answered by a British voice. I remember saying, 'Is this John?' And he said 'What of it, luv?' Then another voice came on the line. It was Mal Evans."[18]

The roadie was sorry that Paul was unavailable, but said she was welcome to call back the next afternoon.

"Do you just talk to anybody that comes through?" she asked.

Mal replied, "No, obviously not."

He later wrote that she seemed like a nice girl and he had enjoyed talking to her. The next day, Georgeanna telephoned the Warwick, as instructed, and Mal answered. When he learned that she had tickets to the Beatles' upcoming gig in Chicago, he suggested she stop by after the show and meet the band. "We seldom ever get a chance to talk with a true American," Mal added. "It's always celebrities."[19] Georgeanna and Mal were soon chatting like old friends.

A few days later, the entourage was reminded of the dark side of Beatlemania, of how easily the fervor of simple autograph seekers can develop into violence. As it happened, the Beatles were in Texas on August 19 for a pair of shows at the Sam Houston Coliseum. The band's plane landed in Houston, met by a crowd of two thousand impatient fans. "Christ, they've broken through," John said, glimpsing fans swarming over the tarmac. The quick-thinking pilot managed to cut the engines before anyone was mangled by the propellers, but "as the plane shuddered to a standstill, the youngsters couldn't wait. They clambered all over the plane—onto its wings, its tail section, and over the still warm engines. They hammered on the aircraft's windows and screamed and shouted to the Beatles inside, 'We love you, we want you.'"[20]

For more than half an hour, the Beatles and their entourage were trapped inside the plane. Eventually, security officials managed to round up a forklift truck and empty the marooned passengers. But now the Beatles were standing exposed at the top of its platform. Mal could only stand with them and watch, helpless, as all manner of "confetti, handbags, cigarette lighters, shoes, and lipsticks were hurled by the excited youngsters to express their adulation."

Eventually, the forklift made its way to a waiting phalanx of limousines. As the members of the band and their entourage dropped to the ground, Brian Epstein fell awkwardly to the tarmac, badly injuring his spine, which required treatment. Safely ensconced in the hotel, an infuriated Lennon vented his anger to Mal and the others. "This always bloody well happens in Texas," he exclaimed. "I told Brian before we left that we should double-check the security arrangements for Houston."[21]

After the first Houston show, the police chief finally admitted defeat. Wiping his brow with a handkerchief, he lumbered up to Mal and said, "Well, I guess you were right Mr. Evans. I'm bringing in another 40 men for the second show."[22] The police even managed to locate an armored car to transport the Beatles back to their hotel.

For Mal, the trip to Houston wasn't a total loss. At one point, he found time for a shopping excursion, purchasing a black felt cowboy hat, its outer band decorated with six metal discs, each sporting an arrow. With his adoration for the Old West, Mal simply couldn't resist buying the item—a vintage hat from the Stelzig Saddlery, a company that dated back to 1870.

The next day, the band and their entourage flew to Chicago for a pair of gigs at Comiskey Park, home to the White Sox. Georgeanna Lewis attended the second show, accompanied by her mother and two friends. As discussed, she made her way to the Sahara Inn, hoping to meet the Beatles.

There, she and her group joined thousands of screaming fans jam-packed into the hotel's lobby. Georgeanna waded through the mass of humanity to reach the concierge. "Do you have a message for Georgeanna Lewis?" she asked. In response, the concierge handed her a piece of paper inscribed with a telephone number. "When I called that number, Paul McCartney answered, and I was like, 'if I die right now, it's okay. I've talked to Paul McCartney.' I tried to act very calm, 'May I speak to Malcolm Evans.' He said, 'Just a minute.'"[23]

When Mal got on the line, he told her that he was delighted that she had made the trip and that he would come down to the lobby to retrieve her. "You don't know what I look like," he added. "I'm wearing a red sweater, and I'm tall—six foot three. I look like a Greek god." Moments later, Georgeanna watched as Mal exited the elevator into the lobby with a big grin on his face. He whisked Georgeanna and her group up to the sixth floor, where George was clomping around in a pair of flip-flops; John was walking through the room with a microphone to record the proceedings, followed by Ringo, who was clad in polka-dot pajamas. Georgeanna recalled that she talked to Mal about the Beatles' fan clubs and how they were popping up across the globe. "I said, 'Do you have a fan club?' He started laughing really hard. And I said, 'Well, you should!'"[24]

Moments later, Mal returned with Paul, who said, "Which one of you birds is starting a fan club for Mal? This is great, Mal. It's just what you need." But "there's only one thing I've got to warn you about," Paul added. "Mal's a bigger fan of Elvis Presley than he is of us. Apart from that, you'll find he's quite normal." Grabbing a stray paper bag and a pen, Georgeanna began conducting an impromptu interview with Paul, scrawling his answers on the bag like a reporter. As Mal recalled, Paul "chatted on to the delighted girls and told them how I had joined the Beatles over two years previously, when they were playing at Liverpool's Cavern Club." Paul told Georgeanna that "at the start, Mal was just a bouncer at the club. I think he got the job so that he could hear us for nothing. We hired him for his own protection." During the interview, Georgeanna enumerated the roadie's vital statistics: "Malcolm Evans, wife Lily, son Gary," she wrote, adding a reference to Mal's "rugged, handsome good looks" and listing his measurements as six foot, three inches tall and 205 pounds.

In the end, Georgeanna and her group stayed until the pre-dawn hours of the morning. Before she left to make the drive back to Indianapolis, she and Mal exchanged addresses. Georgeanna recalled thinking, "This is not going to amount to anything."[25]

By the next evening, the whole shebang had shifted northwest, to Minneapolis, where the Beatles performed at Metropolitan Stadium. Larry Kane recalled that after the show that night, Mal and Neil went into their usual routine, screening potential female candidates for the post-gig party. But this was one night, Kane pointed out, when their "talent scouting" failed—at least, when it came to John, who later confided to the reporter that the women he met "didn't want to have a go at it."[26] Even so, in Mal's memory, the Beatles' Minneapolis jaunt—as with Las Vegas the previous year—brought the tour perilously close to the sort of scandal that might have left a lasting scar on the band's reputation.

Late that night, as Mal and the group watched television in their suite at the Leamington Motor Lodge, the police raided the premises. "We believe you are harboring teenage girls," the senior officer shouted as other officers confronted the Beatles and their entourage. "We want them out!" The only nonresident in the suite was a blonde teenage girl who was watching television with the boys.[27]

Mal discovered that there was a lively party that night at the Leamington, but it wasn't in the Beatles' suite. Apparently, a conman had lured a slew of teenage girls into a suite on a different floor, promising that the Beatles would be joining them. Soon, the suite was bustling with young girls, who eventually spilled out into the corridor. A door-to-door search by the authorities resulted in the Leamington being emptied of all nonresidents, including the boys' blonde visitor.

After sealing off the motel, one of the police officers accosted Mal, saying, "This is a respectable town, and we aim to keep it that way. We don't want you limeys and your shenanigans here." That's when Mal had had enough. "We've done nothing to give you that impression," he countered. "We're getting the blame for other people's behavior. We travel all over the world, and we always try to avoid situations like this. What can we do about it?" The policeman gave Mal a dirty look and said, "You could always try performing somewhere else."[28]

Incredibly, things seemed to only get worse the next day, when the Beatles and their entourage came in for a landing in Portland. Aboard the plane as it made its final descent, Mal watched in horror as Paul exclaimed, "Hey, look! We're on fire!" At that, "everyone leapt up and looked out of the windows on Paul's side," Mal recalled. "My first thought was that the engine might explode as we landed and set the whole plane alight, but just then, the aircraft pilot, Captain Bill Marr, feathered the engine"—that is, turned the propeller blades in the direction of flight, to create a low-drag condition—"and the trail of smoke thinned a little." At one point, as the plane leveled off at 22,000 feet, John became distraught and made a leap for the cabin door, only to be stopped by an imposing Mal, against whom the Beatle crashed with a thud. After a safe landing in Portland, "there was no happier nor more relieved bunch of people in the world that day than us."

Like the boys—George especially—Mal could be, at times, a nervous flier. Not surprisingly, the band and their entourage began to talk about what would happen if an accident or other mishap claimed one of the Beatles. "We'd never go on, Mal," said Paul. "We're a family, and we're all very close to each other. If it ever did happen that either of us was out of action for any time, we'd shut down the shop and call it a day. We wouldn't like doing it, mind you, because life is a ball of fun for us right now. But it would be the end of the Beatles, that's for sure."[29]

A few days later, the group alighted in Los Angeles for a brief hiatus before the Beatles played a pair of gigs at the Hollywood Bowl. "We were all heading for a fabulous mountainside retreat that the Beatles had hired—for $10,000 a week!—and where we all hoped for a little peace and quiet,"[30] Mal later wrote, but as it turned out, the sojourn in Southern California would be something altogether different.

Situated at the end of a cul-de-sac in Benedict Canyon, the estate the Beatles had rented was owned by actress Zsa Zsa Gabor and seemed, at first, to be a secure location. That afternoon, the band and their entourage enjoyed a pleasant and restful day around the lavish pool, floating for hours on the cool blue water, sunbathing on the patio, and sipping American beer. But it wouldn't last. "My heart sank later that evening when I saw on the TV screen loads of shots of the bungalow," Mal later wrote, "and newscasters giving out the full address of the Beatles' hideaway. They might as well have printed maps of the place and distributed them in the street, for as soon as the word got out, it started a series of fantastic pilgrimages seven miles up to the mountains by hundreds and hundreds of Beatle fans. They walked, they hitch-hiked, they borrowed cars, crammed themselves into all kinds of vehicles—anything that would get them to the place where they just might get a glimpse of their idols."[31]

14

THE ELVIS SITUATION

So began one of the strangest series of events in Mal's, and the Beatles', story.

As always, the roadie quickly fell into a routine. At Benedict Canyon, he and Alf would often wake up early, enjoy a quick swim in the pool, and then begin patrolling the Gabor estate. "You could see the girls up in the hills with their binoculars watching us," Alf recalled. "They probably thought it was the boys. What a shock they must have had when they realized it wasn't."[1] Meanwhile, the home endured a barrage of Hollywood stars and showbiz personalities. With his penchant for being starstruck, Mal was delighted by the parade of glitzy visitors, although several overstayed their welcome.

One of the regular uninvited guests was twenty-five-year-old actor Peter Fonda. During one of his visits, John and George experienced their second brush with LSD, the notorious hallucinogen championed by counterculture guru Timothy Leary. Back in April 1965, John, George, and their significant others had been duped into taking the drug at the Bayswater home of a dentist friend who had covertly spiked their coffee with it. At the house in Benedict Canyon, George's acid trip proved frightening, prompting Fonda to comfort him. "I remember sitting out on the deck of the house with George," the actor recalled, "who was telling me that he thought he was dying. I told him that there was nothing to be afraid of and all that he needed to do was relax. I said that I knew what it was like to be dead because, when I was 10-years-old, I'd accidentally shot myself in the stomach and my heart stopped beating three times while I was on the operating table because I had lost so much blood." Ringo went along for the ride, but Paul and Mal avoided taking the drug—at least, for the moment, that is.[2]

That same week, the band and their entourage met twenty-seven-year-old

Ken Mansfield, West Coast promotions manager for Capitol Records, during a press event. Having briefly traded their Benedict Canyon retreat for Studio A in the famous Capitol Records Tower, the Beatles received gold records for the American sales of the *Help!* soundtrack. After the press conference, they invited Mansfield to join them the next day in Benedict Canyon. "Here I am," Mansfield later recalled. "I'm the suntanned dude in a Cadillac convertible. I'm Mr. California to them, so they wanted to know things about Mulholland Drive, Grauman's Chinese Theatre, and some of the other Capitol artists. Ringo wanted me to introduce him to Buck Owens, and Paul wanted some Gene Vincent records."[3]

Sitting poolside the following day with the Beatles, Mansfield observed, in a kind of awe, as Mal managed the hordes of young women attempting to scale the walls of the estate. Mansfield had no illusions about why he had been invited to Benedict Canyon that day. "The reason I had such a great and warm acceptance with the guys from the get-go was because of Mal's immediate blessing," said Mansfield. "They trusted him, he trusted me, and it was that simple. In those days, you didn't get anywhere near the Beatles unless you first passed muster with Mal or Neil."[4] As they sat around the pool, he recalled the sight of "Mal busily working the periphery of the pool area, where the kids were making it to the top of the walls of the estate and coming down on the other side. Mal would gently spray them with the garden hose, lift them up over his shoulder, and carry them out to security at the end of the cul-de-sac. And the whole time, the kid would be looking over Mal's shoulder, hoping to wave to a Beatle."[5]

For Mal, it was generally easy work, handing wayward fans over to law enforcement. Not surprisingly, he bonded with the sheriffs staffing the Benedict Canyon security. They were so impressed with the roadie that they gifted him with an honorary sheriff's badge. Occasionally, though, he would find himself becoming distraught over the level of some fans' desperation. "From time to time," he wrote, "I wandered out to the gates to tell the kids they were wasting their time and ought to go home. As always, I felt a bit sorry for them, and I took them a few jugs of coffee to take the chill off."[6]

Given his fascination with the King, Mal understood the fans' plight. But while the Beatles fans' dreams of meeting their idols in Benedict Canyon were continually dashed, Mal was on the precipice of finally seeing his own dream of doing so come true. On the night of August 27, he and the boys met none other than Elvis Presley at the King's Bel Air mansion. The thirty-year-old superstar was in town for the film shoot associated with *Paradise, Hawaiian Style*.

Prior to his coveted meeting with the King, Mal spent time with Colonel Tom Parker at his Paramount Studios office, where the roadie was lavished with gifts, including a gold-plated cigarette lighter and, to his utter glee, a white bathrobe emblazoned with "Girls! Girls! Girls!" Mal not only appreciated Parker's generosity, but recognized that the Colonel possessed "one of the most astute showbiz brains in America," adding that "he has wrung every dollar he can out of the Elvis situation—and who can blame him?" As Mal was lounging in the Colonel's office that day, the telephone rang. "That was a news agency, Mal," Parker said. "It looks as though word has got out about Elvis and the boys meeting tonight. There's a story in the London *Daily Mirror*. Now Reuters wants confirmation." At that moment, Mal's heart froze. "For a moment, I thought Parker was going to call the whole thing off."[7]

But the Colonel wasn't to be deterred. With the so-called Memphis Mafia—a group of Presley friends and employees who served and protected the King—at his beck and call, Elvis's manager instigated a complex system by which they changed vehicles several times before arriving at Benedict Canyon. As the Colonel looked on, Mal, Neil, Tony Barrow, and the Beatles ducked into a black limo with Alf sitting behind the wheel. "For once," Mal later quipped, "John, George, Paul, and Ringo were ready to leave on time, and they climbed into the waiting cars at the bungalow bang on the dot."[8] Shouting, "Roll 'em!" out his car window, Alf followed the Colonel's vehicle as it snaked its way through Hollywood, the convoy followed by a police motorcycle unit. By 10 p.m., the motorcade had arrived at Elvis's house at Perugia Way. Incredibly, the Colonel's plan had worked.[9]

NME's Chris Hutchins was there the night Mal and the Beatles made their way inside Elvis's Bel Air home: "Elvis and Priscilla were sitting in the center of the horseshoe couch in the den—the King and his secret bride-to-be cozily at home," Hutchins wrote. "He was wearing a red shirt and close-fitting black jerkin, the high Napoleonic collar rising above his sideburns. Priscilla was pure Hollywood starlet: her black bouffant towered above her forehead and she was heavily made up with thick black mascara, midnight blue eyeliner, red blusher and Heartbreak Pink lipstick." As Mal, Neil, Alf, and Tony followed the Beatles, they couldn't have possibly missed the members of the Memphis Mafia standing around the room in all their glory. At least nine-men strong, they doubled the Beatles' entourage.[10]

Naturally, Mal was beside himself, feeling a combination of reverence and utter shock. "If there is one day in my life I shall never forget," he wrote, "it is the day when the two biggest phenomena in showbiz met for the one and only time." After being served a large Scotch and Coke by one of the King's minions, Paul beckoned Mal to meet his idol in the flesh. "Presley turned, and we shook hands. 'This is your number-one fan, El,' said Paul. 'And he's with *us*.'" Mal was thunderstruck by the sound of the King's "strangely quiet voice" as he said "Sure pleased to meet you" to the roadie.[11]

As the evening progressed, Mal marveled at Elvis's luxurious home, with its well-stocked cocktail bar and lounge, its thickly carpeted rooms, and, in the den, a massive fireplace with a copper chimney disappearing into the

The Colonel presenting Mal with a "Girls! Girls! Girls!" bathrobe

ceiling at the center of the great room. "Pretty soon the record player was working full blast," Mal wrote. "Elvis played a whole lot of albums, many of them the Beatles, but modestly, perhaps, did not play any of his own. The noise was terrific, the drinks were flowing, the talk was animated, and, as I say, it was just like being at home with the lads from Liverpool."[12]

Mal later opined that "so casual and informal was this party that not even a photograph was taken." Eventually, Elvis picked up a bass guitar that was plugged into an amp positioned near the television set. "He began to strum away on the thing, playing quite ably, but he insisted that he was only learning," Mal wrote. "Keep practicing, fella, you'll get to the top yet," Paul quipped. As Mal looked on, "the most fantastic impromptu unrecorded sessions of all time" ensued when "El found some guitars for John, George, and Paul and a set of bongo drums for Ringo, and they began to make the place rock with an hour of improvised beat music. It was fabulous."

And that's when it happened: "There was only one hitch during the little concert the boys put on," Mal later reflected.[13] Nobody had a plectrum. "Mal's got a pick," said Paul. "He's always got picks. He carries them on holidays with him."[14] Crestfallen that he had neglected to bring his well-traveled doctor's bag, along with its ready supply of guitar picks, Mal scurried to the kitchen, where he fashioned pieces of plastic cutlery into makeshift plectrums.

As the evening continued, more guests began to arrive. "Elvis played the genial host," Mal wrote. "He himself sipped iced water all night, since he neither drinks nor smokes and was at pains to make sure that everyone enjoyed themselves." Ringo and Mal tried their hand at pool, losing four straight games to members of the Memphis Mafia, while "John lost nine dollars at roulette with Colonel Parker and Brian Epstein, who had joined us on getting back from New York." In one of Mal's favorite memories of that night, John pretended to be a reporter:

> Once, when I was talking to El, sitting on a settee, John came screaming up to us and jabbed an imaginary microphone under El's nose and began to fire off a string of meaningless questions—which I must say were a pretty accurate take-off of some of the daft things that interviewers ask at our own press conferences.

"What are you going to do when the bubble bursts, Elvis?" he asked. "What toothpaste do you use? What time do you go to bed? Do you like girls? Who's your favorite artist?"

"Yeah, yeah," chuckled El. "I've heard 'em all before."[15]

By 2 a.m., the party had begun to wind down, and the Beatles and their entourage said their goodbyes. As they climbed into their limo, Tony remembered Mal's face "glowing with happiness" because Elvis, his cherished rock 'n' roll idol, had called him "sir."[16] It hardly mattered to the roadie that the King addressed nearly everyone that way.

The Beatles wrapped up their Benedict Canyon hiatus with a pair of gigs at the Hollywood Bowl. At the conclusion of the second show on August 30, Mal observed in amazement as "girls flung themselves into the moat dividing the stage from the vast open auditorium of the Bowl, and as soon as the boys dashed off the stage, colossal fountains were switched on full blast to deter the more determined moat swimmers from reaching the battlements of the stage, so to speak." It made for a bizarre scene, to be sure, but nothing could have prepared them for the onslaught the next day in San Francisco.[17]

The Beatles' first show at the Cow Palace erupted into a near riot, with the bandmates enduring a relentless fusillade of jelly beans, teddy bears, and the like. At one point, a security guard was even knocked unconscious after being hit in the head by a bottle. In the end, more than two dozen girls had to be hauled offstage, while a male fan managed to breach the scaffolding behind Ringo and make a run at his kit. After the conclusion of the first show, Mal wrote, "somehow, the Beatles managed to eat a meal backstage with Joan Baez, who had travelled from Los Angeles with us, and country and western–style singer Johnny Cash looked in for an hour. But the atmosphere was tense and electric, and, for once, the Beatles were not looking forward to their next show."[18]

And that's when things got worse. As with the afternoon show, the venue was jam-packed for the nightcap. Perhaps even more troubling, local radio stations had already shared harrowing stories of the earlier gig during their broadcasts. Fearing a repeat of the afternoon's grim spectacle, Mal double-checked the crash barriers and the exits, feeling cautiously optimistic when he observed that "a solid wall of police was posted in front of the stage."

In the end, it hardly seemed to matter. The Beatles opened the concert with "Twist and Shout," and "it seemed as if the whole building rocked as the teenagers began to spill forward," Mal wrote. "I could see the crash barriers starting to give way under the weight of the onslaught, and, determined though they were, it looked as though the police lines must collapse."[19]

In advance of the second show, Mal had been especially concerned about the fifteen-foot-high wire-mesh fence behind the stage. Incredibly, the fans "just hoisted each other up and clambered over, oblivious to cuts, bruises, and broken limbs as they fell from the top. Paul was almost torn off the stage by a girl who grabbed him, while another nearly hauled Ringo from his drums." As the show devolved into out-and-out mayhem, "Nell, Alf, myself, all the GAC officials, and even Brian Epstein were now on stage, trying to protect the boys, keep the show going, and throwing off the stage intruders as they kept coming." And that's when Captain David Hansen, the San Francisco Police chief, shouted to Mal, "If we don't get this lot under control, we'll have to stop the show."[20]

By this point, the stage and its immediate environs had taken on the look of a battle zone. "Unconscious teenagers were being dragged out of the audience," Mal wrote, "and we hauled them on to the stage for safety. Some were in a terrible state, bruised, battered, cut and unconscious. Their clothing was torn and their hair disheveled. We put them backstage, where the casualties mounted into the hundreds as the show went on. A chain of policemen organized to get them to the first aid center." At one critical juncture, a fan hurled a metal folding chair onstage. Eventually, the situation became simply too dangerous for the band to continue. "It's no good," Captain Hansen told Brian. "You'll have to cut the show. Only one more song."[21]

As the casualties mounted, Mal prepared to usher the Beatles to safety. "Sobbing girls lay slumped against the walls or huddled in the corners," he wrote, "and I caught a glimpse of Joan Baez trying to revive some of them with smelling salts. Every artist in the show was backstage helping out and trying to get the fainting youngsters back on their feet."

When the concert mercifully ended, the Beatles dropped their instruments, ran from the stage, and climbed into an enclosed freight truck to make their escape. Afterward, "pandemonium broke out in the auditorium," Mal wrote, "and I thought the whole place was going to collapse around us. But somehow, the police managed to keep the tide at bay, all the exit doors were thrown open, and people were hustled out. The scene behind them was of devastation, with seats overturned, people still trying to get onto the stage and more people fainting."[22]

By the next morning, the Beatles and their entourage were winging their way back to London. But the perils of the band's second North American tour would not be so quickly forgotten. For his part, Brian Epstein would chalk up the chaos and violence to lax security. But it was more than that, Mal realized. He had long felt that there was a dark side to Beatlemania, that not all the attendant hysteria could be understood as the simple by-product of fandom.

Back home, Mal's reunion with Lil and Gary was tempered by the infrequency of his correspondence and by the odd scraps of paper his wife had discovered in his suitcase—addresses and telephone numbers, invariably written in a feminine hand, from the "pen pals" he would meet on the road. Mal brushed off their significance, but Lil knew better. "It used to break my heart," she recalled.[23]

There was simply no brushing off the family's financial difficulties that autumn. Mal was determined to fill the household's meager coffers. With the experience of meeting Elvis and the Beatles' recent tour fresh in his mind, he hatched a plan to write his memoir—to tell the band's story from his perspective at the center of the vortex. Working with Michael Borrisow of Southern News Services out of Maidstone, Kent, Mal dictated a 37,000-word manuscript entitled "Beatles—U.S.A." Not willing to risk his relationships with the boys—even if it meant earning some much-needed side income—he ensured Borrisow that he had the Beatles' express approval to proceed with the project. And, indeed, each of the boys had provided him with a pithy foreword to his story:

Paul McCartney
Malcolm always was a talented boy, he has worked hard, and, if he works well this term, I feel sure he'll move up a class. I knew him

when he was nothing and he was still unassuming and a great one with the kiddies. Yes, I would recommend him for a post in your organisation without another word.

I would, before I close, like to thank all the people who have made all this possible: the Post Office of Liverpool, the patrol attendants along England's long roads, and most of all Lily of Allerton.

Thanking you,
Paul

Ringo Starr

Malcolm, Malcolm, now let me see, Malcolm at least it will be the truth when you read what is written by Malcolm.

Malcolm, good Malcolm, nice Malcolm.
Ringo

George Harrison

If we paid Mal more money, then he probably wouldn't need to do things like this book. But seeing as he does need the money, and also with Mal being along on every trip with us, the book naturally is more factual than had someone else written it. Therefore, I hope I enjoy reading it as much as you do.

George

John Lennon

Dear Malcolm,
I hope you get better soon and also your devoted servant (?)

Yours actually,
John

P.S. I like the drawings, too.[24]

Having gathered an assortment of tour photographs by Leslie Bryce as potential illustrations—and a film still from *Help!* depicting Mal in his star turn as "Channel Swimmer"—Borrisow presented the roadie's story to the whimsy of the commercial marketplace. And there it languished, bereft of any takers.

That was okay, though. For the next few weeks, Mal and the Beatles enjoyed a welcome break from the spotlight—save for Ringo and Maureen, who welcomed baby Zak on September 13, 1965. On October 9, John's twenty-fifth birthday, Mal, Neil, and the whole crew reunited for a party celebrating the opening of Lionel Bart's musical *Twang!*

Then it was back to work with George Martin at Abbey Road. With the label demanding material for the Beatles' new LP in advance of the holiday season, there was no time to spare. As Martin later recalled, "Coming to the studio was a refuge for them. It was the time and place when nobody could get at them. The strange hours for their sessions were really necessary because of the frenetic life they were forced into. Just look at what they used to pack into a year; tours here and overseas, TV, radio, press, and general promotion. Recording was important but it had to be squeezed in between everything else, and they enjoyed recording much more than touring. They got fed up with the vulnerability of it all—the continual pawing—and needed to escape from time to time."[25]

Mal was busier than ever during the production of the new album, which would be christened *Rubber Soul*, a punning title (a play on rubber-soled shoes) Paul had coined to reflect the admitted inauthenticity of English R&B—or "plastic soul." The Beatles' instruments were becoming more diverse by the day—George had taken up the sitar, for example, and Paul had begun using a full-bodied Rickenbacker bass in the studio—requiring Mal to expand his relationships with the London instrument vendors in order to maintain easy access to spare parts and enhancements. There was also the matter of the band's gear, which had taken a beating back in the States. Given the state of their stage equipment, they would receive a much welcomed gift from Vox that November. "Vox have just delivered a new set of amps to the Beatles," *Beat Instrumental* reported. "The old ones were still functioning perfectly, but their cases had received so many knocks on their travels that they had begun to look shabby."[26]

Mal would receive a few knocks of his own during one late-night session at EMI Studios. As events would show, the increasing fervor he had observed during the recent American tour was not an isolated phenomenon. Ever vigilant when it came to the boys, Mal recalled the time "we were recording in Number 2 studio, when a crowd of girls tried to break in through the double soundproof doors leading to outside. I thought I could get them out if I talked to them, so with security holding the inner [door], I slipped into the small room between the doors. Of course, with both doors closed, it was pitch black, so there I was fighting for survival as they jumped all over me, literally tearing my shirt off my back. Last time I did that, I can tell you!"[27]

In late October, the Beatles took a break from the *Rubber Soul* sessions to attend a ceremony at, of all places, Buckingham Palace. Back in June, Queen Elizabeth II had announced that the band would be awarded the MBE (for "Member of the Most Excellent Order of the British Empire") for service to the nation, marking the first time pop stars would receive an accolade usually reserved for military veterans and the like. In advance of the Queen's investiture of their medals, the boys gathered at Mal and Neil's flat, which was swiftly becoming their regular rendezvous point and was the site of a recent photo session with photographer Leslie Bryce. It had even emerged as a kind of makeshift storage unit for the bandmates: John Fanning recalled visiting the Montagu Mews West flat and coming upon, to his astonishment, a "cupboard that was ankle deep in gold records."[28]

After lazing about at Mal and Neil's place, the boys were driven by John's chauffeur, Les Anthony, to the palace in the Beatle's shiny Rolls-Royce Phantom V. Officially, the group was being recognized for their contributions to British commerce. But beyond their considerable economic achievements during a time when their country was suffering under the dark clouds of a protracted financial crisis, the Fab Four had imbued the nation with the bright colors of hope.

By the mid-1960s, the group existed in a swirling vortex of new movements in music, art, literature, and fashion. And London was its epicenter. The so-called Swinging Sixties drew a new youth culture into the capital. In remote places, young people were imagining new lives for themselves in faraway London among the capital's evolving intelligentsia. In an interview with a tiny seaside newspaper, nineteen-year-old Arwen Dolittle and her eighteen-year-old friend Amanda Hawkins—both from a remote hamlet in southwest England—complained about the lack of youth-oriented activities available there. Arwen and Amanda were planning, they told the reporter, to take the extraordinary step of leaving their quiet hometown behind for the allure of London.[29]

That same autumn, Mal and Lily had learned that Lily was pregnant with their second child. She later traced the baby's conception to the *Help!* premiere back in July, when she spent the night with her husband at the Montagu Mews West flat. With Mal's frequent and prolonged absences, Lily's family had proven invaluable—especially her fifteen-year-old niece, Shan, who often stayed with her and Gary in Mossley Hill. Living only a few miles away in Wavertree, Fred and Joan Evans were also regular visitors at Mal and Lily's home on Hillside Road, chipping in whenever they could as Lily's pregnancy progressed.

On the day after their investiture at Buckingham Palace, the Beatles were back at it in the studio, which was quickly emerging as Mal's working address, given the large amount of time the band spent there crafting their music. The length of their sessions had been increasing rapidly, often requiring Mal to be at EMI Studios at all hours of the night—on call for a meal, to restring a guitar, or for virtually any odd job the Beatles imagined. Not surprisingly, the folks at EMI were only too happy to oblige the group in their creative efforts. "We were given very much *carte blanche* with Studio 2, but didn't really chuck people out," George Martin later recalled, "although there were times when pressure was brought to bear and somebody who had the studio booked was told that the Beatles wanted it. I didn't approve of this at all, but sometimes the boys would steam-roller people. EMI contributed to this by demanding product, and we were often unfairly accused of being arrogant."[30]

Martin was under formidable pressure to bring *Rubber Soul* to completion in time for an early December release date. As with *Help!*, the new LP found the Beatles expanding their musical palate. On John's moving "In My Life," for example, Martin himself overdubbed a baroque piano solo. "I love 'In My Life,'" Mal later remarked. "It's my all-time favorite. Something magical about it."[31]

On November 11, the Beatles spent some fifteen hours in the studio in a breakneck effort to finish the album. And it was on that day that Mal was invited to participate in the magic-making for the very first time. As the group completed work on "You Won't See Me," Paul hit upon the idea of including a Hammond organ overdub at the tail end of the song. At Paul's instruction, Mal depressed an organ key for the last several measures of "You Won't See Me." The boys had great fun compiling the LP's liner notes, which cheekily included a credit for "Mal 'Organ' Evans."

Given the tight deadline, stress naturally mounted during the *Rubber Soul* sessions. "Things get tense, sometimes even between close friends," Mal recalled, "and recording is not the easiest thing in the world, you know, especially when you've got four people with different ideas, and you've got to jell them all together in one direction." At a certain level, Mal understood that he was, in a sense, mothering the band members. "I was always making tea, sandwiches, or scrambled eggs," he said, "just doing anything to look after them, to make sure we kept them working well. The whole thing was, 'You make the music, and I'll do anything in the world to make you comfortable.'"[32] Mal realized the intrinsic value of this effort—of keeping the Beatles well fed for a long night in the studio—but he also began to recognize a second role he had come to play in the Beatles' creative lives, a role that allowed him to quell their divisions and drive them back together when creative tensions ran high.

Mal recalled walking "into the control room one night, and the air was electric. You could cut it with a knife, everyone was snarling, and I just walked in and dropped the tray of cups, and they all turned round and said, 'Hey, look at the dummy!'" For Mal, this was the moment of success, the instant when the boys "had a common enemy. They had gotten diverted, and so I broke the ice." Quite suddenly, "they were all joking and laughing. Cups were all over the floor, and they went back into the music again," he wrote. "I didn't mind," he added. "While they were laughing at you, they couldn't be shouting at you."[33]

A few days after the "You Won't See Me" session, George Martin and the band put the finishing touches on *Rubber Soul*, which was set to be released simultaneously with their latest single, "We Can Work It Out," backed with "Day Tripper" on the B side. Knowing that the Beatles intended to perform "Day Tripper" on the upcoming British tour, set to begin on

December 3 in Glasgow, Mal fashioned a bespoke tambourine, removing its outer skin, inserting an internal rod, outfitting the instrument with an additional "ching ring," and attaching the tambourine to a cymbal stand.[34]

As Mal and the Beatles made their way north to Scotland, *Rubber Soul* was released to nearly universal acclaim, singled out by many music critics as a clear elevation of the band's sound and creativity. In faraway California, the Beach Boys' Brian Wilson took special note of Mal's contribution to "You Won't See Me," writing, "There's an organ drone in there, a note that's held down for the last third of the song or so. Those were touches they were trying, almost art music."[35]

By the afternoon of December 3, as Mal made final preparations onstage, the Beatles had already decided—privately with Brian and among their innermost circle—that this would be the final tour of their homeland. "By the end of 1965," Ringo recalled, "the touring started to hit everybody. I remember we had a meeting during which we all talked about how the musicianship was going downhill, never mind the boredom of doing it; going away and hitting all those hotels."[36]

Mal was of two minds about the decision. On the one hand, he adored the opportunity to revel in the Beatles' company anytime, but especially on the road, day after day, when they shared meals together and behaved, as he later wrote, like a "family unit."[37] On the other hand, he had also witnessed how seemingly ordinary fans could lose themselves, in an instant, and become capable of virtually anything, even, occasionally, violence.

15

THE FAMILY WAY

For Mal and the Beatles, the nine-day tour must have seemed like old times. For one thing, the band and their entourage took to the motorways, rather than depending on the air travel that had dominated their touring days of late. Having loaded up the Commer van with the group's equipment—including seven guitars, two each for John and Paul and three for George—Mal left for Glasgow a day early. With Alf behind the wheel, Neil and the boys piled into the Austin Princess the next day. The chauffeur was responsible for lashing two additional guitars—a Rickenbacker and a Gretsch Country Gentleman—to the back of the Austin Princess. John and George, respectively, had been using the guitars during one last pre-tour rehearsal the previous afternoon at Mal and Neil's flat.

Somewhere in the vicinity of Berwick-on-Tweed, not far from the border between England and Scotland, disaster struck. Alf realized there was a problem when a lorry driver began flashing his lights. When Alf brought the Austin Princess to a halt to find out what all the fuss was about, he was greeted by the incredulous truck driver. "Didn't ya hear it fall off?" he implored the chauffeur. As it turned out, the spare Country Gentleman had fallen off the back of the limo a few miles back, while Alf was driving the Princess through a particularly bumpy patch of road.[1]

A distraught George looked on in disbelief as Alf and Neil gathered up bits of the destroyed guitar along the motorway. "About 13 lorries went over it before our chauffeur could get near it," he recalled.[2] Ironically, the stray pieces of broken guitar came in handy a few days later. When Paul broke one of the machine heads on his Höfner violin bass, Mal was able to use the spare parts from the ruined Country Gentleman to make the repairs.

In Liverpool, where the group was set to play the Empire Theatre, tensions had been ratcheted up by a local controversy involving the fate of the Cavern Club. During the post-Beatles years, the basement club had seen a steep decline in attendance. An accountant by trade, owner Ray McFall had been a notoriously lackluster businessman; things had recently come to a head when the city council required sanitation and drainage improvements to the club, expenses McFall simply couldn't afford. On the afternoon of the Empire Theatre gig, the Beatles were approached by well-meaning fans who were campaigning to save the Cavern from closure. For his part, Paul liked the idea of transforming the club into a permanent local attraction, although John felt less charitable, bluntly remarking that "We don't feel we owe the Cavern anything physical."[3] Salvation would come, at least temporarily, in the form of local restaurateur Joey Davey and his partner Alf Geoghegan, the father of longtime Cavernite Debbie Geoghegan (now Greenberg).

With a hometown gig in the offing, the Beatles and their entourage had been understandably besieged by ticket requests from friends and family. Prominent among their guests was Ringo's beloved mother, Elsie, along with George's parents, Harry and Louise, and his fiancée, Pattie Boyd. Lily was on hand, too, supporting her husband and enjoying a rare night out. *NME*'s Alan Smith had been embedded with the group for the duration of the tour, taking special note of the fans' subdued behavior that night at the Empire. "Even in the 'Pool,'" Smith wrote, "I noticed a quietening down of audience reaction compared with previous concerts. I'm not knocking in any way—I just think the group's fans are getting a bit more sensible lately. There was tons of thunderous applause to compensate for the lowered screaming decibel rate!"[4]

Even so, the constant rain of jelly babies continued unabated—as usual, mucking up the band's gear and requiring hours of post-concert attention from Mal. At the Newcastle gigs, fans had supplemented the sticky candies with "gonks," egg-shaped novelty toys distinctively adorned with frizzy hair. Although tiny in size, the gnomelike gonks were capable of leaving a welt on their victims. In Sheffield a few days after the Empire performance, Paul was struck in the eye by a hard candy, which resulted in his blinking uncontrollably throughout the show.

Prior to the gig, Mal surprised John with the gift of an antique banjo. Knowing that John's late mother, Julia, had played the instrument, the roadie simply couldn't pass up the purchase during a recent shopping trip in Chester, even throwing in a copy of *Amateur Banjo Tutor* for John's reference. And that's when Mal pointed out the signature—"George Formby" was scrawled on the headstock. Cradling in his arms a banjo that had once belonged to Liverpool's vaudevillian legend, and one of his and George's most cherished idols, John couldn't believe his good fortune.[5]

The tour came to a close with a pair of shows at Cardiff's Capitol Theatre on December 12. During the break between sets, Mal and the Beatles dined on bangers and mash in their dressing room and, to the roadie's great joy, watched a Western on television. As it happened, the audience for the nightcap—one of their final gigs in their homeland before a paying audience—was considerably more raucous than the earlier show. At one point, Mal raced into the fray after a fan leapt up onstage and lunged for Paul and George before being restrained by security.[6] Reflecting on the tour, Smith pronounced—perhaps prematurely—that "crazy Beatlemania is over, certainly." Adding that the latest concerts had been free of riots and other mayhem, Smith opined that "Beatles fans are now a little bit more sophisticated than Rolling Stones followers."[7]

As Neil and the band traveled back to London with Alf behind the wheel, Mal stayed behind in Cardiff to painstakingly load their gear into the Commer van. While he drove through the night, the Beatles attended a Christmas party at the Scotch of St. James nightclub. Much later that same evening, Paul tried acid in the company of twenty-year-old Guinness heir Tara Browne. The next day, the Beatles' inner circle met up to consider their plans for 1966, which included a world tour set to begin in Munich in June. In a bold move, the boys unanimously rejected film producer Walter Shenson's pitch for a third United Artists movie to succeed *A Hard Day's Night* and *Help!*. Entitled *A Talent for Loving*, the screenplay called for the Beatles to play Old West characters. Hence, there would be no new Beatles film in the coming year, exploding Brian Epstein and George Martin's plan for two LPs and a movie per annum.

And there wouldn't be a holiday residency, either, which left Mal free to spend his first nonworking Christmas at home since 1962. The winds of change were clearly in the air. With a fortnight of rest splayed out ahead of him, Mal likely experienced a shock to the system, although he was, no doubt, excited by the opportunity to finally play Father Christmas for Gary. He also found time to catch up on his correspondence, sending out a raft of holiday cards and season's greetings, one of which was posted to a quiet street in Indianapolis. To her great surprise, Georgeanna Lewis received a letter from Mal. "That Christmas I got a card from him, a really cute drawing," she recalled. "So I tried writing him. We carried on a correspondence for quite some time."[8]

On January 6, Mal and the Beatles were back at it, having convened with George Martin at Bayswater's Cine-Tele Sound Studios for one of the strangest sessions of their recording career. Their task was to carry out touch-up work on the ragged audio from their August 1965 performance at Shea Stadium, which BBC One intended to release as a documentary film on March 1. Knowing that the audio had been captured in a cavernous stadium in front of some 55,000 fans, Martin had deliberately chosen the studio because of its high level of reverb, figuring that much of the band's distorted performance would necessitate rerecording.

Things started out normally enough, as Mal set up the Höfner bass so that Paul could begin noodling around while he waited for the others to arrive. Within the hour, John, George, and Ringo made the scene, strolling into the studio empty-handed. Realizing that their instruments hadn't been delivered, the roadie experienced a sudden frisson of fear.

With no time to spare, he sprang into action, calling in favors at Sound City. With Alf in tow, he raced across town to the music vendor, where, to his great relief, the proprietors loaned the Beatles a complete set of instruments, allowing them to begin "sweetening" their Shea Stadium recording.[9] For the most part, the boys were able to overdub new instrumentation and vocals into the mix, save for Ringo's live performance on "Act Naturally," which was so badly distorted that Martin simply patched in the original master recording and camouflaged it with prerecorded crowd noise. When the Shea Stadium film was broadcast that March on BBC One, Mal was delighted to see himself on the little screen, standing plain as day behind Ed Sullivan as the TV host delivered his introduction in front of the hordes of screaming fans.

As Mal had the previous year, Martin was coming to realize the boys' increasingly precarious position while touring. "By 1966, the Beatles were in a car that was going downhill very fast," he later recalled. "This is not to say that their career was going downhill; but they were a media juggernaut that was increasingly out of their manager Brian Epstein's control—and everyone else's, for that matter. It wasn't so much that somebody was pressing the accelerator too hard; it was that nobody had their foot on the brake."[10]

On January 21, 1966, Mal and Neil attended George and Pattie's nuptials at the Epsom Registry Office in Surrey, with Paul serving as best man. The roadies stayed overnight at the newlyweds' Esher home, observing Paul as he became steadily drunk and waking up to the aroma of a home-cooked breakfast courtesy of the bride and groom. For the bride's part, Mal was welcome company on any occasion—he was, for Boyd, "a big cuddly bear" who "always had this little smile and soft, soft eyes."[11]

That spring, the Beatles began working on their new album with Martin at EMI. With twenty-year-old engineer Geoff Emerick behind the mixing desk, the band started with an experimental song by John that went under the working title "Mark 1" and that would eventually be called "Tomorrow Never Knows," after another "Ringo-ism." John wanted Martin to manipulate his voice for the song, instructing the producer to "make me sound like the Dalai Lama chanting from a mountaintop."[12] He even asked Martin if it were possible to suspend him from the ceiling by a rope so that his voice would swell in volume and intensity as his body swung above the microphone. But Martin understandably demurred at the thought of hanging the Beatle by a rope under any circumstances. At one point, Paul brought a series of tape loops into the studio for inclusion in John's surreal composition. Along with Neil and Alf, Mal found himself helping Geoff feed the tape loops into the studio's machines to create a swirling sound collage. "It was a great laugh," Alf recalled, "and we were all falling about. John was being just as silly, and wanted to pile the furniture up, so he could stand at the top, and pretend he was singing from the mountains, along with his monks."[13]

A few days later, Mal took a break from the studio to pick up a selection of new, more powerful amplifiers for the Beatles' upcoming world tour. Constructed from a hybrid transistor and valve design, the Vox 4/7 Series amps featured variable controls that would exert an immediate impact upon the band's creative work in the studio. The 120-watt, shoulder-high amps made for bulky, cumbersome gear. With Alf in tow, Mal transported the amps to EMI Studios in the Commer van. "I don't know how he is going to manage them, as they are so big," Alf recalled. "He says the boys need some more power to get over the noise of the crowds."[14]

With the powerful amps in place in Studio 3, the Beatles began work on "Paperback Writer," their new single. By this juncture, "the Roll" continued unabated. With the addition of the double A-sided "We Can Work It Out" and "Day Tripper," the group had notched eleven consecutive number one U.K. hits. As Ringo and Neil played chess in a corner of the studio, Paul and John created new sounds with the assistance of Martin and Emerick—both for "Paperback Writer" and its B side, "Rain," which featured backward vocals. Meanwhile, Mal kept the team fueled for the lengthy session. "Right on cue at the end of the fourth take," *Beatles Book* editor Sean O'Mahony wrote, "Mal emerged into the studio laden with tea, biscuits and something very special—toast and strawberry jam. Everything was immediately dropped and a sudden swoop was made on the toast and jam."[15]

During the April 16 session, Alf sensed that the roadie was becoming increasingly ill at ease—and he soon found out why. "Mal was hanging around looking all lost," Alf observed. "I understand how he feels, because his wife, Lily, is expecting soon, and he's quite nervous about it all. We had a chat about family life and life with the Beatles. He's been with them a lot longer than me."[16] After the session ended around one thirty in the morning, Mal and Neil returned to their flat, only to be awakened by a telephone call from Liverpool Maternity Hospital reporting that Lily had just given birth to a daughter. For the next several hours, Mal shared the news far and wide.

By two thirty in the afternoon, the roadies were back in the studio, with Mal prepping the band's afternoon snacks.

"Ah you've got the tea then," said Ringo, as Mal strolled into the studio with a tray.

"I've got a daughter too," Mal replied.

"You've what?" John exclaimed. "What are you doing here then?"[17]

With that, the boys insisted that Mal return forthwith to Liverpool to

Mal with infant Julie

be with his wife and baby daughter. Given his association with the Beatles, a *Liverpool Echo* reporter was dispatched to cover the story. "We are going to call her Julie Suzanne, but she will be known as Julie. She's our first daughter and we are both thrilled to bits. We already have our boy, Gary, who's now four and a half."[18]

Within a few days, Mal was back in the Beatles' orbit. On April 21, with his four-day-old daughter still in the hospital with Lil, he was at EMI Studios, where the band was recording the basic rhythm track for "Taxman." "I'm in the recording studio at this moment," Mal wrote to his wife, "and the noise is deafening when they are playing, but one gets used to it eventually, and it really is an unoffensive noise at that." When he arrived at the studio that day, a fan outside presented him with a little pair of booties in honor of Julie's birth. "It was so nice to see you and Julie on the weekend," Mal wrote Lily. "I must be the luckiest man in the whole world for I have you and Gary and Julie to love and that in itself is a wonderful thing, but to be loved by three wonderful people is something that no amount of money will buy." He signed his letter with a series of playful initials reflecting his multitudinous roles:

L.H. (Loving Husband)

B.R.M. (Beatle Road Manager)

C.S. (Channel Swimmer)

O.P. (Organ Player)

F.O.T. (Father of Two)[19]

Mal penned a second letter to Lily on April 29. At this point, his wife was being nursed back to health by a revolving door of relatives and friends. While their daughter's birth, in contrast to Gary's, had been without complications, Lily's postnatal condition was dire. As Mal later recalled, "Lil was to have a bad time also with our second child, Julie Suzanne, spending several months partially paralyzed after the birth, but there was a lot of courage and determination in that wonderful five-foot [body] of hers."[20] Julie's birth clearly found Mal longing to be back in Liverpool, as he expressed in his letter to Lily, yet he never strayed from the excitement he felt over his Beatles-related duties: "I have all the love in the world for you and Gary and Julie," he wrote. "My thoughts at this moment are jumping all over the place, and it's very hard to put love and how I feel for you down on paper—but I think you know how sincere I am." He concluded the letter with a reference to a "big day on Sunday at the *NME* Poll [Winners'] Concert. Wish me luck. First public appearance of Mal since last November—still trying to decide what stage suit I will wear. But joking apart, I'm really nervous about the whole thing—so please have me in your thoughts, won't you?"[21]

On May 1, Mal was road-managing his first show since Cardiff back in December. It was also the Beatles' initial opportunity to try out the new Vox amps in front of an audience—in this case, at the ten-thousand-seat Empire Pool in Wembley. The occasion was the annual *New Musical Express* Poll Winners' Concert. When they took the stage that day, the Beatles topped a roster of all-stars that included the Rolling Stones, the Who, the Yardbirds, the Spencer Davis Group (featuring Stevie Winwood), the Small Faces, Roy Orbison, and Cliff Richard and the Shadows. In order to ensure their safe arrival, Mal and Neil devised a ruse in which the Beatles disguised themselves as culinary staff, wearing white aprons and chefs' toques, and entered the venue through the service doors.

The trouble began when the Stones finished their set. As John, Paul, George, and Ringo prepared to take the stage, *NME*'s publisher, Maurice Kinn, announced that the Beatles wouldn't be performing until after the awards ceremony. "We're not waiting," Lennon barked. "We're going on now." The Beatles were England's reigning superstars—the world's, really—and there was no way they would be playing second fiddle to the Stones. Kinn explained that he was powerless to concede to John's wishes, having made a prior agreement with Andrew Loog Oldham, the Stones' manager. After a bit of wrangling, Brian agreed to Kinn's demands, although he countered that ABC-TV would not be allowed to film the Beatles' set. "You can't do this to us," Lennon roared at Kinn. "We will never appear on one of your shows ever again."[22]

And they wouldn't. When they concluded their performance, the boys tossed their awards into the waiting arms of Mal and Neil before hurling themselves into Alf's limo for a quick getaway. As for the new Vox amps, Mal was suitably impressed with their potency. The Beatles had turned in a blistering set at the Empire Pool, the fracas backstage no doubt fueling their passion, and the extra wattage had served them well. The next day, Alf eavesdropped as Brian fumed about the bad tidings in Wembley, suggesting that it had marked the Beatles' final live performance. The chauffeur surmised that he would be out of a job after the upcoming tour, as would Mal and Neil, presumably. In what world would a band working strictly in the studio require roadies?[23]

By mid-month, the Beatles had put the final touches on their latest project, which would be entitled *Revolver* during a brainstorming session in West Germany on their upcoming tour. In order to promote the release of the attendant single "Paperback Writer," Brian hired American director Michael Lindsay-Hogg, who had helmed several episodes of *Ready Steady Go!*, the popular ATV music program. Lindsay-Hogg was understandably nervous about meeting the band prior to the video shoot at Chiswick House, a lavish estate on the western outskirts of London. To his great relief, Mal set about calming the director's anxiety. "He made your heart happy," Lindsay-Hogg later recalled. "He was sending out calm vibes. He knew what was going on in my head. My first impression of him was just of this gentle, kind, sensitive man who is built like a bodyguard."[24]

On June 1, Mal not only participated, but also took a leading role, in the most unusual Beatles recording session to date. That night in Studio 2, John came up with the idea of adding sound effects to "Yellow Submarine," a playful children's song, with Ringo handling lead vocals. The result was a twelve-hour, marijuana-infused session. After the dinner break, the Beatles invited a bevy of friends to EMI Studios, including the Rolling Stones' Mick Jagger and Brian Jones, along with Marianne Faithfull, Mick's new girlfriend, and Pattie Boyd. John was particularly intent on recording the sound of his voice underwater. "First, he tried singing while gargling," Geoff Emerick recalled. "When that failed (he nearly choked), he began lobbying for a tank to be brought in so that he could be submerged." That's when Emerick hit upon the idea of recording John's voice using a submerged microphone.[25] As if on cue, Mal produced a condom from the bowels of his doctor's bag.

"Well done, Malcolm!" John exclaimed. "After all, we don't want the microphone to be getting in the family way, do we?"[26] The roadie succeeded in waterproofing the mic by enclosing it inside the condom and then dunking it in a water-filled milk bottle, which had been helpfully supplied by Neil. When the underwater experiment failed, Martin observed as "Mal Evans evolved an ingenious method by which the words were spoken by John through his guitar amplifier."[27] Afterward, the Beatles and their friends began raiding the trap room, the closet beneath the staircase in Studio 2 that was brimming with an odd assortment of sound effects. Mal remembered "bashing chains in a bucket of water for sound effects and shuffling sand."[28] The bizarre session concluded when he began marching around the studio with a bass drum strapped to his chest, as the raucous band gathered up behind him, conga style, singing the song's catchy chorus.

On June 14, the Beatles turned to a new composition, entitled "Here, There, and Everywhere." Written primarily by Paul at John's Weybridge estate earlier that month, the song had been inspired by the Beach Boys' "God Only Knows," a standout track on their new LP, *Pet Sounds.* Mal recalled the moment Paul debuted "Here, There, and Everywhere" for him.

"Neil Aspinall and I were staying in a hotel in London," he said, "and we had been up rather late, until about seven o'clock in the morning, and we were really whacked out. And at nine o'clock, there is a bang at the door and jolly ol' Paul comes in with a smile from ear to ear. 'Good morning lads. Thought we'd come and have breakfast with you.' 'Oh sure, Paul,' we replied. Then he said, 'I've got this song of mine and I'm stuck for a line.' So, he sits down, plays it for us, and sings it."[29]

When Paul reached the end of the tune, a phrase began to materialize in Mal's mind. "I'm very eye-conscious," he recalled, "and the line I came up with was 'watching her eyes, and hoping I'm always there.' I'm very proud of that." In a notebook that he carried around during this period, Mal described "Here, There, and Everywhere" as a "lovely song," adding that he was alone with Paul on the studio floor when he recorded the lead vocal. Paul complained about his performance—"He thinks it too 'fruity,'" Mal wrote, but "I don't."[30] As composers, Lennon and McCartney often accepted—even asked for—assistance in crafting their lyrics. Sometimes, it would simply be a matter of trying to capture the word on the tip of the songwriter's tongue. "Other people don't necessarily give you a word or a line," said John, "they just throw in the word you're looking for anyway."[31]

A case in point occurred at EMI Studios back in late April, after Mal had returned from Lily's bedside in Liverpool. The Beatles were working on a new song, entitled "Eleanor Rigby," yet another tune Paul had begun at Weybridge. When they gathered in the studio to record the song, Paul still hadn't completed the lyrics. As John later recalled, "we were sitting around with Mal Evans and Neil Aspinall, so he said to us, 'Hey, you guys, finish up the lyrics.' Now I was there with Mal, a telephone installer who was our road manager, and Neil, who was a student accountant, and I was insulted and hurt that Paul had just thrown it out in the air. He actually meant he wanted me to do it, and of course there isn't a line of theirs in the song because I finally went off to a room with Paul and we finished the song."[32] In this instance, John was clearly incensed at what he felt was his partner's cavalier attitude toward their creative process. But the example also demonstrates Lennon and McCartney's porous songwriting practices. Similar to the manner in which Paul sought Mal's aid in completing the lyrics for "Here, There, and Everywhere," John would often consult with Neil in crafting the final lines of his songs.[33]

By the time the Beatles completed work on "Here, There, and Everywhere" in mid-June, Mal had less than a week to prepare for the upcoming world tour, the first two legs of which would take them to West Germany, Japan, and the Philippines. His notebook bespeaks a whirlwind of last-minute preparations, ranging from making an inventory of the boys' stage outfits to ensuring that his doctor's bag was fully stocked; he even references the amount of toothpaste and toothbrushes they would need for the trip. He made a circuit of the London instrument vendors to maintain his ready supply of guitar leads, guitar and bass strings, drumsticks, and the like. And he made a special point of checking and double-checking the voltage on the Beatles' Vox amps and Vox Continental organ, which he dutifully loaded into the Commer van for transport to Heathrow.[34]

As usual, Mal's dirty, road-worn equipment van had been decorated with the Beatles' names scrawled in lipstick. According to *The Beatles Book*, as a favor to the roadie, "four fans, who had been waiting patiently outside for autographs, spent an hour cleaning it down for Mal. But no sooner had they finished and departed with many thanks from the Beatles' Road Manager when a new bunch of autograph hunters arrived and started writing new slogans on it."[35] With the instruments stowed, Mal tended to his most important duty, ensuring that there was a handful of spare plectrums in his shirt pocket at all times. After the fiasco with Elvis in Bel Air, there was simply no way the roadie would be caught flat-footed again.

At 11 a.m. on June 23, 1966, Mal, the band, and the rest of the entourage boarded the plane for the flight to Munich. And that's when Mal's anxiety got the better of him. A premonition of overwhelming force took hold of his being: "I knew at that moment I was going to die," he wrote. In a flourish, he started composing a hasty last will and testament–cum-prayer. "I am male, name Malcolm Frederick Evans, married to a truly adorable wife, Lily," he began. "I have so much to live for. My wife and I, I guess worship (excuse me Lord) our son Gary, four and a half years, and Julie Suzanne, now nearly 11 weeks old." He continued: "I have prayed to God and meant it, a thing I have not done since very young. Lily, I love you," he added. "Please tell our children some of the bad things about me, for this way, I will appear a human being, not perfect in so many ways, not perfect in any way, but God's child who loves his fellow man."[36]

As the plane prepared for takeoff, Mal wrote, "I feel quite calm about dying, and I hope that I can face death thinking not of myself, but of my loved ones. God knows my sins, please forgive me. I only hope I have never hurt anyone. I have hurt Lily and Gary, I know, but my love has grown with every passing moment." And with that, Mal felt the power of the jet's "racing engines, sliding forward, pressed back in my seat, wheels are off the ground." And in a final flourish, he wrote, "Love me back to you, Lil, Gary, and Julie. I love you."[37]

16

WE LOVE YOU, BEATLES!

"Having landed safely at Munich," Mal wrote, revealing a sudden faith in providence, "I know now that I will always travel safely by plane."

The next afternoon, after the roadie had prepped the stage, the Beatles opened the tour with a pair of shows at Munich's Circus-Krone-Bau. In stark contrast to the band's gigs on the 1965 American tour, the West German fans were fervent but not riotous. In Mal's view, the heightened police response was disproportionate to the audience's behavior. "I was disgusted at the brutality handed out to fans for showing just plain enthusiasm," he recalled. "I can still see one young boy who got excited, standing up, shaking his arms and letting it all hang out, being grabbed by four policemen, hustled through the crowd, and savagely kicked down the steps backstage."[1]

While in Munich, Mal and the Beatles had never felt more isolated, increasingly keeping to themselves, even eschewing the mad all-night parties that characterized their previous tours. Instead, the Beatles and their minuscule entourage sat in their hotel rooms, often playing cards to pass the time. And, of course, Mal's dope bag was never too far away.

The roadie understood the bandmates' sense of languor and isolation. During the West German leg of the tour, the rest of the entourage journeyed by train between shows. "I spent several lonely nights in the various cities," Mal wrote, "travelling the following day on my own, the reason being that police insisted the train leave right after the show and, of course, it was impossible to join them in time, having to break down and take care of the equipment." Even so, he was surprised later, in Hamburg, when the Beatles didn't celebrate on the famous Reeperbahn, the center of the city's nightlife, after their show at Ernst-Merck-Halle. After all, Hamburg had

Brian in a railway car en route to West Germany

been, in many ways, the making of them as bona fide performers. "The whole town was expecting the Beatles to go to the Star Club and celebrate," Mal wrote. "I feel that if they had, the party would have lasted for the next two weeks."[2] Instead, the bandmates were content to meet up with their old friends backstage and call it a night.

With West Germany in their rearview mirror, the band and their entourage embarked on a thirty-hour flight to Tokyo, where they were set to play the famed Nippon Budokan arena. Their journey would take even longer thanks to a typhoon, which forced them to wait out the storm in Anchorage, Alaska. When they were back on the plane, Tony Barrow recalled, "instead of the usual poker game started by Mal, they all gathered in the forward lounge of the aircraft to drink Scotch and Cokes and play 'Dictionary,' a game they claimed to have invented to pass the time on such excursions. To get things rolling, Mal would read out an obscure word from his pocket dictionary, and the assembled players would make up crazy definitions for it, and once they were read out loud in turn to much laughter, the best one was chosen by voting."[3]

During the flight, Mal penned yet another letter to Lily. "Thinking of you so much this trip," he wrote. "You know when you get busy, work takes a lot of your thinking up. But this time you and the children are never out of my thoughts for very long, and I never realized I could miss anyone and feel so upset about being apart as I do when I think of you."

For the first time since undertaking his great rock 'n' roll adventure, Mal had begun to doubt his choices. Nearly nine years into his marriage and with two children at home, he concluded that "[I] guess I really am ready to settle down to being a family man, or perhaps now I feel that I have grown up and realize what and who are really important in my life, and that is your love and [for] you to love me."[4] The notion that he was finally "ready to settle down" was, by any measure, an extraordinary admission on his part.

Once the group landed, Mal was determined to soak up Japanese culture. Neil later recalled that the roadie was the first member of the Beatles team to try a cup of sake, although he may have preferred something stronger.

"What does it taste like, Mal?" Ringo asked.

Paul, Mal, and Alf en route to Tokyo

"It's not really like wine," he replied. "It's *definitely* not like Scotch," Mal proclaimed.

To which, John said, "That gives us a very clear idea. Thank you, Mal!"[5]

After the Beatles deplaned in Tokyo, the entourage was immediately struck by the level of security Japanese authorities had amassed—with forty armored personnel carriers at their disposal and more than thirty thousand uniformed police lining the route from the airport to the Tokyo Hilton, where the band occupied the Presidential Suite.

They soon learned that a local controversy had erupted over the band's upcoming performance at the Nippon Budokan, which had been constructed to host martial arts competitions for the 1964 Olympics. The Beatles were set to be the first rock band to play the arena, which was considered a national shrine. With numerous death threats reported in advance of the group's appearance there, the Japanese government was determined to avoid any national embarrassment related to the Beatles' visit. For this reason, the band and their entourage were prohibited from making any excursions, given the overriding fear of an international incident involving their safety. With the prohibition on sightseeing, the Japanese promoter regaled the group with a private party in his suite. "We all were delighted to enjoy the company of half a dozen very striking Geisha girls," Mal recalled, "each one of them like a beautiful painting, or flawless piece of porcelain."[6]

For his part, the roadie managed to slip out of the hotel, and it wasn't long before Paul decided to join him on his excursion. But when they attempted to leave the Hilton, the two were almost immediately intercepted by police, who insisted they conduct their outing in the company of plainclothes detectives. With their newly appointed security detail along for the ride, Mal and Paul were treated to a tour of the Meiji Jingu Shrine and a portion of the Imperial Palace grounds before a posse of photographers tracked them down, and in short order, they were hustled back to the Hilton.

As for the concerts themselves, the Japanese fans were especially subdued, with some three thousand police on hand to supervise ten thousand fans. Standing backstage, Mal and the Beatles watched as the officers filled up the front rows—both on the floor of the arena and in the upper balconies—only then followed by the Budokan audience, who quietly took their seats behind the lines of security. "There was heavy police presence,"

Neil recalled, "and the audiences were unusually quiet. For the first time in a long while, the audience could hear [the music]. There was no loud screaming, which came as a surprise: the band suddenly realized they were out of tune, and they had to get their act together." For the Beatles, the whole experience was "a bit of a shock."[7]

Mal felt a considerable shock of his own when, for the first time in recent memory, his stage setup partially failed. At one juncture, Ringo's cymbal stand began to loosen, slowly cascading toward the base of his drum riser. Mal was understandably sick to his stomach over the lapse, no matter how minor. But there was nothing that went wrong in Tokyo—much less, in the entirety of their experience on the road—that could have remotely prepared them for Manila.

On the morning of July 3, the Beatles and their entourage left for the Philippines by way of Hong Kong. "Manila was our next port of call on our way back to England," Mal later remembered, "and it was here, for the first time in my life, I was to experience real fear." As it turned out, things were cockeyed from the outset. After attending their usual post-arrival press conference, John, Paul, George, and Ringo were hustled out of a rear entrance and taken to the harbor, where they were ushered aboard a motor yacht.

"It was really humid, it was Mosquito City," George reported, "and we were all sweating and frightened. For the first time ever in our Beatle existence, we were cut off from Neil, Mal, and Brian Epstein. There was not one of them around, and not only that, but we had a whole row of cops with guns lining the deck around this cabin that we were in on the boat. We were really gloomy, very brought down by the whole thing."[8]

Incredible as it may seem, things would actually get worse. After Brian succeeded in securing the Beatles' return to the mainland, they ensconced themselves in the opulent Manila Hotel for the night. What the members of the band's entourage didn't know was that the Beatles had received an invitation from Philippine president Ferdinand Marcos and First Lady Imelda Marcos requesting their appearance at Malacañang Palace at eleven o'clock the next morning. Only, Brian and the Beatles never laid eyes on it. After the incident at the British embassy in February 1964, official requests for the Beatles' presence were routinely ignored. Instead, the group went about their business in Manila, performing the first of two shows for some

35,000 spectators at José Rizal Memorial Stadium and another audience of 50,000 later that same day. Things seemed normal enough at this point. "The audience was purely and simply Beatles fans," Mal recalled, and both shows were "received with a wonderful warmth they get from their fans everywhere."[9]

For the moment, the band and their entourage hadn't felt any blowback from having snubbed the First Lady, save for scathing news reports on Filipino TV. That night, the promoter arranged for a lavish party at the hotel, with numerous prostitutes on hand to cater to the boys' needs. "At one point in the evening's festivities," Mal wrote, "I opened Neil's door to his darkened room where he was sleeping peacefully, having retired early with a headache, and pushed a young lady in to keep him company. Now Neil didn't want to know at all, and she was to exit about five minutes later, leaving Neil with some sort of terrible social disease!"

On the morning of July 5, Mal began to sense trouble when a pistol-packing member of the promoter's staff requested autographed pictures of the Beatles. "I was in the middle of explaining that I had given away most of the photographs," Mal wrote, "keeping a few for the plane crew on the way home, when I was cut short by the same gentleman brandishing a gun in my face and repeating the demand. I couldn't give them to him fast enough. This was the prelude to a morning of terror."[10]

Mal could feel the tension rising as he sought out a truck to transport the luggage and gear to the airport. "The feeling in the air was that nobody wanted to be associated with us," he wrote. "On arriving at the airport, I was informed by the police on duty that I couldn't park near the airline gate, but in the normal parking area like ordinary people. Their attitude being, 'who do you think you are?'" When the band and their entourage arrived at the airport, Mal discovered that no one would help them, save for the KLM airline attendants, who processed their baggage.

Everything went to hell when they began making their way to the international lounge, only to be intercepted by a dozen Filipinos. "It was obvious that they were looking to cause trouble, and quite prepared to beat the hell out of us, because of the fiasco the previous evening with the First Lady," Mal wrote. "They were standing on our toes, jabbing us with elbows, generally giving us a bad time, and the last thing we could do was hit back. Up to that point, they were just a nuisance and making us feel very uncomfortable. I would give my right arm for any of those boys, but under these circumstances, it was most inadvisable to retaliate in any way whatsoever. To stand there and see my beloved Beatles treated so roughly was heartbreaking to me."[11]

It was chauffeur Alf Bicknell, of all people, who could no longer contain himself. Daring to strike back at the assailants, he was viciously attacked, ending up flat on the airport floor with a pair of cracked ribs. Despite his large size, Mal sustained numerous blows, as did Ringo, who was knocked down with a swift uppercut and crawled away as assailants kicked him. Things seemed to get worse as the group approached customs, where John and George were punched and kicked. Paul managed to avoid the brunt of the violence by sprinting ahead. Along with Alf, Brian suffered the most, sustaining a sprained ankle during the mêlée. At one point, Mal realized he was bleeding from his leg.

Mal would never forget the surrealness of walking across the tarmac after the violence they had experienced back in the terminal. The ruffians were still in evidence, hurling insults and epithets as the Brits made their way to the waiting KLM jet. But the fans were there, too, shouting "We love you, Beatles!" and tossing bouquets of flowers at their feet.

Once on board the plane, "sitting in the seats and fastening seat belts," Mal wrote, "we all gave a sigh of relief, thinking we were safe on neutral territory. We were all shaking, beads of fear running down our faces. It's the moments like this [when] the thought of home and loved ones fills your mind."

And that's when immigration officials boarded the plane, demanding that Mal and Tony follow them back to the terminal. In that instant, Mal wrote, "I knew I was never going to see the friendly skies of England again. Visions of being thrown in jail and left there to rot passed through my mind, and as I walked past Brian's seat, I bent down and said to him, 'Brian, please tell Lil, Julie, and Gary that I love them.'"[12]

Back in the terminal, Mal and Tony were led ever deeper into the building. "Tony and I walked as close to each other as possible," Mal recalled, "getting some small crumb of comfort from each other's company." In the immigration office, they found themselves once again at the whimsy of the mob, being jostled, pushed, and shoved as customs officials demanded they fill out new immigration forms. As television crews recorded their every move, the two struggled to complete the forms, their hands visibly shaking in terror.

And then, just like that, they were being led back to the plane, once again experiencing a strange gauntlet of violence and insults on the one hand and the warmhearted goodwill of the assembled Beatles fans on the other. After some forty intense minutes away from their friends, Mal and Tony were back in their seats. "The last words we heard before the doors closed were, 'We love you, Beatles,'" Mal wrote.[13]

On the way back to England, the KLM jet made a stopover in Delhi to refuel. Led by George, the group opted to stay behind for a few days to decompress after their experience back in the South Pacific and to experience Eastern culture up close. But for once, Mal wasn't having it. "The Beatles were so relieved at getting out of Manila alive, I felt they wanted to stick together," he wrote, "but home was calling me." Incredibly, his longing to spend precious moments with new baby Julie and the rest of his family overmatched his typical yearning to be with his beloved Beatles. Besides, he would be back on the road with the boys in a month for their third U.S. tour.

In Mal's absence, the group made a crucial decision after Neil let it slip that Brian was already planning concert tours for 1967. "Nobody can hear a bloody note anyway," said John. "No more for me. I say we stop touring."[14] On July 8, the rest of the group arrived back in London, where George joked to a reporter that "we're going to have a couple of weeks to recuperate before we go and get beaten up by the Americans."[15]

Mal's restful stay in Liverpool was to be short-lived. In the days before the U.S. tour was set to begin, the American magazine *Datebook* republished an interview that the *London Evening Standard*'s Maureen Cleave had conducted with John back in March. "Christianity will go. It will vanish and shrink," John had said, adding, "We're more popular than Jesus now; I don't know which will go first—rock and roll or Christianity."[16] In the ensuing days after the July 31 *Datebook* article, radio stations across the American Bible Belt sponsored "Beatle-burnings," elevating John's remarks into an international controversy.

For Mal, the whole business was much ado about nothing. "I can't read John's mind," he wrote, "but to my way of thinking, whenever we did a show on a Sunday in any city, there would be many more people in the audience to see the Beatles than there would be attending church. I know at the time religious authorities were generally complaining about the empty churches and lack of support from their parishioners."[17]

The 1966 American tour began with the Beatles' most unusual press conference on record. On August 11, the day before the band's show at Chicago's International Amphitheatre, John attempted to quell the storm: "I wasn't saying whatever they're saying I was saying," he explained. "I'm sorry I said it really. I never meant it to be a lousy anti-religious thing. I apologize if that will make you happy. I still don't know quite what I've done. I've tried to tell you what I did do, but if you want me to apologize, if that will make you happy, then okay, I'm sorry."[18] So began what John would later describe as the "Jesus Christ Tour," a planned eighteen-show jaunt across North America that would conclude on August 29 in San Francisco.

Sixteen-year-old Victoria Mucie had been on hand that day in Chicago, hoping to cover the press conference for *Teen Life* magazine. A Kansas City native, Victoria had attended the band's September 1964 press conference and, in the ensuing years, had interviewed such acts as Gerry and the Pacemakers, Herman's Hermits, and the Dave Clark Five. During the Beatles' 1965 tour, she had attended the Shea Stadium concert and, with her *Teen Life* press pass in hand, had gained entrance to the Toronto press conference. After narrowly missing the press conference in Chicago, she prepared to go to an early dinner with her father, Dick Mucie, a Kansas City physician. And that's when she saw Mal get into an elevator at the Astor Tower Hotel.

"So, of course, I jumped in after him," Victoria recalled, "and he said, 'What floor?' And I said, 'Well, I'm on eleven, but I'd rather go to twenty-seven,' and he's like, 'I'm on twenty-seven,' and I'm thinking, 'You really think I don't know that?' I told him about the press conference and how I was supposed to [have] be[en] there. And he said, 'Well, the boys are exhausted, but if you can stay around until tomorrow, they should get up around eight o'clock, and you can have your interview.' Then he asked where I was going. I said I was going to meet my dad; we were going to dinner. And he said, 'May I come with you?'"

After sharing a convivial dinner with Victoria's father, who retired early, Mal and Victoria returned to the hotel and went up to the twenty-seventh floor. When they arrived in the Beatles' suite, Victoria observed that all the doors were closed, leading her to assume that the bandmates had turned in for the night. "Mal was very sweet," she recalled, "and we talked and we talked, and we sort of made out." And while she was unable to meet the Beatles the next morning to do an interview, she exchanged contact information with Mal. And later that year, the letters from her new pen pal began arriving, elegantly adorned with "this beautiful British handwriting."[19]

Beyond the chaos and the controversy, Mal was confronted with the usual series of challenges that accompany a big-time rock 'n' roll tour. The supporting acts included the Ronettes, the Cyrkle, the Remains, and Bobby Hebb, who had recently landed a major hit with "Sunny." In contrast with previous American tours, Mal had extra hands at his disposal: a professional photographer and singer-songwriter, Ed Freeman, was serving as a roadie for the Remains while Mike Owen worked in a similar capacity for the Cyrkle. Having joined the tour as a favor to the Remains' Barry Tashian, Freeman was a novice roadie at best, helping out Mal and Mike by tuning all the acts' guitars. As for the threats of violence that emerged in the wake of John's "Jesus" remarks, Freeman admitted that "I was probably too stoned to be more than normally cautious." Like others before him, he observed in awe as Mal, without the benefit of assistance, picked up the Beatles' amps in his arms. "That's how he got them onstage," Freeman recalled. "He would just grab them, put a hammerlock on them, and lift them up single-handedly. There was no way any normal human being could do that."[20]

Vern Miller, the twenty-one-year-old bass player for the Remains, developed a healthy respect for "people like Mal and Neil and Brian," who seemed "devoted to the well-being and the well-oiled machine that was necessary for the Beatles' success." Miller recalled that Epstein, in particular, was "very precise. He knew what he wanted. One night, he got mad at Neil because Neil set out the wrong color suits for what Brian thought the lighting of that night's stadium would require." At the same time, Miller could see the Beatles starting to become exhausted with that level of precision. "I remember being on a plane," he recalled, "and John had to change his pants before he deplaned with the rest of the group. Brian wanted the Beatles to present a cohesive look, and John was grumbling, saying, 'Why do I have to change my pants?'"[21]

As for Mal, Vern remembered the Beatles' roadie as a bigger-than-life character. "He was jovial," Miller said. When it came to prepping and tearing down the stage, there was no question that Mal was "the senior guy." Even so, he could party as hard as anyone, according to Vern. During the tour, the roadie had taken to carting around a violin case, which he called his "sin kit." An alcoholic complement to his dope bag, the sin kit usually held a bottle of booze. But Mal's appetites for vice didn't stop there. "I remember sitting across the aisle from him on the plane, on one of the flights, because we all shared a chartered jet," Vern said. "And I remember seeing Mal with this cute little reporter on his lap bouncing up and down.

Mal protecting Paul from fans rushing the stage at San Francisco's Cow Palace

So, he was a pretty uninhibited kind of guy. And apparently, this reporter was a pretty uninhibited kind of young lady."[22]

During that first night in Chicago, Mal listened in horror as the Vox amps seemed to be turning on and off. He sussed out the problem in ten minutes flat, discovering that fans in the balconies were dancing on the power cables, thus causing the interruptions. A few nights later, in Toronto, he neglected to bring the boys' stage outfits to the Maple Leaf Gardens venue, having left them on the plane. Commandeering a limo, Mal later wrote, he "drove like hell for the airport, calling ahead on the car radio so that they would have the plane's baggage compartment open for me. We also had a police escort because of the traffic conditions. Half the time, we were riding the pavement and the grass verges. Such was the status of the Beatles, [that] the police worked wonders, getting me back to the stadium just in time to meet the Beatles as they left the dressing room to go on stage."[23]

In Cleveland, the entourage encountered their first crowd-control issue of the tour. On this occasion, the trouble began when Paul, with seven numbers remaining on the Beatles' set list, erroneously introduced "Day Tripper" as the band's final song. Mistakenly believing that the group was about to depart Cleveland Stadium, the crowd began pressing forward, eventually breaking through the police cordon and forcing the Beatles to suspend the concert for half an hour until security could be restored.

During the band's American sojourn, reminders of John's remarks in *Datebook* were always in evidence. In Washington, DC, five white-hooded members of the Ku Klux Klan paraded outside the stadium in protest of the Beatle's perceived blasphemy. The next day, during the band's stay in Philadelphia, Mal found a spare moment to pen a letter to Lily. He was ebullient in his own celebrity. "Lil, it's amazing how many people know me over here," he wrote. "I know it sounds big-headed, but nearly all the fans know me, and it's terrific how many know about Gary, and say, 'how is your wife and baby daughter?' I get a big kick out of it."[24]

While this tour had been arguably less riotous than the Beatles' 1965 visit, the August 19 concerts in Memphis gave the entourage cause for concern. Mayor William B. Ingram had sponsored a resolution by the City

John, Mal, and Paul backstage at Munich's Circus-Krone-Bau

Council proclaiming that "the Beatles are not welcome in Memphis," and adding, "We of the commission feel it is our duty to protect Memphians against the Beatles' use of the public Coliseum to ridicule anyone's religion."[25] The group's route to the Mid-South Coliseum was thronged with protesters holding "Beatles Go Home" signs, and the local Ku Klux Klan picketed the venue. Mal recalled that "in the warm sunshine outside the Coliseum, [the white supremacists'] white shrouded anonymity did not strike fear in the heart, just looked daft."[26]

At the conclusion of the afternoon concert, Mal embarked on a rock 'n' roll pilgrimage to Graceland. Sadly, the King was not in town, but to Mal's good fortune, Elvis's father, Vernon, lived on the grounds. "Plucking up courage," Mal wrote, "I knocked on Vernon Presley's door, thrilled when I was invited in and offered coffee and cookies. The two topics of conversation being Presley on my side, and the Beatles from his family's."

While the Beatles' afternoon show had occurred without incident, the band's evening performance was markedly different. As George sang "If I Needed Someone," a loud bang reverberated in the arena. A cherry bomb had been tossed onstage. In that moment, Mal later wrote, "I could see the four Beatles look at each other to see if either of them was bleeding, thinking for sure somebody had been shot."[27] Incredibly, the group went on playing without so much as missing a beat.

Standing backstage, the entourage felt a palpable sense of relief, grateful to be nearing the conclusion of their southernmost gig. But they weren't out of the woods just yet. "The next town after Memphis was Cincinnati," Mal later wrote, "and it was here that I was nearly electrocuted."[28]

Mal and Paul in Tokyo

17

BABOONS, VERY MANY

When the tour rolled into Cincinnati for a nighttime show at Crosley Field, dark clouds were quite literally looming on the horizon. That afternoon, Mal received a visit from Georgeanna Lewis, who had made the two-hour drive from Indianapolis with her mother. "It's really good to see friends who are really friends!" he announced when he caught sight of them. Georgeanna spent the afternoon with Mal at the Vernon Manor Hotel, where the group had reserved the entire sixth floor. At one point, she observed Paul lying "flat down on the bed, fully clothed, zonked out to the world."[1]

The highlight for Georgeanna occurred while she was talking with Mal about *Revolver*, the new Beatles LP, which had been released Stateside on August 8. "One of my favorite songs right now is 'Here, There, and Everywhere,'" she told him, recalling that the roadie literally stopped in his tracks, "looked down, and said, 'Oh, that's your favorite song, luv?'" Then he proudly reported that "I helped Paul with the lyrics." Georgeanna would never forget walking the hotel's hallways holding hands with Mal and singing "Here, There, and Everywhere."[2]

When Mal arrived at Crosley Field later that afternoon, he discovered that the stage had been left uncovered during a recent downpour, with the potential for additional rain in the forecast. Everything onstage was soaked. "I went out to test all the equipment one more time," he recalled, "and was thrown on my back by a heavy electrical shock."[3] When he recovered his senses, he located Epstein in the dressing room, warning him that if the show went on that evening, "it could mean putting the Beatles' lives in danger." Brian countered that "it's a heavy decision, and I hate to disappoint all those wonderful fans out there." Mal changed tack, taking a more forceful tone, perhaps the only time he had dared challenge Brian. "Think of the disappointment all the fans would experience if one of the Beatles was to be killed," he exclaimed.[4] Epstein took the roadie's advice to heart and canceled the evening show, rescheduling it for the next day at noon.

Unfortunately, the rain followed the boys to Busch Memorial Stadium in St. Louis the following day. Although the stage had been covered throughout the downpour, the rain managed, slowly but surely, to reach the band's equipment. As a failsafe measure, Mal stationed Ed Freeman in front of the main power connection, which he had wrapped in towels to keep it dry. Ed was instructed to keep his eyes on the performers and to cut the power to the stage at the slightest hint of trouble. Fortunately, for him and the Beatles, Freeman never had to pull the plug.

After the St. Louis show, the Beatles piled into a steel-lined truck. As they slid around in the vehicle's bed, Paul finally agreed with John's suggestion, in the wake of the Manila fiasco, that they end the madness and stop touring. Apparently, Busch Memorial Stadium had been the last straw for McCartney—"The worst little gig we'd ever played at." In Paul's memory, "George and John were the ones most against touring; they got particularly fed up. So we agreed to say nothing—but never to tour again."[5] For his part, Brian was crestfallen at the idea of putting the Beatles' touring days behind them. Mal, too, was dispirited at the thought of no longer sharing in their brotherhood, no longer feeling part of their world.

After a modest reprise of their Shea Stadium triumph on August 23, the Beatles made a final West Coast swing, setting up temporary digs at a rented house in Beverly Hills. On August 25, the boys flew north for a pair of shows at the Seattle Center Coliseum. The first concert hadn't sold out, but the second show was packed to the rafters. Sixteen-year-old Ann Wilson was there, along with her younger sister, Nancy. The future members of the rock band Heart reveled in the experience, committing to memory every moment, no matter how seemingly minor. In addition to the musicians' forest-green suits, Ann Wilson vividly recalled the image of John chewing gum for the entirety of the Beatles' set and the instant George broke a string during "Nowhere Man." But her most lasting memory of the day occurred prior to the Beatles' performance. "Here's this empty stage," Ann said. "The tension is running high as everyone waits for the show to begin. And suddenly, here's this big guy, Mal Evans, carrying the famous bass drum with 'The Beatles' on it onto the stage to set it up. The roof just blew off the place with the roar of the crowd. Everybody knew Mal!"[6]

The band's penultimate gig, at Los Angeles's Dodger Stadium, ended in near-pandemonium when some seven thousand fans broke through the fence separating the stage from the audience. Forced to hide out in a safe room inside the stadium while the crowd dispersed, the Beatles were eventually ushered away in an armored car.

On Monday, August 29, the group played their last concert at San Francisco's Candlestick Park—although it very nearly didn't come to pass. In fact, the show had originally been scheduled for the Cow Palace, the Beatles' regular Bay Area venue, but the promoters had selected Candlestick Park instead, hoping for a larger box office. Their gambit failed when they managed to sell only 25,000 of the venue's 42,500 seats.

But in the hours leading up to showtime, the burning issue turned out to be the stadium's natural-grass surface. "The Beatles were to perform surrounded by a box of wire mesh for protection," Mal recalled. "The means for leaving after the performance to be an armored car stationed behind the stage." The trouble began when Candlestick Park's groundskeeper refused to allow the roadies' equipment van to travel across the infield, plunging Mal into a heated argument with stadium officials. Eventually, Mal acquiesced, carrying the band's gear from the dugout to the stage. At the same time, the groundskeeper also refused to permit the armored car carrying the band members to travel across the infield.

Backstage, Mal observed Brian "looking very worried and tense, talking to himself as much as anyone nearby; I heard him say, 'I'm not going to let my boys' lives be endangered.'"[7] But like Mal, Brian eventually yielded, fearing that the crowd would have torn the place apart if he had insisted on canceling the show. After the concert, which concluded with Paul shredding his vocal cords for one final pass at "Long Tall Sally," the Beatles raced across the infield to their waiting armored car.

After the concert, Mal stood alone amid the tumult, as fans and security streamed by him, oblivious to the Beatles, who had already made their escape. With Ed Freeman and Mike Owen in tow, he began breaking down the stage, disassembling the gear, and stowing away the instruments for transport back to London. In the post-concert hubbub, Ed found himself briefly alone with Ringo's bass drumhead, with the famous descended-*T* logo emblazoned across its face. For his part, Ed had no idea that the group was abandoning life on the road, possibly forever. "Had I known," he said, "I might have done things differently, because after we had packed up all of the instruments, the Beatles' drumhead was still lying there on the stage. I thought, 'Oh, for Christ's sake. I don't want to unpack the whole goddamned drum kit and stick this thing inside. Then I thought, 'I could just take it as a souvenir, you know?' But then I realized it would be wrong. They'll need it again for the next tour, right? So I unpacked the whole goddamned drum kit and stuck the drumhead back in there. But had I known, I might have kept it after all!"[8]

On August 30, the band and their entourage returned to London, and for the first time in years, the Beatles—that "four-headed monster"—went their separate ways. George planned to enjoy an extended stay in India to pursue his growing interest in Eastern music and philosophy. Ringo was ready to settle into family life with Maureen and their new baby, Zak, at Sunny Heights. Back in July, John had accepted a role as "Private Gripweed" in Dick Lester's upcoming feature film, *How I Won the War*, which was set to begin principal photography in West Germany and Spain in September. For his part, Paul was content to undertake a driving tour of France's Loire Valley in his sporty Aston Martin DB6, going incognito and playing the part of "a lonely little poet on the road with my car."[9]

As for Mal, *The Beatles Book* reported that the roadie "has been spending a few weeks off with his wife and two children in Liverpool, but he pops down to London regularly and visits any of the boys who are at home to make sure that their equipment is in good order and also to find out whether they want him to get any more instruments from any of the manufacturers."[10]

In truth, life in Mossley Hill was not so simple for the roadie. Mal had become used to living his life in compartments, as his sister June feared he would, and those compartments were beginning to spill over into one another. Lily later recalled discovering "letters from girls saying how wonderful [Mal] was. I would find them when I emptied his suitcase to do his dirty washing. They upset me. I'd say, 'Why can't you throw them away before you come home?'" All Mal could do was hang his head and tell her the letters didn't mean anything to him.[11]

During the Beatles' post-touring interregnum, their music continued to lord it over the charts. In the United Kingdom, "the Roll" had grown to fourteen consecutive chart-toppers with the addition of "Paperback Writer" and, most recently, the double A-sided "Yellow Submarine" backed with "Eleanor Rigby." In recent months, Mal had been approached by Sean O'Mahony, the editor of *The Beatles Book*—who wrote under the pen name "Johnny Dean"—about writing a regular column for the fanzine, which had been published monthly since 1963. With an array of cameras at his disposal, Mal would provide photographs for the rag, along with a series of articles to be known as Mal's Diary and, in some instances, Mal's Page. "I had always had a liking for writing and, as a means of communication, I thought it was wonderful that the twistings and turnings of ink on paper should be understandable to so many people," Mal later wrote. Besides, with "talking not being one of my better subjects," he was eager to gauge his ability with the written word.[12] As luck would have it, the subject of his first column for *The Beatles Book*—a safari, no less—would present itself in a matter of weeks.[13]

As a novice writer, Mal was no doubt buoyed by Paul's inclusion of his lyric in "Here, There, and Everywhere." Although he admired the Beatles one and all, he put special stock in Paul's opinion. Having gained some measure of confidence over his contribution to that song, Mal had begun writing poetry. Perhaps a bit overwrought, his first effort as a writer betrayed an inner claustrophobia, suggesting that he was trapped inside a veritable prison of language: "I am every animal ever put into captivity, / Pacing, slithering, swinging in my new false environment, / I feed, sleep, to dream of childhood games." In the world of his poem, Mal describes hypocrisy as "a collar that strangles me," ultimately "denying me the clean fresh draughts of thought / That would lift me above the other animals." In concert with his longing for the whimsy of "childhood games," he concludes with the image of his kitelike heart yearning to fly yet remaining unsatisfied, earthbound by gravity.[14]

For Mal, this untitled poem may be the purest confession of his predicament—his grappling with meeting the obligations of adulthood

(Lily and the kids), on the one hand, and giving in to his overwhelming desire for the consequence-free delights, of the flesh and otherwise, that came with the Beatles' fame, on the other.

By late October, Paul had grown bored with his solo journey on the Continent, and by prearrangement with Mal, he agreed to rendezvous with the roadie to continue his sightseeing tour. At 7 p.m. on November 12, Mal met Paul under the Grosse Cloche tower at the doors to the Saint-Eloi Church in the center of Bordeaux. "I arrived amidst pouring rain, booked in a small hotel, and was standing by the designated pillar," Mal recalled, "when, at precisely 7 p.m., [I] heard a small voice behind me going, 'pssst, pssst.' It was Paul."[15]

With a Michelin map as their only guide, the two were off on their merry way. Their plan was to travel to Almería, Spain, where John was filming *How I Won the War*. Taking turns behind the wheel of the Aston Martin, Mal and Paul spent the day sightseeing, with the Beatle "going mad, as usual, with his movie camera, using roll after roll of film wherever we went," Mal wrote. As they neared the border between France and Spain, they went antiquing, with Paul purchasing an old lamp "like something out of *Aladdin*" and Mal happening upon a double-barreled shotgun he simply couldn't pass up. As it happened, he wouldn't possess the weapon for very long. Spanish customs officials balked at allowing him to transport the shotgun into their country. Reasoning that the officials "thought maybe we were old-fashioned revolutionaries," Mal left the weapon in the hands of the proprietor of a French border café.[16]

Driving into Spain and through San Sebastián, Madrid, Córdoba, and Málaga to Torremolinos, they each shot footage with their Canon home movie cameras, capturing images of the Playa de la Concha, in San Sebastian, and a statue of a shepherd at Pancorbo, in the province of Burgos. From their hotel balcony, they filmed gorgeous sunsets and golden waves crashing onto the shore. At one point, Paul sent a postcard to Ringo: "Dear Rich and Mich, and Zak, Tiger, Donovan, Daisy, and all at Sunny Heights: We're going through Spain for a bit, not understanding a word, but having fun. Lousy weather, but lovely indoors. Paul and Mal. Available for social functions."[17]

The duo spent the first Spanish night in San Sabastian before making

Mal posing with his shotgun from Kenya and a holstered pistol

their way to Madrid. And that's when calamity struck. With Mal behind the wheel during a blinding snowstorm, the Aston Martin hit a patch of ice and went careening off the road. In addition to documenting their every move through photographs, Paul had carted along a portable cassette recorder, which was running throughout the accident. "As we went off the road, dropping about four or five feet into a frozen field," Mal recalled, "Paul was heard to shout over the cassette, 'We're crashing—watch your head, Mal!' This [is] accompanied by various rumblings, bangings, as the car came to a stop. There's a minute's silence on the tape, followed by two breaths being let out very slowly."[18] The two friends had narrowly escaped disaster.

By this juncture, they had learned that John was no longer in Spain, having returned to London with his wife, Cynthia, and Neil. "How do you fancy our going on a safari?" Paul asked. With whimsy on their side, they booked a flight to Nairobi by way of Seville, Madrid, and Rome. The night before their departure, Mal penned a hasty letter to Lily. "One of these days," he wrote, "we will have a nice holiday on the continent," adding that "I want to share so much with you, nay I would share the world with this fair maiden." In closing, he wrote, "I know, Lil, how lucky I am to have you. I will really, really try to not be grumpy and bad-tempered in future, for I don't want to lose any of you."[19]

With a ten-hour layover in Italy, Mal joined a busload of tourists on a sightseeing trip to St. Peter's Basilica, while Paul stayed behind at the airport. Mal would never forget gazing in awe at the *Pietà*, "my favorite piece of sculpture in the whole wide world."[20]

Arriving in Nairobi, Mal and Paul were greeted by their Kenyan driver, Moses, who transported them to Tsavo National Park, where Paul booked them into a lodge under his assumed name, "Hunt Hanson." During their stay in Tsavo, Paul was accosted by a group of British soldiers, who began making disparaging remarks about the Beatles. Not backing down from their barbs, he joined the servicemen in a friendly game of poker. Apparently, the hours of matching wits with the likes of Mal, Neil, and Alf had paid off. Paul managed to win handily. But "being the good sport he is," Mal observed, he "gave them their money back."[21]

The next day, they enjoyed a guided tour of Amboseli National Park, with its stunning views of Mount Kilimanjaro. One night, with Moses behind the wheel, they came face-to-face with a massive bull elephant standing on the side of the road. "He completely ignored our flashing headlights, the sounding of our horn," Mal recalled, "so it was fingers crossed, foot down, and zoom pass it! The elephant must have had the shock of its life, for it immediately gave chase. I'm not sure if it was the same elephant getting his own back, but the next morning, our hut started shaking like mad. We thought it must be an earthquake, but it was just an elephant scratching its back on the corner of the hut. When you get an itch, tree or hut, who cares!"[22]

During their photo safari with Moses, Mal was especially taken with a pride of lions he and Paul happened upon in the park. "The strange thing with a lion," he wrote, "is that he does seem to be a lazy sort of character, and very often, it's the lioness who goes out and makes a kill for the cubs. Apparently, what happens is that one of the lionesses looks after all the cubs while the others are hunting. We filmed a reunion when the lioness returned, and on greeting the auntie who had minded the kids, the two of them acted like kittens, rolling over, playfully punching and nipping each other."[23]

For their last night in the bush, Paul booked them into the Treetops Hotel, the British royal family's favorite Kenyan lodgings. Built into a copse of fig trees, the lodge was modeled on the concept of a treehouse, with branches snaking their way through the guest rooms. In his Treetops brochure, Mal recorded the animals that he observed during their stay, including a rhinoceros, two warthogs, three giant forest hogs, and, next to the word "baboon," he wrote "very many." After a sumptuous meal, Mal and Paul retired to the veranda, where they watched as "amazingly agile baboons, babies clutched to their bosoms, clamored for tidbits from the visitors." The next morning, as the pair prepared to make the return trip to Nairobi, they encountered a troop of baboons while making a final pass through the jungle. In the cool light of day, Mal found the baboons to be off-putting, even dangerous. "Those baboons can be nasty little bastards," he wrote, "what with their large canine teeth and bright red arses!"[24]

Back in Nairobi, Mal and Paul spent the night at the local YMCA, where, in the middle of the night, Mal woke up to the sensation of a small black snake wriggling across his shoulder. Nursing a long-standing fear of snakes, he counted to nine—his lucky number—and hurled himself out of bed. In so doing, he landed on Paul, who was sound asleep in the next bed.

The next day, as they spent their last moments in Kenya, Mal recorded "a very simple memory" of his beloved Paul sitting among a group of schoolchildren. "Paul was getting a great kick out of just chatting to them," said Mal, who thought about the improbable cascade of events that had brought him to this place. "If John hadn't finished his film early," he realized, "those kids would have never met a very thinly disguised Beatle at the Nairobi YMCA, and I wouldn't have had a most memorable 10-day safari holiday."[25]

On November 19, Mal and Paul boarded their return flight to London. During the nine-hour journey home, Paul began imagining what lay in store for the Beatles, what the next chapter might hold. He later recalled that during the flight, "I got this idea. I thought, 'Let's not be ourselves. Let's develop alter-egos so we're not having to project an image which we know. It would be much more free.'" After all, he had enjoyed the relative freedom that traveling incognito over the past few months had afforded him. With that, he turned to Mal, with whom he "often bantered words about," and asked him to "think of names" for the Beatles' new alter egos.[26]

In Paul's memory, "we were having our meal, and they had those little packets marked 'S' and 'P.' Mal said, 'What's that mean? Oh, salt and pepper.' We had a joke about that. So I said, 'Sergeant Pepper,' just to vary it, 'Sergeant Pepper, salt and pepper'—an aural pun, not mishearing him, but just playing with the words." The conversation turned to the fancifully named musical groups of the moment—like Country Joe and the Fish, Big Brother and the Holding Company, and Quicksilver Messenger Service. This led Paul to "Lonely Hearts Club," the Beatle recalled. "I just strung those together rather in the way that you might string together Dr. Hook and the Medicine Show."[27]

In Mal's recollection, they had first settled on "Doctor Pepper's Lonely Hearts Club Band" as the name of the fictitious group, only to realize that "Dr. Pepper" was already a registered trademark. This necessitated additional brainstorming, which produced "Captain Pepper" before the duo finally arrived at "Sgt. Pepper's Lonely Hearts Club Band." Mal's involvement might very well have ended there on the plane had it not been for unforeseen events in Paul's life.

Within a matter of days after their return to London, the Beatles were back in the studio to record their next single. Mal and Neil were on hand when, on November 24, John debuted "Strawberry Fields Forever" at EMI Studios. With its surreal lyrics and psychedelic mélange of instruments, the song was a game-changer for the band. As a harbinger of things to come, Paul played its distinctive intro on the Mellotron Mark II with the flute stop deployed. Mal had helpfully lugged the "sampled keyboard" instrument over to EMI from John's Weybridge estate. He would later share in the recording of the backing track, chipping in a tambourine part. He was there, too, on November 25, when the Beatles taped their annual fan club message, with Mal contributing his voice to the pantomime entitled "Everywhere It's Christmas."

In the early days of the group's post-touring life, their roadies, far from seeing their roles diminished, seemed to be even more present in the Beatles' world. As the bandmates' style and grooming began to take on the look and feel of Swinging London, so, too, did Mal's and Neil's. That December, as the Beatles plied away at "Strawberry Fields Forever" and Paul's "Penny Lane," Mal was captured on film as he ascended the studio steps with Paul. Resplendent in his Carnaby Street finery, the roadie—in stark contrast to his clean-shaven look during the touring years—now sported a handlebar mustache. *Beat Instrumental* took special note of the changes to the Beatles' and their entourage's appearance: "Neil and Mal have both grown mustaches along with the Beatles. Mal's is different, though, from the other five. It's a great mutton-chop effort, which makes him look like a Victorian guardsman." The music magazine's writers also observed a marked shift in Mal's and Neil's duties: "They started off by splitting the work so that Neil handled most of the personal details and Mal the equipment side. But the distinction has got very blurred since, and nowadays they share the same jobs."[28]

One of those jobs involved chauffeuring the Beatles around the city. After the conclusion of the American tour, Alf Bicknell had left the Beatles' employ to work for other celebrated clients, making room for Mal behind the wheel of the Austin Princess. In November, Mal drove Brian, Neil, and the group to the relaunch of the Bag O'Nails as a members-only club on Kingly Street. For Mal and Paul in particular, "the Bag" was quickly becoming a regular haunt after late-night Beatles recording sessions.

In January 1967, Mal accompanied Paul and Ringo to see the Jimi Hendrix Experience perform at the basement club. The star-studded audience included the likes of Mick Jagger and girlfriend Marianne Faithfull, Eric Clapton, Donovan, and the Who's Peter Townshend. After the show, Townshend recalled observing Hendrix in the throes of a flirtation with Faithfull, much to Mick's chagrin. "In the end, Jimi himself broke the tension by taking Marianne's hand, kissing it, and excusing himself to walk over to Paul and me," Townshend recalled. "Mal Evans, the Beatles' lovable roadie cum aide-de-camp, turned to me and breathed a big, ironic Liverpudlian sigh. 'That's called exchanging business cards, Pete,'" Mal quipped.[29]

That same month, Mal's duties expanded yet again after Paul abruptly fired his housekeeping staff at his 7 Cavendish Avenue residence. McCartney had moved out of the Ashers' home the previous year, having bought a house just a few blocks away from EMI Studios. When he learned that Mrs. Kelly, his housekeeper, and her husband, George, his butler, intended to sell their story to an Australian magazine, Paul promptly dismissed the couple. With Jane Asher off on a six-month North American tour with the Old Vic Theatre company, Paul invited Mal to move in with him at Cavendish Avenue.

Having taken on myriad roles, the Beatles roadie could now add "housekeeper" to the ever-expanding list. By early February, he had settled in as Paul's temporary flatmate, carrying out cooking, cleaning, and gardening duties. For the roadie, it was a dream come true. He loved all the Beatles, of course, but he reserved special esteem for Paul. If there was a drawback, it came in the form of McCartney's beloved—and soon to be massive—Old English sheepdog, Martha. Mal was fond of pets generally, but Martha could be quite a handful, literally. Paul had purchased the dog as a puppy from a Buckinghamshire breeder in 1966, originally naming her Knickers, after she had an accident in his lap. After his girlfriend recoiled at the name, Paul took to calling the puppy Martha.[30] When it came to Mal's housekeeping, Martha proved to be an ongoing nuisance. "One thing we both did laugh about was coming home from sessions or filming late at

Julie with Martha, Paul's beloved sheepdog

night," he recalled, "and finding that his dog, Martha, had crapped either in his bed or mine, quite indiscriminately!"[31]

Mal's quarters at 7 Cavendish Avenue were located in the basement, but his favorite part of the house was the third floor, where Paul had assembled a sumptuous music room. "We were to spend many pleasant evenings in that little room at the top of his house," Mal wrote. The space was filled with instruments, but its centerpiece was "a very gaily decorated piano." Painted by Simon Posthuma and Marijke Koger—Dutch artists who would adopt "the Fool" as the name of their collective—the piano had been designed by pop artists Dudley Edwards and his partner, Douglas Binder, in October 1966. Because of its psychedelic imagery, Paul took to calling the instrument his "magic piano."[32]

Not surprisingly, Lily was despondent over Mal's new living arrangements, especially after having recently spent the Christmas holidays with him in Liverpool. She accused her husband of "kowtowing" to the Beatles. In his diary, Mal admitted that her anger was "a terrible blow," but at the same time, he wrote that he wanted to do "everything" for the group—thus only underscoring his wife's concern over his low place in the Beatles hierarchy. "He was always at their beck and call," Lily said. Still, when it came to the Beatles' efforts at monopolizing her husband's time, she understood: "He was a nice fella to have around," she recalled, "so much so that it could provoke little jealousies within the band." And when it came to Mal, his housemate, Paul, was currently winning the sweepstakes.[33] Mal continued to fret over Lily's disappointment in him, but he began to fashion a solution to his family's ills, reasoning that they should join him in London in a house of their own.

On January 27, 1967, Paul started working on a new song with Mal that the roadie came to refer to as "Where the Rain Gets In." The composition found its roots, at least initially, in Paul's first brush with homeownership, with Mal having discovered a leak in the ceiling of the music room. The next day, according to Mal, the two continued refining the tune—"Hope people like it," he wrote in his diary. After making progress on "Fixing a Hole," as the song would become known, the duo turned their attentions toward "Sgt. Pepper's Lonely Hearts Club Band." In Mal's recollection, the song was "the brainchild of two people keeping each other company at a painted piano." As the duo made quick work of the tune, Mal became increasingly elated at the prospect of becoming a published songwriter. Not only did the song "sound good," but "Paul tells me that I will get royalties on [it]—great news, now perhaps a new home."[34]

By late January, Mal and the Beatles had begun working on the promotional spots for "Strawberry Fields Forever" and "Penny Lane." The films were shot at Knole Park in Sevenoaks, Kent, under the direction of Peter Goldmann and produced by Tony Bramwell. As they watched the proceedings unfold, Mal snapped a series of photos. Meanwhile, Neil pitched in with some ideas about how to transform *Sgt. Pepper* into a concept LP of sorts. As Neil later recalled, "I said to Paul, 'Why don't you have Sgt. Pepper as the compère of the album? He comes on at the beginning of the show and introduces the band, and at the end he closes it.' A bit later, Paul told John about it in the studio, and John came up to me and said, 'Nobody likes a smart-arse, Neil.'"[35] On the second day of the promotional shoot, Paul insisted on bringing Martha along, which meant that Mal was tasked with "washing her bum" so as not to foul the interior of the Austin Princess—and, back in London, he resolved to purchase some "doggie ex-lax" to minister to the dog's irritable bowels.[36] He was also contending with ongoing security problems at 7 Cavendish Avenue, where the girls who habitually hung outside the gates were managing to make their way inside.

On January 29, Mal and Paul worked in the music room yet again, this time putting the finishing touches on "Door"—the working title for "Fixing a Hole." A few days later, back in Sevenoaks, Mal donned a "flunky's uniform" trimmed in gold braid and complete with powdered wig for the production of the "Penny Lane" video, in which he plays the part of a waiter.[37] The whimsical song depicts a host of neighborhood characters, including a convivial barber, a pretty nurse, and a banker with a motorcar much like that owned by Mal's sister Barbara's husband, Eric Hoyle, who managed a bank in Penny Lane during this era and, like the character in the song, regaled his friends and relations to no end about his fancy automobile. At one point, they shot footage around the Penny Lane bus roundabout in Liverpool, which afforded Mal the opportunity to visit his Mossley Road home for the first time in weeks. "Have been away from home many years now," he wrote in his diary, "hope the kids will recognize me."[38]

To Mal's great delight, on Wednesday, February 1, the Beatles brought "Sgt. Pepper's Lonely Hearts Club Band" to life in the studio. By this point, it had emerged as the title track for the group's new album. "*Pepper* became a theme, I would say, right at the beginning," said Ringo. "Paul wrote a song with Mal Evans called 'Sgt. Pepper.' I think Mal thought of the title. Big Mal, super roadie!"[39] The next evening, with the group having completed the basic track, Mal and Neil sang backing vocals on the song's chorus.

Any hopes that Mal might have nursed about public recognition for his songwriting efforts with Paul would be short-lived. "We were driving somewhere late at night," he recalled. "There was Paul, Neil Aspinall, and myself, and the driver in the car, and Paul turned round to me and said, 'Look Mal, do you mind if we don't put your name on the songs? You'll get your royalties and all that, because Lennon and McCartney are the biggest things in our lives. We are really a hot item, and we don't want to make it Lennon-McCartney-Evans. So, would you mind?'" The sudden change of heart might have been a blow to any other person, but Mal didn't mind. "I was so in love with the group that it didn't matter to me. I knew myself what had happened."[40]

John during the making of *Sgt. Pepper's Lonely Hearts Club Band*

18

SWIRLING SILVERY SHIMMERY WORLDS

On Friday, February 10, 1967, Mal was tasked with decorating the cavernous Studio 1 for an unprecedented event in the Beatles' story. The occasion was the recording of a forty-piece orchestra for "In the Life Of," the working title for "A Day in the Life." Back in January, the Beatles had recorded a basic track for the song. After performing the first few verses, John announced that "I don't know where to go from here." Knowing his partner wanted a bridge for the song, Paul good-naturedly offered up a solution: "Well, I've got this other song I've been working on," he announced.[1]

To accommodate the orchestral build-up to the future Paul section, George Martin gave Mal instructions for the first take for a potential "middle eight," or bridge. As the producer later wrote, Mal's "job was to count down the 24 bars in the middle of 'A Day in the Life' that were still blank. Why 24 bars? *Why not?*" As with John's vocal, Mal's counting was overladen with echo, which increased as he counted ever higher until the climax of the twenty-fourth bar, which Mal accentuated with the sound of a ringing alarm clock. As engineer Geoff Emerick later recalled, there "happened to be a windup alarm clock set on top of the piano—Lennon had brought it in as a gag one day, saying that it would come in handy for waking up Ringo when he was needed for an overdub."[2]

With Paul's middle eight now in place, Martin prepared to superimpose the orchestration onto "A Day in the Life" on February 10. The Beatles had decided that this wouldn't be any ordinary session, but rather, an *event*. The task of filling the twenty-four bars that Mal had counted out back in January fell squarely on George Martin's shoulders. "I asked John for his ideas," the producer recalled. "As always, it was a matter of my trying to get inside his mind, discover what pictures he wanted to paint, and then try to realize them for him. John said, 'I want it to be like a musical orgasm. What I'd like to hear is a tremendous build-up, from nothing up to something absolutely like the end of the world. I'd like it to be from extreme quietness to extreme loudness, not only in volume, but also for the sound to expand as well.'"[3]

With a secret plan up their sleeves, the boys instructed the players to don formal wear for the evening session. Meanwhile, Mal drove to the nearest novelty store, where he purchased an assortment of silly hats, rubber noses, clown wigs, bald head pates, gorilla paws, and a hefty supply of clip-on nipples. To set the mood for the classical musicians, John reasoned that "if we put them in silly party hats and rubber noses, maybe then they'll understand what it is we want. That will loosen up those tight-asses!"[4] With a film crew on hand to capture the proceedings, Mal had gussied up Studio 1 with party favors galore. As for himself, he donned a face mask with a balding head, funny eyes, and a bulbous nose. His diary reflected the whimsy of that most unusual and unprecedented occasion: "LIGHTS! CAMERAS! ACTION! BALLOONS?"[5] John's "musical orgasm" was nearly complete.

The next day, flush with the triumph of the previous evening's session, Mal made the two-hundred-mile drive up to Liverpool, dead set on completing a long-promised makeover of Julie's bedroom. In addition to finding time for tea with his parents at Waldgrave Road, he picked up a load of furniture—"Some real nice stuff," including a plum Welsh dresser—that Neil had purchased for their flat. On Monday, February 13, with a trailer hitched to the Super Snipe estate car, Mal drove out of Liverpool. "Kept 40 MPH all the way down till a mile along the M1," he wrote, when a "police car pulled me over [and the officer] said, 'we have clocked you doing 68–70 over the measured mile.'" Mal protested, in vain, that he had topped out at 40, but the cops weren't buying it. "Oh well," Mal wrote in his diary, "that's show business. This is my third offense in three years—keep your fingers crossed for me."[6]

With Epstein and EMI clamoring for new Beatles product, "Strawberry Fields Forever," backed with "Penny Lane," was released in Great Britain on February 17 and went on to sell more than 2.5 million copies and to dominate the U.K. and U.S. airwaves. Then, incredibly, the double A-sided single stalled at number two, unable to assume the number-one position on the U.K. charts. George Martin later surmised that each side of the single had canceled the other out. And then there was the issue of English balladeer Engelbert Humperdinck, who, with "Release Me (and Let Me Love Again)," had come out of nowhere to deny the Beatles their thirteenth straight U.K. chart-topper. While he was clearly disappointed about losing "the Roll," which ended at twelve, Martin described "Strawberry Fields Forever"/"Penny Lane" as "the best record we ever made."[7]

In a rare effort to keep the home fires burning, Mal returned to Mossley Hill on the very next weekend. Paul came along that weekend, with Martha in tow, planning to stay with his father, "Jim Mac," at Rembrandt, the home Paul had purchased for his dad on the Wirral. But any goodwill Mal may have hoped to engender with his family that Saturday was all for naught. "NIGHTMARE STARTS HERE," he scrawled in his diary. "Lil and I just battled all over the weekend." With husband and wife on emotional tenterhooks, especially regarding the family's precarious financial picture, Mal left Hillside without saying goodbye, but Lil wasn't having it: she called Jim Mac's house just in time to catch her husband before he made the drive back to London with Paul. Mal recalled that "the last time we parted in bad words, I crashed and nearly died."[8]

That Wednesday, February 22, Mal woke up early, fought back his pride, and traveled to NEMS, where he asked Brian to provide him with a personal loan in the amount of £500 to ease his family's economic pain. The paperwork was completed in time for Mal to rendezvous with the Beatles at EMI Studios, where they finally brought John's dream of a "musical orgasm" to fruition.

John and Paul's original plan had been to conclude "A Day in the Life" with a gigantic om in the form of a hummed E-major chord. The result had been uninspiring, sending the Beatles back to the drawing board to create a more momentous conclusion for the song. Working in Studio 2, Martin instructed studio personnel to gather up as many pianos as they possibly could. The idea was to perform a thundering piano crash. "To get as strong an attack as possible, everyone decided to play standing up instead of sitting down," Emerick recalled. "John, Mal, and George Martin each stood behind a different piano, while Ringo and Paul shared the out-of-tune

Steinway upright."[9] McCartney took charge of the proceedings and counted the players in for take one:

> **Paul:** Have you got your loud pedal down, Mal?
> **Mal:** Which one's that?
> **Paul:** The right hand one, far right. It keeps the echo going.
> **John:** Keep it down the whole time.
> **Paul:** Right. On four then. One, two, three . . .

The ninth take was selected as the best, with the resulting chord punctuating "A Day in the Life" in unforgettable style.

By then, the band was working around the clock on the *Sgt. Pepper* LP. Even so, they were always ripe for diversions. On February 23, for instance, Mal noted that "Paul has [an] appointment with a Japanese lady who wants to photograph his bottom," referring to thirty-four-year-old conceptual artist Yoko Ono, who had met John at an exhibition at the Indica Gallery back in November.[10] In 1966, in the States, Yoko and her husband, Tony Cox, had made a short film consisting of celebrity derrieres, and they were eager to repeat the exercise in Great Britain. With John and Paul firing on all their creative cylinders, George and Ringo were often left with nothing to do. The drummer would later joke that he learned how to play chess during the album's production.

The staggering difference between Mal's bifurcated life, in Liverpool and Swinging London, was never more apparent than on the week of March 1. From one day to the next, Mal played the role of consummate family man, washing the car and tending to his nest. But within a matter of hours, he had shifted personae yet again for a brush with the drug du jour. That night, Mal finally breached the chrysalis, joining Neil and the Beatles as the last member of their group to try LSD.

It all started at the Bag O'Nails, where he and Neil were hanging out with their American friend Steve, who said, "Here's some acid for you and the boys." Later that night, after getting their fill of "the Bag," they made their way to Montagu Mews West. (With Jim Mac in town for a visit, Mal was taking a break from 7 Cavendish Avenue, to allow father and son their privacy.) "We were at the flat, and had several friends over, drinking, listening to music, and I happened to be sitting in one of the bedrooms with the guy who had given [the acid] to me," said Mal. He would remember turning to Steve and saying, "Eat me, and I'll grow big!" And that's when he started tripping. "It was incredible," he said. "If you're going to take acid, this is the only way to do it—unprepared, with no pre-conceived ideas."[11]

As with so many LSD users before him, Mal engaged in a rigorous postmortem in which he searched for evidence of the changes the acid had wrought. Had it, indeed, opened his mind? Was he no longer the person he had been before? While it had been an "enjoyable" trip overall, he experienced several micro-incidents along the way that gave him pause. "For example, I became lucid at one point and thought I must be insane, but explained to myself that it was alright, because I had a beautiful family who would come and visit me," he wrote. "Another time I thought I must be a drug addict, but knew I had a lot of friends who would look after me, and keep me supplied—so the world was okay."[12]

Neil couldn't help needling his flatmate—even during his time of great vulnerability and self-discovery. "One funny part about the trip was Neil ringing to Paul to tell him that I had taken it," Mal recalled. "Now Paul's father was staying with him at the time, and he was horrified at the idea, Paul carefully explaining to him that it didn't change your personality—I would be the same as I ever was." Still, as Mal's trip continued to spiral, Neil never left his friend's side.

Mal described the experience as "very colorful," adding that it was "nice to have Neil there, [I] met myself for the first time—an acid test." Even hours later, Mal was still tripping. In the shower, he imagined his hair flowering in "flying silver whirls" as "swirling silvery shimmery worlds surround me." Afterward, he got dressed, perceiving his workaday clothes as a kind of poetic refrain—a "shining garment" that "filled the air with soundless noise / Living, breathing hair dissolving, / Stand serene, filled with poise."[13]

For members of the Beatles' inner circle, the opportunity to observe Mal during a full-blown acid trip must have been too hard to resist. Later that day, Jim Mac and Paul, along with Martha, turned up at the flat, followed by George. Harrison, in Mal's LSD-bathed perception, appeared to be holding an "armful of flowers and singing of India." By the next day, the acid in Mal's system had fully dissipated, but much to his surprise, he discovered that psychedelia had fully taken hold of him, that he *had* been changed by the experience. "Now I had always been sober in my dress and appearance," he wrote, "but that morning, I just wanted to wear the brightest things I could find, so I arrived at Paul's house to pick him up for the session, walking in on Paul's dad with a six-foot-wide smile, wearing a multitude of colored scarves, ties, and socks!"[14]

As March rolled on, the boys began to make quick work of the *Sgt. Pepper* LP. A deadline of sorts had materialized for the album's completion. On April 3, Paul planned to surprise Jane Asher, who was still on tour with the Old Vic in North America, to celebrate her upcoming twenty-first birthday. By the beginning of March, Geoff Emerick and the other members of EMI's staff were starting to feel the pressure. "By the end of the album, it wasn't unusual for sessions to start at midnight and finish at dawn, which put a strain on all of us," the engineer recalled. "We sometimes suspected that Mal Evans was putting something in our tea to keep us awake, but we never found out for sure. I doubt very much if he ever dosed us with acid—it wouldn't have been very helpful to the Beatles if we were tripping in the control room!—but I suppose it's possible that he might have occasionally spiked the tea with a mild upper."[15]

Meanwhile, as the Beatles were putting the finishing touches on the new LP, Mal and Neil were consumed with a project of immense complexity. Working with pop artist Peter Blake and Jann Haworth, Blake's creative collaborator and wife, the band had envisioned an ambitious cover design, and Mal and Neil were tasked with bringing together the various elements—costumery, photographs, props, even landscaping, of all things—for the tableau being constructed in the studio. Haworth vividly recalled Mal's good-natured attitude during their lengthy sessions to stage the cover art. "He was a very sweet person in a world of poseurs," she said. "Where everyone else seemed fractious and self-serving, Mal was laid-back and genuine."[16]

And in the midst of everything, Mal and Neil took on the guise of moving men, transporting household items for Ringo and Maureen down from Liverpool to Sunny Heights. Up in Liverpool, Gary joined his father as he loaded up the trailer with furniture. They were accompanied by Neil, who was driven over to Mossley Hill by his girlfriend, Mona Best, and their

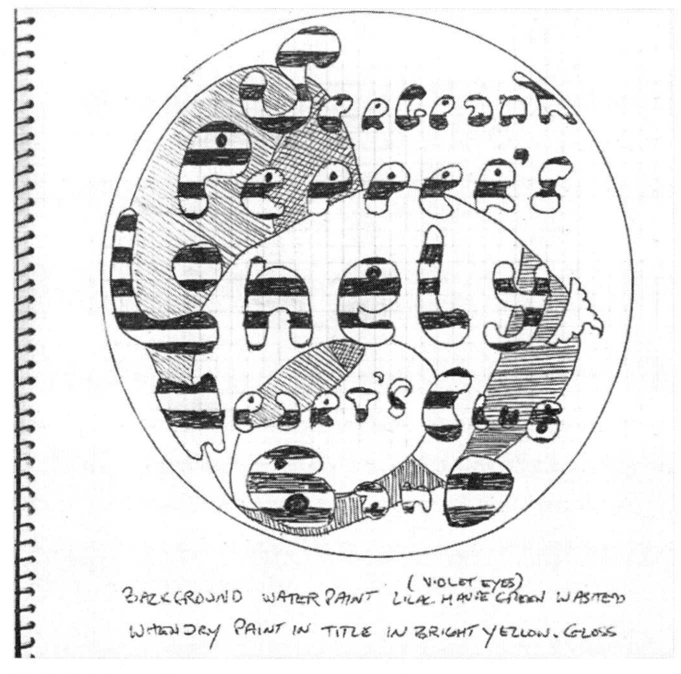

Mal's *Sgt. Pepper* logo

five-year-old son, Roag, who played in the yard with Gary. Before he made the return trip to London, Mal gazed at Gary in wonder, contemplating his good fortune. "Love him," he wrote in his diary, "think I'd give my life for him—hope I would."[17]

At the same time, Mal made a point of speculating about his motives for keeping a diary in the first place. "Do I write this for other people to read?" he wondered.[18] Was the act of journaling about his emotions and experiences a performance for somebody else's benefit? Was the roadie maintaining his diaries for posterity?

19

SOCKS, MAL!

Even with the Beatles' touring years seemingly behind them, there was always a flurry of activity in Mal's and Neil's lives. In early March, with Paul having hired a new housekeeper at Cavendish Avenue, Mal rejoined Neil in relocating from Montagu Mews West to nicer digs at Fordie House on Sloane Street. As always, both men were still expected to be at the Beatles' beck and call in the studio.

On March 7, Mal unloaded furniture and a piano for Ringo at Sunny Heights. But what a difference a single day can make in Beatle World. Later that evening, he and Neil found themselves gathering up, of all things, EMI-embossed rolls of toilet paper around the studio. As it happened, John, Paul, and George were attempting to fashion homemade kazoos with paper and combs for "Lovely Rita."

Incredibly, EMI's toilet paper was a subject of regular conversation among Mal and the Beatles. George Harrison was an especially strident critic. George Martin later recalled that the band's lead guitarist "complained frequently to the EMI management about the horrible slippery hardness of its loo paper. (Each sheet had the legend 'Property of EMI' stamped across it!) He said it was okay for wrapping round a comb and blowing through, but as to using it for what it was intended, you could forget it!"[1]

When they weren't carping about the toilet paper's quality, Mal and the boys managed to use rolls of it to stage an elaborate prank. The occasion was beloved sound engineer Ken Townsend's recent promotion to EMI's manager of technical operations. Mal set the antics in motion when he telephoned Townsend in his office, bluntly informing him that the Beatles required his immediate presence in the studio in order to register a complaint. By the time he joined them in Studio 2, the mild-mannered engineer was shaking with fear. "Bloody hell!" he thought to himself. "I've never had a complaint from the boys before." Worse yet, the last thing he needed in his new managerial role was trouble with EMI's most important clients.[2]

With that, Townsend later recalled, "I went into the control room of Studio 2," where Mal and the Beatles were standing around the mixing desk with stern looks on their faces. John piped up first, rebuking Townsend because "the toilet paper is too hard and shiny. And it's got EMI, Ltd., stamped on it. If you don't do something about it," John continued, "I'm going to contact Sir Joseph Lockwood," he said, referring to the vaunted chairman of the EMI Group.

"Oh dear," Townsend thought. "I'm going to take this seriously." It was only after he contacted studio head Allen Stagg and the two managers succeeded in discarding all the studio's toilet paper and replacing it with a "nice, soft tissue" that Townsend realized what had happened, that it had all been a big "wind-up" arranged by Mal and the Beatles to celebrate his promotion.[3]

As the *Sgt. Pepper* sessions continued apace, Mal worked increasingly longer days, barely managing to squeeze in a few hours of sleep. During the same week that they worked on "Lovely Rita," he and Paul pulled all-nighters at the Bag, while making time to take in the latest movies with John and Neil—including *The Night of the Generals*, with Peter O'Toole—and browsing the wares at the Chelsea Market, where Mal bought a slew of multicolored scarves. When he wasn't hauling more furniture down from Liverpool or attending sessions for "Getting Better" and "She's Leaving Home," he was preparing dinner (shellfish and rice) at 7 Cavendish Avenue for the boys and Neil before a late-night session with Sounds Incorporated to overdub the brass and woodwinds on "Good Morning Good Morning."

During a March session for "Lucy in the Sky with Diamonds," Mal laid out the morsels that comprised the Beatles' favorite snacks: an array of candy (including Mars bars and Smarties) and a crate of Coca-Cola. While John, Paul, and George wrangled with the new tune, Ringo tucked into his first course—Heinz Baked Beans on toast prepared by Mal in a frying pan on a portable electric burner. A reporter and photographer from *Life* magazine were there to watch the proceedings, and when the reporter saw what Ringo was eating, he remarked, "My God man, you can't eat that!" He seemed to have believed the superstar drummer snacked on nothing less than caviar. Ringo stopped the conversation with the reporter flat, exclaiming, "Did you?"[4]

While they expected Mal and Neil to provide a steady supply of weed, the band had clear expectations when it came to their own comportment while in the studio. Barry Miles, co-owner of the Indica Gallery and a frequent Beatles confidant, recalled that the boys "had a policy of no cocaine, no LSD, or anything that would blur their senses. Even alcohol was frowned upon because they found that it made them lazy and not want to try one more take to get something right." Still, when it came to visitors—rock glitterati along the lines of Mick Jagger and David Crosby—the Beatles were unfailingly hospitable. In addition to setting up folding chairs for the bandmates' guests, "Mal Evans established a little commissary of his own where he dispensed soft drinks, alcohol, Wagon Wheels, Penguin bars, and other snacks."[5]

Miles recalled that Mal was quite attuned to the boys' desires, culinary and otherwise. "John in particular, liked to have his every wish fulfilled. He only had to say, 'Apples, Mal,' at 3 a.m., and Mal Evans would drive to the wholesale fruit and vegetable market at Covent Garden and return with a box of fresh Golden Delicious." Miles marveled at Mal's "astonishing fund of knowledge," remembering that he "once overheard John mutter 'Socks, Mal!' and an hour later Mal appeared in the studio with a dozen different pairs of brightly colored socks. Where Mal found them in the middle of the night is a mystery."[6]

With barely more than two weeks left to complete *Sgt. Pepper*, Mal joined one EMI Studios session after another, catering to the boys' every need and being asked on several occasions to take up an instrument. For "With a Little Help from My Friends," he played the cowbell, while, performing in tandem with Neil, he tried his hand at the bass harmonica on "Being for the Benefit of Mr. Kite." The former song went under the working title "Bad Finger Boogie," after John, nursing an injury to his forefinger, was forced to play the piano using his middle digit.

With John, Ringo, and Neil in tow, Mal spent several hours at the Bag on March 15, where he knocked back numerous pints—and, apparently, multiple slices of pie, to boot—with Bill Collins, a Liverpudlian roadie. Earlier in the evening, Bill had been Mal's guest at the session for George's "Within You Without You." During a break, he regaled Paul and Mal with stories of the Iveys, a Welsh rock band he was managing. In keeping with the boys' taxing lifestyle during the early months of 1967, the party didn't break up until 5 a.m.

By mid-March, Mal and Neil were spending most of their time at photographer Michael Cooper's Chelsea studio, where the album cover was being painstakingly assembled. In Blake and Haworth's vision, the group's fan base of "lonely hearts" would be arrayed behind them, including the likes of Mae West, Bob Dylan, Edgar Allan Poe, and Karl Marx. Blake and the Beatles "had a list of the people they wanted standing in the background," Neil recalled, "so Mal and I went to all the different libraries and got prints of them, which Peter Blake blew up and tinted. He used them to make the collage, along with the plants and everything else you see on the cover."[7] In preparation for the shoot with the bandmates, Mal ferried the boys to Berman's West End costume shop for the fittings associated with the four Beatles' psychedelic, Day-Glo military uniforms. Period photographs depict Mal hulking about with a scarf around his neck like an oversize tailor.

Meanwhile, he and Neil began seeking permission to use the images from the still-living subjects, whose portraits were pasted onto hardboards and placed in the background of the shot. When it came to the photo releases, Mal wrote, "we got some very interesting replies. Several famous people not making the front cover because they wanted money, but most everybody we talked to thought it was a wonderful idea, being only too pleased to be counted a Beatles friend."[8] Even so, Brian Epstein was deathly afraid of the litigation that might result from the album cover's imagery, going so far as to suggest that the LP be released in a plain brown wrapper.

At one point, the images of Jesus Christ and Adolf Hitler were slated to be featured on the cover, only to be jettisoned to avoid any religious furor, on the one hand, or deplorable taste, on the other. In Mal's memory, "Everybody contributed ideas to the cover, including Neil and I, and it was not until the album was due for release that Paul pointed out to me that I hadn't included Elvis. This was a bitter blow to me, and I can't imagine why it didn't happen."[9] A painting had originally been commissioned from

Mal posing on the *Sgt. Pepper* set with, from left to right, Jann Haworth, Mohammed Chtaibi, Peter Blake, Andy Boulton, Trevor Sutton, Nigel Hartnup, unidentified Madama Tussauds employee, and Michael Cooper

Simon Posthuma and Marijke Koger, to accommodate the LP's gatefold design, only to be rejected in favor of a group portrait shot by Cooper. The discarded image, a stunning concoction of futurism and fantasia in the spirit of their age, was subsequently given to Mal by John.

On the evening of March 21, Mal and Neil joined the Beatles for a session at EMI Studios, where the Beatles intended to work out the vocal arrangements for "Getting Better," a song inspired by drummer Jimmie Nicol's oft-quoted remark during the early days of their inaugural world tour. Beatles biographer Hunter Davies was at the session that night, along with Ivan Vaughan, the boyhood friend who had introduced John and Paul back in July 1957.

It was George Martin who first noticed that John seemed out of sorts. As the producer later recalled, "I was standing next to John, discussing some finer point of the arrangement to 'Getting Better' when he suddenly looked up at me. 'George,' he said slowly, 'I'm not feeling too good. I'm not focusing on me.'" And that's when the strangeness of the moment hit the Beatles' producer: "This was a pretty odd thing to say, even for John. I studied him. I'd been oblivious to it until then, but he did look pretty awful—not sick, but twitchy and strange."[10]

That's when Martin suggested that John join him on the flat roof of Studio 2 for a breath of fresh air. "It was a beautiful clear night," Martin said. "John took a deep breath, and, with a bit of a lurch, took a couple of steps towards the edge of the building. I grabbed hold of his arm: it was a good 50 feet to the ground. We stood there for a minute or two, with John swaying gently against my arm."[11] At this point, Martin left John alone on the roof, having grown eager to get back to the session. Moments later, Paul and George, sensing trouble, hurried up to the roof to rescue their mate before he fell to his death.

Having learned that John had accidently ingested an LSD tab, mistaking it for an amphetamine, Paul and Mal called it a night and took their tripping friend to Cavendish Avenue. Wanting to keep his ailing mate company, Paul took an acid tab of his own—only his second pass at the hallucinogen—while Mal remained sober in order to look after them. After several hours, Paul decided to hit the hay, reasoning that "it's like with drink. That's enough. That was a lot of fun, now I gotta go and sleep this off. But of course you don't just sleep off an acid trip, so I went to bed and hallucinated a lot in bed. I remember Mal coming up and checking that I was all right. 'Yeah, I think so.' I mean, I could feel every inch of the house, and John seemed like some sort of emperor in control of it all. It was quite strange."[12]

That weekend, leaving his mates to their own devices, Mal made another hasty visit to Liverpool, where he took Super 8 film footage of Gary trundling off to school. By this point, Mal had floated the notion in earnest of moving his family to London. For her part, Lily was reluctant, fearing that she would lose her support system of friends and relatives. Infant Julie was simply too young to care, while Gary seemed positively torn—not wanting to upset his life by moving to the big city, but at the same time, loving his father and wanting to be with him all the time. "If only I could retain that love," Mal wrote, seeing himself as childlike both in Gary's eyes and in his own.[13]

Mal was flush with inspiration that weekend and began penning a seafaring adventure poem for his son, who played a starring role in the narrative, commanding a ship on the briny sea:

The afternoon was pleasant and the crew just loafed about,
Using old electric irons to catch the golden trout
That fluttered in the evening breeze and left you in no doubt
As to who they loved the most.
'Twas Gary, Captain Gary, who was the perfect host.[14]

Mal could barely contain his emotions for the boy. But his rush of sentimentality didn't stop there. Before he made the return trip to London that Monday, he composed a paean to his wife, extolling his good fortune and his family in glowing terms. "Each day is a seven-day weekend with you. Time is a peacock, full of color and excitement—with you," he wrote in his notebook. "I was always lucky, I guess, never had been poor or rich, or neither would be. I blessed myself with a pretty good woman, beautiful and fair of face, and who was to grace our home with a prettiness and handsomeness in the form of my son and my daughter. He—five years tall, and she 11 months small and crawling." In a final emotional push, he concluded that "the lust for one and enjoyment of the others in our family made me a complete 'I.' That it shall remain is my constant prayer, for I have not known tragedy with family, but only in my mind and imagination, times have been many when I visualize my son or daughter or wife injured or crippled, but is this a guilt compensation for being happy. I hope writing this will rid me of it for good—for I love."[15]

When the date of the *Sgt. Pepper* cover photo shoot finally arrived—"BIG PHOTO SESSION TONIGHT! I'VE GOT EVERYTHING CROSSED," Mal scrawled in his diary—Mal's breakneck efforts with Neil paid off handsomely. The iconic photo proved an arresting sight, the perfect emblem for marking the Beatles' place as the high priests of psychedelic culture. "Photo session last night turned out gear," Mal wrote the next day. At the last moment, he had situated a "a flower vase with a fat little soldier" in the foreground of the cover image, having purchased the porcelain figurine earlier in the day at the Chelsea Market.[16] In the shot, the bandmates clutch a quartet of musical instruments while posing around a bespoke drum skin that had been painted by fairground artist Joe Ephgrave.[17]

After the Beatles exited the photo shoot, Mal and the artists and photographers working behind the scenes, including Haworth, Blake, and Cooper, posed among the "lonely hearts" to commemorate the occasion. Mal had rarely felt so connected to the Beatles' creative efforts, having shared his musical ideas earlier in the year with Paul at Cavendish Avenue and, now, having participated so fully in the production of the *Sgt. Pepper* cover art.

In early April, as Mal and Paul made final preparations for their State-

Mal during the *Sgt. Pepper* sessions

side visit to celebrate Jane Asher's birthday, the Beatles brought the *Sgt. Pepper* recording sessions to a sizzling conclusion with a hard-rocking reprise of the title track. Prior to the session in Studio 1, Mal and Neil set up the drums and amplifiers in a concert formation. The result was one of the tightest recordings on the album.

Meanwhile, with springlike warm weather now gracing the capital, Mal found himself regularly corralling fans both on the studio steps and in front of 7 Cavendish Avenue. At one point, he enjoyed his "own personal adventure" while chatting with fans in front of the studio. Suddenly "hearing a lady shout that she had her purse snatched, I chased [the culprit] and caught him, holding him until the police arrived." Several weeks later, after he and Paul had returned from America, they were not so lucky: "Paul's house was broken into by some of the fans," Mal wrote, "and two copies of the album [were] stolen, weeks before the release date, [with] strangely enough, a London radio station after that playing the whole album, claiming an exclusive pre-release."[18]

As it turned out, the new LP would receive a premature debut all right—courtesy of the Beatles themselves. On a spring morning that April, Mal, Neil, and the boys showed up on the doorstep of Mama Cass Elliot's London apartment, having stayed up all night at the studio. In their hands was an acetate of *Sgt. Pepper's Lonely Hearts Club Band*. As Neil later recalled, Elliot "had a great sound system. Her flat was in a block of houses, back to back, really close together, and we put the system on a window ledge and the music blasted through the neighborhood. All the windows around us opened and people leaned out, wondering. It was obvious who was on the record. Nobody complained," he added. "People were smiling and giving us the thumbs up." Mama Cass returned the favor in the form of Owsley Stanley's "White Lightning" LSD, generously sharing it with her guests. As the acid took hold of them, Neil recalled, "John and Mal went for a bus ride (something we never usually did) and stayed on the bus until it turned round and came back."[19]

Mal would look back on his experiences during the *Sgt. Pepper* sessions as being among his most engaging days with the band, with whom he felt deeply connected, willing to do virtually anything to support their art. Incredibly, when the LP was released to the world that June, their status—

already iconic in so many ways—would grow even larger. "*Sgt. Pepper* was certainly the most colorful album cover they produced," he wrote, "and psychedelia was running rampant, mirrored in [the bandmates'] very colorful cars, houses, and clothes. Not forgetting, of course, the songs. For the Beatles, like the good songwriters they are, take their living experiences and communicate it to the people through the medium of their songs."[20]

The LP would emerge as yet another high-water mark for the Beatles. But outside his bountiful pride in the boys and in his association with them, Mal would experience a quiet sense of regret. When the album hit the shops, as Paul had forewarned, "Lennon-McCartney" were listed as the authors of "Sgt. Pepper's Lonely Hearts Club Band" and "Fixing a Hole," and, "unfortunately for me," Mal wrote, "I was to receive no credit, and as it turned out, no royalties."[21]

20

MYSTERY TOURS

After spending a few hours on a layover at Paris's Orly Airport, Mal and Paul made the long flight to the American West Coast. It was precisely the sort of adventure the roadie enjoyed most—feeling a sense of deep camaraderie and of being indispensable all in the same breath.

As it happened, the journey itself took nigh on twenty-four hours. Arriving in Los Angeles on the evening of April 3, the pair were briefly delayed while Paul sorted out some visa issues before Mal received his first taste of luxury. After winding their way through customs, they enjoyed "a casual stroll to our waiting Lear Jet," Mal wrote, "and high-ho for San Francisco, where we would saunter atop Nob Hill."[1]

In San Francisco, Mal and Paul were confronted with unexpectedly chilly weather—including the Bay Area's first snowfall in forty-two years. But as tourists working on a short calendar, they were on a mission. "Paul and I went out shopping, buying records and taking pictures of the famous Golden Gate Bridge," Mal wrote.[2] And then it was off to observe a Jefferson Airplane rehearsal at the Fillmore Auditorium. That February, the band had released their *Surrealistic Pillow* LP, complete with such standout tracks as "Somebody to Love" and "White Rabbit." Guitarist Marty Balin would never forget the moment Mal made his entrance: "We were sitting there playing at the old Fillmore, in comes this guy Mal, suit and tie, and we're all hippied out."

Adopting a formal tone, Mal announced that "Master Paul McCartney would like to meet with you."

Flabbergasted, Balin replied, "Oh, well send him in!" In truth, Balin "didn't know if this guy was real or a joke. So he went out and in comes Paul."[3]

Paul jamming with Jefferson Airplane's Jorma Kaukonen and Paul Kantner

Afterward, the Beatle joined Balin and bassist Jack Casady at their Oak Street apartment for an impromptu jam session, while Mal stood in the doorway snapping photographs of this mid-sixties rock 'n' roll summit. The Britons smoked some weed with their new North American friends, during which Paul produced an acetate of *Sgt. Pepper*, which he was eager to share with the likes of Balin and Casady, if not the world.

And then Mal and Paul were off on yet another Lear Jet ride—this time, to Denver, where the Old Vic Theatre company was on a brief hiatus from its North American tour of *Romeo and Juliet*. During the flight, Mal marveled at the plane's agility, especially as it made its descent into the Mile High City. "[Forty-one thousand] feet at 650 miles an hour!" he exclaimed. "These must be one of the most maneuverable planes in the world, for they seem to drop vertically from that height down to the airport—quite exhilarating."[4]

The two were met in Denver by Associated Press sportswriter Bert Rosenthal, who had lent Paul his house for the duration of his stay. Meanwhile, Mal booked himself a room at the nearby Driftwood Motel. As he prepared for Jane Asher's surprise birthday party that evening at a swanky

Denver hotel, he was interrupted by a phone call from Paul, who was nervous about the security at his borrowed lodgings. "I bade a taxi to take me over there," Mal recalled, "gave it the twice over, then arranged to meet Paul and Jane at the hotel entrance, getting the pair of them in without any hassle, but quite a few photographers, including our old friend Harry Benson, followed the birthday cake in! It was a delightful party, the Old Vic Theatre Company really mixing, and we had a right old 'do.'"[5] The roadie even managed to photo-bomb a few of the shots, awkwardly leaning across the dining table as Jane admired her birthday cake.

The next day, Mal enjoyed the most memorable day of his American jaunt—outside the luxuriant Lear Jet, that is. With Jane behind the wheel of their car, she, Mal, and Paul found themselves in the heart of the Rocky Mountains. For the Liverpudlians, the experience made for "a real magical mystery trip, pulling off the road and parking amongst the so green trees, walking down a rocky gorge to a tinkling river, which was to take us for a ride to wonderland," Mal recalled. "It was a warm, lazy day, and so were we, finding it strange to walk through snow which lay around in twinkling

Paul relaxing in the Rocky Mountains

confusion, treading the virgin whiteness with naked feet, as many reincarnations of man must have done before us."[6] As usual, Mal snapped plenty of pictures, including a photo of the young couple looking coy during a private moment on their hike in the Rockies. That afternoon, Mal reverted to form. Never being one to ignore a body of water, he took a plunge into the icy river for a bracing swim.

That night, Jane prepared a meal for the three of them in Rosenthal's kitchen. Mal and Paul were agog over a concept they had hatched in the Rockies earlier that day. As usual, the roadie and the Beatle had been glued to their Canon film cameras, which inspired Paul to consider making a Beatles home movie of sorts. "The idea going at that moment is for some sort of mystery tour, where everybody boards a coach with no idea of their destination," Mal wrote, "the tentative title being *Roll in for the Mystery Tour*. This develops over our stay and *Magical Mystery Tour* is born. The magic giving us free reign [*sic*] to do all the silly things we wanted to."[7] Together, they hatched the concept of a Sharrabang trip—indeed, much like the one Mal himself had taken back in October 1961 to see the Blackpool Illuminations.

In Paul's memory, "When we were kids, you'd get on a bus, and you didn't know where you were going, but nearly always it was Blackpool. From Liverpool, it was inevitably Blackpool, and everyone would go, 'Oooo, it was Blackpool, after all!' Everyone would spend time guessing where they were going, and this was part of the thrill. And we remembered those."[8] With the Sharrabang concept in place, Paul suggested that the television movie mimic the acid-soaked activities of author Ken Kesey and the Merry Pranksters, who had embarked upon a cross-country journey of the States in a vintage International Harvester school bus arrayed in psychedelic colors.

The next afternoon, as Jane starred in a matinee performance for the Old Vic, Mal and Paul went exploring in the Central City environs, sightseeing around the old Boodle Mine and getting their rental car stuck in the mud that had accompanied the spring thaw. At one point, Mal snapped a photo of mustached Paul sunning himself on the hood of the car. That night, they ate dinner at "Paul's Café," an irresistible choice, of course, for the two men. Afterward, they hoisted a few drinks at the Gilded Garter.

Paul and Jane in the Rockies

As the two took in the performance of a local band, the lead vocalist asked, "'Are you two folk singers? I know your faces from somewhere.' Maybe I looked like a country singer," Mal wrote.

"The following morning, I phoned for a cab in order to pick Jane up and take her to the airport, leaving Paul asleep, but the manager of the hotel I was staying in wouldn't let me leave without paying the bill—maybe I also looked unscrupulous!"[9]

Prior to leaving Colorado, the duo drove out to Red Rocks, the spectacular amphitheater on Denver's western outskirts, where the Beatles had performed during their first American tour, in August 1964. After Paul paused to sign a few autographs, they visited a local Native American trading post before catching a flight to Los Angeles.

As usual, Mal couldn't have been more chuffed with the experience, writing that "we left Denver in Frank Sinatra's Lear Jet, which he very kindly loaned us. A beautiful job with black leather upholstery and, to our delight, a well-stocked bar."[10] They were met at the airport by Derek Taylor, who was now handling PR for the Beach Boys and other West Coast rockers, and his wife, Joan.

Mal and Paul had missed Derek considerably, especially his urbane wit and inherent goodwill. They enjoyed hanging around the Taylors' swimming pool and playing with the couple's daughters. For his part, Derek was happy to hear that things were looking up in the Beatles' camp, particularly for the members of their inner circle. "They seem to be a very tight six group now in England—the four Beatles and Malcolm and Neil," he recalled. "Mal and Neil are also involved creatively, suggesting things and being listened to." With their touring days seemingly behind them, at least for the foreseeable future, the group appeared to have found a working routine, which pleased Derek to no end. "Mal said that life had never been easier for him, that the Beatles were absolutely beautiful to be near, and there were no rows, no irritability, no put-downs, and no boredom," he wrote. "Everyone is just doing sort of little things that they want to do. Everyone has their own thing. Whatever that means. That's what he said."[11]

During their last night in L.A., Mal and Paul went over to Michelle and John Phillips's Beverly Hills home, where they sat around sipping wine. At one point, Paul split for a Beach Boys recording session. After several hours had passed and many bottles were emptied, McCartney returned with Brian Wilson in tow. Before the roadie knew it, Michelle and John had produced a variety of instruments for an impromptu hoedown. Mal played guitar on "On Top of Old Smokey," with Paul trying his hand at cello and, later, the flügelhorn. To Mal's chagrin, Brian "put a damper on the spontaneity of the whole affair by walking in with a tray of water-filled glasses, trying to arrange it into some sort of session."[12]

The next morning, during their return flight to the United Kingdom, Paul became increasingly occupied with the idea of working on the new project. At one point, he borrowed a notepad from a flight attendant and began composing the lyrics for "Magical Mystery Tour." As Mal looked on, Paul started drafting a rough schema for the movie, a circle divided into eight segments to accommodate a sixty-minute television program.

When they arrived back in London, "we were surprised to see a whole crowd of photographers," Mal recalled, "but they were waiting for Oscar-less Lynn Redgrave, who had irritated me somewhat by her laughing and shouting [on the plane] on the way over. I stayed as close to Paul as I possibly could," Mal added, although his efforts had nothing to do with protecting the Beatle's safety. Rather, they were a clumsy attempt to ensure he was photographed along with such A-listers as McCartney and Redgrave. He tried as hard as he possibly could, "but Paul still got photographed by himself!"[13]

As always, Mal and Paul were confronted with a flurry of activity back in England. On April 19, NEMS engineered a solution to the Beatles' looming tax problems by overseeing the formation of "Beatles and Company." Replacing "the Beatles Limited," which had been formed in June 1963, this new entity counted but four principals in John, Paul, George, and Ringo—along with two employees in Mal and Neil. With the creation of Beatles and Company, the band would not only stave off a massive loss of

Mal and Paul return from the United States

their existing capital to the Inland Revenue (the U.K. version of the IRS), but also ensure that their earnings were channeled back into their new legal partnership, which, in turn, would be taxed at a lower, corporate rate. It was a masterstroke of business acumen, but the Beatles had much bigger game in mind. And it was right there, hidden in plain sight on the back cover of *Sgt. Pepper's Lonely Hearts Club Band*: "The Apple."[14]

On April 21, Mal, Neil, and the Beatles were back at EMI Studios to apply one last flourish to the *Sgt. Pepper* LP, a coda that consisted of only a few seconds, yet required an all-night session to produce. Barry Miles later recalled that during the marathon session, the Beatles "stood around two microphones muttering, singing snatches of songs, and yelling for what seemed like hours, with the rest of us standing round them, joining in. Mal carried in cases of Coke and bottles of Scotch. Ringo was out of it. 'I'm so stoned,' he said, 'I think I'm going to fall over!' As he slowly toppled, Mal caught him and propped him neatly in a chair without a murmur. In the control room, no one seemed to notice."[15] At John's suggestion, Martin appended the sound of a dog whistle, an eighteen-kilocycle note that would be largely inaudible to humans.

With Martin and Emerick engaged in postproduction duties for *Sgt. Pepper*, the boys turned their attention to a pair of projects, including *Magical Mystery Tour*, which Paul would shortly unveil, and a feature-length cartoon based upon *Revolver*'s "Yellow Submarine." Both projects would require new Beatles music, with the former calling for Mal and the bandmates to take on the guise of filmmakers. For the *Yellow Submarine* animated film, which was being developed by King Features Syndicate, the band was tasked with delivering new material, a string of songs—mostly "rejects" in the Beatles' minds—that over the next several months grew to include "It's All Too Much," "All Together Now," "Hey Bulldog," and "Only a Northern Song," a holdover from the *Sgt. Pepper* sessions.

Magical Mystery Tour was a different story altogether, having already been slated by Paul as the natural follow-up to *Sgt. Pepper*. As John later recalled, Paul "set *Magical Mystery Tour* up and had worked it out with Mal Evans, and then he came and showed me what his idea was, the story and how he had it all, the production and everything. George and I were sort of grumbling, you know, 'Fuckin' movie, oh well, we better do it.'"[16]

At first, *Magical Mystery Tour* was slow to get under way, which was not uncommon as the group shifted gears into a new project. "Beatles sessions were always very hectic for the first few days, I think due to the fact that everybody was a little nervous getting in the studio again after a break," Mal recalled, "and they certainly kept me hopping! I would get requests from the four of them to do six different things at one time, and it was always a case of relying on instinct and experience in awarding priorities. They used to be right sods for the first few days until they realized that everything was going to go smoothly, and they could get into the routine of recording again."[17] With *Magical Mystery Tour*, Mal was especially eager to trace the project's progress, particularly given his role in its gestation.

This was certainly the case with the April 25 session, when he found himself acting as amanuensis as Paul worked out the lyrics for the "Magical Mystery Tour" track. That evening, Hunter Davies observed as Paul "played the opening bars on the piano as Mal Evans wrote down the title in a schoolboy hand. Paul said, 'trumpets, yes, they'd have some trumpets,' a fanfare to go with 'Roll up, roll up for the Magical Mystery Tour.' Mal had better write that down; it was the only line they had. Paul also told Mal to write down DAE, the first three chords of the song. Mal sucked his pencil and waited, but nothing more came."[18]

That night, the boys recorded the song's basic track, with Mal and Neil chipping in with percussion, including Mal reprising his work on the cowbell. Afterward, Paul invited his mates to try their hand at free association to complete the lyrics for "Magical Mystery Tour." Earlier that day, he had tasked Mal with canvassing the London bus stations to find posters advertising mystery trips, hoping that they might borrow phrases that could be redeployed in the song. But it had all come to naught, and Mal returned to EMI Studios empty-handed, forcing Paul to improvise. "Just sing out any words and phrases that you can think of," said Paul. "Not of course *any* words, but stuff that might be shouted out by someone wanting people to roll up and go on a coach ride, such as 'Invitation,' 'Reservation,' 'Satisfaction Guaranteed.'"[19]

That same week, Mal and Neil joined the Beatles at the Bag, where the roadies were charged with ferreting out "possible items for the 'Coach Show,'" they recalled. "Basically, it was agreed that the plan should be 'all-inclusive, non-exclusive.' This meant trying to fit into the show something for everyone, as wide a variety as possible."[20]

As April came to a close, Mal's family joined him at the Fordie House lodgings he shared with Neil. The family weekend in London was not without its traumas. On Sunday, Lil answered a knock at the door and came face-to-face with Victoria Mucie, the cub reporter for *Teen Life* and one of Mal's American pen pals.

Now seventeen, Victoria was in town with her father, Dick, the Kansas City physician, ostensibly to audition for drama school, although, in truth, she had just wanted to see London—and Mal. In a recent letter to her, Mal had scheduled a visit for Monday, presumably after his family had returned to Liverpool. Father and daughter were staying at the nearby Carlton Tower, on Sloane Street, only a block or so away from Fordie House.

Victoria had been eager to see the roadie, thinking to herself, "'Why don't you just pop by and say hello?' So, I knock on the door, and his wife opens the door, and I was really shocked, because I didn't know he had a wife. And he came to the door, and he said, 'My family is visiting this weekend from Liverpool.'"[21] In a kind of stunned shock, Victoria beat a hasty retreat, promising to see him the next day. Naturally, she had plenty of questions—namely, "'Why didn't you tell me that you were married?' And he said, 'It's different in England.'" To her late-teenage mind, Mal's excuse sounded reasonable. "Okay, that makes sense to me," she thought. "It's a cultural thing."

That week, she hung out most every day with Mal at Fordie House, where she "started seeing these little scraps of paper around with song lyrics on them, and that was the first that I knew that he was actually helping contribute to some of their songs." At night, Victoria and her father enjoyed meals at Alvaro, an exclusive eatery on King's Road that catered to the rich and famous. The chef and proprietor, Alvaro Maccioni, was the culinary toast of Swinging London. Mal had provided Victoria with an unlisted telephone number that allowed her to gain entrance to the restaurant, where, in her memory, "Alvaro kept the curtains drawn as if it was some kind of speakeasy.[22]

"My dad and I ended up going there almost every night," she recalled, "and we saw Terence Stamp, Jean Shrimpton, Michael Caine, Brian Jones, and then, one night, football player turned actor Jim Brown," who recognized Victoria's father from his NFL days. "I'm just sitting there thinking, I'm seventeen, I'm from Kansas City, how can this possibly be happening?"

While Mal was off doing odd jobs for the Beatles, Victoria donned her *Teen Life* reporter's cap and met the Yardbirds, who gave her a tour of London, making sure to show her the grocery stores they had purchased for the day "when this is all over," they said, referring to their rock 'n' roll careers. "And I remember thinking, 'You're a really big band. This is never gonna be over.'"

That Thursday night, Victoria and her father joined Mal at the Bag, where the roadie coyly announced that "there's somebody I want you to meet." Victoria recalled following him through "this big, dark club way into the back, and suddenly there's Paul McCartney, who says, 'Hello, Vicky.' And I'm thinking, 'I could die now and my life would be complete.' And then we sit down, and Paul orders drinks, and he says, 'Scotch and Coke, three doubles.' And I'm thinking, 'I'm seventeen. I've never had a single.'" Poignantly, during her conversation with the Beatle, she remembered looking over at Mal, and "I could tell that he was really happy because he knew what he was doing for me. You know, he knew he was giving me this memory that would last forever."[23]

Victoria and her father returned to the club the very next evening. After all, "it seemed like such a magical place." Her effort was almost immediately rewarded when she caught sight of John. "I went up to John and told him I was Mal's friend, and that I was from Kansas City. And he immediately held up his hands like he was holding a baseball bat, and he said, 'Kansas City baseball,'" obviously remembering the band's outlandish fee for a single night's performance during their North American tour back in 1964. "We spoke briefly," she said, "because I didn't want to feel like a fangirl." Much later, as the Bag prepared to close down, she was touched when John made a special point of stopping by her table to bid her good night.[24]

For Mal—and, in truth, the waiting world of music fans—the highlight of the coming month would be Brian Epstein's bravura press launch for *Sgt. Pepper* at his Chapel Street home on May 19. For the group—having been out of the public eye, save for the release of the "Strawberry Fields Forever"/"Penny Lane" single—it was a coming-out party of sorts. Underscoring the gravity of the press party with a sly reference to Greta Garbo, *NME* trumpeted the banner headline "Beatles Talk Again!" "John Lennon walked into the room first," *NME*'s Norrie Drummond wrote. "Then came George Harrison and Paul McCartney, followed closely by Ringo Starr and road managers Neil Aspinall and Mal Evans. The Beatles had arrived at a small dinner party in Brian Epstein's Belgravia home, to talk to journalists and disc jockeys for the first time in many months."[25]

One of the guests that night was American rock photographer Linda Eastman, who had first met Paul four nights earlier at the Bag, where Georgie Fame and the Blue Flames were topping the bill. Linda later remembered that she and Paul "flirted a bit" before heading out to yet another club, the Speakeasy—where they heard Procol Harum's "A Whiter Shade of Pale" for the first time. They concluded the evening at 7 Cavendish Avenue, where Linda recalled being "impressed" to see her future husband's prized trio of Magritte paintings.[26]

Later that month, Brian threw a housewarming party at Kingsley Hill, his Sussex country house. As it happened, Mal and Neil would be dramatically late to the proceedings, having dropped acid during the drive there and losing their way among the rural backroads. The two friends ended up driving around the countryside for hours, finally arriving at Kingsley Hill at six the following morning. In an especially bizarre moment, Neil recalled stopping at a rural police station to ask for directions while Mal studied a road map on the walls of the constabulary. In Mal's acid-soaked haze, the highways and byways depicted there began to take on surreal colors. He could only stare at the map in a kind of drug-addled disbelief, muttering "Oh, wow, man" over and over as Neil attempted to corral his wayward friend and resume their strange journey.[27]

For the Beatles—John especially—the housewarming party offered the opportunity for an acid-drenched weekend in the country. By this point, he had grown deeply attached to Owsley's White Lightning, even going so far as to arrange for his own regular supplier to smuggle the drug into the United Kingdom in film canisters.

The next day, with Mal's family in tow, the festivities continued in Weybridge, with the Evanses shuttling between the Lennons' Kenwood estate and Sunny Heights, the Starkeys' abundant spread at the bottom of

St. George's Hill. Mal never tired of visiting Ringo's manse, which featured its own mirrored pub, "The Flying Cow"; a private cinema; and nine immaculately terraced acres, including a waterfall, a go-cart track, a koi pond, and a secret garden highlighted by a hedgerow maze.

For Gary, the experience was truly magical. When he wasn't climbing up to the treehouse at Sunny Heights or goofing around with Ringo, who took movie footage of him playing the guitar, the boy spent hours playing with four-year-old Julian Lennon at Kenwood, where, like his father, he had grown especially fond of John's aboveground swimming pool. Gary took special pleasure playing with the Lennons' cat, Mal, which John had good-naturedly named after "you know who."[28] As for John, he spent most of the time in bed, according to Mal's diary, no doubt floored by his latest shipment of White Lightning.[29]

By the time he drove the family back to Liverpool at the tail end of May, Mal felt himself ailing precipitously. On the evening of June 1, while

Mal and Gary posing with the Starkeys' kitten at Sunny Heights

working a Beatles session at De Lane Lea Studios in Soho—EMI Studios was unavailable—he began to see telltale "spots on his face."[30] By the next evening, he was contending with a full-blown case of the measles. Mal raced home to Liverpool in his Humber Super Snipe. In short order, Gary came down with his own case of the itchy rash. "Mum and dad got me a kid's doctor's set," he later recalled, "with a plastic syringe and stethoscope—all in a white plastic carrying case."[31]

During his recuperation at Hillside Road, Mal received a typewritten condolence letter from John, in which the Beatle adopted the Joycean style particular to his bestselling books, *In His Own Write* (1964) and *A Spaniard in the Works* (1965). Making nonsensical jokes throughout, John pulled out all the stops—spelling errors and misnomers included—to cheer up his bedridden mate, including the message that however black Mal's clouds may be, they're not as black as John himself. The letter ended with a cryptic postscript sending love to Lil and Gary but also to the other children he said Mal seemed to have.[32]

By the time Mal had recovered and made his return to London, Neil and the band were caught up in the fervor associated with the Beatles' upcoming appearance on *Our World*, an international television simulcast slated for June 25. The program was the brainchild of BBC producer Aubrey Singer and had been some ten months in the making. But true to form—and, as always, notoriously busy—the boys waited until a fortnight before the event to settle on a song, which they would subsequently perform live in front of hundreds of millions of viewers. After they selected John's "All You Need Is Love," George Martin insisted that the band prerecord a backing track to avoid any last-minute glitches. "We're going to hedge our bets," he told the group. "When we go on the air I'll play you the rhythm track, which you'll pretend to be playing. But your voices and the orchestra will really be live; and we'll mix the whole thing together and transmit it to the waiting world like that.'"[33]

On June 14, the Beatles assembled at Olympic Studios, in Barnes, to make their first pass at recording "All You Need Is Love," with John and his mates working out the song's structure in real time. To facilitate their efforts, Mal mapped out the head arrangement for the song in his notebook.[34] On the Friday before the simulcast, Brian Epstein interrupted their rehearsal to recommend that they release "All You Need Is Love," backed with "Baby, You're a Rich Man," as their next single, both to take advantage of *Our World*'s status as a truly global event and to cash in on what could be the greatest and most visible pop song debut in the history of the record business.

As Martin had feared would happen, the telecast on Sunday, June 25, suffered a technical glitch. Just moments before the broadcast, he learned that *Our World*'s producer had lost all contact with the studio. "I was on the verge of hysterical laughter," Martin later recalled. "I remember thinking: 'If we're going to do something wrong, we might as well do it in style in front of 200 million people.'"[35] To Mal and the band's great relief, "All You Need Is Love" proved to be a triumph, with the single shortly taking its place atop the U.K. charts. "Strawberry Fields Forever," backed with "Penny Lane," had been an anomaly. The Roll had roared back into life.

Having completed "All You Need Is Love," the boys would go on a hiatus from the recording studio that lasted some two months. But they were hardly idle during this period. That July, as *Sgt. Pepper* took its place as the de facto soundtrack for the Summer of Love, the Beatles embarked upon a most unusual summer of their own making.

With John taking the lead in his acid-washed state, the boys had decided to establish their own hippie commune on an island in the Aegean Sea. As Neil later recalled, "The idea was that you'd have four houses with tunnels connecting them to a central dome."[36] Naturally, there would also be accommodation for Mal and Neil. On July 22, the group—which included John, Cynthia, and Julian; Paul and Jane; George, Pattie, and her younger sister, Paula; rounded out by Ringo, Mal, Neil, and Alistair Taylor—left London for Athens. Lily and the children had been invited to join them, but they had to bow out because their passports weren't in order. For his part, Brian missed the trip because of the recent death of his father, Harry, for whom the Beatles' manager was sitting shiva. The trip would prove a relatively short adventure for Neil and Ringo, the latter of whom was eager to return to be with Maureen, who was expecting their second child.

In Athens, the group was squired around the city by Alexis Mardas, a former TV repairman–cum–crackpot inventor who had wriggled his way into John's good graces with outrageous promises of such technological wizardry as a secret substance he would deploy to erect a force field around their homes, wallpaper speakers, and other dubious electronic gadgetry. And with Magic Alex, as John had dubbed him, there was always the promise of more to come.

With Neil and Ringo still in tow, Magic Alex led the Beatles and their entourage on a guided tour of the countryside. Mal recalled traveling in "a convoy of cars, a big Mercedes, and a couple of huge old American taxis headed for the beach. For three hours, we drove through the countryside in the pleasant hot sunshine, until suddenly, we realized that the taxi carrying Paul, Jane, and Neil was not following. Apparently, the extreme heat had been too much for [their car], and on turning back, we found them surrounding the taxi, with thick black smoke pouring out of the engine, which all but caught fire."[37]

Mal couldn't help noticing that the Greek tourist board "always seemed to be one step ahead of us," thanks to Magic Alex, who had been tipping off his compatriots about the Beatles' presence. "Two musicians, flute and guitar players, entertained us after lunch," Mal recalled, "with everyone dancing, Ringo, with such wild abandon, cutting his ankle." When they reached the seaside, Mal naturally took a swim, which left him with a thorn in his foot. A comedic scene ensued in which Paul and Neil held Mal's legs while Jane attempted to remove the thorn. The hilarity emerged when it became apparent that it was Neil's foot to which Jane was tending, all the while "wondering why [Mal] didn't flinch!"[38]

The group rounded out the afternoon with a shopping trip in which Ringo, still smarting from his injured ankle, attempted to outmaneuver the crowds by waiting until they followed John and the rest of the group into one shop and then exploring another all by his lonesome. Eventually, Ringo's plan backfired, and "he was caught on his own with dozens of photographers and a large number of American visitors surrounding him, overhearing one of them say, 'Say, isn't it crazy—we travel all the way from Chicago and find Ringo in a Greek shoe shop!'"[39]

A few days later, the band and their entourage began tooling around the Aegean in a hired yacht, the MV *Arvi*, searching for the Beatles' island utopia. The luxurious boat featured twenty-four berths, an eight-person crew, along with a chef and two stewards. Thanks to Magic Alex, a large crowd gathered on the dock at sunset to bid the group farewell.

"That night, it being so warm," Mal recalled, "I slept on the upper deck of the boat next to John, the two of us talking and enjoying the night air before sleep was to overcome us." Mal reveled in "wonderful warm days with George playing a banjo that I had taken with me and which he had previously painted, with a large face on the skin and the Hare Krishna mantra on the back." The whole experience "was dreamlike, the white foam rushing from the bow down to either side of the ship, the hazy mountains in the distance, all of us sitting up front chanting the mantra. The Greek mountains seemed to have no past and no future as we sailed by, only an eternal presence, evenings spent looking for flying saucers amongst the cold, icy points that glittered in the sky."[40]

When they finally arrived at their destination, Aegos Island, which comprises some three hundred thousand square meters, the boys discovered a rocky expanse "occupied by what seemed to be a million crickets."[41] Any disappointment they may have felt was immaterial; John and George had spent most of the journey tripping on acid courtesy of Mal's dope bag. For his part, Mal thoroughly enjoyed the holiday in the Aegean, luxuriating in its beautiful clear waters at every opportunity. With an American trip in the offing, George and Pattie departed Greece on July 29. John and Paul insisted that Mal join the couple on the return flight to England and bring back Lil and his children to share in their Aegean adventure.

But before Mal could make the return trip to Greece with his family, John and Paul had flown back to England. Despite their misgivings about the habitability of Aegos, the boys instructed Alistair to make the purchase anyway, earning a modest profit when they flipped the property a few months later. Not wanting to disappoint Lil and the children, John invited the Evans family to spend a few weeks at his home in Weybridge. While they were there, Lily's father, William White, succumbed to a heart attack at age sixty-seven. Over the past few years, Mal had shared with her how intimidating John could be, so Lil was surprised when the Beatle brought her a cup of tea, let down his guard, and showered her with consolation.

Like Mal, Lily would always remember John's tender gesture. "It's very hard at times like these to give verbal comfort to anybody," Mal wrote, "but John was fantastic, and I knew that he gave Lil a lot of comfort in her hour of need—something I have always blessed him for." Shortly afterward, Mal and his family made their sad return to Liverpool, "where we were to receive a most beautiful letter from Brian Epstein, offering his condolences and sympathy."[42]

August passed by in a hush, with Mal sticking close to Liverpool for a change and Lily navigating her life in the wake of her father's death. Together, the Evans family returned to London toward the end of the month.

On August 22, the band had begun working on "Your Mother Should Know," a tune that Paul had slated for the television special. The session was held that night at London's Chappell Recording Studios. Mal was on hand, of course, and the boys enjoyed a rare visit from Brian Epstein, who was still languishing in the aftermath of the loss of his own father.

Mal visiting John at Weybridge

With the Beatles planning to travel to Wales to attend Maharishi Mahesh Yogi's ten-day seminar on Transcendental Meditation later that week, Mal and Lily happily accepted George and Pattie's offer to house-sit for them at Kinfauns, their Esher bungalow. The Beatles had come into the fifty-year-old holy man's orbit during his recent lecture at the Hyde Park Hilton, and they were enthralled with the opportunity to learn more about Eastern philosophy at the feet of the master.

As for Gary, visiting the Harrisons' place was easily one of his favorite experiences in his young life. Back in July, he had joined his father at Kinfauns, where they assisted George and twenty-nine-year-old Klaus Voormann, one of the Beatles' longtime friends dating back to their Hamburg period, as they repainted the bungalow in the psychedelic colors of the day. For his part, Voormann was struck by Mal's "beautiful, sunny" attitude. Not surprisingly, the two men became fast friends. "Mal was a marvelous, fantastic person. I loved him to death." The German musician would soon come to learn that Mal was "the right man for the right job when they needed him the most."[43] As for the painting of Kinfauns, that August, *The Beatles Book* reported that "all the white parts of the outside walls [were] now adorned with beautiful floral designs. George did a bit of the painting himself, and Mal dropped in to lend a hand, earning himself a plate of baked beans on toast for his enthusiastic brushwork!"[44]

For Gary, the possibility of taking up a brush to paint somebody's house—at their invitation, no less—was nothing short of a dream come true. His visits to Kinfauns, while few and far between, made for some of his most cherished childhood memories, but the visits there didn't always go so well. As Pattie later recalled, on one trip, Gary fell into a sour mood and swiftly transformed into a "naughty boy," haphazardly playing with the pendulums on the cuckoo clock that George hung in the bungalow's kitchen. In short order, the boy succeeded in breaking the clock. For her part, Pattie was secretly thrilled because "I never liked it anyway," but the incident left Mal understandably flush with embarrassment.[45]

On Friday, August 25, the Beatles and their Mal Evans–less entourage trundled off to Euston Station, where they boarded the train for University College in Bangor, Wales, the site of the Maharishi's upcoming seminar. For once, Mal stayed back with his family while everyone else—Neil, the Beatles' girlfriends, even Brian, who was scheduled to join them on Monday—picked up the slack. But that Sunday, as the roadie settled in for another amiable day in Esher with his family, their euphoria was cut brutally short by a telephone call.

Brian Epstein was dead.

21

THE FIFTH MAGICIAN

Brian had been found in his elegant bedroom at Chapel Street, having died of an apparent overdose. He was just three weeks shy of his thirty-third birthday. His death followed a lengthy period of depression that had gone back at least as far as August 1966, when the Beatles decided to end their touring days.

"The official verdict," Mal wrote, "was misadventure. A lot of people have said that Brian had committed suicide, and you know how rumors tend to spread. I will never believe that, for though Brian and I were not very close, I did feel we were friends." Indeed, the two men had been at odds on more than one occasion, but Mal knew full well that it had been Brian who had brought him into the Beatles' fold, first as bouncer and later as roadie. More than that, Mal understood implicitly Brian's indissoluble bond with his beloved Beatles, the kind of connection the roadie continued to nurture in his own way. "He had too much to live for to take his own life," Mal concluded. "He was a lonely person in many ways, but the Beatles were his pride and joy, and I know he would have lived for them, if not for himself."[1]

As it happened, Mal and the Beatles didn't attend Brian's funeral, which was held in Liverpool on August 29, a full calendar year after their performance at San Francisco's Candlestick Park. If the boys had been present, the event would have devolved into a media circus, which would have been a cause for even further distress for Epstein's mother, the recently widowed Queenie.

The implications of Brian's death loomed large in the band's universe.

Mal en route to Brian's wake with, from left to right, Pattie, George, Neil, and Paul

"I knew that we were in trouble then," said John. "I didn't really have any misconceptions about our ability to do anything other than play music. And I was scared. I thought, 'We've fucking had it.'"[2]

To his great credit, Neil recognized that the Beatles were suddenly walking on thin ice. "There was a meeting of the six of us—the four boys, Mal and I," he recalled, "and they realized they didn't have a single contract for anything with Brian; not with a record company, not with a film company—Brian had them all." The situation, he added, "didn't make them vulnerable, but it did make them realize that they had to get it together. Suddenly the lunatics had got hold of the asylum. There were several different sets of advice coming in at them about what they should do, but they decided they needed an office and an organization of their own. And that's really why they expanded Apple." Most important, "they decided they had to keep on trucking," said Neil, using a popular expression of the period borrowed from a Robert Crumb cartoon. "They had to find a way forward out of the malaise."[3]

Six weeks after Brian's death, Mal, Neil, and the Beatles attended a memorial service for their fallen manager at the New London Synagogue, located at 33 Abbey Road, scant blocks away from EMI. Mal drove Paul,

George, Pattie, and Neil to the service, their crestfallen faces captured for all time by the lens of Clive Limpkin, a photojournalist for the *Sun*. George Martin's most poignant memory of that day involved seeing "the Beatles coming into the synagogue, their faces white and pinched still with shock. Out of respect for Brian, they were all wearing yarmulkes. They had all washed their hair for the occasion, and the little round caps kept slipping off, falling to the floor. Wendy Hanson [Brian's former assistant], who was standing behind the Beatles, had to keep picking their yarmulkes up and fixing them back on to their mop-tops. Somehow, that made me feel so sad, sadder than anything."[4]

During the intervening weeks between Brian's death and his memorial service, Paul had briskly set in motion the plans for *Magical Mystery Tour*. In his vision, it would be a multicolored psychedelic feast for the eyes and ears. Having gathered the Beatles and their inner circle into his Cavendish Avenue music room, he resurrected his circular scheme for bringing the television special and its attendant soundtrack to fruition. Mal later set the scene, recalling Paul hunched in front of his typewriter, "using a very overworked finger, putting down a list headed 'Main Points.' Underneath,

Mal posing with the *Magical Mystery Tour* bus

coach tour (three days) with people on board, week beginning September 4th, cameramen, sound, cast, driver, hotels to be arranged for two nights, *Magical Mystery Tour* emblem to be designed, yellow bus to be hired (September 4–9), microphone system in bus. Must be all-around vision, tour 'staff,' driver, courier, hostess, bus destination, Cornwall? After bus, Shepperton Studios one week." On a separate sheet of paper, Paul "typed out a list of arrangements to be made. 'Write outline for script, engage cast, decide when shooting starts, sets for studios, fix completion date.'"[5]

If only things had been so simple. "As we came close to filming time," said Paul, "we all realized that each of us had very specific ideas about the show, and the best way to make sure that our ideas came out as we wanted was to direct and edit ourselves. So if we're not satisfied with anything in the finished film, we have only ourselves to blame."[6] But as the project began to get under way that September, Neil had no illusions about the Beatles' prospects for success as movie impresarios. "We went out to make a film," he said, "and nobody had the vaguest idea of what it was all about."[7]

To get things quite literally rolling, Mal was tasked with locating the motor coach that would serve as the group's mobile soundstage. He leased the vehicle—a sixty-two-seat 1959 Bedford Val Panorama Elite, license number URO 913E—from the coach company Fox of Hayes, after Alistair Taylor spotted the behemoth bus during a recent vacation with his wife, Lesley, in Eastbourne. Alistair would never forget the day he first laid eyes on it. "I was tucking into roast beef and two veg when a coach pulled into the hotel car park," he recalled. "I leapt to my feet and kept yelling 'I found it! I found it!' before dashing out into the driving rain, leaving Lesley looking bemused. I stood on the car park, getting drenched, staring at this acid yellow and vicious blue coach. It was perfect."[8] To complete Paul's vision, Mal and Neil hastily painted the *Magical Mystery Tour* logo on posterboard, which they affixed to the bus's side.

Already a week behind in terms of Paul's original outline, the film production commenced in Allsop Place, behind the Baker Street tube station, on Monday, September 11, although it was delayed for two hours after Mal and Neil's posterboard kept sliding off the coach's flank thanks to gusts of rainy, windy weather that morning. The film shoot lasted a fortnight, with the "Mystery Tour" portion of the movie snaking across the West Country in Devon and Cornwall, followed by three days devoted to filming bikini-clad women at Newquay's Atlantic Hotel. Given the unplanned nature of the production, the Beatles were forced to shoot much of the movie at the RAF West Malling military base, a decommissioned airfield near Maidstone, Kent. The site consisted of disused runways, where they would shoot the "I Am the Walrus" video, and a parcel of empty airplane hangars, one of which was converted into a ballroom for the dance hall sequence that accompanied "Your Mother Should Know." Meanwhile, the film's striptease scene took place at Soho's Raymond Revuebar.

"For the first couple of days when we went out in this big bus full of people," said Paul, "we all took things easy, and we let everyone get to know what it was all about. After a while, they were as enthusiastic as we were."[9] Most of the folks aboard the brightly painted coach were extras whom Mal and Neil had hired after flipping through the pages of *Spotlight*, a casting magazine, and picking the most eccentric characters of the lot. Only a few actors were specifically cast, including Nat Jackley (as Happy Nat the Rubber Man), a music hall comedian whom John admired, and Victor Spinetti (as Recruiting Sergeant), the Welsh actor who had appeared with the boys in *A Hard Day's Night* and *Help!* Other standouts included larger-than-life accordion player–cum-actress Shirley Evans (as Accordionist), Ivor Cutler, who played the inimitable Mr. Bloodvessel, and Jessie Robins, who starred as Ringo's widowed auntie.

Paul's twenty-year-old hairdresser, Leslie Cavendish, was among the passengers who boarded the coach that morning, a motley group that included thirty-three actors, a smattering of Beatles Fan Club secretaries, and other friends and hangers-on. As he made his way to the bus, Cavendish asked if they were going to see the Blackpool Lights.

"I don't know," Paul replied. "It's a mystery!"

While Mal wrangled the film crew nearby, Cavendish climbed aboard the coach, which "seemed like the kind of fantastical vehicle that might take you flying over the moon. We all piled inside enthusiastically, and then, as we were setting off, Neil gave each of us five pounds to cover our food-and-drink expenses on the way."[10]

Cavendish had first met Mal back in 1966, when he began cutting Paul's hair. By the advent of the *Sgt. Pepper* sessions, he was also grooming the roadie's thick locks and neatly tailored sideburns. The hairdresser recalled that Mal maintained a highly visible profile throughout the production, especially given the increased proximity Beatles fans enjoyed as the coach made its way across southwestern England. "If a fan tried to touch a Beatle, they had much less of a chance with Mal Evans in the way," he said. "The funniest thing about it, though, is that he didn't have an aggressive approach. That was the weirdest thing. He was a big guy, of course, always smiling, but you couldn't get around him."[11] While much of the footage they shot was ultimately left on the cutting room floor—the film was supposed to run only sixty minutes, after all—the Beatles always managed to have a good time.

Not surprisingly, the *Magical Mystery Tour* bus swiftly became the toast of southwestern England. "People were lining both sides of the road in Teignmouth," the roadie proclaimed to a reporter from *Disc and Music Echo*. "Police were called in to hold them back. It was back to the days of Beatlemania."[12] When they reached the village, they discovered that their hotel was "jammed with cameramen, reporters, and sightseeing holiday makers, and until the early hours of the morning," Mal recalled, "I spent quite a lot of time evicting fans who had broken into the hotel."[13]

It wasn't very long before the coach proved too wide and cumbersome for the narrow British roadways. In Dartmoor, as it traveled toward the tiny village of Widecombe in the Moor, the vehicle became stuck on a little stone bridge, which, sadly for the Beatles and company, was four inches narrower than the coach. A traffic jam naturally ensued, and the bus driver was forced to retreat onto a nearby expanse of grass in order to map out a different route.

Thanks to the inclement weather—and the village bridge—the production was already behind schedule. To make up for lost time, Mal recalled, they "did a lot more filming inside the bus, establishing the professional characters in the film, Paul writing, and improvising dialogue as we go along. A lot of my time after the day's filming seemed to be overcoming the work of weather and fans, spending hours late at night pasting *Magical Mystery Tour* posters on the sides of the bus." The next morning, Mal woke up, disillusioned by the work of some unsavory fans during the night. "George was very upset," he wrote, "because somebody had broken into the bus and pinched his favorite old denim jacket, and anybody who has had a denim jacket for years, finally getting it down to the right faded color, will understand how he felt."[14]

In Mal's favorite sequence of the film, he plays the role of "Fifth Magician," starring alongside his four beloved mates in their laboratory. The scene begins with John, in voice-over, announcing that "beyond the blue horizon, far above the clouds in a land that no one knows, live four or five magicians who spend their days casting wonderful spells. Come with me now into that secret place where the eyes of man have never set foot!" In yet another scene, Mal makes a cameo appearance, along with Neil, when they have their pictures taken by "Little George," the Photographer (played by George Claydon), who emerges from behind the camera's hood wearing a lion's head.

On October 1, the cast and crew returned to West Malling to film the climactic ballroom scene. Some two hundred dancers were on hand to create the requisite pomp for "Your Mother Should Know," the movie's grand finale. But before they could begin the film shoot, the portable generators gave out, stranding hundreds of extras with nothing to do until the generators could be repaired.

For Mal's part, his frustration began to boil over. "It took three hours for the highly paid generator mechanic to decide it couldn't be fixed, every five minutes saying it would be ready in five minutes," he wrote, "and it was several more hours before a replacement generator could be brought from London."[15] As they awaited the new generator, an idea began to percolate: the dancers' impatience might be allayed by a few autographed photos of the Beatles. Even years later, assistant producer Gavrik Losey would recall the perilous moment he began walking into the crowd of dancers with only a handful of signed photos for distribution. Mal tried in vain to stop him from entering the mêlée, saying, "Don't go out there!" Alas, it was too late. Losey recalled that "I went out there, then I went under. They went for me. The crowd—these girls in their sequined dresses—I went under! Mal pulls me out from underneath and says, 'I told you so!' and picks me up under his arm and pulls me back into the security area."[16]

With the television movie scheduled to make its BBC debut on Boxing Day, December 26, 1967, Mal and the boys had no time to spare. Having amassed more than twenty hours of footage, the Beatles worked with film editor Roy Benson at Norman's Film Productions, in Soho. Originally, two weeks had been allotted to edit the film, but the process eventually stretched into eleven weeks, with Paul taking a lead role in the postproduction process. Mal recalled that working at the editing facility "was not without its lighter moments. One of them being a constant visitor, a permanently inebriated gentleman called Billy, well known for dancing the streets of Soho with a bottle of wine on his head. Plying him with a bottle or two, we would encourage him to leave, but in the end, this more than likely was the reason for his constant visits!"[17]

Incredibly, Mal and Neil were forced to hire the bus again shortly after the *Magical Mystery Tour* editing process had begun. "When John and Paul were editing the damned thing," Neil recalled, "they found out that nobody had filmed any linking shots. There wasn't one shot of the bus from the outside." To remedy the situation, "Mal and I got the bus out again, put all the posters on the side, and drove off into the sunset. We stopped by a little gypsy camp. I got a couple of children to wave at the bus going past, and because there was nobody on board, I told the bus driver to drive fast. We did those shots with the bus driving up and over the camera, then of it going away. So, now we had a few links."[18]

When they weren't carrying out postproduction activities on behalf of *Magical Mystery Tour*, the band was in the studio, working on "Hello, Goodbye," their next single, along with recordings for the soundtrack. That November, with Mal serving as a member of the technical crew, they filmed several different versions of a promo film for "Hello, Goodbye" at the Saville Theatre, including footage of the bandmates donning their Day-Glo *Sgt. Pepper* uniforms.

To complicate matters even further, they continued to shoot new footage for *Magical Mystery Tour*. In late October, Paul turned to Mal as they listened to a playback of "The Fool on the Hill," and said, "Does this song need a short?" For his part, the roadie disagreed. "Well, you're wrong, mate," said Paul. "Get us on the night flight to Nice, and we'll shoot something up on the cliffs there at dawn."[19]

On October 30, Mal gathered up an armload of camera equipment and met Paul at the airport. "Well, Mal, ready for a holiday in the South of France?" the Beatle said. "Do you think Alistair Taylor has brought my passport?"[20] Mal and Paul managed to make their way to the Hôtel Negresco in Nice, without Paul's passport and with very little in the way of money. After unsuccessfully scouting locations, they sought out diversions for the evening, finally deciding to try out a psychedelic club on the city's Promenade des Anglais. Having grown perilously low on funds, and awaiting money to be wired from London, Mal negotiated a line of credit with the club.

Early the next morning, he and Paul, along with cameraman Aubrey Dewar, continued their quest for the perfect location, especially hoping to incorporate the sunrise into the video short. "Driving to the top of the mountain along those twisted, tortured, narrow roads did nothing to help the hangovers we were all suffering from," Mal recalled. "The results though were well worth the effort, the sunrise excellent, with me taking some incredible still pictures, only to find at the end of the day that the film had torn in the camera, so was completely blank."

That night, they returned to the psychedelic club, still planning to take advantage of their credit line. In the intervening hours, "news about Paul's visit to the club the previous night had spread, and the place was jammed," Mal wrote. "Now Paul, being a generous sort of person, had built up quite a bar bill."[21] And that's when the manager demanded immediate payment.

Mal attempted to explain the pair's unusual circumstances, while also drawing the manager's attention to Paul's celebrity. "You either pay the bill, or I call the police," the manager replied. "It certainly looked like we were going to end up being thrown in jail," Mal wrote. "It was ironical, sitting in a club with a millionaire, unable to pay the bill. After many phone calls, we were able to contact the owner of our hotel, who very generously guaranteed payment."[22]

Fortunately, thanks to Dewar, they managed to capture sterling footage of Paul gamboling atop the mountainside and walking along the promenade, a splendid backdrop for "The Fool on the Hill." Incredibly, though, the boys hadn't yet completed the principal photography for *Magical Mystery Tour*. With video accompaniment still required for George's "Blue Jay Way," they gathered at Sunny Heights on November 3, where they shot images of each Beatle playing a white cello in Ringo's garden, followed by the bandmates

Paul playing drums on the *Magical Mystery Tour* set

kicking and headbutting a football on the Starkeys' lawn. In quite possibly the strangest instance of the entire production, they shot footage of a close-up of Mal's bare chest, onto which a sequence from the West Malling shoot was projected. Stranger still, the next scene depicts the Beatles in the act of watching the images they had just recorded, courtesy of Mal's chest. And with that, the film shoot finally concluded, allowing them to continue their editing work unabated in Soho.

That autumn—smack-dab in the middle of the multitudinous activities that comprised his workaday life—Mal succeeded in moving his family, lock, stock, and barrel, to the London suburbs. The roadie had originally planned to buy a house in Weybridge, with easy access to the Lennon and Starkey abodes, but try as they might, Mal and Lily couldn't come up with the extra £2,000 they needed to close the deal, so they settled for more modest accommodation in Sunbury-on-Thames.[23]

Located at 135 Staines Road East, the sixty-three-year-old house was only a few yards away from Kempton Park Racecourse, which undoubtedly appealed to the man of the house. For Mal's purposes in particular, the home was ideally located, being just seventeen miles from EMI Studios and Paul's place on Cavendish Avenue, seven miles from the Harrisons' home in Esher, and six miles from John's and Ringo's Weybridge estates. The Sunbury property featured four bedrooms and a rear garden. With the sale of their house back in Liverpool, Mal and Lil netted £331, a tidy sum in that day. To close the deal on their new home, the Evanses took out a mortgage for £5,163.

And with that, Mal's dream of bringing his family in closer proximity to his work life had seemingly come true. And for a while, at least, it was Lil's dream, too. Living in the same metropolitan area as her husband meant she could finally take advantage of his opportunities to hobnob with celebrities.

In early November, the Evans family was invited to celebrate Guy Fawkes Night at Sunny Heights, where they would socialize with the Beatles and their families, complete with a traditional bonfire and fireworks display to awe the children. Ringo later recalled that he and John "went and bought all these fizzy [fireworks]. We'd smoked a lot of herbalized stuff, so we didn't want anything really loud. We were doing this whole setup and sitting around, relaxing a little, and we went outside to give the babies this big show, and everything we bought just exploded! Exploded! What the kids must have thought, I don't know, because the grown-ups were going 'Ow! Ow! Aaaagh!' We were so shocked we had to go back inside."[24]

If there was an early casualty of the family's relocation, it was six-year-old Gary, who transferred from Liverpool's Dovedale Primary School to Sunbury's Kenyngton Manor, which still had air-raid shelters arrayed around its athletic fields. From the outset, he was plagued by the regional differences separating a Northern Englander's experience from life in the capital. "I was bullied at school over my accent," Gary recalled. "But I was pretty stoic about it, even when I was 'slippered' [spanked] for speaking Scouse [Liverpudlian] in school." Not surprisingly, he learned very quickly to keep to himself and to speak only when he must, lest he reveal his Liverpool accent.[25]

By this point, Gary no longer admired the Beatles in quite the same way he had back in his father's early days as their roadie, when the boy would dance with abandon to the sounds of "From Me to You" playing on the radio. "The Beatles were a riotous noise around my dad," he said, the express reason he was so rarely able to spend time with Mal. "I didn't even regale my friends at school about the Beatles," Gary recalled. "If I went round to George's house on a Sunday, I didn't go to school on Monday and brag, saying 'I was hanging around George's house yesterday.' Even when I was attending a drama class and 'Yellow Submarine' came up, I didn't bother saying, 'Hey, you know, my dad contributed to that song.'"[26]

At times, his association with the world's most famous foursome even moved him to embarrassment. That spring, John had famously arranged for his Rolls-Royce to be repainted in a psychedelic pattern, and Mal would often drive the flashy vehicle around town on errands. "Sometimes I found it all a bit too much," Gary recalled. "I'd be picked up from school by my dad in Lennon's psychedelic Rolls-Royce. He'd be wearing a cowboy hat, surrounded by kids. I thought, 'I don't need this.'"[27]

That November, Mal and the Beatles gathered in Studio 3 to record the band's annual Christmas message. As in previous years, it was distributed via "flexi disc"—a thin, flexible vinyl sheet that made it easy to include sound with printed material—through the Beatles Fan Club. The latest installment, entitled "Christmas Time (Is Here Again)," featured the usual holiday-inspired shenanigans and tongue-in-cheek British humor.

Mal arrived late to the November 28 session, having been ensconced in a pub with one of his mates. His tardiness left Ringo in the lurch, forcing the drummer to set up his own kit for the first time in years. The roadie arrived just in time to record a short piece called "13 Amp," a reference to the United Kingdom's standard thirteen-watt fuse. For his appearance, Mal acted the part of the mythical Ravelers' roadie, adopting a mannered Scottish accent for the occasion. The record's liner notes identified him as "Malcolm Lift-Evans," with production duties credited to "George (Is Here Again) Martin." The record also included the cryptic phrase "Another little bite of the Apple."

When it came to Mal's next gig on Ringo's behalf—an all-expenses-paid trip to Rome to film *Candy* and the opportunity to rub elbows with the world's biggest movie stars—nothing could stop the roadie from arriving at the airport on time. For Mal, the *Candy* set offered a moveable feast of A-list celebrities. Richard Burton's mere presence meant that his wife, Elizabeth

Taylor, would be in his orbit, along with the mighty Marlon Brando and "Candy" herself, seventeen-year-old Swedish sex kitten Ewa Aulin. Mal gleefully played the role of social secretary for Ringo and Mo, arranging a lunch date with Burton and Taylor followed by a weekend on the superstar couple's yacht, moored in the harbor at Anzio. The quintet left Rome in a pair of Rolls-Royces—Burton and the Starkeys riding together, with Taylor and the roadie tagging along behind.

At Anzio, they were joined by Brando—"Marlon Brandy," as the actor was affectionately known by Burton and Taylor. The yacht, the *Kalizma*, was the veritable picture of luxury, her name deriving from the couple's three daughters, Kate, Liza, and Maria. Brando, Burton, and Taylor were household names, of course, but Ringo was a *Beatle*, and Mal could scarcely contain his pride as the group listened to *Sgt. Pepper* and *Magical Mystery Tour* aboard the yacht: "All of the party are avid Beatles fans, and for me, it was a delight to see Elizabeth, Richard, and Marlon (holding the [album's] sleeve) sitting on the sofa reading the words whilst the LP played."[28] The next morning, Mal enjoyed an unforgettable stroll on the beach with Brando, whom he had known only as a flickering image on the silver screens of Liverpool's grand cinemas. As Burton and Taylor walked their dogs, "Myself and Marlon then took a trot along the sand, amongst the spray, stopping and sitting occasionally to talk. I must admit, he was nothing like the image I had of him, being a most sensitive person."[29]

But Mal's dream European vacation wasn't over just yet. In Rome, he was flabbergasted to see his image on a newsstand, posing with the cast of *Magical Mystery Tour* on the cover of the December 14 issue of *Rolling Stone.*

While the Starkeys made their way back to Sunny Heights to be reunited with their children, Mal made a detour to Paris, where the annual UNICEF gala benefit was being held at the Palais de Chaillot. Burton, Taylor, and Brando were in attendance, along with John and George and their wives, who had flown in for the occasion to sit at the feet of the Maharishi, with whom they enjoyed a private audience in the yogi's suite at the Ritz on the Place Vendôme. The Beach Boys and Ravi Shankar provided the evening's entertainment, but the most pressing Beatles news coming out of Paris arrived in the latest issue of *Billboard.*

The scoop, supplied by the magazine's international correspondent Ni-

Mal in Rome

gel Hunter, reported that "The Beatles plan to visit their transcendental meditation mentor, Maharishi Mahesh Yogi, in India January 25 for a three-month course at his Himalayan academy."[30] Apparently, the group would be continuing their studies, which had been interrupted back in August with Brian Epstein's untimely death.

Meanwhile, to mark the occasion of *Magical Mystery Tour*'s upcoming television debut, the Beatles held a boffo affair on December 21 at the Royal Lancaster hotel. Several hundred guests, including the full cast and crew, were among the attendees, all decked out in colorful and inventive costumes. "There were cowboys galore, myself included of course," Mal wrote, along with "nuns, several Charlie Chaplins, Paul and Jane arriving as the Pearly King and Queen, Ringo a Regency dandy, Maureen, a red Indian princess. John arrived as himself in a lot of leather gear, with George looking great in an Errol Flynn outfit, complete with tights and a sword, Pattie perfectly dressed as an Eastern princess."[31]

Dinner began fashionably late at 9 p.m.—a "delightful, full scale, pre-Christmas dinner, with turkey and pudding," Mal noted—followed by dancing; then entertainment from the Bonzo Dog Doo Dah Band, who had performed their song "Death Cab for Cutie" during the movie's strip-tease scene; and then a visit from Father Christmas himself (as played by actor Robert Morley). And then everyone settled in for a special showing of *Magical Mystery Tour*—pointedly in color and on a large screen. "It was what it was, and nothing it didn't pretend to be," Mal wrote, "a vehicle for Beatle music and fantasy. I loved it, as did the other people there."[32]

Not everyone in the Beatles' camp felt so positive about the movie. Peter Brown, Brian's trusted NEMS assistant, had seen the finished product and recommended that they mothball it, even suggesting that they write off the whole bloody business (which included some £40,000 in production expenses) and move on with their lives.

Five days later, on Boxing Day, *Magical Mystery Tour* made its British television debut—this time, in black and white and on small screens across the nation. So much for a multicolored, psychedelic feast for the eyes and ears. The reviews were devastating—indeed, they were the first collectively unenthusiastic notices the Beatles had experienced. "The bigger they are, the harder they fall. And what a fall it was," James Thomas wrote in the *Daily Express*. "The whole boring saga confirmed a long held suspicion of mine that the Beatles are four pleasant young men who have made so much money that they can apparently afford to be contemptuous of the public." Meanwhile, the *Daily Mirror* ridiculed *Magical Mystery Tour* as "Rubbish . . . Piffle . . . Nonsense!"[33]

But the music, as always, was stellar. With Mal and Neil listed as "Editorial Consultants (for Apple)," the soundtrack was released as a double-EP [for "extended play"], topping the British record charts, along with the single "Hello, Goodbye" backed with "I Am the Walrus." The Roll was alive and well.

Meanwhile, back on the weekend of November 11, the group's artist friends Simon and Marijke, known collectively as "the Fool," had begun painting a gigantic psychedelic mural on the corner of Baker and Paddington Streets in Marylebone, London. As the stunning image began to take form, it revealed the figure of a Native American chieftain in all his multicolored glory. The Fool hadn't bothered to apply for a license to paint the mural or obtained consent from the local council to undertake the venture, but these were seemingly trivial matters for the moment.

On December 7, with the mural in full bloom overhead, the Beatles had opened the Apple Boutique at 94 Baker Street. As was typical of goings-on in Beatle World, a massive crowd began congregating outside the retail shop, which specialized in fashion garments and accessories for Swinging London. The throng eventually grew so large that even Simon and Marijke couldn't make their way inside, where John, George, and their wives were holding court. John's boyhood friend Pete Shotton and Pattie's sister Jenny had been tapped as managers for the store, where apparently everything was for sale—even down to the furniture and the fittings. In Paul's words, the Apple Boutique would be a "a beautiful place where beautiful people can buy beautiful things." That's right: the boys were entering the rag trade.

Not surprisingly, rumors began running rampant about the Beatles' business empire and what direction it might take. With good reason, some critics were quick to question the Beatles' decision to try their hand at commercial enterprises outside their primary area of expertise. And what was this Apple business, anyway? Music fans and record company insiders alike had taken note of the Beatles' hints throughout the year. Early reports had been circulating about the formation of such entities as Apple Music and Apple Records, with some even going so far as to suggest that Mal and Neil—the band's road managers, no less—would be appointed to executive-level positions.

The cat was let out of the bag in a December 23 article in *Billboard*, which quoted longtime Beatles insider Terry Doran. "The Beatles were discussing the formation of their own label sharing the name of Apple in 1968," he announced. "The foursome has used the trade name for a company, Apple Holdings, which controls the music company, a newly opened boutique, and a production company."[34]

There it was. In one way or another, Mal's ever-growing portfolio was poised to expand yet again. Would he be anointed "Malcolm Frederick Evans, record company exec"?

22

MANAGING DIRECTOR?

Mal really hadn't seen it coming. Along with the likes of Neil and Alistair Taylor, he had joined the boys for a meeting in Brian's old boardroom at NEMS to divvy out the responsibilities associated with their new venture, vague as it may have been at the time. One of the group's first orders of business was to right an old wrong and bring Derek Taylor back into the fold. And that's when it happened.

The notion of Mal's acting as talent scout, as Apple's inaugural A&R man, seemingly came out of the blue. Mal later recalled "Paul turning to me at one point, saying, 'What are you doing these days, Mal?' 'Well, Paul,' was my reply, 'not a whole lot—things are pretty quiet, aren't they?' "Okay then, you'll be the Managing Director of Apple Records."[1]

Admittedly, Mal had no idea what a managing director did, but he didn't waste any time trying to figure it out. To his mind, the brief was ineluctably clear: seek out and sign new talent to the fledgling Apple Records label. "The previous December, the Apple Boutique had opened on Baker Street," he wrote, "and I was ensconced on the top floor auditioning new talent for Apple Records—aspiring singers and musicians passed through my ears in that lonely office at the top of the building. I would record their efforts, and wanting to keep that personal touch going, I would write to them in my very own handwriting, feeling that typewritten notes did not have the feel of Apple about them."[2]

Not surprisingly, Mal began to receive unsolicited material almost immediately. "Typical was the singing cowboy," he wrote, "with photographs showing [the Apple aspirant] stripped naked to the waist, sitting on a horse with a large dog at his side, informing us that when he rode onto the stage,

John during the "Lady Madonna" video shoot

Paul during the "Lady Madonna" video shoot

leapt to the floor and started singing, he would bring the house down! I believe him—but it wasn't quite what Apple was looking for."

Even during the new label's earliest days, an ethic developed that Apple would be the place where raw, inexperienced artists would get a fair shake. Mal liked to joke that "I had been whistling and singing around the halls of EMI recording studios for many years and never been discovered! On writing that," he added, "I'm thinking of those early days on the road, when I first drove the Beatles. Now I did like to entertain myself by singing and, at one point forgetting who was sitting behind me, burst into song, only realizing when John piped up saying, 'Do you know you sound like Dean Martin, Mal? Come on, give it to us again!'"[3]

But when it came to his new role at Apple, Mal put all joking aside. The man who was always good for a laugh was hell-bent on transforming himself into a serious person, the kind of bloke who could make the most of the unique opportunity that lay before him. Simply put, it was high time for him to trade in his dope bag for a briefcase. From the beginning, Mal had been determined to devote all his energies to Apple Corps, the umbrella firm that would oversee several subsidiaries that, in the boys' original vision, would grow to include Apple Records, Apple Retail, Apple Publishing, Apple Electronics, Apple Films, and Apple Studios.[4]

With the shape of Apple Corps only just beginning to materialize, Mal had lunch in a Marylebone pub with Alistair Taylor, whom the boys had appointed as general manager, hoping to glean as much as he possibly could about the company's business model. And within a few days, he learned that his new role had already been modified, albeit in a most unwelcome fashion. "Apple Records to be run by Derek Taylor and yours truly as Co-Managing Directors," Mal scrawled in his diary. "This is a complete new venture for me, but with effort and help from my friends all will be successful." Noting that Derek's return to London had been set for March 31, 1968, Mal began sketching out several key "Points for Apple Records," including matters associated with distribution and record pressing (and how these aspects would interface with EMI, Apple Records' U.K. distributor), as well as cover and label design for the subsidiary's products.[5]

He soon discovered that when it came to talent scouting, he wouldn't be left to his own devices. Over the Christmas holidays, Paul had finally pro-

Mal's various attempts at designing an Apple Corps logo

posed to longtime girlfriend Jane Asher, ending rampant speculation over the glamourous couple's plans. Having learned that her twenty-three-year-old brother, Peter, was taking a break from his work as a member of Peter and Gordon—the duo that scored an international hit with the Lennon-McCartney tune "A World Without Love"—Paul helpfully suggested that his future brother-in-law produce records for Apple. From the outset, Peter shared Paul's vision regarding the ethical, even humanistic possibilities of Apple, "a new kind of label with a much more generous and respectful attitude towards artists than was current at the time."[6] So, Asher naturally accepted the offer.

The next day, Paul upped the ante, saying, "Well, why don't you become the head of A&R?"

Peter replied, "Sure, great. I'd love to," figuring that "this was the way Apple was being set up at the time. The only other person appointed to Apple Records in any capacity was Mal Evans, who was there in a General Manager capacity."[7] And Peter certainly had no issues when it came to the prospect of working closely with Mal. Over the years, he had become friendly with the roadie, if for no other reason than when it came to the Beatles, "he was always there. He didn't say much, but he was extremely affable," Peter recalled. "You got the impression that he was solid, that he was reliable." Most significantly, "you realized that his affection for the Beatles was unquestionable. He wanted to be invaluable," Peter added, "and he *was*."[8]

But the new A&R man also recognized a subtle, albeit key difference in Mal's approach to life with the Beatles versus that of his longtime counterpart, Neil. Peter didn't really get to know Neil until he joined Apple, but he could tell that Mal—in his steadfast devotion to the boys—was "reactive, that he would do what he was asked to do." Through his sister, Asher knew that the two men had previously held different roles in Beatle World, with Neil acting as tour manager and Mal working as the equipment-lugging roadie. In Peter's view, "Neil was much more proactive, while Mal was the guy who, when a Beatle said he wanted something, made sure it happened, whereas Neil was the guy who would figure out what a Beatle wanted before he even knew it."[9]

With Apple adding personnel by the day, space was already at a premium. On January 22, 1968, the company had entered into a one-year lease for offices on the fourth floor of 95 Wigmore Street, in the West End, which would serve as the inaugural headquarters of Apple Corps, if only temporarily. Mal celebrated by ordering a desk for the first time in his life. By the time that his office furniture arrived on February 1, however, the Apple staff had already been under fire from the other Wigmore Street tenants for playing records during business hours. Not being able to listen to music, to scout out potential talent for Apple Records, was a professional handicap Mal simply couldn't afford, and the complaints left him having to shuttle back and forth between Apple's operations on Baker and Wigmore Streets.

Still, nothing, it seemed, would blunt his determination to make this new opportunity work. Drawing upon his skills as a sketch artist, Mal even tried his hand at designing a logo that captured the essence of Apple

Corps. "They had been looking for something to express the feeling of being completely self-contained, as all facets of the business they were involved in would be gathered together under one roof," he recalled. Ultimately, he fashioned three candidates for his colleagues' consideration, including a design that featured a bulbous uppercase orange "A" outlined in the shape of a green apple; a circular design with the word "APPLE" writ large in bold, pink letters set against a yellow background; and, finally, a burgundy capital "A" set against a green apple. Any consideration that Mal's drawing might possibly have received would be short-lived. "Paul had a Magritte painting of an apple," Mal said, "and everybody agreed it would be the ideal logo for the Beatles' new company."[10]

Working out of the Wigmore Street office, Mal and Neil didn't waste any time in transforming Paul's vision into reality. Richard DiLello, Apple's twenty-two-year-old American "house hippie," recalled a meeting that the former roadie–cum–record exec held with London adman Gene Mahon. "Neil told Gene that he wanted a photograph of an apple for a record label," said DiLello. "Well, that seemed simple enough. Suddenly on the pickup—in that one instant—[Mahon's] flash came to him! It was one of those illuminating rushes in which the entire design universe opened up. 'Listen,' he said, 'why don't we have the A-side of the record as a completely whole apple with no writing on it whatsoever. On the B-side, we can have an apple sliced in half with all the label copy.'" In DiLello's memory, "It was the ultimate Acid-Purist design concept for a record label. Neil and Mal looked at him and nodded silently," knowing genius when they saw it.[11]

After a few weeks of listening to unsolicited material in his Baker Street office, Mal decided to take matters into his own hands. He had originally hoped to sign the Perishers (formerly known as the Seftons), whom he had known from his friendship with bass player Norm Bellis. The Perishers had even gone so far as to cut an acetate for their song "How Does It Feel?" Unable to drum up any interest for the group at Apple, Mal recalled his March 1967 meeting with Bill Collins at the Bag. He had wanted the opportunity to hear the Iveys, the Welsh band Collins had been so high on. Fortunately, he wouldn't have to wait for very long. On Monday, January 22, he got things rolling during a lunch with Bill. Two days later, Mal shared his intentions with Peter, Neil, and Paul during a series of meetings at Apple. He also learned, although he had not yet begun to panic—trusting in the boys, as he did, to have faith in him—that Apple Records was now "Derek, Peter, and Mal."[12] Scarcely a month earlier, the job had seemingly been his alone.

By Thursday, January 25, Mal was on his way with Bill to see the Iveys perform at the Marquee, a trendy Soho club on Wardour Street. In Mal's memory, the roadie recalled Peter Asher joining him that night at the Marquee. Iveys bassist Ron Griffiths would never forget the moment Mal entered the club. "We had just finished our regular 'wind-up-the-audience-and-have-a-laugh-with-them' stint when this giant bloke came up at the end with Bill. We recognized him because we'd seen pictures in the magazines from years gone by. We were thrilled to bits because that was the nearest we'd got to the Beatles at that time."[13] But, apparently, Peter had already seen enough. According to Mal, "when the Iveys had finished their first set, Peter gave them the thumbs down, telling me that they weren't worth listening to, and didn't stand a chance of making anything of themselves."[14]

But Mal wasn't throwing in the towel just yet: "'That's what you think, Peter boy,' I said to myself. I had just got that funny feeling up my spine, and that's something I always acknowledge, so I stayed for the second set, which indeed was a lot better." At this point, Mal decided to believe in himself, to trust in his instincts. "After the show, I played executive, buying [the Iveys] and their manager, Bill Collins, a round of drinks," he wrote. "My mouth tends to run away with me when I get enthusiastic about something, but what I like, the public likes."[15] Mal pointedly avoided resorting to any showbiz bluster—no "the Iveys will be bigger than Elvis" or any such drivel—but if he knew one thing as well as anyone, it was the sound of a hard-driving rock 'n' roll band working a crowd. Over the years, he'd paid his dues at the Cavern and then some.

A few nights later, Mal treated Bill and the Iveys to dinner, hoping to continue grooming them as his first major Apple signing. Ron Griffiths remembered that "we were up 'til all hours of the morning playing our demos." Mal was impressed not only with their sound, but also with the fact that, like his cherished Beatles, the Iveys composed all their own music. Mal "couldn't get over the variety of songs," said Griffiths. "We were pouring drinks and he started to pass a joint around. He was the first person to ever make it available to us. I didn't enjoy it." At this point, the joint came around to Pete Ham, the band's lead singer and guitarist, who was wary of smoking weed. But it was a different story when it came to Tom Evans, the Iveys' guitarist. "Tom certainly got into it," Griffiths recalled.[16]

On January 30, Mal had a chance meeting with Bill at a Marylebone pub. Over lunch, they began discussing the contours of a potential Apple deal for the Iveys. Taking a leap of faith—or perhaps after being prodded by Mal—Bill went for broke and named his terms. In Mal's memory the Iveys' manager said that a "contract with EMI should be percentage of top to cover overheads, i.e., artist fee [for] pressing and distribution, and promoting, etc. Then remaining percentage to be split 50/50 between record company and Apple."[17] All in all, it was pretty standard stuff.

But what Bill didn't know was that Mal had already struck out back at the office, where he was playing the Iveys' demo reel to virtually anyone who would listen. He had shared the recordings with Mike Berry, a new member of Apple's publishing team, who had worked at Sparta Music and was already a convert to the Iveys' sound. As with Mal and Bill, Mike was impressed with the grassroots popularity the Welsh group had already stoked—and without a record deal, no less. Taking up the banner for Mal, Mike recalled "telling my Apple Publishing partner, Terry Doran, that the Iveys were going to be our first signing. I gave Paul McCartney my personal Iveys demo tape, but Paul said he didn't see anything in it."[18] And so began an ongoing saga in which Mal would, time and time again, prime the pump for the Iveys, hoping to impress the boys—Paul, especially—about the Iveys' incredible potential. "For six months," Mal recalled, "I brought tapes into Apple, playing them for the fellas and being rejected." But as time wore on, he became ever more determined. "I had mentally dug my heels in, determined to prove to all these people that I was right."[19]

Meanwhile, it was slowly dawning on Mal that having his family in such close proximity wasn't necessarily making his life any easier, that the carefully maintained compartments of his life were beginning to spill over into one another at an alarming rate. Worse yet, though his new role had proven to be a stimulating addition to his life, his duties as the Beatles' equipment manager hadn't even remotely ebbed, looming even larger now that his family lived in the metropolitan area. In fact, the boys still relied upon his jack-of-all-trades contributions to make their lives work, both creatively and personally.

For Gary, the New Year had started off on a sour note. The Christmas holidays had been a respite from the schoolyard bullies who maligned him for his Northern accent. On the day he was scheduled to return to Kenyngton Manor, he comforted himself with the knowledge that the Easter holidays were only a few months away.

Meanwhile, Mal went on high alert after Lily missed her period and believed herself pregnant. They were barely making ends meet as it was. How could they possibly afford another mouth to feed? Meanwhile, the boys were gearing up for a series of recording sessions in advance of the India trip, which was now to commence, for Mal at least, on February 15. As he began making plans to receive his pre-travel inoculation, Mal discussed with John the possibility of taking Lil and the children along with him to India. If nothing else, going to the Maharishi's distant ashram on the banks of the Ganges would excuse Gary from school for a while.

By mid-month, Mal's work with the boys was back in full swing. On Saturday, January 13, he made an appointment with Paul to bring Ringo's drum kit from EMI Studios to 7 Cavendish Avenue so he could practice his percussion skills. Gary was determined to come along, at one point disappearing upstairs inside the Evanses' Sunbury home to don his "visiting Paul outfit," which consisted of new trousers, socks, and shirt, along with a decorated handkerchief strategically positioned in his breast pocket. "Will you smooth my hair before I go into Paul's house?"[20] Gary asked his father.

That afternoon, Mal set up the kit in Paul's basement, knowing full well that he would be transporting it back to the studio the very next day for the Beatle's recording session with a crack lineup that included Paul on drums, Jeff Beck on guitar, Paul Samwell-Smith on bass, and Nicky Hopkins on keyboards. For the occasion, the makeshift band recorded a cover version of the Bee Gees' "And the Sun Will Shine" at EMI's Studio 3 with former Manfred Mann front man Paul Jones taking lead vocals, along with "The Dog Presides," which would comprise the single's B-side. The session marked Peter Asher's debut in the producer's chair.

That same day, Mal was scheduled to attend a press reception for the psychedelic rock band Grapefruit, an Apple Publishing client and one of the first signings for the new venture by subsidiary head Terry Doran. The band's handle had been suggested by John as a nod to the book of the same name by conceptual artist Yoko Ono, with whom the Beatle had become close friends of late. After the conclusion of the session for "And the Sun Will Shine," Mal was expected to join Doran and other Apple colleagues for the presser. In an express effort to align his priorities, the roadie ultimately skipped the event, heading home to Sunbury to share the evening meal with his family. In his diary, Mal chided himself, writing that "Gary cries when I say I won't make it for dinner."[21]

On February 4, Mal and the Beatles made their return to EMI Studios, where the boys took their first pass at John's ethereal "Across the Universe." After completing work on the song's basic track, Paul concluded that the recording would benefit from soprano harmonies. When he approached the regular gaggle of female fans congregated outside the studio gates to see if anyone could hold a high note, sixteen-year-old Lizzie Bravo and seventeen-year-old Gayleen Pease replied in the affirmative. A few minutes later, Mal ushered the young women into the studio, where they were understandably astounded to be not only inside the famous facility, but also performing on a Beatles record, for which they sang, "Nothing's gonna change my world."

Hailing from Rio de Janeiro, Lizzie had been in London since the previous spring, having arrived during the *Sgt. Pepper* sessions. On her very first day at EMI Studios, she caught glimpses of the bandmates, Brian, and Mal, whom she had gotten to know while standing vigil outside the studio walls. As with so many of the Beatles devotees who made the pilgrimage to St. John's Wood, she quickly discovered that Mal was a fan himself, idolizing the boys almost as much as, if not more than, the fans themselves did.[22]

A week later, Mal met Yoko Ono for the first time when the Japanese artist observed the Beatles' recording session for "Hey Bulldog," one of the numbers slated for the *Yellow Submarine* feature cartoon's soundtrack. During the session, Mal played the tambourine on the rocking new tune, which was filmed by Tony Bramwell and his team for a promotional video. Images of the band performing "Hey Bulldog" were redeployed for "Lady Madonna," the group's next single. As events would demonstrate, Yoko's attendance hadn't been a mere afterthought. John fully intended to invite her to join the Beatles and their entourage for their upcoming trip to India.

Yoko had even gone so far as to attend a recent Beatles meeting to make final preparations for the trip, but John lost his nerve after she jumped into his Rolls-Royce in front of Cynthia and demanded a ride home.

For his part, Mal intuited John's growing feelings for the artist, and the roadie made sure he was unfailingly polite and welcoming to Ono during the "Hey Bulldog" session. He may not have been able to close the Iveys deal—at least not yet—but he knew a thing or two about showing hospitality. And he was determined to see that Yoko received it.

23

POVERTY THROWS A SMILING SHADOW

On February 14, Mal traveled to India—pointedly, without his family. The expense of transporting the entire Evans clan to the subcontinent would have been simply too exorbitant. His salary had certainly improved since Brian hired him, growing from an initial £25 per week in August 1963 to £30 in October 1964, when Alf Bicknell joined the team. By 1968, Mal was taking home a weekly wage of £38, which presumably had been augmented through incremental salary increases to keep pace with inflation. In 1968, he earned an annual salary of £1,976, in comparison to the average Briton's take-home pay that year of £1,144.[1] By most families' standards, Mal and Lily were doing well. But Mal's appetites had grown by leaps and bounds during that same period; he had become accustomed, in short, to living like a Beatle. Besides, after having to pay back their January 1964 Paris expenses to NEMS in monthly installments, Lil was likely disinclined to tax her household budget again in that fashion.

The day of the flight began in a torrent of emotion for Mal, who bade farewell to Gary as the boy was heading to the playground with his new friend, Barry. "Arm in arm, off they went," Mal recalled, feeling "quite choked" as he observed the boys walking away. After gathering the Harrisons' and the Lennons' luggage from their homes—for which he paid £195 in excess-baggage fees—Mal boarded Qantas flight 754 to Delhi, carrying John's guitar for safekeeping. He was in for a long journey, especially with "only five first-class passengers" and "no lonely blondes to chat up," he wrote. Having performed his role as advance man, securing cars and other necessities for the 150-mile drive to the ashram, Mal awaited the Harrisons' and Lennons' arrival.

With very little press lying in wait at the airport, the roadie was able to ferry both parties to Rishikesh, the site of the Maharishi's ashram in the northern state of Uttarakhand, by early afternoon. "Our arrival at the ashram was perfect," he wrote, "with Maharishi to greet us with kind words and tea, very welcome indeed."[2] The Maharishi made a point of explaining the nature of the Beatles' visit to the current crop of students at the ashram's fifteen-acre complex. "Please remember," he said, that "I have offered these young people a quiet refuge from being celebrities. I promised them they would not be molested in any way by news seekers. Please do not have any cameras near them, do not ask for their autographs, and treat them no differently than anyone else here."[3]

Almost immediately, Mal settled into a tranquil routine. The rooms were to his liking—"No creepy crawlies have I seen anywhere"—and the vegetarian meals were refreshing. His quarters at the ashram were suffused with "a nice smelling incense burning," he wrote to Lily.[4] Each day's schedule included a pair of ninety-minute lectures, scheduled for 3:30 p.m. and 8:30 p.m., respectively. Mal was eager to learn more about Transcendental

Mal in Rishikesh

Meditation, having grown to adore Paramahansa Yogananda's *Autobiography of a Yogi*. He had first read the book, originally published in 1946, at George's suggestion. For Mal, the yogi's life and search for spiritual wisdom provided him with a ready fount of inspiration.

The only blemish on Mal's Eastern experience occurred on the second day, when "the press really tried knocking down the gates into the ashram." The Maharishi's staff immediately summoned Mal, who, at first, was respectful of the journalists, quietly explaining that the Beatles wanted to be left alone. But the press soon tested his patience, especially when "an Indian reporter told me, 'no bloody foreigner is going to stop me in my own country.'"[5]

Suddenly, Mal's temper got the better of him. But in the spirit of the ashram and the Maharishi's teachings, he turned the other cheek and went back to his quarters. In the weeks ahead, Mal attempted to mollify the scrum of journalists by delivering daily press briefings of the dullest sort—reporting, in blasé fashion, that the boys had eaten, meditated, and slept. Afterward, there were fewer media incursions at the ashram, save for the occasional photojournalist who would shinny up a tree in a brazen attempt to capture the Beatles' images with a telephoto lens. Fortunately, Mal's experience with the Indian press was an aberration. He quickly came to admire the Indian people, later writing that "'poverty throws a smiling shadow' just about sums up my feeling for the majority of the people I met during my stay in India. For the most part, poor and hard-working, they always seem to face life with a smile and fortitude I envied."[6]

On Monday, February 19, Mal made a return trip to the Delhi airport to retrieve the Starkeys, who were traveling with Paul and Jane. As he awaited the couples' arrival, he bought "a one-stringed instrument and a sort of banjo" for George's twenty-fifth birthday in six days. The excitement of his reunion with Paul and Ringo turned out to be short-lived. As he and the Maharishi's disciple Raghvendra placed garlands upon the shoulders of the new arrivals as they deplaned, Ringo said, "Mal, my arm's killing me; please take me to a doctor right away." The convoy found its way to a local hospital, where Mal attempted to secure immediate treatment for the Beatle, only "to be told curtly by the Indian doctor, 'He is not a special case and will have to wait his turn.'" But Mal refused to leave Ringo's condition unattended, "so off we go to pay a private doctor ten rupees for the privilege of hearing him say it will be alright."[7]

That Sunday, the ashram prepared to celebrate George's birthday. Mal and Raghvendra drove to nearby Dehradun to pick up a birthday cake for the Beatle; it was decorated with white icing and adorned with pink and white flowers, with embossed gold lettering reading, "Jai Guru Deva and Happy Birthday George." Together, Raghvendra and Mal took a horse-drawn taxi through the city, stopping to purchase balloons and fireworks for the party. "While walking through the streets on my own at one point," Mal recalled, "I was followed by a laughing, smiling bunch of children who seemed to think I was amazing. I guess it was being tall, white, and blonde that did it!"[8]

At the party, the guests were serenaded by Indian musicians, and balloons and streamers were hung from the party tables and the banyan trees. In a moment that touched his heart, Mal recalled that "garlands were given to everyone present, and these we placed on George, who nearly disappeared under the mound of flowers! George then gave some of them back to us, and when he came to give me one, we ended up with a garland around each of our necks, but linked together, which a local photographer said meant 'real affection.' Then George and I collapsed on our knees laughing, which really brought on the party spirit."[9]

Mal reveled in the feeling of community he experienced at the ashram. When they weren't attending the Maharishi's lectures, John and Paul were happily strumming their acoustic guitars, composing new songs with great abandon, often having been inspired by the holy man's teachings. As always, Mal ensured that all his mates enjoyed their stay. Knowing Ringo's history of childhood stomach ailments, the roadie went to Rishikesh every morning to gather fresh provisions so he could prepare breakfast for the drummer.

When he wasn't serving the boys, Mal found time to indulge his own creative impulses, which had likely been inspired after a songwriting session with Donovan. The Scottish musician had recently arrived, in the company of "Gypsy" Dave Mills, an English artist, and Mills's girlfriend, Yvonne. Working with Donovan, Mal helped craft the breezy, evocative lyrics of "The Sun Is a Very Magic Fellow," which would be included on the singer-songwriter's upcoming LP, *The Hurdy Gurdy Man*. And Donovan wasn't the only artist of note to make his way to the Maharishi's retreat. Actress Mia Farrow and her sister Prudence had also ventured to the ashram in order to attend the holy man's celebrated Transcendental Meditation seminar.

At one point, Mal composed a song entitled "I'm Not Going to Move," the lyrics of which describe the "perfect peace of mind" he had obtained through the auspices of meditation, a transcendence that had motivated him to become a better person: "Lord, I want to be your man, / Follow your eternal plan." But the search for nirvana could occasionally be illusory, as the roadie learned shortly before he left the ashram. "One night, I thought my meditating was reaching a very special new depth," he wrote. "I could see flashing lights around me in the darkness, although my eyes were closed. Then, when I opened one eye to peep, I realized I'd been fooled." To Mal's great surprise, "Raghvendra was flashing a torch at me through the window. He'd read the PLEASE DO NOT DISTURB sign on my door and thought this would be the most polite way of drawing my attention!"[10]

As February wore on, the ashram was abuzz with the news that a tiger had made a human kill only about a half mile away from camp. Mal watched in awe as the Beach Boys' Mike Love, having been inspired to make his own Rishikesh pilgrimage after attending the UNICEF gala back in December, decided they should confront the animal. "Mike Love and myself, full of peace," Mal wrote, "marched off into the jungle to tell him off about it! Luckily, all we found was our own pleasant company amidst a delightful setting."[11]

The excitement increased when the son of socialite Nancy Cooke de Herrera, one of the Maharishi's most devoted followers, arrived to join his mother from the States. A fervor developed around the ashram after the young man, Rik Cooke, made plans to go tiger hunting. "We thought this a complete contradiction to the peacefulness and serenity that meditation gives, but off he went," Mal wrote. "The first day, with a blood curdling scream, the tiger leapt out of the underbrush onto the back of the elephant carrying this young man. [Cooke] was very shaken by this experience, but not enough to discontinue the hunt. The next day, he must have been giving off delicious vibrations, for the tiger ignored the goat staked out as bait and climbed the tree in order to get [Cooke] again. This was too much, and [Cooke] returned to the ashram in abject misery suffering from every known tropical disease, which we all thought was just penance."[12] John would commemorate the farcical episode in "The Continuing Story of Bungalow Bill," one of numerous songs he composed while in Rishikesh.

On March 1, the ashram was abuzz with news of a very different sort when Ringo announced to Mal that he and Mo were ready to make their return to England. "We're missing the kids, and Maureen doesn't like the flies," Ringo admitted. The drummer confided in Canadian student and budding filmmaker Paul Saltzman that Maureen, every night before they went to bed, insisted that Ringo hunt down any flies or bugs in their bathroom and bedroom. A cover story was concocted that claimed Ringo had grown tired of the vegetarian cuisine at the ashram, but this was a ruse.[13]

With the Starkeys' impending exodus in the offing, others quickly joined in for the ride back to Delhi, including Saltzman, Gypsy Dave, Yvonne, and Mal, who not only arranged for the taxis, but also squired Ringo and Mo back to the city. Before they made their departure, though, the Maharishi arranged for a group photo to commemorate the Beatles' sojourn at the ashram. The holy man played the part of director, organizing where everyone would sit while flowers and garlands were draped about the students. "Let everyone outside the ashram see how happy your meditations are making you!" he said. "Ready! Now everyone look happy!" Saltzman recalled that the entirety of the experience was festive, "like a class photo for everyone to take home."[14] Not long afterward, the images of the Maharishi and his celebrated students, with John and Mal sitting stage left, made their way around the world.

On March 3, Mal led the taxi caravan out of Rishikesh. Ringo later recalled that "we just drove into Delhi, got a ticket, and that was it. We stopped off in Tehran, and this bloke from the airline came up and said, 'Excuse me, are you one of the Beatles?' I said, 'No' and he just walked away, and that was that. I guess we're not too big in Tehran!"[15] Mal followed suit six days later, making the long flight back to London on March 9. With the Easter holidays coming up—and Gary looking forward to a break from the bullies at Kenyngton Manor—he seemed to be getting his priorities right.

Safely ensconced in Sunbury in the bosom of his family, Mal learned that the alarm bells over Lil's potential pregnancy had been for naught. He had returned to sociopolitical unrest in the capital, highlighted by a riot in Grosvenor Square in which ten thousand people protested the war in Vietnam. While Mal abhorred the war in Southeast Asia, he was particularly distressed over the mistreatment of law enforcement. In his diary, he opined that the protest had "developed into a little war of its own. Ironical that they should use violence to protest against violence. British police are the finest in the world," he added. "They stood firm and were not tempted to use any more violence than was necessary!"[16]

With the riots and protests only ratcheting up, Mal attended to Apple affairs in the Wigmore offices. After sending flowers to George's fifty-seven-year-old mother, Louise, in Liverpool as a belated birthday present, Mal felt the onset of an out-of-body experience. "I have been standing in the lift at Apple with a middle-aged regular business man," he wrote, "and a strong feeling came over me [that] life is a game, a game where I make the rules to fit me, and when I die, none of this around me now will exist."[17]

Sitting at Neil's desk—his partner had flown out to Delhi in his stead, to join the Beatles remaining in India—Mal indulged his reverie, attempting to work through as much in his mind as he could. He felt as if he were

Mal, far right, in a group photo at the ashram

"re-enacting a film script using fragments of things I have seen in the past. The right type of desk, the reception hall seems to be just right, as though I have planned it all. Have I really built all these buildings and modelled these people, my beautiful family, to order—an order I once knew a long time ago?" Grasping with a newfound "strong awareness of self," he wondered if "this is death, and I'm playing to amuse myself till birth?"[18]

Mal would also think back fondly to the Beatles' remarkable creative output during their stay in Rishikesh. Their music had flowered like never before, and the roadie had enjoyed the privilege of observing their art as it manifested in real time. Months later, Paul would tell him about a song he had begun composing in the ashram, outside Mal's earshot. After many hours of uninterrupted meditation, the Beatle said, he had experienced a vision in which the roadie stood before him, gently repeating words of succor and comfort, saying, "Let it be. Let it be."[19]

24

BIG, CUDDLY, CHEERFUL, AND SEXY

When Mal took his monthlong sojourn in Rishikesh, he wasn't merely fulfilling his standing obligations in Beatle World. Surely, he had wanted to impress the boys and was eager to take full advantage of his opportunity with Apple Corps, which had been a frequent subject of conversation—even among the relative peace and tranquility of the ashram. But his trek to the Indian subcontinent had deeper roots than the protection of his turf where the Beatles were concerned. In truth, Mal had been running from something that had its roots in the latter months of 1967.

At some point that autumn, twenty-one-year-old Arwen Dolittle had found her way into the roadie's orbit. Things might have started up between them near the seaside, as the *Magical Mystery Tour* bus made its way through Devon and Cornwall. Or it might have been slightly later—at a pub in the city perhaps, after she had left her rural hometown behind for a clerical job in London—when Mal first caught sight of the blonde, blue-eyed beauty. At this point, *where* he had made her acquaintance didn't really matter. By the time Mal had deplaned in London, Lily's pregnancy scare was the least of his problems: Arwen was five months along with his child.

It is impossible to know what Mal was thinking during this period. For the most part, his diary references to the young woman are vague and infrequent. The roadie's life, as usual, was a veritable whirl of Beatles business. And with his family now living nearby, he likely found it more difficult to conceal his movements. Besides, he wouldn't have been the first unfaithful husband to simply stand pat and hope the problem went away, that it would somehow magically resolve itself.

When Mal returned to Sunbury that March, changes were afoot. John's chauffeur, Les Anthony, had kindly gifted Gary and Julie with a pair of rabbits, leaving Mal with the task of installing wooden hutches in his family's backyard. Originally, the kids named the bunnies, both males, Bernie and Priscilla. Belatedly realizing that Priscilla was a boy, they renamed him Snowy, to match his soft white coat. Unlike the kids' pet guinea pigs, Sweet Pebbles and Nicola, the rabbits frustrated Mal to no end, frequently managing to slip out of their cages and run loose.[1]

At Apple, things were moving quickly in spite of John and George's having remained at the ashram. On March 24, Paul and Jane had made their return with Neil and newly minted Apple Films head Denis O'Dell, carrying with them the news that the next Beatles film would be an adaptation of J. R. R. Tolkien's *The Lord of the Rings*. But the larger issue for Mal involved the fate of the Iveys. Bill Collins was understandably itching for an answer, having seemingly discussed contract terms nearly two months earlier. For his part, Collins had been managing the Welsh band since July 1966, and in the ensuing years, they had given up their day jobs to try their luck as professional musicians. Collins was eager to move the Iveys' career forward, and Mal still seemed their best bet.

Back in January, of course, Mal had been managing director of Apple Records, shortly to become co-managing director with Derek, and now having been bumped down to *co*-co-managing director with Derek and Peter Asher. For his part, Bill promised to provide Mal with more Iveys demos to share around the office, where Peter was making news of his own with American singer-songwriter James Taylor. Asher would never forget his first encounter with Taylor's demo reel, which included "Something in the Way She Moves." He recalled being bowled over, thinking that "this is one of the greatest things I've ever heard in my life."[2] Having been tipped off about Taylor from guitarist Danny Kortchmar, a former member of the singer's defunct band, the Flying Machine, Peter was keen not only to sign the American musician, but moreover to get him into the studio posthaste.

By mid-April, George and John and their wives had left Rishikesh, departing after scandal erupted in the ashram over the Maharishi's alleged sexual advances toward his female students. As the remaining two Beatles left camp, John began composing a scathing new tune, later entitled "Sexy Sadie," about the hypocrisy he had witnessed on the subcontinent.

Meanwhile, Mal and Neil were preparing to unleash the bandmates' Apple concept upon a waiting world. Richard DiLello was excited to watch it all unfold. In his estimation, the two Liverpudlians occupied a key source of power in the whole enterprise, and he described Mal as a "top Beatle attaché and road manager, just a shade to the right of Neil Aspinall in the psychological Apple hierarchy."[3]

From DiLello's perspective, it was the addition of Derek Taylor—who made his triumphant return to the Beatles' fold on April 1—that had imbued Apple with the energy and vision it sorely needed. "Neil Aspinall and Mal Evans might have known them the longest," the house hippie wrote, "but Derek Taylor was the one who had the articulate and immediate human touch. From the very beginning, he was the one who had injected the energy into his employers' wishes to mold this nonstop schizophrenic dreamboat into reality. Almost singlehandedly, he had created and sustained all the aspirations that the young Apple had announced so confidently."[4]

On April 18, Apple's inaugural advertising campaign hit the print media. In a concept dreamt up by Paul, the ad featured Alistair Taylor decked out as a beleaguered one-man band. "This man has talent," the ad copy proclaimed. "One day he sang his songs to a tape recorder (borrowed from the man next door). In his neatest handwriting he wrote an explanatory note (giving his name and address) and, remembering to enclose a picture of himself, sent the tape, letter, and photograph to Apple Music, 94 Baker Street, London, W.1. If you were thinking of doing the same thing yourself—do it now! This man now owns a Bentley!"[5] The response was predictable—and overwhelming. Within a fortnight, hundreds of would-be Apple artists deluged the Baker Street offices with their wares.

That same month, Victoria Mucie had returned to London to continue her studies. Now eighteen, she was eager to resume her friendship with Mal, later admitting that "there were times I thought I was in love with him. He was the sweetest guy, and he was so understanding. And I know that he met hundreds, if not thousands, of young women. But he was writing me letters." But much had changed since Mal last saw Victoria: she had entered a dark period involving a lot of family upheaval and was no longer the easygoing spirit who had visited the British Isles the previous year with such carefree abandon.[6] And it was in this state of mind that she invited Mal over to her flat, having decided to seduce him.

If you're going to seduce somebody, you wear lingerie—or so Mucie told herself. But in her youthful naïveté, she believed that "lingerie" simply referred to sleepwear. "So, I wore this granny gown," she said, "and he came over, and I'm sure he just thought, 'This kid is so pitiful.' But we sat up and talked for a long time. They had just been to India, so we talked about meditation and the meaning of life. And I remember this last thing that he said to me, which I'll never forget. He said, 'I've been everywhere, and I've done everything, and that spirituality, man, that's really all there is, ain't it?"[7]

Victoria could never have known the crossroads at which Mal had found himself in that pivotal month. Like the proverbial time bomb, one of his extramarital affairs had placed his marriage and family life in jeopardy, and his professional life seemed to be simultaneously skyrocketing and deflating before his very eyes. He seemed determined, this time, to straighten out his domestic life and be the husband Lil deserved.

In the intervening years, Victoria would come to understand Mal's place in the Beatles' universe as the driving force behind his actions. "I realized that Malcolm lived to please those guys, just like Hare Krishnas live to please their guru. It's like, 'I'm going to scrub the banisters, and I'm going to get down on my hands and knees and polish these steps. And then I'm going to do it again, because I want to serve the guru. That's how I believe Mal felt about serving the Beatles. They were his guru."[8]

And if serving the Beatles meant making Apple the success of which they dreamed, then Mal would be damned if he didn't try to make the Iveys work. To his mind, the Welshmen deserved to be the fledgling label's first signing. To keep the pressure on, Mal encouraged Collins to provide yet another demo reel, bringing the total to four at this juncture. On May 6, Mal shared the recordings with Peter and Derek. For his part, Peter gleaned a significant difference between the latest demos and the band he had heard perform back at the Marquee. "This is a really good, solid band," he thought. "And they've got some good songs, certainly worth making a record. It wasn't quite the same as I felt about James [Taylor], but I thought the Iveys were very good."[9]

Derek couldn't help comparing the Welshmen to bands represented among the barrage of tapes arriving on Apple's doorstep, concluding that "the Iveys had an extremely melodic, professional, coherent sound. It stood out amongst all the other tapes that were coming in. And it sounded like a record, which was the best test." Mal knew that the key to closing the deal involved having a Beatle in his corner, and to his delight, Paul thought the latest reel was a winner, saying to Mike Berry in Apple Publishing, "Have you heard the new Iveys tape? It's fucking great!"[10] But, to his credit, Mal didn't want to stop with Paul, who still wasn't sure the Iveys had the capacity to land a hit record. The roadie wanted *everyone's* support.

Mal went back to Collins and asked for yet another demo reel, and on May 21, he threw down the gauntlet to his Apple colleagues. Peter recalled that Mal made an impassioned speech on the Iveys' behalf before walking out of the room. Having heard the latest demos, "Paul admired them," said Peter, and "George and John liked the new tapes. And we all liked Mal. So there was no hesitation. They became Mal's baby."[11] While Mal felt he had been forced to go to extraordinary lengths to plead the Iveys' case, the evidence seemed to suggest, in retrospect, that the group was destined to receive an Apple deal on the strength of his support alone.

When it came to the contract's terms, Mal had set the Iveys up for a strong start. The three-year agreement called for a minimum of twelve new songs per year. At one point, Collins discussed the particulars of the deal with George, who waxed nostalgic, saying, "Tell you what Bill, you're not going to get ripped off like we were getting ripped off in our day. With us, you get 5 percent, and you don't pay for production costs." Collins was elated, believing that it was a fantastic deal.[12]

With the Iveys on the Apple roster, Peter Asher wasted little time in seeking out a producer for the Welshmen. In an internal memo, he wrote that "they are a group that Mal Evans found. They have not made records before, but they have made several demo tapes, some of which are extremely good and impressed John Lennon and George Harrison considerably." Peter was keen on tapping Denny Cordell for the job, given the producer's track record, which included Procol Harum's smash hit "A Whiter Shade of Pale." After getting a positive response from Cordell, Peter sent him "a copy of the two [Iveys] songs that he liked best, and I think he is prepared to do a deal for the production of at least one single by them. Obviously, if this is a success, he will do more, and I think that in the hands of an expert group producer like Denny, they could do very well."[13]

By this point, Paul had begun to champion an artist of his own in Mary Hopkin, a teenage Welsh singer who had landed a strong showing on *Opportunity Knocks*, a popular British TV program of the day that highlighted amateur talent. On the strength of recommendations from English supermodel Twiggy and her manager, Justin de Villeneuve, Paul tuned into the program and subsequently lobbied for Hopkin to receive an Apple recording contract. Ultimately, it was Mal who closed the deal—no doubt delighted to have fulfilled Paul's expectations. The challenge, as he discovered, was to convince Hopkin's father that Apple was the right label for his talented daughter. Mal remembered talking Hywel Hopkin into "allowing Mary to sign her contract in a room at Trident Studios," where "her affairs [were] handled by a lawyer from her hometown, Ponterdawe [*sic*] in Wales. Some of the clauses he wrote into the contract gave us a smile or two—one of them being that we would never force Mary to perform in the nude!"[14]

With several acts in the mix—the Iveys, James Taylor, Mary Hopkin, and the biggest prize of all in the form of the Beatles themselves—Apple was ready to take its show on the road. On May 11, Mal joined John and Paul for the grand announcement in New York City. The entourage included Neil, Derek, and Magic Alex, the newly minted head of Apple Electronics. During their five-day visit, John and Paul set up digs at the Upper East Side apartment of their American attorney Nat Weiss, while the others were left to their own devices. Derek later recalled the "mad, bad week" being fueled by the unexpected addition of a hallucinogen called Purple Holiday, which left John and Paul in a mild, distanced stupor throughout the interviews and press conferences Derek had lined up for Apple's bravura coming-out party.[15]

Paul, in particular, recalled feeling uncomfortable throughout that strange week. "I had a real personal paranoia," he said. "I don't know if it was what I was smoking at the time," he added, but "for some reason, I just felt very uneasy about the whole thing; maybe it was because we were out of our depth. We were talking to media like *Fortune* magazine, and they were interviewing us as a serious economic force, which we weren't. We hadn't done the business planning; we were just goofing off and having a lot of fun."[16]

When Mal wasn't sitting in on press interviews with John and Paul at the St. Regis hotel or sailing around the Hudson with the boys on a Chinese junk, he attempted to effect his usual friendly demeanor and play tourist. And on the outside, it seemed to have worked. Writing a puff piece for *Eye* magazine, Lillian Roxon described Mal as "big, cuddly, cheerful, and sexy. If America bit him, his twinkling eyes told you, he would not hesitate to bite it right back."[17]

In truth, Mal's state of mind was nothing of the sort. He was an absolute wreck. His marriage was increasingly beset by an internal cold war, there was an out-of-wedlock baby on the way back in London, and his role at Apple appeared to have been built on a foundation of quicksand, shifting by the day and threatening to suffocate him. Writing in his diary that week, Mal made a meager attempt at philosophizing about his current predicament. "Fear is knowing the right answer," he observed, "while hoping it's the wrong answer." But it also occurred to him that the concept of fear might be something even more problematic, that "fear is not [even] knowing the right answer."[18] Had his moral compass become so broken that it was too late to reorder his misplaced priorities?

Magic Alex, John, Mal, and Paul arriving in New York City to promote Apple

25

THE GRINNING GIANT

On May 15, the Apple Boutique finally succumbed to local pressures, with the Beatles agreeing to whitewash the Fool's mural in a surrender to propriety. To George's mind, "that's just typical of the narrow minds we were trying to fight against. That's what the whole Sixties Flower-Power thing was about: 'Go away, you bunch of boring people.' The whole government, the police, the public—everybody was so boring, and then suddenly people realized they could have fun. Once we were told we had to get rid of the painting, the whole thing started to lose its appeal."[1] Losing money at an alarming rate—perhaps as much as £200,000 during its brief period of operation—the Apple Boutique was slated for closure on July 31.

In a press release, Paul attributed the decision to a shared commitment to the company's core vision. "Our main business is entertainment—communication," he said. "Apple is mainly concerned with fun, not with frocks. We want to devote all our energies to records, films, and our electronics adventures. We had to refocus." On the evening of July 30, the refocusing began when the Beatles and their significant others selected a few last-minute goods for themselves from the shop. "It was quiet when we slipped in," Mal wrote, "feeling much like thieves in the night, for even though it did belong to them, there was that feeling of not wanting to be caught. I know myself I was very hesitant about touching anything, expecting at any minute for alarms to sound. But overcoming this diffidence, I proceeded to stuff everything I could lay my hands on into large bags. This second phase ended when I realized that none of the [clothes] I'd put into the bags would fit my large frame, so I proceeded to put everything back, keeping an Apple watch for myself."[2] The next day, the Beatles flung open the doors of the shop to the public for a madcap giveaway in which the police were called, as in Beatlemania days of old, to quell the near-riot that ensued.

For Mal, refocusing had become the order of the day at Apple. In New York City, John and Paul had met Ron Kass, the thirty-three-year-old American music exec who had managed Liberty Records' European operation. Kass had come highly recommended from Capitol, who handled the group's American distribution for EMI, so the Beatles were all ears. As a leader, he exuded sophistication, cool, and competence, elements the boys saw as essential to their brand. With the Apple Boutique hitting the skids so precipitately, and John and Paul fresh off their New York City charm offensive, a new launch for Apple seemed a vital next step.

Until one of the Beatles deigned to tell him otherwise, Mal could take some solace in being managing director of Apple Records. Peter was clearly in place as A&R head, and Derek had assumed the role of Apple Corps' press officer. A solid roster of new talent was beginning to emerge with the Iveys, James Taylor, and Mary Hopkin on board. For his part, George Harrison was excited about signing twenty-four-year-old Jackie Lomax, whom the Beatles knew from their Merseybeat and Hamburg days as a member of the Undertakers. Most recently, the Cheshire-born singer and guitarist had been a member of Brian's stable, recording a trio of singles for CBS with the Lomax Alliance, his backup band. And Paul was eager to bring the Black Dyke Mills Band to Apple. A British institution, the brass band from Yorkshire dated its origins as far back as the early nineteenth century, and Paul saw them as a vehicle for recording his instrumental "Thingumybob."

Eager to continue scouting out new talent—to land something that would really impress the boys—Mal had set his sights on Luan Peters, the stage name for Carol Ann Hirsch. A trained actress and singer, Peters (as "Karol Keyes") had previously served as front woman for the Big Sound, specializing in throaty, blues-driven vocals. In contrast with the Iveys, her résumé already included a dynamite stage presence, and her soulful cover version of Ike and Tina Turner's "A Fool in Love" had been released by Columbia in 1966. Mal figured that if he provided Peters with the right repertoire—a Paul McCartney original would fit the bill nicely—she would make an admirable addition to Apple's growing stable.

During the same period in which Mal struggled to maintain his position at Apple, he found himself sidelined yet again by his *other* job. Since May, the Beatles had been back at EMI Studios to record their long-awaited follow-up LP to *Sgt. Pepper*. As always, this meant the roadie would be in high demand, possibly for months on end, to tend to their needs, personal and professional alike. When things got rolling with the new record at the tail end of May, Mal was greeted by twenty-one-year-old American Chris O'Dell, a new face in Beatle World. O'Dell had come to London by way of Derek, whom she had briefly worked for as his driver only a few months earlier in Los Angeles. She was now working in the Apple offices at Wigmore Street, filling in here and there for members of the staff and doing odd jobs. "The first day I was there," she recalled, "John and Yoko were sitting in reception, followed by Paul. And of course, Mal was there. They were just starting *The White Album*, so he was there every day organizing things for the studio."[3]

For Chris, Mal was "approachable," which was vital for the young woman as she attempted to navigate her new environs. "It was kind of weird being in this world," she recalled, "because for American kids at that time, the Beatles were kind of unreal. I was definitely a Beatles fan, so suddenly being dropped into this world where these people are actually walking around and talking was pretty mind-boggling." Fortunately for O'Dell, Mal was there, "like this big teddy bear and very Liverpudlian, and we got to know each other very quickly."[4] At the time, all she knew about him was that Derek referred to him as "'chief bodyguard.' What that meant, I'd soon learn, was that you had to get through Mal—a burly guy who took his job seriously—to get anywhere near the Beatles. That worked out well for Mal, because all the young women who threw themselves at the Beatles ended up bouncing off Mal, who was more than happy to entertain them."[5]

After a few days at Apple, Chris asked Paul if she could visit the studio to see the Beatles at work. "In my naïveté, I didn't know that you weren't supposed to do that," she said. For his part, Paul instructed her to "talk to Mal." It was a mantra she heard over and over again during her days at Apple—"Talk to Mal." So, she did, and the roadie invited her to a session at EMI Studios. That night, as she waited outside the studio, "Mal was very friendly and very nice. We chatted about all kinds of things—Apple goings-on, the weather, what he had [had] for dinner—but he never once mentioned going into the studio. After a while, I realized Mal was just passing the time and had no intention of taking me back inside with him." Chris was understandably disappointed, feeling she had been led to believe she was welcome at EMI. "I could have asked him straight out—'Can we go to the studio now?'—but he knew why I was there, and I had some pride, after all. I was also afraid that if I asked him outright, he'd explain the 'rule' about not having visitors in the studio, and I'd never get inside."[6]

And knowing Mal's reputation as the group's chief procurer back in their touring days, Chris was also slightly concerned that he might start coming on to her. But her worries proved to be short-lived. Moments later, John's boyhood friend Pete Shotton arrived on the scene, informing Mal that he was needed inside. With Mal having left to tend to the boys' needs, Pete asked Chris if she'd like to join him inside Studio 2, and within a matter of minutes, she was standing among John, Paul, and George on the studio floor, providing staccato handclaps, along with Pete, for "Revolution 1."[7]

By this juncture, the war raging in Vietnam had become a regular staple of conversation in the studio. Shotton remembered being present one evening when he and the boys were discussing the recent student antiwar demonstrations breaking out across Europe and North America. "If I had the chance," Mal brusquely interjected, "I'd just shoot the whole bloody lot of them!" Shotton recalled that the Beatles responded with good-natured boos and catcalls, surprised by their friend's staunch support of the authorities.[8]

On Friday, June 7, the boys took a break from their new record, which they had begun referring to as the "double album," given the considerable amount of material they had composed in Rishikesh. For Mal, the break meant traveling with George to California, where the Beatle was joining Ravi Shankar to film a scene in *Raga*, Howard Worth's documentary film about the Eastern classical music guru's life and work. With mounting pressures both at home and at Apple, Mal was eager to get away, scrawling in his diary, "the adventure starts here."[9] With Ringo in tow, along with Pattie and Mo, the trip must have seemed like old times for the roadie—he played hours of card games on the plane with the two Beatles, hobnobbed with celebrities, and acted the part of tourist without a care in the world.

With the film shoot taking place in nearby Big Sur, Mal and the group stayed in Pebble Beach, at the Hotel Del Monte, where the roadie, always on the lookout for celebrities, was delighted to learn that Bing Crosby was also in residence. As they settled into their luxurious accommodation, George practiced his sitar, with Mal playing the role of equipment manager. Given their proximity to Pebble Beach's world-famous links, "George suggested a round of golf," Mal wrote, "and it was fantastic! If any sightseers had spotted George, they'd have never connected him with the Beatle of the same name. Picture him standing there, enormous sunglasses beneath an orange trilby with bright orange suit to match, golf club clutched in his fist, seated in the middle of a green in this crazy little go cart!"[10]

The next day, Mal accompanied George to the coastal Esalen Institute, marveling at the lush scenery as Worth filmed Ravi in the act of teaching George a new raga, as the traditional melodic patterns in Indian music are called. As the cameras rolled, Mal wrote, "They just sat there with their sitars, very informally and without any rehearsal or planned dialogue."[11] The next day, Worth filmed establishing shots of George and Ravi walking along the cliffs, while Mal snapped several still photographs of the musicians and of Pattie, who was lounging serenely in the California sun. They concluded their vacation in Los Angeles while staying at actor Van Heflin's Brentwood home. Mal enjoyed the opportunity to witness bona fide Hollywood hijinks when they visited Peter Tork's Laurel Canyon home, where the Monkee was swimming with several naked women when they arrived. Later, George and Ringo played in a jam session, with Tork on piano, Peter Asher on bass, and David Crosby on guitar.

The group then flew to New York City, where they stayed at the Drake Hotel, in which Jimi Hendrix and Eric Clapton were also ensconced. For Mal, one of the trip's great highlights involved taking Ringo and Mo to Hendrix's intimate club performance at the Scene, where the guitar god played a duet with jazz flutist Jeremy Steig. Mal also accompanied George and Eric to Manny's Music, the city's go-to shop for musical instruments, where the Beatle landed "a lovely big, fat Gibson Jumbo, Country and Western style."[12]

The trip was just what Mal had most desired—a diversion from his real-life troubles back in the United Kingdom and a chance to meet new people along the way. One of those new faces was twenty-seven-year-old singer Harry Nilsson, who had released his debut LP, *Pandemonium Shadow*

Show, with RCA back in December. The album included Nilsson's clever reworking of the Beatles' "You Can't Do That," in which Nilsson referenced eighteen other Beatles songs in the innovative, multilayered mix.

Later that month, Paul made his own trip to the American West Coast, to attend Capitol Records' annual convention, which was being held at the Beverly Hills Hilton on June 20. Tony Bramwell was there, too, along with Ron Kass, who had recently been appointed president of Apple Records. At the convention, as Bramwell recalled, Paul announced the Beatles' intention to release their work on the new label and then did "the old meet-and-greet" with top Capitol executives. After the presentation, which Tony described as a "PR masterpiece," the two returned to their bungalows, where they were surprised to see Linda Eastman, the enchanting photographer from the *Sgt. Pepper* launch party. "She had a joint in one hand and a beatific smile on her face," said Tony. "Paul immediately detached himself from the circus surrounding him and took Linda aside. As I looked across the room, I suddenly saw something happen. Right before my eyes, they fell in love. It was like the thunderbolt that Sicilians speak of, the *coup-de-foudre* that the French speak of in hushed tones, that once-in-a-lifetime feeling."[13]

Ken Mansfield was also at the convention, where he worked with Paul and Ron, helping them to position Apple among Capitol's growing roster of subsidiaries. At one point, Mansfield marveled at Great Britain's remarkable impact upon popular music.

"Gosh," he said to Paul, "I'd really like to come to London someday."

Paul responded with mild surprise. "Haven't you been to Europe?" he asked.

Later, when Mansfield ferried Paul, Ron, and Tony to the airport, Paul made a point of removing a medallion he had been wearing around his neck and placing it around Mansfield's. "Next time I see this, it'll be in London, maybe?" A few weeks later, Mansfield received a call from Ron, who invited him to England to serve as Apple's U.S. manager.[14]

The news of Ron Kass's appointment as president of Apple Records didn't surprise Mal in the slightest. He had been in an emotional and professional freefall virtually since Paul first asked him to take on a leadership role with the new label. For a long while, he had felt that "Apple was getting away from me. My term as Managing Director of Apple Records was short-lived. The Beatles then got real about the whole thing and brought in professional people. I didn't mind, knowing it was for the good of the company, but not being a pushy sort of person, [I] felt I had no real status in Apple, apart from being buddy and pal."[15]

As it turned out, one of those professional people wasn't having it any longer. Mike Berry was at his wit's end trying to get Apple Publishing off the ground. "From the time I had joined Apple in January of '68," Berry said, "I had been frustrated. I remember I lost out on signing one writer because a Beatle was never around to get anything approved. One of his songs that I really wanted went Top Five. Finally, we had this meeting between the Beatles and everyone from all the departments. McCartney chaired the meeting. We all agreed we had to get more communication going on all levels. It was decided that Derek Taylor would be a go-between coordinator for everyone to help get things done. The next day, I wanted to talk to Derek about getting something going for the Iveys, and I was told he had gone to Los Angeles. I said, 'This place is not working.'"[16] Having become disillusioned, Berry returned to his old stomping grounds at Sparta Music, where he was promoted to a directorship.

No one was really surprised—least of all Mal—when Neil was eventually appointed managing director of Apple Corps. Outside of Mal's concern over his diminishing role at the new company, nobody really seemed to care about their title. As Derek later recalled, "Whatever anyone outside chose to call his role" was relatively inconsequential, "for really none of us had any title then, except when we were negotiating to have one, because Sir Frank or Lord Kenneth, or whoever Apple were negotiating with, liked our side to have titles too." The title of artists relations officer was ultimately bestowed upon the roadie, whom Derek referred to, without animus, as "Mal, the grinning giant."[17] In stark contrast, Derek described Neil as having "a face like a death mask of Alexander the Great."[18]

Perhaps because of his studies in accountancy, or his longevity with the Beatles' inner circle, or even his shrewd hardheadedness, it made perfect sense for Neil to serve as managing director. Mal understood the internal logic, too, writing that Neil "is a go-ahead person, taking full advantage of any situation that arises, even to the point of the office that we [later] shared being known as his office."[19] When it came to comparing the two men's strengths and proclivities, Peter Asher saw Neil as canny, as "much more standoffish," the sort of fellow who "sat in his office and kind of ran things." Meanwhile, "Mal was very outgoing and laughing and friendly—he embraced people." In terms of their different personalities, Peter opined, "I imagine it was always like that," as far back as their early years together, if not earlier still. Neil "did the business stuff," but Mal "did everything else—*he was there.* If the Beatles went out of town, Mal went, too. He was everywhere."[20] Mal understood *that,* too. "I was arrogant in my own way about my relationship with the Fab Four," he later wrote, "feeling secure in our mutual friendship—quite used to standing in the wings, and helping to put the show on the road."[21]

That July, as Apple's administration grew beyond him, Mal took solace in his place in the Beatles' ecosystem. He may not have had a fancy title, but he had *them.* "All four of the lads have this nice manner which makes you feel good and [that] nothing is too much trouble," he wrote—charitably adding, "so has Ron Kass."

On July 5, Mal drove to 7 Cavendish Avenue to pick up Paul and John for a session at EMI Studios, where the boys were set to resume work on the ska-infused "Ob-La-Di, Ob-La-Da." Paul greeted the roadie saying, "We've been talking and decided that you're the straightest guy in the organization." Later that night, as the session got under way, Mal transcribed Paul's words for posterity, adding that "I'm writing it down because it pleased me so much."[22] He couldn't possibly have missed the irony that, to John and Paul's way of thinking, *he* was somehow the straightest of the lot. They very likely had no idea that the carefully nurtured compartments of his life were threatening to overflow, one into the other, with perilous consequences in nearly every direction.

With Neil taking on greater responsibility as managing director of Apple, Mal's duties as Beatles roadie–cum–equipment manager–cum–personal assistant seemingly doubled overnight, and it quickly became apparent that he needed an assistant of his own. One arrived in the form of Kevin Harrington. With his telltale shock of red hair, Kevin had begun working at NEMS as an errand boy at age sixteen. He first met Mal and Neil prior to the Beatles' third and final American tour, in August 1966, when the two Beatles insiders arrived at the NEMS offices to pick up some travel visas.

"They walked in with an air of confidence," Kevin recalled. "Mal and Neil were inseparable. For them, it was never about working for the Beatles—it was a vocation. They lived and breathed the Beatles." Not long afterward, Kevin was sent on an errand to Montagu Mews West. When he showed up, Mal and Neil invited him inside, where he observed the two men rolling hundreds of joints and painstakingly loading them into empty cigarette cartons, which they would encase in cellophane, for the band's upcoming tour. "I must admit," said Kevin, "I thought that was pretty nice. Those guys were cool."[23]

By the summer of 1968, Harrington was working out of Apple's Wigmore Street offices. One evening, Mal telephoned him and asked the errand boy to drop off salad and sandwiches for the boys at EMI Studios. Kevin didn't know it at the time, but he was already auditioning to be Mal's assistant. The next day, Mal invited him to visit the studio during a Beatles session. Kevin would never forget the image of Mal pulling up in his Humber Super Snipe—"a real old beast of an estate car." When they arrived at EMI, Mal provided the younger man with a breezy tour of the studio, making sure to stop by the basement canteen. By the time they reached Studio 2, Harrington recalled that "my legs were shaking. I was really worried because it was a no-go area." During his NEMS days, he was reminded, time and time again, that "nobody gets into the studio." For Kevin, it was "a mystical place. And so, when we walked in, I couldn't believe it. I just said, 'Whoa,' and my knees were knocking out of sheer nerves."[24]

The next day, Mal met Kevin at Wigmore Street. "Want to come and work with me in the studio with the boys, with the equipment?" he asked Harrington. "I'll show you what to do." With Kevin joining the inner circle, Mal took him on a tour of the instrument shops, such as Sound City on Shaftesbury Avenue, where they could replenish the boys' supplies of strings, drumsticks, and plectrums. A few days later, Mal hazed the new recruit, sending him off to Sound City to round up an "electric plectrum" for George's acoustic guitar. Fortunately, the salespeople at Sound City were in on the joke, even going so far as to send Kevin to another instrument shop in search of the nonexistent item.[25]

Not surprisingly, Mal taught Kevin about serving *all* the Beatles' studio needs, including the finer points of separating the leaves from the seeds when rolling a proper joint. Later that summer, Kevin earned his driver's license and drove Mal's Humber estate car on an errand to score some pot. "Mal introduced me to my first drug dealer," the young assistant later recalled, "a lovely Caribbean man who lived in Notting Hill. I used to buy an ounce a week for £11, and was told by Mal to put it down on expenses as 'sweets.'" On two separate occasions, Apple's Wigmore Street bookkeeper questioned Kevin about the amount he was spending on sweets—that is, until Harrington told Mal about the hassle he was getting from the accounting department. The next time Kevin turned in his receipts for sweets, the bookkeeper merely smiled.[26]

By this point, Apple's Wigmore Street offices simply wouldn't do. An internal memo of July 10 updated staff about the new terms of the building's lease, which strictly prohibited playing music from tape recorders and record players and even musical instruments at any time on the premises. "If there are any complaints from our superior landlords who are above us," the memo stated, "or our landlords who are below us, we can be sued for breach of our lease."[27] For a firm like Apple Corps, such stipulations were untenable.

Alistair Taylor later recalled that when the boys and Apple leadership began looking for solutions, they considered some fairly outlandish concepts. "The original idea that was put to me was that they would buy an estate and we'd all live on it," said Alistair. "There'd be a big dome in the middle, which would be Apple, and then there'd be four corridors leading to four large houses, one for John, one for Paul, one for George, and one for Ringo. And around the estate, there would be other houses, sort of gardener's domes, and we'd live in there. One way and another, a good time would be had by all. Well, the reality was that they did not try and buy an estate because, land being what it is, the nearest place we could get was Norwich, and nobody could see us running a record company out of Norwich, crazy though we were."[28]

In the end, they settled on a compromise, purchasing a five-story building at 3 Savile Row, in London's garment district, for the princely sum of £500,000. While some staff would remain at Wigmore Street until the lease expired, Savile Row swiftly assumed its place as Apple's headquarters. Even so, the Beatles and their staff's penchant for playing music—even going so far as to perform it on occasion—rankled the folks in stately Mayfair. "We had some very snobby neighbors in Savile Row, and the boys used to love to wind them up," Alistair wrote. "Whenever we had a new piece of music to listen to, which was pretty often given our business, they always made sure the windows were wide open and the volume was turned right up. We would get telephone calls from our frightfully upper-crust neighbors demanding, 'I say, could you turn that awful racket down,' and the Beatles would roar with laughter."[29]

On July 17, Mal and the boys made the familiar trek to the London Pavilion for the premiere of *Yellow Submarine*. After treating the feature

Mal, Paul, John, and Lily at the *Yellow Submarine* premiere

cartoon as a secondary consideration for much of its production, the Beatles were delighted by the outcome, right down to their spirited cameo at the end. For Lily, it marked one of the rare occasions when she was able to participate in her husband's life among the glitterati. The future stars of Apple were there—James Taylor and Mary Hopkin—along with the Rolling Stones' Keith Richards and members of the Bee Gees, Cream, and Grapefruit. Ringo and Mo were there, as were George and Pattie. Paul conspicuously went stag, while John was in attendance with Yoko, having unceremoniously replaced Cynthia, in his life and in his bed, with the conceptual artist. In terms of their personal lives, the ground beneath the Beatles' feet was shifting.

The simple act of getting to the cinema that evening had been a trial for Mal and Lily. The weekend prior to the gala premiere had witnessed a marital struggle, with husband attributing the malaise to his exhaustion, on the one hand, and, in a chauvinistic gesture, to his wife's menses, on the other.[30] Mal's seemingly indefatigable efforts to please the boys had become—not surprisingly, in retrospect—more complicated in their post-touring days, requiring him to be constantly behind the wheel, shuttling among their manses, or putting in increasingly longer hours in the studio.

As the couple rushed out of the house to meet the Beatles in time to tread the red carpet for *Yellow Submarine*, Lily was injured carrying two-year-old Julie down the stairs. Determined to go play with her older brother, the toddler had leapt out of her mother's arms, rewarding Lily with a nasty bump on the nose.[31]

The trip into London may have been harrowing—and paparazzi photos captured Lily's throbbing red proboscis for posterity—but an anxious night out was the least of her family's problems. By now, despite living in the same city as Mal, Lily knew that she and the children would always come second. "And it was very hurtful," she later said. Mal would ditch the family for even the slightest hint of Beatle business, and "I would cover up for him, saying, 'Daddy has to be away for work.' One day, we were all ready for a family outing to the zoo," she recalled, "when George rang to ask Mal for a guitar string. Instead of insisting on taking his kids out, he drove off to see George. I couldn't bear to see the disappointment on [the children's] faces."[32]

Still, Lil had to admit she enjoyed the perks, however rare, that came with living in the Beatles' orbit. "I had my share of the high life," she acknowledged. That summer, she and Mal were invited to a private screening of *Rosemary's Baby*, courtesy of Mia Farrow, who held the roadie in great esteem after their time together in Rishikesh. Mal recalled that "Lil and I arrived several minutes after it started, due to heavy traffic. Standing in the darkened viewing theatre, and seeing two empty seats, we climbed across people's toes, and filled them." Soon, Lil began nudging her husband. "Look who I'm sitting next to," she whispered. "We could hardly contain ourselves with excitement at sitting next to Robert Mitchum," said Mal. They came to realize that the actor had secreted a stash of whiskey glasses beneath his seat for the occasion. At one point, Lily recalled, Mitchum "mistook my foot for a glass and said, 'sorry, ma'am.'" When the lights went up after the show, Lily, proving she could be nearly as starstruck as her husband, became excited to see that Yul Brynner and Clint Eastwood had been sitting in front of her during the screening.[33]

As always, Mal attempted to make up for his shortcomings at home. And it was Gary, more often than not, who stood by his side, ready for

Gary posing with Martha and the band at Cavendish Avenue during the Mad Day Out

anything despite spending years coming in second to the Beatles. Take July 20, for example, when father and son drove into the city to the West End's Odeon cinema to see the hottest movie in town. "Big event of today was Gary and myself going to see *2001: A Space Odyssey*," Mal wrote in his diary. "Trick photography and color really lovely, storyline rather weak, and the end—forget it. Very colorful, but nothing. Gary thought it a great film but did not understand the ending."

On July 28, Mal had something even grander in store for his son. That Sunday, he squired Gary around London during one of the most unforgettable days in Beatles history—the photo session that has come to be known as the Mad Day Out. It was a magical day for Gary, who relished the opportunity to observe his dad at work with the world's most famous foursome. A quintet of photographers was on hand—Stephen Goldblatt, Tom Murray, Ronald Fitzgibbon, Don McCullin, and Tony Bramwell—along with Mal, who was working the beat for *The Beatles Book*. Naturally, Yoko was there, too, along with twenty-four-year-old American newcomer Francie Schwartz, Paul's new girlfriend; his solo appearance at the *Yellow Submarine* premiere had been no accident—things were over, once and for all, with Jane Asher. Mal had made Francie's acquaintance under traumatic circumstances, having been summoned to 7 Cavendish Avenue in the middle of the night after the fans who kept vigil outside Paul's house dognapped Eddie, McCartney's Yorkshire terrier. "Mal had to go to the police station to get him back," Francie recalled. "The girls insisted they wouldn't release the dog unless Paul came. I talked to them on the phone, and somehow they returned the poor thing. Paul was less upset than I was."[34]

The Mad Day Out photo session comprised seven different locations across Greater London. After alighting at Thomson House, on Gray's Inn Road, home to the *Times*, the group shifted to the Mercury Theatre, in Notting Hill, where the boys posed with a parrot and, later, behind a large sign reading "International Theatre Club." With a little encouragement, Gary stepped into the frame, standing in front of the imposing sign. At one point, as the photographers and the Beatles prepared for another shot, Gary played in a vacant lot, inexplicably pushing a sizable piece of lumber around while Mal busily snapped photos of him. The session continued at Highgate Cemetery, North London, as well as Old Street, where the boys climbed atop a concrete island at the center of a bustling roundabout. At St. Pancras Old Church and St. Pancras Gardens, they posed with Gary around a park bench, later stopping for photos in front of the church's arched doorway.

At this point, Don McCullin, one of the photographers, suggested that the Beatles and Yoko pose among the crowd of onlookers who had gathered behind a nearby railing. The assemblage featured several children, including one particularly cheeky boy who stood front and center with nary a care in the world. But Gary wasn't having it, refusing to join the tableau; he was part of the Beatles' entourage, after all—not some nameless bystander.

Moving on to East London, the Beatles were photographed in and around the Wapping Pier Head building. There, John, donning a camo jacket, played dead as the others solemnly collected around him.

At sunset, they concluded the Mad Day Out back at Cavendish Avenue, where Paul posed with Martha inside the geodesic meditation dome gracing his backyard. They were later joined by the others, including Gary, who vividly recalled the experience of sitting for a photo with the Beatles and the giant, floppy Martha. As he contemplated how to situate his body, he remembered intentionally looking away from the camera that day, having noticed that John and Paul were nonchalantly, even dreamily staring into space. Gary achieved a similar effect when he caught sight of a stone Buddha inside the dome's perimeter. "I'll just look at that for a few seconds," he thought to himself.[35]

The next day, Monday, July 29, Mal joined the Beatles in Studio 2 for rehearsals and early takes of Paul's new composition, "Hey Jude." The comforting song had found its roots in McCartney's recent visit with John's five-year-old son, Julian, a casualty of his parents' impending divorce. Expectations were high for the song to be the first Beatles single since "Lady Madonna," released back in March. For Mal and Kevin, "Hey Jude" marked another long night in the studio, with the boys not wrapping things up until around four o'clock the next morning. In his diary, Mal wrote, "Strange night indeed. Lil phoned in the start of it. Didn't phone back." It was a cryptic remark, to be sure. But the next line in his diary was anything but subtle: "Arwen had baby boy on Saturday evening [July 27], 6 lbs., 13 oz."[36]

Listed as "Malcolm" on his birth certificate, the infant had been delivered at Charing Cross Hospital. His mother's profession was listed as "secretary," her residence as "11 Narcissus Road," two miles away from EMI Studios in Northwest London. The birth certificate didn't name a father for baby Malcolm. At some point later that summer, Mal would visit mother and child, gifting the boy with an oversize teddy bear from Harrods.[37]

26

TO RULE IS TO SERVE

By August 1, Mal and the Beatles were in the final stages of recording "Hey Jude" at Trident Studios, where George Martin and the boys had access to an eight-track desk, as opposed to the four-track machines at EMI. "Towards the end of the evening we decided to make double use of the 40 musicians by asking them if they'd like to do a bit of singing and clap their hands," Mal wrote in *The Beatles Book*. "They were quite pleased to oblige, and the entire orchestra stood up, clapped, and sang their 'la-la-la' bits under Paul's close supervision!"[1] Privately, he felt that Paul "sometimes came on a bit heavy in the studio, perching on a high stool, working [the Beatles] hard when he wasn't upstairs on the intercom."[2] As for "Hey Jude" and the forty-piece orchestra, not everyone, it seemed, was happy to share their voices on the chorus. One of the musicians reportedly left, complaining that "I'm not going to clap my hands and sing Paul McCartney's bloody song!"[3]

Meanwhile, Ken Mansfield finally earned his trip to London, joining Mal, Neil, Ron Kass, and other members of Apple's leadership team for strategy sessions at the Royal Lancaster hotel. The boys were there, too, Mansfield recalled, "so this was a pretty important meeting. There was nothing frivolous about it all—very serious business." They were mapping out the future of Apple Corps, including the upcoming bravura release, on August 30, of "Our First Four," a special collection comprising the inaugural singles for the Apple Records label: the Beatles' double A-sided "Hey Jude" backed with "Revolution," Mary Hopkin's "Those Were the Days," Jackie Lomax's "Sour Milk Sea," and the Black Dyke Mills Band's "Thingumybob."

During a break in the proceedings, Mal and Neil led Mansfield into an adjoining room. The idea, it seemed, was to have a quick smoke, but the menu didn't include Mal's Senior Service cigarettes. Once alone with him, they presented the new recruit with a hashish-laced joint before taking a few tokes themselves. "Now this was something I wasn't used to doing," Mansfield recalled, "and those two got me pretty stoned." When the break ended, Mansfield returned to the Apple meeting wafting on the fumes of Mal and Neil's joint. "Unfortunately," said Mansfield, "that's when John started showing me these pictures—nude pictures of him and Yoko. So, my head was just spinning." And that's when Mansfield learned, courtesy of Paul, that the whole business—the weed, the naked pictures—was part of an elaborate initiation. "I think Mal and Neil got a big kick out of that," said Mansfield, "especially because I didn't really do drugs."[4] He later learned that the photo he had been holding would become the notorious cover shot for the upcoming release of John and Yoko's *Unfinished Music No. 1: Two Virgins.*

On August 9, the Iveys finally made it into the studio to record their debut single, albeit without Denny Cordell in the producer's chair. After trying his hand at a few Iveys sessions, he had turned the band over to Tony Visconti, a twenty-four-year-old American transplant serving as Cordell's apprentice. As Mal looked on, the Iveys made short work of "Maybe Tomorrow," an emotional ballad composed by guitarist Tom Evans. Visconti later recalled that "they gave me what they'd worked out, and I wanted to put orchestra on top of it. I wrote the parts, played them on the piano, and asked if they liked it. I think they were so much in awe they were going to get violins, they basically just said, 'Great. Go ahead as it is.'" The band felt especially buoyed after Paul listened to one of the playbacks, saying, "I think you've got a hit there."[5]

Later, after they mixed "Maybe Tomorrow" for the song's commercial release, Mal took the Iveys, Visconti, and Bill Collins out for dinner and drinks at the Bag to celebrate.[6] Excited at the prospect of transforming the Iveys into reliable international hitmakers, Mal began plotting the course of their career and, to their delight, contemplating the production of their first album. Meanwhile, he introduced them to Swinging London and squired them to Beatles sessions, where they could observe their idols at work. He even turned them on to LSD. "Mal gave us our first acid," said drummer

Mike Gibbins. "He called it Strawberry Fields Forever." Tom Evans was especially smitten with the experience. "I know where I'm going now," he said. "Acid taught me that."[7]

With the Beatles' double album entering its latter stages of production, George invited the Evans clan to join his family on a four-day cruise in the Aegean Sea. The party set sail on the MV *Arvi*, the same luxury yacht they had chartered during their 1967 search for an island commune. With Twiggy and Justin de Villeneuve in tow, the *Arvi* sailed around the island of Corfu. During the cruise, Twiggy, George, and the Beatle's mother, Louise, took turns reading Rupert Bear tales aloud to Gary and Julie.[8] As they sailed around the Aegean, the group supped on sumptuous meals of barbecue-roasted lamb, while watching George and Mal gleefully swing out on tree ropes and drop into the ocean waters below. As for the children, Mal recalled, "we just put life-jackets on the kids and threw them into the sea. They couldn't swim, but they had a marvelous time."[9] In addition to playing cards, sunbathing, and water-skiing, members of the party took sightseeing trips to the islands of Hydra and Paxos, where they visited the port city of Gaios. At one point, Mal snapped a photo of George, Pattie, and the children posing around a statue of Georgios Anemogiannis, the Greek revolutionary hero who, in 1821, sacrificed his life to the cause of Greek independence. But the cruise wasn't all fun and games. Gary recalled his parents' icy relationship at the time, their frequent rows, and his father's strange disappearances for hours on end.[10]

On August 21, Mal and George made the return flight from Athens to London, still reveling in the warmth of their Aegean sojourn, although George was feeling a touch fluish. That evening, they returned to EMI Studios, where John was putting the finishing touches on "Sexy Sadie," his acidic paean to the Maharishi. That same night, Paul sat at the studio piano and regaled Mal with a snippet from "Let It Be," the dream song that he had begun composing back in Rishikesh. Paul had previously sung the tune's rudimentary lyrics to him while they were sitting in the car outside 7 Cavendish Avenue, but this was different. For the roadie, it was thrilling to hear the then lines "When I find myself in times of trouble, Mother Malcolm comes to me, / Whispers words of wisdom, let it be."[11]

If Mal and George felt refreshed after their recent vacation, it wouldn't last. The next day, August 22, all hell broke loose. Prior to the recording session, Ringo abruptly quit the band. Mal observed the incident as it unfolded in real time, writing in his diary that "Ringo has gone off drums."[12] George Martin's business partner and longtime colleague Ron Richards had seen it coming, later recalling that "Ringo was always sitting in the reception area waiting, just sitting there or reading a newspaper. He used to sit there for hours waiting for the others to turn up. One night he couldn't stand it any longer, got fed up, and left."[13]

When they heard what had transpired, the remaining Beatles attempted to carry on with the recording session. Paul unveiled a new rocker that had found its genesis in Rishikesh, called "Back in the U.S.S.R.," a Cold War parody of the Beach Boys' "California Girls" and Chuck Berry's "Back in the U.S.A." As the song evolved in Studio 2, John, Paul, and George each took a turn behind Ringo's drum kit. As the Ringo-less band attempted to plot its way forward, everyone agreed to keep the situation "hush-hush," according to producer George Martin, who had observed the group's increasingly corrosive internal politics all summer.[14]

As Mal and Kevin would shortly learn, the EMI Studios rumor mill leaked like a sieve. A few nights later, they were sitting in the studio's reception area, having a smoke, when a strange man, drunk and apparently a drummer, lumbered into the building. "I've come to play with the Beatles," he announced, having heard that Ringo had quit the group. Mal stood up and approached the much smaller man, telling him that "Ringo hasn't left the Beatles. He's just on holiday." Mal began chatting up the fellow, every few moments taking a step toward the exit, with the man following his lead. "It was a slow progression," Kevin recalled, but within some twenty minutes, Mal had succeeded in gingerly removing Ringo's would-be replacement from the premises, walking him straight out of the studio carpark, and even pausing to share a smoke with him from the roadie's handy pack of Senior Service ciggies.[15]

"It was absolutely amazing," Harrington recalled. When Mal returned to the reception area, Kevin couldn't help but ask him, "Why didn't you just pick him up and send him out?" If it had been Neil instead of Mal, the assistant reasoned, Aspinall probably would have said, "Fuck off and get out," lacking the patience for such a long, drawn-out exercise.

As he considered Kevin's question, Mal shook his head slightly, saying, "If I had done that, then the bloke would have gone back and told his mates, 'What a bunch of bastards those guys are.' Instead, he walked away, really happy, thinking what a nice bunch of people we are. What we do reflects on the band. *It's about the band.*" For Kevin, the episode made for "an amazing sight, just to sit there and watch Mal doing his thing." But more important, he added, "It was a really good lesson."[16]

Fortunately, Ringo's hiatus from the group proved short-lived. On August 27, he made his return to EMI Studios, where Mal had adorned his drum kit with a cascade of flowers to welcome him. That night, George Harrison was producing a session for Jackie Lomax, who was recording "You've Got Me Thinking," backed by an all-star lineup that featured Eric Clapton on guitar, Klaus Voormann on bass, and Ringo behind the drums.

That same month, Neil married twenty-four-year-old Suzy Ornstein in a hastily organized ceremony at the Chelsea Registry Office. The daughter of George "Bud" Ornstein, the late chief executive of United Artists, Suzy had first met Neil during the production of *A Hard Day's Night* and *Help!*, and the two later became reacquainted after a chance meeting at a party in 1967. After the couple shared their nuptials, with Magic Alex serving as best man, Peter Brown threw an impromptu party that evening at a King's Road restaurant, with Paul, Ringo and Mo, and Mal there to celebrate the glad tidings.[17] The Beatles wouldn't allow Neil's marriage nor his recent ascendance at Apple to go unremarked. Later that year, Brown arranged for the boys to buy the newlyweds a posh flat in Knightsbridge.[18]

With Ringo back in the fold, the Beatles returned to Twickenham Film Studios on September 4 to shoot promotional films for "Hey Jude" and "Revolution." Directed by Michael Lindsay-Hogg, the promos were slated for broadcast on David Frost's popular British talk show, *Frost on Sunday*, and on the American variety show *The Smothers Brothers Comedy Hour*. Save for the vocals, the Beatles mimed their performances in front of Lindsay-Hogg's cameras. After capturing "Revolution" on tape earlier in the day, the group performed "Hey Jude" that evening in front of a live studio audience that had been helpfully rounded up by Mal and Kevin. Having canvassed potential guests outside EMI Studios, the two had tried to ensure a wide cross-section of ages, ethnicities, and professions. In order to increase the number of attendees, Mal had recruited twenty students to pass out leaflets around the city.

Each prospective audience member was provided with a typewritten, cryptically worded invitation asking them to "take part in a TV performance by the Beatles." Participants were also instructed to "confirm that you recognize that you will be part of a studio audience, do not object to being seen in the television program, and that you agree that you do not wish to be paid for your appearance in the program," although refreshments would be provided gratis. In order to avoid any unwanted guests, attendees were instructed to meet beforehand at the Grosvenor Hotel, where a motor coach would be waiting to take them to the studio.

In the end, Mal and Kevin managed to corral more than three hundred willing participants for the film shoot. Mal wasn't taking any chances with so many fans on-site, instructing Kevin to stand guard behind Ringo's drum kit in case anyone began trolling for souvenirs. After treating the fans to tea and sandwiches in Twickenham's commissary, Mal led the lucky attendees into the studio.

Standing directly in front of the makeshift stage that day, twenty-year-old American student Joel Soroka had procured his ticket while sitting on the upper level of a double-decker bus. Between takes, Soroka observed a tambourine resting beside Ringo's riser. And that's when he caught Ringo's eye, and the drummer gestured toward the tambourine, willing Soroka to have a go at the instrument. "I had a little bit of hashish earlier that night," Soroka admitted, so "I was a little high. Maybe that reduced any inhibitions I might have had."[19] Accepting Ringo's dare, Soroka picked up the tambourine and began banging it in time as "Hey Jude" transitioned into the famous coda that concludes the song. As if on cue, dozens of other attendees followed in his wake, congregating around the Beatles in the process.

That's when Mal hatched an idea. As Lindsay-Hogg and the Beatles set up for the next take, Mal announced to the audience, "When the chorus comes on, we want everybody to come towards the camera slowly. Don't rush. Surround the stage and sing the chorus. It's a party. You're having a good time, look happy."[20] And that's exactly what they did. Following Soroka's lead, the assembled fans good-naturedly congregated onstage, mingling among the bandmates for a spirited sing-along during the song's coda. Quite suddenly, Lindsay-Hogg had his dream take for "Hey Jude." "My plan was to start on a close-up of Paul and then slowly introduce the other band members," the director recalled. "Then we got to the beginning of the chorus and the next shot, a wide one, was filled with people."[21] It was pure magic.

Mal felt buoyed by his efforts at Twickenham. Working with Lindsay-Hogg and Kevin, he had brought off the arrangements for the film shoot without a hitch. And though he was enormously busy, he had succeeded in leading the Iveys to their first milestone, the release of "Maybe Tomorrow," slated for mid-November, as Apple's fifth single. He may not have been managing director, but he was confident he was making a contribution to the larger cause of Apple Corps, which was more important to him than titles, anyway. Mal's emotions soared even higher a few days after the film shoot, when Paul took him aside and proclaimed that "without you, I'm a mole on a mountain."[22] For the roadie, it simply couldn't get any better.

By this juncture, the boys were nearing the finish line with the double album they had begun back in May. To be entitled *The Beatles* and featuring a stark white cover design in contrast with *Sgt. Pepper*'s festival of psychedelic colors, the LP, within days of its November release, would become known the world over as *The White Album*.

As usual, Mal enjoyed plenty of opportunities to perform on the album. He provided handclaps on "Birthday" while Pattie and Yoko sang backing vocals. For "Dear Prudence," recorded during Ringo's hiatus, Mal sang harmonies along with Jackie Lomax and Paul's cousin John. For "What's the New Mary Jane," which didn't make the album's final cut, he played a handbell and provided various other bits of percussion.

But Mal's most raucous performance by far was on "Helter Skelter," which, in the roadie's words, Paul had performed "in his screaming rock voice."[23] For the song's cacophonous backing track, Mal chipped in with a trumpet part while John played, of all things, the saxophone. Neither man had the first clue about how to play their respective instrument, of course, but that aspect only heightened the song's inherent madness. At the end of one particularly rowdy take, Ringo hurled his drumsticks across the studio, shouting, "I've got blisters on my fingers!"

"They were completely out of their heads that night," recalled engineer

Brian Gibson. "But as usual a blind eye was turned to what the Beatles did in the studio. Everyone knew what substances they were taking, but they were really a law unto themselves in the studio. As long as they didn't do anything too outrageous, things werc tolerated."[24]

As John, Paul, and George Martin prepared to conduct the final mixing and sequencing sessions for *The White Album*, Mal joined George and Pattie Harrison for an extended American jaunt to work on Jackie Lomax's debut LP. For Harrison, the American visit meant several concentrated days in a Los Angeles studio, where he hoped to complete Jackie's album. When Mal left Lily and the children back in Sunbury, he figured he would be away for a fortnight, possibly three weeks at most. Ultimately, the trip took more than seven weeks—in the process, pushing Mal, and particularly Lil, to an emotional brink.

The stakes were much higher for Jackie Lomax, whose debut single, "Sour Milk Sea," had stalled despite solid reviews in the music trade papers. In contrast with the Beatles' "Hey Jude" and Hopkin's "Those Were the Days," both of which were chart-toppers or near toppers, "Sour Milk Sea" had barely registered a dent in the British and American marketplaces. Mal's copy of Apple's cumulative U.K. record sales for the week of September 12 made a strong case in point: a fortnight after its release date, "Hey Jude" had sold 395,565 copies, and "Those Were the Days" had netted 127,125 copies; meanwhile, the Black Dyke Mills Band's decidedly unhip "Thingumybob" was outselling the comparatively au courant "Sour Milk Sea," moving 6,307 units to Jackie's 5,829. Hence, the trip was an important coming-out party for Jackie, with several U.S. press junkets scheduled, along with an appearance at the Music Operators of America's annual convention and trade show at Chicago's Sherman House. And Mal would be there every step of the way.

As Mal introduced Jackie to American media and industry players that October, he was joined by Ken Mansfield. "When we were working with Apple," Mansfield recalled, "we had fun at our jobs. Mal was this big old lovable guy. But when it came to Jackie's press tour, Mal told me that he would treat Jackie as if he were one of the Beatles, that [Lomax] would receive that level of treatment. In that situation, where anything could happen, Mal wasn't just somebody's gofer. He was steady as a rock, taking nothing for granted and being prepared for any eventuality." In one of Mansfield's favorite memories from his time with Mal and Jackie, the three men were lounging in a Cleveland club when the musician was on the verge of being accosted by a hostile fan. Lomax and Mansfield hadn't seen the man as he approached from across the club, but Mal clearly had. The two men were both surprised, therefore, when the roadie, without even breaking their line of conversation, suddenly stood up and put himself between the man and Jackie. "Mal just unfolded himself," Mansfield recalled, "using his size to make this guy think twice about his intentions. It was just incredible."[25]

But as it turned out, the trip wasn't all business. During a stopover in Cincinnati, Mal and Jackie attended a concert by Janis Joplin and Big Brother and the Holding Company. Mal was astonished when, halfway through her act, "Janis stopped the band, asked for all the house lights to be put out, and wheeled a television set to the middle of the stage. It was the Smothers Brothers' show, and the Beatles were featured playing their new record 'Revolution,' bringing a lump to my throat and really blowing my mind." When the Beatles' promo had concluded, the TV was wheeled offstage and the concert resumed. Later that night, Mal and Janis got drunk and watched television in her hotel room. With Jackie in tow, Mal also took in shows by the Statler Brothers, Sonny James, and a "larger-than-life Johnny Cash."[26]

When the press tour arrived in Indianapolis, Mal made a point of telephoning Georgeanna Lewis, now twenty. "My God, what happened to you?" he exclaimed over dinner. "You grew up. You're beautiful!" For her part, Georgeanna appreciated his kindness, while making sure he knew she had a steady boyfriend whom she intended to marry. As they walked to her car, "Mal started kissing me, and I didn't resist that much. It stirred some feelings, and he knew it." She reminded him, "You're still married. You have a family," adding, "You live in another world. You don't live in the world I live in. You probably do this all over the place. If it's not me, it's somebody in Texas or England or somewhere else." That's when Mal went for broke, suggesting that Georgeanna meet up with him later that week in New York City. And the next day, in spite of everything, she agreed.[27]

After a stopover in Philadelphia, Mal, Jackie, and Mansfield arrived in New York City on October 17 for a few more interviews and business meetings before they would make their rendezvous with George on the West Coast the following week. As promised, Georgeanna flew in from Indianapolis, spending the weekend with Mal at the Americana Hotel. He pulled out all the stops, taking her to see *Hair* on Broadway. She recalled "sitting dead center on the front row, with naked people flying above our heads." During the musical's raciest scenes, Mal squeezed her hand with all his might, having grown uncomfortable at subjecting the young woman to such tawdriness.[28]

When Mal was away in meetings with Jackie and Mansfield, Georgeanna enjoyed free rein with their limo, seeing the sights from the vantage point of a luxury automobile. At night, she and Mal shared a bed at the Americana. "Did I sleep with Mal? Yes, I did," said Georgeanna. "Did we consummate? No, we didn't. He was very loving and very passionate, but all I could think was 'How many mes are there all around this world?'" Feeling pangs of guilt, she pointedly asked the roadie about his wife.

"I don't have a marriage anymore," he told her. "We have an understanding. I haven't been around much, and it's been hard for her—for me. It's been hard on everyone." As she looked on, Mal grew ever more serious. "I didn't see this life coming to me," he told her. "I never thought I'd be anywhere but Liverpool all me life. It's been a good life, but it's also been hard. There's no regular life anymore—it's gone."

By the time they said their goodbyes at the airport, Mal was his usual jovial self, promising to stay in touch. For her part, Georgeanna felt that the roadie "was searching for something in life, and that it might have been in Indianapolis with this crazy girl who wanted to start a fan club for him."[29]

In California, with the press tour behind him, Mal allowed himself to release every restraint. Most nights, he attended Jackie's recording sessions with George at Sound Recorders. But when he wasn't in the studio, his life devolved into seemingly nonstop drunken debauchery and the consumption of junk food. He was sharing a house with George in Beverly Hills, where his diet consisted almost entirely of pizza. "The sessions tended to go on late, and, as the nearest available food was a pizza stand near Sound Recorders, every night was pizza night," he wrote. "To this day, I can't look a pizza in the face." At their rented home, Mal took to ogling the staff. "While we were staying at the house," he added, "I did what I reckoned to be one of my best deals. I traded a 40-year-old maid for two 20-year-olds, Gayleen and Mona being very decorative additions to the household."[30]

Mal and George spent considerable time in the company of Alan Pariser, one of the architects of the Monterey Pop Festival and the manager of Delaney and Bonnie and Friends, an R&B revue starring husband-and-wife duo Delaney and Bonnie Bramlett. Pariser squired Mal around Southern California, showing him the sights and introducing him to the region's growing rock 'n' roll culture. On November 10, Pariser provided Mal with one of the great highlights of his North American jaunt when he took him shooting on the Malibu beach at sunset. Mal was impressed with Pariser's arsenal, which included a replica 1892 Winchester rifle and an 1887 Colt .48 revolver. Steadying the Colt in his burly hands, Mal hit a tin can at a hundred yards. "Would you believe it?" he scrawled in his diary.[31]

As his time in the States wore on, Mal became increasingly anxious about telephoning his wife and family back in Sunbury. During that first month, he posted the occasional letter—that is, when he wasn't dining out with Frank Sinatra; going to parties in Laurel Canyon, where he and George met up with R&B stars Delaney and Bonnie; or observing, in a kind of awe, as George Harrison and Eric Clapton composed "Badge" in a bungalow at the Beverly Hills Hotel. On October 17, Mal finally managed to put pen to paper, writing that "every night I lie here and want you to be with me. I miss you so much it hurts, and my eyes fill with tears as I think of you and Julie and Gary. I love you all, with my all, and feel I never want to be separated from you again."[32]

But in the very next breath, Mal wrote that he and George would be remaining Stateside for at least another month, to spend the Thanksgiving holidays with Bob Dylan and his family in Woodstock, New York. As the days rolled by, he still couldn't muster the courage to call Lily, perhaps fearing her reprisal for his staying in the States for several more weeks. "Lil, why don't I ring you?" he wrote in his diary. "[I] keep making excuses to myself as to why I shouldn't. I think I'm frightened you will shout at me."[33] A week later, as November came to a close, Mal finally broke down and telephoned his wife. To his great despair, she told him that she could no longer take it, that she wanted a divorce. That night, he took to his diary.

"Lil, what are you doing? This trip has made me realize what you and the children mean to me."[34]

In Woodstock, when he wasn't gazing in amazement as Dylan and the Band jammed with George, Mal busied himself playing with Bob and Sara Dylan's children. He also found the time to write one more letter to Lily. "I'm going to try and be what you want me to be," he said. "Forgive me my bad ways, Lil, and I'm yours forever."[35]

Before leaving Woodstock, Mal made a point of telling Dylan that "George had always thought of him as a good friend." Dylan replied, "I think of George as a good friend," then added, to the roadie's utter glee, "I think of you, Mal, as a *really* good friend." When he considered his budding friendship with the folk singer, Mal concluded that, "obviously, children were our common denominator. I found throughout my life that to make any friend, you have to find this common denominator, whatever it may be, work, play, children, politics, sex, or collecting old socks. If you have something in common, it's the opening gambit to knowing each other."[36]

On November 30, Mal finally returned to Sunbury, where Lil seemed genuinely happy to have him back home. Any residual warmth he felt after learning that his wife no longer intended to divorce him was diminished, however, when he returned to Apple during the first week of December. For her part, Lily had long believed that the Beatles were jealous when it came to her husband's seemingly boundless supply of energy and goodwill on each of their behalves. Mal himself was acutely aware of the special relationship he shared with Paul, the Beatle with whom he was, to his mind, undoubtedly the closest, but he also understood Paul's psyche best, and recognized that his friend "seemed to have the attitude of a North of England mill owner." In one especially painful instance, Mal recalled Paul "turning to me and saying, 'you are my servant. You do as you are told.'"[37]

Mal felt shaken to the core. "'I've never been anybody's servant,'" he replied, "always feeling in my heart that I worked *with* the Beatles and never *for* them." In his anger and hurt, Mal sought out John's advice. "They also lead who serve," Lennon told the roadie, paraphrasing the famous line from John Milton's Sonnet 26 (1673), "They also serve who only stand and wait."[38] During the First and Second World Wars, generations of Britons had found solace in Milton's words as they awaited their loved ones' return from the horrors of some faraway military front. Flush with John's guidance, Mal took to his diary, transforming the Beatle's words of wisdom into a poem:

Don't take my weakness
Give me your strength
Don't give me your weakness
Take my strength

To rule is to serve
To lead is to follow
I'll serve and follow you
And take you to love.[39]

For Mal, John's good counsel made all the difference, calming him after what he felt to be a personal affront.

As 1968 came to an end—a year in which he had tried in vain to remake himself as a record executive—Mal was fortunate to still be in residence at 135 Staines Road East, all things considered. Lily's mistrust of her husband had reached a fever pitch. By this point, she wasn't just finding "silly groupie letters" in his suitcase, but also the occasional stray pair of knickers and other telltale signs of infidelity.[40] She recognized that Mal was being seduced—and had been for some time—by overwhelming forces, impulses with which she could hardly begin to compete. "One minute he would be in Hollywood," she said. "The next day he'd be back here cleaning out the rabbit hutch."[41]

As for Apple Corps, the Iveys' "Maybe Tomorrow," the subject of so much anticipation at Apple for Mal and Ken Mansfield especially, had fallen well short of Mal's fondest expectations. Mansfield had ordered some four hundred thousand copies of the single for the American marketplace, while working overtime to generate airplay and reviews for the Welshmen. In the end, the American release notched a number sixty-seven showing, with more than three hundred thousand copies of the single going unsold. *The White Album*, meanwhile, had made its maiden U.K. chart appearance at number one on December 7 and was still lording over the charts with no end in sight. "Hey Jude" had not only extended the Roll, but had succeeded in

The Evans family at the Apple Christmas party

becoming the year's bestselling single by a wide margin. An office Christmas party was thrown to celebrate a productive year and usher in a new one.

Adorning the walls of Apple's new digs at 3 Savile Row were John Kelly's stunning portraits of John, Paul, George, and Ringo that accompanied the release of *The White Album*. Also there, posing below Kelly's photographs as the Christmas party rolled on, were Mal, Lil, Gary, and Julie, with smiles that seemed to go on forever.

Mal with Ken Mansfield

27

SEE YOU 'ROUND THE CLUBS

By the dawn of 1969, Mal had grown lumpy and unkempt—a far cry from his days on the road, when lugging amps and wrangling fans kept him fit and trim despite his voracious appetites. With the Iveys' "Maybe Tomorrow" struggling on the charts, Mal was eager to return to the studio to record new material, possibly even an LP. But so were the Beatles, who, buoyed by their interaction with Mal and Kevin's studio audience, had fashioned a system by which they would film their rehearsals in advance of making their triumphant return to the stage. The *Get Back* project, as it came to be known, was under way.

On January 2, Mal and Kevin delivered the Beatles' instruments, amps, and attendant gear to Twickenham's cavernous number-two soundstage. When they arrived in the Apple van, mobile recording equipment was already in place, courtesy of EMI, and Lindsay-Hogg's film crew, led by Tony Richmond, was raring to go. To provide his documentary's audience with a bird's-eye view of the Beatles' preparation, Lindsay-Hogg supplemented his two-camera team with a pair of Nagra tape recorders, which had been strategically placed, audio vérité style, around the studio to capture the group's interactions as the live performance unfolded.

As a nod to cinema realism, Lindsay-Hogg's opening shot depicts Mal and Kevin as they unload the Beatles' equipment onto the bare stage, pointedly focusing on the image of Ringo's former bass drumhead, complete with the descended-*T* logo of days gone by. As it turned out, Paul was ninety minutes late that day, having forgone a lift with Mal in favor of public transportation. As Mal explained, "At half eight that morning, between bites of breakfast, I'd telephoned round all four fellows to remind them it was getting up time and they were due at Twickenham by eleven. On that first day Paul was last to arrive—half an hour after noon!—having come by underground, then local train, then taxi from Hampton Court station. He'd meant to do the entire journey by public transport but, knowing he was late, he chickened out and caught a cab rather than wait at the bus stop!"[1]

Determined to make a splash with their new concept, the Beatles and their circle engaged in hours of discussion about *where* to stage such a momentous event. "There had been a lot of suggestions as to where the show should be filmed," Mal wrote, "but two characteristics were needed for the location. One was to be acoustically sound, the other important factor, of course, being appealing to the eye. At one point it was suggested that we do the show in Africa, where we could find some sunshine. And I very nearly got to fly out with producer, Denis O'Dell, to view an old Roman theatre on the shores of Tripoli, but that fell through."[2]

At Twickenham, Mal attempted to settle into his standard studio routine, maintaining the equipment, prepping tea and toast for the group, and being a general source of goodwill. When he wasn't meeting the boys' culinary needs or transcribing their lyrics in real time, he was chipping in with an instrument—sometimes of a most peculiar vintage. On January 3, Paul discussed the potential instrumentation for "Maxwell's Silver Hammer," a new number that had its origins in one of the Maharishi's lectures at the ashram. "Originally, I was trying to get a hammer, which we might get Mal to do," said Paul. "A hammer, like on an anvil. A big hammer on an anvil—you can't make it with anything else. Bang, bang!" Four days later, as the Beatles were rehearsing the song, Paul suddenly announced, "Mal, we should get a hammer," before adding, almost as an afterthought, "and an anvil."[3] For a moment, Mal seemed perplexed by the unusual request. Not bothering to ask any questions, though, he simply shrugged and went about the business of fulfilling Paul's wishes during their upcoming break. By the time the boys returned from lunch, Mal had rounded up an anvil from a West End outfit that specialized in theatrical props. With the anvil in place, he soon learned that Paul expected him to bang the rented hunk of steel during the chorus of "Maxwell's Silver Hammer."

The next day, Mal and the Beatles continued rehearsing the song. Between iterations, Mal transcribed the number's evolving lyrics onto Apple

Corps letterhead. At the same time, he jotted down performance notes to guide his efforts on the anvil. At this point, "Maxwell's Silver Hammer" included a prominent section featuring John whistling, an aspect in keeping with the tune's dance hall origins. Later in the session, George kindly requested another run-through of the song's ending for Mal's benefit, realizing that the roadie was having trouble keeping time during the song's relatively tricky coda.

That same day, as Paul prepared to lead a rehearsal of "Let It Be," John suggested that he modify the lyrics, which had originally referred to "Mother Malcolm." "Change it to Brother Friar Malcolm, and then we'll do it," said John. "Would be great. Brother Malcolm."[4]

With Mal as his amanuensis, Paul also took a pass at "The Long and Winding Road," an impassioned ballad he had unveiled a few days earlier at Twickenham. Mal admired the fledgling song, which he likened to *The Wizard of Oz*, especially the movie's central motif involving the Yellow Brick Road and finding one's way back home. After admitting that he hadn't seen the Hollywood classic, Paul sought Mal's advice about the lyrics. As the roadie transcribed the words, McCartney asked him to consider the placement of the phrases "don't leave me *standing* here" and "don't leave me *waiting* here." Moments later, Paul fell into an impromptu Elvis imitation, prompting Mal to remind the boys that January 8 had marked the King's thirty-fourth birthday. Hearing this news, John stood at attention and delivered a formal salute.

But the Beatles' spirit of creativity and camaraderie proved short-lived. During lunch on January 10, all hell would break loose when George abruptly quit the band. Mal was eating with Lindsay-Hogg in the canteen, just a flight of stairs up from the studio floor, when "George walked up to the table and said, 'I'm leaving. I'm going home.'" According to Lindsay-Hogg, Harrison then said, "See you 'round the clubs," and made a hasty exit. In his diary, Mal recorded the incident in his typically understated manner, writing that "George got in his car and drove away."[5]

During lunch, Harrison had apparently shared heated words with John out of Mal's earshot—and beyond the capabilities of Lindsay-Hogg's Nagra recorders—although the roadie pointedly saw things slightly differently. George wasn't merely going back to Esher. In his mind, he was leaving the band. "There were several factors involved in his decision," Mal later wrote. "One was that George wasn't particularly keen on the idea of making a television film, the other being personal differences with Paul—the latter being the most decisive. George felt that Paul was encroaching on his contribution to Beatle recording sessions. In the past, each Beatle had added his own tasteful coloring to the recorded picture, but of late, Paul wanted George to paint by number, several times picking up his own electric guitar and saying, 'Play it like this.' To me, it was a put down on George's ability as a guitar player—I personally considered him one of the best in the world. Of course, everybody has their own favorites, and technically, they may be better, but for me, George's playing always had a lot more feeling, a lot more soul."[6]

For Mal, any scenario in which the Beatles were not intact as a foursome was unacceptable. He admired George's discretion, writing that "the parting was done quietly and tactfully, but of course, to the press people who were hanging around the studios, it was a juicy bit of information which was played up out of all proportion."[7]

What surely rankled the roadie the most was John's behavior after George had left Twickenham. "I think that if George doesn't come back by Monday or Tuesday, we'll have to get Eric Clapton to play with us," said John. "The point is: if George leaves, do we want to carry on the Beatles? I do. We should just get other members and carry on."[8] As if to underscore the malaise that greeted George's absence, that day's session ended with a cacophony of improvised jamming, including a strained rendition of *The White Album*'s "Martha My Dear" during which Yoko provided a screeching solo, yelling John's name over and over. Meanwhile, Paul simply played on, seemingly unfazed by the chaos around him.

Despite the turmoil at Twickenham, Mal saw George in the flesh that evening. The occasion was an orchestral session for "King of Fuh," an irreverent novelty recording by twenty-eight-year-old American singer-songwriter Stephen Friedland, who recorded his work under the name Brute Force. The song had begun life as a poem, but by 1967, Friedland had built a melody around the lyrics, and in late 1968, he recorded a demo of the song at Olmstead Studios on Fifty-Fourth Street in Manhattan. Given the composition's controversial lyrics—which weave a melancholy tale about a mythical monarch, the "Fuh King"—Friedland knew implicitly that "King of Fuh" would be a tough sell for most record labels. By this time, of course, the Beatles had invited musicians the world over to share their music for consideration by Apple. Drawing upon a connection with Tom Dawes, cofounder of the Cyrkle, one of the opening acts on the Beatles' previous tour, Friedland managed to get his demo for "King of Fuh" into the hands of Nat Weiss. To Friedland's great fortune, Weiss played the demo for George, who decided that the tune was perfect for release by Apple.[9]

On the evening of January 10, with the other Beatles seemingly in his rearview mirror, George rendezvoused with Mal at Trident to oversee the session devoted to the "King of Fuh." On hand were eleven string players from the Royal Philharmonic. In his role as artists relations officer, Mal handled the postproduction communications with Friedland. A few weeks after the orchestral session, he penned a letter to the songwriter: "Dear Brute Force," he wrote. "I was at the session when we added the strings," and "when we finished we played the vocal track as well. It was terribly funny, for the whole orchestra fell about laughing and really enjoyed the whole thing."[10]

After an ill-fated group meeting at Ringo's new Brookfield estate on Sunday, January 12, the Beatles began contemplating a George-less future for the band. That Tuesday, as the band's prospects for moving forward continued to remain in doubt, John and Yoko sat down for an interview with Hugh Curry, a reporter with Canada's CBC-TV. Photographer Richard Keith Wolff, who was on hand for the midday interview at Twickenham, couldn't help noticing Mal's lingering presence that day. "You could sense that he was discreetly checking that John was all right." For Wolff and the members of Curry's crew, it shortly became apparent that John was high on heroin.

As the interview progressed, the Beatle grew pale and increasingly restless, eventually saying, "Excuse me, I feel a bit sick," which prompted Curry's team to stop recording. Not missing a beat, Mal swooped in to rescue his fallen comrade, who vomited off-camera.[11] Lennon and Ono had been experimenting with heroin since at least November 1968, when Yoko miscarried. "We were in real pain," Lennon later remarked, and their understandable misery in the wake of the loss of their baby, whom they had named John Ono Lennon II, had led to the couple's protracted heroin abuse. The overpowering drug habit left them debilitated for the balance of 1968 and the early months of 1969, if not longer. "The two of them were on heroin," said Paul, "and this was a fairly big shocker for us because we all thought we were far-out boys but we kind of understood that we'd never get quite that far out."[12]

Meanwhile, a collective sense of relief over the Beatles' future would shortly arrive in the form of a compromise struck on January 15: George would consent to return to the fold if the others agreed to abandon Twickenham and the idea of the bravura concert gimmick in some foreign locale. He suggested transforming their latest material into the germ of a new LP. For the others, it was a no-brainer, really. Ringo had no interest in going

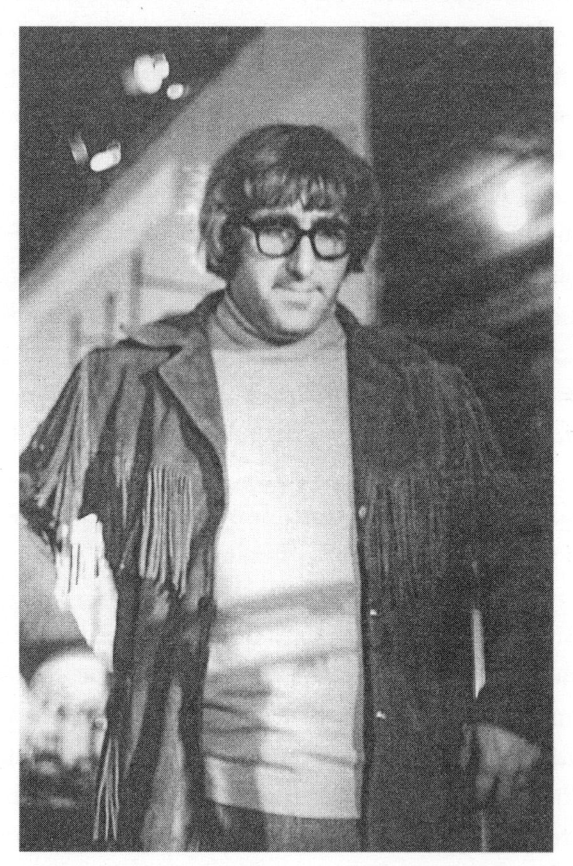

Mal coming to John's rescue during the Canadian TV interview

abroad—he was set to begin filming *The Magic Christian* with Peter Sellers at Twickenham in early February. Besides, if the Beatles knew how to do anything, it was to make an album. Lindsay-Hogg could simply refocus his film's subject to documenting the group's creative process. "Having gone through the whole phase of recording with 40-piece orchestras and added session musicians," Mal wrote, "the feeling in the air was that it would be nice to make a group album again."[13] *Get Back* might just be that record.

And things might have resumed the following week at the newly completed Apple Studios, located in the basement of 3 Savile Row, had it not been for Magic Alex. George held serious misgivings about the so-called electronics wizard, whom he later described as "the biggest disaster of all time. He was walking around with a white coat on like some sort of chemist but didn't have a clue about what he was doing."[14] Worse yet, Magic Alex had made bold promises about the innovative recording facility he had been cooking up in the Apple basement. He envisioned a multitrack studio befitting the Beatles, one that would be unrivaled the world over. With eight-track recording coming into vogue, Magic Alex vowed to provide the group with double that capacity, even if he didn't quite understand what that meant. "It was a 16-track system," said George, and Magic Alex "had 16 little tiny speakers all around the walls. The whole thing was a disaster and had to be ripped out."[15] With the Beatles now working with a self-imposed deadline of January 31 for completing the project, George Martin leapt into action, liaising with EMI to install portable equipment in Apple Studios to make the facility functional in the near term for Glyn Johns, the hotshot young soundman who had been handling production duties for the film shoot.

As an unexpected bonus, Billy Preston, now twenty-two, stopped by the studio at George's invitation. The keyboard player was in town playing with Ray Charles, and George sensed that Preston's presence might make a difference in the Beatles' attitude. To Mal's mind, the fact that the group had known Billy from their Hamburg days didn't hurt. "Straight away there was 100 percent improvement in the vibe in the room," said George. "Having this fifth person was just enough to cut the ice that we'd created among ourselves."[16] George's gambit paid dividends almost immediately. John, who had been especially apathetic that January, lobbied for Billy to become the fifth Beatle on a permanent basis, although Paul wasn't having it. "It's bad enough with four!" he countered.[17]

With Billy Preston in tow, the Beatles began rehearsing their new material in earnest. While George Martin had been sorting out Magic Alex's technical snafu, Mal and Kevin had transported the band's gear to the Savile Row basement, including Paul's Blüthner grand piano, which was tuned and ready for the next stage of the project. In a matter of days, a collection of songs began to materialize, including such numbers as "Get Back," "Two of Us," "I've Got a Feeling," and "Don't Let Me Down," with the group making progress on "Let It Be" and "The Long and Winding Road."

The sessions at Apple Studios were convivial in comparison to the Beatles' dour days back at Twickenham. In one memorable instance, the band's rehearsals were interrupted by the welcome appearance of Linda Eastman and her six-year-old daughter, Heather. Paul's relationship with Francie Schwartz had proven to be short-lived. Paul wasted little time rekindling his relationship with the American photographer. Not long afterward, Linda and Heather had moved to London, where they joined Paul in his Cavendish Avenue residence. During the session at Apple Studios, precocious Heather stole the show, even coaxing Mal into dancing with her as Lindsay-Hogg's cameras rolled. For the roadie, it was pure heaven. "Most mornings, the Beatles would limber up playing most any kind of song, and several interesting jam sessions were recorded," said Mal, who felt nostalgic for his early days with the band at the Cavern. "Playing all the old skiffle songs, Paul at one point saying, 'This is for you, Mal,' the band going into a string of early Elvis hits."[18]

Seeking a climax for the documentary, Lindsay-Hogg championed the idea of staging a concert on the roof of 3 Savile Row. To the director's mind, a climactic show on the roof offered the perfect "payoff" for the documentary. With Mal and Kevin in tow, Paul and the director scouted out the roof. In Mal's experience, the site would need to be reinforced in order to support the Beatles and their gear. With the concert slated for Wednesday, January 29, Mal hired a consulting engineer to assess the roof that Monday. He concluded that in its present state, it would support only five pounds per square inch. To ensure the players' safety, the engineer recommended using scaffolding to erect a more solid platform. They also reinforced the rooftop itself by hauling wooden planks up from the street via a series of pulleys.

Chris O'Dell recalled being unable to concentrate on her work in her top-floor office, where workmen were erecting steel poles to provide structural support from below.[19] Meanwhile, Mal was tasked with arranging for a helicopter to provide aerial shots of the concert, along with images of the expected crowd along the streetscape. "Who knows," Mal concluded, the "police might try to stop us."[20]

The original date for the Rooftop Concert was scrapped due to inclement weather, forcing Lindsay-Hogg and the Beatles to go with Thursday, January 30, as their makeup date. The show almost didn't come off. For one thing, George recoiled at the notion of performing around the "chimneys." For Mal and Kevin, the typically simple act of setting up the gear, while sometimes onerous, proved to be a herculean task when it came to the rooftop. In truth, Kevin recalled that "it was ridiculous—all of this up and down, up and down on the lift to haul the equipment up from the basement." The real trouble occurred when it came to transporting Paul's bass amp and Billy's keyboard up the narrow staircase just below the roofline. "There was no way I could get those pieces of gear around and over the bannisters that led to the entrance," said Kevin. "It would not happen."[21]

With time running out ahead of the show, Mal took matters into his own hands, disassembling the skylight atop the staircase to allow Kevin to cart the last bits of gear up to the roof and then hastily restoring the whole business in time for the concert. Even so, George continued to pooh-pooh the idea of performing upstairs in the wintry wind. "We planned to do it about 12:30 to get the lunchtime crowds," Lindsay-Hogg later recalled, but "they didn't agree to do it as a group until about twenty to one. Paul wanted to do it and George didn't. Ringo would go either way. Then John said, 'Oh fuck, let's do it,' and they went up and did it."[22] Given the frigid conditions, twenty-year-old EMI sound engineer Alan Parsons had purchased women's stockings from Marks and Spencer as DIY microphone coverings. As for the helicopter, "the law wouldn't allow us to fly over London," Mal wrote, "and it was too late to go out and borrow a balloon, another idea they came up with."[23]

Finally, there was the issue of where the audience would congregate,

Mal on the Savile Row rooftop with Metropolitan Police constables

beyond the expected bystanders five stories below. Mal placed a wooden bench against the chimney to accommodate special guests. With Yoko and Mo already planning to attend, he figured he could round up a few more lucky folks to enjoy a ringside seat at the Beatles' Rooftop Concert. Ken Mansfield would never forget looking up to see "Mal Evans looming over me," having come to invite him up onto the roof. "We had become close friends in a very short time, and he had that look on his face that said he was going to share something special with me. Mal was very childlike to those who knew him, and his invitation was akin to the way kids want to share something really cool with their pals."[24]

Wearing a white trench coat to stave off the cold, Mansfield took a seat beside Chris O'Dell, who had been invited upstairs by Tony Richmond on the pretext of her serving as his "assistant."[25] Not everyone was happy that day. Leslie Cavendish made an effort to win a place on the roof, but Mal wasn't budging. "Sorry Leslie, there's just a handful of people allowed on the roof," he said. "There's hardly any space, with all the equipment. But frankly, it's pretty cold and windy out there. You're better off inside anyway." Cavendish was surprised, having believed that he and the roadie were close.

"Mal could be a tough nut to crack," Leslie reasoned, wondering about his motives for selecting Mansfield instead.[26] Neil was absent that day, having been hospitalized for acute tonsillitis.

By the time the Beatles stepped out onto the roof, everything seemed to be in place. Only Ringo, it seemed, was miffed. "Mal, you nailed me down in the wrong place!" he exclaimed, referring to the positioning of his drum kit on the wooden platform. After a few hasty adjustments from Mal, Ringo was ready to roll, and the bandmates launched into their first, tentative rendition of "Get Back."

For anyone lucky enough to observe the proceedings as they unfolded atop 3 Savile Row, the group must have offered an incredible sight. In order to fight the cold, John had donned Yoko's fur coat, while Ringo wore his wife Maureen's red raincoat. Paul and George flanked John, their standard formation from days of yore, while Mal looked on from the wings. As that most improbable show got under way, he was ready for anything.

28

PISSPOTS ON A JOURNEY

Given Mayfair's conservative bent, Lindsay-Hogg predicted that the police would make their arrival on the scene in response to noise complaints. He asked Mal to act as the Beatles' liaison with the Metropolitan Police, a role he gladly accepted. "Mal was the one who gave us the extra, I would say, ten to twelve minutes of songs up on the roof," Lindsay-Hogg recalled, "because he figured out what to do about the police. He was our front man."[1]

The director had been spot-on about the police. "The day we filmed on the roof of Apple was to cause quite a lot of excitement," Mal wrote. "The Beatles had only just started playing when the switchboard of the Savile Row police station was jammed with dozens of calls from irate neighbors, most of them very stuffy businessmen who had offices adjoining Apple. It got so bad that the police arrived at Apple, where we had a booth with one-way glass installed, filming the comings and goings of everybody who entered."[2]

Mal attempted to waylay the police officers through a combination of small talk and smoking breaks, but nineteen-year-old constable Ray Dagg wasn't having it. "They insisted they had so many complaints that we would have to stop the show or at least turn the sound down," said Mal. "I went away for five minutes, had a crafty smoke, and came back asking if it was any better. The Beatles wanted to record at least half a dozen songs on the roof for the finished film, and I was gaining as much time for them as possible, but after several such excursions to the cellar, the police insisted on going to the roof of Apple." As they made their way upstairs in the lift, Dagg announced that Mal was under arrest, even going so far as to write the roadie's name in his book. He also informed Mal that "if I didn't switch off the power to the amplifiers, they would arrest the Beatles and take them down to the police station. I felt that this would have been a silly thing to let happen."[3]

When they stepped out onto the roof, Mal made one last effort to keep the peace. "I switched off the power starting with George's amplifier just as they were about to break into a new number." His gambit immediately failed when "George got a right cob on and turned around, demanding to know 'What the fuck are you playing at?' I switched the amp on again, they played that last number and decided that they had pushed the filming to its limits and finished." After completing the last of several versions of "Get Back" that afternoon, John turned to the audience sitting below the chimney and proclaimed, "I'd like to say thank you on behalf of the group and ourselves. I hope we passed the audition."

Fortunately, Mal didn't end up taking a ride to the police station. "Paul, being the perfect public relations man that he is, apologized profusely to the police and got me off the hook," the roadie later wrote. "The mission had been accomplished and is set on film for posterity."[4]

With the forty-two-minute concert in the books, Mal and the Beatles returned to their basement studio the next day, polishing off renditions of their new repertoire for the planned *Get Back* LP. Lindsay-Hogg filmed the proceedings, including "Let It Be" and "The Long and Winding Road," the album's principal ballads. Paul had recently warned Mal that he was making a key alteration to the lyrics of "Let It Be." As the roadie later recalled, they had been sitting in the car outside 7 Cavendish Avenue in the pre-dawn hours of a very rainy London morning. Just before he went inside, Paul told him that he planned to change "Mother Malcolm" to "Mother Mary," "in case people get the wrong idea."[5] Even so, during the session that day at 3 Savile Row, at least one of the takes for "Let It Be" featured Paul singing "Brother Malcolm." In truth, Mal didn't care in the slightest. Whether it was "Mother Malcolm," "Brother Malcolm," or "Mother Mary," he simply adored the song, believing it to be one of Paul's finest compositions.

While January had ended in triumph, with the band succeeding in bringing a host of new songs to fruition despite their tensions earlier in the month, February—for Mal at least—proved far less successful. On February 1, the Beatles met with Allen Klein, the notorious and scrappy New York businessman who had made his name by winning a large advance for the Rolling Stones at a crucial moment in their career. He was determined to do the same, if not more, for the Beatles, whom he had been planning to manage for the past several years—even when Brian Epstein was still among the living.

The meeting with Klein had seemed convivial enough, although Mal noted in his diary that Ron Kass had seemed particularly shaken afterward. A few days later, a conversation with Paul threw Mal into a full-blown crisis. "Paul is really cutting down on the Apple staff numbers," he wrote in his diary. "I was elevated to office boy, and I feel very hurt and sad inside—only, big boys don't cry." He admitted that "the reason for writing this is ego; you see, I thought I was different from other people in my relationship with the Beatles, and being loved by them and treated so nice, I felt like one of the family. Seems I fetch and carry."[6]

Mal's psychological tailspin wasn't just about status. "I found it difficult to live on the £38 I take home each week and would love to live like [the Beatles'] other friends who buy fantastic homes and have all the alterations done by them and are still going to ask for a rise. I always tell myself—everybody wants to take from [them], be satisfied." In his heart, Mal knew that he deserved a wage increase, but characteristically, he opted to leave things in the hands of fate. "Try to give and you will receive," he told himself. The bitter truth was that "I have about £70 in my name, but was content and happy loving them as I do, [and] nothing is too much trouble because I want to serve them." He ended the diary entry by enumerating his devotion to the Beatles like a mantra:

I want them,
I need them,
I love them,
Feel a bit better now—ego?[7]

It was against this backdrop that Arwen Dolittle likely gave up on Big Mal serving as a father to their infant son. Since leaving the hospital, she had reared Little Malcolm in her cramped lodgings in West Hampstead. At some point, around the age of six months, he was put up for adoption, leaving her care lock, stock, and barrel, with Mal's teddy bear as the baby's only consolation. Mal's diary would enumerate lunches and telephone calls with the young woman at various points across 1969, but eventually, Arwen chose to move on, putting the whole painful episode behind her.[8]

To improve what he perceived as his fading status at Apple, Mal was determined to bring the Iveys back into the studio to continue plugging their career. A victory for one of the label's key signings could make all the difference, he thought. Mal was still smarting over the inability of "Maybe Tomorrow" to make a meaningful dent in the charts. "This must surely be one of the most beautiful records that [the Iveys] ever released," he wrote. "But unfortunately, in the record business, good music doesn't always sell."[9]

By this juncture, Mal realized that, like the Iveys, he was at a crossroads, lamenting in his diary that they were all just "pisspots on a journey."[10] And the Iveys were feeling it, too. They had already recorded several new songs with producer Tony Visconti, but according to Mal, the band believed that Visconti "was pushing them into a direction that they didn't want to go. He was an excellent producer, of that there is no doubt, at that moment in time being involved with T. Rex. But the group was not happy with him and turned to me." To Mal, it made perfect sense: "Because of our strong friendship, the group asked me if I would produce them. I was a little taken aback at first, never having done that before, but as they pointed out, I had spent an awful lot of time in recording studios with the greatest recording artists in the world," he added, "and some of it must have rubbed off!"[11] Visconti later admitted to being caught unaware. "It took me completely by surprise," he said. "I remember Mal being around at a lot of our sessions. I loved the man—he was such a nice guy—but I questioned his qualifications. I was crushed. I loved working with the band."[12]

With Mal behind the console at Trident, the Iveys recorded several new songs across February and March. Together with the material Visconti had produced the previous autumn, they had plenty of songs to fill out their first Apple LP, which they entitled *Maybe Tomorrow*. A cover photograph of the band in Golders Green, their regular stomping ground, was commissioned. At the same time, Mal tasked Bramwell with shooting a promo film for the title track. In a nod to the early days of the Beatles, the roadie insisted that the Iveys wear matching suits. As a subtle form of protest, the Welshmen turned their collars up in defiance. "Mal Evans was a bit overprotective of them," Tony Bramwell recalled. "He thought they were the next Beatles, and he pushed them as the new Beatles before they were ready for it."[13]

Mal personally took charge of *Maybe Tomorrow*'s planned American release, and he adorned the album's cover with a framed photo of daughter Julie among individual photos of the Iveys. By early April, he was sitting in the producer's chair, preparing the Iveys' album for distribution and hoping that it would improve his standing at 3 Savile Row. All he needed now was a green light from Ron Kass.

That same month, Mal took comfort in hanging out with Gary, his steadfast buddy despite everything. With Lil and Julie in tow, they made time to go to the cinema, their favorite pastime, where they saw the newly released *Chitty Chitty Bang Bang*. On the way home from the movies, they drove by Snakey Lane, the location of the Kempton Park water treatment works that was the stand-in for Scrumptious Sweets in *Chitty Chitty Bang Bang*. Even years later, whenever he happened to pass by Snakey Lane, Gary would think fondly about going to the cinema with his dad.[14]

As March 1969 got under way, Mal ferried John and Yoko in the Beatle's white Rolls-Royce Phantom V to Lady Mitchell Hall, in Cambridge. The event marked the couple's artistic debut, with Yoko taking lead vocals and John providing musical accompaniment. The couple invited Mal to be part of the proceedings, strategically positioning him onstage between themselves and the audience. "John was playing, holding the guitar close to the speaker creating feedback," Mal wrote, and "Yoko was doing her voice modulating. I think the two of them together create an incredible sound, in the way the guitar and the voice complement each other. While driving them there, it was Yoko's idea that I should sit on the stage in front of them, and stare at the audience. Her feeling being that in most shows, the audience stares at the stage, so why shouldn't the artists get their own back? I sat in my little chair with an alarm clock set to go off in half an hour to mark the end of the show, the audience's reactions to this being wide and varied. Some people would look you in the eye, others would get embarrassed and look away, and I would catch some people staring at me when they thought I wasn't looking. It was an interesting venture on my part and a thrill to be on the same stage with two fine artists."[15]

Meanwhile, Paul and Linda were on the verge of getting married, having zeroed in on a mid-March ceremony at the Marylebone Registry Office. Mal recalled a conversation with Paul in early March as they left Apple at the end of the workday. "'What do you think, Mal, should I get married?' My answer being: 'Well, Paul, I can't make your mind up. But look at me, been married 11 years [and I] wouldn't have it any other way.' Whether that influenced him at all, I don't know."[16]

On March 11, the day before the wedding, Paul and Mal were walking in Mayfair when they ran into Carol Bedford, a member of the "Apple Scruffs." Comprised mostly of young women, the Apple Scruffs had taken to keeping vigil outside 3 Savile Row, EMI Studios, and 7 Cavendish Avenue, among other Beatles-centric locales. When a photographer snapped a photo of Paul and Carol standing together, the Beatle dispatched Mal to chase down the shutterbug and seize the film, which the roadie promptly did.[17]

While Linda and Paul had considered canceling the blessed event after a last-minute spat, they met with Mal and Peter Brown bright and early on March 12 to make the trip with daughter Heather to the Marylebone Registry Office. Mal and Peter were ready to serve as the couple's witnesses, along with Paul's brother, Mike, who was traveling down by train from Birmingham to act as best man. Unfortunately, the train broke down, delaying Mike's arrival by several hours. When he finally made it to the Registry Office, he expected the wedding to have already concluded.

"Where the hell have you been?" Paul asked.

Mike couldn't believe they'd waited.

"You're the best man, you sod," Paul said to his brother. "Let's go and get this done!"[18]

Things never being quiet in the Beatles' world, Mal stayed up late tending to the Harrisons on the evening of Paul and Linda's wedding. As he scrawled in his diary the next morning, "Big drama, last night about 7:30 p.m. Pattie rang the office from home for George to say, 'eight or ten policemen including Sergeant Pilcher had arrived with search warrants looking for cannabis.'"[19] Sergeant Norman Pilcher had been making a name for himself by busting British pop stars for drugs, having arrested John and Yoko the previous October. George was merely the latest casualty, later conjecturing that the bust had been timed to coincide with Paul's nuptials that same day.[20]

John and Yoko made fresh headlines on March 20, when they staged

Mal with Linda, Paul, and Heather after the McCartneys' wedding

their own wedding, near the Rock of Gibraltar, followed by a "Bed-In for Peace," a nonviolent protest of the Vietnam War that they held in their Amsterdam Hilton room. As was his wont, John transformed the entire saga into a new composition, entitled "The Ballad of John and Yoko." With George traveling abroad and Ringo on the set of *The Magic Christian*, John and Paul took a stab at the song at EMI Studios on April 14. John Kosh was there, having recently been appointed Apple's creative director.

Kosh had heard stories of "gloom and doom" about the Beatles' relationships, only to discover that John and Paul—two men who were supposedly not even speaking to each other—"were having great fun making truly joyous music."[21] With Paul sitting behind the drums and overdubbing his bass part, John handled the lead vocals and guitars. During a break in the session, John could be heard saying, "Go a bit faster, Ringo!" with Paul good-naturedly replying, "Okay, George!" The second take broke down, momentarily bringing a halt to the proceedings. "Un string avec kaput, Mal," said John, with the roadie coming to the rescue.

The elation Mal felt after the session for "The Ballad of John and Yoko" grew by leaps and bounds on April 30, when John and Paul invited him to help complete "You Know My Name (Look Up the Number)," a comedic revue they had begun two years earlier after the conclusion of the *Sgt. Pepper* sessions. Working at EMI Studios, Mal added sound effects by running a spade through gravel. "We had these endless, crazy fun sessions, and eventually we pulled it all together," Paul recalled. "We just did a skit—Mal and his gravel. I can still see Mal digging the gravel. And it was just so hilarious to put that record together. It's not a great melody or anything. It's just unique."[22]

Meanwhile, Mal continued working behind the console, coproducing "New Day" with Jackie Lomax. The groovy number featured the Merseybeats' Billy Kinsley on bass, Tim Renwick on guitar, Chris Hatfield on piano, and Pete Clarke on drums. When "New Day" was released as a single later that spring, the production was credited to "Jackie and Mal." Making a name for himself as a soundman had become Mal's capital objective, but he knew that accomplishing that end meant overcoming the built-in prejudices of the Beatles and other members of their inner circle who perceived him strictly as a roadie or, worse yet, a gofer.

"I had been their road manager for too long," Mal lamented, "and there's no way that the Beatles could see me in any other capacity. From here on to the end of my career as their road manager, I had to fight every step of the way. What would have happened if Ringo had listened to critics saying, 'You're not an actor, Ringo, you're a drummer.' Or had told George or John, 'You're not guitarists, you're electricians, or whatever.'" Mal also recognized that, in many ways, he had only himself to blame for his status in the Beatles organization. "In my relationship with the Beatles, I was not interested in credit," he wrote. "I put a lot of ideas and thought into the projects the Beatles got involved in, but I was so in love with the group," he added, that as far as he was concerned, receiving explicit credit hadn't been necessary.[23]

But when Mal did receive credit, even tangentially, things seemed to go badly for him. With British and North American releases for the *Maybe*

Tomorrow LP tentatively scheduled for July, but ultimately scrapped, Apple released pressings of the album in Japan, West Germany, and Italy in the fall. The liner notes made special mention of Mal's efforts on behalf of the group: "We the Iveys dedicate this album to Mal." The gesture infuriated Ron Kass, who deemed it "childish" while also maligning the album's cover design.[24] When it came to the liner notes, there was a hint of truth to Kass's concerns. In addition to highlighting his own production credits, Mal had taken some liberties, assigning some tracks as having been arranged by Mal Evans and John Barham. "That was a bit naughty of Mal," said Barham. "He was a lovely guy, but he had nothing to do with the arrangements."[25]

It was in this frame of mind that Mal made what, in retrospect, could only be described as a strategic blunder. The blowback he was experiencing as the Iveys' in-house Apple advocate and all-around cheerleader had been taking its toll. On April 24, he confessed to George that the "situation with [the] Iveys [was] getting a little too heavy for me." He took things a step further, admitting to the Beatle that "I'm broke." Mal added that he felt "really miserable and down because I'm in the red, and the bills are coming in, poor old Lil suffers, as I don't want to ask Apple for a rise." As usual, he felt guilty for even thinking about a salary increase—this time, because the "fellows are having a tough time as it is." With his own financial outlook in a death spiral, Mal contemplated going so far as to share his predicament with Allen Klein and ask the gruff businessman to provide a thousand-pound loan to help out the Iveys, who were languishing in their own budgetary straits.[26] Mal's capacity for vulnerability and engendering empathy in others was easily his strongest suit. But with Klein, it could only be interpreted as a sign of weakness, as a chink in his adversary's armor.

As serious as Mal had been about elevating record production among his portfolio of duties—or, more troubling yet, about addressing his mounting financial woes—it was shortly to become a secondary concern. That May, Glyn Johns and George Martin had begun working in earnest to mix the LP, which was tentatively titled *Get Back, Don't Let Me Down, and 12 Other Songs*. The single "Get Back," backed with "Don't Let Me Down," had been released in April, generating another chart-topper and being deservedly credited to "The Beatles with Billy Preston." EMI was understandably eager for another long-player to follow in its wake. The Beatles had begun working on new material at Olympic that May, including "You Never Give Me Your Money," a complex, intensely autobiographical song cycle about the perils of fame and growing older.

It was at Olympic on Friday, May 9, that the Beatles arrived at loggerheads over the appointment of Allen Klein as Brian's successor. Only a week earlier, John had informed *Disc and Music Echo* that Klein had no intention of becoming the group's manager, only that he was "simply doing a job for us. If he does something, he gets paid. If he doesn't, he isn't."[27] But by the ninth, there had clearly been a change of heart. At this point, John, George, and Ringo favored Klein to serve as the group's manager, while Paul was eager for his new in-laws, attorneys Lee and John Eastman, to receive consideration for the role. That night, as Mal observed in a kind of horror, the three other Beatles cornered Paul at Olympic, insisting that he join them in appointing Klein not only as their business representative, but also as managing director of Apple Corps, supplanting Neil. In Paul's memory, they said, "You've got to sign a contract—he's got to take it to his board." Paul countered, saying, "It's Friday night. He doesn't work on a Saturday, and anyway Allen Klein is a law unto himself. He hasn't got a board he has to report to. Don't worry—we could easily do this on Monday. Let's do our session instead. You're not going to push me into this."[28]

Paul finally began to lose his cool when the others accused him of creating needless roadblocks, of favoring his in-laws, which seemed like a conflict of interest. As Paul recalled,

> They said, "Oh, are you stalling? He wants 20 percent." I said, "Tell him he can have 15 percent." They said, "You're stalling." I replied, "No, I'm working for us; we're a big act." I remember the exact words: "We're a big act—the Beatles. He'll take 15 percent." But for some strange reason—I think they were so intoxicated with him—they said, "No, he's got to have 20 percent, and he's got to report to his board. You've got to sign now or never." So I said, "Right, that's it. I'm not signing now."[29]

Years later, Paul reflected on the incident that night at Olympic. "That was the night we broke the Beatles," he told historian Mark Lewisohn.

Mal's drawing of an infuriated Paul at Olympic Studios

"Really, that was the big crack in the Liberty Bell. It never came back together after that one."[30]

For Mal, the whole sordid business was nothing short of heartbreaking. Seeing his beloved Beatles in all-out turmoil was beyond his ken. That night, when he sat down to record the day's events in his diary, words simply wouldn't suffice. Instead, he sketched the image of Paul going apeshit at Olympic Studios, screaming at the top of his lungs as his precious Beatles—*Mal's precious Beatles*—were being torn asunder.[31]

29

SUN WORSHIPPER

For the past eight years, Mal had steadfastly protected the Beatles, relying on his imposing physique and fueled by unequivocal devotion to the boys. But the schism inside the band he had witnessed at Olympic had effectively rendered his powers moot. From Mal's perspective, Allen Klein seemed determined to make things worse.

Alistair Taylor had been suspicious of Klein's motives from the outset. "He had all the charm of a broken lavatory seat, but he did have a reputation for being a ruthless businessman," Taylor recalled. "I only ever once had a conversation with Mr. Klein. I met him on the stairs one morning and I said, 'Good morning, Mr. Klein.' And he grunted. It was not a lot to base your opinion on, I know, but could this curt, unshaven, overweight guy really be the new Brian Epstein? I thought not."[1] In short order, Klein would fire Alistair, the Beatles' "Mr. Fixit."

Knowing Klein's plans for trimming the fat at Apple, the Beatles themselves had provided the New Yorker with a list of untouchable employees. Alistair clearly hadn't been on it, and neither had Ron Kass, who was let go shortly afterward. Not surprisingly, Magic Alex never stood a chance of surviving the purge. When an audit revealed that the inventor had cost Apple more than £180,000, Klein made short work of the former TV repairman. Klein's analysis of the Apple books also disclosed that two company cars had disappeared without a trace, while various payments for "erections and demolitions" had in fact been disbursed to prostitutes.[2]

Having seen the writing on the wall, Peter Asher would take his leave that June, resigning to pilot James Taylor's career. Asher didn't mince words, later informing the press that he had thrown in his lot with Apple because "its policy was to help people and be generous," but with Klein, he added, those days were gone, along with the "original feeling" of goodwill on behalf of musical art.[3]

Meanwhile, a theory had developed among the Apple ranks that Klein's decisions about redundancies were motivated by a desire to weed out the company's strongest, most admired personalities—especially those who had nurtured a closeness with the Beatles themselves. At a crucial juncture that same month, Klein went off list and began taking steps to fire Mal and Neil.

The Beatles wasted little time in rescuing their chief lieutenants. Losing such stalwarts was simply unthinkable. The two were reinstated forthwith, albeit with a certain irony: In spite of their various titles over the years, Mal and Neil didn't actually work for Apple, and Klein didn't have the authority to fire them. Outside their four world-famous bosses, Mal and Neil were the sole employees of Beatles and Company, falling outside the range of the American's axe.

For his part, Mal's brief tenure on the chopping block didn't leave a scar. After all, he had already been consigned to "office boy." Likely perceived by Klein as an eminently greater threat than his oversize colleague, Neil wasn't so lucky, having been demoted from his lofty position as Apple's managing director to a kind of glorified personal assistant[4]—at least, for the time being.

Tony Bramwell had also been among the ostensibly sacrosanct list of untouchables, a group that included Derek Taylor and Jack Oliver, who had assumed Kass's role as president of Apple Records. But Tony held nothing but disdain for Klein and what he perceived as the new managing director's true motives for trolling the Apple waters. "He wanted to get rid of everybody so he could cook the books and milk the company dry," Bramwell said. "He spent his days conspiring about how to get rid of us, whispering about everybody behind their backs to John and George, who thought he was some kind of New York financial genius. Klein's tentacles were long. He tore everything apart."[5] Tony understood the need to jettison the likes of Magic Alex, but he was especially embittered over Klein's ideas about closing shop when it came to Apple Publishing. From Tony's perspective, the publishing arm was already on a strong trajectory, with a number of lucrative properties under its belt. Besides, Tony knew where Apple's loss-leaders had been all along, blaming John and Yoko for their personally exorbitant spending sprees despite the Beatle's protestations to the contrary. Bramwell also had a bird's-eye view of Apple's extravagance in terms of catering and liquor expenses, which, by any measure, were substantial.[6]

Meanwhile, Mal continued to come to grips with the recent bad tidings in Beatle World, desperately trying to hold it all together. As if overnight, Apple had transformed from a place of possibility and, yes, frivolity, into a ghost town where the survivors tried to keep their heads down and, most important, their jobs intact. And then there were the boys themselves. A cold war of sorts had developed after the showdown at Olympic. As Tony later recalled, "People like myself and Neil Aspinall and Mal Evans would constantly be getting calls from one of the Beatles, asking us to do something but not tell the others." When it came to 3 Savile Row, "One week Paul would be in the office, the next it would be John and Yoko ruling the roost. It was difficult for those of us who'd grown up being faithful to them, and who suddenly found ourselves having to play them off against each other, behind each others' backs."[7]

From a Mal's-eye view, things seemed much worse than even that. Mal had given everything he had, elevating the Beatles over Lil and his children to meet the boys' needs. With the summer looming, the roadie was beside himself with dread and despair. He was no longer the nexus in the group's world, the rallying point for moving their lives and their projects forward, for letting the good times roll. But when it came to gleaning the vital intelligence that had allowed him to sustain his insider position all those years, he was, for the first time, forced to rely on others—in this instance, the Apple Scruffs.

To describe the tightly knit Scruffs as groupies would be to dishonor their cause. Their collective had begun its life keeping tabs on Paul, their favorite Beatle and—because he lived only a hop, skip, and a jump from EMI Studios—the most accessible. And they were willing to go to extremes that Mal couldn't even begin to contemplate—he being a lover of a hot meal, a warm bed, and every possible creature comfort. They also had an information-gathering network that put Mal's best efforts to shame. The Apple Scruffs "had their sources," Tony said. "One of these sources was probably, and for the most part unwittingly, Rosie, Paul's housekeeper. When Rosie went out or went shopping these girls used to go into Paul's house."[8] It's rumored that they knew exactly where Paul hid his spare key, and when his security system was activated, that they perfected the art of disabling it—but some Apple Scruffs deny this ever happened.

When their idol Paul grew cross with them over the intrusiveness of their surveillance activities and their petty theft—they would often take turns wearing the clothes they had looted from his bedroom—the Scruffs would invariably blame the roadie. The girls would explain to Paul that Mal had forcibly thrown them down the steps of EMI Studios as they kept their vigil; or, to win back his favor, they would demonstrate how they had hoodwinked the security measures at 7 Cavendish Avenue. Paul had taken to describing the Scruffs as "the Eyes and Ears of the World," and, to Mal's great chagrin, the nickname wasn't that far off the mark.[9]

Eventually, Mal would develop a vital relationship of his own with the Scruffs, although he had his detractors—namely, Carol Bedford, a peripheral member of their scrum and a George aficionado who later claimed that Mal tried to put the moves on her. Apparently, Mal had continued to approach women in the Beatles' universe in the same transactional manner in which he and Neil had "auditioned" willing fans during the band's touring years.[10]

Another Apple Scruff recalled a similar instance when Mal's attempts to cozy up to the Scruffs went terribly wrong. Apparently, he had crawled under one of the girls' blankets and "touched something he shouldn't have." With that, the offended Scruff came flying out from under the blanket yelling, "Who do you think you are, Paul McCartney?" On another occasion, Mal flirted with an Apple Scruff, indicating that he would be willing to have sex with her.

"I'm not chicken!" he exclaimed.

"We're not the ones laying the eggs," she coolly replied.

After that, Mal managed to keep the peace with the Scruffs, even developing a mutually valued friendship with them. Indeed, when they realized "he wasn't a danger," the Apple Scruff reported, they became especially close with the roadie. "He would let us sit in his car occasionally to get out of the cold," she said. Later, when "a drunk guy messed with me" outside Trident, she was rescued by Mal, who found a safe place for her to hang out in the studio. She would never forget Mal coming to fetch her later that night, when "George was about to leave, so I wouldn't miss him."

Ultimately, Mal came to understand the Scruffs because, like him, they were überfans. It was a kinship that existed above everything else, even sex or money or fame. He adored the boys, and so did the girls who lay in wait for them. He made sure the Scruffs were able to attend the Twickenham "Hey Jude" shoot back in September. And when a prized photo of Jim Mac was stolen from Paul's house at 7 Cavendish Avenue, Mal had helped negotiate the keepsake's return. The Apple Scruffs were especially touched by his protectiveness of them, which verged on the same level of concern he had for the Beatles. "Mal made it his mission to keep popping outside when the boys were recording to make sure we were safe," the Scruffs recalled. "He was in truth the consummate gentleman, and he was like a protective big brother, and we loved him for it."[11]

By June 1969, Mal and the Scruffs alike were buoyed by the news that the Beatles were returning to EMI Studios to undertake a new album. For the time being, the *Get Back* project was on hold. "The fellows listened together to the final tapes of all the *Get Back* LP recordings after they got back from their various business and holiday trips abroad," Mal reported to *The Beatles Book*. "They realized that it would be much more appropriate to hold back this whole set of recordings so that they could form an LP which would go out at the time their TV documentary is shown in Britain and America."[12]

But as Mal well knew, delaying the release of *Get Back* hadn't merely been about marketing synchronization. No matter how many times Glyn Johns tweaked the mix, John and Paul simply didn't like the album. For his part, Mal not only enjoyed *Get Back*, but found the concept of the band getting back to their roots enticing. In *The Beatles Book*, he described the unreleased record as "the Beatles with their socks off, human Beatles kicking out their jams, getting rid of their inhibitions, facing their problems, and working them out with their music. During and in between most of the tracks, you will hear lots of studio-floor conversation, each of the fellows chatting, preparing for the next number, shouting comments up to the control room. On other albums, this type of ad-lib stuff has been cut from the tapes before putting the tracks on disc. This time, everything is left for you to hear—just as it happened."[13] The ragged nature of the LP might not have appealed to the Beatles themselves, but Mal loved it, warts and all.

As far as making a brand-new album was concerned, the band was scheduled to return to EMI Studios with George Martin that July. For the first time since August 1963, neither Mal nor Neil would be there, having planned an old-school double family vacation together beginning in late June, in the Algarve, Portugal. This time, there would be no yachts or motor coaches or jet planes. It was more than that: in Mal's world, when it had come to choosing between the Beatles and his family, the boys had won out every single time—that is, until June 1969, when he opted to spend time with Lil and the kids instead.

Before he left London, though, Mal transacted one final piece of business. On June 25, he made a last-ditch effort to convince Allen Klein—the very person who had recently attempted to fire him—to provide the Iveys with an advance on their production expenses. Going for broke, Mal even went so far as to ask Klein to sign him to a production contract for his work with the Iveys and others. All in all, it was a risky gambit, but also a remarkably canny one. Instead of recoiling from Klein like the other Apple survivors, Mal was making a good-faith effort to negotiate with him. And there was reason to believe—as events would demonstrate over the next several months—that his risk might very well pay off, that he had wandered into the lion's den and escaped with his life.

Having rented a villa in Portugal, the Aspinall and Evans clans set out for the coast in their two personal cars. For the two families—and for Mal and Neil, in particular—the respite away from London simply couldn't have come at a better time. Gary enjoyed playing with Neil's son, Roag, with little Julie tagging along as they explored the pristine beaches of the Algarve. Meanwhile, Mal was in desperate straits. The interpersonal tremors at Apple and among the Beatles had taken their toll on him, and he was searching for something, *anything*, to soothe his aching psyche. Solace arrived in the form of a seaside revelation.

"I am, by nature, a sun worshipper," Mal recalled, "and no matter how hot it gets, I can stay out in the sun. One particular afternoon, having the beach to myself, everybody splitting to take a siesta, I went for a stroll feeling in a great philosophical mood and talking out loud to myself and to God." Heavily bearded and bedraggled, Mal shouted to the heavens, "If you're really there, God, show me a sign." He had taken special notice of the signs already in evidence—"the heavy afternoon, [the] small waves lapping the beach, the never-ending cries of the sea gulls, piercing the hot sunshine, but still I was asking for another."[14]

No, Mal needed something more than a pleasant walk along the beach. He needed genuine proof to elevate his soul. "God, if you're here with me," he proclaimed, "make the cliffs fall down." After strolling another twenty yards, Mal suddenly heard a "thunderous, crashing roar." Up ahead, "a large portion of the cliffs had fallen down. It scared the living daylights out of me, I can tell you, but in my own mind, it reassured me and strengthened my faith in a supreme being."[15]

Mal was buoyed by what he witnessed along the seaside all right, but his newfound providence was to be short-lived. After the beach was hit by a flash flood, he listened in horror as Lily ran up to him, saying that "Roag can't find Gary anywhere." Mal couldn't believe his ears. "The first thing my imagination did was to put him in the water fighting for his little life and shouting for me," he wrote. "I shouted his name and searched the waves until we found him playing in a safe pool of water."[16]

A few days after briefly losing sight of Gary during the squall, Mal and Lil became concerned when Julie began to develop a fever. Their mild alarm turned into all-out fear when she seemed to lapse into a coma late one evening. A Portuguese doctor advised that her condition may have resulted from something she ingested—or, more distressingly still, perhaps it was typhoid fever. By the time they made their return to Spain, doctors had ruled out typhoid. "It wasn't until we had driven back to Madrid that she came out of it," Mal wrote.[17]

That Sunday, the Evans and Aspinall clans spent the day in Madrid, where they watched the television coverage of the Apollo moon landing together. With Julie on the mend, the two families made their way back into France via the Spanish border. As luck would have it, they were crossing at the same customs post Mal and Paul had visited back in November 1966, when the roadie had to leave his newly purchased shotgun in the hands of the proprietor of a French border café. Amazingly, the weapon was still there waiting for him three years later. Perhaps providence was still on Mal's side, after all?

By the afternoon of Wednesday, July 23, Mal was blissfully back in the Beatles' fold, refreshed after his monthlong respite in the Algarve. His relationship with his family seemed to be back on track, and the camaraderie with Neil was as strong as ever. And the Beatles' music he heard that day was stupendous, including "Come Together," with its funky groove, and the then-named "Ending," a sizzling rock 'n' roll revue. During his absence, the boys had crafted a multipart medley that went under the working title of "The Long One." The concept had been instigated by George Martin, who was eager for the band to attempt a longer-form, symphonic work.

While Mal was away in the Algarve, things had eroded precipitously in the Iveys' universe. Klein's ascendancy at Apple had left in jeopardy the U.K. and U.S. release dates for *Maybe Tomorrow*. And by that July, the album had been mothballed. Still treading water in the Apple Records promotion department, Tony Bramwell blamed Klein for gumming up the works in terms of issuing new releases. "I think he put the stops on it because he was saying, 'We're not going to issue any more records until I sort out this mess,'" he recalled. "Apple really wasn't a mess as far as we were concerned. But a lot of things stopped. I think a Billy Preston single got held up, along with a Mary Hopkin record." As U.S. label head for Apple, Ken Mansfield hadn't even been consulted over the decision to scrap the Iveys' debut LP. "I didn't even get to hear it," he said. "We weren't involved in that decision. A lot of things came down with no explanation." To Mansfield's mind, Klein may have jettisoned the project for the simple reason that Ron Kass had been so keen to support the Iveys.[18]

It was in this state of mind, and under these conditions, that Iveys bassist Ron Griffiths and guitarist Tom Evans took to the pages of *Disc and Music Echo*. "We do feel a bit neglected," Griffiths said. "We keep writing songs for a new single and submitting them to Apple, but the Beatles keep sending them back saying that they're not good enough." He added that "the Beatles haven't offered us any of their songs, but then we're not really expecting them to."[19] As it turned out, Griffiths's public fit of pique did not fall on deaf ears.

Shortly after Mal's return from the Algarve, Paul took matters into his own hands. Contractually obligated to provide three songs to *The Magic Christian* soundtrack, he recorded a demo for "Come and Get It" on July 24 at EMI Studios. In the space of an hour, he performed all the song's instrumentation, including double-tracked lead vocals, instructing Mal to share the acetate with the Iveys. With Paul in the producer's chair, the Iveys later joined the Beatle at EMI to learn the song and commit it to tape. While they were there, Tom Evans recalled seeing John and Yoko. At one point, "Lennon stopped and looked over at Paul, bowed his head, and said, 'Oh wise one, oh sage, show us the light.'"[20]

Mal was there, too—but not merely as the band's chief supporter. He played a mean tambourine, working the percussive instrument so hard that he ended up with a case of "dead thumb."[21] Meanwhile, Paul was ineluctably clear that the Iveys' version of "Come and Get It" needed to be recorded exactly like his demo. And, with only a slight shift in tempo, it was. Suddenly, the Iveys had their next single ready for release to coincide with *The Magic Christian*'s December premiere. With Paul McCartney in their corner, Klein couldn't possibly derail their next single.

With the Beatles working long hours at EMI Studios, Mal was in his element. As always, he kept the boys well fed and their instruments in tip-top shape, while making time to cavort with the Apple Scruffs and other assembled fans outside the studio. As the hours ticked down on July, the real action was occurring inside the studio, where Mal was doing his part to help the band complete the medley and, indeed, the album. Several potential titles were still under consideration at this juncture, including *Four in the Bar*, *All Good Children Go to Heaven*, *Turn Ups*, and *Inclinations*.[22] On July 30, tape operator John Kurlander prepared a test mix of "The Long One," including a recent version of Paul's "She Came in through the Bathroom Window," based upon the Apple Scruffs' Cavendish Avenue burglary. During the prelude to the song, John can be heard playfully joking with Mal in the studio. At Paul's express instruction, Kurlander had deleted the acoustic ditty "Her Majesty" from the mix. "I'd been told never to throw anything away," he recalled, "so after he left, I picked it up off the floor, put about twenty seconds of red leader tape before it, and stuck it onto the end of the edit tape."[23]

One of Kurlander's abiding memories of that summer's sessions involved staying up late with Mal, who would ferry each day's recordings over to Apple, where, in turn, disc cutter Malcolm Davies would create lacquer acetates for the band's review. From his experience with the Beatles, Kurlander knew that "Mal [Evans] was entrusted very much with lots of duties, and some were very sensitive. But perhaps the most sensitive duty of all involved transporting their unreleased music around the city."[24] On July 31, Mal began his workday at 3 Savile Row, where he picked up the acetates from the July 30 session and drove them over to EMI Studios. When he returned for his next shift that afternoon, Kurlander was stunned to discover that "Her Majesty" was still in the medley—precisely where he'd left it, some twenty seconds after the conclusion of "The Long One." When the boys played the acetates, they loved the song's placement. "The Beatles always picked up on accidental things," said Kurlander. "It came as a nice little surprise there at the end."[25]

By August 5, the conundrum over the new album's title had been settled. A late entry in the sweepstakes had been *Everest*, in reference to engineer Geoff Emerick's preferred brand of cigarettes. Not surprisingly, the boys scuttled the idea when the suggestion was made, preposterous as it may have seemed, of traveling some five thousand miles to Tibet to shoot the cover photo. Besides, said Paul, "You can't name an album after a ciggie packet!"[26] It was he who finally broke the logjam. "I don't know how I thought of it," he said. "*Abbey Road!* It's the studio we're in, which is fabulous; and it sounds a bit like a monastery."[27]

Mal adored the new title, especially as an homage to the studio where the boys had made their name. For him, *Abbey Road* affirmed the Beatles' larger creative achievement—and the potential, despite their recent spate of interpersonal and business-related tensions, for reaching even greater heights. "Sgt. Pepper is alive and well and living in Abbey Road," Mal wrote in his diary, arguably a tad overoptimistic considering the events at Olympic back in May.[28]

In his role as Apple's creative director, John Kosh was summoned to refine the album's cover design. Working from Paul's sketch of the four Beatles crossing Abbey Road, Kosh coordinated a cover shoot with photographer Iain Macmillan for Friday, August 8. At Kosh's suggestion, Mal canvassed London's public works department for information about the lettering on the street signs along Abbey Road, so the designer could match the font. Earlier that same week, as Mal held the traffic at bay, Macmillan took Polaroid test shoots of Kevin Harrington, Apple's Steve Brendell, and various studio personnel walking back and forth across the zebra crossing a few yards away from the studio entrance.

Meanwhile, the boys continued recording—often commandeering multiple studios at a time during postproduction. *Abbey Road* was the product of numerous innovations, including EMI's newfangled TG12345 eight-track mixing desk and the Moog synthesizer, which featured prominently on songs like John's "Because" and George's "Here Comes the Sun." Paul

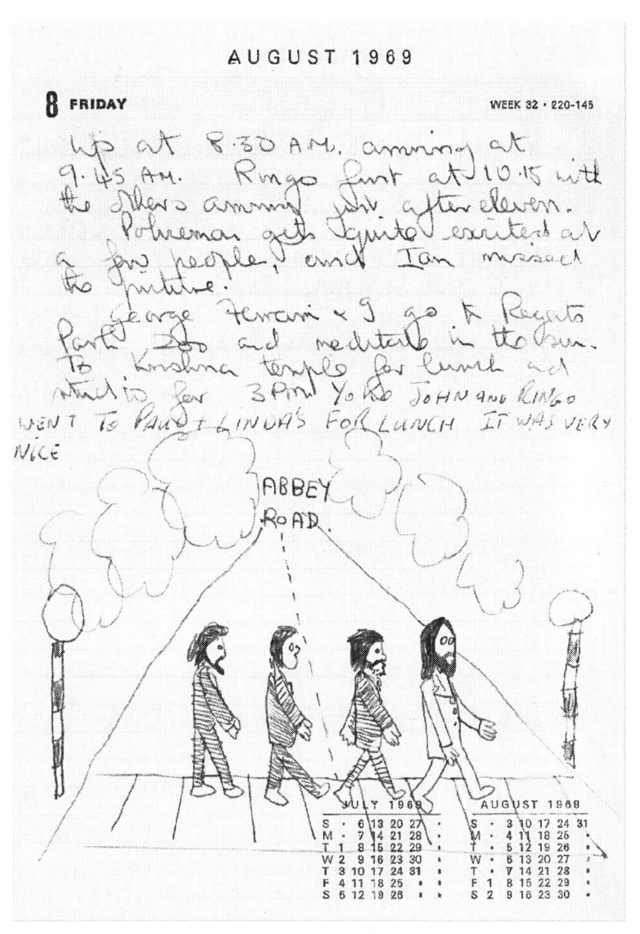
AUGUST 1969

8 FRIDAY WEEK 32 • 220-145

Up at 8.30 A.M. arriving at 9.45 A.M. Ringo first at 10.15 with the others arriving just after eleven.
Policeman gets quite excited at a few people, and Ian missed the picture.
George Ferrari & I go to Regents Park Zoo and meditate in the sun. To Krishna temple for lunch and returned for 3PM. YOKO JOHN AND RINGO WENT TO PAUL + LINDA'S FOR LUNCH IT WAS VERY NICE

ABBEY ROAD.

JULY 1969					
S	·	6	13	20	27
M	·	7	14	21	28
T	1	8	15	22	29
W	2	9	16	23	30
T	3	10	17	24	31
F	4	11	18	25	·
S	5	12	19	26	·

AUGUST 1969						
S	·	3	10	17	24	31
M	·	4	11	18	25	·
T	·	5	12	19	26	·
W	·	6	13	20	27	·
T	·	7	14	21	28	·
F	1	8	15	22	29	·
S	2	9	16	23	30	·

Mal's drawing of the *Abbey Road* cover shoot

overdubbed a selection from the complex electronic instrument on "Maxwell's Silver Hammer," which the group completed during Mal's absence in Portugal, with Ringo handling hammer and anvil duties in his place.

Unfortunately, the Beatles also had days like August 7, when moments of pure majesty became interspersed with maximal interpersonal stress. On the eve of Macmillan's cover shoot, Mal and the bandmates gathered in the Studio 2 control booth to listen to playbacks of "Come Together." Yoko was visible on the studio floor below. As George and the others looked on from their vantage point in the control room, Yoko crept across the room and helped herself to one of the guitarist's digestive biscuits. "That bitch!" George yelled. "She's just taken one of my biscuits!" With that, a shouting match broke out in the booth as John attempted to defend his wife.[29]

Incredibly, despite everything, the group managed to shift the mood from disastrous to sublime in the blink of an eye. Later that same day, John and George put aside their differences to record a fusillade of guitar solos to realize "Ending"—now going under the title "The End"—to fruition. To capture the moment, Mal set up the guitarists' amps on the studio floor, much as he had for the "Sgt. Pepper" reprise two years earlier, when he had arrayed their gear in concert formation. With George on "Lucy," his Gibson Les Paul Standard, and John and Paul playing their Epiphone Casinos, each guitarist tore off a two-bar solo, trading their licks in a virtuoso performance. What had begun as another dark day in Beatle World had resulted in an unexpected triumph. Perhaps the spirit of Sgt. Pepper was alive and well in EMI Studios, after all.

By Friday, August 8, Kosh felt the pressure to complete the album's cover design. "We were working under a deadline," he recalled. "We had to go to press, and the album was already late, as far as EMI was concerned."[30] Mal's workday had begun that morning at eight thirty. For nearly two hours, he fretted over a white Volkswagen Beetle with license number 28IF that threatened to spoil the shot. Unable to have the vehicle towed away, he threw up his hands in defeat. And with that, the Beatles were summoned.

As the London Metropolitan Police cleared the area of traffic, the boys walked single file across the street. John was up first, having donned a stark white suit; followed by a dark-suited Ringo; a tieless, shoeless Paul; and George, a vision in blue denim. After taking a few passes across the zebra crossing, with Mal sketching the boys for posterity in his diary, the Beatles took their leave. The cover shoot was in the books.

With a few hours to kill until their afternoon recording session commenced, Mal and George went to the London Zoo, where the two men meditated together in the afternoon sun. For the next few hours, they wandered around the cages and animal houses, concluding with a stroll around Regent's Park. But for Mal, the most extraordinary thing was that during that whole time, not a single person recognized his famous companion.[31] After years of standing out among the crowd for their long locks, the Beatles had fallen into the norm in Hippie London, where flowing tresses had become the fashion.

As always, a deadline loomed. Racing against the clock, Mal assisted George Martin in staging a mammoth overdubbing session for the *Abbey Road* album on August 15. Working in cavernous Studio 1, the producer supervised orchestral tracks for songs associated with "The Long One," including "Golden Slumbers," "Carry That Weight," and "The End." Meanwhile, Mal joined the EMI Studios crew that was desperately trying to keep the complex session together. As engineer Alan Brown recalled, "We had a large number of lines linking the studios, and we were all walking around the building with walkie-talkies trying to communicate with each other."[32] Later that day, Martin turned to "Something" and "Here Comes the Sun." Mal watched in amazement as Harrison performed a live guitar solo for "Something" in Studio 2 along with Martin's orchestra, playing across the hall in Studio 1.

On Friday, August 22, Mal joined the bandmates at Tittenhurst Park, John and Yoko's new estate, in Ascot, for a photo session. He had every expectation for a pleasant day in the country, with the forecast calling for sunny skies. Incredibly, John's new digs were even more regal and grandiose than Kenwood. Purchased for £145,000, Tittenhurst Park included a twenty-six-room main house, a Victorian-era assembly hall, a Tudor cottage, a chapel, servants' cottages, and assorted other outbuildings amid neatly kept rolling lawns, gardens, and a cricket pitch. Along with Mal, the day's attendees included the band and Yoko, Derek Taylor, a heavily pregnant Linda McCartney, and Paul's sheepdog, Martha. As for the photographers, Derek had invited twenty-three-year-old American photographer Ethan Russell, who had taken photos of the Beatles during the January *Get Back* sessions, and the *Daily Mail*'s popular sports reporter Monte Fresco. A professional photographer in her own right, Linda would join in the shutterbug fray, as would Mal, who had brought along his trusty Pentax for the occasion.

"It was just a photo session," Ringo later recalled. "I wasn't there thinking, 'Okay, this is the last photo session.'"[33] But it would be. For Russell, who had already spent hours photographing the band earlier in the year, "the vibe was strange." As the Beatles posed for him that day, Russell registered a feeling of discontent in the air, especially when it came to George, who, in the photographer's memory, never so much as cracked a smile.[34] For his part, Mal took dozens of photographs, which he planned to submit for consideration by Sean O'Mahony at *The Beatles Book*.

As usual, the Beatles were stylishly dressed. For the occasion, Mal gladly contributed to their look by sharing his black felt hat with John, who had taken a liking to it. Lily had used a purple scarf to tastefully decorate the hat's band. It was the very hat Mal had purchased back in Houston in 1965 from the Stelzig Saddlery, a vintage accessory that complemented George's wide-brimmed cowboy hat for the shoot. Ringo wore a paisley scarf, while Paul sported a nondescript dark suit, tieless in the style of the recent *Abbey Road* cover shoot.

As the group meandered from place to place on the estate, Mal snapped a few dozen photos, showing deference to Russell, Fresco, and Linda as the professional photographers on the shoot. If he had known that the Beatles' remaining time together could be tallied in a handful of hours, he might have behaved differently that day.

Fresco managed to get the final picture, capturing Paul and Ringo in the act of waving goodbye, rather fittingly, for his camera. At the end of the shoot, Mal hung around for a while, listening to a fresh acetate of *Abbey Road* with the band and Yoko. He might have stayed longer, relishing the company of his beloved Beatles, but, as always, he had to get back to the city. When you worked for the boys, there were always plenty of errands to run.

Mal and Neil in Portugal

30

BADFINGER BOOGIE

For Mal, the momentous events of September 1969 would be a veritable blur. But first there was the Isle of Wight Festival. Joining John, George, and Ringo and their wives, Mal and Lil took the children on a road trip to the island in the English Channel. In addition to Bob Dylan's headlining appearance at the festival, the group of friends played several rousing sets of tennis by day, punctuated by star-studded parties at night. Along the way, the Beatles played acetates of *Abbey Road*, proudly showing off their new LP for scores of lucky listeners—many of whom commented about George's standout tracks in "Something" and "Here Comes the Sun."

For Gary Evans, visiting the Isle of Wight was a dream experience—traveling by hovercraft from the mainland, watching Ringo arrive by helicopter from London, being allowed to stay up until midnight, and being gifted a harmonica from Bob Dylan, who called Gary his "best mate."[1]

Paul didn't make the trip. He was back in London with wife, Linda, who had given birth to a daughter on August 28. The new arrival was christened "Mary" in honor of the Beatle's late mother.

Meanwhile, the Beatles' lingering tensions finally caught up to them during a meeting among John, Paul, and George at 3 Savile Row on September 10. As Mal and Neil observed, John took particular issue with what he perceived as Paul's megalomania, saying that "if you look back on the Beatles albums, good or bad or whatever you think of 'em, you'll find that most times if anybody has got extra time it's you! For no other reason than you worked it like that."[2] For Mal, the conversation must have been pure agony. He idolized Paul, who bore the brunt of the meeting's vitriol.

In his own defense, Paul protested that he had "tried to allow space on albums for John's songs, only to find that John hadn't written any."

John wasn't having it. "I don't want to think about equal time," he said. "I just want it known I'm allowed to put four songs on the album, whatever happens."

John felt that George deserved the same consideration, but George countered, saying, "I don't particularly seek acclaim." He simply wanted an equitable forum for his songs.[3]

Paul wanted the Beatles' working relationship to continue without change or deference to John's and George's wishes. "When we get in a studio," he said, "even on the worst day, I'm still playing bass, Ringo's still drumming, and we're still there, you know."

With the idea of recording a new album seemingly off the table, John suggested that they produce a Christmas single instead. After all, he reasoned, their annual holiday fan club record would be due before long. When this idea was met with silence and indifference, John soberly concluded, "I guess that's the end of the Beatles."[4]

As horrible as the experience must have been for Mal, panic hadn't set in just yet. During the past fifteen months, Ringo and George had quit the band at various times, only to be coaxed back. On Friday, September 12, as Mal was leaving 3 Savile Row to catch a performance by the Iveys at the RAF's Brize Norton base in Oxfordshire, he overheard John talking about an upcoming trip to Canada. "Having well-pricked ears," he wrote in his diary, "I leapt in with me leads and plecs," volunteering to serve as roadie for the Plastic Ono Band's debut performance the next day at Toronto's Rock 'n' Roll Revival festival.[5]

Mal was eager to help out. "The Beatles had not appeared on stage for over three years," he wrote, "and personally, I missed the excitement of the tours tremendously." The only problem was that John and Yoko didn't have a backing band. In short order, Mal rounded up Klaus Voormann and Alan White to play bass and drums, respectively. "John and Yoko particularly wanted Eric Clapton to make up the fivesome," said Mal, "but we couldn't get [a]hold of him, even though we worked through the night phoning everyone we knew."[6]

The next morning, Mal commandeered a limo to pick up the musicians, hoping against hope that he would be able raise Clapton in time. Twenty-year-old studio musician White recalled the sight of Mal arriving to take him to the airport. "Here was this lovable, cuddly guy," said White. "Just like a big bear."[7] Fortunately, at the last minute, Clapton's gardener was able to get the message to the guitarist, who joined the band and their entourage for an afternoon flight to Canada. "That's when it hit me," Mal wrote. "None of the people who were due to make the concert that night had ever played together before. How on earth were they going to get a show together before they went on stage that night? John had obviously thought about it too, because he and Eric walked to the back of the plane after a quick snack to have their first rehearsal. Ever tried rehearsing in the back of a Boeing 707 with electric guitars—and with no amplification?"[8]

When they arrived at Toronto's Varsity Stadium, Mal "began to feel all the tremendous excitement of the old touring days." John felt it, too, turning in an energetic set that concluded with John and Yoko's "Give Peace a Chance." "This is what we came for, really," John announced to the twenty-thousand-strong audience, "so sing along!" For Mal, the whole

John and Yoko in Toronto

concert was a revelation, underscoring his longing to return to the road. When they had finished playing, he wrote, "all the boys placed their guitars against the speakers of their amps and walked to the back of the stage. And when the feedback started to build, John, Klaus, Alan, and Eric lit ciggies. Then I went on and led them off stage, finally walking on to switch off their amps, one by one. It was over. I loved every minute of it."[9]

Time and time again over the past few years, Mal had attempted to remake himself, only to encounter roadblocks at nearly every turn. But road-managing a band came naturally to him. When he was on tour or prepping a band for a one-off gig, he felt peerless, as if he could do anything all by his lonesome. That night in Toronto, Mal felt as if he had come full circle. "I'll always remember turning around during the performance on stage," he wrote, "and finding Gene Vincent next to me with tears rolling down his cheeks. He was saying, 'It's marvelous. It's fantastic, man.'"[10] Suddenly, it was May 1963 again, and Mal was back in the Cavern Club, dying to catch a glimpse of Vincent in all his glory. And now they were together again, just six years later, although for Mal, it must have seemed like a lifetime.

For John, it may have been as simple as the confidence he gained that night at Varsity Stadium. Or perhaps it was the resistance Paul had demonstrated a week earlier, when John proposed four songs apiece on the next Beatles LP for the band's three primary songwriters. In any event, it all spilled out during a meeting at Apple on Saturday, September 20. When it came to the band's future, John could simply no longer contain his emotions.

Mal and Allen Klein were there, along with Yoko, Neil, and the boys. For his part, George was on speakerphone from Cheshire, where he was visiting his ailing mother. The topic at hand was a new agreement with Capitol, which Klein was understandably eager to ink. As Mal observed, Paul began to enumerate the group's upcoming opportunities, including a series of intimate gigs and a possible television special. In each instance, John said, "No, no, no," before telling Paul, "Well, I think you're daft." Eventually, he blurted out that he wanted a "divorce."

"What do you mean?" a stunned Paul asked.

"The group's over," John replied. "I'm leaving."

At this point, Paul recalled, "Everyone blanched except John, who colored a little, and said, 'It's rather exciting. It's like I remember telling Cynthia I wanted a divorce.'" The typically unflappable Allen Klein was flummoxed by the sudden turn of events, quickly intervening and demanding absolute secrecy to avoid upsetting the Capitol agreement. John acceded to the manager's demands. "Paul and Allen said they were glad that I wasn't going to announce it," he recalled, "like I was going to make an event out of it. I don't know whether Paul said, 'Don't tell anybody,' but he was damned pleased that I wasn't. He said, 'Oh well, that means nothing really happened if you're not going to say anything.'"[11]

Afterward, Mal and Paul returned to 7 Cavendish Avenue, where they retreated to the garden, still trying to process what had transpired back at 3 Savile Row. Paul remained hopeful that John might change his mind, that the Beatles would continue unabated. But Mal knew better. The September 20 meeting was different. As with George, Mal had reasoned that "all of them had left the group at one time or another, starting with Ringo." But when "John came into the office and said, 'the marriage is over! I want a divorce,' that was the final thing. That's what really got to Paul, you know, because I took Paul home and I ended up in the garden crying my eyes out."[12]

The trauma Mal felt in Paul's garden that afternoon might have been even more acute had the roadie not been so desperately busy. Within a matter of days, he would be working a solid week in the service of John's "Cold Turkey," intended as a Plastic Ono Band release. In terms of the Beatles' future, Mal came to recognize, as with Paul, that Klein's veil of secrecy imbued the whole episode with a level of unreality. If it wasn't public, then perhaps it wasn't true. And if it wasn't in the public consciousness yet, then John might yet change his mind. After all, he had been known to be mercurial.

That Thursday, Mal was back at EMI Studios, where John led the Plastic Ono Band's rehearsal of "Cold Turkey," with Clapton on guitar, Voormann on bass, and Ringo behind the drum kit. Unlike George, who thought John was grandstanding, Ringo was the least affected by Lennon's outburst back at 3 Savile Row. He had realized the extent of the band's malaise for quite some time. "On a lot of days, even with all the craziness, it really worked," he reasoned. "But instead of working every day, it worked, say, two days a month. There were still good days because we were still really close friends, and then it would split off again into some madness."[13]

As for "Cold Turkey," John had originally presented the song as the next Beatles single, only to be rebuffed by Paul and George, who didn't cotton to a song about heroin withdrawal. After working in EMI's Studio 3 for several days, John began to doubt the quality of the recording, which led him to move the whole shebang, with Mal providing the muscle, to Trident on September 28. After recording a solid take in the Soho studio, John and Yoko returned to EMI the next day. Working with Geoff Emerick, they mixed "Cold Turkey" for release.

With the Beatles on hiatus, and perhaps permanently so, Mal turned back to the Iveys with a vengeance. Paul's "Come and Get It" had given the Welshmen new life, and the Beatle had produced the band performing "Rock of All Ages" and "Carry on Till Tomorrow" to fulfill his obligations for *The Magic Christian* soundtrack. With the *Maybe Tomorrow* LP on the shelf, Mal knew the group needed to maximize the success of the soundtrack. Over the next few months, he mixed several songs for the LP, which was slated for a January 1970 release as *Magic Christian Music*, a standalone album of Iveys tunes as opposed to a standard movie soundtrack. That autumn, Mal also helped the band weather a key personnel change after bassist Ron Griffiths resigned. In addition to being a family man, Griffiths had missed several recording sessions due to illness, and, with the band on the verge of potentially bigger and better things, he had become a liability.

When Mal wasn't working with the Iveys, he was looking for new opportunities to demonstrate his talents. The chance to work with a new band arrived in the form of singer-songwriter Rod Lynton, who fronted a group called Rupert's People—their name an homage to the Rupert Bear tales. Mal had known Lynton from the London music scene, along with Rod's fellow bandmates Dave "Dai" Jenkins, the former Iveys rhythm guitarist; bassist Ray Beverley; and drummer Steve Brendell, who had worked at Apple as a personal assistant for John and Yoko.

A preternaturally empathetic person, Mal was well aware of the band's hard-luck story. Back in 1967, Lynton had written a song with Chris Andrews entitled "Hold On," which they arranged with the assistance of organist Matthew Fisher. During the songwriting session, Lynton introduced the musicians to his original song "Reflections of Charles Brown," based on Bach's "Air on the G String." As Lynton prepped the song for release,

Fisher joined the group Procol Harum, with whom he performed "A Whiter Shade of Pale," which, like the Rupert's People song, was based on Bach's familiar tune. The Procol Harum recording became a smash hit, of course, leaving "Reflections of Charles Brown" in a kind of also-ran status and Lynton in a state of bitter disappointment.[14] Eager to help his friend and improve the fortunes of Rupert's People in the bargain, Mal produced the band's next single, "Water to a Stone," composed by Lynton and Beverley. To the roadie's delight, the music press compared the song favorably to Steppenwolf's "Born to Be Wild."

Meanwhile, with the looming release of *Magic Christian Music*, the Iveys visited the long-standing issue of their name. Mal and Bill Collins believed that "the Iveys" had run its course as the band's handle. Besides, they were often confused with the Ivy League, a British trio that had notched several hits in the mid-sixties. "We were told many times that the Iveys was a stupid name," Tom Evans recalled. "We had great arguments with people about it. Finally, we realized the name was a disadvantage." With Mal acting in his capacity as artist relations officer for Apple, Bill Collins and the Iveys proffered several names for consideration. "We used to write out a list," said Evans, "and we'd get it down to 10, then three, and maybe one guy would like it and another wouldn't. Or we'd like it, and the record company wouldn't."[15]

A number of names were under deliberation, including "Fresh," "the Glass Onion," "Tendergreen," "the New," "the Old," and "Hyena's Nose." Paul and John were surveyed, too, suggesting "Home" and "Prix," respectively. Eventually, the Iveys found themselves under the gun. Apple was preparing *Magic Christian Music* for release, and there was no time to lose. The solution came courtesy of Neil Aspinall, who was sitting with Mal and Bill Collins in a Mayfair pub called the Thistle, there to celebrate Neil's twenty-eighth birthday. "I was asked to suggest something. Badfinger just popped in my head," said Neil, recalling "Bad Finger Boogie" as the working title for "With a Little Help from My Friends."[16] That November, twenty-two-year-old Liverpudlian Joey Molland auditioned for a spot with the Iveys, who were still reeling from the loss of Griffiths. To accommodate the new guitarist's membership in the band, Tom Evans took over bass duties.

During this same period, Mal shuttled between stage-managing *Sentimental Journey*, Ringo's debut solo LP, and, with Neil, compiling a promotional video for "Something," George's first Beatles A side. Recorded in October 1969, the short was shot on location at the Beatles' homes, with George and Pattie strolling among the gardens at Kinfauns; Paul and Linda cavorting with sheepdog Martha on their Scottish farm; John and Yoko dark-robed and solemn at Tittenhurst Park; and Ringo and Mo tearing about Brookfield on their motorbikes. With the footage under their belts, Mal and Neil returned to 3 Savile Row, where Neil edited the individual sequences into an illusory whole.

On October 11, Mal celebrated Gary's eighth birthday in unforgettable style, staging a massive fireworks display in the family's Sunbury garden. *The Beatles Book* marked the occasion—not only the birth of the eldest child among the Beatles' inner circle, but also the manner in which Mal's good intentions could go horribly awry. "When they came to let off the roman candles," *The Beatles Book* noted, "Mal decided it would make a good display—something like a big fountain—if they stuck all the candles into one of the apple trees before they lit them. But he'd forgotten how powerful roman candles are and as soon as the touch-paper had burned down, the neighbors were startled to see red, blue, green, and yellow balls of fire hurtling past their windows. [Mal's] immediate neighbor was a bit upset to find that a couple of his apple trees had been set on fire!"[17]

That fall, Ken Mansfield visited London for the first time since Allen Klein's Apple bloodletting. Afterward, he penned what he later described as his "first fan letter," though it was "not directed to a person or an act, but instead is aimed at a concept and those that make up the heart and soul of that concept." The concept, of course, was Apple. Addressing the letter to Mal, Mansfield lamented the sad state of affairs at 3 Savile Row, where he said he could sense the discontent. Hoping to buoy his friend's spirits, Mansfield remarked that the Beatles and their supporters are a source of warmth with the ability to do great things. Clearly referencing Klein, Mansfield added that he was distraught over how things could go wrong when the wrong individuals get involved. The purpose of the letter, he concluded, was to say that he cared and that he was always happy to help in any way.[18]

Mal was hardly the only person who could benefit from Mansfield's glad tidings. Not surprisingly, Paul, by this juncture, had become estranged from his fellow Beatles, a situation that dated back to the blowup at Olympic in May. John's divorce announcement had left Paul in a fierce depression, which he nursed that autumn in Scotland with a steady diet of liquor. To make matters worse, he had become the target of the bizarre "Paul is dead" rumors that forced him into the curious position of having to defend his own existence. Despite the ridiculous "death clues" uncovered by overzealous fans, the media attention had become so profuse that Paul eventually submitted to a *Life* magazine cover story entitled "Paul Is Still with Us." When he finally emerged from his stupor, he and Linda returned to 7 Cavendish Avenue, where the Beatle began contemplating a solo career.

That December, George renewed his acquaintance with Delaney and Bonnie and Friends, having seen them perform at the Royal Albert Hall, with Eric Clapton chipping in on guitar. George had been so moved by the concert that he agreed to accompany Delaney and Bonnie on tour. "Several days later, he asked me to join him on the road," Mal wrote, "a request I willingly complied with. This was certainly one of the easiest gigs I had done, for George is very self-sufficient and looks after himself most of the time. And with one guitar and amplifier to look after, I was on easy street. We were to play Liverpool on this tour, four years since that day when George last trod that Empire stage as a member of the Beatles."[19]

As with the Plastic Ono Band's Toronto set back in September, Mal was delighted to reprise his familiar role of roadie, especially when it came to the hijinks associated with a rock 'n' roll tour. After one especially raucous night with Delaney and Bonnie and Friends, "things got a little out of hand and a beer fight ensued, everybody ending up soaked to the skin with liberal quantities of ale—all in good fun, mind you. At one point, Eric dared me to pour a pint of beer over the yet untouched George. I chickened out, and at the last minute poured it over myself, much to the amusement of all concerned, but it wasn't long before George was also covered. The hotel management and staff were very tolerant of the whole affair, but did present us with a bill for several hundred dollars the following day to cover the cost of cleaning the carpets."[20]

That same month, Mal unexpectedly served as roadie for the Plastic

Ono Band's appearance at the Lyceum Theatre on the Strand. The day after returning to London from George's adventures with Delaney and Bonnie, Mal had received an urgent telephone call from Kevin Harrington, who had been asked by John and Yoko to road-manage the Lyceum concert, which was being held as a benefit for UNICEF. "This was to be Kevin's first solo gig and he was terrified," Mal wrote. "I understood exactly how he felt, and though tired from the trip, took over the whole proceeding." Entitled Peace for Christmas, the gala event featured a massive "WAR IS OVER (IF YOU WANT IT)" banner above the stage and John and Yoko sharing the spotlight with George, Eric Clapton, Klaus Voormann, Alan White, Billy Preston, Keith Moon, and Delaney and Bonnie, among a host of other top-flight musicians of the day.

Mal was forced to work double-time to bring the event off. "I had to provide three drum kits and as many percussion instruments as I could lay my hands on," he wrote. "Chaotic it may have been offstage and behind the scenes, but the onstage performance made all the hard work and headaches worthwhile."[21]

Incredibly, after a multiyear hiatus from acting as a roadie, Mal had returned to his element with a vengeance.

31

DOUBLE AGENT

It was around this time that Mal began working for Paul in a clandestine fashion, cloaking his movements so as not to arouse the attention of any other Beatle and to stay under the radar with the folks at Apple. He even kept his activities on Paul's behalf from Neil. On December 26—the two-year anniversary of the *Magical Mystery Tour* television debacle—Mal unloaded a Studer four-track recorder at 7 Cavendish Avenue. Outside of him and a few folks at Apple and EMI, nobody knew that Paul was going it alone musically with Linda, which was exactly how the Beatle wanted things—at least for the time being.

Recording an album in this fashion proved to be the perfect balm for Paul's depression. With periodic visits from his loyal manservant Mal, who would ferry instruments and fresh four-track tape over to 7 Cavendish Avenue, Paul began to enjoy the homespun nature of his post-Beatles life.

Meanwhile, Mal rang in the New Year—indeed, the new decade—accompanying Bill Collins and the newly christened Badfinger to a taping of *Top of the Pops*, where the band lip-synched a performance of "Come and Get It" for a studio audience. That month, Mal would be proud to learn that "Come and Get It" was selling some four thousand copies per day. Eventually, the song would notch a top-five showing for Badfinger on the U.K. charts. After nearly two years of toil, the band was finally getting their just deserts.

But nothing was better than working a Beatles session. On January 3, 1970, for the first time in months, Mal met the boys at EMI Studios. They were contractually bound to release a soundtrack album in tandem with Lindsay-Hogg's documentary, which was now going under the title *Let It*

Be. On this day, Paul, George, and Ringo convened in Studio 2 with George Martin, who was celebrating his forty-fourth birthday with the band that had made his name. John was absent, having taken an extended vacation with Yoko in Denmark.

As the band prepared to record "I Me Mine," George acknowledged John's absence with a wry reference to the popular British band Dave Dee, Dozy, Beaky, Mick, and Tich: "You all will have read that Dave Dee is no longer with us," he joked, "but Mickey and Tich and I have decided to carry on the good work that's always gone down in Number 2."[1] They called it quits at 11:30 p.m., when the studio's eight-track machine began to "take up smoking," Mal wrote in his diary. This gave him the perfect excuse to join Lil at a party that evening hosted by musical instrument impresario Ivor Arbiter. He arrived just in time to enjoy a lovely Chinese meal his wife had plated for him.[2]

Mal and the three Beatles returned to EMI Studios the next day for a bravura fourteen-hour session to complete work on "Let It Be," which for the roadie now rivaled "In My Life" in his affections as his favorite Beatles song. That afternoon, George, Paul, and Linda would add harmony vocals to the group's original January 31, 1969, performance of the tune—"aahing and oohing," Mal scrawled in his diary.[3] Mary Hopkin had originally been scheduled to join them on backing vocals, but she had been waylaid at the last minute.[4] That same day, George would try his hand at a new guitar solo, while Martin arranged an overdub featuring two trumpets, two trombones, and a tenor saxophone. As the night wore on, Ringo and Paul added percussion to the mix, along with another, still-more-sizzling guitar solo courtesy of George. As one of Paul's crowning achievements from Rishikesh, "Let It Be" was, for all intents and purposes, complete. That afternoon, Mal had picked up the acetate for "You Know My Name (Look Up the Number)," which had been slated as the upcoming single's B side.

With new versions of "I Me Mine" and "Let It Be" at his disposal, Glyn Johns began compiling yet another mix of the *Get Back*–cum–*Let It Be* soundtrack for the Beatles' consideration. A few days later, Mal shared an acetate of the LP with Paul at Cavendish Avenue, where he had arranged for Doug Ellis, the manager of Sound City, to offer a private demonstration of a slew of left-handed guitars for the Beatle. Ellis had known Mal for years as a welcome presence in his shop on Shaftesbury Avenue. "He was about nine feet tall," he recalled. "A good bloke." The Sound City staff adored Mal's roguish ways, and they would often nip off to the pub for a quick pint with him after he had transacted his Beatles business. On one occasion, Mal gifted Ellis with a set of the boys' autographs, although "he'd probably signed them himself," the store manager joked.[5]

Keen on finding new guitar sounds for his solo record, Paul tried out a Fender Telecaster and a Gibson Firebird during the demonstration. For Mal, Doug's demo proved a welcome distraction after a brutal day with George at 3 Savile Row. "I'm going to embarrass you now in front of your friends," Harrison had announced in front of Apple staff. "John Barham arranged the tracks on the Badfinger album that you take credit for." Apparently, the error Mal had made during the previous spring—and for which Ron Kass had chided him—had reared its ugly head yet again with the release of *Magic Christian Music*.

"Well, I guess he did embarrass me," Mal later reflected, "but it should not have been on the album—me as arranger, that is." Refusing to let the issue go, Mal admitted that he still felt as though he had conducted the arrangements, reasoning that he had merely used Barham in the same fashion that George had used other people's arrangements for Jackie Lomax's LP.[6]

If Mal experienced any lingering sting from George's admonishment, it didn't register in his diaries. As usual, he found plenty of projects to divert his attention, including a new venture with Neil, who had steadily turned to drink in the days since Klein's ascension and the Beatles' hiatus and potential disbandment.[7] Working together, the two erstwhile road managers began compiling *Scrapbook*, an audio history of the Beatles for which they narrated their memories into a Nagra tape recorder.

Meanwhile, at George's instigation, Mal had started stage-managing recording sessions for Billy Preston's Apple debut, for which George and Ringo served as the keyboard player's backup band. To occupy his mind during one particularly lengthy session at Olympic, Mal had purchased a plastic "saddle gun" kit for a few pounds in a nearby shop. It was a replica of a Winchester rifle—a far cry from the genuine article that Alan Pariser had shown him a few years back in Malibu. Indulging his fascination with the Old West, Mal glued the scale model weapon together and proudly hung it on his living room wall, near the children's baby pictures.

As January 1970 came to a close, Mal began drifting into an emotional slide that had been developing over the past several years. "Seem to be losing Paul," he wrote on January 27. "Really got the stick from him today. He let me down," and ominously added "Fixing a Hole," "Pepper," and "Directorship" to a growing list of disappointments. Apparently, the conversation had turned yet again to the issue of Mal's servile role in Paul's life, with the roadie believing their association was bounded by friendship and love. "A servant serves," Mal wrote, but "he who serves is not always a servant," he added, echoing John's philosophy from December 1968. "Love is as sharp and piercing as a sword," Mal reasoned, "but as the sword edge dulls—you sharpen it. So love's keenness needs honing—needs honesty."[8]

Indeed, it was Paul's heartbreaking honesty with regard to Mal's role in his life that had been affording the roadie such discomfort. Meanwhile, as he motored all over London, carrying out the Beatle's secret errands, he found much-needed relief in a 3:30 p.m. telephone call from John, who wanted Mal to arrange for a session that night with legendary American producer Phil Spector at the helm. Apparently, John had woken up that day and composed "Instant Karma! (We All Shine On)," which he was eager to commit to tape. One of Mal's first calls was to Alan White, who remembered that the roadie didn't mince words. "Get your drum kit together," Mal said, "and get yourself down to the studio as quickly as possible. John wrote a song this morning. He wants to record it today and release it next week."[9]

By 7 p.m., Mal had assembled the musicians at EMI Studios. With John on lead vocals and piano, George on electric guitar, Klaus on bass, and White on drums, the group quickly compiled a basic track, with adornments from Billy Preston on Hammond organ and Mal playing the chimes. When John began fashioning the idea of a chorus, Mal and Billy went to Hatchetts Playground, a hip Piccadilly Circus nightclub, where they rounded up a group of revelers to join Yoko and Allen Klein on backing vocals. For Mal, the "Instant Karma!" session was pure magic. Within the space of a single evening, the recording was in the can.

On February 11, Mal joined John and Yoko for a lip-synched performance of "Instant Karma!" on *Top of the Pops*, with the roadie, clad in a beige suit and a light-green tie, playing the tambourine. By this juncture, Mal's long-standing relationship with Paul was in freefall. A few days earlier, he had been awakened by a 1 p.m. telephone call from the Beatle. It went "something like this," he wrote in his diary:

Mal: Yeah?

Paul: I've got time at EMI over the weekend. Would like you to pick up some gear from the house.

Mal: Great, man. That's lovely. Session at EMI?!

Paul: Yes, but I don't want anyone there to make me tea. I have the family—wife and kids there.

Mal: [*thinking to himself*] Goes my poor head, "Why????"[10]

By the next week, Mal found himself behind the wheel of the Apple van, moving Paul's gear from EMI Studios to Morgan Studios, another Northwest London facility where Paul could work incognito. At one point, Neil cornered Mal about Paul's surreptitious recording sessions, demanding to know more. "Where's Paul?" he asked, to which Mal tersely replied, "Not telling you."

In other instances, Mal ordered a Mellotron for Paul, while keeping him fully stocked with plectrums and other gear. In late February, Paul asked Mal to move everything back to EMI, where he was set to record "Maybe I'm Amazed" in Studio 2. For Mal, everything came to a head at 7 Cavendish Avenue, when "my long love, Paul, to whom I had devoted so many years of loyalty, turned around to me and said, 'I don't need you anymore, Mal.'"[11]

It is difficult to imagine a more crushing blow for Mal during his many years of service to the Beatles. He had clearly elevated Paul to a kind of hero status, marveling in his talent and reveling in the opportunity to be his friend. "I was heartbroken and very distressed, for someone to whom I had given so much love and dedication all those years saying that to me was a bitter blow. Paul was making his first solo album on which he was to play most every instrument himself, and he had asked me to set up all the equipment at EMI for him before he delivered his parting message."[12]

Years later, Mal would ascribe a more gracious motive to Paul's brusque effort to shun him. "Looking back," he wrote, "I have a greater understanding of what he was saying to me, realizing that it must have been very hard for him to put in words." Mal consoled himself, writing that "we really did like each other, and we still do to this day." But Mal had come to believe that the turmoil in the Beatles' business lives—namely, Paul's alignment with his in-laws versus the other bandmates' throwing in their lot with Klein—was behind the schism in his relationship with Paul. "It was the only thing he could do," Mal concluded. "Paul couldn't ask me to sit on the fence." To Mal's mind, Paul was merely attempting to stave off any sense of embarrassment for the roadie, hoping to avoid forcing him into a position where he would have to side with one Beatle over another. "And so he was honest with me," Mal wrote, "surely the mark of a true friend."[13]

At virtually the same moment that Paul was pushing him away, Mal was enjoying a greater affinity with the other Beatles, especially George. That February, George and Pattie invited Mal to see their future home, a lavish estate in Henley-on-Thames called Friar Park. Construction on the manor house had begun in 1889 at the behest of Sir Frank Crisp, an idiosyncratic London lawyer who transformed the sixty-two-acre property into a splendid Gothic retreat, replete with elaborate gardens featuring gnomes and other statuary and even a scale model of the Matterhorn. In the decades since Crisp's death in 1919, Friar Park had undergone a slow decline into decrepitude. George and Pattie had considered purchasing the property for at least a year; finally, in January 1970—with his bank account flush after the American chart-topping success of "Something"—George was ready, plunking down £140,000 for the estate.

On February 15, Mal joined George and Pattie for a tour of Friar Park. Like George, he could glimpse the property's potential. At one point, Mal snapped a shot of the Beatle walking in front of the main house. In the photograph, George seems dwarfed by the mansion, which has fallen gray after years of neglect, many of its windows long since broken, surrendering the interior to the elements. As he imagined a potential future for Friar Park, George floated the notion of Mal and his family living in a house on the estate. "I really would feel a friend for life," Mal wrote in his diary.[14]

Before the day was out, George proudly showed off the giant earthmovers in place to repair Sir Frank's lagoons, good-naturedly posing atop one of the machines as Mal captured the moment with his Pentax. George returned the favor as Mal posed in front of one of Sir Frank's engravings on the exterior of the main house. It depicted a robed monk atop a plinth, holding a frying pan with a pair of holes in its basin; the legend read, "Two Holy Friars." Like George, Mal adored Sir Frank's wordplay, which was on display in nearly every nook and cranny of the property—from the "Don't Keep Off the Grass" sign before the great lawn to the words arrayed above the windows of the gardener's shed: "Yesterday—today—was tomorrow" and "Tomorrow—today—will be yesterday."

In mid-March, Mal assisted George and Pattie as they began moving their belongings from Kinfauns to Friar Park. Years later, Gary recalled walking inside the mansion, unnerved by the spooky, unlit corridors as his father searched in vain for a working light fixture. A few days later, Chris O'Dell hosted a housewarming party of sorts in honor of Pattie's twenty-sixth birthday. "The party was a great success," Chris recalled. "Ringo and Maureen, Paul and Linda, John and Yoko, Derek and Joan, Neil and Suzy Aspinall, Klaus and Christine Voormann, and Peter Brown were all there." As always, Mal was in evidence, supping on wine and hors d'oeuvres and joining his friends on an eerie tour of Sir Frank's secret caves beneath the property. Flashlights in hand, the partygoers made their way through the dark, rocky tunnels. At one point, someone laughed and said, "This is a real magical mystery tour."[15] The gathering at Friar Park that night proved to be a convivial one—a great success, indeed. But for Mal and the Beatles, it was also the last. John, Paul, George, and Ringo would never be under the same roof together again.

On April 10, with his first solo album about to hit the shelves, Paul let the cat out of the bag. "PAUL IS QUITTING THE BEATLES," the *Daily Mirror* headline trumpeted. While John, George, and Ringo had maintained radio silence for nearly seven months, Paul had gone public about their disbandment. For his part, Mal heard the announcement on his car radio. This time, the sorrowful tidings didn't end in a fusillade of tears, as they had back in September in the Cavendish Avenue garden. His deteriorating experiences with Paul since January had well prepared him for a new, post-Beatles world.

At Apple, Derek Taylor issued a press release, attempting to sow seeds of optimism in the face of so much doom and gloom in the press and among the band's legions of fans: "Spring is here and Leeds play Chelsea tomorrow and Ringo and John and George and Paul are alive and well and full of hope. The world is still spinning and so are we and so are you. When the spinning stops—that'll be the time to worry. Not before. Until then, the Beatles are alive and well and the Beat goes on, the Beat goes on."[16]

As with everyone connected with the group, Mal would be inundated with questions about the breakup for the rest of his days. The roadie traced the seeds of the dissolution back to 1966, reasoning that "the end of touring was the beginning of the end for the Beatles and their personal relationships with each other. While they were together, facing a common enemy, which in their case was the boredom of travelling, the crowds, being locked up in hotel rooms, all of which looked alike and could be anywhere in the world," Mal wrote, "the pressures of having to perform night after night to the best of their ability kept them together as a family unit."[17]

To Derek's mind, it had simply come down to a matter of survival for the boys, for whom the desires of superfans like him and the other members of their inner circle were no longer enough. "Neil and Mal and me and Peter, we were there because we wanted to serve the Beatles," he wrote. "We were heavy fans, so are all the people around them; I guess the whole world is and the miracle is not that the Beatles survived the world's adoration (they didn't, they took a powder to end the pain), but that Lennon and McCartney and Harrison and Starkey had the wit and the wisdom to cling to the good earth and not fall off."[18]

Taylor had grown to admire Mal immensely, seeing in him a survivor of sorts as the Beatles sailed the bumpy seas of touring and world superstardom before going into business for themselves with Apple and then out the other side into disbandment and détente. To Derek's mind, Mal was well positioned to make something out of the new landscape, writing that "Mal Evans (Neil's companion when they were managing the road before the job got its own title and its own dignity and its truly fascinating place in the complexities of touring, in other words before we heard the word 'roadies') is still at Apple and still one of the greatest roadies the world has ever known. But more than any of us he found a way to adapt to changing times and he became a record producer, played parts in movies, and he is willing to serve if he may, and there is nothing nobler than real service, I believe."[19]

On April 1, Mal had worked the final Beatles session at EMI Studios. The only band member in attendance that day was Ringo, who sat behind his kit in Studio 1 during producer Phil Spector's orchestral superimpositions for "The Long and Winding Road," "Across the Universe," and "I Me Mine." Working from Richard Hewson's orchestral scores, John Barham had created choral arrangements for "The Long and Winding Road" and "Across the Universe." The soundtrack LP, with production credits ascribed to Spector, George Martin, and Glyn Johns, featured a pair of American chart-topping singles in "Let It Be" and "The Long and Winding Road." Meanwhile, "Let It Be" fell short in the United Kingdom, notching a number two showing and closing the book on Martin's "Roll," which had concluded with "Get Back" and "The Ballad of John and Yoko," the band's last U.K. number one song.

It was an extraordinary accomplishment, by any measure—one that Mal could quantify over hundreds of hours of devoted support at EMI, nourishing the boys with tea and nosh, maintaining their gear in tip-top shape. Indeed, when it came to the studio, Mal was "Mother Malcolm" to the nth degree.

That May, when Lindsay-Hogg's *Let It Be* documentary finally premiered at the London Pavilion, Mal and Lil made the trip into the city, joining Neil and Derek and their wives for one last opening night. The Beatles, of course, were nowhere in evidence, leaving their innermost circle and business associates to toe the line. "We felt miserable and guilty at sharing in something so innately untruthful, as celebrative as a première," Derek later wrote, "for we knew that grim as the worst moments in the film may seem, the real facts and abstractions were terrible."[20]

For Mal, seeing himself on the silver screen provided, as always, an unabashed thrill. Not surprisingly, the roadie's turn with the anvil on "Maxwell's Silver Hammer" quickly emerged as a favorite scene among viewers. "When the fans heard about this," Mal wrote, "they presented me, all gaily wrapped, with a silver hammer of my very own, which pleased me to no end."[21] The Beatles may have ended, but Mal was destined to be a star.

On Mal's thirty-fifth birthday, the Apple Scruffs joined in on the fun, anointing him as the cover story for the May 1970 issue of their monthly newsletter, with the words "Happy Birthday 'Maxwell'-Mal!" emblazoned above a drawing of the roadie preparing to pound a birthday cake—with a hammer, of course. As with Derek, Mal was an honorary, card-carrying member of the Apple Scruffs. And thanks to George, he was poised to enjoy plenty of face time with the Scruffs over the next several months. Having stockpiled dozens upon dozens of songs, "the Quiet Beatle" planned to return to EMI Studios with Spector to produce his first post-disbandment LP.

At first, Spector proved to be an able coproducer for George, attending sessions and providing guidance on the implementation of his much-ballyhooed "Wall of Sound" recording technique. But as the summer wore on, the American took to drinking heavily for the first time, gradually losing his effectiveness and returning Stateside to find his bearings.

In terms of musicians, George had envisioned a large ensemble of players coming together for the occasion. Working with Kevin Harrington, Mal stage-managed nearly the entirety of the album, a three-record set to be entitled *All Things Must Pass*. As part of his duties, he took copious notes regarding the tracks and performers—no easy feat. "I went to a couple of sessions," EMI engineer Alan Parsons recalled, "and every time a musician came in, George would tell them to go find a guitar and join in."[22] When work began in earnest on *All Things Must Pass*, George invited Pete Ham and Tom Evans from Badfinger to serve as his backing band, which also included, at various times, the likes of Ringo, Eric Clapton, Peter Frampton, Bobby Whitlock, Klaus Voormann, Carl Radle, Gary Wright, and Jim Gordon.

Yet, as always, Mal's duties weren't restricted to maintaining George's studio diary. With so many musicians involved, there were plenty of mishaps to be remedied. During an impromptu take of "Get Back," George can be heard summoning the roadie to clean up a spill on the studio floor: "Mal, get a mop and another glass of orange juice!" Peter Frampton later recalled working with Mal, whom he recognized on sight, during the *All Things Must Pass* sessions. "He was a gentle giant and a teddy bear," he said of the roadie. "He was a lovely guy and in his way was almost as famous as the Beatles."[23]

When it came to Badfinger, Mal was determined to find success for the band with Apple. Nearly a year earlier, as he prepared to travel with Neil on their dual-family vacation to the Algarve, he had pitched the idea of a production contract with Klein. While the American manager hadn't approved the idea, he also pointedly hadn't declined the pitch, either. With Badfinger riding high after the success of "Come and Get It" and *Magic Christian Music*, Mal felt that the time was nigh to make his move.

That February, Ringo had taken a stab at a new number called "You Gotta Pay Your Dues," which had originally been offered to Badfinger. Eventually retitled "It Don't Come Easy," the propulsive rocker roared to life with Ringo's lead vocals. Produced by George, "It Don't Come Easy" included a tambourine part by Mal, along with Badfinger's Pete Ham and Tom Evans on backing vocals. After the session concluded, Mal and engineer Ken Scott took turns overdubbing themselves on lead vocals. "I have no idea whatever happened to those mixes," Scott wrote, "but I'm pretty sure no one will bootleg them, luckily for all."[24]

On April 18, barely a week after the Beatles' disbandment made international news, Mal brought Badfinger back to EMI Studios, where he produced four new tracks by the group, including standout compositions in "No Matter What" and "Without You." More than a year after Allen Klein's purge, Jack Oliver had managed to hang on to his role as president of Apple Records. As with other folks in the organization, he was keenly aware of Mal's background as a roadie and understood implicitly how it served as a yoke when it came to professional advancement. But Oliver was also open to seeing Mal in a new light. "Mal was the gentle giant, a lovable person," he later remarked. "Everybody loved Mal, especially the Beatles, but sure, everyone was a bit dubious about him as a record producer. That always happens when you see someone walk out of the role you're used to seeing them in. But as long as what comes out of the studio sounds good, it really doesn't matter who does it."[25]

When Pete Ham played the demo for "No Matter What," Mal was blown away, confident that Badfinger had a solid hit on their hands. A collaboration by Ham and Tom Evans, the soaring ballad "Without You" wasn't that far behind. In nearly the same instant, Bill Collins was Stateside, making the acquaintance of Stan Polley, a shrewd negotiator who, for all intents and purposes, seemed to be the hard-nosed advocate the band sorely needed. Sure, they adored Collins, but he was weak on the business aspects of their affairs, so they agreed to a deal with Polley that gave him full, irrevocable authority to negotiate all contracts on their behalf.

Mal with Badfinger: from left to right, Tom Evans, Pete Ham, Mike Gibbins, and Joey Molland

On May 13, Mal led Badfinger through a new, high-octane rendition of "No Matter What" at EMI Studios, with John Kurlander and Richard Lush handling engineering duties; everyone was thrilled with the results. Guitarist Joey Molland later recalled that people in the Beatles' circle had been accustomed to "seeing Mal as the roadie, as a bit of a buffoon, really. But he wasn't like that in the studio. He was very workmanlike. He stayed on the studio floor with us and even had a voice in the arrangement."

During the session, the composition that had begun life as a plaintive acoustic tune now radiated with electric power and rock 'n' roll swagger. "I made up the guitar solo on my Firebird," said Joey. "It was a slurring solo, doubling up the notes, bending them, and picking them normally." During a break, the guitarist took the opportunity to glance into the closet beneath the Studio 2 stairwell. "There was an old lap steel sitting there, and I was just noodling on it." Liking what they heard, Mal and Joey's bandmates suggested he play the lap steel guitar over his existing Firebird solo.[26]

As "No Matter What" continued to evolve in the studio, Mal recommended several Beatlesesque adornments, including a healthy dose of ADT (or "artificial double tracking") on the introductory guitar part and as an enhanced, or "Leslied," sound effect on Joey's Firebird.[27] For the recording, Mal and the band even concocted a false ending to afford "No Matter What" some panache. When the session concluded, "We were real happy," Joey recalled. "It sounded like us, but at the same time it sounded like a record. We were knocked out."[28]

But when it came to putting "No Matter What" out as Badfinger's next single, the folks at Apple balked. "We all believed in it," said Mike Gibbins. "Mal believed in it. But Apple thought it wasn't a good single."[29] Mal remembered struggling to earn the boys' approval: "When I went to the Beatles and Apple in general saying I felt 'No Matter What' should be released as a single, I came up against stiff opposition, all four Beatles telling me that it was not worthy." George had been especially disparaging, cautioning Mal, "It's your neck. If you want to stick it out, don't blame us if it gets chopped off."[30] Longtime Beatles engineer Geoff Emerick had listened to the recordings Mal had presented and deemed them "lackluster," concluding that "no amount of enthusiasm and urging from Mal could get them, or any of the Beatles, to change their minds, and so the tapes just sat on the shelf."[31] Determined to prove his mettle as a record producer, Mal wasn't about to give up on "No Matter What," which, to his ear, sounded like a bona fide hit.

Meanwhile, based upon the success of "Come and Get It," Badfinger had been invited to represent Apple Records at Capitol's annual convention, scheduled for that June near Honolulu's Waikiki Beach. As it turned out, the Capitol convention would prove to have long-lasting implications for Mal's professional ambitions. For the most part, he was excited by the prospect of showing off the band and, as a bonus, sunning himself in the tropics. But there was trouble brewing among Badfinger's inner circle, and in retrospect, Mal may have been caught unaware by the political tides turning against him.

When it came to the upcoming trip, Apple had provided funding for Badfinger to transport one additional person to Hawaii, and given that they were expected to perform, the band naturally selected their roadie, Ian "Fergie" Ferguson. "The group decided that I should be the one," Fergie recalled, a decision that was met with derision by Badfinger's manager. "When Bill [Collins] was told, he went absolutely bananas!" Fergie added. "He couldn't handle it."[32]

Collins later maintained that he had an issue not with Fergie's being invited to the convention, but rather, with Mal's plans to make the trip to Hawaii. By this point, Collins had concluded that Mal intended to usurp his role with Badfinger and take over as their manager. On the day of their departure, Collins attended a breakfast meeting with the band, Fergie, and, as luck would have it, Stan Polley. As Badfinger prepared to make the long flight to Honolulu, Polley intercepted Collins and told him he should go to the convention regardless of whether he had been officially invited. Collins was livid, telling Polley, "I should be with them. There's a ticket for me. There's a hotel room for me. But Mal Evans is taking it; and no one is saying a word about it!"[33]

The notion that Mal, as a key player at Apple, was in some fashion preventing Collins from going to Hawaii was ridiculous. Perhaps out of compassion for the manager—or in a brazen effort to solidify his own place in Badfinger's political ecosystem—Polley offered to pay Collins's airfare. When he arrived at the convention hotel, Collins claimed that Mal seemed surprised to see him in Honolulu, which, to the manager's mind, lent further credence to his hypothesis that Mal harbored less than scrupulous motives for attending the convention. "I'm sure he wanted to take the band away from me," Collins said. "He was shocked to see me there." For the life of him, Collins couldn't understand that Mal was lobbying to be the band's *producer*, and had been for quite some time. Indeed, prior to their journey to the South Pacific, Mal had helmed twenty-five sessions on behalf of the group.

Beverley Ellis, Pete Ham's girlfriend, chalked up Collins's behavior to unchecked paranoia. "Mal Evans was a big huggy bear. All of the group had a really good relationship with him," she recalled. "Mal had done it, he'd met everyone, and Bill didn't have to worry that Mal was after something.

So the only reason Mal could have for hanging with the group was that he really did like them."[34] With Collins and Fergie in tow, Mal was delighted to squire Badfinger and their entourage around the convention floor among the numerous contacts he had cultivated during his Beatles years.

At one point, the group attended a reception with Allen Klein. Var Smith, a thirty-year-old Capitol employee, was there, too. He recalled that Klein acted arrogantly throughout the convention. "He had this swagger about him," said Smith, "and he was carrying a golf putter. He would poke people in the chest with the putter to emphasize whatever he was talking about. He was just a big bully."[35] During the reception, Mike Gibbins witnessed a sight he would never forget. "Allen Klein was sitting in his lounge chair, talking to everybody," the drummer recalled, "and his balls are hanging out of his Bermuda shorts. Nobody said anything, but everybody was smiling."

Unfortunately, the band's performance at the convention proved to be no laughing matter. With Mal leading the way, the bandmates naturally logged plenty of beach hours. "The day had started out overcast," said Fergie, "and no one thought they would get sunburned." When they were finally ready to play their set, Mal and the members of Badfinger had been ravaged by the sun. "Tom and Joey's shoulders were so burnt that they couldn't even put their guitar straps on," Fergie remembered. "They played the whole set sitting down!"[36]

By the time the band and their entourage returned to London, Collins's suspicions had reached a fever pitch. The manager had convinced himself that bassist Tom Evans, one of Mal's best mates, was part of the plot to unseat him—and possibly even Klein himself. Not long afterward, a meeting was convened at Apple to map out Badfinger's future. Klein and Derek Taylor were in attendance, along with Collins, Geoff Emerick, and Tom Evans. Collins later described the gathering as a "big brouhaha." The manager took the opportunity to make his case, grandstanding about his role in Badfinger's ascendancy. In Collins's memory, Mal scarcely uttered a word and "nearly put his foot through the floor." As for Klein, Collins believed he had knocked the Beatles' manager off his "pomp and circumstance" pedestal.[37]

Emerick remembered things somewhat differently from Collins, whom he described as "very paranoid, constantly protecting his position, and extremely manipulative." Worse yet, Emerick perceived an additional threat that may have escaped Mal's notice. "Aggravating the situation was the fact that the group had added a new member—Joey Molland—who seemed to me to be just as paranoid and manipulative as Bill," said Emerick. "They soon fell in league with each other, and the next thing Mal knew, he was being called on the carpet by Allen Klein. The poor guy—all he had done was introduce the group, who were nobodies at the time, to the most famous recording artists in the world and gotten them a record deal." The meeting finally came to an end when Klein, disgusted with the whole business, appointed Emerick as the band's producer. Geoff was happy to take on Badfinger as a client, but he hated the fashion in which Mal, his longtime colleague and friend, had been treated. "It was a nasty, embarrassing meeting," Emerick recalled. "Now [Mal] was being forced out, not just because he hadn't been a very good producer, but because Bill Collins thought that [he] was out to take his job as manager!"[38]

Mal was understandably brokenhearted by the outcome of the meeting, having been severed from Badfinger's musical affairs henceforward. Gibbins could barely contain his disgust, later remarking that "Mal Evans never wanted to take over the band. That was Bill's paranoia. He just wanted us to do good, and Bill was protective of his position. Mal was our buddy. We used to spend time at his house with his wife and children. Mal never wanted Bill out of the picture."[39] Tom Evans's girlfriend, Marianne, attributed Mal's motives to nothing more sinister than a desire for friendship. She and Tom had met Mal and Lily at one of the Apple parties, becoming fast friends with the couple and sharing Sunday dinners at their place in Sunbury.[40]

As for Molland, he vehemently denied Emerick's assertion about his role in the fracas. "Mal was a softie, just a great guy," said Molland. "He just liked to help people. He was concerned about the band to the point where it alienated Bill. And that messed up his relationship with the band."[41]

When it came to assigning blame regarding the unfortunate turn of events in his life, Mal didn't pull any punches. "My career as Badfinger's record producer was brought to an abrupt end by Mr. Allen Klein, who verbally stabbed me in the back," he wrote. "Bill Collins and I had known each other for many years, and I always thought we were close friends, but suddenly, after I had been disposed of, Bill told me Allen suggested that I wanted to take over as personal manager for the group. This was the furthest thing from my mind, but such was Bill's paranoia that he readily believed it and was instrumental in coming between me and the group."[42]

Although the various players and their roles in Mal's undoing as Badfinger's producer may have been hazy, Emerick was sure of one thing without reservation: "As a talent scout, Mal was a success. Badfinger clearly had musical ability, and, like the Beatles, they were blessed with not one, but two lead singers and songwriters—Pete Ham and Tom Evans."[43]

32

HITMAKER

Sadly, Mal would come to understand the nature of paranoia firsthand as work proceeded on *All Things Must Pass*. With Badfinger seemingly lost to him, he threw himself headlong into his work with George—so much so that he began to perceive Kevin Harrington, of all people, as a threat.

"During *All Things Must Pass*, I started to feel like Mal was excluding me from George as he was the only one left working," Kevin recalled. After nearly two years of working side by side with his mentor, he felt as though he had been demoted. "I was pissed off at Mal because he started to treat me like his personal assistant," Harrington said. In one especially painful instance, he found himself ensnared in a rather childish power move by Mal, who ordered him to "make me some tea." Kevin knew full well that Neil would never have asked Mal to prepare a cuppa for him. Kevin made the tea, only to watch as "Mal would take it off me and give it to George. It felt like Mal had put a cloak 'round George and I had been excluded."[1] Worse yet, the incident reeked of desperation.

Fortunately for Kevin, a chance opportunity presented itself during the *All Things Must Pass* sessions that the young roadie simply couldn't resist. Derek and the Dominos—comprised of Clapton, Whitlock, Radle, and Gordon, key session players on George's album—planned to take their show on the road that August, and they were in desperate need of a road manager. For Kevin, it was a dream opportunity. After serving as Mal's assistant for the past few years, he had been privy to hundreds of stories about the ramshackle, no-holds-barred life of a rock 'n' roll tour. By this point, Harrington didn't simply "want to go on the road," he recalled. "I *needed* to go on the road."[2] For him, touring with Derek and the Dominos would be a trial by fire, but thanks to Mal, he was fully prepared for anything that came his way. At Mal's recommendation, he had even taken to keeping a spare plectrum in his wallet, recalling what had happened on that fateful day in August 1965, when Elvis and the Beatles held their impromptu jam session and there were no guitar picks in evidence.

When Mal wasn't fretting over his place in George's universe, he found time to make several standout contributions to *All Things Must Pass*. For the hit single "What Is Life," he turned in a driving tambourine part. He can also be heard on "Ballad of Sir Frankie Crisp (Let It Roll)," singing "Oh, Sir Frankie Crisp" in a deep monotone. He made an appearance, too, on "It's Johnny's Birthday," a bonus track George had concocted to celebrate John's upcoming milestone. For it, Mal sings along with engineers John Leckie and Eddie Klein, their voices arrayed against the sound of a wobbly fairground organ.

Later, on October 9, Lennon's thirtieth birthday, George presented the recording to John in Studio 3, where Mal was working a session with Ringo and Phil Spector for the *John Lennon/Plastic Ono Band* LP. For Mal, it must have seemed like a Beatles reunion of sorts—almost, that is. He was still feeling the sting of Paul's rebuff, but as with legions of fans the world over, he longed for a Beatles reconciliation.

That July, Mal was interviewed for a special issue of *Beat Instrumental* devoted to the "Roadie Scene." When he was queried about the Beatles' future, he bristled with hopefulness, stating, "I think they will record again, and I can also see them doing a show again, but never the sort of tour they did before." When he was asked about the secret behind his longevity as the Beatles' roadie, he credited his survival to "Animal cunning. I'm just nice!"[3]

In easily the tenderest moment in the making of *All Things Must Pass*, George recorded "Apple Scruffs" as an ode to the young women who kept vigil for the boys, demonstrating their steadfast devotion through all manner of inclement weather. Gill Pritchard recalled the moment when she and the other Scruffs first learned about the song. "We used to curse the Beatles sometimes under our breath whenever it was too cold or they ignored us," she said, "and that night it was particularly cold and we were particularly miffed. It was about 6 a.m. and me and Carol Bedford, who was a big George fan, Lucy, Cathy, and Margo were all outside EMI Studios. Mal Evans had been looking out through the letterbox every so often. He opened the door and said, 'Come inside girls, George wants to see you.'"

To the Scruffs' delight, "We were ushered into the control room of Studio 3 and George said, 'Sit down, I've got something to play you.' He was very nervous, pacing up and down. He put this track on and we all went gooey. We all just looked at each other. It was unbelievable." Pritchard remembered that "we were so moved we went home in a daze that morning and made him a giant wreath of flowers. When we gave it to him he said, 'Well you had your own magazine, your own office on the steps, so why not your own song?'"[4]

Meanwhile, Mal and Neil continued to work on *Scrapbook*, their homespun history of the Beatles. By this point, the concept had been expanded to include both audio *and* visual elements and rechristened as *The Long and Winding Road*. To this end, Neil had been feverishly gathering film clips of the boys. For him, the project proved therapeutic. Mal had certainly experienced his own ups and downs after the Beatles' disbandment, but Neil was enduring a difficult time of his own, having been at the boys' beck and call since February 1961. Klein's tyrannical control of Apple had understandably left Neil in a state of depression. He had figured so prominently in fulfilling the Beatles' vision of Apple Corps, only to see it vanquished by the New York City accountant's draconian moves. Indeed, Mal would often seek him out for a friendly drink during this period, only to discover that Neil was already drunk or stoned.

At Apple, Neil's assistant, Steve Brendell, who doubled as the company's film and tape librarian, had begun cataloging hundreds of hours of audio and video for the project. Brendell later recalled setting up a 16 mm film projector so that Neil and Mal could screen footage on the former's office wall.[5] By August, the music press had learned about the making of *The Long and Winding Road*, even going so far as to speculate, erroneously, that the documentary would be in cinemas that Christmas.

Although the film's release date may have been up in the air, the project proved to be a source of great joy for Mal and Neil, who spent long hours working on the documentary at 3 Savile Row. Apple secretary Barbara Bennett recalled one memorable occasion when she happened upon the two Beatles insiders hard at work on the project. "On opening the door, I saw Neil and Mal sitting by the fire recording memories for *The Long and Winding Road* film," she said. "I was just about to walk through and suddenly looked down, right in front of me screwing on the carpet was one of our press officers, hump death came to mind, so I closed my eyes and jumped over them." Entranced in their documentary project, "Neil and Mal were oblivious."[6]

Mal was hardly oblivious when it came to a crucial meeting among Klein, John, and Phil Spector over financial disbursements. That summer, he simply couldn't escape the stress emanating from 3 Savile Row. One morning, he woke up in a cold sweat after experiencing a vivid dream about Brian Epstein. "He was as large as life," Mal wrote. As the dream unfolded, the roadie could only stare at the fallen manager in confusion, muttering, "But you're dead." Eventually, as Mal became used to the reality of the apparition, he begged Brian's ghost to provide insight into the current Apple malaise, exclaiming, "Give us a clue as to what we should do!"[7]

Things weren't much better for the roadie in the corporeal world. With Mal in tow at a July 1970 summit in London—pointedly held before Phil Spector returned to the States after completing basic recording sessions for *All Things Must Pass*—tensions flared when John and Phil began questioning Klein about money matters. According to Ruth Ellen Carter, Allen Klein's secretary at the time, her boss "told Spector [that] he was running the show, not him." When John informed Klein that he had no right whatsoever to the money in question, [Klein] responded to [John] by "slapping [him] across the face, calling him several names. . . . When Mal attempted to intervene, "he was hit over the head with an umbrella" by the irate manager. Klein left soon after, "making several threats." Carter later observed that "Mal must have exercised considerable restraint—as he could have lifted Klein off the ground with one hand and at least given him a good shake!"[8]

That autumn, Mal would enjoy an unexpected moment of vindication thanks to Allan Steckler. Klein had appointed Steckler to look after Apple's North American interests after the departure of Ken Mansfield, who was eager, like Mal, to try his hand at production and artist development. Naturally, Steckler's work brought him into Badfinger's orbit. During a recent visit to London, Steckler recalled, "I heard the finished tracks they'd done with Geoff Emerick. I didn't hear anything I thought could be a single. There were some good songs, but they were not commercial tracks." Fortunately, "Badfinger told me they had some tracks in the can they'd done with Mal, but nobody seemed to care for them. So I listened to those tracks, and I just loved 'No Matter What.'" Smitten with the song's hit potential, Steckler told Badfinger, "That's going to be your next single!"[9] Under Steckler's direction, Apple hastily assembled a promotional video for "No Matter What." As the leadoff single from Badfinger's *No Dice* album, "No Matter What" was released on November 6, 1970, with Mal receiving sole production credit.

By this point, Apple's publicity arm had all but shut down, with Derek Taylor and Richard DiLello seeking out new opportunities elsewhere. Tony Bramwell led the office's skeleton crew, attempting to stir up interest in "No Matter What" wherever he could possibly find it. "I got them on the album spot for *Top of the Pops*," Bramwell recalled. "They did a few numbers; it seemed to crack open the floodgates."[10]

Bramwell's efforts paid off handsomely, with "No Matter What" landing a top-five showing on the U.K. charts. For his part, Mal was downright chuffed. "If you hear the sound of a trumpet, dear reader, it's mine," he later wrote. "I'm blowing it with what I feel is justifiable pride." As for Ken Mansfield, the onetime Apple exec simply couldn't let the moment pass, writing, "Let this be my first fan letter to you. It's nice to know that the good guys do win once in a while."[11]

As 1970 raced to a close, Mal threw himself headlong into stage-managing the *John Lennon/Plastic Ono Band* album, which would prove to be one of the most difficult projects of his career. Back in April, John had undergone "primal scream therapy" at the hands of Dr. Arthur Janov, who assigned considerable weight to the untimely death of John's mother, Julia, in July 1958 for its long-term effects on his psyche. "Janov showed me how to feel my own fear and pain," John remarked at the time. "I can handle it better than I could before, that's all. I'm the same, only there's a channel. It doesn't just remain in me, it goes round and out. I can move a little easier." But there was a side effect to the therapy, John cautioned, that could make some people uncomfortable. "Before, I wasn't feeling things," he said. "I was blocking the feelings, and when the feelings come through, you cry."[12]

That fall, John poured this torrent of raw emotion into the making of his new album. During the sessions, Mal and Ringo were beside themselves with concern. "We'd be in the middle of a track and John would just start crying or screaming, which freaked us out at the beginning," Ringo recalled. "But we were always open to whatever anyone was going through, so we just got on with it."[13]

In one of the album's most dramatic moments, John recorded "God," an impassioned paean to the Beatles and the 1960s, in which he sings, "The dream is over." The song featured Billy Preston on a thundering grand piano and Ringo behind the drums. As always, Mal provided "tea and sympathy," John's reference in the LP's liner notes to the title of the 1956 American film in which actress Deborah Kerr, as a prep school coach's wife, provides comfort and consolation to a distressed student. As usual, Mal's assistance wasn't merely limited to tea service and goodwill. During the recording of a cover version of Lonnie Donegan's "Lost John," John broke a string, crying out "I'm defunct!" and summoning Mal to the rescue.

Meanwhile, *All Things Must Pass* stormed onto the record charts, catapulting to number one on the strength of George's blockbuster single "My

Mal posing by the gates of EMI Recording Studios

Sweet Lord." It would be in this environment, with George and John earning widespread critical acclaim for their first post-Beatles solo albums, that Paul filed a lawsuit in the High Court to dissolve the band's partnership. "I don't mind being bound to them as a friend," he explained to the *Evening Standard*'s Ray Connolly. "I don't mind being bound to them musically because I like the others as musical partners. I like being in their band. But for my own sanity we must change the business arrangements we have. Only by being completely free of each other financially will we ever have any chance of coming back together as friends. Because it's business that has caused a lot of the split."[14]

George and Ringo were particularly distraught after hearing the news. Far from being crestfallen, John and Yoko traveled to Japan to put some distance between themselves and the legal onslaught that had begun brewing back in London. Much to his own surprise, Mal was oddly sanguine about the sad tidings involving his beloved Beatles. The chart success of Badfinger's "No Matter What" had invested him with newfound confidence in his potential as a record producer, and life in Sunbury had, to his mind, never been better. He had done relatively little traveling that year, which had drawn him and Lil closer than they had been in years. While he and George were putting in long hours conducting postproduction work on *All Things Must Pass*, she had prepared meals for them and brought them by the studio.

When he wasn't in the studio, Mal was spending the lion's share of his time with his family, rather than palling around with the Beatles, other members of rock's glitterati, or assorted hangers-on. During the same week in which Kevin Harrington departed for his new life as a roadie with Derek and the Dominos, Mal had enjoyed a tender moment with four-year-old Julie, who came downstairs in the middle of the night to announce that she had ridden her bicycle, complete with training wheels, all the way to a family friend's house. "That's great," Mal had said, "the first time you've been out on your bike. That's lovely. I'm going to put it in my diary." She replied, "How can you? It won't fit!"[15] That October, Mal had even made time to attend his sister June's production of *The Pickwick Papers*, by the Young People's Theatre troupe. As the family made their way back home that evening, Gary uttered the word "arse," earning a stiff rebuke from his parents, who informed him that the term was socially unacceptable. As if on a dare, the boy proceeded to use the offensive word in a sentence and prove his parents wrong. "Arse is a nice home, arse is," he told them.[16]

Spending more time at home afforded Mal the opportunity to indulge his children, and in turn, they were able to get to know their father, who had been absent as much lately, if not more so, than he had been during the Beatles years. As usual, the Evans clan celebrated Guy Fawkes Night with Ringo's family, with Gary taking the lead in setting the fireworks off while Mal supped on sausages. Meanwhile, Mal and Julie discovered that one of the neighbors behind their garden built model trains as a hobby. Straining for a closer look, "I climbed over the fence with Julie to see them—this was a bit difficult with gun belt and Winchester rifle, mind you!" That December, Gary doted on his father, learning how to make coffee and then serving it up to him on a tray. He's "fantastic," Mal wrote, "and I love him." And then there was Julie, "who dances and sings in my heart."[17] That Christmas, Mal even enjoyed a seasonal pleasantry courtesy of Phil Spector, of all people, who gifted him with a personal check, writing "please have a drink on me and know how very much I have appreciated your kind and generous help this past year!"[18]

By the advent of 1971, Apple's wayward refugees seemed to be tighter than ever. In early January, Mal and Lil hosted a jaunt to the London Zoo for Gary and Julie. Their guests included the Aspinalls, along with Ringo and his sons, Zak and Jason. At the same time, something ugly was beginning to stick in Mal's craw. "No Matter What" was in heavy rotation on the radio airwaves, and Mal had learned from his colleagues at Apple that it was selling three thousand copies a day. In his diary, Mal wrote, "[I] feel hung up about not producing Badfinger at the moment, having put so much time and effort and belief into them." He still couldn't fathom how the band had been "taken from me" just as they were beginning to find genuine success. He added, as an afterthought of sorts, perhaps to console his aching soul, that "all things must pass!"[19]

But Mal had been fooling himself. His tremors of self-pity and anger hadn't passed. On the morning of January 13, 1971, he watched *Top of the Pops* on the telly in his Sunbury living room. There they were—Badfinger performing "No Matter What," the song he had produced and for which he had fought, tooth and nail, to see released on the label that, at a certain level, he had helped found. At some point that morning, he had resolved to drive to Golders Green and perhaps confront the boys from Badfinger about his place, or his significant absence, in their ecosystem.

Eventually, he must have thought better of his half-baked plan, stopping instead at the BBC Club on Great Portland Street, where he indulged in a bout of heavy drinking with a side of fish and chips. It was in this sorry state that Lil managed to get word to him that he needed to rush back to Sunbury. Straining to understand his wife's anxious words through a miasma of alcohol and fried food, Mal came to learn, improbable as it must have sounded, that Gary had shot someone.

33

HAPPY CRIMBLE!

Given his affection for the Old West, Mal had purchased several BB guns, including a rifle and a pair of pistols. Father and son would often practice firing the air-powered guns in the family's backyard in Sunbury by setting up paper targets at the far end of the garden, which ran the length of their house and dead-ended into a ten-foot-high fence.

On that fateful January afternoon in 1971, Gary had set up a target for some shooting practice of his own. Even years later, he would vividly recall how dangerously close he had come to killing Keith, the older brother of his best friend, Barry. "When Keith popped his head over the fence," Gary recalled, "I was startled." Mal's son had been caught up in the act of taking his shot, and he yelled at Keith to "get down or you might get hit." Keith had curtly replied, "No," which seemed even more confounding to Gary. "God knows what went through my mind," said Gary, but "much to my everlasting chagrin, I discharged the BB rifle, and [the projectile] hit Keith just above the bridge of his nose."[1]

In an instant, Keith collapsed back into his own yard, and all hell broke loose in the Evans household. Lily fell into an understandable panic—had Gary just murdered a kid from the neighborhood?—and the mayhem had plunged Julie into tears. Within a matter of minutes, Lil was certain that Keith would survive, that it was only a flesh wound. Better summon Mal, though. Firearms were his department.

Gary didn't need his father to rush home, drunk and stinking of fish and chips, to interpret what had transpired in the back garden. "I, and more important, Keith really got away with one there," said Gary. His friend could easily have lost an eye—or, worse, suffered intercranial injury and died. Although Mal recalled sending his son early to bed as punishment, Gary remembered things differently. "My dad let me know in no uncertain terms how naughty I had been, and I was grounded for quite a while." But Gary's brush with the awful potential of gun violence didn't end there.[2]

"Fast-forward to 1981, when I am a sapper [combat engineer] in the Territorial Army," Gary said. "I am standing on the range waiting to fire my nine-millimeter submachine gun, when the guy standing next to me inadvertently fires off a round that narrowly missed my right ear. The NCO in charge of the range ordered everyone to make their weapons safe, and then he told the guy to my right what he thought of him in a very robust way." Later, the fellow who had mistakenly discharged the round apologized to Gary, who replied that "these things happen." But Gary knew better. "If he had hit me with the nine-millimeter round, I would have been shot dead."[3]

No, these things didn't just happen. And Mal knew that as well as anyone. In recent years, he had learned plenty about causality, that some folks were "go-ahead" people like Neil, who tried to make things happen, while others, people very much like *him*, were victims of circumstance who, more often than not, had to take what they could get, had to wait their turn.

And by 1971, Mal had been doing an awful lot of waiting. For the roadie, time seemed to pass differently in ex–Beatle World. With Paul seemingly out of the picture, the roadie's time was wide open and available for John, George, and Ringo to exploit at their pleasure. At times, Mal acted very much like a shuttlecock, sporadically ricocheting from one former Beatle's racquet to another, often in an unsteady rhythm that left him back in Sunbury waiting for the phone to ring.

Take Ringo, for example, who was determined to accelerate his film career. That February, Mal joined the drummer-cum-actor on the set of *200 Motels*, Frank Zappa's surreal take on life on a rock 'n' roll tour. For the film, Ringo played Larry the Dwarf, Zappa's irreverent doppelgänger. Mal essentially served as Ringo's driver, ferrying him back and forth to Pinewood Studios in Buckinghamshire. At Pinewood, Mal became reacquainted with the Who's madcap drummer Keith Moon, whom he had known as an on-again, off-again drinking partner during Swinging London's heyday. Outrageously dressed in a nun's habit, Moon's character chases a harp-carrying

Ringo in *200 Motels*, at one point, racing through an orchestra pit inside, of all things, a concentration camp.

When he wasn't whiling away the hours with Ringo and "Moonie" on a suburban soundstage, Mal shuttled between sessions with John at Ascot Sound, Lennon's newly minted home studio at Tittenhurst Park; and with George at EMI Studios, where the Quiet Beatle was working on an album with Ronnie Spector. At Tittenhurst, Mal joined in the rousing chorus on a new peace anthem entitled "Power to the People." And when it came to the Ronnie Spector sessions with George at EMI, Mal stumbled into a peculiar rock music footnote. With a backing band that included Badfinger's Pete Ham and piano great Leon Russell, George put Ronnie through her paces as lead vocalist for "Try Some, Buy Some," a leftover composition from the *All Things Must Pass* sessions. Mal unwittingly served as the catalyst for the single's B side "Tandoori Chicken," when he left to get Indian takeout. Working with Phil Spector, George hastily concocted the number while they waited for Mal to return with their meals. "It's a 12-bar thing done on the spot with Mal our roadie and Joe the chauffeur," George recalled. "We did it in one take, with a lot of scat singing in the middle. It's hysterical."[4]

While a ringing telephone on Staines Road East invariably meant that Mal was on the verge of being called away on ex-Beatle business, this wasn't always the case. Lil would never forget picking up the receiver on Easter weekend. "It was a shock," she recalled. "This man said, 'Hello, this is Elvis. Is Mal there?'"[5] Naturally, Mal was surprised when Lily called him out of the bath to answer a telephone call. He rushed down the stairs, dripping wet and clad in nothing but a towel. On the other line was the King himself, calling to wish Mal and his family a Happy Easter. Afterward, Mal was so overwhelmed by the experience that he smoked a cigar to calm his nerves.

While Mal was making his usual tour among London's recording studios that spring, Harry Nilsson was tracking *Nilsson Schmilsson* with producer Richard Perry at Trident. Nilsson's career had been on overdrive since the release of his cover version of the Beatles' "You Can't Do That." He had scored an international hit with "Everybody's Talkin'," while composing the hit single "One" for Three Dog Night. As he searched for the next vehicle for his soaring voice, Nilsson heard Badfinger's "Without You" at a party in Laurel Canyon, assuming that it was a Beatles song that had somehow escaped his notice. When he learned otherwise, he and Perry set about recording the Pete Ham–Tom Evans composition. In Nilsson and Perry's hands, the song took on an impassioned, heartbreaking tone, superbly enhanced by Paul Buckmaster's orchestral arrangement. When Nilsson's take on "Without You" was released that October, it would change all their lives—Badfinger's, Nilsson's, even Mal's.

Back at Tittenhurst, things were moving apace for a new Lennon album, to be entitled *Imagine*, which was already expected to include "Jealous Guy," a reworking of "Child of Nature," from the Beatles' time in Rishikesh. Badfinger's Tom Evans and Joey Molland were on hand, playing acoustic guitars for "Jealous Guy" and proving that when it came to landing a gig with an ex-Beatle, Mal's Rolodex was worth its weight in gold. Later, when John needed an additional guitarist to round out a session, Mal remembered his old friend Rod Lynton, from Rupert's People. Lynton would never forget receiving a cryptic telephone call from Mal, who asked the guitarist if he was free. "Is there a party? Are we gonna go out drinking?" Rod asked.

For his part, Mal remained coy, saying, "Just have your guitars ready."

"But who am I playing with?" said Rod, pressing the roadie for more information.

"Don't ask any questions," Mal tersely replied. "You're in the deep end now."

The next thing he knew, Rod was strumming his acoustic guitar with John Lennon at Ascot Sound Studios, performing on such classics as "Crippled Inside" and "Gimme Some Truth."[6]

John and Yoko's assistant, Dan Richter, was there, too. He would never forget the onset of the *Imagine* sessions, when Mal turned up with a brick of fine Afghani hash. Richter remembered thinking, "Well, that's going to keep everybody cooking while we make the album." He was amazed by Mal's capacity for meeting the bandmates' every need. At one point, John confided in Dan that Mal "'was amazing. He knows every police chief in all of the major cities throughout the world—absolutely anywhere we played.' John absolutely loved him. Actually, I've never met anybody who didn't love him."[7]

For Mal and the former Beatles, working outside the friendly confines of EMI Studios in a place like Lennon's Ascot Sound Studios necessitated certain changes to how the boys conducted their business—especially when it came to studio musicians. With everyone toiling on Apple's dime, Mal had been tasked with paying for *everything*—session players, bar tabs, meals, lodging, transportation, you name it—out of petty cash. This meant he was carting around more pound notes than ever before, always at the ready to meet the boys' needs, whenever they happened to arise and whatever they happened to be. And as events would demonstrate, their "needs" could cover just about anything.

Meanwhile, thanks to John, Mal had managed to land his first production gig in more than a year—since "No Matter What," as if the roadie needed reminding. The occasion was a recording session for "God Save Oz," a song inspired by a Metropolitan Police's "Obscene Publications Unit" raid on the editorial offices of *Oz*, an underground magazine that specialized in satire, humor, and politics. Unable to fund their defense on obscenity charges, the publication's editors set up "the Friends of Oz" to cover their legal costs. Eager to come to the magazine's aid, John composed "God Save Oz," pledging the royalties to the cause of a free and independent press. He even provided temporary lodging in one of Tittenhurst Park's outbuildings for the editors, who came to be known as the Oz Three.

In truth, producing the "God Save Oz" session meant that Mal would be handling a gamut of duties. Twenty-year-old Charles Shaar Murray was on hand to play rhythm guitar, having contributed to the controversial issue of *Oz* that had landed the magazine in so much trouble. He recalled working with "the legendary Mal Evans as gear guru and general all-purpose facilitator and problem-solver." Murray found himself in need of Mal's services almost immediately, as "my first contribution to the creative festivities was to break a string. 'Don't worry,' said Lennon, 'we'll see if we can get Mal to change it.'"[8]

When he wasn't effecting minor guitar repairs, Mal was ferreting out studio musicians for "God Save Oz," which would be styled for release as "God Save Us." Later, when it became apparent that contractual obligations would prevent John from appearing as lead singer on the record, Mal recruited Bill Elliott from a Newcastle band called Half Breed to rerecord John's original vocal track. After working the faders and completing the track in a swift four takes, Mal turned to the post-recording festivities, concocting a veritable feast for the musicians—and he paid for it with mounds of petty cash from his bulging wallet.

"Musical chores eventually completed," said Murray, "a stupefyingly fabulous buffet magically appeared, comprising everything from cold roast beef and chicken to delicious pastas and exquisite little vegetarian messes, all accompanied with bottles of vintage wines, lakes of beer, and bales of serious weed."[9] As Mal well knew, there was nothing magical about the hastily assembled smorgasbord. But as far as he was concerned, it was all in a day's work.

That May, as recording continued on John's *Imagine*, Mal was called back to EMI Studios, where George had brought Badfinger into the studio to produce the band's next album. For Mal, it would be a mercifully short stint in the presence of his former Welsh mates, as he was scheduled to fly out with Ringo to Rome, where the drummer was set to star in *Blindman*, Ferdinando Baldi's spaghetti Western du jour. Knowing that he would be available for only a handful of sessions, and determined that George have the benefit of an equipment manager, Mal rehired Kevin Harrington, who had recently wrapped up his gig as roadie for the short-lived Derek and the Dominos. Clapton's latest band had burned out almost as quickly as they had emerged, touring behind their LP *Layla and Other Assorted Love Songs* and collapsing into alcohol- and heroin-fueled disarray.

The escape hatch of his upcoming Italian jaunt with Ringo was a source of great relief for Mal. How many sessions, really, could he withstand as Badfinger's manservant, as a mere hanger-on? As it turned out, George arrived at the sessions brimming with inspiration. When it came to producing Pete Ham's bombshell composition "Day After Day," Harrison was intrigued by the song's nifty slide guitar part. At one point, he turned to Joey Molland and asked if he could play guitar on the song, too. Joey gladly stepped aside, giving George and Pete Ham a wide berth, saying, "No, man. Sure, go ahead." What else could he do? "I mean, this man's a Beatle," Joey recalled. "He's a hero."[10] With Harrison's arresting guitar arrayed against Leon Russell's gentle piano, "Day After Day" had all the makings of a can't-miss hit.

By the time George and the band completed work on "Day After Day," Mal was long gone, having ensconced himself with Ringo in the opulence of Rome's Grand Hotel. "While we were there," he recalled, "I was to be given a part in the film, which delighted me to no end, for having been a Western freak all my life, my ambition of course was to star in a Western, and a bit part is a step in the right direction, isn't it?" By day, Mal and Ringo attended a rigorous horse-riding school, where the riding master put them through their paces, with the roadie thrown from his steed several times. By night, the two friends hit the town, bruises and all. In his eternal quest for stardom, Mal enjoyed the excitement of being with a well-known personality like Ringo, "for there are a breed of freelance photographers called 'paparazzi,' and it seemed every time we went to a restaurant to eat, the manager would phone them; they would then come bursting into the restaurant taking pictures, the manager indignantly having them thrown out, after, I'm sure, he had received a large tip."[11]

A few weeks later, Mal and Ringo joined the cast and crew on the *Blindman* set in Almería, the same Spanish city where, five years earlier, John had starred as Private Gripweed in *How I Won the War*. Almost immediately upon arriving, Mal suffered bouts of insomnia, accented with extended

Mal and Ringo astride horses on the set of *Blindman*

periods of abdominal distress. His physical trauma begat insecurity, which drove him to write home to his family for reassurance: "Don't ever stop loving me, Lil, Gary, and Julie, for you are the most beautiful people, the most important people in my life."[12]

Meanwhile, on the set of *Blindman*, Ringo played Candy, an outlaw in love with a rancher's daughter. For his cameo, Mal played Honey, one of the grimy cohorts of a double-crossing bandit played by none other than Allen Klein, who was coproducing the film. Mal despised Klein, of course, still holding him responsible for the debacle involving Badfinger and his own record producer ambitions. But for the film shoot, Mal seemed more than willing to extend an olive branch to the notorious Apple boss. For one thing, he relished the chance to play a whoring, gun-toting desperado under any circumstances. Besides, Klein had rented a yacht for the duration of their stay on the Andalusian coast, the ideal lure, in Mal's estimation, when one was "trying to pull the chicks."[13]

Mal's transcendent experience on the *Blindman* set might have continued unabated had it not been for the distressing call he received from the folks back in Liverpool. His sixty-six-year-old father, Fred, had suffered a succession of heart attacks and fallen into a coma; he was not expected to survive. "I can picture the scene now," Mal later wrote, "sitting in my bedroom in the hotel, looking out over the beautiful blue sea, sparkling in the warm sunshine, and crying my eyes out."[14] Even so, the roadie didn't make any plans for a hasty return to England.

As he had since the India trip, Mal had traveled with his well-thumbed copy of Paramahansa Yogananda's *Autobiography of a Yogi*, which he consulted in his hour of need. "This time," he recalled, "I opened it on the page where Yogananda talks about his own father dying. I laid back in my easy chair and started to read, then I had the most incredible experience. It was as though Yogananda came to me. I didn't hear anything, didn't see anything, but felt a beautiful warm glow as though he was breathing inside me saying, 'Don't worry, your father will be alright.'" Not missing a beat, Mal phoned home, announcing to his family that Fred would be making a full recovery. With nothing left to do but pray—rushing to his father's bedside would be senseless, after all, given what had been prophesized in his vision—Mal awaited the inevitable good news from Klein's yacht on the Spanish coast. Not long afterward, Fred took the expected turn for the better, in Mal's words, "making what can only be called a miraculous recovery."[15]

Fred's phenomenal recuperation in Liverpool simply couldn't have been timed better, allowing Mal the luxury of a few extra days lounging on the beach and prepping for his scene with the abhorrent Klein. Their cameos called for them to feign sleep in bed beside a well-endowed actress, with Mal's hand resting on her breast and Allen using her belly as a pillow. In his bravura moment, the script called for Mal to rise up out of bed, cross to a nearby window, and proclaim, "Take your sisters to the miners, Blindman!"

For several days in advance of shooting the scene, the other, vastly more experienced actors on the set had relentlessly hazed Mal, predicting that he would botch his lines. But Mal wasn't having it, impressing American actor Lloyd Battista into serving as his dialogue coach. Meanwhile, Ringo heroically came to his friend's aid, volunteering, in a moment of sublime role reversal, to act as Mal's "road manager for the day," tending to his makeup, sating his hunger, and plying him with coffee and tea on the set. In the end, a determined Mal delivered his lines perfectly, admitting that "it was a good day for me, for I love being in front of the camera."[16]

That same month, as Mal and Ringo were cavorting on the set of *Blindman*, George had traveled to L.A. to work on the *Raga* soundtrack with Ravi Shankar. The Indian classical musician related his distress over the news out of Bangladesh, where more than 7 million refugees had been devastated by cyclones, torrential rains, and a resulting cholera epidemic. Meanwhile, more than 250,000 Bengalis had been slaughtered at the hands of the Pakistani army, resulting in a humanitarian disaster of epic proportions.

Resolved to use his celebrity to bring some measure of relief to the Bangladeshis, George spent some six weeks assembling a supergroup of musicians to perform a pair of benefit concerts that August at New York City's Madison Square Garden. During the week prior to the shows, Mal and George moved into the Plaza Hotel to make final preparations. With Klein acting as promoter, the event was billed as "George Harrison and Friends." The special guests included Ringo, Shankar, Bob Dylan, Eric Clapton, Billy Preston, Leon Russell, and Badfinger. With Mal in tow, George visited John and Yoko's suite at the St. Regis Hotel, hoping to convince them to take part in the benefit. Unfortunately, George's goodwill mission turned into a shouting match with his old friend. John later blamed himself for not participating, saying, "We nearly went, and Yoko would have gone. It was me. I was just too paranoid." As for Paul, he simply couldn't fathom performing at an event associated with Allen Klein. Besides, "If I'd turned up and John had turned up, then the headlines 'round the world would have screamed, 'The Beatles Are Together Again.'"[17]

Given the enormous complexity of the benefit concerts, with so many musicians and their instruments being bandied about onstage in quick succession, Mal enlisted Kevin Harrington to serve as his fellow roadie. Kevin recalled that "I used to get butterflies in my stomach whenever I got a new gig," but with an event of the magnitude of the Concert for Bangladesh, he now experienced those butterflies tenfold.[18] In addition to working with his former assistant, one of the great highlights of the concert for Mal involved seeing Badfinger's Pete Ham perform "Here Comes the Sun" as a duet with George. "I was proud to see a guy I thought of as my protégé standing alongside another dear friend in the limelight, which he richly deserved."[19]

Not surprisingly, given the buzz that accompanied the benefit's origins, the Concert for Bangladesh sold out quickly, leaving some fans heartbroken that they weren't able to score tickets. Lynda Dearborn, an avid Beatles fan from Maine, had traveled to New York City, desperate to see her idols in the flesh at Madison Square Garden. Her disappointment was tempered by her regular interactions with Mal, whom she encountered outside the Plaza Hotel during the run-up to the benefit. "Mal was exactly the person we had read about—friendly, outgoing, enjoying people and the experience," she recalled. Dearborn also remembered observing Neil coming and going that weekend. Mal's longtime comrade was clearly still reeling from the dissolution of Apple in Klein's unruly hands. "He ignored all of us and our questions," she said. "We were disappointed in him. The difference between him and Mal was night and day."[20]

A few days after the concerts, Mal and George visited John and Yoko at the St. Regis Hotel, where the couple had set up shop on the seventeenth floor. They had even hired a new personal assistant in twenty-year-old May Pang, who had been formerly employed in Allen Klein's New York City offices. With Dylan in tow, John and George conducted an impromptu jam session at the St. Regis. In a matter of a minutes, any rift between the two ex-Beatles had healed. All was right with the world.

On September 1, with the Concert for Bangladesh in the books, George proudly authorized a check to UNICEF for nearly $250,000. His humanitarian effort had paid off handsomely. He would later commemorate the event by awarding each of the concert participants a medallion; Mal took to hanging his around his neck from a leather strap. But the real bonanza for UNICEF and the refugees was yet to come: that December, Capitol Records reported receipts totaling $3.8 million for advance sales of *The Concert for Bangladesh* live album. But what Mal didn't know—couldn't have known—was that he would never road-manage another gig again.

In the days after George's triumph at Madison Square Garden, Mal made his way to California, where he was set to rendezvous with Lil, Gary, and Julie for their annual August vacation. Inspiring his envy, his family had flown over from the United Kingdom on a Boeing 747; Mal's opportunity to take flight on one of the jumbo jets, complete with its distinctive hump, would have to wait. Meanwhile, Ken Mansfield invited the Evans clan to stay at his home in L.A. For Gary and Julie, it was a dream vacation. Mansfield lived alone in a large, secluded house in the Hollywood Hills; more important, the house featured a giant swimming pool. "Gary and Julie practically lived in that pool. Every night they looked like prunes," Mansfield recalled. "To them, everything was so California, just like they had seen in the movies. The weather was sunny and incredible all the time."[21] When they weren't playing in Mansfield's pool, the kids were at the beach or whiling away the hours at Disneyland.

Gary was especially taken with the nearby Houdini Estate, which had been owned by escape artist Harry Houdini until his untimely death in 1926. The estate's pool was where Houdini had practiced many of his most daunting illusions. And speaking of illusions, while they were in Southern California, Mal performed a disappearing act of his own, often being away from Mansfield's home for hours at a time. Gary remembers witnessing his mother's growing suspicion that her husband was out seeing other women.

While her older brother may have had affection for magic and illusion, five-year-old Julie was wild about cows, squealing with delight when Mal returned with none other than a cowgirl outfit. Earlier that year, she had regaled her father with the very first joke she had committed to memory. "Why do cows wear bells?" she asked her dad. "Because their horns don't work!"[22]

Later that month, Mal made the return flight to Heathrow in his family's company, alighting in Sunbury for several weeks before immersing himself in Beatle World yet again. With George busy wrapping up loose ends on the Bangladesh project, Mal joined the latest Apple signees—American brothers Derrek and Lon Van Eaton—at Apple Studios, where Klaus Voormann was producing the singing duo's debut album. During a break in the sessions, Lon recalled observing Mal and Klaus taking to the studio's piano, where they worked on one of the roadie's original compositions, a sweet little ditty that went by the title "You're Thinking of Me."[23]

On October 1, Mal joined George in a pair of first-class berths on the SS *France*. They made their crossing aboard the luxury liner from Southampton to New York City. The two friends enjoyed themselves immensely, partying at all hours in the ship's lounge and taking primitive selfies in the mirrors of their staterooms. But when they landed at the Midtown pier a few days later, George was all business—at least, when it came to work. With Mal and Neil toiling beside him, he put in long hours poring over footage from the Madison Square Garden shows for a film version of *The Concert for Bangladesh*. Meanwhile, at their suite in the Plaza Hotel, George proved he hadn't left his randy self completely behind. "I was being entertained by a young lady late one evening," Mal wrote, "when George rushes into the darkened room, stoned out of his mind, tearing the bedclothes off, shouting, 'My turn next—come on, give us a bit!'" Mal gave way to the Beatle, concluding that "apart from that, I was the one that got screwed."[24]

On October 9, Mal and Neil took a break from working on the Bangladesh film to attend John's thirty-first-birthday party at a hotel in Syracuse, where Yoko was staging her *This Is Not Here* exhibition at the Everson Museum of Art. The star-studded gathering included Ringo and Mo, Phil Spector, Eric Clapton, Klaus Voormann, and poet and counterculture hero Allen Ginsberg. The partygoers enjoyed several sing-alongs, including a stab at George's "My Sweet Lord" and a good-natured take on Paul and Linda McCartney's recent hit "Uncle Albert/Admiral Halsey." One of the evening's highlights involved an impromptu version of "Attica State," an

Mal on the deck of the SS *France*

ad-libbed anthem devoted to the recent prison riots over living conditions and human rights violations.

Meanwhile, as Mal carried out ex-Beatles business Stateside, Lily grew impatient with her husband, who had become incommunicado yet again. "I hope there is a letter from you tomorrow," she wrote, "as you have been gone 20 days, and it just seems one hell of a time." Things were especially difficult for his wife at night. After Gary and Julie go to bed, "it just hits me, and I feel all alone, and I really hate it."[25]

As usual, Mal wasn't ready to return to Sunbury just yet. That November, he would pull another disappearing act, skipping out on an Evans family tradition and missing Ringo's annual Guy Fawkes festivities for the first time in years. To Mal's way of thinking, he had good cause. In a moment that portended pure joy, he made plans to attend Elvis's November 8 performance in Philadelphia. For Mal, it was a can't-miss concert; for one thing, he had never seen the King play a gig, and to make it even more thrilling, he had been given seats near the stage by his lady friend from the Philly radio station. "It was magic," Mal wrote. "Suddenly he's on stage, and a fan's 15-year-old dream comes true! Elvis was singing just for me!"[26]

As the set list unfolded that evening at the Spectrum, Mal found himself in seventh heaven. Debuting his white "snowflake" jumpsuit that night, Presley turned in drop-dead takes of "Are You Lonesome Tonight," "Suspicious Minds," and Simon and Garfunkel's "Bridge over Troubled Water."

Back in London, Mal's Apple duties finally reached their nadir. The most recent assignment was the kind that, in the moment, had all the earmarks of fun. But from a longer view, it was nothing short of absurd that Mal, who had once been the titular head of Apple, would find himself trolling the streets of London tossing foam apples at innocent bystanders. Earlier that year, the company had lost yet another one of its stalwarts in Tony Bramwell, who was subsequently replaced in the Promotions Department by A&R man Tony King. As the new guy in an office beset by downsizing and an increasingly uncertain future, King quickly assessed the lay of the land as far as Apple business went. "Where there was a Beatle," he recalled, inevitably "there was Mal."[27]

Ringo's driver, John Mears, later recalled working the strange holiday assignment with Mal. "I remember it was coming up to Christmas '71 and we had hundreds of foam Apples, each of which featured the words 'Happy Xmas from Apple' on its leaf." Overwhelmed by the ridiculousness of his mission, Mal stepped outside onto Savile Row and began hurling the foam keepsakes at passersby, shouting, "Happy Crimble!" With bags of foam apples left to distribute, Mal and Mears jumped into John's white Rolls-Royce and began tooling down Regent Street, throwing them at unsuspecting pedestrians. "It was mad," said Mears.[28]

As the holiday season began gaining momentum, so, too, did Harry Nilsson's cover version of Badfinger's "Without You," selling millions of copies in the United Kingdom and the United States alike, eventually earning Grammy Award nominations in multiple categories. No less than Paul, a consummate hitmaker in his own right, pronounced Nilsson's version "the killer song of all time."[29] Richard Perry would shortly become one of the hottest producers in the business. "It was a different record for its time," said Perry. "It was a big ballad with a heavy backbeat, and although many artists have cut songs like it since, no one was doing it then."[30]

And now "Without You" was promising to generate enormous royalties for Badfinger—the likes of which composers Pete Ham and Tom

Evans could scarcely imagine. As Nilsson's cover version lorded it over the airwaves and they counted the days until the money began rolling in, the songwriters were overcome with pride. Originally debuted for Mal back in April 1970, "Without You" had been proof positive that Badfinger, a band he had championed before they were passed around Apple like a well-worn hat, could go toe-to-toe with the finest songwriters of the day.

As 1971 drew to a close, Mal and the family spent Christmas Eve at Roundhill, the Starkeys' estate in London's Highgate suburb. For Gary, it would be an unforgettable night, primarily for a moment he would contemplate for decades to come. What really stuck in his craw was a two-word phrase uttered by the Beatle's six-year-old son, Zak. It was something Gary had never really considered before, but after that night, he couldn't get it out of his mind. "You're poor," Zak told him matter-of-factly. And when Gary didn't react boisterously enough, the younger boy repeated his words, as kids tend to do, in rapid succession: "You're poor! You're poor! You're poor!" For his part, Gary was flummoxed. "It hadn't resonated before," he said, "that we might be poor."[31]

But what really got to him was the possibility that his dad, who had been so central to the Beatles' fame, could suffer from something as mundane as money troubles. Obviously, Roundhill was enormous in comparison to the Evans house in Sunbury; anyone could see that. But Gary and his sister never seemed to want for anything. Besides, as far as Gary was concerned, his dad was the veritable reincarnation of Superman. Only recently, as they drove toward the Kew Bridge on their way to the M1, he and Mal had passed a car with smoke pouring out of its front end, and without breaking a sweat, Mal made a wide U-turn and pulled up alongside the wounded vehicle. Gently removing a fire extinguisher from the driver's side of the Super Snipe, he had ambled over to the other car, motioned for the driver to release the hood, and in what seemed like a single motion, emptied the powdery contents into the car's front end, extinguishing the engine fire in one fell swoop. Turning on his heel, he then gave an amiable wave to the driver and hopped back into the Super Snipe with his son.[32]

34

MALCONTENTED

Mal had long prided himself on being an affable bloke, a lovable rogue who was always up for a good time. But in the early months of 1972, he was anything but. That January, he experienced his first interaction with Bill Collins since the debacle with Allen Klein in the wake of the Capitol Records convention. Mal had recently been dispatched to work as a "trainee engineer" at the refurbished Apple Studios in the 3 Savile Row basement. And lo and behold, his first session would involve his old friends from Badfinger.

Working as a trainee was a welcome nod—likely at George's instigation—to Mal's long-standing ambition to act in some capacity behind the mixing desk. Knowing that he'd shortly be seeing the lads, who were set to begin working on their next album at Apple with Todd Rundgren in the producer's chair, Mal figured he'd pay a visit to Golders Green—only to have the misfortune of encountering Collins in the band's stead.

Not surprisingly, Mal was chagrined to be in close proximity to the Badfinger manager, who "bullshitted me again with the same story of two years ago." Mal had paid dearly for Collins's paranoia. And it hardly mattered that the manager's unhinged emotional state had been stoked by Klein. The fact was, the roadie's career had suffered, and Mal, who had scored a genuine top-five hit as a producer, had been forced to start all over again.

Despite his pleas to the contrary, Collins's paranoia was clearly still in full bloom. The moment Mal left Golders Green, the manager telephoned Badfinger at Clearwell Castle, their deluxe new rehearsal space, and hastily called a meeting to poll the boys about whether, in the roadie's words, "they should object to [Mal] doing the sessions." But Mal had no intention of forgoing his upcoming opportunity at Apple Studios. As far as he was concerned, Collins was nothing more than a "silly old git."[1]

Sure enough, Mal was in attendance on Monday, January 17, when Badfinger convened with Rundgren at Apple to contemplate their follow-up LP to *Straight Up*, the album that had spawned a hit single in "Day After Day." With Nilsson's "Without You" now burning up the charts, there seemed to be nothing but an upside when it came to Badfinger. While Rundgren led the band through renditions of "The Winner" and "I Can Love You," Mal worked with veteran engineer Phil McDonald at Apple Studios, who was teaching the roadie the basics of audio engineering. By his second day, McDonald had shown Mal how to conduct a drop-in—an editing technique in which a musician or vocalist adds to or corrects an existing recording. In addition to getting a crash course in the newfangled Dolby noise-reduction technology, Mal learned the ins and outs of microphone and amplifier placement in the studio setting. He clearly experienced a few missteps, too—making a note to himself in his diary that, for best results, he should depress the Play button a split second before hitting Record.

As it happened, Mal worked in the service of Rundgren and Badfinger for only a couple of sessions. With professional recording space at a premium in London during that era, Apple Studios was booked solid with plenty of guinea pigs for the trainee. American singer Doris Troy was on hand to record a follow-up album to her 1970 debut LP, for which Mal had taken an arresting cover photograph of the musician seated at a piano. Troy had enjoyed chart success in the 1960s with the R&B classic "Just One Look," which her Apple release had failed to duplicate, thanks to the label's increasingly lackluster promotional efforts. Even so, she was willing to give Apple another try. As January came to a close, Mal worked under the tutelage of Ian Samwell, who was producing a record by English singer Linda Lewis. Working with Samwell and McDonald, Mal added the preparation of lacquer acetates to his skill set.

But, seemingly, no matter what he did, or with whom he worked, Mal couldn't shake the specter of Badfinger in his life. That Friday, he learned that an event had been held in the band's honor without his presence. He didn't waste any time in confronting Tony King, Apple's new A&R head, about what he considered a breach of etiquette. "Had words with Tony King about last night's celebration dinner for Badfinger, to which I was decidedly not invited," Mal wrote in his diary, "with much eloquence."[2] For the life of him, he simply couldn't—*wouldn't*—understand why he continued to be frozen out of Badfinger's universe.

Fortunately, the roadie was still a welcome fixture in Ringo's world. That February, Ringo brought "Back Off Boogaloo" to Apple Studios. He had taken previous stabs at recording the catchy song, with George handling production. Now, with Mal working as both trainee engineer *and* road manager, they remade "Back Off Boogaloo" with Gary Wright on piano, Klaus Voormann on bass, Alan White doubling Ringo's drum part, and George turning in a madcap slide guitar solo. Kevin Harrington was on hand, too, at one point "nobly washing shit off of George's shoe" after the guitarist had trod into the studio from Savile Row. As they overdubbed background harmonies from Wright, Jean Gilbert, and Madeline Bell, Mal learned how to sync the various tracks together—that is, when he wasn't dispensing session fees to the musicians from petty cash.[3]

Released a month later, "Back Off Boogaloo" notched the only hit song by any of the former Beatles that year, taking shrewd advantage of "T. Rextasy," which had drawn comparisons to the throes of Beatlemania. "Back Off Boogaloo" had been inspired by glitter rock star Marc Bolan, the lead singer of T. Rex, who was known to pepper his conversation with the word "boogaloo." Bolan was also the subject of the *Born to Boogie* concert film Ringo was directing on his behalf. In March, with Mal by his side, Ringo had shot the film at Wembley's Empire Pool, after which Mal and Bolan had attempted to escape the waiting throng by exiting the venue in an ambulance. For the roadie, it was as if he had been transported back to 1964, when fans the world over wanted a piece of the Beatles and it was his job to protect the boys.

Only, when it came to Bolan—and, more pointedly, the act of physically protecting his asset—Mal simply didn't have it in him anymore. T. Rex's producer, Tony Visconti, was on the scene, later recalling that "the fans went berserk when they saw Marc appear at the stage door with only Mal at his side. The commotion made me come out of the mobile, and I could quickly see that Mal and Marc were in trouble." The ambulance ruse had clearly failed, and the fans—some five hundred teenage girls—were on the verge of tearing Bolan to shreds. Visconti remembered that they "were behaving like a pack of wolves at this point and were trying to drag Marc into the crowd. I pushed through the mob and got to the other side of Marc and shouted to Mal, 'Let's go!'" As they edged closer to the waiting ambulance, "we were being kicked and scratched; many hands with sharp fingernails were trying to clasp our grip on Marc. Some girls were getting in and ripping pieces from Marc's clothes; some even managed to uproot some curly locks from his scalp." When they finally managed to reach the safety of the ambulance, Bolan fell into a fit of laughter, unaware of how close he'd come to severe physical harm—and possibly worse. But Mal didn't recover so quickly. He was "petrified," Visconti later wrote.[4]

Mal's tutelage as an engineering trainee met an abrupt end when he was asked to consider producing a record by Half Breed, a band that had operated out of Newcastle since 1970. As with aspiring artists the world over, the group had posted a demo to 3 Savile Row, and Mal had been especially taken with the quality of their songwriting, particularly when it came to twenty-one-year-old musicians Bobby Purvis and Bill Elliott. He had previously worked with Elliott during the sessions for "God Save Oz." Intrigued by the chance to produce Half Breed, Mal traveled to Newcastle, where he recorded one of their local gigs. "I had taken tapes down to Apple and was talking very highly of them," he wrote, "and it was agreed that they would be signed. The only provision Ringo [was] making was that they had to get another producer other than myself, but God bless them when they turned down his offer, preferring to have me produce them and go with another record label."[5] Rather than expressly doubting Mal's production skills, Ringo had clearly hoped to steer him away from another heartbreaking situation along the lines of Badfinger.

Chuffed by Purvis and Elliott's unwavering faith in him, Mal immediately began setting his sights on producing Half Breed, even going so far as to begin designing a logo for them. When the band broke up that summer, Mal didn't miss a beat: he signed Purvis to management and publishing contracts, hoping Elliott wouldn't be too far behind. At this point, the two had rebranded themselves as a duo. "Groups and egos got in the way," Purvis recalled, "so we formed Splinter. Mal was delighted; it's what he wanted from the start."[6]

That summer, Purvis bunked with Mal and his family in Sunbury, hoping that living near London would help jump-start his career. One evening, Mal returned from a session in the city only to find Purvis sitting at the piano attempting to work out a structure for a new song that went under the title "Another Chance that I Let Go." Mal observed that Purvis didn't seem to be making progress on the tune. "I sort of put him down a little bit," Mal recalled, "saying I didn't like the song. So the next night, I came home and he just picked up the guitar. So I thought to make things better, I'll join in and sort of took over."[7] With Mal's über-romantic, gushing lyrics in place, the song swiftly evolved into "Lonely Man." But it wasn't merely constructed out of sappy, lovestruck clichés. In a moment of autobiographical revelation, Mal's lyrics struck at the heart of his malaise—or, at the very least, the fount of his self-reflection during the post-Beatles years: "Maybe being a lonely man was my destiny, / Holding on to what's past and gone means so much to me."

As the summer of 1972 got under way, Mal and Lily made a point of seeing his parents more often. Fred's health scare had given Mal serious pause—he was troubled about not only his father's mortality, but also the fleeting nature of his own. That June, he drove his parents down to London to see *The Catching of the Querle*, his sister June's latest play for the Young People's Theatre, in which she played three different roles—and very convincingly, in Mal's estimation.

Fred and Joan's visit would take a turn for the worse back in Sunbury, where, one morning, Mal's temper got the better of him. Lil had prepared poached eggs—Mal's favorite—but her husband was fifteen minutes late for breakfast and, by that point, his meal had gone cold. Gary would never forget the moment his father had the temerity to complain about the state of his breakfast. In her understandable anger, Joan reprised the cutting phrase she had delivered on the eve of Mal's wedding back in 1957. "Lily deserves better than you," she had proclaimed, sticking up for her daughter-in-law. Only, this time, Mal didn't take the remark in stride. "Fuck off!" he said, a fiery retort that chilled Gary to the bone.[8]

Before driving his parents back to Liverpool, Mal made a point of trying to make things right by taking the whole family for a day trip to coastal Littlehampton. Naturally, Fred and Joan enjoyed their time with their grandchildren in the seaside town. Mal and Fred did a little surf fishing, during which Mal's father extracted a fossil from the sandy beach. That night back at Staines Road East, as the children prepared for bed, Mal briefly lost his composure and became cross after Julie neglected to kiss her grandfather good night. "Silly of me," he wrote, chiding himself in the pages of his diary.[9]

That August, Mal and Lil made another go of it with Fred and Joan, who joined the Evans clan for a family vacation in Cornwall. This time, Mal was determined to experience a stress-free holiday with his loved ones, to become more centered in his approach to life's vicissitudes. As they prepared to make the trip west, he dashed off a couplet in his diary: "Got no ties, got no strings, / Nothing to bind me to earthly things."[10] As an added bonus, the inclusion of Mal's parents in the family's holiday plans helped to defray the cost of their visit to the Cornish coast. For their part, Fred and Joan didn't mind helping out, happy to enjoy an extended getaway with their grandchildren.

By that summer, Zak Starkey's Christmas Eve pronouncement to Gary had proved to be a reality Mal understood all too well. With the Beatles in the throes of receivership, the accounting trail had dredged up Mal's unpaid loan, issued by Brian Epstein way back in February 1967, in the amount of £500.[11] With Mal having no means of covering the expense, the loan was charged against royalties he had earned through Apple Corps. This meant that any monies he was owed for his work on "No Matter What" would be deducted until the loan had been repaid in full. All in all, it was a generous repayment plan for a loan that Mal had essentially ignored for the past five years—and for which he wasn't being asked to account for the considerable interest that would have accrued during that period.

Mal returned from Cornwall just in time to begin work stage-managing George's follow-up LP to *All Things Must Pass*. Much of the new album would be recorded at Apple Studios, although plans were already in motion to build a state-of-the-art home studio at Friar Park by demolishing and enlarging several rooms inside the mansion.

When he wasn't working George's sessions at 3 Savile Row, Mal had taken to spending his free hours drinking with Ringo and Harry Nilsson at Tramp, their pub du jour. Given the blockbuster success of "Without

You," Nilsson had returned to London to work with Richard Perry at Trident on his next album, *Son of Schmilsson*, slated for a September release. The American singer, in no hurry to return to L.A., had recently hatched a plan to star in a movie with Ringo called *Son of Dracula*. But mostly, he just wanted to drink with Mal and Ringo.

When it came to making his next album, to be titled *Living in the Material World*, George was under considerable pressure—and Phil Spector's deteriorating condition was making matters worse. George and Mal had difficulty wrangling the producer into doing his job. Even getting him to the studio had become a chore. "Phil was never there," George recalled, "I'd go along the roof at the Inn on the Park [hotel] in London and climb in his window yelling, 'Come on! We're supposed to be making a record.'"[12]

Outside Spector's shenanigans, the sessions proved to be highly professional and, for the most part, relaxing. At George's request, Mal kept incense burning at Apple Studios and EMI Studios, to maintain the vibe. The usual coterie of musicians was on hand, including such standouts as Nicky Hopkins, Gary Wright, Klaus Voormann, and Jim Keltner. As always, Mal dispensed cash payments to the musicians, maintaining careful records in his diaries as the sessions mounted up—along with the costs. *Living in the Material World* was proving to be an expensive undertaking. Session men like Keltner were now charging exorbitant fees for their efforts, and EMI's top brass, including managing director Len Wood, were taking notice and giving Allen Klein grief. Apple's director, in turn, made sure that grief was passed down to Mal and then some.

That November, Ringo's annual bonfire night was bigger and better than ever. In addition to the usual crowd—the Harrisons, Starkeys, Evanses, and Aspinalls—hard-drinking types like Harry Nilsson and Marc Bolan made the scene. For Gary, Guy Fawkes Night would be a rite of passage. In a fit of preteen pique, Zak Starkey had caused a major ruckus when he set off a parcel of fireworks prematurely, leaving Gary to take on the role, as Mal described it in his diary, of "chief firework setter-offer."[13]

As always, Mal's duties were manifold. On a quiet early December evening, twenty-three-year-old American tourist Phil Hilderbrand and his friend Tom loitered outside EMI's Abbey Road facilities, hoping to glimpse one of the former Beatles in the flesh. Eventually, the two fans decided to take fate into their hands and sneak inside the building. Hilderbrand recalled "walking straight past the receptionist, who said, 'Stop, you can't go back there!'" Mere steps away from the doors to Studio 2, "we were grabbed by the back of our coats with our feet dangling. Mal Evans had us. He carried us to the front door, kicked it open, and threw us like rag dolls down the front steps. 'Don't ever come back!' Mal snarled." As the two Americans righted themselves in the carpark, they looked up to see the incensed roadie. He was dressed in an ivory shirt with a button-down collar and black slacks, his familiar goateed face glaring at them beneath his Beatles haircut.[14]

As 1972 raced to a close, Mal had something new roiling around his mind—and it wasn't trespassers or the soaring costs of George's new LP. In the wake of "Lonely Man," he had been composing more lyrics than ever before—his diaries and notebooks were bulging with potential songs. He determined that it was time to stop waiting for other people to divine his future, and he began working out the figures on what a career as a professional songwriter might look like, imagining the quarterly residuals he would earn for his labors. And to make that happen, he resolved to create his own publishing venture. It would be called—in deference to the Beatles' shout-outs to him back at the Cavern Club more than a decade earlier—Malcontent Music.

As postproduction work continued into the New Year, with the roadie putting in long hours at Trident with George, Mal's lyrics began taking on an increasingly maudlin tone. He was ready to begin his new creative life, but it seemed impossible to shed the old one. For one thing, he needed the money. Sure, his £38 weekly wage covered the mortgage at Staines Road East, but it didn't seem to stretch as far as it used to. And for another thing, his loyalty to the ex-Beatles—George and Ringo, mostly—dominated his time and energies. Their wishes were inevitably his commands, a situation that seemed impossible for the roadie to shake. As George's remixing sessions trudged forward, Mal wrote, "Seems I've been building castles made of cards, / Now it seems—instead of dreams— / Some fucker kicked the table!"[15]

As luck would have it, George was preparing to produce a feature film entitled *Little Malcolm and His Struggle Against the Eunuchs*. Based upon a stage comedy George and Pattie had seen back in February 1966 at London's Garrick Theatre, *Little Malcolm* was set to star John Hurt in the title role. Naturally, George was on the lookout for soundtrack material. Thanks to him, the boys from Splinter were cast to perform in *Little Malcolm* during a nightclub scene. With Half Breed having gone kaput, Mal had continued putting his efforts into making Splinter a reality. Later, when George was editing the film, he turned to Mal and asked, "The song they are singing is really beautiful—who wrote it?" Mal could scarcely contain himself when he announced that Bobby Purvis had written the music and that he himself had penned the lyrics. At first, George couldn't believe what he was hearing. Mal Evans, his roadie, had written a song—and one that was as beautiful and as stirring as "Lonely Man"?

Flush with excitement over the band and its catchy tune, George resolved to produce a single version of Splinter's "Lonely Man" and synchronize its release with the premiere of *Little Malcolm*. But it wouldn't be anytime soon. The Apple Films production turned into a protracted, two-year odyssey, its fits-and-starts nature associated with the precariousness of the Beatles' post-breakup finances, which had necessitated Apple's being placed in receivership. But the important part, as far as Mal was concerned, was that George had lavished unqualified praise on his song. Quite suddenly, after indulging his creative energies over the past several years, the longtime Beatles roadie felt validated.

Which is why Mal jumped at the chance to join Ringo in Southern California that March. Perhaps he could fashion an opportunity to build a platform for his songwriting ambitions? Working at Sunset Sound Recorders in Hollywood, the drummer was set to make his first album since 1970's *Beaucoups of Blues*—and with the hotter-than-hot Richard Perry in the producer's chair, no less. Mal had a plan up his sleeve, one he would implement from the very first day in the studio with Ringo, where he was expected to stage-manage the LP. He was determined to ensure that Ringo's triumph was also *his*, that he would do more than merely provide "tea and sympathy" to his rock 'n' roll betters.

Mal with Splinter: Bill Elliott, left, and Bobby Purvis

35

PANDORA'S BOX

As it happened, Mal's plan unfolded on the very first day of the sessions for Ringo's new LP. On the afternoon of March 4, 1973, Ringo took his inaugural pass at a cover version of Randy Newman's "Have You Seen My Baby?" with the usual suspects in attendance—Nicky Hopkins, Jim Keltner, and Beatles buddy Klaus Voormann. No sooner had they rehearsed the song than Mal suggested they try their hand at the latest incarnation of "You're Thinking of Me," the Mal Evans original he had played with Klaus back in September 1971.[1]

With Ringo taking lead vocals on the warmhearted tune, the all-star session band joined in, supplemented by Harry Nilsson, who provided organ accompaniment. The session concluded with Ringo and the band jamming on a new version of "You're Sixteen," the Sherman Brothers' 1960 hit with Johnny Burnette. But for Mal, most of the evening was a blur. "You're Thinking of Me" had come off beautifully that night at Sunset Sound! Was it even remotely possible that a Mal Evans composition might finally see the light of day?

As the sessions continued, Ringo made his way through one catchy song after another, including the disco-tinged "Oh My My," the hard-rocking "Devil Woman," and the tender "Photograph," which he had cowritten with George. At the same time, Mal was growing tired of the regular parade of musicians who played on George's and Ringo's records, believing they were exploiting the ex-Beatles' generosity. Indeed, their fees seemed to increase precipitously with each new album. At one point, Mal described the guest studio musicians as "the usual star-studded yawning cast—well, familiarity does breed contempt. I love Ringo so much it really pisses me off when people take advantage of his easy-going nature."[2]

After he arrived in Los Angeles, Mal picked up his usual wad of petty cash at the Capitol Records Tower—and on March 10, not long after retrieving a jet-lagged George from LAX, he was separated from it.

That night, back at the Beverly Hills Hotel, Mal rode the elevator up to his floor only to be greeted by a strange sight. As he stepped out of the lift, "a rather tall gentleman lurking by the elevator door asked me for the time, and on saying '8:45,' thought it strange that he should shout in a loud voice, 'Time goes by quickly, doesn't it?'" As Mal continued on his way, "I turned the corner to find two gentlemen walking towards me, and the click of a door closing behind them as they came down the corridor immediately told me that I had just been robbed." Sure enough, the three men had burgled his hotel room of some $1,500 in petty cash, along with a stray £200. Against his better judgment, Mal chased after the culprits, but by the time he reached the lobby, they were long gone. In a crude attempt to allay the roadie's fears, "Detective Deegan, who was put in charge of the

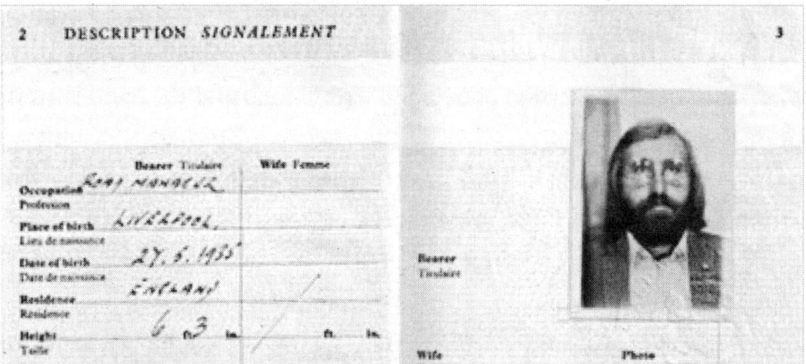

Mal's 1973 passport

case, assured me that they are not usually armed in hotel jobs and would most likely have just beaten me up."[3]

As the sessions for his album progressed, Ringo fell ever deeper into full-on alcohol abuse. Mal chalked it up to "Ringo being his inimitable happy self." But it was more than that. "One night at the studio," Mal wrote, "he gets through a quart of Southern Comfort and crashes in the control room. So, as on several occasions with the fellows, I had to pick him up, carry him to the car, and take him back to the hotel." That same night, after the two had returned to the Beverly Hills Hotel, David Bowie telephoned with an invitation to a party. "It was like a battle cry to an old war horse—a quick wash of the face, and Ringo was off and running to enjoy the party!"[4] Mal could only stand back and marvel at the Beatle's remarkable stamina.

For Mal, outside of "You're Thinking of Me," the highlight of the production involved a March 13 session when John arrived on the scene. In the history of the ex-Beatles, very few, if any, recording sessions would rival the events of that night, when Ringo sang John's "I'm the Greatest" with no less than John, George, and Klaus working as his studio musicians. For Mal, the eight-hour session was pure joy. "Ringo, John, Klaus Voormann, and myself grouped around a piano in the studio to put the finishing touches on the song," Richard Perry recalled. "Then someone called me out of the studio to say that George was on the phone. 'I hear there's some recording going on,' George said. 'Can I come down?' So I said to John, 'George is on the phone and wants to come down to record with us. Is it okay?' 'Hell, yes,' John said. 'Tell him to get down here right away and help me finish this bridge.' George arrived, and without saying a word, he joined in on the same wavelength we were on. He played guitar and John played piano, and they complemented each other perfectly. There was the Beatles magic unfolding right before my eyes!"[5]

Back in London, Paul and Linda would belatedly get into the spirit, contributing "Six O'Clock" to the album, which was now set to be entitled *Ringo*. The LP wouldn't be a full-fledged Beatles reunion, but it already promised, even in its unfinished form, something akin to the next-best thing.

The thrills continued a few nights later, at Sunset Sound, when several members of the Band joined Ringo for "Sunshine Life for Me (Sail Away

Raymond)." The song had been composed by George, who was thrilled to play on the recording session with his Canadian American idols.

With the Quiet Beatle ensconced back in Southern California to produce a Ravi Shankar LP at A&M Studios, Mal moved into George's rented home on Miradero Road in Beverly Hills. Enamored with his new digs, he informed Lily that he planned to stay in California for at least another month, which left his wife in tears during a telephone conversation on March 17. "It's nice to know you miss me and the children," she said, noting that "Gary had a little cry upstairs" after speaking with his dad.[6]

A few weeks later, the Beatles informed Allen Klein that as of April 1, 1973, he would no longer be their manager. The ex-Beatles felt the brunt of the change almost immediately. "George's days were certainly full," Mal wrote, "what with meetings during the day with lawyers to try and sort out his business, the first item on the agenda was hiring new cars, Allen having cancelled the ones we already had." Always a keen observer of natural coincidence, Mal couldn't help noticing that "the night Allen Klein was told he was no longer their manager, a bird fell out of a tree right next to my bed, and I got a lot of pleasure out of caring for this baby bird by feeding it milk and bread, keeping it alive until it was big enough to fly. When I phoned home and told my boy Gary a storm was taking place, he immediately christened the bird 'Stormcloud.'"[7] Not long afterward, John was asked why Klein had been given the boot. "Let's say possibly Paul's suspicions were right, and the time was right," Lennon admitted.[8]

With postproduction work for *Living in the Material World* well in hand, George tasked Mal with stage-managing the photo shoot for the album's gatefold design. The concept called for a contemporary update on Leonardo da Vinci's *The Last Supper*, with a coterie of rockers wining and dining to their heart's content, while surrounded by the trappings of material wealth and excess. Depicting George flanked by Ringo, Jim Horn, Klaus Voormann, Nicky Hopkins, Jim Keltner, and Gary Wright, the picture was shot in front of a mock-Tudor mansion by notorious Hollywood glam photographer Ken Marcus. "For the picnic photo, Abe Sommers [*sic*] generously allowed us to use his house and grounds," Mal wrote, referring to entertainment lawyer Abe Somer, "and whilst shooting this scene, where else but in Los Angeles could somebody say, 'Wouldn't it be great to have a nude chick sitting in the window of the house,' and 10 minutes later, there's a nude chick sitting in the window of the house!"[9]

More important, bunking with George would occasion a life-changing event for Mal, one that would have him reconsidering the trajectory of his career plans in dramatic fashion. During the week of April 17, 1973, after Ringo had returned from his rendezvous with Paul and Linda at the Apple studios, the musicians reconvened at Sunset Sound to complete the basic tracks for the *Ringo* LP. By this juncture, a concept of sorts had emerged in which John's "I'm the Greatest" would introduce the album. In order to provide a counterpoint, Ringo needed a grand finale to bring the record to a close. Mal felt that he had the makings of that very song in "I'm Not Going to Move," an unfinished composition he had begun in Rishikesh five years earlier.

"It was late one night, and I had this song going round my head," Mal recalled, "and I asked George if he would help me out with the chords, because I don't play very well. He started playing on the piano, it developed, and this is what it turned out to be. Ringo was surprised by it, I suppose."[10] That same week, Ringo and his studio band recorded the basic track for Mal and George's cowritten song, "You and Me (Babe)," with Ringo on drums, Klaus on bass, George on electric guitar, Nicky Hopkins on electric piano, and songwriter and record producer Vini Poncia on acoustic guitar. With Mal's lyrics, Ringo provided his listeners with a warm sendoff into the night, where he'd be sure to keep on partying, a pastime very much shared by the song's primary composer:

Now I want to tell you the pleasure really was mine.
Yes, I had a good time, singing and drinking some wine.
And when the sun sets in the sky
And you close your weary eyes,
I'll be in some nightclub, getting high, that's no lie.

As it turned out, the burglary of the petty cash was only the beginning of Mal's problems that spring. Sometime after George alighted in Southern California, Mal had gone out with a girl known only as Pandora. Most likely her dancer name, Pandora worked at Pips, a private discotheque and backgammon club that had recently been founded by L.A. real estate mogul Stan Herman and *Playboy*'s Hugh Hefner. During their date, Mal had taken Pandora to the Rainbow Bar and Grill; afterward, a highly inebriated Pandora wrecked her car outside George's rented house, which required a hospital stay for a fractured skull and brought a swift end to her evening out on the town with a certain roadie.

Then, on the night of Friday, April 13, an ominous date in Mal's book, a heavily sedated Pandora decided to visit George's house again, this time with some friends while the Beatle was away. Mal came home later that evening to learn that George's house had been burglarized. Fortunately, Ravi's master tapes were still on the premises, but to Mal's horror, the thieves "had stolen George's cherry red Gibson guitar, the very one that had been a present from Eric Clapton, and which meant so much to him." This was none other than George's much-cherished "Lucy," on which Clapton had played for "While My Guitar Gently Weeps" and which George himself had deployed for "Revolution" and "The End."

Knowing the tendencies of guitar thieves, Mal began telephoning instrument stores and pawnshops across the region. Sure enough, Lucy had been purchased by Whalin's Sound City, but to Mal's dismay, she had been resold only a half hour before he phoned the shop. As George continued his work with Shankar at A&M Studios, Mal remained glued to the phone, trying to ascertain the guitar's whereabouts.

Things might have ended there had it not been for Pandora's guilty conscience. She telephoned Mal, explaining that she had gone to George's house, hoping to hear one of the recordings he had made with Ravi. Instead, "what had been a desire to listen to a song had gotten out of hand," Mal wrote, "her companions ignoring all her pleas and stealing everything they could lay their hands on. It was just as well, I found out, that I hadn't interrupted that particular scene, for one of the guys was carrying a gun, and had told her at the time if either I or George showed up, he'd blast us with it."[11]

And that's when things got weird. "The night she phoned me about it," Mal continued, "I drove around to her apartment finding her very distressed and upset about what she'd done. There was a friend of hers sitting on the sofa, and after I had been there several minutes being my usual understanding self, the guy stood up and showed me a huge knife that he had been holding behind his back, saying, 'If you'd have walked in here and had a go at her, I would have stuck you with this.'" For a split second, Mal fell into a state of shock, before righting himself and saying, "Don't ever pull a knife on me unless you intend to use it."[12] His moment of bravado must have impressed the thug, who volunteered to accompany him to the house where the rest of his thieving friends lived.

Quite suddenly, Mal found himself living the plot of a real-life B movie. With the knife wielder in tow, he prepared to bust into the crooks' hideout. "It all seemed like a dream to me," Mal wrote, "standing outside the door in the early dawn, knocking and stepping back to either side of the door until somebody answered." Making his way inside, Mal found himself face-to-face with a pair of rough-and-tumble types, who were guarding a houseful of stolen property. "The two guys really tried to give us a rough time," he continued, "and I was sure scared as hell. Especially on opening a cupboard and finding the gun laying there. My friend, without more ado, picked the gun up, aimed it at one of the guys' heads, and on being told it wasn't loaded, said, 'You better be right, pal,' as he pulled the trigger."[13] In a twist of fate or providence, the gun wasn't loaded.

Mal's hard-boiled crime tale continued in the company of Detective Deegan, to whom he reported that they had managed to recover all the stolen goods from George's rented house, save for Lucy, which was still nowhere in evidence. Hoping to avoid seeing Pandora in handcuffs—at least for burglary—Mal had elided her role in the theft. Even so, he wasn't entirely sure his bluff worked as far as the detective was concerned. "I'm sure he knew something had happened other than what I [had] told him, could only take my word for it, and the case was closed," Mal wrote. "In spite of my not pressing charges and taking the matter any further, my girlfriend's guilty conscience pushed her to the point of attempting suicide."[14] Pandora was subsequently admitted to the psychiatric ward at UCLA Hospital.

But alas, the saga didn't end there. Nearly a month later, Mal picked up Lucy's scent after talking to a pair of roadies for Canned Heat, the hippie band that, in the late 1960s, had scored international hits with "On the Road Again" and "Going Up the Country." Having heard that a Mexican national named Miguel Ochoa had innocently purchased Lucy at Whalin's

Sound City, the roadies volunteered to fly down to Mexico to retrieve the instrument as a favor to George. Mal believed that the plan had a reasonable chance of success, given the Canned Heat roadies' solid connections with Mexican authorities.

The plan imploded when Ochoa learned that the guitar in his possession belonged to none other than the world-famous George Harrison of Beatles fame. Besides, to his mind, he had bought the instrument legally from Whalin's Sound City and owned it fair and square. At this point, the roadies suggested that other sorts of pressure could be applied to Ochoa. "We even got an offer to have him killed for $20," Mal wrote, "which horrified both George and I, refusing of course to have anything to do with that."[15] Fortunately for Mal, his conscience guilty thanks to his association with Pandora, Ochoa agreed to swap Lucy for a guitar of a similar age, make, and color. Working with Norman Harris, an L.A. collector, Mal managed to find a suitable guitar for the exchange.

But closing the deal with Ochoa proved just as complicated as seemingly everything else involved with Lucy's disappearance. "Negotiations never did proceed smoothy," Mal wrote, "because every time we complied with his demands, he asked for something extra, and it ended up costing George the price of a similar guitar, same price mysteriously having tripled overnight, plane tickets for two to Mexico, and the price of a bass guitar." Fortunately, price was no object for the Quiet Beatle, and after forty-three fretful days, Lucy was back in the hands of her rightful owner.

The next day, Mal celebrated his thirty-eighth birthday—and Lucy's recovery—at the Beverly Hills Hotel in fine style. Lounging by the pool, he was "surrounded by a veritable bevy of bikini clad beauties soaking up the one hundred and four degrees the day was offering. That evening, I was to enjoy, in the company of George, Ringo, and friends, Lakshmi Shankar's delightful singing in a concert of Indian music."[16]

A few days later, Mal returned to Sunbury after a three-month absence. It was by far the longest stretch of time he'd been away from his family—a month longer, in point of fact, than his 1968 American jaunt, which nearly ended with Lil's filing for divorce. By any measure, the trip home was a disaster. No sooner had he arrived than Lil found photos in his luggage of him with other women. In his diary, Mal lamented that "Lil and I fight in front of the children. Gary gets really upset and cries. Julie seems unconcerned, but she is a lot younger." Incredibly, he appeared to have talked his way out of any further confrontation—at least for the moment.

The next day, the couple enjoyed a "beautiful day" with the children at the Chessington Zoo. Perhaps thinking better of having made his return to the bosom of his family, Mal beat a hasty retreat to L.A. In total, he had spent fewer than eighty hours back in England that week. "I felt so sad walking away from Gary at the airport," he scrawled in his diary. "Please don't stop loving me, son. May God protect you always."[17]

The urgency of Mal's sudden return to Southern California was belied by entries in his diary. During his first week back in the States, he lounged on a Malibu beach, gazed at the smog hovering over L.A., and watched hours of mindless television. He finally got back to work on June 16—Lil's thirty-seventh birthday—when he and George drove out to the Record Plant West, located at 8456 West Third Street, to book studio time for remixing Ravi's album.

When Chris Stone and Gary Kellgren founded the Los Angeles branch of their New York City Record Plant in 1969, they were determined to transform it into rock music's showpiece recording studio, the place where the industry's shining stars came to play, see, and be seen. By 1973, the complex on Third Street featured three deluxe studio spaces with sixteen-track mixing desks, a jacuzzi, and private hotel–like suites with names like "the Rack Room," with S/M-style ropes and winches; "the Sissy Room," with over-the-top flowery décor; and "the Boat Room," with a nautical theme. The complex even boasted a Las Vegas Room, complete with pinball machines and other games of chance. The Record Plant West had also become famous for its regular Sunday night jam sessions, hosted by the Jim Keltner Fan Club. The latter was so popular of late that George, in a nod to the drummer's place in the zeitgeist, referenced it on the back cover of *Living in the Material World.*

While there, Mal studied the photos on the Record Plant's Wall of Fame, consisting largely of portraits of the facility's comely female staffers. That's when he caught sight of a shot of a beautiful strawberry blonde wearing a micro-bikini and an elaborate headdress. A few inquiries led him to discover that she was Francine Hughes, the twenty-four-year-old manager of the Record Plant West. In industry lingo, Fran ran "the Book," which was essentially the studio calendar. Being a booking agent meant acting as the studio's nerve center. And when you worked at a high-caliber facility like the Record Plant, running the Book meant juggling the lives and work of the industry's most talented and sought-after artists, producers, and engineers. It was also how Stone and Kellgren made their livelihood and kept their costly studio mecca on a paying basis.

After he saw her picture, Mal knew he wanted to take Fran out. "But at that particular time, I was a large, overweight, hairy roadie, with quite a magnificent beard. Now, Francine was quite used to people trying to pull her"—he wrote, using the English slang for "hit on"—"for very obvious reasons, so she didn't take to me at first."

Having grown tired of listening to his friend prattle on about the studio's eye-catching manager, George decided to take matters into his own hands. "For Christ's sake," he said to Fran, "go out with him just one night," adding, with a well-practiced smile, "or you're fired!"[18] Fran Hughes may

Fran Hughes's photo on the wall of the Record Plant

have been responsible for the Book, but George was a Beatle, and he had just delivered an ultimatum.

Fran agreed to accompany Mal to a party at Peter Asher's house. As Mal recalled, she "got quite drunk, mainly I'm sure to escape from me and any intentions I might have on her." But Mal played his cards carefully. "I was the perfect gentleman, as always, never making any advances, taking her home safe and sound."[19] His gambit must have succeeded, because Fran agreed to see him again after he returned from his upcoming trip to England.

36

FOOLS AND DRUNKS

Mal may have been the "perfect gentleman" in his comportment with Fran, but his diary suggests that prior to returning to London in late July, he had, at the very least, fallen in love with her. "The hands of fate brought us together," he wrote, "and tied the knot of love forever 'round my heart."[1] This time, Mal returned to England with a greater sense of purpose—and it pointedly did not involve Lil and the children.

Back in the States, Mal had received clear assurances from George that Splinter was on the verge of a major opportunity vis-à-vis the *Little Malcolm* soundtrack. On the strength of "Lonely Man," George was interested in producing Splinter's debut album, which he intended to record at his newly completed Friar Park home studio. Mal had also begun making further preparations for his new life as a professional songwriter. Inspired, no doubt, by George's fervent response to "Lonely Man," he had begun churning out lyrics at a remarkable rate. With "You and Me (Babe)" set for a late-autumn release on the *Ringo* LP, and with "Lonely Man" not far behind, he moved forward with a renewed sense of confidence. In a mid-July diary entry, he pointedly started designing a personal logo.

In short, he was a man both in love and on a mission. What could possibly go wrong?

To his credit, Mal refused to rest on the laurels of "Lonely Man" and "You and Me (Babe)." He was determined to continue refining his craft, even going so far as to seek out famed songwriter Jimmy Webb at his home in Encino, California, for mentorship. The composer behind such classic tunes as "Galveston," "Wichita Lineman," "Up, Up and Away," and "MacArthur Park," Webb recalled Mal's frequent appearances on his doorstep.

"Songs were difficult for him," said Webb. Even so, Mal "made agonizing but steady progress as a songwriter."[2] And the results were there, as Mal slowly but surely honed his ability to turn a memorable phrase or to capture an emotion.

When Mal wasn't writing lyrics in his diary and notebooks, he was studying all the angles, attempting to get the best possible deal for Splinter in advance of their autumn recording sessions. With Apple Records set to expire with the Beatles' partnership, George was eager to sign the duo to a contract with his fledgling Dark Horse label, which he intended to announce in 1974 as a subsidiary of A&M Records. At the same time, though, Threshold Records was vying for the band's services, making a late push to land the South Shields duo for its label.

As usual, Mal kept up his correspondence with his voluminous roster of pen pals, sending postcards by the bushel across the United Kingdom and abroad—and Fran had moved swiftly to the top of his list. Amid it all, on August 4, he made time to attend Bill Collins's wedding. At sixty, the Badfinger manager, despite marrying a much younger woman in twenty-four-year-old Toni McMahon, was beginning to feel his age. As far as Collins went, Mal—possibly buoyed by the spirit of new love—was happy to let bygones be bygones. And he was always happy to see the boys from Badfinger, who attended the outdoor wedding that weekend. After all, Klein was out of the Beatles' picture, having earned his just deserts.

In recent months, Collins had been fielding barbs from the bandmates, who were wondering when their riches would finally materialize. From their vantage point, it looked like Collins was on easy street, having footed the bill for his fancy and, no doubt, expensive wedding. And then there was Stan Polley, the business manager who had complete authority over the group's finances: he was living like a king while the boys still resided in "scumbag" houses despite spearheading hit singles like "Come and Get It," "No Matter What," "Day After Day," and, the most lucrative of them all, Nilsson's "Without You."[3]

Meanwhile, having completed principal photography on the *Little Malcolm* film, George began compiling the movie's soundtrack. To get things rolling, he convened Splinter at Apple Studios that summer for his first pass at "Lonely Man." As Big Mal looked on, beaming with pride, his song came to life in the 3 Savile Row basement, with Elliott and Purvis fronting an all-star band featuring George and Pete Ham on guitars, Klaus on bass, and Jim Keltner, of the eponymous fan club, on drums. Having toiled for years to find a vocation outside of being the Beatles' roadie and all-around manservant, Mal had the great pleasure of witnessing not one, but two of his original compositions in production.

That August, the Evans family undertook their annual vacation—this time, traveling to Majorca, the Spanish island and tourist mecca in the Mediterranean Sea. They had passed through the Balearic Islands a few years earlier, and Mal was eager to do some scuba diving. During the holiday, Gary felt something peculiar in the air when it came to his father, as if something were "off-kilter." Mal had booked an afternoon of sub-aqua adventuring for Gary and himself, but when they arrived at the scuba club, they were met by a large group of German tourists, who had inexplicably been given priority over them, despite Mal's reservations.

As he drove his son back to the hotel, Mal "looked as miserable as sin," according to his son. On the cusp of turning twelve, Gary had trouble believing that his father's gloomy state had anything to do with the German tourists who had usurped their scuba reservations. "My dad was with us in body, but his mind was elsewhere. He was far away." Later, after they

Lily posing in the Evanses' Sunbury garden

returned to Sunbury and Mal prepared to fly back to L.A., Gary put the question to his father. "You're going to leave us, aren't you?" he asked him as the two stood in the back garden. Mal ruffled Gary's hair, saying, "Don't be silly, son."[4]

Gary was right, of course, about his father's standoffishness. Mal was lovesick over Fran Hughes and desperate to return to Southern California. But first, he had to ensure that Splinter, as promised, made it into the studio with George. After some last-minute haggling, Dark Horse Records won the Splinter sweepstakes, with Threshold falling out of contention for the deal.

One afternoon, as he was having coffee with Bobby Purvis, Mal was surprised when the musician said, "Hope George does a good job on the album." To Mal's mind, it was an incredible thing to say. "I had to larf," he scrawled in his diary.[5] The Quiet Beatle had just notched three consecutive chart-topping LPs in a row in *All Things Must Pass*, *The Concert for Bangladesh*, and *Living in the Material World* and, at that very moment, his latest single, "Give Me Love (Give Me Peace on Earth)," was in heavy rotation.

George had originally intended to begin work with Splinter in early October, but delays in the completion of his home studio at Friar Park pushed their maiden session back until Halloween. Over a fortnight, he and the band managed to cut fourteen tracks, including a new version of "Lonely Man," which George produced over an eight-hour session on November 12. With Mal on hand in a supporting role, Splinter couldn't have asked for a better backing band, with George on guitar, Gary Wright on piano, the ever-reliable Klaus on bass, and Jim Keltner on drums. A few days later, George took to the studio to begin work on his own LP, which Mal was happy to stage-manage, if only briefly. In advance of the session for "Ding Dong, Ding Dong," Mal even dropped by the music shops on Shaftesbury Avenue to pick up strings for "Rocky," George's psychedelic Strat.

Meanwhile, when he wasn't ironing out contract details for Splinter with Denis O'Brien, George's business manager, Mal was gearing up for his return to Los Angeles—and to Fran, he hoped, at the end of the month. His heart was clearly in California, as evidenced by his diary. At one point, he decorated his "ME" monogram with a line of poetry, "No greater life has a man than to give his love to another"—a crude rendering of John 15:13:

"Greater love hath no man than this, that a man lay down his life for his friends." But on that very same page, in a less lofty poetic vein, he simply gushed, "Love is a flower that blooms in the warmth of your smile. With you, a day is a garden of smiles."[6]

On the eve of his flight back to the States, Mal returned to Gary, the subject that had brought him to recording events in his life in the first place, back in January 1963. In stark contrast to everything else in the decade-long history of his self-reflection, he crafted a strange, dark, apocalyptic poem:

I'm killing you, son, and you know not why.
The clowns perform as the audience dies,
And my mother tuts about the wallpaper on a bombed site.
She is blind to the destruction about her.

I'm taking my family to be burned,
And stroke my son's head,
And love him.

Life's a car rally with the whole human race going here and there,
Looking for clues as to which direction to go.[7]

For the moment, it seemed, Mal felt certain of his destiny. Lil must have sensed a change in the air, too. Frustrated by her husband's inconsistent role in the family's life—or, perhaps, simply hoping to take the pressure off an inflation-ravaged household budget—she landed a job as a typist at Hallite Seals. Located just two miles away from Staines Road East, near Hampton Court Palace, the company manufactured hydraulic seals, gaskets, and other rubber and plastic components. But, in truth, Lil didn't care what they made. It was a job.

As far as Gary was concerned, it made a difference in his life, too. The family's finances had become so tight that he and Julie qualified for free school meals. Gary's grandmother had recently told him, "You should count yourself lucky—all the toys you've got." But Gary saw things differently, thinking, "I'd rather not have all the toys and spend more time with my dad."

Before he left for the States, Mal asked Gary what he'd like him to bring back when he returned for the Christmas holidays. Fumbling for an answer, Gary went with the American version of Monopoly, the popular Parker Brothers board game. But then he said what he couldn't verbalize to his grandmother: "I'd rather spend more time with you."[8]

By the very next week, Mal was back in L.A., where he was set to rendezvous with John. Things had gone terribly awry in the Lennon household in the years since John and Yoko ensconced themselves in the St. Regis. What John would later describe as his Lost Weekend—a nod to the 1945 Billy Wilder film noir classic of the same name—began in the summer months of 1973. Yoko had kicked John out of the Dakota, their fortress-like apartment building on Central Park West, after his drinking and public debauchery grew out of control. During the Lost Weekend, "I was just insane," John admitted. "I've never drunk so much in my life, and I've been drinking since I was 15. But I really tried to drown myself in the bottle, and it took an awful lot. I don't seem strong physically that much, but it just seems to take an amazing lot to put me down. And I was with the heaviest drinkers in the industry."[9] Those drinkers grew to include the likes of Ringo, Harry Nilsson, Keith Moon, Alice Cooper . . . and Mal.

Yoko had pointedly sent John on his journey in the company of May Pang, the Lennons' twenty-two-year-old assistant. With his lengthy background as the Beatles' watchdog, Yoko had originally considered Mal for the role,[10] but he had been absent from New York City that summer when the crucial decisions were made. After John confessed his attraction to the beautiful young woman, sending him away in her company had made perfect sense. Pang had ably served as Yoko's assistant and as production supervisor on her avant-garde films, and Yoko felt she could count on her loyalty.

Not surprisingly, May was initially aghast at the thought of such an unconventional, even unethical, arrangement with her employers. "It'll be great," Yoko told her. "He'll be happy. It's cool." But as far as Pang was concerned, the idea of being with another woman's husband was anything but cool. "It was wrong," Pang remembered thinking, "and I wanted no part of it."[11] All that changed, of course, when John made his move, proving simply too much for Pang to resist.

That same spring, Mal received a much-welcome telephone call from Paul, who was prepping Wings for their first proper British tour, a twenty-one-show jaunt over two months. The five-piece band was heading out onto the road in support of their *Red Rose Speedway* album. Paul hired Mal as a consultant to assemble a team of roadies and other technical crew in advance of the tour.[12] For Mal, it was his first opportunity to work with Paul in the past few years, and he jumped at the chance to be of use to his old friend. Lucky fans who attended the first show, on May 11 at Bristol's Hippodrome, caught up with Mal at a nearby pub, where he was distributing *Red Rose Speedway* badges.

During this same period, Ringo and Harry Nilsson procured Mal's jack-of-all-trades services, having finally convened their film production for *Son of Dracula*. The loosely constructed plot featured Ringo as Merlin and Nilsson as "Count Downe," the son of the late Count Dracula, King of the Netherworld. A raucous party scene called for the appearance of Count Downe's rock 'n' roll band, which featured Bobby Keys on saxophone, Peter

Ringo and Mal

Frampton on guitar, and Led Zeppelin's John Bonham on drums. At one point, they ran out of instruments for the musicians to play onstage, and Mal left for his car. Frampton's jaw dropped when the roadie returned moments later with an armful of vintage Beatles guitars, including John Lennon's famous jet-black Rickenbacker Capri. Frampton happily played the guitar for the scene, awestruck to discover a set list still taped to the instrument's neck.[13]

Back in Southern California, Mal fell into his familiar routine again, reacquainting himself with the L.A. set. On one unforgettable occasion, he joined John and May Pang on a promotional jaunt for Lennon's *Mind Games* album. Apple rep Susan Markheim hired a limo to squire her guests around the greater Los Angeles area to visit radio stations. But when John caught a glimpse of Markheim's canary-yellow 1966 Ford Mustang, he couldn't resist riding in the sports car instead. Markheim would never forget the image of John, May, and big Mal cramming themselves into her tiny automobile. "It was the first time I met him," Markheim recalled, and "Mal was so kind, so special"—even as he forced his massive, wayward body into the Mustang's cramped interior.[14]

After years of working at the behest of record labels large and small, Ken Mansfield had decided to go into business for himself. That fall, Mal attended the launch of Mansfield's Hometown Productions, a new venture that would cater to the evolving "Outlaw" country music genre. The gala event, held at Mansfield's ranch in Malibu Canyon, was attended by George and Pattie and Jack Oliver. It would be one of George's last appearances with Pattie, who would shortly leave him for Eric Clapton. Other guests included Franco-American singer and actress Claudine Longet, Leonard Nimoy (aka "Mr. Spock" of *Star Trek* fame), and Mansfield's close friend, country singer Waylon Jennings, one of the central figures in his new business.

Mal and Mansfield's friendship took on even greater import during this period. As Mansfield later recalled, "Mal and I became the Englishman and the cowboy riding hard herd on the Sunset Strip until the sun came up many mornings."[15] With Nilsson having made his return to L.A., the three men became fast friends—drinking hard, staying up all hours, and basking in the excitement of the region's burgeoning music scene.

Mal had two primary objectives in mind for his sojourn in Los Angeles:

First, at Neil's suggestion, he planned to serve as John's road manager for a new album of rock 'n' roll standards the Beatle intended to record with Phil Spector. John was initially sheepish about bringing Mal onto the project, telling Neil that "Mal's mainly working with George and Ringo these days—he won't want to come out here and work with me." Neil knew this wasn't true, and he urged Mal to help John see the light—which he did at the first opportunity, fixing a series of November and December dates to get the Beatle's new LP under way. When it came to the new record, Mal was especially wary of Spector, whose behavior had become increasingly erratic since the heady days of "Instant Karma!"

Mal's other objective, of course, was to pursue a romantic relationship with Fran Hughes. As it happened, things there would be fast-tracked, unexpectedly, when calamity struck. Mal had been up for three days straight with Harry Nilsson, who was ostensibly helping him stage-manage John's new album with Spector, currently under the working title *Back to Mono*. In truth, working with Mal gave Harry an excuse to go on a seemingly uninterrupted bender. After dropping John and May off following their latest recording session at A&M Studios, Harry suggested that he and Mal hit the highway in Mal's rented Cadillac and see where the road took them.

"We had a lovely day on the beach," Mal recalled, "watching penguins play golf, fishermen in boats, birds lighting on their heads. It's an acid test for any friendship, getting high from lack of sleep, and the considerable amount of booze we'd both been drinking—I being a Southern Comfort man and Harry sticking to his brandy."[16] Later that day, Mal and Harry went to dinner with a pair of young couples they had met at the beach. This was followed by a show at Cal's Corral—a gathering spot in Huntington Park for country-and-western singers and musicians—where an Elvis impersonator performed a thrilling set of the King's early hits into the pre-dawn hours. Not surprisingly, Mal and Harry, riding high from sleep deprivation and too much to drink, got lost trying to make their way back into the city.

On the morning of November 30, Nilsson caught sight of an all-night restaurant. As Mal looked on, "Harry proceeded to demolish a large breakfast, and I, on the sight of it, went outside, spewed, and fell asleep on the passenger side of the car. The next thing I'm aware of is the sound of ambulances," Mal wrote, "bright red lights flashing, and two policemen pulling me out of the wrecked Cadillac."[17] Apparently, Harry had commandeered the vehicle during Mal's slumber and then proceeded to fall asleep himself, behind the wheel, totaling the Caddy and nearly costing the two friends their lives in the process.

At the hospital, Mal received fifteen stitches above his left eye, while Harry required several stitches in one of his cheeks. Initially, there was some concern that Mal might lose vision in his left eye. For Mal, there must have been "a guardian angel looking out for fools and drunks," he reasoned after learning he would retain his sight. "It must have been funny for the hospital staff," he added, "because when they were stitching me up, I remember lying on the table chanting the Hare Krishna mantra, feeling no pain whatsoever, but poor old Harry was having a terrible time on the next table, shouting and kicking."[18]

Mal recuperated at the Beverly Wilshire hotel, but he wasn't alone in his hour of need. "After dropping Harry off at his apartment," Mal wrote, "I phoned Francine and told her what had happened. She immediately took a day off from work, came over to the hotel and nursed me. I really believe that young lady saved my sanity that day, lying in bed, aching in every bone, black and blue all over, hardly able to move." Thanks to Fran's beneficence, Mal began to recover, slowly but surely. "She fed me, bathed me every hour, and brought me 'back to life.'"[19]

Fran Hughes may have possessed the sweet bloom of youth, but she was anything but naïve. And she had big plans when it came to her life and work; she always had. In 1968, when she was eighteen, she quit school after a year at Philadelphia's Temple University and moved to New York City. She knew she had the talent and the brains to make it. With her looks, she became adept at landing modeling gigs. "But then I got too skinny," she recalled. "I kept blacking out," she said, having starved herself to maintain a Twiggy-thin weight of a hundred and five pounds.[20] After stints as a secretary at *Billboard* magazine and as Morris Levy's assistant at Roulette Records, she took a job in the front office at the Mirasound recording studio, home at the time to such big-name acts as Led Zeppelin, Vanilla Fudge, and the Edwin Hawkins Singers. Bobby Hughes was working there, too. A skilled engineer—his résumé already included credits with the likes of Simon and Garfunkel and Barbra Streisand—Hughes was outfitting the facility with sixteen-track capabilities when he met Fran. The scuttlebutt around Mirasound was that Bobby was gay, but Fran didn't care. She fell for the handsome engineer, and the two got married. With her organizational gifts and natural chutzpah, she saw their dual-career livelihood as a challenge—a project of sorts.[21]

Knowing a good thing when he saw it, Chris Stone hired the power couple away from Mirasound and installed them at the Record Plant's operations on 42nd Street in Manhattan.[22] By this point, Fran was integral to Stone and Kellgren's business, having been part of the studio's operations since its inception. It was she who had famously welcomed Jimi Hendrix to the building in 1970, when the guitar god was working on his *Cry of Love* album. As Hendrix prepared to leave the studio for the last time, Fran remembered giving him a pound of weed as a sort of bon voyage. It seemed that "nobody had ever given him a gift," she recalled, and "the concept that it was a giving gesture made him break down in tears."[23] And when Stone and Gary Kellgren founded the Record Plant West, Fran and Bobby made the cross-country move. By this point, Fran was the bigger catch, having perfected the fine art of booking a top-flight recording studio for maximal profit.

After the birth of baby Jody in 1971, Fran found her marriage to Bobby faltering when he could no longer resist the flourishing Southern California gay scene. Ever forward-thinking, Fran didn't look back, purchasing for herself a duplex just east of Beverly Hills, at 8122 West Fourth Street, within easy walking distance of the Record Plant. Nestled in a quiet residential neighborhood, it was a cozy home for mother and child, with a modest balcony above the front stoop. Today, the locals describe the area in real estate speak as "Beverly Hills adjacent," but in the early 1970s, it was known less elegantly as "the Flats."[24]

After catching Mal's eye, Fran determined to make the roadie the subject of her latest project. He was hell-bent on finding success in the recording industry, and with her contacts and resourcefulness, she was just the partner to make it happen. In the weeks and months to come, the two took their place as the Record Plant's "It Couple," partying with the leading artists of the day, horseback riding on the beach, hanging out with the ex-Beatles when they were in town, and living it up SoCal style.

Fran recalled that when she first met Mal, she wasn't afraid to take risks. "I was a daredevil," she said. "I sky-dived."[25] Thanks to his budding relationship with Fran, Mal became a fixture at the Record Plant—much to Stone and Kellgren's delight. He seemed to know everyone in the business. Besides that, the two were hoping the roadie might convince the former Beatles—Paul especially—to record their latest tracks at the Third Street complex.[26]

Outside of getting to know Fran, Mal took great pleasure in spending long hours in John's company, enjoying the Beatle's undivided attention, as opposed to sharing him with Paul, George, and Ringo. "It was fascinating," said Mal, "because John was talking to me like I was a songwriter, and that was incredible. For the first time, John and I really communicated, whereas, when it was the four of them, John was always the hardest to talk to. I always thought that when John stopped insulting me, we had fallen out as friends." But, he added, referring to John's teasing, "The more he likes you, the more he takes the mickey out of you."[27]

Yet, as Mal soon discovered, working with John during this period would prove to be a chore—incomparable, in fact, to their touring years together, when the Beatles were often confined to the relative safety of a hotel suite. When he was in L.A., John could often be found at the Sunset Strip's Rainbow Bar and Grill, which had emerged as his de facto headquarters during the Lost Weekend. With musicians like John, Harry, Ringo, Moonie, Alice Cooper, and Micky Dolenz adopting the Rainbow as their regular watering hole, they had taken to calling themselves the Hollywood Vampires, a nickname that evoked the night hours they spent guzzling hooch in the bar's loft space.

On one of his most harrowing evenings in Los Angeles, Mal had accompanied John and Phil Spector to the Rainbow. At one point, John walked Phil to his car, assuring Mal that he would return shortly. "About a half hour goes by, and I start worrying and go outside looking for John—no sign," Mal later wrote. "I'd lost track of a Beatle for a day. What had happened, I found out the following evening, was that when he'd seen Phil off, a few hippie fans of his took him in tow, and John, who had just moved into a flat, couldn't remember the address, nor his or my phone numbers. [John] eventually turn[ed] up, but not before I'd had a few irate words

Ringo, Mal, and John with Bobby Womack

from Yoko, who phoned me from New York shouting, 'I thought you were John's bodyguard—why don't you guard his body?'" At a loss for words, Mal admitted that "I never really thought of myself as a bodyguard to anybody, but I suppose over the years that had been part of the gig. Anyway, they were all grown up, with very strong minds of their own as to what they wanted to do, and I certainly didn't expect them to hold themselves accountable to me."[28]

That December, as work on *Back to Mono* proceeded, John and Phil shifted their project to the Record Plant West. The change of recording studios had nothing to do with Stone and Kellgren's amenity-rich facilities and everything to do with John's and Phil's antics having gotten them evicted from A&M. At one point, Harry Nilsson and Keith Moon, in a drunken stupor, had urinated onto the studio's recording console, leaving the electronics in an ungodly mess. In a letter to Phil entitled "A Matter of Pee," John wrote that neither he nor May should be expected to mind adult rock stars, and that he was about to join Record Plant in frustration.[29]

Mal was delighted by the change of venue, but within a remarkably short period—only a few sessions, really—John's Lost Weekend would leave its mark on the Third Street facility. As for Phil, nobody in the business had any illusions about the producer's condition. "He was batshit crazy," said Fran, who pointed out that the industry tolerated Spector only because he was a legendary hitmaker of yore.[30]

Things began innocently enough after John and Phil completed their December 11 session at the Record Plant West, where they took a pass at Chuck Berry's "You Can't Catch Me." As Mal looked on, the two men, drunk to the gills, were horsing around the Las Vegas Room. In a nod to the early days of Beatlemania, John decided to hop onto Mal's back for a piggyback ride. Unfortunately, Phil opted to get in on the act, too. Mal's physical dexterity in late 1973 was a far cry from that of the early 1960s, and he had difficulty sustaining the weight of two men atop his aching back. As always, Mal observed, "Phil goes a little too far," and in the ensuing ruckus, "he karate-chopped me on the nose, my spectacles went flying, and I got tears in my eyes I can tell you. I turned around with a real temper and told Phil, 'Don't ever lay another finger on me, man.'"

And that's when Phil, "maybe to reestablish himself in his own eyes," Mal thought, pulled out a handgun. To the roadie's surprise, the producer "fired it off under our noses, deafening us both, the bullet ricocheting around the room and landing between my feet."[31]

John was understandably incensed, exclaiming to Phil, "If you're gonna kill me, kill me, but don't take away my hearing—it's me living!"

Until that moment, Mal and John had believed that Spector's handgun was a toy. At one point earlier in the evening, Phil had cocked the trigger and aimed the weapon at John's head. As a result of the incident in the Las Vegas Room, "John's fear of guns generally was doubled."[32] For his part, Mal vowed to stay clear of Phil. He would attend the recording sessions in deference to John, but that was it.

In nearly the same instant that Mal decided to banish Phil from his world forever, he and John were hustled off to Gary Kellgren's house for a lavish going-away party in honor of Mal, who was preparing to make his return to Sunbury. For the occasion, Phil had arranged for Mal to receive "a beautiful large cake, which must have measured four feet by three feet, so nicely decorated with a large bottle of Napoleon brandy, [and] a lot of comic figures like Superman and Batman," Mal wrote. The sumptuous dessert was inscribed, "To Mal, my pal, love, Philip."

As it turned out, the madcap producer's greatest gift to Mal that night came in the form of his absence. "Phil, to show the most understanding side of his nature, did not come to the party," said Mal. "He knew if he had, he'd be outrageous and spoil it for me. But he set it up and didn't come—a true mark of affection from a friend."[33] The party came to a sudden close, though, when John, having grown blind drunk, planted a telephone into the sticky remains of the cake.

All in all, "It was to be a nice, warm, friendly weekend to send me off to a very cold England," Mal wrote.[34]

37

SO WHAT?

From Mal's vantage point, leaving the warmth and sunshine of Southern California for dour, wintry England was always jarring—like traveling backward in time from the glitz of Technicolor into grainy black and white. Or, put another way, it was like leaving the urgency and relevance of Hollywood behind for the sameness of family and the suburbs and their rabbit hutches.

For Gary, Mal's return to Sunbury that December was no different from any of his father's recent visits. Playing to form, Mal still seemed distant and, at times, was temperamental—especially when it came to his interactions with Lil. The only discernible change involved the mottled left side of his face, which was still healing from the car wreck back in November. Fortunately, Mal had remembered to bring Gary's American Monopoly set, and his son—who had developed a fascination for maps and the idiosyncrasies of places—enjoyed seeing Atlantic City's streets and avenues sprouting up where, in his U.K. version of the game, London landmarks such as the Strand and Trafalgar Square once stood.

On Christmas Eve, Mal drove the family over to Neil and Suzy's house to celebrate the holidays. As far as Neil was concerned, with Allen Klein and his awful regime having been sent packing at last, there was plenty to celebrate. A few days earlier, Mal and Lily had joined Neil and the remaining members of the Apple staff for a Christmas party in Covent Garden, marking a return to normalcy of sorts after enduring years of Klein's scorched-earth policies. Neil had continued his private toil as resident historian, still hoping one day to loose *The Long and Winding Road* upon Beatle World.

As they drove back to Sunbury that night, Gary received a bitter reminder of the state of his parents' marriage. From the backseat, he could

Julie, Mal, and Gary

glean the sounds of his father's dismay—"For fuck's sake, Lil," he heard his father say, no doubt in response to his mother's litany of grievances. There it was again, Gary thought. The F-word, the crown prince of expletives to his twelve-year-old ear. "Oh dear," he said to himself in the darkened car. "This is the end."[1]

Only, it wasn't. When Mal gathered his belongings to make the return trip to Los Angeles, things were strangely normal. It was Friday, January 4, 1974. Even years later, Gary would think back to that day, sifting among his memories for clues. But there was nothing there, really, to expose in the light of the present. It was only the familiar image of his father heading off to work for the Beatles—or at least a subset thereof—in some foreign locale. Same old same old.

Upon returning to L.A., Mal began shacking up with Fran almost immediately. Her two-bedroom duplex, while modest at 1,700 square feet, was plenty big for the couple and Jody, her and Bobby's precocious toddler. Not surprisingly, affable Mal had quickly befriended his girlfriend's ex-husband.

When it came to shop talk, Bobby, with his engineering background, could more than hold his own. And the roadie, having worked for the Greatest Show on Earth, bar none, had no end of tales to tell.

And the New Year was about to gift Mal with the ending to a tale that had so long eluded him: bona fide creative success. Sure, "No Matter What" had cracked the vaunted top ten in the US of A, but he had been robbed of that achievement thanks to Klein's backroom cruelty and Bill Collins's rampant paranoia. Mal's deliverance would arrive, finally, on the wings of the *Ringo* LP.

The album had originally been slated for an early fall release, only to be delayed—in a shrewd move, all things considered—to afford artist Tim Bruckner with much-needed extra time to complete a brilliant *Sgt. Pepper*–like cover that arrayed the cartoon images of Ringo's supporting cast, including Big Mal, gold sheriff's star proudly affixed to his chest, festooned

Fran and Mal's Fourth Street duplex

around the "Starr" of the show. With the public clamoring for a Beatles reunion, the *Ringo* LP was the next best thing.

With a pair of chart-topping singles in "Photograph" and "You're Sixteen," *Ringo* was a runaway hit, earning gold record status from the Recording Industry Association of America. This meant that Mal, as the cowriter with George of "You and Me (Babe)," was entitled to some golden hardware to display on the wall of Fran's second-floor bedroom, which was slowly emerging as the storehouse for his memorabilia.

The inclusion of "You and Me (Babe)" on Ringo's blockbuster LP meant that in terms of pure mechanical royalties, Mal and George were each entitled to an equal 5 percent share of the residuals. For the time being at least, Mal's £38 weekly wage seemed like chicken feed. As a songwriter, Mal had long dreamt of hitting the big time, and with the success of the *Ringo* album, he was on his way. But he wasn't the only person who had benefited from riding the drummer's coattails. No less than John Lennon dashed off a telegram to Ringo: "Congratulations. How dare you? And please write me a hit song."[2]

As it happened, Mal's first few months back in Southern California would be absolutely dominated by John, who, at times, was in a full-blown alcohol- and drug-fueled personality crisis as he attempted to navigate his post-Yoko life with May. His latest challenge involved rekindling his relationship with his son, Julian, now ten, who was visiting L.A. in the company of John's ex-wife, Cynthia. By this point, John hadn't seen the boy since 1971, when he and Yoko left the United Kingdom behind for New York City. For her part, Cynthia was delighted to catch up with Mal, who had been such a fixture during her marriage to John. "While Julian was with John and May, I spent time with Mal," she recalled. "John had asked him to keep me company and show me around. It was good to see him again." And true to his word, Mal made sure Cynthia had a good time. "He took me to a great Mexican restaurant," she recalled, "introduced me to Tequila Sunrises, and drove me all round Los Angeles."[3]

On January 14, with Mal and Cynthia in tow, John and May squired Julian around Disneyland. As always, Mal was game for anything, joining Julian on the Mad Tea Party attraction, where the pair spun around in a giant teacup. Though out of his element, John managed to enjoy the experience, thanks to a drug-infused euphoria. As their holiday in Southern California came to an end, Cynthia and Julian spent their last evening at Fran and Mal's place on Fourth Street, where the couple hosted a dinner party. Naturally, Fran pulled out all the stops. "I was raised like that," she said. "When people come over to your house, you make sure they have a good time."[4]

During the party, Cynthia confided in Mal that she felt awkward in John's presence. "Mal, ever the supportive Mr. Fix-It, wanted to help. It seemed to work. While Mal poured the drinks, John and May sat down with me and we chatted." The convivial event seemed to make a difference. "At last I saw a glimmer of hope that things would ease," Cynthia recalled. "For the first and only time since our divorce, John seemed to put aside his guilt and embarrassment and relax with me. John reminisced about Liverpool and old friends and asked me to give them his love."[5]

But that wasn't all Cynthia noticed that night in Fran's duplex. It didn't take an amateur sleuth to figure out that the roadie had taken up with another woman. "I'd known his wife, Lil, and their two children—they used to come to Kenwood—so I was sad to hear that he'd left them and was living in LA with a new girlfriend," Cynthia said.[6] For his part, young Julian had been led to believe they had been guests in the home of Mal's "cousin," as opposed to his girlfriend. And this was precisely what the boy told Lily a few weeks later in her kitchen, when he and his mother stopped by Sunbury for a visit with their old friends.

"Julian was playing drums with wooden spoons on biscuit tins," Lil recalled, when he suddenly announced that Mal had planted "a great big kiss" on his cousin. When Julian left to join Gary and Julie, who were watching television in the family room, Cynthia took advantage of the opportunity to console Lil, who knew full well that Mal didn't have a cousin living on the West Coast of the United States. "She is just a smut on your nose," Cynthia told her. "Just wipe her off."

Unbeknownst to Mal, the cat was out of the bag. Lily realized that her husband hadn't departed Sunbury for yet another in a long line of Beatles-related business trips. He'd left her for another woman. And "she was more than a smut," as Lily came to learn.[7]

Meanwhile, Mal had been busy contending with the fallout from John's deteriorating condition. On January 12, while Cynthia and Julian were seeing the sights in L.A., John and May had dinner at the restaurant Lost on Larrabee, in the company of Jim Keltner and session guitarist extraordinaire Jesse Ed Davis. At some point during dinner, an inebriated John affixed a Kotex sanitary napkin to his forehead, an appendage he continued to wear when the group relocated to the Troubadour nightclub for a set by Ann Peebles. Eventually, the group settled in for the night in attorney Harold Seider's duplex near the Hollywood Hills, where John and May were staying at the time.

All hell broke loose when Davis, who had been matching John drink for drink, began biting at John during a mêlée in the kitchen. In his shock, John reacted by clocking Davis in the head with a bottle of Coca-Cola, leading other members of the party to believe he had accidentally killed the guitarist. In the ensuing noise and mayhem, one of Seider's neighbors had apparently called the police. May and John answered the door to find a bevy of policemen, guns drawn. When the cops realized who John was, and having ascertained that Davis was still among the living, the officers relaxed, even going so far as to make chitchat with the famous musician who, only moments before, had been a possible manslaughter suspect.

"Are the Beatles ever gonna get back together again?" one of the officers inquired.

"You never know," John replied, still attempting to regain control of his senses.[8]

With his wad of petty cash at the ready, Mal was tasked with arranging for repairs to Seider's condo. Meanwhile, John and May checked into the Beverly Wilshire hotel, where the Beatle continued his drunken harangue. No stranger, of course, to John's hard-partying lifestyle, Harry Nilsson remembered a particularly madcap evening at the hotel when he spotted Mal attempting to console John, lost to another bender. "One night he was crying on Mal Evans's shoulder, saying, 'I was always a good boy. I was always a good boy,'" Nilsson recalled. "And Mal said, 'Right brother, you were always a good boy.' And I told him, 'What is this horseshit? Stop being a baby. You're being a baby.' 'Well, if you don't like it, you can get the fuck out!' John yelled. 'Well, all right,' and I slammed the door, and I was crying." Feeling rejected by John, one of his idols, Nilsson became "so pissed off [that] I took a bottle of whiskey and threw it through what I thought was his little window, but which turned out to be a 17-foot high window in the Beverly Wilshire Hotel." For Nilsson, it was just another incidence of "overlapping madness" that typified his life with John and Mal during this era, "but Jesus, it was a good time."[9]

Ensconced in Fran's world, Mal began to imagine a new life for himself beyond the long shadow of the Beatles. He and Fran had even discussed the possibility of applying for his green card and earning permanent U.S. residency. Flush with success in the wake of the *Ringo* LP, he began contemplating hanging up his shingle as a professional songwriter. And he owed much of his newfound confidence to Fran, whose daredevil, forward-thinking nature had buoyed his spirits.

When Fran met the roadie, she had been immediately struck, like everyone, by his larger-than-life presence. "But inside, he was just a child," she recalled, "he had no self-esteem." It didn't take a therapist to realize that "when the Beatles split up, he lost his identity."[10] Fran was determined to build Mal back up, to help him realize his dream of making a name for himself outside the Beatles. Besides, she was in love with the guy. She hadn't realized that he was still married to Lil when they met, assuming that, like so many jet-setters of the day, he was caught up in a trial separation on the road to divorce. But the fallout after their dinner party with Cynthia and Julian changed all that. "I didn't know that Mal hadn't told his family about us," said Fran. "I mean, that's terrible."

After Lily confronted Mal, during a telephone call, about having an L.A. girlfriend, he retreated into his already broken self-esteem. "Everything had been fine until then," Fran recalled. "He was so disappointed with himself for having let his family down." In her typical no-nonsense fashion, Fran cut to the chase: If he was going to wallow in misery about what he'd wrought back in Sunbury, there was an easy solution. "Then just go home—go back," she told him.[11]

But Mal wasn't willing to do that. And it came down to a variety of reasons, including his unerring loyalty to the boys and his own plans for embarking on a new career. But as usual, he was living his life at cross-purposes: he wanted to be with Fran, to enjoy their SoCal lifestyle together; yet, at the same time, he longed for his family back in England. If he were being truly honest with himself—and he rarely was—he would have had to admit that his recent yearning for life back on Staines Road East had been rekindled only *after* Cynthia and Julian spilled the beans on him, that his current psychological malaise was rooted in his guilt over being found out as much as in anything else. It was a difficult pill to swallow—the idea that he wasn't "affable Mal" in everyone's eyes, that Lil and his children had good reason to be upset and disillusioned by his selfish behavior. As Fran had so clearly recognized at the outset, he really was an overgrown child lost inside that gigantic body.

On Valentine's Day, Mal and Fran took a break from their troubles and attended Bob Dylan and the Band's concert at the L.A. Forum, the latest stop on the American folk hero's 1974 tour. The couple took in the show from one of the exclusive Forum Club boxes, where they sat with Ringo and Chris O'Dell. At one point, Mal's carefully honed roadie sense kicked in, and he began to notice a man crawling along the floor of the arena toward Ringo. "Watch this," Mal announced to his girlfriend. A shocked Fran observed as he attempted to stop the insurgent fan by pressing his foot upon the man's outstretched leg. Despite Mal's considerable weight coming down on him, the fan succeeded in crawling alongside Ringo and began chattering away to the Beatle, seemingly oblivious to the pain in his leg. This must be a real Beatles fan, Mal recalled thinking, because "he didn't even flinch."[12]

If Mal wasn't going to bite the bullet and go back to his wife and family, Fran reasoned, then he had damned well better resolve to make the most of his life in the here and now. In the meantime, ex-Beatle World reared its head in the form of a new project involving John and Harry. At this point, the *Back to Mono* production had gone on hiatus after Spector's reckless behavior finally caught up with him in the form of a harrowing car accident. Barely escaping with his life after being catapulted through the windshield of his Rolls-Royce, he had required some seven hundred stitches. As for Harry Nilsson, his latest record, *A Little Touch of Schmilsson in the Night*, had hit the charts with a thud, and he was eager to recapture the glory days of his "Without You" era. As his drinking buddy and bosom companion, John offered to serve as producer on the singer's next album. Thanks to Spector's penchant for driving while intoxicated, John had plenty of free time on his hands.

For Harry's album—which went under the working title *Strange Pussies*—John intended to pull out all the stops for his friend, and this meant procuring the services of Mal to stage-manage the production. After the drunken debauchery associated with *Back to Mono*, there was little doubt that *Strange Pussies* would be no easy feat. Knowing Harry's hard-drinking proclivities, John reasoned that the best way to proceed would be to ensure that the album's motley group of participants lived under the same roof for the duration of the project. Their salvation arrived in the form of an opulent seaside estate in Santa Monica.

As it happened, they had passed that way before. Mal had recently driven John and May along the Gold Coast, where the roadie had been pulled over for speeding. Although May was terrified about what might transpire in the presence of the California Highway Patrolman, Mal played it cool, gesturing toward the famous musician in the passenger seat and gently telling the officer that they were in a hurry to keep an important appointment. Within a matter of minutes, they were once again on their way, with the patrolman, mesmerized after having observed an honest-to-goodness Beatle in the wild, letting them off with a warning.

On the advice of Ringo's personal lawyer, Bruce Grakal, John and May toured the Spanish-style mansion on Palisades Beach Road, easily the most storied address among California's Gold Coast abodes. Constructed in 1926, the home had been the brainchild of legendary Hollywood mogul Louis B. Mayer. The estate had earned a notorious reputation in later years, after it was purchased by actor Peter Lawford and his wife, Patricia (née Kennedy). As John already knew, in the early 1960s, 625 Palisades Beach Road was the site of President John F. Kennedy and Marilyn Monroe's love nest.

When it came time to move into the rented house, John and May took the master bedroom for themselves, with Lennon quipping "so this is where they did it," referring to Kennedy and Monroe's seaside assignations.[13] The other bedrooms at the estate were allotted to Harry, Keith Moon, and Klaus Voormann, with the estate's library—complete with President Kennedy's portrait on the wall—converted into a bedroom for Ringo, who was in town to escape his failing marriage to Mo. For the purposes of recording *Strange Pussies*, RCA Records had blocked off studio time for John and

Harry at the Record Plant, which was just fine with Mal, who enjoyed an easy commute from Fran's duplex.

For those associated with *Strange Pussies*, the project was doomed from the start, with John and Harry earning international headlines after being kicked out of the Troubadour for disorderly behavior after heckling the Smothers Brothers earlier that same month. For Mal especially, working on Harry's album was nothing short of a disaster. For one thing, most of the players subsisted in a state of perpetual drunkenness worsened only by the lines of cocaine being doled out. It didn't help that the other principal musicians—saxophonist Bobby Keys and guitarists Jesse Ed Davis and Danny Kortchmar—were world-beating partiers in their own right. Along with May, a lifelong teetotaler, Mal struggled to keep the troops in order and working toward the common goal of righting Harry Nilsson's career. When the sessions devolved into chaos, which they invariably did, Mal would throw up his hands in defeat and join the revelry.

By April, Mal wasn't sure that John could even bring the album in for a landing. For one thing, Harry, as Nilsson confided in the roadie, had ruptured one of his vocal cords during an early session. Desperate to see the album through at any cost and regain his previously stellar career, Nilsson had concealed this fact from John, even as the quality of his vocal output eroded with each day. For another, the *Strange Pussies* production had begun to take on the pretensions of a rock 'n' roll joke. There was no way, for example, that RCA would approve of *Strange Pussies* as the album's title, but Harry and John plowed ahead anyway.

For Mal, the album achieved its zenith on March 28. In many ways, that evening alone should have given *Strange Pussies* the kick in the ass it sorely needed. But the players simply weren't up to it. That night, none other than Paul and Linda had strolled into the Record Plant. Ever the sentimentalist, Mal was overcome by emotion at the sight of John and Paul together for the first time since Pattie's March 1970 birthday celebration at Friar Park. Unfortunately, the music they made that night was a different matter altogether. In truth, Mal couldn't have asked for a more talented assemblage of musicians under a single roof. The great Lennon and McCartney were on hand, of course, along with Nilsson, Davis, and Keys. Better yet, they had been joined that evening by Stevie Wonder, who chipped in on keyboards. With nary a drummer in sight, Paul strode behind Ringo's empty drum kit, joining John and a series of ragged lead vocals on such chestnuts as "Lucille" and "Stand by Me." For their part, Mal and May made half-hearted efforts at percussion. After several sloppy attempts at finding a groove, the musicians mercifully called it quits. What might have been an unexpected Lennon-McCartney triumph had ended in an amateurish, desultory jam.[14]

For Mal, the sunny afternoon of March 29 would bring pure magic in contrast with the previous evening's lackluster proceedings. The McCartney clan showed up out of the blue, this time with daughters Heather, Mary, and Stella in tow, and Mal was thrilled at the prospect of seeing John and Paul together again—twice in the span of two days, no less. And he was by no means disappointed, observing the two old friends reclining on the patio together and, later, walking along the beach, with May, Linda, and the McCartney brood trailing along behind them. "Nice to see him and John together," Mal scribbled in his diary later that month.[15]

When Mal returned to John and May's Gold Coast estate the following Saturday, he arrived with purpose in his step. He had decided that today, April 6, 1974, would mark the end of his employment with the Beatles. It was high time he made Malcontent Music a reality. Fran had been right all along: Either put up or shut up. Stake a claim on his future as a songwriter and talent scout, in California, or hit the bricks, wipe away his tears, and return, hat in hand, to Sunbury and the rabbit hutches. He was ready, finally, to elevate his own hopes and dreams above the Beatles' welfare. It was a difficult prospect for Mal, having become accustomed for more than a decade to sublimating his own needs and desires—and even those of his estranged wife and kids back in London—behind those of John, Paul, George, and Ringo.

By this juncture, nothing would alter the resolve Mal had built up in recent months. Having made up his mind, the only thing left for him to do was inform his famous employers. His diary entry for the day spoke volumes in its simplicity. There would be no absent-minded doodles, no chitchat about the weather. It was all business. In truth, Mal had brought Fran and Jody along for ballast, although his girlfriend had every expectation of enjoying a rollicking good time. After all, she and her daughter would be spending quality time with a Beatle. To their surprise and delight, they would end up getting *three.*

As they strolled into the rented manse, Mal caught sight of John and May, followed closely by Ringo. And not long afterward, the McCartneys returned to 625 Palisades Beach Road. For Mal, it was nothing short of a godsend. At the same time, he had the most history with Paul, which upped the difficulty considerably. Mal comforted himself with the knowledge that by day's end, the terrifying work of resigning from the Beatles' employ would be largely complete.

Girding his courage, Mal sought out John first. To his relief, the Beatle was sitting alone by a table in the living room. "I told him that I felt it was time for me to become my own person and do my own thing," Mal later recalled. He had to admit that "doing his own thing" wasn't entirely clear in that moment. "For too long, I had been resting on my laurels," he told John, "not doing anything constructive for them nor myself except on a personal level, and I would never stop doing that, no matter what." And with that, Mal braced himself for John's reaction.

Without missing a beat, John piped up, saying, "It's about time, Mal. I was wondering when you would come to it. You're certainly capable of standing on your own two feet now, and I wish you all the luck in the world. If you ever need me, I'll be there," he continued, "and I know your songwriting will develop into a career for you."[16]

As it happened, Ringo's reaction was more difficult to gauge. In Mal's memory, the two old friends "sat together at the bottom of the garden, just lying back in the sunshine." When Mal informed the drummer of his decision, Ringo went quiet. By contrast, Paul proved to be eminently more receptive, taking Mal in a warm embrace and saying, "Good on you, lad. I know you'll be very successful—you deserve to be." For Mal, Paul's words were a welcome relief. After all, he had elevated Paul to a kind of hero status over the years. Later that night, as Mal shared Paul's reaction with Fran, he couldn't help but think about the time, four years earlier, when, after announcing the Beatles' disbandment, Paul told him, "I don't need you anymore." To Mal's mind, he had just accomplished the same thing, telling the former bandmates, one by one, "I don't need you anymore."[17]

The next day, Mal repeated the act with George, whom he telephoned at Friar Park. In truth, he didn't really know what to expect, thinking in advance that the phone call could go in any number of directions. Busy conducting a recording session in his home studio with Splinter, George had little time for pleasantries. "So what?" he remarked, before ringing off and leaving Mal to contemplate the silence at the other end of the receiver.[18] Clearly, George held his doubts about Mal's capacity for actually leaving his employment with the Beatles. In an unusual instance of self-confidence, Mal took George's reaction in stride. And for the briefest of moments, Mal's plans for making a convivial break from his old life seemed to be working.

That Sunday evening, he and Fran joined John, May, and a bevy of other friends for a seafood dinner at the Crab Shell, a bistro on Venice Beach. Harry was there, of course. He confided in Mal that Ringo had stayed up with him drinking well into the night and weeping as he took in the full measure of Mal's decision. "Now that Mal's left," Ringo had cried to Harry, "the Beatles are really over."[19]

Keith Moon was there, too. After dinner, he bought several rounds of Brandy Alexanders. Over drinks, the Who's raucous drummer confessed to Mal that he wanted to record a solo album, although nobody seemed to take him seriously as a front man. As Mal listened, Keith "got very emotional and was crying the blues," remarking that "everybody is doing solo albums, even Ringo, and he's a drummer. I've been trying to do one for years, but no one will work with me because they think I'm crackers. Would you produce me, Mal?"[20]

Quite suddenly, Mal had his first client. And true to his word, he began pursuing his post-Beatles life that Monday, when he kept an appointment with Wayne Berry, an L.A. songwriter who was hoping, with Mal's guidance, to land a deal with A&M Records. And then there was Wes Farrell. Back in the 1960s, Farrell had composed such hits as "Boys" (with Luther Dixon), which had become a concert staple for Ringo during his Beatles days, and "Hang On, Sloopy," which had topped the American charts for the McCoys in 1965. But for Farrell, the 1970s had been relatively lean, save for his "C'mon Get Happy" landing the spot as theme song for television's *The Partridge Family*. Hoping for a new beginning of his own, Farrell was looking to Mal as a potential songwriting partner to help reignite his career.

But by Tuesday afternoon, Beatle World had already managed to draw

Mal back into the fold. It happened rather subtly at first, with Ringo asking Mal to round up some maracas and tambourines for an upcoming session. By the end of May, Mal was serving as Ringo's production assistant, stage-managing his new LP, *Goodnight Vienna*, the much-anticipated follow-up to the drummer's blockbuster *Ringo* album. With Richard Perry overseeing production at L.A.'s Sunset Sound, Mal had easily slipped back into his old life, satisfying a Beatle's every whim, from tuning and prepping the instruments to hitting up the local bistros for late-night sandwiches and beverages.

For Mal, the very idea of failing at his quest, of moving one step forward and two steps back, left him understandably melancholy. Outwardly, he remained determined to make his name as a songwriter, dutifully jotting down lyrics in his diary and recording demos in his spare time. And, on a positive note: his weekly wages never ceased, meager as they were; he was living rent-free on Fourth Street and, when he wasn't ferrying the Beatles and their friends around in rental cars, driving Fran's car free of charge. Yet, inwardly, he knew the score: undoing the Beatles' spell would be no easy feat. But, he consoled himself, at least he had Fran.

On May 27, Memorial Day, Mal celebrated his thirty-ninth birthday.

Mal target-shooting with the Winchester rifle

Enjoying a seaside party hosted by Ringo, he was nearly moved to tears when the drummer gifted him with a beautiful stone necklace. For her part, Fran presented her boyfriend with a Swiss Army knife and, to Mal's great joy, a Winchester repeating rifle.

Ever since his target practice with Alan Pariser's Winchester in Malibu back in 1968, Mal had wanted one of his very own. For the roadie, owning the rifle transported him back to his simpler childhood days, a time when he was beholden to no one but his imagination—a world in which the pull of adulthood's loyalties and obligations held little sway.

But that was a long time ago. The gun Mal held in his hands in May 1974 was no pellet-firing toy. Fran's gift was the genuine article.

38

TELL THE TRUTH

"It was all good till it wasn't," Fran was fond of saying, "which is kind of like life." And Mal and Fran had plenty of good times, especially when it came to John, May, and the folks at the Santa Monica estate. "We were such a tight group," she recalled. "We were always together." One of Fran's favorite memories involved the daily appearance of "Baron von Moon," Keith's alter ego. As she and Mal lounged around the pool with the others, Baron von Moon would appear on the balcony, monocled and costumed in a full-length leather coat, albeit without any trousers, greeting his fellow houseguests with a fusillade of German. "Oh my God," said Fran, "the tears would be running down our faces."[1]

When they weren't hanging out with John, Harry, and the other rock 'n' roll refugees, Mal and Fran enjoyed taking Jody to the beach—Santa Monica's Ocean Park was one of their favorite haunts. Naturally, Mal always had time for anything vaguely related to the Western lifestyle he so coveted. With Fran's blessing, he would take the Winchester out to the game lands and shoot at tin cans with Harry, George, or any number of friends who had an afternoon to kill. In addition to the .30/30 Winchester Lever-Action Rifle, Mal often went target shooting with his .22 Colt Woodsman pistol. He and Fran also enjoyed horseback riding, with Mal donning his wide-brimmed cowboy hat to get into character. During one unforgettable Mother's Day, they went riding in remote Beachwood Canyon, with the Hollywood sign looming above them. Before they left the stables, Fran had been given a stern warning about her horse, which hadn't yet been "rein broken." Always the daredevil, she pushed forward anyway, falling off the untamed animal and breaking her collarbone. As she lay immobilized on the trail, even Big Mal couldn't rescue her. Eventually, she had to be airlifted out of the canyon.[2]

And sometimes the good times weren't quite as convivial as they may have seemed in the moment. "I remember one particular day at the beach in Malibu," said Fran. "We were watching this whole scene unfold, which we felt was made up of people and stuff. But then later we realized that it was just birds that we [had] been seeing, not tourists milling around the beach. We were *that* fucked up." Then there were the times when Mal would get drunk and fall into a depression, often taking Valium to soothe his aching conscience and get some sleep. Inevitably, he would become crestfallen about "being torn between his family back in England and staying in L.A. with me," Fran recalled. "In those moments, life just got too hard for him. But

Mal and Fran

as soon as other people would come around, he had the ability to morph into this happy-go-lucky person no matter what was happening in his life."[3]

And her boyfriend had proven to be especially adept at donning this happy mask in the company of Beatles fans. He lived for the occasions, fewer and fewer as time marched on, when fans would spot him, often recalling his cameo in *Help!* "I have always had an affinity with Beatles' fans," Mal wrote, "and in the years since the film has been made, it has grown stronger on hearing 'White Cliffs of Dover, Mal,' and turning to see a grinning Beatles' fan."[4]

That same spring, John and Harry flew to New York City to put the *Strange Pussies* project to bed. RCA Records rejected the title out of hand, forcing Harry to rename the album *Pussy Cats*. Mal would receive credit as production assistant for having provided his usual brand of "tea and sympathy." As a sophomoric nod to their proclivities at the time, the LP's cover would feature a not-so-veiled rebus that spelled out the word "drugs."

While they were in the city, John and Harry spoke at an April 28 March of Dimes benefit in Central Park. Seizing the moment, New Jersey native Mark Lapidos met up with John at the nearby Pierre Hotel that same day and pitched the concept of a Beatles fan convention. "Sitting down in the hotel suite," Lapidos recalled, "I told him about my idea for a convention for Beatles fans. To mark the tenth anniversary of the band coming to America, we would watch the Fabs' films, enjoy presentations by special guests and music experts, listen to live music, and buy and sell Beatles items. It would be something for everyone. Lennon gushed with excitement about the idea, exclaiming, 'I'm all for it. I'm a Beatles fan, too!'"[5]

Back in California, Mal seized the moment for himself. At Fran's urging, he had rededicated himself to acting as a talent scout while continuing to refine his songwriting craft. After all, he had discovered no less than Badfinger and Splinter, an impressive record by any measure. That May, Mal attended an artist showcase event for a Beverly Hills band called Silverspoon. After working together over the past several years, the group felt it was high time they made their move. They knew they were on the precipice of finally landing a big break. Prior to the showcase, "We had never done anything," keyboard player Blair Aaronson recalled. "*Literally.*" And by this point, they had developed a reputation as a bunch of slackers. Area nightclub manager Rodney Bingenheimer had taken to saying, "Silverspoon talks the biggest game in town."[6]

Mal attended the band's showcase in the company of Record Plant engineer Bob Merritt. Held at Studio Instrument Rentals, the production services outfit on Sunset Boulevard, the invitation-only event was limited to top producers, engineers, and label execs. The band comprised the sons of actors—hence, their name, which nodded to being "born with a silver spoon in one's mouth." Hardcore Beatles fans to a man, the group featured Joey Hamilton (son of comedian Carol Burnett) on lead vocals, Jimmy Haymer and Stephen Gries on guitar, Chas Sandford on bass, Aaronson on keyboards, and Miguel Ferrer on drums. As the son of actor José Ferrer and singer Rosemary Clooney, Miguel had the finest pedigree of the lot, although the others were no slouches. Haymer's father, Johnny, was a well-known TV actor who had a recurring role on *M*A*S*H.*

As showcases go, Silverspoon's performance left a lot to be desired. From the beginning, they were doomed. A garage band in every sense of the term, the sextet had very little live experience among them. Things got off to a terrible start when Joey, the front man, came down with a bad case of stage fright. "He just stared down the audience," Aaronson recalled. "It was crazy. And Stephen, who was a bit of a space cadet anyway, went into his guitar solo, which was supposed to be eight bars. Instead, he just put his head down, with his hair flopping above him, and played for at least a minute before we finally got his fucking attention." But the worst part, Aaronson said, occurred during the very first number. "I come in on the bridge, and I hit the organ, and nothing happened. I hit the Start switch and hit the chord again, forgetting that it took like thirty seconds for the keyboard to warm up. It was horrible."[7]

But as after-parties go, the Silverspoon showcase was a smashing success—one Mal clearly enjoyed immensely. The partiers convened at the Continental Hyatt House—"the Riot House" in local parlance. "It was a madhouse, wall to wall people," Haymer wrote. "It was total debauchery at the Riot House—sex, drugs, and rock 'n' roll. My brother Robbie was there watching his big brother snort a white powdered substance in a closet, where the mirrored doors had been recently ripped off, with Mal and two big breasted bimbos." And they weren't alone. "There were groupies and rock wannabes in all shapes, sizes, and colors—mingling, eating, smoking, and drinking."[8]

Given their performance that night, the musicians were a little surprised when Mal telephoned their manager, Larry Gordon, and invited Silverspoon to join him at the Record Plant. With Merritt in tow, Mal announced that they were interested in producing the band. In short order, they set about recording demos at the Record Plant. "We would begin our demo sessions at odd hours, usually around two or three in the morning," Haymer recalled, "because we had to wait for a studio to become available. The hardest part was always cleaning up and rolling the cables at seven or eight in the morning, after we were dead tired, but Bob Merritt was like a sergeant-major, and we had to listen or risk being excommunicated from the studio, our Shangri-La."[9]

The boys in Silverspoon weren't convinced that Mal had solid production chops, "but we didn't care. He had Beatle stories that nobody else had, and we listened attentively." They enjoyed a special kick when he would say, "I used to have four brothers, John, Paul, George, and Ritchie, but now I have 10, Joey, Jimmy, Stephen, Chas, Blair, and Miguel." The boys enjoyed a laugh when Mal "used to pronounce Miguel's name like it had a 'w' instead of the 'u,' sounding like 'Migwell.' It didn't get much better than that."[10] When they weren't recording demos with Mal and Bob, the wide-eyed bandmates enjoyed being mesmerized by the likes of Harry, John, and Ringo trolling the halls of the Record Plant.

After they had recorded the basic tracks for Silverspoon's demos, Mal and Bob called the guys back to the Record Plant for a meeting. Mal was seated behind the desk in Chris Stone's office. "Now you boys can do whatever you want," he began, "but if you want Bob and myself to continue with this project, I feel we need to make some changes in the rhythm section. Sorry, Miguel, but I feel we need a different drummer, and Chas, you just don't have the 'Spoon' vibe." At this juncture, Silverspoon had a choice to make. "We could pull up our apron strings, band together, and tell Mal and Bob to go stick it where the sun don't shine," Haymer wrote, "or we could go along with the politics of the situation and continue the journey without Chas and Miguel. We chose option number two."[11]

While Mal may not have admired the sound of the band's low end, he held deep admiration for its primary songwriters in Jimmy and Stephen, especially when it came to "You Hurt Me So." To Mal's ears, the song, with its tale of romantic woe, had the makings of a hit record. He made several tweaks to the arrangement, saying, "It needs a harmonium just like we used on 'We Can Work It Out.' That was all we needed to hear to get our Beatle juices flowing," Haymer recalled. In truth, they would have done cartwheels if the roadie had asked them. "Are you kidding?" said Haymer. "This was one of the guys who was there in the studio with John and Paul."[12]

With the basic tracks and vocals completed for "You Hurt Me So," Mal and Bob went about the business of mixing the song for release. By the group's estimation, the recording "was sounding good but not great. Something was missing." One evening, when Mal and Bob were away from the Record Plant, twenty-five-year-old engineer Mike Stone joined Silverspoon in the studio. As the nephew of the facility's co-owner, Chris Stone, Mike had plenty of experience working behind the console. Impressed by the song's direction, he tried his hand at remixing "You Hurt Me So" to give it more oomph. "He had that 16-track machine humming with the compression pumping away like gangbusters," Haymer wrote. "It sounded brilliant, hands down the best mix this novice band had ever been a part of." But now the bandmates had a fresh dilemma on their hands: "How could we play it for Mal and Bob without some egos being badly bruised?"[13]

During this same period, Mal continued to press forward with his budding songwriting career, seeming to catch a break when he met Norman Kurban, a songwriter with an impressive list of credentials and his own publishing outfit, Circus Wheels Productions. In the late 1960s, Kurban had cut his chops at the Pasadena Playhouse, where he fashioned a parlor trick that never failed to impress: he could play Beethoven's *Moonlight Sonata* while simultaneously reciting the Gettysburg Address.[14] By the time he met Mal, the twenty-seven-year-old composer had already made a name for himself creating arrangements for such popular artists as Rita Coolidge, Buddy Miles, and Kris Kristofferson, one of Ken Mansfield's Outlaw country stars. But his biggest coup had been composing and conducting the strings for Carole King's *Rhymes and Reasons* LP, less than two years removed from her blockbuster *Tapestry* album. His arrangement graced King's hit single "Been to Canaan."

To Mal's way of thinking, Kurban could be the perfect songwriting partner, a seasoned arranger who could bring his lyrics to life in song. "I play very bad guitar—three chords," Mal admitted. "Musically oriented yes, but not a guitarist. I'm a lyricist." He enjoyed working with Kurban and liked to boast about the composer's status as a musical prodigy. "He was 11-years-old when he conducted his own symphony, played by the London Philharmonic in Germany for a big convention," Mal liked to tell people, "and he won first prize with it. He's the musician."[15]

As usual, Kurban had come into Mal's life via Fran, who was intrepid when it came to helping folks make contacts in the business. "Francine thought that his music and my lyrics should go together," Mal wrote, "telling each of us at different times that the other was right for him."[16] When the two men met, Mal took a liking to the musician almost immediately. Ironically, as Fran got to know Kurban, she started to think the songwriter was a little on the strange side, that he had a dark personality. Even so, she couldn't deny his talent as a pianist. As was his wont, Mal became fast friends with the composer, quickly involving himself in the musician's life. When he wasn't dreaming up new tunes with Kurban at his place in the Valley, the bigger-than-life roadie would spend hours teaching the pianist's seven-year-old son, Andy, how to play chess.[17]

With his career on the move, Kurban had incorporated Circus Wheels in January 1973, working out of a sixth-floor office across the street from the Rainbow, at 9200 Sunset Boulevard. The office's primary tenant was thirty-eight-year-old David Mook, an A&R man who had worked for several record companies before founding a music publishing agency and going out on his own. In addition to Kurban and Circus Wheels, Mook lent space to the roadie and Malcontent Music, betting that they would generate future returns in the form of hit songs and publishing rights. To afford his clients regular opportunities to share their wares, Mook kept the place buzzing with budding producers, A&R men, and other potential collaborators.

Mal knew that having a steady cowriter who could handle the musical end of things was essential. One of the team's earliest collaborations involved an unpublished song about Mal's traumatic car accident with Harry, especially the part about his nearly losing his sight. Their latest project involved setting Mal's poem "Family Tree" to music. While the majority of his lyrics concerned romantic topics associated with finding (and losing) love—in keeping with the sappy Top 40 radio hits of the mid-1970s—Mal embraced an especially personal subject in "Family Tree." Indeed, in stark contrast to his earlier writings, no set of lyrics spoke more deeply of his personal conundrum. When it came to the conflicting emotions tearing Mal apart, "Family Tree" got to the heart of the matter: the pull between Mal's competing needs to derive professional satisfaction and personal gratification in the heat of the moment versus nurturing his husband and father role and shouldering the attendant obligations of family life:

I wonder what the future holds
Now that I'm fast and fancy free.
Have I destroyed my happiness
Cutting down my family tree?

In addition to teaming up with Kurban, who had begun fashioning rudimentary chords for Mal's lyrics for "Family Tree," the roadie had considerably widened his professional and social circles through Fran, the Record Plant, and, as always, his association with the ex-Beatles. Replenishing his supply of petty cash often brought Mal to the Capitol Records Tower at 1750 Vine Street, as did his work on many of the boys' solo projects. His close connection with Capitol's most prestigious clients imbued him with considerable prestige whenever he entered the building. As Var Smith, now a project manager in the advertising division, recalled, "The Beatles made so much money for Capitol that they quite literally paid all of our salaries for a long, long time. There's the old cliché about making money hand over fist. Well, at Capitol, the Beatles did that."[18] Over the years, Mal had become acquainted with numerous folks within the Louis Naidorf–designed tower resembling a stack of phonograph records. But when it came to rock's FM radio heyday, there was nothing like the crew who roamed the building's corridors in the 1970s, when the money was big, the music was hot, and there was a high tolerance for the creative types who made it all happen.

In time, Fran would come to lament the many ways in which California "changed" Mal during this period—an era in which the common denominators seemed to be vats of alcohol and bowls of cocaine. Fran was certainly no stranger to the rock 'n' roll lifestyle, but she had her limits. She could party with the best of them, but she had to think about her daughter's welfare, of course, not to mention her high-powered job at the Record Plant. "There were a lot of drugs in California," she said. "It was easy and free. Cocaine would pick you up and make you feel good about yourself." But how would the drug affect Mal, who, in Fran's words, "could never believe in himself"?[19]

At Capitol, an entire subculture existed to keep the record label humming. At the center of the action was Janet Nichols, a vivacious PR woman with purple streaks in her brown hair. Known in the Capitol corridors as "Janet Planet" because of her spacey behavior, Nichols would amuse staff and visitors alike by roller-skating around the building. "She was a pretty, pretty lady," engineer Richard Digby Smith recalled. "Just kind of wild, kind of crazy."[20] Janet Planet worked for Dennis Killeen, who ran Capitol's advertising division out of the tower's ninth floor.

Killeen vividly recalled the November day in which Mal squired Ringo up to the roof of the tower to shoot a promotional video for his *Goodnight Vienna* LP. For the album's cover art, Ringo's face had been superimposed over the body of actor Michael Rennie from the 1951 sci-fi classic *The Day the Earth Stood Still.* To evoke the cover art's space opera feel, Killeen staged a helicopter shoot to capture Ringo, wearing a form-fitting space suit, waving from atop the tower. Killeen would never forget the image of Mal, "the big, burly guy" accompanying Ringo as they walked out toward the roofline. The ad man was particularly concerned because they had brought along Harry Nilsson to the shoot. Clearly intoxicated, Harry was conspicuously clad in a brown bathrobe. Knowing that Nilsson "was having a little coke problem at the time," Killeen wanted to complete the shoot as quickly as possible before the singer tumbled to his death from the roof of the tower.[21]

Killeen's ninth-floor advertising team included John Hoernle, the label's forty-six-year-old art director, and Joanne Lenard, his twenty-seven-year-old secretary. A bearded, charismatic sort, Hoernle had designed numerous album covers for the likes of Linda Ronstadt, Buck Owens, Merle Haggard, and Grand Funk Railroad. He had recently completed the cover art for Yoko's *Feeling the Space* LP. Although Hoernle's productivity had waned in recent years due to his inveterate drinking—the art director was known to keep several bottles of hooch in his Capitol office—Killeen valued his ability to work in a pinch, to be able to hit deadlines and fulfill requests on short notice.

By the time Mal had become friendly with Hoernle and Lenard, the coworkers had become an item. For her part, Lenard vividly recalled the Capitol Tower being abuzz one afternoon when Mal squired John, George, and Ringo down the landmark building's corridors. "I was sitting across from the elevators when they arrived," she remembered. "It was such a wonderful moment, and Mal was very sweet, walking them around and introducing them to everybody."[22]

Digby Smith recalled socializing with the couple and Mal at their log cabin in Laurel Canyon, where Hoernle and Lenard would throw large parties. During their get-togethers, Mal would relate "amusing and sometimes shocking tales of his Beatle days, all of us listening to music, sitting around the piano, laughing and smoking" and drinking until the early hours.[23] As project manager, Var Smith worked closely with Hoernle and observed the art director's downfall firsthand. "He had prestige and status at Capitol," said Smith. "He was well liked, did a good job, and was affable. Everybody liked him. *A lot*."[24] But eventually, it all caught up with Hoernle—the drinking, the cocaine—and he would be drummed out of Capitol. Embarrassed by the implosion of his career with the record label, Hoernle preferred to say that his ouster was "political."[25]

During his years in the Capitol Tower, Var Smith had seen a lot of artists and employees fall victim to excess. He grew fond of citing the conventional wisdom that "cocaine heightens your personality. If you're an asshole, then cocaine turns you into a bigger asshole."[26] In Mal's case, his increased dependence upon the drug, compounded at times by his excessive drinking, left him in a precarious state in which his low self-esteem became exacerbated; his innate need to please, more acute. And when he became depressed, his capacity for self-pity could feel overwhelming.

As he had promised Moonie over Brandy Alexanders back in April, Mal fully intended to produce the drummer's solo LP, but it would be no easy feat. It was apparent from the very first recording—a cover version of the Beach Boys' "Don't Worry, Baby"—that Moon's near-constant state of inebriation would be an overarching challenge. Blair Aaronson was there for the first session, which took place in the Record Plant's Studio C, with Harry, Ringo, and John Sebastian, the founder of the Lovin' Spoonful, on hand. Thanks to Mal, Aaronson contributed a pipe organ part to the recording. "But it was all downhill from there," he later recalled. With the basic track completed, Blair was tasked with standing beside Moon as he recorded his lead vocals. His job was to hold a vitamin jar–size parcel of cocaine aloft while blowing puffs of coke into the singer's throat, which he believed would enhance the quality of his performance. It didn't.[27]

That September, Mal joined Keith at the Whiskey a Go Go, where Dick Dale, King of the Surf Guitar, was holding a weeklong residency. A devoted fan of the musician, Keith was determined to get Dale to play on his record. For his part, Dale seemed only vaguely aware of the Who, much less Moon. "I was in the middle of a song," the guitarist recalled, "when he walked up on stage with Mal Evans. Keith was stoned and grabbed the mic right out of my face and said, 'Dick Dale, I'm Keith Moon of the Who!' Then he told me—and everyone else—that he'd got John Lennon and Ringo on his solo album, and if Dick Dale didn't play on it, he'd junk the whole project.'"[28]

The very next day, Mal duly conducted a session at the Record Plant, with Dale performing on a cover of "Teenage Idol," the old Ricky Nelson hit, with Moonie taking lead vocals. Working on the Moon project had afforded Mal plenty of opportunities to showcase his friends, including, at times, Norman Kurban and Silverspoon's Jimmy Haymer, who had joined Aaronson in the makeshift backup band. As one of the performers on "Teenage Idol," Haymer recalled that Dale "played a gold Stratocaster with a gold metallic pick-guard." Yet it soon became clear that even with top players like Dale on the scene, nothing could salvage the project—not even Mal's penchant for engendering goodwill. Moon's legendary substance abuse was wreaking havoc on the LP, which, at Ringo's suggestion, was now going under the title *Two Sides of the Moon*. In late September, Mal continued to press forward, producing Keith's take on John's "Move Over Ms. L," for which the roadie fashioned a horn arrangement.

Reaching back to his Beatles days, Mal suggested that Moonie try his hand at singing John's "In My Life." For his part, Mal was delighted with the result. "One of the tracks on the album I'm really pleased with is 'In My Life,'" he said. He even sent a rough mix of Moon's version to the Beatle, who was back in New York City with May. "I got a beautiful little card back from him, saying 'That's the best version of "In My Life" I have ever heard in my life.' So, really, that was for me, the ultimate as being a producer."[29] As far as Mal was concerned, it would have to be.

Within a matter of days, the entire project had imploded, leaving the roadie as odd man out. Mal would later describe the impasse as the result of a "falling out" between him and Moon. But Haymer recalled things differently. "Not only was Mal having to deal with his own demons of depression and anxiety," he said, but "there was also a rift on the *Two Sides of the Moon* record. A battle for control of the project was being formulated by the dark side, and they were influencing Keith and his party to make a change. Mal was fired from the project."[30]

A war of words emerged in which Mal claimed he had managed to coax reasonable performances out of Moon despite the drummer's near-constant state of inebriation. Moon would counter, arguing that Mal's substance abuse exceeded his own—which was saying something, given Keith's reputation as rock's most uninhibited, unrestrained party animal. Mark Volman, formerly one of the vocalists for the Turtles, witnessed the whole awful business. "There were a lot of great musicians involved with that album," he said. "It also gave us a chance to work with someone we loved very much, which was Mal Evans. Mal Evans produced that album the first time around. We did a whole album, and then it got turned in and the record company turned it down." After MCA dismissed Mal, engineers Skip Taylor and John Stronach stepped in to produce the LP. By Volman's estimation, they reproduced some 90 percent of *Two Sides of the Moon*, with very little discernible difference. "There was just some re-recording of some more musical things and some different mixes and things of that nature," he said.[31]

Ironically, several of the principals involved in finishing the album, including Taylor, would admit that the drugs flowed even more freely after Mal's departure. For Haymer, observing his friend and mentor's fall from grace was difficult to fathom. "Everything went downhill fast from there," he recalled. "Mal sank even deeper into his depression, then locked himself in his room with nothing but his Elvis records and [his] Western gun collection."[32] Later that same year, Mal would get the opportunity to confront Moon face-to-face at Jim Keltner's New Year's Eve party. Taking responsibility for his betrayal of the roadie, "the drummer from the Who offered me his chin, saying, 'Hit me right here, Mal, and let's get it over with.'" But Mal wouldn't go there, opting for benevolence instead. "I kissed him on the cheek, which really did his head in. For he had told Fran halfway through the album, 'If it hadn't have been for Mal taking my head out of my arse, I would have been dead in six months.'" Mal found solace in Moonie's admission, believing that "everybody needs something creative to do in their life, and I had given him a new lease on his."[33]

Unbeknownst to Mal, the despair he was experiencing as the Moon production collapsed was nothing in comparison to the tragedy he had wrought back in Sunbury. On October 11, Gary turned thirteen. By this juncture, his family had endured more than ten months of Mal's abandonment of them, save for occasional fawning letters to the children. To try to mend his ways and bring some joy to his son on his special day, Mal made a cassette recording in which he offered the boy sincere wishes for the coming year. Harry had even chipped in a cassette tape recorder as Gary's gift. But any goodwill Mal hoped to deliver was quickly undone that morning as Gary listened to the recording over breakfast with his mother and sister. To his incredible pain and embarrassment, the tape didn't end with his father's birthday greeting. Apparently, Mal had recycled the cassette, and as Gary and his sister prepared to go to school, they heard the unmistakable sounds of Fran fellating their dad. The boy's only solace was the knowledge that his eight-year-old sister didn't understand the sounds emanating from the tape player.[34]

Mal's spirits were lifted, if only briefly, that November, when George Harrison and Ravi Shankar's concert tour rolled through L.A. Mal felt a rush of pride at the Forum as his beloved Beatle performed a raft of classic tunes the roadie had witnessed in their infancy: "Something," "While My Guitar Gently Weeps," "In My Life," "Give Me Love (Give Me Peace on Earth)," "My Sweet Lord." The whole evening was an embarrassment of riches. Mal was joined at the concert and its after-party by twenty-two-year-old Laura Gross, a budding rock journalist. After seeking out the roadie for a print interview, the Cal State Northridge grad and KCSN radio deejay had become tight with Mal and Fran, emerging as a truly bright light for the couple in what had been an otherwise arduous autumn. When Mal first met Laura, they hit it off right away. "I know you and I are going to be really good friends," he told her.[35]

A forward thinker to a fault, Fran was never the kind of person to wallow in her own misery, and after the *Two Sides of the Moon* debacle, she was not about to allow her boyfriend to drift unconsolably. Her plan for Mal's absolution, when it occurred to her that winter, was nothing short of brilliant. An avid reader, Fran had enjoyed Norman Mailer's recent bestselling biography of Marilyn Monroe. Always interested in connecting the dots, Fran knew that Mailer's book had been repped by well-known Beverly Hills attorney Harold Lipton, who was doubly famous as the brother of *The Mod Squad*'s Peggy Lipton. Coincidentally, Mal had met the actress a decade earlier, at a garden party hosted by L.A.'s Hemophilia Foundation. Better yet, Peggy's lawyer brother had succeeded in landing a fat advance from Grosset and Dunlap for *Marilyn: A Biography*. And while nobody would ever have confused Mal for Mailer, the roadie had an amazing story to tell about his life with the four lads from Liverpool.

When Fran broached the idea of his writing his memoir, Mal clearly perked up, and he wasted little time before sharing the concept with Ringo, assuring the drummer that, no matter what, "I wouldn't put you down." To his great credit, Ringo didn't accept this approach, telling Mal, "Look, if you don't tell the truth, don't bother doing it." So Mal resolved to do exactly that with his memoir. "It will be the truth," he said. "There will be a few things they'll be mad about, but it'll be the truth. It's not meant as a derogatory thing, it is just what happened." Besides, he reasoned, "The book is going to be a good book because I only had a good time."[36]

But life in Beatle World—even ex-Beatle World—had never been quiet. And no sooner had Mal determined that he would tell his story than another momentous event occurred some 2,500 miles away, in Florida. On December 29, at Walt Disney World's Polynesian Village Resort, John, with Julian and May Pang as his witnesses, affixed the final signature to the band's dissolution papers. The Beatles were over.

39

CRYING IN A HOTEL ROOM, NY

On January 9, 1975, in a private hearing, the London High Court formally dissolved the group's partnership. The Beatles and Company no longer existed, and with its demise, Mal and Neil fell into the ranks of the unemployed.

For the past several years, Neil had been caught in his own depression, a demoralizing period only exacerbated by drink and drugs. "He barely survived," said Tony Bramwell.[1] Even Neil's much-cherished documentary had fallen by the wayside. As with the Beatles themselves, *The Long and Winding Road* was in mothballs. So, too, was the dream of Apple Corps.

True to her nature, Fran wasted little time in booking an appointment for herself and Mal with Harold Lipton. The fifty-four-year-old attorney was working out of the Beverly Hills offices of the white-shoe law firm Kaplan, Livingston, Goodwin, Berkowitz, and Selvin. "Harold was an old school, New York film and literary lawyer," newly minted attorney John Mason recalled. "He came and joined our firm around 1972 as Senior Counsel." With Fran's chutzpah and Mal's incredible story as a vaunted Beatles insider, the project was a fairly easy sell, one that Lipton readily accepted. An agreement was struck in which Lipton would receive 10 percent of the book's royalties for the first million dollars in gross sales, with another 5 percent thereafter.[2] Lipton proposed a trip to New York City that spring to audition publishers for Mal's story. All the roadie had to do was write it.

With the terms in place, Lipton tasked Mason with handling the legal arrangements. Fresh out of UC Berkeley, the twenty-eight-year-old attorney was eager to develop a reputation in entertainment law. "I was a wide-eyed young lawyer," he recalled, "mesmerized by someone who'd had the experience that Mal Evans had."[3] As it happened, Mason had briefly worked with Mal and Fran back in October 1974, when he put together a standard managerial contract so that Fran could be compensated at the rate of 20 percent for handling Mal's business affairs and creative opportunities.[4]

As he got to know him better, Mason happily joined Mal in the couple's Fourth Street bedroom, where the attorney was treated to a grand tour of the roadie's memorabilia. As Mal began to remove items from various trunks, Mason could scarcely believe his eyes. Suddenly, he was in the presence of thousands of photographs, lyric sheets written in the Beatles' hands, Mal's stack of diaries dating back to 1963, and a pile of Super 8 films. "I'm sitting there speechless," said Mason. "When it came to the Beatles, I just wanted to know more. I didn't even have the adjectives to describe what the group meant to me. They had produced some of the greatest—if not *the* greatest—sounds and songs that had ever been created. And all of a sudden, I am here with this guy who was with them every step of the way, the guy who drove them around from gig to gig. It was a lot to take in."[5]

As his friendship with Mal grew, Mason good-naturedly took on legal assignments for the roadie. He was happy to work pro bono with the understanding that future, larger deals might pay dividends. One of the first tasks he completed was to formalize Mal's agreement with David Mook for the use of his office space on Sunset Boulevard. As it happened, working with Mook would prove to be one of the strangest assignments of Mason's legal career. When he prepared the boilerplate contract for Mook's review, the music publisher insisted on a single alteration: "I want a clause in there that says, exactly, 'Everybody agrees not to fuck David Mook.'"[6]

Whether it was a brazen effort to appear younger for Fran or, perhaps more likely, to coalesce among the sun-kissed Californians, Mal had taken to tinting his hair blond. His new look—complete with a wispy, blow-dried haircut—was in vogue in late March 1975, when Paul held a wrap party in Long Beach on the *Queen Mary*, the retired ocean liner and bravura tourist destination. His star-studded gala marked the completion of the LP *Venus and Mars*, Wings's follow-up to the blockbuster *Band on the Run* album.

In just a few short years, Paul had amassed an impressive string of hit singles and chart-topping albums with his newly minted band, swiftly surpassing the commercial solo successes enjoyed by his former bandmates.

Mal with Denny Laine, George, and Olivia Arias aboard the *Queen Mary*

Mal and Fran were there that night, in the ocean liner's Grand Salon, rubbing elbows with hundreds of industry stalwarts. For her part, Fran had styled her hair in a fashionable perm. With live music provided by Professor Longhair and the Meters, guests included Cher, Bob Dylan, Michael Jackson, Marvin Gaye, and Jimmy Webb, who shared a table with Mal and Fran. For the roadie, the evening's great highlight occurred when George arrived with his new girlfriend, twenty-six-year-old Olivia Arias. By the next day, images of Paul and George caught in a warmhearted embrace would be broadcast across the globe, with Mal looking on from his place in the background, beaming from ear to ear.

After his experience working on *Two Sides of the Moon*, Mal was in no hurry to return to record production. But this didn't stop him from hanging out with Silverspoon. He got a kick out of sharing stories about the early Beatles with the guys—and they, in turn, loved hearing tales about the "windscreen incident" and the euphemistic "200 miles to go." If Mal held any ill will over the band's having remixed "You Hurt Me So" with Mike Stone, he certainly didn't let on. Haymer had begun to see Mal as "a frustrated songwriter. I think that one of the reasons he liked to work with us was because we had shown an interest in his original material. Most of his songs were about retaining peace of mind and meditation."[7] At one point, Silverspoon had become especially taken with "I'm Not Going to Move," Mal's composition that was born in Rishikesh and rewritten with George as "You and Me (Babe)." For a while, they had toyed with the idea of recording the song themselves, but as with so many things that came the band's way, they never got around to it. "It's incredible how many opportunities we got," Aaronson lamented, "and we fucked every single one of them up."[8]

For Silverspoon, privileged scions of Hollywood's elite, the diversions of drug and drink were just too seductive. Aaronson would never forget the night he celebrated his twentieth birthday at the Record Plant, the band's favorite haunt. After watching his girlfriend imbibe a massive dose of THC, Aaronson opted to follow suit. The drug's high came on like gangbusters, sending him in a headlong rush into the studio's jacuzzi to calm his nerves. He was joined there by Mal, who intuited the younger man's stress and paranoia. To comfort him, he shared the story of the vision Paul had experienced while meditating in the Maharishi's ashram, when the roadie came to the Beatle during his time of trouble and gently urged him to "let it be."[9] More than a continent and seven years away, Brother Malcolm had come to the rescue yet again.

Mal was in good spirits that spring, making preparations, with Harold Lipton and Fran, to travel to New York City to woo potential publishers for his memoir. As a show of good faith, he had solicited letters of support from the boys, just as he had for "Beatles—U.S.A.," for Southern News Services back in 1965. Mason supplied a form letter for Mal to share with the ex-Fabs, which they followed, more or less, in their replies.[10] The Beatles' letters—short and sweet to a man—had begun to arrive over the past several weeks. The one from George, who penned his approval on February 25, his thirty-second birthday, politely wished Mal success with the project,[11] while John's noted that he'd been dying to read Mal's diary for years and warned "Make a buck, but don't fuck it . . .".[12] Paul gave his agreement "as long as you tell 'em how lovely I am",[13] while Ringo's more formal confirmation of permission wished Mal well while also requesting to read the book ahead of publication.[14]

With all the pieces falling into place, Lipton crafted the book pitch with Mal and Fran. Their original plan was to entitle the memoir *200 Miles to Go*—Mal's idea, no doubt, in deference to his most cherished Beatles memory. When it came to winning over the big publishing houses, Lipton surely felt they had a number of aces up their sleeve. The notes from their pitch document enumerated several morsels, including 2,500 unpublished photos of Mal and the Beatles, access to Mal's personal diaries, and "13 years of memorabilia," as well as his and the boys' artwork and sketches. When it came to the timing of the publication, Lipton saved his canniest move for last. The pitch doc referenced Bill Sargent's recent multimillion-dollar offer to stage a Beatles reunion, suggesting the possibility of the band's gathering for a gala concert "within six months."

Under the heading "What We Want," Lipton stipulated hardback publication of Mal's memoir with one of the "top houses," along with a guaranteed advance and the promise of high-quality paper and photo reprinting services. The list of possible publishers was a who's who of the key players of the day, including Random House; Putnam; Simon and Schuster; Delacorte; Doubleday; and Grosset and Dunlap. The document concluded with a final nugget, which suggested that Mal had two additional writing projects for consideration: a "Hallmark Hall of Fame–style" short story and *Roadie*, a novel "based on fact" about the "seamier side of life" associated with a pop group.

While Mal's short story existed only as an outline at this point, *Roadie* had been under way for the past few years, possibly even as far back as the late 1960s. And it was "seamy" all right, telling salacious tales about an unnamed, mythical rock 'n' roll band at the crest of their fame. All in all, the pitch doc made for a tantalizing proposal, one in which Lipton must have felt supremely confident, given the public's ongoing interest in anything to do with Beatle World.

With the New York City sojourn fixed for late May 1975, Mal made time for a quick visit to London. With Julie's ninth birthday looming on April 17, he planned an impromptu visit at Sunbury. After all, he hadn't seen his children—much less Lil—since January 4, 1974. But, not surprisingly, he had an ulterior motive for traveling to the United Kingdom: he had been invited to sit for an interview with David Frost for an upcoming television special devoted to the Beatles' legacy. Frost had already lined up interviews with other insiders, including George Martin, Derek Taylor, and Dick Lester, while also booking English singer-songwriter David Essex and Americans Chuck Berry, Bobby Vinton, and Andy Williams to provide expert commentary on the group's influence on popular music. There was no way Mal was going to miss out on such an opportunity. Besides, Frost's production team had promised to put him up in five-star digs at the Park Lane Hotel.

During his interview with Frost, Mal giddily took a walk down memory lane, sharing tales of his role as "Mother Malcolm" in the origin story for "Let It Be" and reliving the sadness that came with the end of the Beatles after John asked for a divorce back in September 1969. When Frost inquired about the reasons behind their disbandment, Mal observed that "the group became too small to contain all four of them." All in all, it was a superb, albeit brief interaction. Mal even allowed himself a sheepish smile when Frost made reference to his upcoming memoir.[15]

On its face, the trip had been a brilliant idea. Mal could enjoy the best of both worlds: reveling in Frost's spotlight, on the one hand, and being reunited with his children, whom he missed desperately, on the other. Having telephoned his estranged wife in advance, he concocted a scheme to surprise his daughter by picking her up in Sunbury and driving her to school. How surprised, indeed, she might have been had it worked out.

But this was Mal, of course, who, when it came to his family, had always managed to create havoc. After the interview with Frost, he had plenty of time to get a good night's sleep and drive out to Sunbury early the next morning to pick up Julie. Instead, he decided to go out for drinks with David Essex after they had filmed their spots for the TV special. For celebrity-conscious Mal, hanging out with Essex must have seemed like a rare and irresistible privilege. England's reigning pop idol, Essex had landed a number one U.K. hit the previous November with "Gonna Make You a Star." Later that night, sloshed to the gills, the roadie returned to his fancy room at the Park Lane, where he overslept the next morning, missing his morning rendezvous with Julie on Staines Road East. His daughter was brokenhearted when she learned she had been jilted—and Lil was furious.

Incredibly, Mal enjoyed yet another in a long line of second chances when his wife allowed him to stay at the Sunbury house for a few days, hoping that close proximity would give him the opportunity to spend quality time with his children. At one point, he slipped into bed with Lil, hoping for "a little horizontal refreshment." It turned out that Lil was game—she still loved the guy, after all. But in keeping with his proven capacity for snatching defeat out of the jaws of victory, Mal ruined the postcoital vibe when he slinked off to sleep in another room. Understandably, Lil felt used. "It really cut her up," Gary recalled.[16]

A few days later, Mal packed his belongings to make the long flight back to the States. Before he left, he watched a movie on television with Gary—the 1969 World War II action flick *The Thousand Plane Raid*. As for Lil, who had girded herself for her husband's departure, she later recalled saying their goodbyes in the back garden, where she was tending to the hedges. Incredibly, Mal pitched the concept of an open marriage. "He told me he loved me," Lil said, "but [that he] was besotted with Francine. He wanted to live six months with me, six months with her." Choking back tears, Mal said, "Fran needs me." But his wife wasn't taking the bait. "I said we couldn't," Lil recalled. "I was quite calm when I said, 'You had better go, then.'" For her, the situation was undeniably clear: "I was always second fiddle to the Beatles—and now to this new girl. I felt very sad."[17] Mal and Lil had violated their marital pact—"always leave home smiling," they had promised each other back in 1957—for the last time.

Not long after he returned to Southern California, Mal learned the horrible news that Pete Ham, Badfinger's gifted singer-songwriter, had died by his own hand in Weybridge. By this juncture, Badfinger had fallen into a precarious position thanks to Stan Polley, who had wrested complete control over the band's finances from Bill Collins and relegated Bill to a secondary role in the group's management. After Badfinger's Apple deal expired, Polley had negotiated a contract with Warner Bros. Records, which called for a sizable advance. In the ensuing years, it became clear that Polley had absconded with the funds, leaving the band members essentially penniless. Having grown despondent about his ability to earn a livelihood, Pete had hanged himself on April 24. In his suicide note, he wrote, "I will not be allowed to love and trust everybody. This is better, Pete. PS: Stan Polley is a soulless bastard. I will take him with me."[18]

Mal was shaken to the core when he learned the terrible news from

Tom Evans, Pete's longtime bandmate and fellow composer of "Without You," the song that had earned so many accolades for Badfinger yet, at the same time, had plunged them into financial and legal wrangling over unpaid royalties. The power-pop group Mal had discovered back at the Marquee in 1968 was suddenly over. In May, Warner Bros. canceled its agreement with Badfinger, and the band quietly dissolved—a far cry from the enormous promise Mal had witnessed in them when they were at the height of their powers.

In late May, as David Frost's *A Salute to the Beatles: Once Upon a Time* TV special made its debut on ABC's *Wide World of Entertainment,* Mal and Fran joined Lipton in New York. For her part, Fran was excited to meet with the city's most vaunted literary houses. She had conceived of the idea behind Mal's memoir and succeeded in landing Lipton. Now the project was on the verge of being made real. "It was fabulous at the time," she recalled. "It turned out to be a nightmare, but it certainly didn't start out that way." As they made their way through the publishing houses, Mal's insider's narrative generated considerable interest among buyers. But Grosset and Dunlap always had an inside track on making the deal, given Lipton's long-standing relationship with the imprint, and especially after the success of *Marilyn: A Biography.*

Bob Markel, Grosset and Dunlap's editor in chief, was eager to hear Mal's pitch that May day at the New York Life Building, the massive, golden-spired complex at 51 Madison Avenue. At the time, Markel was riding a wave of success that included the publication of Bob Dylan's *Tarantula,* a work of experimental prose poetry, in 1971. When it came to Mal, the editor was particularly drawn to the roadie's treasure trove of previously unseen Beatles photographs, which portended strong sales for a book in the pop music sector.

As director of the publisher's Contracts, Copyrights, and Permissions Department, Alyss Dorese recalled that Markel harkened back to a time when "publishing was a gentleman's game prior to having become corrupted like Hollywood." In Markel's heyday, "publishing was a fantastic industry." But Dorese could already glimpse the winds of change, which were shortly set to transform the book business into a bottom-line world bent on making the next big celebrity acquisition.[19]

Given Markel's old-school mind-set, he was excited to see Mal's collection for himself. Years later, he recalled a convivial afternoon with Mal, Fran, and Harold Lipton in which they perused the roadie's impressive stockpile of Beatles memorabilia in the living room of the Fourth Street duplex. In Markel's memory, that was all he needed to see. With a Beatles insider's story in the offing, supported by unique documents and photographs, he was ready to tender an offer for Mal's memoir.[20] For his part, Lipton was delighted with the terms for the book, which was referenced in the contract as "Untitled Work on the Beatles." The agreement called for Mal to author a fifty-thousand-word manuscript and compile one hundred photographs and other illustrations to be delivered to Grosset and Dunlap on Leap Day, February 29, 1976. When it came to brass tacks, Markel offered a generous $15,000 advance—$5,000 more than Lipton had netted for Mailer only a few years earlier—with Mal set to receive an additional $10,000 when he produced the manuscript in the New Year.

But something strange had transpired back in New York City, something known only to Mal. On the evening of Tuesday, May 20, 1975—possibly hours after meeting with Markel—Mal had taken to his notebook, which oddly comprised looseleaf paper crudely embossed with the image of Mickey Mouse. It was, by any measure, a cryptic admission to be making at such a time, in such a place:

I was born August 3rd, 1963, in Liverpool
Died May 20th 1975, crying in a hotel room, NY[21]

August 3, 1963, was the date of the Beatles' final performance at Liverpool's Cavern Club. Was Mal experiencing premature seller's remorse at the thought of betraying the Beatles in his memoir?

By the time the agreement with Grosset and Dunlap was firmly in place, Mal was well into the writing process. When Fran had first hatched the plan, Mal knew he had neither the patience nor the ability to sit in front of a typewriter and pound out his story. Then he remembered John Hoernle, the former art director at Capitol, and John's girlfriend, Joanne Lenard, and he resolved that "they would be the perfect combo to put this together." Mal struck a deal with the couple, offering to pay $500 a month for clerical services, courtesy of Lenard, along with professional assistance with his book's illustrations, courtesy of Hoernle, who would act as the project's art director.[22]

He also promised Hoernle and Lenard a percentage of the book's royalties. Over the next few months, Mal's tendency to offer friends and colleagues a share of his profits would seemingly get out of hand. The agreement with Grosset and Dunlap called for him to receive a fluctuating royalty rate of between 10 and 15 percent of the hardcover sales, with a sliding rate of 6 to 10 percent related to paperback sales. As his agent, Lipton would be entitled to a 15 percent share of these monies, with Fran receiving 20 percent of Mal's take for her managerial work on his behalf. But Hoernle and Lenard were hardly the only people to which Mal had promised a share of his royalties. That November, in a moment of ridiculous generosity, he ceded 1 percent of his gross earnings to David Mook. In a handwritten letter to the music publisher, Mal attributed his largesse to "the initial excitement generated by you about the project" and, better yet for Mook, wrote that the project "does not require any further involvement on your part."[23]

For their part, Hoernle and Lenard rose to the challenge of working on Mal's behalf. Across much of 1975, the roadie had been filling a notebook with anecdotes regarding nearly every aspect of his life with the Beatles. But he didn't stop there. He also followed to the letter Ringo's dictum to "tell the truth." While he rarely seemed to betray the boys' trust or confidence in his notes, he exposed numerous brutal truths about himself and the defining choices he had made in terms of his sexual experiences and his family life.

His voluminous notebook in hand, Mal transformed his memories into writing prompts and then, aided by a portable cassette recorder, began dictating his memoir aloud. Lenard dutifully recorded his words in her stenographer's books in Gregg shorthand, the cursive notetaking technique, and then transformed the shorthand into manuscript pages by collating her steno books with Mal's cassette recordings. The two had employed this process since early May—even before Lipton had an agreement in place with Grosset and Dunlap. That summer, Mal would hold fourteen dictation sessions with Lenard, producing a few hundred manuscript pages along the way. Naturally, the subject matter was heavily skewed toward his heady years in Beatle World.

Intriguingly, an analysis of his 1975 notebook suggests that Mal didn't initially plan to include autobiographical details from his pre-Beatles years. In its original form, his memoir would have been set in motion by the "windscreen incident" of January 1963—as if to insinuate that his pre–Fab Four life was somehow secondary to his experiences with the boys, that he had somehow been "born" in that instant. The 1975 notebook also reveals that he never intended to write about the Beatles' 1965 American tour, which he had already explored in detail in "Beatles—U.S.A.," his ill-fated project with Southern News Services. His plan all along, as he explained to Markel, had been to insert the text of "Beatles—U.S.A." into his memoir.

While Lenard made steady work of processing Mal's recordings and her steno notes, the summer of 1975 turned out to be a stormy experience for the Record Plant's onetime "It Couple"—and also for Fran, who was fired as booking agent for the studio. In her memory, Mal's out-of-control behavior, particularly his alcohol and cocaine binges, had contributed to "blowing up her job." In his own observations, Blair Aaronson saw things differently. He had been tasked with handling the union paperwork for Silverspoon's Record Plant sessions, and when the guild called him onto the carpet for not filing the group's studio documentation, he checked with upper management. "Apparently, Fran had been blowing off a lot of the paperwork for the sessions." Reading between the lines, though, Aaronson concluded that the Record Plant "may have just used that as an excuse" to rid themselves of their Mal-and-Fran problem. "It could have been as simple as she and Mal were using so much blow in the studio that they just wanted it to stop," Aaronson reasoned.[24]

Whatever the pretext for her firing may have been, Fran was out of work. The practical implications of this were considerable: she was now chief breadwinner, responsible for making rent and her car payments. The effects of her job loss were immediate and very personal for the former booking agent, who lamented, "I was devastated. I was unemployable. I was humiliated."[25] The woman who had been steadfastly managing her boyfriend's demons over the past two years was suddenly in a world of trouble of her own.

40

DEAD LETTER OFFICE

As one of the couple's closest friends, Laura Gross witnessed the fallout firsthand as Mal and Fran's cocaine consumption worsened seemingly by the day. An inveterate teetotaler who had seen her share of drug-addled rock stars, Laura had made it crystal clear that she valued their friendship but wouldn't stick around when the drugs came out.

During this period, Gross was teaching elementary school by day as she worked to jump-start her rock journalism career in her free time. She

Laura Gross

Mal with Harry Nilsson

especially adored Fran's four-year-old, Jody, and remembered the cute relationship Mal had developed with the girl. "They were definitely buddies," she said. When Jody answered the phone—inevitably, one of the Beatles calling for Mal—she would announce "in this nasally voice, 'Malcolm Frederick, telephone.'"[1]

Laura warmly recalled watching episodes of *Gunsmoke* with Mal and Fran. Given his yen for Westerns, Mal never missed the long-running network television show starring James Arness as Marshal Matt Dillon, a fearless, principled Dodge City lawman. Mal would often wax poetic after watching the show, which typically ended in a big shootout in which Marshal Dillon bested the bad guys. "That's how I want to die," Mal liked to say, "going out in a hail of bullets."

Laura adored her evenings in their company all right, but whenever Fran called up Louise, their drug dealer, Gross would swiftly take her leave. She had seen the way drug abuse tended to wrest control of her friends' lives over the years, and she wanted no part of it. That summer, while dining out with the couple and Harry Nilsson, she had observed the two men retiring to the bathroom, time and time again, to get another hit of coke.[2]

As the awful summer of 1975 wore on, Joanne Lenard compiled the latest draft of Mal's manuscript, which the roadie pointedly concluded with his resignation from the Beatles in April 1974. As with the recent, ominous note he had penned in May in a New York City hotel room, Mal clearly perceived his memoir—and hence, the contours of his life story—as being bookended by his years with the boys between January 1963 and April 1974. As a coda to the book, he intended to include the lyrics of "In My Life," his most cherished song by the boys.[3]

The first draft of *200 Miles to Go* amounted to some 55,000 words, slightly exceeding the stipulation of his agreement with Grosset and Dunlap. At this juncture, Hoernle kicked into gear, working to create negatives for the illustrations Mal had chosen to include in the book. During this period, Lenard had been in close correspondence with Shelli Wolis, Bob Markel's assistant, about selecting a vendor for producing the images, a relatively expensive undertaking in those pre-digital days. Among twelve finalists for the job, a Hollywood outfit called Schaeffer Photo Supply won the sweepstakes, setting up a line of credit with Wolis and Grosset and Dunlap that September. Acting on Mal's behalf, Hoernle created thirty negatives for *Magical Mystery Tour*, three for *A Hard Day's Night*, five for *Blindman*, and twenty-seven "miscellaneous" images from Mal's life with the boys.

Not surprisingly, one of the miscellaneous negatives depicted Mal in his Channel Swimmer role for *Help!* Hoernle prepared a mockup of the image, which he proudly shared with his twelve-year-old daughter, Erika. She recalled her father's excitement over the quality of the photo reproduction and about working with Mal on his memoir. Hoernle's daughter often joined him at Fourth Street, and Mal learned about the time she had tagged along with her father in 1973 when, in his role as Capitol's art director, he presented John Lennon with the proofs for his *Mind Games* cover art. Naturally, meeting a Beatle had been a special day for the girl, who remembered Lennon muttering "Fantastic" as he gazed at Hoernle's handiwork. For the cover, Hoernle had assembled a hand-cut photo collage that featured an image of John symbolically striding away from Yoko, who was depicted as a distant mountain. Touched by Erika Hoernle's memory of meeting Lennon during his Lost Weekend days, Mal reached into his treasure trove of memorabilia and gifted her his signed copy of John's book *In His Own Write*.[4]

That August, Lipton signed the final contract with Grosset and Dunlap on Mal's behalf, clearing the way for him to receive the first, hefty installment of his advance. By that point, the news had made the rounds in Beatle World and beyond that Mal Evans would be publishing a memoir. While John had unhesitatingly lent his support to the project, he couldn't help making a snide comment in a letter to Derek Taylor. Mocking what he assumed to be the mundanity of the roadie experience, Lennon wrote that "Mal's releasing his diary . . . 'Tues: 1965: got up, loaded van' . . . should be a laugh." Having returned to home and hearth with Yoko in the Dakota, John also referenced seeing Derek and Mal being interviewed on Frost's Beatles special back in May, noting that the roadie had "dyed his hair and reveals his chest to anyone!"[5]

That month, Mal had received a letter from Mark Lapidos, who was on the verge of hosting Beatlefest '75: Welcome to Pepperland at the Commodore Hotel, near Grand Central Station. In addition to offering to cover Mal's expenses, Lapidos assured him that the Fest "would be a most enjoyable experience reliving Beatlemania for one weekend with 8,000 old and new Beatles fans. The stories and memories you could relate to the fans would create a natural high all over New York City."[6] For Mal and Fran, the trip made perfect sense. They were gearing up for an eventual marketing campaign for *200 Miles to Go* anyway, and the Fest would allow Mal to begin honing his shtick for a book tour. As news of Mal's memoir began to spread widely, he had also received an offer from the American Program Bureau to hawk his story on the potentially lucrative lecture circuit. In short order, John Mason inked a deal with the Chestnut Hill, Massachusetts, outfit.

In early September, with Jody in tow, Mal and Fran flew out to attend the Fest. Shortly before they made the cross-country flight, Mal received word from Lil that she couldn't see any way out of their protracted estrangement other than divorce. This was hardly welcome news for the roadie, who still preferred—even after his wife had gained full knowledge of his L.A. life with Fran—to keep his two worlds in carefully maintained compartments. If nothing else, he could console himself with the fact that

Lily had contemplated divorce before, only to stand down and keep their family intact—even if that notion was largely illusory by this point. In less maudlin moments, Mal even began to perceive divorce as a means to a different kind of life with Fran. "Mal asked me to marry him when Lily's divorce came through," his girlfriend said. "We had beautiful plans for the future."[7]

As promised by Lapidos, Mal was in for quite a show when he arrived in New York City. For the second year in a row, the event had been met with a highly enthusiastic and very partisan crowd of Beatles fans. Along with famed promoter Sid Bernstein, Mal headlined the fest. That weekend, he was scheduled for a pair of onstage interviews with radio deejay Jim Kerr and to appear on a panel of insiders that also featured Apple house hippie Richard DiLello, May Pang, and Jürgen Vollmer, one of the boys' friends from their Hamburg days and the photographer behind the cover art for John's *Rock 'n' Roll* (formerly *Back to Mono*). In addition to a flea market–style shopping area, Fest attendees enjoyed the rare chance to see

Mal at *Beatlefest* '75

the Beatles' films on the silver screen. For Lapidos, the weekend's highlight involved watching *Magical Mystery Tour* while sitting in the Commodore Hotel's balcony with Mal, who provided a running commentary throughout the screening.[8]

Holding court with Jim Kerr in the Grand Ballroom, Mal was awestruck by the packed house—all these people had turned out to see him in the flesh. He took to the stage wearing a pair of white jeans and his favorite shirt, a country-and-western-style number Ringo and Mo had bought for him a few years back. His carefully selected accessories included his Bangladesh medal, the stone necklace Ringo had given him, and a tiny yellow submarine pin.

The weekend far exceeded Mal's expectations. "It was really a dream of a lifetime," he admitted.[9] For his presentation, "I got together a quarter-hour film from Rishikesh in India where we were meditating, and I thought, 'Well, I'll show this quarter-hour film, talk for 10 minutes, a few questions and answers, and I'll get off as quick as possible!" But it didn't happen that way—not even close. For nearly two hours, Mal held the audience rapt. "They had to drag me off in the end because the audience was so 'pro-me,'" he recalled. "It was wonderful. It was like being a Beatle for a weekend 'cause there were all the autographs, the photographs, and people making a fuss, and getting a lot of attention. You know, it really goes to my head, that sort of thing."[10]

In the Grand Ballroom, Mal good-naturedly took question after question, not wanting the experience to end. When he was asked about Neil, he affectionately described his former fellow roadie as "my best pal" and noted that Aspinall was still toiling away on *The Long and Winding Road* documentary project, which Mal hoped to complete with him one day. At one point, an audience member attempted to draw Mal into the snarl of Allen Klein and the Beatles' financial entanglements, but he sidestepped the question, saying, "I never got too much into their business affairs. I was too busy being friends." And he readily laughed off questions about the absurdity of the "Paul is dead" rumors. "I'm sitting next to the guy, talking to him," said Mal, "and people are trying to tell me that he's dead." And in easily the afternoon's unhappiest instance, he was asked about Pete Ham's suicide. Mal, choked up over the loss, called it a "very sad moment."[11]

As the Fest came to a close that Sunday, Mal took to the stage, playing tambourine and singing along with Northern Song, the house band, which featured New Jersey musicians Teddy Judge, Bob Hussey, and Paul Unsworth. During that last night in the Grand Ballroom, Fran stood alongside her boyfriend, basking in the glow of his excitement. Caught up in the moment, Mal speculated that he might even produce the band, who, in their workaday lives, went under the name Pegasus. He described being onstage as the audience cheered as possibly the greatest thrill of his life. "You couldn't go wrong," said Mal. "People grabbing your legs—it was great. The vibes were so good. Everybody's got just one purpose, and that's to enjoy themselves and to share." As he left the stage that Sunday, he revealed his fondest dream with the assembled throng. "If the Beatles ever get back together," he beamed, "I want to be there!"[12]

But the evening wasn't quite over just yet. Mal and Fran stayed up late that night with Judge, who played his demos for them in their hotel suite. True to his word, Mal was seriously considering Judge and Pegasus for a production deal. And Judge was thrilled at the possibility of working with him. He would never forget playing his compositions for the couple, pausing occasionally as Mal reeled off another story about his former life with the boys. "It was a great night," Judge recalled. "I'm a young kid who was the world's biggest Beatles fan at the time, and here's Mal sharing all of these amazing stories about the group."[13]

Mal, Fran, and Jody rounded out their East Coast sojourn with dinner at Captain Starn's Sea Food Restaurant and Bar outside Atlantic City, where

Mal and May signing autographs at Beatlefest '75

they met up with Fran's parents. Before they boarded their flight for the return trip to L.A., they made time for a quick stop at the Grosset and Dunlap offices in the New York Life Building. Editor in chief Bob Markel was out for the day, but Shelli Wolis was there, excited to meet Mal in person. "He was lovely!" she recalled. Wolis gleefully announced that Markel was planning to publish *200 Miles to Go* in August 1976, as an oversize coffee table book. Better yet, his design team had envisioned cover art featuring a photograph of Mal's doctor's bag from the Beatles' touring days, along with a hand-drawn poster of Mal wearing his wide-brimmed cowboy hat. As always, Mal had come bearing gifts, and he presented Wolis with a signed photo of the boys.[14]

By any measure, Mal's East Coast visit with Fran and Jody was a smashing success. But as always, it never seemed to be enough—the autographs, the photos, the adulation. Back on Fourth Street, everything quickly collapsed on him, leaving him in a deep malaise. Often, Fran would call on others to help out, frequently phoning up Bob Merritt to come over to the duplex and share a comforting word with the roadie. "I used to go over to Franny's and sit and talk with him," Merritt recalled. "Franny would call me up and say, 'Hey, Mal's really depressed. I don't know what to do with him.' So I'd come over and sit down and talk with him and calm him down."[15]

But there were other occasions when Mal couldn't wrest himself from his demons so easily, times when he exacerbated his condition with drink and drugs. And, for the first time, Fran found herself afraid of her boyfriend, whose darkness had never been more acute. It all came to a head one night when Mal, drunk to the gills, began threatening her with his Colt Woodsman pistol, at one point placing the gun against her head before discharging it into the washing machine. When he sobered up, Mal couldn't have been more apologetic, swearing to mend his ways and be the boyfriend she deserved.[16]

Initially, the incident left Fran on high alert, although by the time she saw Laura Gross, she was already cracking jokes about it. "She said, 'Look, he killed the washing machine,'" Gross recalled. "And I said, 'Fran, this isn't funny. You have to make me a promise. You have a four-year-old daughter who lives in this house. You've got a guy who's been erratic and now he's taken a gun and fired it in your home. You have to get rid of every single gun that's in this house, like today or tomorrow.' And she said, 'Oh my

God, you're right.' And I said, 'You have to look me in the eye and promise that you will get rid of the guns in this house.' And she said, 'You know, you're right. I will. I absolutely will.'"[17]

A few weeks later, Mal went out to lunch with Laura and opened up about his troubled state of mind, telling her, "You know, I just don't know what I want in my life. I love Fran, but I think about my family in England, and should I be with them, and I don't know what to do. I'm really at a crossroads, and I'm trying to figure it out." At that point, he reached out to Gross, asking, "Could I just come and live with you for a little while? You know, on the couch, just to get away from everything that's kind of pulling at me and just kind of think things out and be clear."[18]

But, for the life of her, Laura—all of twenty-three at this point—couldn't do it. "I cannot have this man in my house, because he is erratic and had been violent," she said, embracing common sense and suspecting that Fran hadn't confiscated the guns on Fourth Street. Gross told Mal, "I really love you. And I hope you'll understand. And if you don't, I'll be sad. But I can't do it. I can't take the risk. I'm just too concerned about your state of mind and the drug use." And Mal seemed to understand, even agree with, her logic.[19]

At some point that November, Bob Markel must have proffered suggestions to Mal for fleshing out his manuscript further—namely, to amass new material about his pre-Beatles years and reconsider the abruptness of the book's extant "So what?" ending. At the same time, the editor confided in Martin Torgoff, his twenty-four-year-old associate editor, that "he wanted something with more depth, with more pizzazz and juice in the sense of sex, drugs, and rock 'n' roll."[20]

Working feverishly across four meetings in November and December 1975, Mal and Lenard conducted their usual dictation sessions with the cassette recorder rolling. During their conversations, Mal shared numerous stories about his years in Liverpool and Wales, along with a rash of details about meeting Lily and beginning his career as a telecommunications engineer with the GPO. Once she had typed up the new content about Mal's pre-Beatles ascendance, Lenard had accumulated another 7,000 words, bringing the manuscript for *200 Miles to Go* somewhere in the vicinity of 62,000 words (about 250 double-spaced pages). At some point during this period, the book's main title shifted from *200 Miles to Go* to *Living the Beatles' Legend*. From a potential sales perspective, this alteration made perfect sense. After all, the Beatles were the main attraction. A consumer scanning the shelves of their local bookstore would be more likely to pick up a book with the name "Beatles" on its spine than *200 Miles to Go*, which had now been relegated to a subtitle.

For Mal, November concluded with a convivial interview with Laura Gross on KCSN, Cal State Northridge's college radio station. During their conversation, Gross framed Mal's career in relation to the Beatles, suggesting that "being so close to something that was so big, you really were an entertainer in a sense. You definitely were a celebrity, and [for] Beatle fans to this day, Mal is one of the most well known—everybody loves Mal. He's the favorite of all the Beatle fans." Mal audibly blushed, admitting that he possessed a kind of "bullshit exterior" that enabled him to meet people rather easily and make new friends. "I do love people," he told her. "I think that might be my gig all my life—people. I really get on with people generally, you know?" When it came to discussing the newly retitled *Living the Beatles' Legend*, he shared his fondest motive for writing the memoir, which was to win over the boys. "The book is my whole life," he explained to Laura. "I

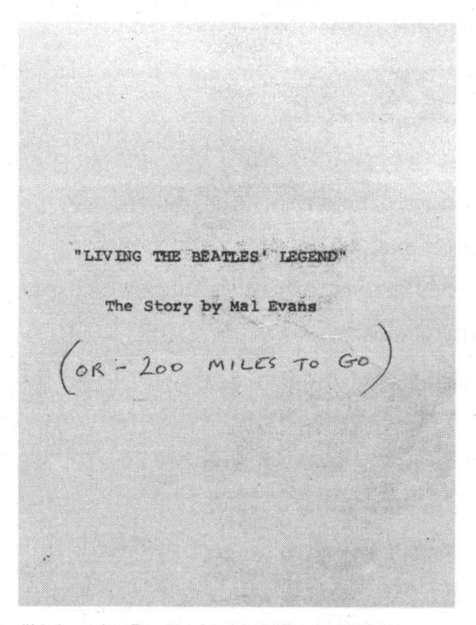
"LIVING THE BEATLES' LEGEND"

The Story by Mal Evans

(OR - 200 MILES TO GO)

"Living the Beatles' Legend" typescript

want the four of them to love my book. That's my whole dream. My whole dream would be realized if they said, 'I love what you're doing.'"[21]

As December got under way, Mal came into the orbit of Joey Molland. The onetime Badfinger guitarist had traveled with his new band, Natural Gas, to Los Angeles, where they were planning to record some demos in advance of landing a record deal. Drummer Jerry Shirley, formerly of Humble Pie, explained the origins of the group's name. "It sounds dumb," he said, "but when you think about it, without any bullshit attached, the only meaning was what the group was going to be—a 'natural gas.'"[22] Rounded out by former Uriah Heep bassist Mark Clarke and keyboard player Peter Wood, Natural Gas responded in the affirmative when Mal expressed interest in overseeing the recording of their demos and possibly working with them further in the New Year. Being persona non grata at the Record Plant, Mal met with the band at Total Experience Studios in Hollywood, with Bobby Hughes, Fran's ex, serving as engineer. Over the next few days, Mal supervised passes at "Little Darlin'," "The Right Time," and, appropriate to the season, "Christmas Song." The band sounded tight and well rehearsed on the demos, and they invited Mal to join them on a late-December conference call with their label, Private Stock.

That same month, Mal had the rare opportunity of seeing not one, but two familiar faces from his Beatles past. Up first was Neil, who seemed in bright spirits, even suggesting that Apple Corps would soon enjoy a renaissance, now that the awful business over the Beatles' partnership had been resolved. Back on May 2, Apple had finally closed up shop at 3 Savile Row, maintaining offices in St. James Place for the foreseeable future. Neil was essentially operating on a skeleton crew that included a few secretaries and accountants to keep the business humming. But he was happy just the same, delighted to be Klein-free and committed to shoring up the boys' legacy.[23]

Several days later, on Sunday, December 14, Mal received a telephone call from Paul. He had seen his old friend a few days earlier, when the Beatle was on a forty-eight-hour layover at the Beverly Hills Hotel. He had flown into L.A. after a Hawaiian vacation with Linda and their children in advance of Wings's spring American tour. Now he was calling from New York City, where he and Linda were visiting with John and Yoko, who had given birth to a baby, Sean, two months earlier, on her husband's

Joey Molland and Mal at Total Experience Studios

thirty-fifth birthday.[24] Laura Gross was at the Fourth Street duplex when the ex-Beatle called. As usual, precocious Jody answered the phone and summoned "Malcolm Frederick."

Mal was ecstatic after ringing off with Paul, who had "phoned me at my home asking me to consider going on the road with him for his upcoming American tour in the spring of 1976." Downright chuffed by the invitation, Mal wrote that "I do feel our friendship is as strong as ever. I certainly admire everything he's done since and will staunchly defend him to the death." Waxing philosophical, he added that "Paul and Linda have come in for a lot of criticism from so-called friends, but in spite of the hurt this must have caused, he carried on to follow his own star—a man to be admired and respected in the profession he has chosen."[25]

That same evening, Mal met interviewer Ken Doyle, a colleague of Laura's at KCSN, to participate in *Full Circle*, a live call-in show at Cal State Northridge. The campus was largely deserted that night, with students having left for winter break. Doyle's pal Rip Rense had tagged along for the occasion, and he recalled Mal's excitement in joining them that night at the studio. Mal referred to having been "locked away for five months" working on his memoir. He was thrilled at the opportunity to talk about the boys. "The Beatles are my favorite subject," he explained. "I can talk for hours and hours." But when the show commenced that Sunday night, Doyle had difficulty raising any callers. Winking at Mal from the sound booth, Rense proceeded to telephone the studio under a host of assumed names, often adopting different voices and accents to sustain the ruse of an active call-in audience.[26]

Inevitably, Rense asked Mal about the possibility of a Beatles reunion. The roadie admitted that seeing the band together would be wonderful. "If wishes made dreams come true," then it would be a near certainty. When Rense commented that he indeed wished that they would reunite, Mal became emotional, saying, "That's lovely to hear you say that. I've got shivers because I believe it, and nothing would make me prouder or more pleased than to hear them play again." Later in the program, when Rense insisted on bringing up the reunion question yet again, Mal answered more enigmatically: "While the four of them are alive—or four of them are dead—then there's still a chance."[27]

Before signing off, Mal admitted his secret ambition to be a performer, even hinting that "I do have secret plans to make an album." He also spoke about having just been in the studio with Natural Gas. "It's been such a beautiful week, such an 'up' week," he said. "I love producing—a very creative side of life." Asked by Rense about the artist he believed would become the 1970s' next "big superstar," Mal proclaimed, "Natural Gas! They're a beautiful group, you're gonna love them, they're nice-looking people, they're nice boys, and they play really good music—good rock 'n' roll music. Put Natural Gas in your tank!"[28]

With the holidays in the offing, Mark Clarke stopped by Mal and Fran's place on Fourth Street for a visit. As Mal showed off his collection of memorabilia and weaponry in the upstairs bedroom—he had recently added a sword to his arsenal—Clarke could tell the roadie was dejected. In truth, he wasn't surprised: "He's just come off the biggest whirlwind in musical history, right?" Clarke said. "Who wouldn't be?"

A few days later, Mal participated in the Natural Gas conference call, which included Clarke, Shirley, manager Bill Cameron, and Private Stock's president, Larry Uttal. As they discussed the particulars of Mal's role with the band, the meeting went sideways after the roadie requested a staggering fee. It seemed a strange request coming from Mal, who had been around the record business long enough to know where things stood. With no other choice, the principals went around the table, voting on whether to approve Mal's request. Everyone—even Clarke, who had been predisposed to help Mal out—voted nay, and the meeting was adjourned.[29]

Joanne Lenard also recalled visiting Mal and Fran during the holidays. To her mind, Mal seemed uncharacteristically subdued, even a little depressed—an unusual demeanor for a person who typically appeared ebullient. She and Mal had decided to take the month of December off before resuming work on *Living the Beatles' Legend* in the New Year. "I think he was mostly sad because of the children," Lenard recalled. "He loved and cared for them so much. I mean, he couldn't stop talking about Gary and Julie. I know that he tried to keep in touch with them. But being apart from them was very hard on him, and he was depressed. But I never in a million years would have expected what happened just a few weeks later."[30]

On Christmas Day, Mal telephoned Lil and the children in Sunbury. At the same time, he had posted a letter to Staines Road East, apologizing to his estranged wife for "being really down on his uppers" as far as sending money home. But "in the new year, I start doing lecture tours," he wrote. "Should be getting about $2,000 a night and traveling all over the country." In lieu of Christmas gifts for Gary and Julie, he had enclosed five-pound notes for each of the children. "Well, love," he wrote in closing, "next year, with a million pounds, then maybe I can come marching home a hero to you all. I love you, Mal."[31]

Sometime that same week, he spoke to Mark Lapidos, thanking him again for inviting him to Beatlefest, "the best weekend of my life." Not only did he expect to come back to the Fest in 1976, Mal explained, but he planned to go to "all of them!"[32]

On December 31, Mal called Sunbury again, wishing Lil and the family glad tidings for the New Year. Gary, who had been felled by a severe case of the flu, vividly recalled lying on the couch and yelling, "I love you, Dad," as Lily spoke with her husband on the living room telephone. With their pleasantries out of the way, she informed Mal that she had made an appointment to consult with a divorce attorney on January 6.[33]

With his wife's pronouncement roiling around his brain, Mal likely telephoned John at the Dakota. In an interview the next day with L.A. radio personality Elliot Mintz, John spoke cryptically about a phone call from a friend who had "just split with his woman." John was worried that this unidentified friend would "hit the bottle like I did," Lennon said, referring to his Lost Weekend apart from Yoko. During the interview with Mintz, John claimed to have counseled this friend to embark on a spiritual path. "That was the advice I gave him," said John, but "he'll probably have to go the hard way. 'Cause he's male, you know, and we express ourselves in those ways and violence and all that."[34]

As 1976 unfolded, Mal and Fran spent a few quiet days at home. He seemed to be holding it together, although he had begun conspicuously instructing her about the duplex's various needs—odd jobs he'd been handling, such as how to properly tend to the fireplace or winterize the car.[35] Then, on Saturday, January 3, things took a dire turn.

That afternoon, Mal telephoned Badfinger's Tom Evans seemingly out of the blue. "If something happens to me," he said, "can you look after Lily?"[36] Then, that evening, Mal asked Fran to witness his will. "He was coked-up at the time," she recalled, so she took his request with a grain of salt. Besides, after the incident with the pistol, it seemed best simply to humor him, to wait out his high until the morning. As Fran sat beside him, Mal began to compose the rudimentary document. "It started off well, but then he just began rambling off into nothing as the drugs kicked in," she recalled.[37]

"Being of sound mind and healthy body," Mal began, "this is my last will and testament." He started by allocating his property, leaving his "guns and books to Gary" and his "Elvis things to Julie Suzanne." He ceded the royalties from his memoir in equal 20 percent shares to Lily, Gary, Julie, Fran, and Jody. At this juncture, the document began to lose coherence. "Please forgive," he continued. "I loved the world, but I can't cope." After affirming his love for "The Beatles, Fran, Lil, Julie, Gary, and Jody," Mal echoed his crude reading of John 15:13 from back in October 1973—this time, writing that "no greater love has a man to give his life for his family."[38]

In perhaps his clearest admission about his state of mind, Mal wrote that "I lost my son and daughter and never stopped loving Lil. Forgive me. I only wanted to be happy and please everybody, but I suffered from so much guilt, I never stopped loving Lily—remember the Pier Head. And loved a photograph of Fran . . . John, George, Ringo, Paul, please think kindly of me. I'll be back to look after you." As he contemplated his final arrangements, Mal expounded on perhaps his fondest hope, the kind that could transpire, as he had proclaimed a few weeks earlier on KCSN, only "if wishes made dreams come true": "If the Beatles love me, please play at my funeral your own brand of rock 'n' roll."[39]

The next day, Sunday, January 4, Mal appeared to have slept off his weary state. "Things seemed normal," said Fran. "He had just taken the Christmas tree down. And then, in just a few hours, it was all over."[40]

The trouble seemed to begin that afternoon, when Mal placed a telephone call to Ken Mansfield. The old friends had spoken only sporadically in recent months, with Mal working on *Living the Beatles' Legend* and

3RD JANUARY. 1976.
Being of sound mind & healthy
body this is my last will and
testament. All my guns and books
to go to Gary, my Elvis stage[illegible]
and Elvis records in fact all my
records to go to Julie Suzanne.
All moneys from royalties past present
and future to be divided in the following
~~manner~~ manner: 20% to my wife
Lily, 20% to Gary Malcolm, 20%
to Julie Suzanne, 20% to Francine
and 20% to Jody [illegible].
All papers relating to the book
"[illegible]" to [illegible] Lily
[illegible] to use as necessary. My
[illegible]

Mal's handwritten will

Mansfield enjoying considerable success as one of the leading progenitors of country music's Outlaw movement. In fact, that very evening, he would attend the *Billboard* Music Awards representing singer Jessi Colter, one of his star clients and the wife of Waylon Jennings. Mal had called just as Mansfield was preparing to leave for the banquet.

Ken could tell that his friend was caught in some kind of "strange euphoria." Mal started right in, announcing that "everything's really great," that he had recently spoken to Paul, and that he himself was about to close a record production deal. Before Mansfield could get a word in edgewise, the roadie continued, remarking that he had recently completed his book and telling Mansfield, "You're really gonna love it!" For Mansfield, the tone of Mal's voice didn't match the ostensibly happy news he was delivering; "there was something underneath it all that wasn't so joyful."

Mansfield finally succeeded in interrupting him: "Mal, are you sure everything's okay? Come on, Mal. Something's wrong, and we need to talk."

After a lengthy pause, Mal said, "Yeah."

Explaining that he had to be at the *Billboard* event on Jessi Colter's behalf, Mansfield fixed a date with Mal for brunch the next morning at Musso and Frank, on Hollywood Boulevard.[41]

Sometime after he completed his telephone call with Ken Mansfield, Mal began looking at Gary and Julie's pictures. "He grew very despondent," Fran recalled. "He started going through all his childhood, crying, and I sat and listened." At this point, he briefly went upstairs. When he rejoined Fran, he announced that he had taken an entire bottle of Valium.

"What are you doing?" Fran asked, as they sat in the dining room.

"I can't have my children," he replied. "They are dead to me, and I want to die."[42]

Figuring that he may have taken the pills in a clumsy attempt to kill himself, Fran reached out for help. At 8:15 p.m., she tried telephoning Laura Gross, who, unbeknownst to Fran, was picking up her mother at LAX. Fran pointedly didn't want to call the cops, fearing that a police record might jeopardize Mal's chances of getting a green card. In her desperation, she called John Hoernle, whose daughter Erika recalled the moment the phone rang: "My dad got a call because Mal was really screwed up. He dropped everything and went over there."[43]

Hoernle arrived at the duplex around thirty minutes later. Attempting to calm her boyfriend, Fran persuaded Mal to lie down in their bedroom on the second floor, while Jody was sound asleep in a rear bedroom. Hoernle followed the couple upstairs. Mal seemed anxious, "really doped up and groggy," Hoernle recalled. According to him, the roadie reportedly said, "Please make sure you and Joanne finish the book."[44]

Shortly after entering the room, Mal took up the Winchester rifle. Feeling apprehensive at the sight of the gun, Hoernle returned to the first floor, while Fran attempted to talk Mal into putting away the rifle. Soon, she was struggling to relieve him of the weapon. But even in his groggy state, Mal was considerably stronger than Fran, who told him that if "you don't give me that gun now, I'm going to call the police." And in that moment, Mal "looked her right in the eye and said, 'Franny, please call the police.'"[45] Unbeknownst to anyone but Mal, the Winchester was loaded with four rounds, one in the chamber and three in the magazine.[46]

Within minutes, Officers David Krempa and Todd Herman, both working out of LAPD's Wilshire Division, entered the Fourth Street premises. Fran announced that "my old man has a gun and has taken Valium and is totally screwed up." With the knowledge that Jody was upstairs, too, the officers prepared to contain the scene. In short order, they were joined by fellow LAPD officers Robert Brannon and Michael Simonsen. With their service revolvers drawn—save for Krempa, who was armed with a shotgun—they made their way upstairs.[47]

By this point, Fran and Hoernle were standing in the front yard; additional uniformed officers had arrived at the duplex. Meanwhile, the officers inside the house were halfway up the stairs. Observing that the master bedroom door was closed, they demanded that Mal walk out with his hands up. When they received no answer, they continued upstairs until they reached the doorway to the bedroom. At this juncture, Krempa set his shotgun on the upstairs landing, fearing their proximity to Jody's bedroom. As he drew his service revolver, Herman kicked at the door, which gently opened into the bedroom.[48]

For the first time, they caught a glimpse of Mal, who was sitting on the floor with his long legs splayed out in front of him. He held the Winchester in his hands, the barrel of the weapon tilted slightly toward the floor. Officer Herman repeatedly ordered Mal to "drop the gun." Finally, the roadie looked in the officers' direction, saying, "No. Blow my head off."

The standoff might have continued unabated had Mal not begun to raise the Winchester toward his shoulder, as if he were preparing to fire it. With that, Officers Krempa and Brannon fired six shots, four of which hit their mark.

Mal slumped backward, killed instantly, mere feet away from the diaries, photographs, and other attendant memorabilia comprising his life's work.[49]

For Fran, the sound of the gunshots was "horrifying."[50] As the officers inside discharged their weapons, the uniformed patrolmen in the front yard forced Fran and Hoernle to the ground to take cover. Meanwhile, an ambulance was idling nearby on Fourth Street, waiting in vain to answer Fran's distress call of a possible suicide attempt in the Flats. Moments later, Jody was carried outside, unharmed, where she was reunited with her mother. Incredibly, the four-year-old had slept through the entire episode.

That night, Fran was taken to the Wilshire Division as a material witness, having left Jody in the care of neighbors. When she was confronted with the issue of processing her boyfriend's remains, Fran was understandably at a loss. But then she remembered the telephone number Harry Nilsson had included in his recent Christmas card. In his grief, the singer drove to Forest Lawn cemetery to make arrangements for Mal's cremation. When Harry asked how his friend's ashes would be transported to London, he was informed that the cheapest method involved a cardboard cylinder. "You'd send a mother the remains of her son in a cardboard box?" an incredulous Harry asked, opting for an expensive-looking urn. Mal's ashes were duly posted to London.

To his surprise, a few days later, Harry received a frantic telephone call from Neil. "Harry, Harry! Where's Mal?" he demanded. The urn had yet to arrive, Neil reported. "He's not here, and his mother's downstairs and his wife Lil is here, and they're all crying. What am I supposed to tell them?"[51]

It was John, weeping and plunged into inconsolable grief in the Dakota, who finally supplied the answer. In a moment of levity Mal would surely have appreciated, the ex-Beatle quipped that his friend must have been lost in the Dead Letter Office.[52]

EPILOGUE

A CELLARFUL OF DUST

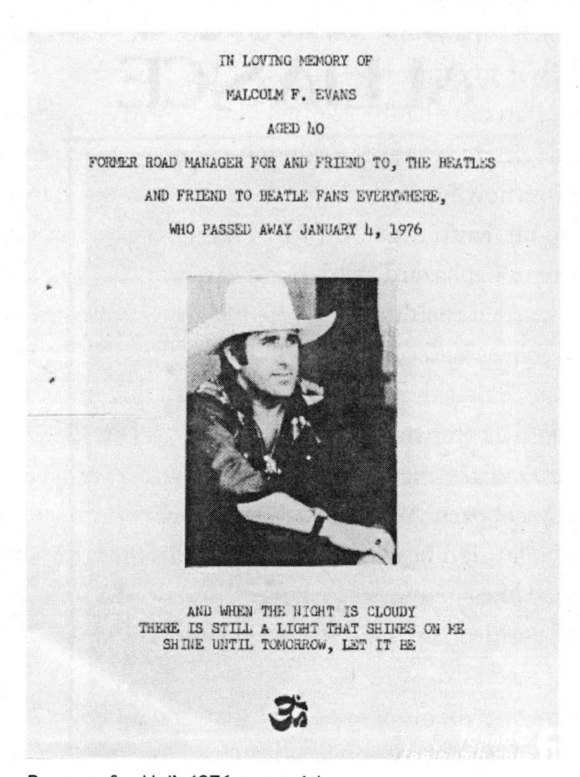

IN LOVING MEMORY OF

MALCOLM F. EVANS

AGED 40

FORMER ROAD MANAGER FOR AND FRIEND TO, THE BEATLES

AND FRIEND TO BEATLE FANS EVERYWHERE,

WHO PASSED AWAY JANUARY 4, 1976

AND WHEN THE NIGHT IS CLOUDY
THERE IS STILL A LIGHT THAT SHINES ON ME
SHINE UNTIL TOMORROW, LET IT BE

Program for Mal's 1976 memorial

In February 1988, a dozen years after Mal's death, Leena Kutti took a temp job with G. P. Putnam's Sons, the New York City publishing house. It would be a short gig for the forty-three-year-old artist, who supplemented her income with odd jobs around the five boroughs. An Estonian immigrant, Kutti had arrived at Ellis Island in 1949, disembarking with her family from the USNS *General Harry Taylor*, a navy transport ship. Like tens of millions of other teens, she watched the Beatles' appearance on *The Ed Sullivan Show* in February 1964, and she was hooked.[1]

The job at Putnam's brought her to the New York Life Building—and more specifically, to the basement. Known as the storage room by the publisher's staff, the dusty basement level was packed to the gills with every possible kind of detritus. It was mostly clerical stuff—paperwork and contracts associated with a century in the life of American publishing. But there were strange things, too, hidden among the attendant accumulation—objets d'art such as paintings, sculpture, and photographs. And Kutti's job, more or less, was to throw it all out.

In 1982, Putnam's had purchased Grosset and Dunlap, and by 1988, when Kutti descended to the New York Life Building's basement, Putnam's offices were overflowing, literally, with material. Assigned to help clean out the storage room, Kutti began sifting through the materials that had accumulated there in haphazard fashion over the decades. Her supervisor, also a temp, told her that their task, essentially, was to empty the basement out. He expected they would consign most of the stuff to the garbage heap, but on the off chance that they found anything of value, those items could be transported to the company's storage facility across the river, in New Jersey.

It was around the second day on the job that Kutti happened upon the four bankers boxes. Almost immediately, she could tell their contents were of particular significance. As she sifted through the boxes, she gazed at what seemed like vintage photographs of the Beatles. And then she found a manuscript entitled "Living the Beatles' Legend: Or 200 Miles to Go." It was an oddly formatted specimen—printed in all caps. As she began leafing through the notebooks and diaries, Kutti was able to ascertain that the boxes must be the property of Malcolm Evans, the Beatles' road manager.

In her excitement, Kutti brought the materials to the attention of her supervisor, who reminded her that they were on a search-and-destroy mission, not a recovery project. But Kutti persisted, informing him "that there's stuff here about the Beatles." Incredibly, the supervisor thought she was referring to insects, which left her even more frustrated. "I guess he just wasn't into music," she said. "I could tell that he was older than I was."[2] But she wasn't giving up so easily. When she insisted that the boxes were the rightful property of Evans's family, the supervisor threw his hands up and sent Kutti to Putnam's corporate offices, where she spoke with Louise Bates in Contracts, Copyrights, and Permissions.

Well over sixty-five at the time she was hired, Bates had stayed on after Putnam's purchased Grosset and Dunlap, becoming one of the industry's doyennes. When Kutti met with Bates in her Midtown office, she could tell the older woman was taking her seriously—but it also became clear that Mal's bankers boxes made Bates uncomfortable. Soon, Bates explained that she would need to check with Legal, and possibly even send the materials out to Los Angeles, to the lawyers who had originally handled the contract.

To Kutti's way of thinking, Bates seemed overly concerned. On its face, this seemed like a simple issue to the temp, with an equally simple solution: by rights, the materials belonged to the surviving family members back in England. That Saturday, February 13, 1988, Kutti decided to take matters into her own hands. Making her way uptown to the corner of West 72nd Street and Central Park West, she stepped up to the copper-plated sentry box adjacent to the Dakota's majestic archway and handed the doorman a sealed envelope addressed to "Ms. Yoko Ono," with "Personal" written underneath. Having written her telephone number in the note, Kutti didn't mince words: "This is regarding some of Malcolm's personal effects," she wrote. "I feel they should be returned directly to the family."

But Kutti didn't stop there. That Monday, she compiled a six-page inventory of the contents of the bankers boxes. As she began to organize

Sat. Feb. 13
Dear Ms. Ono –
Would you know
where to locate
Malcolm Evans
children or his
former wife, I
believe her name
is Lily, and the
children are
Julia & Gary.
This is regard-
ing some of
Malcolm's personal

effects. I feel they
should be returned
directly to the
family. If you
do not know how
I can reach these
people, could
you let me know
who might know
their whereabouts.
I believe maybe
Harry Nilsson might
know. I can be
reached at
0101 (718) 486-6368
Leena Kutti

(2)
and would greatly
appreciate a
response. Sorry
to bother you with
this but I would
like to see this
material in the
right hands.
Sincerely
Leena Kutti

Leena Kutti's letter to Yoko

the materials, they seemed even more tantalizing than before: there was an autographed color photo of Elvis Presley; a signed drawing of Mal by John Lennon; and yet another drawing of the roadie, this one by Paul McCartney, inscribed with the words "To Mal the Van from James Paul the Bass." There were ten Super 8 films in total, with titles like "Family Holiday," "Beatles India," "Africa," "Greece," and "Plane Trip (Paul)."

When Kutti returned to the storage room later that week, with her gig at Putnam's swiftly coming to an end, she discovered that the boxes were no longer in the basement. The temp subsequently met with Bates in her Midtown office, where she discovered all the boxes stacked neatly beside Bates's desk. Again, Kutti couldn't help noticing how uncomfortable and worried Bates seemed, "like she wanted to deal with the stuff and get it over with as quickly as she could." Bates seemed to be particularly fretful about "the lawyers in L.A.," who wanted the materials but didn't want to pay the freight to ship the boxes to the West Coast. For the life of her, Kutti couldn't make sense of this: "They were so worried about the cost that they couldn't begin to understand how important and valuable all of this stuff was."[3]

With a new gig beginning on Monday at Credit Suisse, Kutti realized the clock had seemingly run out. But she had one more card up her sleeve. She made a Xerox copy of the inventory, rifled through the international telephone books at the New York Public Library, and, putting pen to paper, wrote a letter to Lily Evans at 135 Staines Road East in Sunbury-on-Thames. If nothing else, the temp wanted to ensure that Mal's widow knew about the drama playing out in New York City.

What Kutti didn't know was that Yoko had received her message all right. Indeed, by the time Kutti had begun her new assignment in Credit Suisse's 11 Madison Avenue offices, the wheels were already in motion at Gold, Farrell, and Marks, Apple Corps' law firm, which was coincidentally just across the street from the New York Life Building. One of the firm's partners, Paul V. LiCalsi, had taken the lead on behalf of Yoko and Neil Aspinall, who had been appointed executive director of Apple in 1976, in the wake of the dissolution of the Beatles' partnership.

What LiCalsi and his team accomplished in a few short days was a masterpiece of lawyering. When Apple took possession of the bankers boxes, they extracted an agreement from Putnam's to protect Mal's legacy. Putnam's attorney Matthew Martin wrote to Apple, stating that "per our phone conversation of March 14, 1988, this will confirm that neither Grosset and Dunlap nor the Putnam Publishing Group or any of its subsidiaries or affiliates own any copyright or publication rights in and to the untitled literary work on the Beatles (including text, photographs, drawings, memorabilia, and other materials prepared and collected for the work) which was to have been authored by Mal Evans." Most important, Martin added, "please be assured that neither Grosset nor Putnam has any plans or intentions of publishing any material authored or prepared by Mal Evans."[4]

Alas, this had not always been the case when it came to Grosset and Dunlap in the days, months, and years after Mal's death on January 4, 1976. And as it turned out, Grosset and Dunlap hadn't been the only party attempting to bring Mal's story—and his treasure trove of memorabilia—to the marketplace. Within forty-eight hours of her boyfriend's death, Fran packed her bags for a six-week respite with Jody and her parents in Philly. For her, it was a matter of attempting to survive the devastation. At twenty-six, she had to get her life together—and fast—if for no other reason than her daughter.

Even before Fran had left L.A.—before the crime scene had been cleaned up, even—John Hoernle stopped by the duplex to pick up some of Mal's documents and possessions under the pretext of completing the roadie's manuscript for publication. In a June 1976 affidavit, Fran stated that Hoernle and Joanne Lenard took away a large parcel of Mal's materials because they "feared that the house would be looted." "When I was back east," Fran continued, "I told Grosset I would be happy to sit with the writer and help finish the book for Mal. Then I called John [Hoernle] and asked [him] to tell them the good news, and [Hoernle and Lenard] said that the two of them alone were to finish the book and not me. That was the last time we spoke [...] And they're still holding all the Beatles possessions. Now he is holding up the book, six months later. A friend of mine . . ."[5]

Hoernle and Lenard clearly had designs on publishing the manuscript. In a condolence letter to Mal's widow, Lenard wrote, "For the past nine months, Lil, we both practically lived with Mal working on the book and he became a part of us—I don't think either of us have ever had a friendship as close as what we shared with Mal. He spoke of you and Gary and Julie what seems like every day."[6] To her mind, Lenard believed she and Hoernle were honoring Mal's memory by attempting to see his memoir through to publication. Besides, they were just as shell-shocked and confused as nearly everyone else in Mal and Fran's circle. Mal's death just didn't make any sense, Lenard reasoned. "He was always such a happy guy, you know? He had a gentle soul. He was such a wonderful person."[7]

As it turned out, Hoernle and Lenard would shortly stop work on the Mal Evans memoir altogether. Materials were returned to Harold Lipton's office, and the attorney produced a receipt for the following effects:

1. Diaries of Malcolm F. Evans that Mr. Hoernle and Miss Leonard [*sic*] had in their possession for the years 1964, 1967 [*sic*], 1968, and 1970 through 1974.[8]
2. 208 typewritten pages consisting of 23 pages of manuscript which the deceased had dictated to Miss Leonard [*sic*] up to the date of his death, which occurred on January 4, 1976.[9]

Early that spring, Grosset and Dunlap's editor in chief, Bob Markel, dispatched associate editor Martin Torgoff to retrieve the materials from Lipton. As he packaged the memorabilia and manuscripts for transport to New York City, Torgoff recalled "being kind of blown away as I went through his stuff. It was so fascinating to see the pictures."[10] A few days later, he deposited the materials outside Markel's office in the New York Life Building.

Meanwhile, over in Beverly Hills, Lipton had clearly been marshaling his forces. On January 13, he contacted Ringo, entreating the ex-Beatle to help him bring Mal's memoir to the marketplace. The real icing on the cake, Lipton wrote, would be for the drummer "to make yourself available to the writer who will be completing the manuscript," adding "what a wonderful tribute it would be to the memory of Mal."[11] Grosset and Dunlap had tapped award-winning rock journalist David Dalton to complete the project. One of the cofounders of *Rolling Stone* magazine and the author of *James Dean: The Mutant King*, Dalton seemed like the logical choice to finalize the manuscript, with the book now going under the title *The Beatles: A Celebration in Words and Pictures*, with its authorship attributed to Mal Evans and David Dalton. A proposal drawn up by Grosset and Dunlap announced that "the publishers wish to keep Mal's objective sharply in focus and retain his authentic tone and perspective without resorting to material, even if available, that would hold any of the Beatles up to ridicule or embarrassment."

The proposal seemed choreographed to communicate to the Beatles' camp that the publication of Mal's memoir would not be harmful to their reputations, individually or collectively. Even so, Brian Brolly, the managing director of MPL Communications, the organization overseeing Paul's business interests, made inquiries about securing a copy of the manuscript for his client. By this juncture, Lipton, intent on seeing the project to fruition, believed that an essential element involved the Beatles' participation with new interviews. As always, the lawyer was working closely with Grosset and Dunlap, with whom he had a long-standing association. In February, Bob Markel requested Lipton's services in procuring a copy of Mal's death certificate, in order to file an insurance claim to recover the publishing company's advance. That April, to ensure the former Beatles' cooperation, Lipton enlisted attorney John Mason to contact Neil and provide him with the new book proposal. Similar letters were posted to Fran and to Bruce Grakal, in his capacity as Ringo's personal attorney.

Incredibly, Lipton didn't write to Lily Evans until *after* Neil had informed him that the Beatles would not be sitting for interviews with Dalton. In a letter of June 11, Lipton introduced himself to his former client's widow, informing her that "the publisher is still very excited about the book. However, we need some help. I have been endeavoring to arrange for an interview with the Beatles by the publishers to supplement and implement information and experiences recited by Mal. To date, I have not been successful." In closing, Lipton wrote, "I believe the book has excellent commercial and financial potential, but the interviews with the Beatles could make a vast amount of difference in the salability of the book. And now is the time!"[12]

By this point, Grakal—very possibly at Ringo's express instruction—

had demonstrated his role as a key ally for Lil. In March, she enlisted his efforts in recovering Mal's papers and personal effects, a quest that wouldn't end for another dozen years, when Kutti discovered them in the basement of the New York Life Building. While the letters to Lil, Fran, and Neil bespeak of a wish to see Mal's exciting journey with the Beatles in print, Lipton's motives were largely financial. As the de facto agent for the book, he would earn a percentage of its sales. Much later—after all hope of publishing Mal's work with Grosset and Dunlap seemed dashed—Lipton wrote to Lil, whose attorneys had been pestering him about the return of Mal's effects. He calculated that prior to his death, Mal had racked up $20,125 in legal fees and $1,523.75 in legal costs—patently ridiculous sums for negotiating a book deal in that era, especially when the total advance provided for his client had been $25,000.[13] Indeed, to incur legal costs to produce an advance of a similar size would be considered bad business. Yet, in his August 1979 letter, Lipton made it clear that he would help Lily recover her husband's effects, but only after she had handled his outstanding bill to the lawyer.

For Lily, the experience of processing her husband's death, both emotionally and logistically, was nightmarish. Informing Lil of the details of Mal's last will and testament of January 3, 1976—while it had no legal standing—had been accomplished by Neil, who telephoned the LAPD and asked that the details of the will be read aloud to him over the phone so he could assist his friend's widow in her darkest hour. Indeed, Lily would not lay eyes on Mal's will until March 1988, when the Federal Express parcel containing the bounty Kutti had discovered in Putnam's storage room finally arrived on her doorstep.

As far as Lily was concerned, the "Living the Beatles' Legend" manuscript had been the product of a fever dream concocted by her husband—the same man who, in his final letter home, believed he would soon be delivering nightly lectures at $2,000 a pop. In April 1976, Lily had replied to Lenard and Hoernle's letter—not merely to thank them for their condolences, but also to glean vital information. "Malcolm's death is a very big mystery to me as I knew him as a big softie who would not hurt a fly," Lily wrote. "Although he had left me and the children who I know he loved in his own way, I still have a lot of affection for him and cannot understand how he got into such a state." And then there was the matter of the roadie's manuscript: "Perhaps you may be able to help me in obtaining information about the book which Mal was writing and you were so involved in as I would hate for all his efforts to be wasted."[14] But, although they would briefly surface again in the late 1970s, Hoernle and Lenard had already been relegated to bit players in the saga over Mal's memoir and personal effects. Lil would have to take her investigation elsewhere.

Her big chance finally arrived in February 1978, when she and Gary met with representatives from Grosset and Dunlap about the potential publication of Mal's memoir. Gary recalled meeting with his mother and two women at the Savoy Hotel.[15] In her correspondence with her sister Vera, Lily described the upshot of the meeting, during which Jeannie Sakol and Stephanie Bennett, acting on behalf of Grosset and Dunlap, pitched the idea of publishing *Living the Beatles' Legend* in exchange for 25 percent of the proceeds.[16] Harold Lipton, also mentioned in the meeting, would earn 10 percent of the profits, and Hoernle, 5 percent. In error, Sakol and Bennett's financial breakdown listed 25 percent for Fran even though she had already been allotted 20 percent as Mal's manager.

When all the expenses had been tallied, the Sakol-Bennett proposal allowed 15 percent for Lily, albeit with the proviso that any subsequent claims or expenses would come from her end. Indeed, they warned her that "almost anyone who knew Mal could have deposited claims, which only come to light when and if the book is published." Concerned about her sister's peace of mind and worried that she might become ensnared in legal histrionics, Vera counseled Lily against getting into business with the two women, no matter how excited they were about publishing Mal's story. "Small wonder that Jeannie Sakol and Stephanie Bennett were so *enthusiastic*," Vera wrote. "They stand to benefit by 25 percent when you only *might* get 15."[17]

Desperate to avoid any more headaches over the fate of her husband's work, Lily passed on the opportunity. After confronting the many mysteries and entanglements left behind by her husband, who had been dead for more than two years by this juncture, she was flat-out exhausted. During those first awful days back in January 1976, she had struggled mightily to console Gary and Julie, whose father, already estranged, had been wrenched out of the world once and for all.

As it happened, Mal's parents, Fred and Joan, had been staying with their youngest daughter, June, in Greenwich after the New Year when the news of Mal's death arrived. Their daughter Barbara and her family were there, too. When she got the call from Lily, June was with her mother, who said, "He's dead, isn't he?" Moments later, when they shared the news with Fred, he replied, "It should have been me."[18]

Mal's parents and sisters immediately drove out to Sunbury to be with Lily and the children. "As soon as we stepped in the house," Barbara said, "the phone was ringing. Newspaper reporters wanted to know what happened, so we just said, 'no comment,' 'no comment,' 'no comment' because we didn't know what had happened ourselves."[19] In a strange twist of fate, June recalled the terrible irony when all the family members' Christmas cards from Mal began trickling in from the States in the days following his death.

In Sunbury, the house was flooded with condolence calls and letters—perhaps none more poignant than John's. "It is always harder for those left behind," he wrote to Lil. "He was a good man, and I loved him. He always loved you and *never* stopped talking about you and the children." In a postscript for Gary, Lennon wrote, "You are the Man of the house now. Look after your mum."[20]

Not surprisingly, when it came to Mal's parents, the whole awful business was already exacting a toll. Losing their eldest child when he was only forty was bad enough, but Mal's death was now compounded by the blur of headlines. "POLICE TO PROBE BIG MAL SHOOTING," the banner atop their hometown *Liverpool Echo* screamed. It seemed so utterly senseless to Fred and Joan, now seventy and sixty-one, respectively. "Had it all been some dreadful mistake?" they wondered, echoing what would plague Beatles fans and insiders alike for decades.[21] As with the outsize figure of Mal himself, the legends, rumors, and unanswered questions would grow in stature: Had his death been the result of some terrible accident or, worse yet, police brutality? Had the gun been loaded? Perhaps it hadn't even been a rifle at all, but some sort of air gun, a mere child's toy that the coppers had mistaken for a deadly weapon? In his darker moments, Fred would lash out about the Beatles themselves, lamenting that "Malcolm was all right till he met those four lads."[22] The awful experience was compounded, of course, by the misplacement of Mal's ashes. When it came to Mal, even the simple matter of holding a funeral had become a saga in itself.

After six long weeks, Mal's remains were finally located (still encased in Harry Nilsson's expensive urn) on a warehouse shelf at Heathrow. That February, his funeral was held in a private ceremony at the South West Middlesex Crematorium in Hanworth. While the Beatles themselves did not attend—the solemn event would quickly have transformed into a media circus if they had—George provided Lily with £5,000 to cover expenses, and Splinter's Bill Elliott and Bobby Purvis were on hand to pay their respects. The family sprinkled Mal's ashes on the grounds in the shape of a crucifix.[23]

A few days later, on February 26, a memorial service was held at the Church of All Hallows in Allerton, Liverpool. This time, Neil Aspinall and George Martin were in attendance, mourning in the very city where the Beatles had made their name all those years ago. Fred and Joan held a reception afterward in their home at 75 Waldgrave Road. That night, Fred removed the black tie he had been wearing every day since he first heard the awful news about his son. "That's it," he said, some fifty-two days later. "I feel that he's been laid to rest with dignity."[24]

With so little in the way of answers about how Mal had died, Fred and Joan turned their ire on Fran. "It broke my heart when they thought I was responsible for their son's death," she recalled. In an effort to honor her late boyfriend's memory, Fran composed a letter to his parents, sketching out the heartbreaking story of Mal's final hours, including his death. "Don't think poorly of your son," she wrote. "He simply could not face all the realities of life."[25] A few days later, she received a reply from Fred and Joan, acknowledging that they could tell why he had loved Fran so much.[26]

Even so, Mal's sudden loss would reverberate across the decades, leaving nearly everyone in a state of bewilderment, wondering if his death could have been avoided. "It was so crazy, so crazy," said Paul. "Mal was a big loveable bear of a roadie; he would go over the top occasionally, but we all knew him and never had any problems. The LAPD weren't so fortunate. They were just told that he was upstairs with a shotgun and so they ran up, kicked the door in, and shot him. His girlfriend had told them, 'He's a bit moody and he's got some downers.' Had I been there, I would have been able to say, 'Mal, don't be silly.' In fact, any of his friends could have talked him out of it without any sweat, because he was not a nutter. But his girlfriend—she was an LA girl—didn't know him that well. She should not have rung the cops, but that's the way it goes—a thump on the door, 'Where is he? Where's the assailant?' Bang, bang, bang. They don't ask questions. They shoot first."[27]

While Fran and Jody were away in Philadelphia, Laura Gross and Bobby Hughes drove to the duplex to render the master bedroom presentable for their return. Together, they cleaned the bloodstains off the walls and applied putty to the exposed surfaces. Not surprisingly, it was a god-awful, terrible experience. But things were even worse when it came to the area rug covering the bedroom's hardwood flooring. As with the walls, the rug was covered in bloodstains. Realizing they would never be able to salvage the thing, they rolled it up and, given the rug's unwieldy heft, pushed it over the balcony and into the yard below. By the time Fran returned in mid-February, Bobby had reassembled and repainted the bedroom.

Determined to see her friend through her grief, Laura lived with Fran and Jody in the duplex for the next three months, where they mourned the terrible loss together. In later years, an unfounded rumor emerged that Fran had sent Lily a bill for the destruction of her bedroom carpet. In truth, she had written to Mal's widow in the hope of getting some assistance in paying her late boyfriend's outstanding credit card bill.[28]

When it came to the terrible events of January 4, 1976, the LAPD would conduct a post-shooting investigation into Mal's death, which was determined to be a "justifiable homicide." Even so, the department's internal review board would recommend "remediation" for the officers involved in the incident—not a disciplinary measure in the face of misconduct but, rather, a means for encouraging them to be more cautious when engaging high-pressure, unpredictable situations such as the one they had encountered at Fran's Fourth Street duplex. According to the Shooting Review Board's report, the officers "should have taken more time to assess the situation properly"; the report concluded that their decision to enter the residence under such uncertain circumstances "placed the officers in a position of disadvantage and could have resulted in an officer being killed or seriously injured."[29]

Across the decades, Mal's family and friends have memorialized him in numerous ways. For the rest of their years at Waldgrave Road, Fred and Joan kept a framed photo of their son in a place of honor. It was the very same picture—Mal wearing his wide-brimmed cowboy hat—that the roadie had intended to grace the cover of his memoir. As the years passed, the couple learned to cope by raising money for charity. Joan began filling their tight living spaces with all manner of goods to be sold at "jumble" sales. Not surprisingly, Mal's mother earned the nickname "Jumbly Joan."[30]

The extended Evans family, for their part, made a special point of supporting the Alder Hey Children's Hospital in Knotty Ash, not far from where Fred and Joan were married back in 1934. Knowing Mal's unblemished love for children, it seemed an especially appropriate way to honor his memory. Later, after Mal's personal effects were returned to Lily, she would periodically sell some of the fancier pieces of memorabilia at auctions and donate the proceeds to Alder Hey.

But, for the most part, Mal's surviving friends and relatives celebrated him in subtle ways. For the balance of his working life, Ken Mansfield kept a framed photograph of the roadie on his desk, where he could see and remember him every day. It was a picture taken by Jackie Lomax of Mal and Ken together, riding the train to Philadelphia back in 1968.

Kevin Harrington honored Mal, day in and day out, by always having a few spare plectrums on him, just as his mentor had taught him. When he met up with Mal's son at a November 2021 screening of the *Get Back* docuseries in London, Kevin choked back tears as he proudly showed off the plectrums for Gary's inspection.

During the making of the *Beatles Anthology* series in the 1990s, Laura Gross, given her many years of expertise in the industry, was invited to help produce the project's promotional materials. She had grown especially close to Neil and was proud to help promote the *Anthology* documentary, knowing that its genesis had been Neil and Mal's work on *Scrapbook* and, later, *The Long and Winding Road* in the early 1970s. As the documentary was being readied for release, Klaus Voormann's cover art was brought into Neil's Apple office. And there, in a discreet corner of the painting, was Mal's name.

Laura could feel herself beginning to choke up. "Oh, Mal," she said.

"Yeah, I know," Neil replied, as the two gazed at the painting, missing their friend.[31]

But there would be towering moments, too, in which members of the Beatles' inner circle came to grips with Mal's glaring absence from their world. In one unforgettable instance, Gary opened the front door of 135 Staines Road East to find George Harrison on the stoop. It was 1982, and the Quiet Beatle had stopped by the Sunbury house, eager to get something off his chest. As Gary and Julie watched television in the living room, George followed Lily into the kitchen, where he unburdened himself of the guilt he felt at having talked Fran into going out with Mal. "George got the mugs down as I put the kettle on," Lily recalled. "He turned 'round and, with a watery eye, said, 'I'm sorry for what I did to you.'"[32]

While they were in the kitchen, Gary went upstairs and retrieved a pair of guitars that John had given to his father—an early Höfner model from their Liverpool days and a white Vox prototype from the mid-1960s, courtesy of the manufacturer.[33] George had great fun that day playing the guitars for Lily and the kids before leafing through old photo albums and reminiscing.[34]

And then there was the time, in 1989, when Yoko met with Lily, Gary, and Julie in her hotel suite in London, where they shared a meal and talked about old times. Mother and son were grateful, of course, for Yoko's heroic role in making good on Leena Kutti's discovery and swiftly returning Mal's effects to his family after their more than a dozen years in cold storage. In Gary's memory, it was a beautiful evening, although he had been nervous at the outset, self-conscious about his weight at the time. Yoko quickly intuited the source of his anxiety. "Just be yourself," she told him. "Stop trying to look slim for me." For Gary, this made all the difference. "That completely broke the ice," he recalled. As the hour grew late, Yoko made the sad realization that both their loved ones, in one way or another, had been vanquished by gun violence. The group shared a tearful embrace before they left Yoko's suite that night. As with George's visit to Sunbury, Yoko's warmth and generosity helped Gary rethink his dad's role not only in the bandmates' lives, but also in his own.[35]

Gary loved Mal unabashedly, but he never shied away from the reality of his father's lifestyle. Mal Evans lived his life in compartments, one of

Fred and Joan Evans in later years

them reserved for his family and the other for the Beatles. In the former, he reveled in the love of his wife and children, whom he unquestionably adored. In the latter, he lived like a medieval rogue, a freewheeling sort who sucked the marrow out of life at every moment. After his two worlds finally collided in the early months of 1974, he never really recovered. He had been *found out* by his wife and kids in irrevocable fashion, and he could never quite put the pieces back together again.

Mal ultimately lived the way he did—with great deliberateness, often recklessly, and without apology—because he expressly *chose* to do so, step by step. For him, being in close proximity to the Beatles' special brand of stardom trumped the joys and commitments of family. And with nary an exception, when it came to the Beatles versus his family, the Beatles won the sweepstakes every time.

But we won, too. People like Mal and Neil carry out the often invisible work that makes great art of any stripe truly happen. Their efforts on the road and in the studio not only helped to make the Beatles' personal and creative lives possible but also afforded them the space and freedom to produce their unique contributions to world music. In this way, they are no different from Brian Epstein or George Martin, who also played vital, highly particular roles in building the firmament of an art that will eclipse the ages.

Over the years, Mal liked to point out that the reason he got along so well with the fans was because he was one of them. Like the most die-hard among us, he couldn't get enough of his idols. "It was certainly exciting," said Mal about his time with the boys. "I could live on it. It is better than food and drink."[36] And while his addiction no doubt sowed the seeds of his undoing, he wouldn't—nay, *couldn't*—have had it any other way.

Mal in his heyday at EMI Recording Studios

ACKNOWLEDGMENTS

This book simply would not exist without the goodwill and perseverance of Gary Evans, who, for decades, was determined to see his father's extraordinary story told as fully and honestly as possible. Working with Gary and his wife, Vanda, has been one of the great joys of my life. The Evans family has been unfailingly generous with their time and patience. I am indebted to Julie Evans Rossow, Mal's daughter, for never shying away from my requests for more information about her father's life. I owe a similar debt of thanks to Barbara and June Evans, Mal's sisters; and to Shan Morgan, Lily's niece. I am also grateful for the kindness of Ned Ryan, Paul White, Vic Evans, Paul Evans, and Anne-Marie Carlin. This book is humbly dedicated to Lily Evans, Mal's widow, a model of class and resolve.

My sincere thanks are also due to Mal and Lily's extensive circle of friends and colleagues for sharing their memories: Stephen Adamick-Gries, Gary Adante, Nancy Andrews, Blair Aronson, Pete Best, Roag Best, Wallace Booth, Pattie Boyd, Tony Bramwell, Lizzie Bravo, Steve Brendell, Brute Force (Stephen Friedland), Leslie Cavendish, Mark Clarke, Ivor Davis, Richard DiLello, Micky Dolenz, Chip Douglas, Ken Doyle, Linda Easton, Marianne Evans, John Fanning, Peter Frampton, Merle Frimark, Laura Gross, Kevin Harrington, Bill Harry, Jann Haworth, Eunice Hayes, Jimmy Haymer, Leslie Samuels Healy, Derek Hughes, Bob Hussey, Mal Jefferson, Teddy Judge, Larry Kane, Freda Kelly, Tony King, John Kosh, Billy J. Kramer, John Kurlander, Judd Lander, Joanne Lenard, Michael Lindsay-Hogg, Rod Lynton, Ken Mansfield, Susan Markheim, Dave Mason, John Mason, Dana Mazetti, Mary McCartney, Mike McCartney, Vern Miller, Elliot Mintz, Joey Molland, Victoria Moran, Chris O'Dell, May

Pang, Alan Parsons, John Quinn, Johnny Reed, Rip Rense, Fran Hughes Reynolds, Dan Richter, Ethan Russell, Paul Saltzman, Chas Sandford, Bill Schnee, Georgeanna Slaybaugh, Richard Digby Smith, Var Smith, Allan Steckler, Chris Thomas, Ken Townsend, Lon Van Eaton, Klaus Voormann, Shaun Weiss, Alan White, and, last but not least, the Apple Scruffs, especially Carole, Chris, and Sue.

A number of historical witnesses kindly shared their energy and expertise in bringing this book to fruition, including Anita Alexander, Tony Bacon, Peter Blachley, Erika Calvert, Tom Carswell, Pearl Cawley, Rik Cooke, Stan Corwin, Ray Dagg, David Dalton, Andy DiBiccari, Alyss Dorese, Wilfred Frost, Ronald W. Gore Jr., Steve Hale, Tony Hanley, Nigel Hartnup, Phil Hilderbrand, David Kelly, Phil Kenzie, Dennis Killeen, Angela Kurban, Konosuke Kuwabara, Jimi LaLumia, Ray Magee, Bob Markel, Christopher Scarfe, Chris Shaw, Joel Soroka, Martin Torgoff, Rosemary Weeks, Benjamin Whitaker, Ann Wilson, Richard Keith Wolff, and Shelli Wolis.

Similarly, I am grateful for the many colleagues who provided specialized advice, including Tom Adams, McKinzie Brantley, Jane Clemetson, Doug Ellis, Mark Hayward, Angela Leighton-Jones, J. Michael Lennon, Catharine Lynch, Nigel Pearce, Martin Porter, Mark Pringle, Larry Schiller, Mike Sullivan, Ann Swabey, and Nik Wood-Jones.

The world of Beatles scholarship involves a dedicated and unfailingly generous community. I am grateful to so many Beatles writers and thinkers for their steadfast friendship and collegiality, including Jo Adams, Tom Adams, Jeffrey Ainis, Billy Amendola, Farshad Arbabi, Mitch Axelrod, Andy Babiuk, Keith Badman, Julia Baird, Glenn A. Baker, Jennifer Ballantyne, David Bedford, Belmo, Jim Berkenstadt, Tom Brennan, Alison Bumstead, Richard Buskin, James Campion, Peter Ames Carlin, Chris Carter, Harry Castleman, Bill Cermak, Ray Connolly, John Covach, Kathryn Cox, Terry Crain, Martin Creasy, Ken Dashow, Hunter Davies, Melissa Davis, Roger DiLernia, Howie Edelson, Mark Ellen, Scott Erickson, Walter Everett, Roger Farrington, Vinnie Favale, Christine Feldman-Barrett, Tom Fontaine, Tom Frangione, Mike Frontani, Chuck Geneslaw, Rob Geurtsen, Joe Goodden, Fred Goodman, Stefan Granados, Debbie Greenberg, George Gunby, Chuck Gunderson, Nick Hale, Paul Harris, Jonathan Harrison, Piers Hemmingsen, David Hepworth, Tom Hunyady, Keith James, Joe Johnson,

Ashley Kahn, Jude Southerland Kessler, Bill King, Philip Kirkland, Allan Kozinn, Howard Kramer, Peter Lee, Spencer Leigh, Rob Leonard, Gay Linvill, Bob Males, Steve Matteo, Joe Mayo, Ken McNab, Ken Michaels, Wenty Morris, Patti Murawski, Pete Nash, Alan Parker, Andy Pennance, Wally Podrazik, Richard Porter, Hudson Ranney, Tim Riley, Dan Rivkin, Robert Rodriguez, Jim Ryan, Susan Ratisher Ryan, Christopher Sandford, Sara Schmidt, Dave Schwensen, Ken Sharp, Rob Sheffield, Adrian Sinclair, Jeff Slate, Cevin Soling, Brian Southall, Jackie Spencer, Bruce Spizer, Roger Stormo, Tony Traguardo, Steve Turner, David Venturo, Davide Verazzini, Vincent Vigil, Phil Winfield, John C. Winn, Doug Wolfberg, Eddie Zareh, and Stuart Zolotorow.

One of the great joys of living and working in an academic setting involves the opportunity to engage with students and colleagues. For their efforts in transcribing Mal's manuscripts, I am thankful for several graduate research assistants in Monmouth University's Department of English, including Faith Bates, Kaitlyn Lash, Jennifer Rivera, and T. J. Spicer. This book was supported, in part, by a Creativity and Research Grant from Monmouth University. Undergraduate student Carlee Migliorisi deserves particular mention for her remarkable, highly skilled efforts at cataloging the vast number of photographs, drawings, and correspondence in the Malcolm Frederick Evans Archives. A special shout-out to Kurt Wagner, our intrepid university librarian, for whom no research assignment is too small or unworthy. Special thanks are due to Jonathan Clyde and Aaron Bremner at Apple Corps for generously sharing photos from the company's archive.

I am thankful for the encouragement and support of a host of friends and family, including Patrick Alexander, Sheri Anderson, Isabel Atherton, Steven Bachrach, William Baker, Eileen Chapman, John Christopher, Jeff Cook, Brett Cooke, Todd Davis, James Decker, Chris DeRosa, Linda Deutsch, Mona Dooley, Mike Farragher, Furg, Dave Golland, Susan Goulding, Ryan and Chelsea Harshbarger, Pat Leahy, Colleen Lumadue, Justin Lumadue, Jonathan Meer, Nancy Mezey, Dinty W. Moore, Peter and Becca Moran, Carmen Nitsche, Mike Plodwick, Joe Rapolla, Joe Riccardello, Bob Santelli, George and Kathy Severini, Joe Studlick, Bill Timoney, Tortle, David Tripold, Rich Veit, Kurt Wagner, Andy and Melissa Womack, Jennifer Womack, and George Wurzbach.

I am especially grateful to my agent, Matthew Elblonk, whose dedication to ferreting out the truth of Mal's story rivals my own. Matthew, you are an inspiration. Special thanks are also due to Mary Pender of the United Talent Agency and to Matthew's team at DeFiore, including Linda Kaplan, Parik Kostan, and Adam Schear. Likewise, I am grateful for the legal advice and assistance provided by Lee Feldshon, who built the partnership at the heart of the Malcolm Frederick Evans Archives; Eric Berry, for his unparalleled acumen and wry sense of humor; and Mark Burton, who originally paved the way for the project to move forward.

I owe a debt of gratitude to Carrie Thornton at HarperCollins. Her vision and tenacity are deeply appreciated. Carrie's superb team also merits special mention, including Heidi Richter, Megan Wilson, Drew Henry, Angie Boutin, Rachel Meyers, Kyran Cassidy, and Matthew Daddona, as well as HarperCollins U.K.'s Imogen Gordon Clark. A number of folks shared their advice and goodwill throughout the course of this project, including John Bezzini, Ray Brunt, Ken Campbell, Al Cattabiani, Scott Freiman, Katie Kapurch, Jason Kruppa, Mark Lapidos, Chip Madinger, George A. Martin, Dan Matovina, Jacob Michael, Kit O'Toole, Jeff Pollack, Ed Rakowski, Al Sussman, Steve Valvano, Ward Whipple, and my father, Fred Womack, who read multiple drafts with great enthusiasm.

It is impossible to imagine the completion of this book—or any study of Mal Evans, for that matter—without the fearless work of Leena Kutti, who saved the roadie's archives from the garbage heap. And if there is a hero in this story, it is surely Yoko Ono. Too often, Ono, despite her commitment to peace, freedom, and the arts, has served as a lightning rod for critics and naysayers. But in 1988, she accomplished what agents, attorneys, and publishers had failed to do, often intentionally, for more than a dozen years: she put the wheels in motion so that Lily, Gary, and Julie could have access to Mal's legacy. Bravo, Ocean Child.

My work on Mal Evans and the Beatles would simply not be possible without the generosity and friendship of Mark Lewisohn. You are a treasure, and we are all the better for your steadfast efforts at getting the Beatles' story right. Peter Hicks deserves a special note of thanks for sharing more than a decade's worth of primary research with me, as well as for being a fount of inspiration. I am indebted to Simon Weitzman for dreaming up this cockeyed plan in the first place. You, sir, are a mensch. I am grateful, as always, for the efforts of Nicole Michael, my indefatigable publicist and fellow Wonderwallian.

P.S. Thank you for loving me, Jeanine Womack. Thank you for being there. You make everything possible.

NOTES

PROLOGUE: WINDSCREEN

1. George Martin with Jeremy Hornsby, *All You Need Is Ears* (New York: St. Martin's Press, 1979), p. 130.
2. Paul Du Noyer, "Just Out of Shot: Interview with Neil Aspinall," *Mojo* 35 (October 1996), p. 75.
3. Mark Lewisohn, *Tune In: The Beatles—All These Years* (New York: Crown, 2013), p. 584.
4. Lewisohn, *Tune In*, p. 728.
5. Mal Evans, "Diaries," Unpublished, January 20, 1963, Malcolm Frederick Evans Archives (hereafter MFEA).
6. Tony Barrow, liner notes, *Please Please Me*, Parlophone, 1963.
7. Mal Evans, "Living the Beatles' Legend: Or 200 Miles to Go," unpublished manuscript (hereafter "LTBL"), 1976, p. 33, MFEA.
8. Evans, "Diaries," January 22, 1963.
9. *The Talent Spot,* radio script, January 22, 1963; Evans, "Diaries," January 22, 1963.
10. Evans, "Diaries," January 23, 1963, and *passim*; The Beatles, *The Beatles Anthology* (San Francisco: Chronicle Books, 2000), p. 83.
11. Evans, "LTBL," p. 33.
12. Barry Miles, *The Beatles Diary*, Volume 1, *The Beatles Years* (London: Omnibus, 2009), p. 169; The Beatles, *The Beatles Anthology*, p. 83.
13. Evans, "LTBL," p. 33.
14. Miles, *The Beatles Diary*, 1:169.
15. The Beatles, *The Beatles Anthology*, p. 83.
16. Evans, "Diaries," January 23, 1963; Keith Badman, *The Beatles Off the Record: Outrageous Opinions and Unrehearsed Interviews* (London: Omnibus, 2001), p. 48.

CHAPTER 1: A RIGHT LITTLE BASTARD

1. Evans, "LTBL," p. 5.
2. Mal Evans, "Notebook, 1975," p. 104, MFEA.
3. Evans, "Notebook, 1975," p. 104.
4. Author interview with Barbara Evans, January 11, 2022.
5. Author interview with June Evans, June 6, 2021.
6. Author interview with Barbara Evans, May 20, 2021.

7. Evans, "LTBL," p. 6.
8. Author interview with Barbara Evans, January 11, 2022.
9. Evans, "LTBL," p. 5.
10. Frederick Evans, letter to Pat Simmons, April 12, 1976.
11. Author interview with Barbara Evans, January 11, 2022.
12. Author interview with Barbara Evans, January 11, 2022; see Forces War Records, "F. W. Evans, Royal Air Force, Technical Branch," www.forces-war-records.co.uk/.
13. Author interview with Barbara Evans, January 11, 2022.
14. Evans, "LTBL," p. 8.
15. Evans, "LTBL," p. 10.
16. Evans, "LTBL," p. 9.
17. Author interview with Barbara Evans, January 11, 2022.
18. Author interview with Barbara Evans, May 20, 2021.
19. Evans, "LTBL," p. 11.
20. Peter Hicks, interview with Eunice Hayes, November 26, 2019.
21. Evans, "LTBL," p. 11.
22. Author interview with June Evans, June 6, 2021.
23. Evans, "LTBL," p. 12.
24. Evans, "LTBL," pp. 11–12.

CHAPTER 2: FUNFAIR

1. Evans, "LTBL," p. 19.
2. Evans, "LTBL," p. 20.
3. Evans, "LTBL," p. 20.
4. Evans, "LTBL," p. 23.
5. Evans, "LTBL," p. 16.
6. Evans, "LTBL," p. 13.
7. Email from Mike Sullivan, January 21, 2021.
8. Evans, "LTBL," p. 27.
9. Evans, "LTBL," pp. 27–28.
10. Evans, "Notebook, 1975," p. 14.
11. Evans, "Notebook, 1975," p. 13.
12. Author interview with Barbara Evans, January 11, 2022.
13. Author interview with June Evans, June 6, 2021.
14. Evans, "LTBL," pp. 14–15.
15. Evans, "LTBL," pp. 14–15.
16. Evans, "LTBL," pp. 14–15.
17. National Service (Armed Forces) Act, 1939; extended as National Service Act, 1948.
18. Evans, "LTBL," p. 11.
19. Author interview with Barbara Evans, January 11, 2022.
20. Author interview with Mark Lewisohn, December 11, 2021.
21. Evans, "LTBL," p. 28.
22. Evans, "LTBL," p. 28.
23. Evans, "LTBL," pp. 28–29.
24. Author interview with June Evans, June 6, 2021.
25. Peter Hicks, interview with Siobhan Maher Kennedy, December 6, 2021.
26. Email from Billy Maher, November 27, 2021.

27. Evans, "LTBL," pp. 13–14.
28. Evans, "LTBL," p. 17.
29. Evans, "LTBL," p. 17.

CHAPTER 3: A CELLARFUL OF NOISE

1. Author interview with Julie Evans Rossow, January 20, 2022.
2. Author interview with Julie Evans Rossow, January 20, 2022.
3. Lily Evans, Curriculum Vitae, 1982.
4. Author interview with Barbara Evans, May 20, 2021.
5. Author interview with June Evans, June 6, 2021.
6. Author interview with Barbara Evans, May 20, 2021.
7. Author interview with Shirley Ann Morgan, April 22, 2021.
8. Email from Julie Evans Rossow, January 26, 2022.
9. Author interview with Julie Evans Rossow, January 20, 2022.
10. Laura Gross, radio interview with Mal Evans, KCSN FM, November 29, 1975.
11. See www.beatlesbible.com/people/mal-evans, July 17, 2014; email from Anita Alexander, January 21, 2022.
12. Email from Ronnie Gore Jr., August 20, 2021.
13. Author interview with Barbara Evans, May 20, 2021.
14. Evans, "Notebook, 1975," p. 117; author interview with Gary Evans, January 28, 2022.
15. Author interview with Barbara Evans, May 20, 2021.
16. Peter Hicks, interview with Eunice Hayes, November 26, 2019.
17. Gross, interview with Mal Evans, November 29, 1975.
18. Author interview with Shirley Ann Morgan, January 28, 2022.
19. David Frost, interview with Mal Evans, in *A Salute to the Beatles: Once Upon a Time*, ABC-TV, May 21, 1975; The Beatles, *The Beatles Anthology*, p. 85.
20. Author interview with Debbie Greenberg, August 25, 2021.
21. Frost, interview with Mal Evans, May 21, 1975.
22. Author interview with Debbie Greenberg, August 25, 2021.
23. Lewisohn, *Tune In*, p. 584.
24. Julia Baird, *Paul Talks: Paul McCartney in Conversation*, compact disc, 1987.
25. Author interview with Pete Best, July 16, 2023.
26. Neil Aspinall, "The First Official Mal Evans Story," *The Beatles Book* 46 (May 1967), p. 11.
27. Evans, "LTBL," p. 18.
28. Author interview with Shirley Ann Morgan, April 22, 2021.
29. See Vicki Pearce, "Charabanc: All Aboard the Sharrabang!" *Warts and All*, July 20, 2019, wartsandall.blog/2019/07/20/charabanc-all-aboard-the-sharrabang/.
30. Pearce, "Charabanc."
31. Evans, "LTBL," p. 18.
32. Ray Connolly, "Destroyed by the Beatles," *Daily Mail*, April 20, 2005, p. 34.
33. The Beatles, *The Beatles Anthology*, p. 85.
34. Baird, *Paul Talks*.
35. Evans, "LTBL," p. 34.
36. Lewisohn, *Tune In*, p. 514.
37. Evans, "LTBL," p. 34.

38. See Spencer Leigh, *The Cavern Cave: Rise of the Beatles and Merseybeat* (Carmarthen, U.K.: McNidder and Grace, 2015), p. 34; see Ken McNab, *The Beatles in Scotland* (Edinburgh: Birlinn, 2008), pp. 195–96.
39. Author interview with Wallace Booth, August 19, 2021.
40. Peter Hicks, interview with John Quinn, February 16 and May 9, 2020.
41. Peter Hicks, interview with John Fanning, September 27, 2020.
42. See the *Oxford English Dictionary* for "road manager" and "roadie," respectively; Richard O. Boyer, "Profiles: The Hot Bach, Part I," *The New Yorker*, June 24, 1944, p. 30; see also Jenny Fabian and Johnny Byrne, *Groupie* (London: New English Library, 1969).
43. Author interview with Mal Jefferson, March 7, 2021.
44. Lewisohn, *Tune In*, p. 478.
45. Barrow, "Big Mal, the Beatles' Roadie," *The Beatles Book* 180 (April 1991), p. 6.
46. Aspinall, "The First Official Mal Evans Story," p. 11; The Beatles, *The Beatles Anthology*, p. 85.

CHAPTER 4: ROADIE?

1. Evans, "LTBL," p. 36.
2. Tony Bramwell with Rosemary Kingsland, *Magical Mystery Tours: My Life with the Beatles* (London: Robson, 2005), p. 68.
3. Aspinall, "The First Official Mal Evans Story," p. 11.
4. Evans, "LTBL," p. 36.
5. Martin, interview with Lily Evans, 2004.
6. Aspinall, "The First Official Mal Evans Story," p. 11.
7. The Beatles, *The Beatles Anthology*, p. 85.
8. Lewisohn, *Tune In*, p. 675.
9. Lewisohn, *Tune In*, p. 606.
10. Evans, "LTBL," p. 38.
11. Leigh, *The Cavern Cave*, p. 94.
12. Ken Doyle, interview with Mal Evans, KCSN FM, December 14, 1975.
13. Brian Higham, "My Story," *Manchester Beat,* 2012, www.manchesterbeat.com/index.php/my-story/brian-higham.
14. Evans, "LTBL," p. 35.
15. Evans, "LTBL," p. 35.
16. Evans, "Diaries," May 7, 1963.
17. Evans, "Diaries," January 1, 1963.
18. Evans, "Diaries," January–April 1963.
19. Author interview with Shirley Ann Morgan, February 17, 2022.
20. Evans, "Diaries," April 6–7, 1963.
21. See www.beatlesbible.com/people/mal-evans, November 15, 2019.
22. The Beatles, *The Beatles Anthology*, p. 85.
23. Evans, "Diaries," April 9, 1963.
24. Evans, "Diaries," April 20, 1963.
25. Leigh, *The Cavern Cave,* p. 109.
26. Evans, "Diaries," May 4–5, 1963.
27. Evans, "Diaries," January 23, 1963.
28. Evans, "Diaries," May 19, 1963.

29. Evans, "Diaries," May 13, 1963.
30. The Beatles, *The Beatles Anthology*, p. 85.
31. Aspinall, "The First Official Mal Evans Story," p. 12.
32. Author interview with Tony Bramwell, August 6, 2021.
33. Author interview with Booth, August 19, 2021; see McNab, *The Beatles in Scotland*, p. 196.
34. Evans, "LTBL," p. 38.
35. See Parliament's "Average Weekly Earnings" debate of March 21, 1963, in Hansard, vol. 674, cc100–1W, hansard.parliament.uk/.
36. Evans, "Diaries," July 4–5, 1963.
37. Email from Billy Maher, November 27, 2021.
38. Evans, "Diaries," 1963.
39. Philip Norman, *Shout! The Beatles in Their Generation* (New York: Simon and Schuster, 1981), p. 263.
40. Martin, interview with Lily Evans, 2004.
41. Frederick Evans, letter to Pat Simmons, April 12, 1976.
42. Author interview with June Evans, June 6, 2021.

CHAPTER 5: A FREE MAN

1. Evans, "LTBL," pp. 38–39.
2. Author interview with Best, July 16, 2023.
3. Author interview with Lewisohn, January 29, 2022.
4. Leigh, *The Cavern Cave*, p. 113.
5. Evans, "LTBL," p. 40.
6. The Beatles, *The Beatles Anthology*, p. 85.
7. Evans, "LTBL," p. 40.
8. Author interview with Derek Hughes, February 19, 2022.
9. The Beatles, *The Beatles Anthology*, p. 85.
10. Cynthia Lennon, *John* (London: Hodder and Stoughton, 2005), p. 132.
11. Aspinall, "The Beatles and Me! [Part 2]," *16 Magazine* (June 1965), p. 26.
12. Evans, "LTBL," p. 41.
13. Author interview with Derek Hughes, February 19, 2022.
14. Author interview with Derek Hughes, February 19, 2022.
15. Evans, "Diaries," August 30, 1963.
16. Evans, "LTBL," p. 42.
17. Evans, "LTBL," p. 42.
18. Evans, "LTBL," p. 42.
19. Evans, "LTBL," p. 44.
20. Evans, "LTBL," p. 44.
21. The Beatles, *The Beatles Anthology,* p. 85.
22. "Welcome to Mal," *The Beatles Book* 89 (September 1983), p. 14.

CHAPTER 6: THE BIG CLUBBO!

1. Evans, "Diaries," September 11, 1963.
2. Evans, "LTBL," p. 40.
3. Aspinall, "Look What Happened in Just One Year," *Record Mirror*, October 19, 1963, p. 6.

4. Quoted in Bob Spitz, *The Beatles: The Biography* (Boston: Little, Brown, 2005), pp. 427–28.
5. Evans, "LTBL," p. 40.
6. Evans, "LTBL," p. 42.
7. Evans, "LTBL," p. 45.
8. Spitz, *The Beatles*, p. 434.
9. Evans, "LTBL," p. 45.
10. Evans, "LTBL," p. 44.
11. Colm Keane, *The Beatles' Irish Concerts* (Bray: Capel Island Press, 2008), chap. 8.
12. Spitz, *The Beatles*, p. 445.
13. George Gunby, *Hello Goodbye: The Story of Alistair "Mr. Fixit" Taylor* (Belper, U.K.: Yesterday Once More, 2002), p. 16.
14. Billy Shepherd [Peter Jones], *The True Story of the Beatles* (New York: Bantam, 1964), p. 192.
15. Evans, "LTBL," pp. 60–61.
16. Author interview with Barbara Evans, February 18, 2022.
17. Bramwell, *Magical Mystery Tours*, p. 92.
18. Bramwell, *Magical Mystery Tours*, p. 92.
19. Author interview with Bramwell, August 6, 2021.
20. Evans, "LTBL," p. 46.
21. Evans, "LTBL," p. 47.
22. Paul McCartney, letter to Mal Evans, November 1963.
23. Evans, "LTBL," p. 47.
24. Martin, interview with Lily Evans, 2004.

CHAPTER 7: MAL, CRIPPLES!

1. Evans, "LTBL," p. 49.
2. Evans, "LTBL," p. 49.
3. Author interview with Derek Hughes, February 19, 2022.
4. Author interview with Derek Hughes, February 19, 2022.
5. Evans, "LTBL," p. 50.
6. Hunter Davies, *The Beatles: The Authorized Biography* (London: Heinemann, 1968), p. 176.
7. As it turned out, John's Jumbo had been stolen. It was recovered in 2015. See "How John Lennon's Long-Lost $2.4 Million Gibson J-160E Guitar Was Found," *Guitar World*, November 10, 2015, www.guitarworld.com/gear/how-john-lennons-long-lost-24-million.
8. Lewisohn, *Tune In*, pp. 107, 752.
9. The Beatles, *The Beatles Anthology*, p. 142.
10. The Beatles, *The Beatles Anthology*, p. 85.
11. Connolly, "Destroyed by the Beatles," p. 34.
12. Evans, "LTBL," p. 53.
13. Evans, "LTBL," p. 54.
14. See Michael Braun, *Love Me Do!: The Beatles' Progress* (London: Penguin, 1964), pp. 78–79.
15. Evans, "LTBL," p. 55.
16. Author interview with Gary Evans, December 4, 2020.
17. Miles, *The Beatles Diary*, 1:266.

18. Evans, "LTBL," pp. 55–56.
19. Evans, "Diaries," February 1, 1964.
20. Evans, "Diaries," February 4, 1964.

CHAPTER 8: MY FAVORITE ANIMAL

1. Evans, "LTBL," pp. 56–57.
2. See Andy Babiuk, *Beatles Gear: All the Fab Four's Instruments, from Stage to Studio* (San Francisco: Backbeat, 2001), pp. 88–89.
3. Evans, "LTBL," p. 56.
4. Evans, "LTBL," p. 57.
5. Evans, "LTBL," pp. 57–58.
6. Evans, "LTBL," p. 58.
7. Spitz, *The Beatles*, p. 478.
8. Evans, "LTBL," p. 59.
9. Evans, "LTBL," p. 60.
10. Evans, "LTBL," p. 60.
11. Evans, "Diaries," February 21, 23, 1964.
12. Evans, "Diaries," February 24, 1964; see "Case Against Beatles' Company Fails: Manager Was Hurt in Road Crash," *Liverpool Echo*, February 24, 1964, p. 8.
13. Mal Evans, letter to Lily Evans, March 3, 1964.
14. Mal Evans, letter to Lily Evans, March 18, 1964.
15. Evans, "Diaries," March 18, 1964.
16. Evans, "LTBL," p. 48.
17. The Beatles, *The Beatles Anthology*, p. 109.
18. Bramwell, *Magical Mystery Tours*, p. 96.
19. Author interview with June Evans, June 6, 2021.
20. Evans, "LTBL," p. 66.
21. Evans, "LTBL," p. 67.
22. Mal Evans, letter to Lily Evans, April 17, 1964.
23. Evans, "LTBL," p. 68.
24. Evans, "LTBL," p. 68.

CHAPTER 9: THE DEMON

1. Jim Berkenstadt, *The Beatle Who Vanished* (Madison, Wisc.: Rock and Roll Detective, 2013), p. 3.
2. Berkenstadt, *The Beatle Who Vanished*, p. 61.
3. Quoted in Berkenstadt, *The Beatle Who Vanished*, p. 79.
4. Quoted in Berkenstadt, *The Beatle Who Vanished*, p. 62.
5. Evans, "LTBL," p. 68.
6. Berkenstadt, *The Beatle Who Vanished*, p. 62.
7. The Beatles, *The Beatles Anthology*, p. 139.
8. Evans, "LTBL," p. 70.
9. Evans, "LTBL," p. 69.
10. Evans, "LTBL," p. 70.
11. Berkenstadt, *The Beatle Who Vanished*, p. 63.
12. Evans, "LTBL," pp. 71–72.
13. Evans, "LTBL," p. 72.

14. Al Aronowitz, "The Return of the Beatles," *The Saturday Evening Post*, August 8, 1964, p. 28.
15. Berkenstadt, *The Beatle Who Vanished*, p. 106.
16. See Lennon's 1970 interview with Jann Wenner, *Lennon Remembers* (New York: Verso, 2000), pp. 61–62.
17. Glenn A. Baker with Roger DiLernia, *The Beatles Down Under: The 1964 Australia and New Zealand Tour* (Glebe, Australia: Wild and Woolley, 1982), p. 35.
18. Peter Hicks, interview with Eunice Hayes, November 26, 2019.
19. Peter Hicks, interview with Eunice Hayes, November 26, 2019.
20. Evans, "LTBL," pp. 73–74.
21. Miles, *The Beatles Diary*, 1:326.
22. Evans, "LTBL," p. 76.
23. Baker, *The Beatles Down Under*, p. 80; for exemplars of the news coverage, see "Girl Slashes Wrists Near Beatles," *Sydney Morning Herald*, June 24, 1964, p. 1; and "Frantic Teens Rout Cops and Rush Beatles," *Chicago Tribune*, June 24, 1964, p. 45.
24. The Beatles, *The Beatles Anthology*, p. 142.
25. Baker, *The Beatles Down Under*, p. 80.
26. Evans, "LTBL," p. 76.
27. Evans, "LTBL," p. 75.
28. Evans, "LTBL," p. 74.
29. "People Behind the Stars, No. 4: Road Manager Mal Evans," p. 33.

CHAPTER 10: MR. NICE GUY

1. Mal Evans, letter to Lily Evans, July 5, 1964.
2. Mal Evans, letter to Lily Evans, July 5, 1964.
3. Author interview with Gary Evans, July 30, 2021.
4. Another extra can be see lugging an upright bass backstage after the forty-minute mark. This uncredited actor is often mistakenly assumed to be Mal. Studying the individual frames discounts this possibility.
5. Evans, "LTBL," p. 67.
6. The Beatles, *The Beatles Anthology*, p. 144.
7. Christopher Sandford, *McCartney* (New York: Carroll and Graf, 2006), p. 88.
8. Howard Sounes, *Fab: An Intimate Life of Paul McCartney* (Boston: Da Capo, 2010), p. 473.
9. Evans, "Diaries," August 10, 1964.
10. Evans, "Diaries," August 11, 1964.
11. See Babiuk, *Beatles Gear*, p. 138.
12. A. J. S. Rayl and Curt Gunther, *Beatles '64: A Hard Day's Night in America* (New York: Doubleday, 1989), p. 73.
13. Evans, "LTBL," pp. 81–82.
14. The Beatles, *The Beatles Anthology*, p. 188.
15. Evans, "LTBL," p. 77.
16. Davies, *The Beatles*, p. 176.
17. Ivor Davis, *The Beatles and Me on Tour* (Los Angeles: Cockney Kid, 2014), p. 16.
18. Author interview with Larry Kane, December 28, 2021.
19. Larry Kane, *Ticket to Ride: Inside the Beatles' 1964 Tour That Changed the World* (Philadelphia, Pa.: Running Press, 2003), p. 185.

20. Rayl and Gunther, *Beatles '64*, p. 101.
21. Chuck Gunderson, *Some Fun Tonight!: The Backstage Story of How the Beatles Rocked America—The Historic Tours of 1964–1966* (Milwaukee, Wisc.: Backbeat, 2016), 1:51.
22. Georgiana Steele-Waller, *In My Life, So Far . . .* (Glendale, Ariz.: Georgiana Steele-Waller, 2013), p. 11.
23. Author interview with Kane, December 28, 2021.
24. Kane, *Ticket to Ride*, p. 36.
25. Author interview with Kane, December 28, 2021; see Davis, *The Beatles and Me on Tour*, pp. 158–59.

CHAPTER 11: SEVEN LEVELS

1. Kane, *Ticket to Ride*, p. 186.
2. Evans, "LTBL," p. 78.
3. Evans, "LTBL," p. 78.
4. Mal Evans, undated letter to Lily Evans, August 1964.
5. Evans, "LTBL," p. 77.
6. Spitz, *The Beatles*, pp. 535–36.
7. Spitz, *The Beatles*, pp. 535–36.
8. Davies, *The Beatles*, p. 176.
9. The Beatles, *The Beatles Anthology*, p. 157.
10. Kane, *Ticket to Ride*, p. 183.
11. Kane, *Ticket to Ride*, p. 183.
12. Badman, *The Beatles Off the Record*, p. 124.
13. Larry Kane, *Lennon Revealed* (Philadelphia, Pa.: Running Press, 2005), p. 199.
14. Evans, "LTBL," pp. 79–80.
15. Evans, "LTBL," pp. 79–80.
16. Evans, "LTBL," pp. 79–80.
17. Evans, "LTBL," pp. 80–81.
18. The Beatles, *The Beatles Anthology*, p. 157.
19. Debbie Geller, *In My Life: The Brian Epstein Story* (New York: Thomas Dunne, 2000), p. 93.
20. The Beatles, *The Beatles Anthology*, p. 110.
21. Barrow, *John, Paul, George, Ringo, and Me: The Real Beatles Story* (London: Carlton, 2005), p. 137.
22. Author interview with June Evans, June 6, 2021.

CHAPTER 12: CHANNEL SWIMMER

1. "Alf Bicknell: Gary James's Interview with the Beatles' Chauffeur," *Classic Bands*, 1996, www.classicbands.com/AlfBicknellInterview.html.
2. See Evans, "LTBL," p. 41.
3. This number is disputed by music historians who sometimes discount the status of "Please Please Me" as a chart-topper. While the song earned the number one spot on both the *NME* and *Melody Maker* charts, it notched only a number two showing on *Record Retailer*, which later evolved into the official "U.K. Singles Chart."
4. Derek Taylor, "Making a Gold Record," *KRLA Beat*, May 5, 1965, p. 5.
5. James Craig, "The Beatles' Studio Secrets," *Record World*, October 31, 1964, p. 9.
6. Badman, *The Beatles Off the Record*, p. 297.

7. John Lennon and Yoko Ono, *All We Are Saying: The Last Major Interview with John Lennon and Yoko Ono* (New York: Griffin, 2000), p. 173.
8. Hicks, interview with John Fanning, September 27, 2020.
9. Evans, "LTBL," pp. 82–83.
10. Evans, "LTBL," pp. 85–86.
11. Evans, "LTBL," p. 86.
12. Evans, "LTBL," pp. 87–88.
13. Evans, "LTBL," p. 88.
14. Evans, "LTBL," p. 89.
15. Hicks, interview with Fanning, September 27, 2020.
16. Author interview with Fanning, February 17, 2022; in Fanning's memory, Mal's gift from the Beatles came in the form of a new home in Liverpool, but this recollection doesn't cohere with the Evans family's time line: Mal purchased the Mossley Hill property in early 1958, selling it for a modest profit in 1967. For more information regarding the Jaguar, see "Neil's Present," *The Beatles Book*, 18 (January 1965), p. 29.
17. Ray Coleman, "Inside Showbiz," *Melody Maker*, January 30, 1965, pp. 13, 20.
18. Babiuk, *Beatles Gear*, p. 157.
19. The Beatles, *The Beatles Anthology*, p. 167.
20. Geoff Emerick, with Howard Massey, *Here, There, and Everywhere: My Life Recording the Music of the Beatles* (New York: Gotham, 2006), p. 121.
21. Kane, *Ticket to Ride*, pp. 196–97.
22. Kane, *Ticket to Ride*, p. 198.
23. Larry Kane, *When They Were Boys* (Philadelphia, Pa.: Running Press, 2013), pp. 397–98.
24. Evans, "LTBL," p. 91.
25. Dave Hull, "Visitors to Movie Location Tell of Beatlemania Antics," *KRLA Beat*, March 17, 1965, p. 4.
26. Louise Harrison, *My Kid Brother's Band: A.K.A the Beatles* (Morley, U.K.: Acclaim Press, 2014), p. 312.
27. Evans, "LTBL," p. 92.
28. Rudolf Aigmüller [Tony Barrow], "Filming, Curling, and Playing in Austria," *The Beatles Book* 109 (May 1985), p. 36.
29. Evans, "LTBL," p. 90.
30. Evans, "LTBL," p. 90.
31. Martin, interview with Lily Evans, 2004.

CHAPTER 13: GREEK GOD

1. Evans, "LTBL," p. 94.
2. Evans, "LTBL," pp. 94–95.
3. Evans, "My Life with the Beatles," *16 Magazine*, May 1965, p. 11. Tony Barrow later pointed out that he authored many of the *16 Magazine* pieces published "under the signatures of Neil Aspinall and Mal Evans, and with their collaboration," billed as "exclusive from Liverpool, England." See Barrow, *John, Paul, George, Ringo, and Me*, p. 113.
4. Evans, "LTBL," p. 95.
5. Evans, "LTBL," p. 96; in his memoir, Bicknell reported that his ankle, rather than his leg, had been broken during the go-cart outing. See Alf Bicknell with Garry Marsh,

Baby, You Can Drive My Car! (Newcastle, U.K.: Number 9 Books, 1989), diary entry for June 30, 1965.

6. Evans, "My Life with the Beatles," p. 11.
7. Connolly, "Destroyed by the Beatles," p. 34.
8. See, for example, NEMS Enterprises' contract rider for the Beatles' August 18, 1965, performance at San Diego's Balboa Stadium.
9. Mal Evans, "Beatles—U.S.A." (hereafter "BUSA"), 1965, p. 7.
10. Kane, *Lennon Revealed*, pp. 166–67, 169.
11. Kane, *Lennon Revealed*, p. 169.
12. Evans, "BUSA," pp. 16–18.
13. Evans, "BUSA," p. 22.
14. See Dave Schwensen, *The Beatles at Shea Stadium: The Story Behind Their Greatest Concert* (Burlington, Vt.: North Shore, 2013), p. 121.
15. Schwensen, *The Beatles at Shea Stadium*, p. 121.
16. Evans, "BUSA," p. 23.
17. Evans, "BUSA," p. 23.
18. Author interview with Georgeanna Slaybaugh, December 29, 2021.
19. Author interview with Slaybaugh, December 29, 2021.
20. Evans, "BUSA," p. 42.
21. Evans, "BUSA," pp. 43–44.
22. Evans, "BUSA," p. 44.
23. Author interview with Slaybaugh, December 29, 2021.
24. Author interview with Slaybaugh, December 29, 2021.
25. Evans, "BUSA," pp. 51–52; author interview with Slaybaugh, December 29, 2021.
26. Kane, *Lennon Revealed*, p. 176.
27. Evans, "BUSA," pp. 57–58.
28. Evans, "BUSA," p. 68.
29. Evans, "BUSA," pp. 66, 68–69.
30. Evans, "BUSA," p. 73; the rental for the Benedict Canyon estate was actually $3,500, plus a $2,000 deposit. See Gunderson, *Some Fun Tonight!*, 2:103.
31. Evans, "BUSA," pp. 75–76.

CHAPTER 14: THE ELVIS SITUATION

1. Bicknell, *Baby, You Can Drive My Car!*, diary entry for August 26, 1965.
2. Mikal Gilmore, "Beatles' Acid Test: How LSD Opened the Door to 'Revolver,'" *Rolling Stone*, August 25, 2016, www.rollingstone.com/feature/beatles-acid-test-how-lsd-opened-the-door-to-revolver-251417/.
3. Author interview with Ken Mansfield, January 14, 2021.
4. Mansfield, *The Roof: The Beatles' Final Concert* (New York: Post Hill, 2018), p. 105.
5. Mansfield, *The Roof*, p. 105.
6. Evans, "BUSA," pp. 97–98.
7. Evans, "BUSA," p. 117.
8. Evans, "BUSA," p. 117.
9. See Chris Hutchins and Peter Thompson, *Elvis Meets the Beatles: The Untold Story of Their Entangled Lives* (London: John Blake, 2004), p. 166.
10. Hutchins and Thompson, *Elvis Meets the Beatles*, p. 166.
11. Evans, "BUSA," p. 118.

12. Evans, "BUSA," p. 119.
13. Evans, "BUSA," p. 120.
14. Gross, interview with Mal Evans, November 29, 1975.
15. Evans, "BUSA," p. 121.
16. Barrow, *John, Paul, George, Ringo, and Me*, p. 164.
17. Evans, "BUSA," pp. 127–28.
18. Evans, "BUSA," p. 134.
19. Evans, "BUSA," p. 135.
20. Evans, "BUSA," p. 136.
21. Evans, "BUSA," p. 138.
22. Evans, "BUSA," p. 138.
23. Connolly, "Destroyed by the Beatles," p. 34.
24. There were no drawings; see Evans, "BUSA," pp. A–B.
25. Quoted in Brian Southall, *Abbey Road: The Story of the World's Most Famous Studios* (Wellingborough, England: Patrick Stephens, 1982), p. 91.
26. "New Amps for Beatles," *Beat Instrumental* 31 (November 1965), p. 25.
27. Evans, "LTBL," p. 126.
28. Hicks, interview with Fanning, September 27, 2020.
29. After corroborating the facts associated with the role of "Arwen Dolittle" in Mal Evans's life, the author has employed a pseudonym to protect her privacy.
30. Quoted in Southall, *Abbey Road*, p. 92.
31. Doyle, interview with Mal Evans, December 14, 1975.
32. Badman, *The Beatles Off the Record*, p. 201.
33. Badman, *The Beatles Off the Record*, p. 201.
34. Babiuk, *Beatles Gear*, p. 175.
35. Brian Wilson with Ben Greenman, *I Am Brian Wilson: A Memoir* (Boston: Da Capo, 2016), p. 92.
36. The Beatles, *The Beatles Anthology*, p. 199.
37. Evans, "LTBL," p. 109.

CHAPTER 15: THE FAMILY WAY

1. See James, "Behind the Headlines," pp. 13–14.
2. Alan Smith, "Alan Smith Goes on Tour with the Beatles!," *NME* (December 10, 1965), p. 3.
3. Steve Turner, *Beatles '66: The Revolutionary Year* (New York: HarperCollins, 2016), p. 25.
4. Smith, "Alan Smith Goes on Tour with the Beatles!," p. 3.
5. Neil Aspinall, "Beatles Tour Britain," *Fabulous 208* (August 16, 1966), p. 11.
6. Turner, *Beatles '66*, pp. 23, 30.
7. Smith, "Alan Smith Goes on Tour with the Beatles!," p. 3.
8. Author interview with Slaybaugh, December 29, 2021.
9. "Sound City to Beatles' Aid," *Beat Instrumental* 33 (January 1966), p. 25.
10. George Martin with William Pearson, *With a Little Help from My Friends: The Making of Sgt. Pepper* (Boston: Little, Brown, 1994), p. 6.
11. Author interview with Pattie Boyd, February 15, 2023.
12. Emerick, *Here, There, and Everywhere*, p. 8.
13. Bicknell, *Baby, You Can Drive My Car!*, diary entry for April 7, 1966.

14. Bicknell, diary entry for April 12, 1966; see David Petersen and Dick Denney, *The Vox Story: A Complete History of the Legend* (Westport, Conn.: The Bold Strummer, 1993), p. 61.
15. Johnny Dean [Sean O'Mahony], "The 'Paperback Writer' Session," *The Beatles Book* 35 (June 1966), p. 11.
16. Bicknell, *Baby, You Can Drive My Car!*, diary entry for April 26, 1966.
17. Aspinall, "Neil's Column," *The Beatles Book* 35 (June 1966), p. 25.
18. "Daughter for Beatles' Pal," *Liverpool Echo* (April 19, 1966), p. 4.
19. Mal Evans, letter to Lily Evans, April 21, 1966.
20. Evans, "LTBL," p. 18.
21. Mal Evans, letter to Lily Evans, April 29, 1966.
22. Turner, *Beatles '66*, p. 171.
23. Bicknell, *Baby, You Can Drive My Car!*, diary entries for May 1–2, 1966.
24. Author interview with Michael Lindsay-Hogg, December 16, 2021.
25. Emerick, *Here, There, and Everywhere*, p. 120.
26. Emerick, *Here, There, and Everywhere*, p. 120.
27. Badman, *The Beatles Off the Record*, p. 207.
28. Badman, *The Beatles Off the Record*, p. 229.
29. Badman, *The Beatles Off the Record*, p. 223.
30. Badman, *The Beatles Off the Record*, p. 223; Mal Evans, "Notebook, 1966," Unpublished, p. 23, MFEA.
31. Davies, *The Beatles*, p. 276.
32. Lennon and Ono, *All We Are Saying*, pp. 139–40.
33. Davies, *The Beatles*, p. 260.
34. Evans, "Notebook, 1966," pp. 24–26.
35. "Fans Clean Van," *The Beatles Book*, 36 (July 1966), p. 29.
36. Evans, "Notebook, 1966," pp. 16–20.
37. Evans, "Notebook, 1966," pp. 16–20.

CHAPTER 16: WE LOVE YOU, BEATLES!

1. Evans, "LTBL," p. 98.
2. Evans, "LTBL," pp. 98–99.
3. Barrow, *John, Paul, George, Ringo, and Me*, p. 174.
4. Mal Evans, letter to Lily Evans, June 27, 1966.
5. Aspinall, "Beatle Life," *Fabulous 208* (January 21, 1967), p. 6.
6. Evans, "LTBL," p. 100.
7. The Beatles, *The Beatles Anthology*, p. 216.
8. The Beatles, *The Beatles Anthology*, p. 219.
9. Evans, "LTBL," p. 101.
10. Evans, "LTBL," pp. 102–3.
11. Evans, "LTBL," p. 105.
12. Evans, "LTBL," p. 106.
13. Evans, "LTBL," pp. 106–7.
14. Turner, *Beatles '66*, p. 254.
15. Lewisohn, *The Beatles Live!* (London: Pavilion, 1986), p. 195.
16. The Beatles, *The Beatles Anthology*, p. 223.
17. Evans, "LTBL," p. 112.

18. The Beatles, *The Beatles Anthology*, p. 227.
19. Author interview with Victoria Moran, December 13, 2021.
20. Author interview with Ed Freeman, September 5, 2021.
21. Author interview with Vern Miller, August 16, 2021.
22. Author interview with Miller, August 16, 2021.
23. Evans, "LTBL," p. 111.
24. Mal Evans, letter to Lily Evans, August 16, 1966.
25. Gunderson, *Some Fun Tonight!*, 2:234.
26. Evans, "LTBL," p. 112.
27. Evans, "LTBL," pp. 112–13.
28. Evans, "LTBL," p. 113.

CHAPTER 17: BABOONS, VERY MANY

1. Author interview with Slaybaugh, December 29, 2021.
2. Author interview with Slaybaugh, December 29, 2021.
3. Evans, "LTBL," p. 113.
4. Evans, "LTBL," p. 114.
5. The Beatles, *The Beatles Anthology*, p. 227.
6. Author interview with Ann Wilson, March 16, 2022.
7. Evans, "LTBL," pp. 114–15.
8. Author interview with Ed Freeman, September 5, 2021.
9. Barry Miles, *Paul McCartney: Many Years from Now* (New York: Holt, 1997), p. 296.
10. "Everything Ready," *The Beatles Book* 40 (November 1966), p. 29.
11. Martin, interview with Lily Evans, 2004.
12. Evans, "LTBL," p. 51; in later years, Tony Barrow would claim to have ghost-written articles for both Mal and Neil in *The Beatles Book* and elsewhere.
13. See "Mal's Page," *The Beatles Book* 42 (January 1967), p. 25.
14. Evans, "LTBL," p. 116.
15. Evans, "LTBL," pp. 118–19.
16. Evans, "LTBL," p. 119.
17. Ringo Starr, *Postcards from the Boys* (San Francisco: Chronicle Books, 2004), p. 9.
18. Evans, "LTBL," pp. 120–21.
19. Mal Evans, letter to Lily Evans, November 1966.
20. Evans, "LTBL," p. 121.
21. Evans, "LTBL," p. 123.
22. Evans, "LTBL," p. 123.
23. Evans, "LTBL," p. 123.
24. Evans, "LTBL," p. 124.
25. Evans, "LTBL," p. 125.
26. Miles, *Paul McCartney*, p. 303.
27. Miles, *Paul McCartney*, p. 303.
28. "People Behind the Stars, No. 4: Road Manager Mal Evans," p. 33.
29. Pete Townshend, *Who I Am: A Memoir* (New York: HarperCollins, 2012), p. 116.
30. James Tozer, "In Paul McCartney's Arms: The Puppy He Loved So Much He Wrote about Her in the Beatles Hit 'Martha My Dear,'" *Daily Mail*, November 10, 2017, www.dailymail.co.uk/news/article-5071837/In-Paul-McCartney-s-arms-puppy-loved-much.html.

31. Evans, "LTBL," p. 117.
32. Evans, "LTBL," p. 117; Evans, "Diaries," January 19, 1967.
33. Evans, "Diaries," January 27, 1967; Connolly, "Destroyed by the Beatles," p. 34.
34. Evans, "Diaries," January 27 and 28 and February 1, 1967.
35. The Beatles, *The Beatles Anthology*, p. 247.
36. Evans, "Diaries," January 31 and February 2, 1967.
37. Evans, "Diaries," January 29 and February 7, 1967.
38. Evans, "Diaries," February 7, 1967.
39. Badman, *The Beatles Off the Record*, p. 280.
40. Gross, interview with Mal Evans, November 29, 1975; see also Evans, "LTBL," p. 118.

CHAPTER 18: SWIRLING SILVERY SHIMMERY WORLDS

1. Martin, *With a Little Help from My Friends*, pp. 53–54.
2. Martin, *With a Little Help from My Friends*, pp. 53–54; Emerick, *Here, There, and Everywhere*, p. 148.
3. Martin with Hornsby, *All You Need Is Ears*, p. 209.
4. Emerick, *Here, There, and Everywhere*, p. 153; Lewisohn, *The Complete Beatles Recording Sessions: The Official Abbey Road Studio Session Notes, 1962–1970* (New York: Harmony, 1988), p. 96.
5. Evans, "Diaries," February 10, 1967.
6. Evans, "Diaries," February 13, 1967.
7. Martin, *With a Little Help from My Friends*, p. 26.
8. Evans, "Diaries," February 18–20, 1967.
9. Emerick, *Here, There, and Everywhere*, p. 160.
10. Evans, "Diaries," February 14, 1967.
11. Evans, "LTBL," p. 127.
12. Evans, "LTBL," pp. 127–28.
13. Evans, "Diaries," March 1–3, 1967.
14. Evans, "LTBL," p. 128.
15. Emerick, *Here, There, and Everywhere*, p. 142.
16. Author interview with Jann Haworth, July 26, 2022.
17. Evans, "Diaries," March 6, 1967.
18. Evans, "Diaries," March 6, 1967.

CHAPTER 19: SOCKS, MAL!

1. Martin, *With a Little Help from My Friends*, p. 96.
2. Author interview with Ken Townsend, September 27, 2019.
3. Author interview with Townsend, September 27, 2019.
4. Barry Miles, *In the Sixties* (London: Pimlico, 2003), p. 228.
5. Miles, *In the Sixties*, p. 231.
6. Miles, *In the Sixties*, p. 230.
7. The Beatles, *The Beatles Anthology*, p. 252.
8. Evans, "LTBL," pp. 130–31.
9. Evans, "LTBL," p. 130.
10. Martin, *With a Little Help from My Friends*, p. 110.
11. Martin, *With a Little Help from My Friends*, p. 110.

12. Miles, *Paul McCartney*, p. 383.
13. Evans, "Diaries," March 20, 1967.
14. Evans, "Notebook, 1967–1968," p. 8, MFEA.
15. Evans, "Notebook, 1967–1968," p. 9.
16. Evans, "LTBL," p. 130.
17. Mal had earlier tried his own hand at painting a *Sgt. Pepper* drumhead. See Evans, "Notebook, 1967–1968," p. 4.
18. Evans, "LTBL," pp. 126, 130.
19. Taylor, *Those Were the Days*, p. 39.
20. Evans, "LTBL," p. 131.
21. Evans, "LTBL," p. 118. Over the years, Ringo continued to champion Mal's creative input. During an interview in the 1980s with E Street Band drummer Max Weinberg, Ringo remarked that "I'll bet you didn't know that Mal Evans, our roadie, came up with the 'Sgt. Pepper' title. He didn't get the credit, though." See Weinberg with Robert Santelli, *The Big Beat: Conversations with Rock's Great Drummers* (Chicago, Ill.: Contemporary Books, 1984, p. 182); John's boyhood friend Pete Shotton similarly recalled that "it was Mal who not only coined the memorable name 'Sgt. Pepper's Lonely Hearts Club Band,' but also made the invaluable suggestion that this fictitious ensemble be presented as the Beatles' alter-egos—the entire performance as an uninterrupted performance by Sgt. Pepper's 'band.'" See Pete Shotton and Nicholas Schaffner, *John Lennon: In My Life* (New York: Stein and Day, 1983), p. 244.

CHAPTER 20: MYSTERY TOURS

1. Evans, "LTBL," p. 132.
2. Evans, "LTBL," p. 132.
3. Sounes, *Fab*, p. 169.
4. Evans, "LTBL," p. 133.
5. Evans, "LTBL," p. 133.
6. Evans, "LTBL," pp. 133–34.
7. Evans, "LTBL," p. 134.
8. Miles, *Paul McCartney*, p. 350.
9. Evans, "LTBL," pp. 134–35.
10. Evans, "LTBL," p. 135.
11. Derek Taylor, "Paul McC. Was My House Guest," *Teen Datebook* 6, no. 4 (September 1967): 30.
12. Evans, "LTBL," p. 136.
13. Evans, "LTBL," p. 136. Redgrave lost the statuette to Elizabeth Taylor, who won the Oscar for Best Actress for her bravura turn as Martha in *Who's Afraid of Virginia Woolf?*
14. A similar hint would be dropped in the monthly newsletter feature of *The Beatles Book*: "Why are Neil and Mal wearing colorful plastic badges with a drawing of an apple on them?" See *The Beatles Book* 47 (June 1967), p. 4.
15. Miles, *In the Sixties*, p. 232.
16. *Lennon Remembers*, p. 54.
17. Evans, "LTBL," p. 137.
18. Davies, "The Beatles, Part II," *Life* 65 (September 20, 1968), p. 71.
19. Davies, *The Beatles Book* (London: Ebury, 2016), pp. 335–36.
20. Evans and Aspinall, "Magical Mystery Tour," *The Beatles Book* 53 (December 1967), p. 6.

21. Author interview with Moran, December 13, 2021.
22. Author interview with Moran, December 13, 2021.
23. Author interview with Moran, December 13, 2021.
24. Author interview with Moran, December 13, 2021.
25. Norrie Drummond, "Dinner with the Beatles," *NME*, May 27, 1967, p. 2.
26. Miles, *Paul McCartney*, p. 433.
27. Author interview with Kevin Harrington, February 3, 2021.
28. *The John Lennon Letters*, ed. Hunter Davies (New York: Little, Brown, 2012), p. 96.
29. Evans, "Diaries," May 29, 1967.
30. Evans, "Diaries," June 1, 1967.
31. Author interview with Gary Evans, March 14, 2022.
32. John Lennon, letter to Mal Evans, June 15, 1967.
33. Martin with Hornsby, *All You Need Is Ears*, p. 162.
34. See Evans, "Notebook, 1967–1968," p. 18.
35. Martin with Hornsby, *All You Need Is Ears*, p. 193.
36. The Beatles, *The Beatles Anthology*, p. 258.
37. Evans, "LTBL," p. 139.
38. Evans, "LTBL," pp. 139–40.
39. Evans, "LTBL," p. 140.
40. Evans, "LTBL," pp. 140–41.
41. Evans, "LTBL," p. 141.
42. Connolly, "Destroyed by the Beatles," p. 34.
43. Author interview with Klaus Voormann, September 12, 2022.
44. See the monthly newsletter section in *The Beatles Book* 49 (August 1967), p. 4.
45. Author interview with Boyd, February 15, 2023.

CHAPTER 21: THE FIFTH MAGICIAN

1. Evans, "LTBL," pp. 142–43.
2. *Lennon Remembers*, p. 25.
3. The Beatles, *The Beatles Anthology*, p. 268.
4. Martin with Hornsby, *All You Need Is Ears*, p. 165.
5. Evans, "LTBL," p. 152.
6. Badman, *The Beatles Off the Record*, p. 312.
7. Barrow, *The Making of the Beatles' Magical Mystery Tour* (London: Omnibus, 1999), p. 7.
8. Alistair Taylor, "Forward," in Tony Barrow, *The Making of the Beatles' Magical Mystery Tour* (London: Omnibus, 1999), pp. 2–3.
9. Badman, *The Beatles Off the Record*, p. 312.
10. Leslie Cavendish with Eduardo Jáuregui and Neil McNaughton, *The Cutting Edge: The Story of the Beatles' Hairdresser Who Defined an Era* (Richmond, U.K.: Alma Books, 2017), p. 104.
11. Author interview with Leslie Cavendish, December 13, 2021.
12. Badman, *The Beatles Off the Record*, p. 313.
13. Evans, "LTBL," pp. 154–55.
14. Evans, "LTBL," pp. 155–56.
15. Evans, "LTBL," pp. 158–59.
16. "The Making of *Magical Mystery Tour*," DVD featurette, *Magical Mystery Tour* (Apple,

2012). *Magical Mystery Tour* film assistant Andrew Birkin recalled events somewhat differently from Losey. In Birkin's memory, *he* volunteered to sign the autographs after John balked at the task, suggesting that one hundred signed photos had been made available that day as a bribe to keep the dancers on the set. This is at variance with the paucity of keepsakes Losey remembered attempting to distribute. See Birkin, *POV: A Life in Pictures* (Paris: Albin Michel Beaux Livres, 2022).

17. Evans, "LTBL," p. 159.
18. The Beatles, *The Beatles Anthology*, p. 273.
19. Sandford, *McCartney*, p. 147.
20. Evans, "LTBL," p. 159.
21. Evans, "LTBL," p. 161.
22. Evans, "LTBL," p. 161.
23. Email from Julie Evans Rossow, February 27, 2023.
24. Starr, *Postcards from the Boys*, p. 11.
25. Author interview with Gary Evans, April 23, 2021.
26. Author interview with Gary Evans, April 23, 2021.
27. Mark Edmonds, "Here, There, and Everywhere," *Sunday Times Magazine*, March 20, 2005, p. 40.
28. Evans, "LTBL," p. 164.
29. Evans, "LTBL," p. 165.
30. Nigel Hunter, "From the Music Capitals of the World: London," *Billboard* (December 16, 1967), p. 50.
31. Evans, "LTBL," pp. 161–62.
32. Evans, "LTBL," p. 162.
33. Quoted in Badman, *The Beatles Off the Record*, pp. 332–33.
34. "Beatles Firm, Melcher Deal," *Billboard*, December 23, 1967, p. 4.

CHAPTER 22: MANAGING DIRECTOR?

1. Evans, "LTBL," p. 144.
2. Evans, "LTBL," p. 172.
3. Evans, "LTBL," pp. 172–73.
4. While its place in Apple Corps had been clarified in January 1968, Apple Publishing had been signing clients since at least September 1967.
5. Evans, "Diaries," January 19, 1968.
6. Peter Asher, *The Beatles from A to Zed: An Alphabetical Mystery Tour* (New York: Henry Holt, 2019), p. 15.
7. Badman, *The Beatles Off the Record*, pp. 338–39.
8. Author interview with Peter Asher, November 2, 2021.
9. Author interview with Asher, November 2, 2021.
10. Evans, "LTBL," p. 144.
11. Richard DiLello, *The Longest Cocktail Party: An Insider's Diary of the Beatles* (Chicago, Ill.: Playboy, 1972), p. 8.
12. Evans, "Diaries," January 24, 1968.
13. Dan Matovina, *Without You: The Tragic Story of Badfinger* (San Mateo, Calif.: Frances Glover Books, 2000), p. 37.
14. Evans, "LTBL," p. 144.
15. Evans, "LTBL," pp. 144–45.

16. Quoted in Matovina, *Without You*, p. 37.
17. Evans, "Diaries," January 30, 1968.
18. Quoted in Matovina, *Without You*, p. 37.
19. Evans, "LTBL," p. 145.
20. Evans, "Diaries," January 13, 1968.
21. Evans, "Diaries," January 18, 1968.
22. Author interview with Lizzie Bravo, December 5, 2020.

CHAPTER 23: POVERTY THROWS A SMILING SHADOW

1. See Parliament's "Average Weekly Earnings" debate of March 18, 1968, in Hansard, vol. 761, hansard.parliament.uk/.
2. Evans, "Diaries," February 14–16, 1968.
3. Nancy Cooke de Herrera, *All You Need Is Love: An Eyewitness Account of When Spirituality Spread from the East to the West* (San Diego: Jodere, 2003), p. 221.
4. Mal Evans, letter to Lily Evans, February 18, 1968.
5. Evans, "Diaries," February 17, 1968.
6. Evans, "LTBL," p. 166.
7. Evans, "LTBL," pp. 167–68.
8. Evans, "LTBL," pp. 167–68.
9. Evans, "LTBL," pp. 167–68.
10. Evans, "Beatles in India," *The Beatles Book* 58 (May 1968), p. 11.
11. Evans, "LTBL," p. 170.
12. Evans, "LTBL," pp. 170–71.
13. Author interview with Paul Saltzman, June 10, 2021.
14. Evans, "LTBL," pp. 170–71; author interview with Saltzman, June 10, 2021.
15. Starr, "I Want to Lead a Normal Life," *Hit Parader*, September 1968, p. 9.
16. Evans, "Diaries," March 10, 1968.
17. Evans, "Diaries," March 21, 1968.
18. Evans, "Diaries," March 21, 1968.
19. Evans, "LTBL," p. 171; Gross, interview with Mal Evans, November 29, 1975.

CHAPTER 24: BIG, CUDDLY, CHEERFUL, AND SEXY

1. Author interview with Gary Evans and Julie Evans Rossow, March 21, 2022.
2. Author interview with Asher, November 2, 2021.
3. DiLello, *The Longest Cocktail Party*, p. 12.
4. DiLello, *The Longest Cocktail Party*, p. 246.
5. DiLello, *The Longest Cocktail Party*, p. 15.
6. Author interview with Moran, December 13, 2021.
7. Author interview with Moran, December 13, 2021.
8. Author interview with Moran, December 13, 2021.
9. Author interview with Asher, November 2, 2021.
10. Matovina, *Without You*, p. 40.
11. Author interview with Asher, November 2, 2021.
12. Quoted in Matovina, *Without You*, p. 43.
13. Derek Taylor, *Nadolig Llawen* [Apple internal newsletter] (December 1968), p. 33.
14. Evans, "LTBL," p. 146.
15. Derek Taylor, *Fifty Years Adrift* (Guilford, U.K.: Genesis, 1984), p. 327.

16. The Beatles, *The Beatles Anthology*, p. 287.
17. Lillian Roxon, "101 Hours with John Lennon and Paul McCartney," *Eye*, September 1968, p. 33.
18. Evans, "Diaries," May 14, 1968.

CHAPTER 25: THE GRINNING GIANT

1. The Beatles, *The Beatles Anthology*, p. 296.
2. Evans, "LTBL," pp. 186–87.
3. Author interview with Chris O'Dell, May 21, 2021.
4. Author interview with O'Dell, May 21, 2021.
5. Chris O'Dell with Katherine Ketchum, *Miss O'Dell: My Hard Days and Long Nights with the Beatles, the Stones, Bob Dylan, Eric Clapton and the Women They Loved* (New York: Touchstone, 2009), p. 39.
6. Author interview with O'Dell, May 21, 2021.
7. In her memory, O'Dell recalled that the song was "Revolution 9," which seems unlikely, given its distinctly experimental nature.
8. Shotton, *John Lennon*, p. 133.
9. Evans, "Diaries," June 7, 1968.
10. Evans, "Ringo and George in California," *The Beatles Book* 61 (August 1968), p. 24.
11. Evans, "Ringo and George in California," p. 26.
12. Evans, "Ringo and George in California," p. 31.
13. Bramwell, *Magical Mystery Tours*, p. 269.
14. Author interview with Mansfield, January 14, 2021.
15. Evans, "LTBL," p. 149.
16. Quoted in Matovina, *Without You*, p. 43.
17. Derek Taylor, "Apple 1988: A Year for Nostalgia," *Hit Parader*, March 1969, p. 36.
18. Derek Taylor, *Gilet de Sauvetage Est Sous la Siege* [Apple internal newsletter] (November 1968), p. 4. Taylor, in "Apple 1988," notably emended "face like a death mask" to "face like a carving."
19. Evans, "LTBL," pp. 149–50.
20. Author interview with Asher, November 2, 2021.
21. Evans, "LTBL," p. 151.
22. Evans, "Diaries," July 5, 1968.
23. Author interview with Harrington, February 3, 2021.
24. Author interview with Harrington, February 3, 2021.
25. Author interview with Harrington, February 3, 2021.
26. Kevin Harrington, *Who's the Redhead on the Roof? My Life with the Beatles* (Forchheim, U.K.: Apcor Books, 2015), p. 47.
27. Derek Taylor, *Gilet de Sauvetage Est Sous la Siege*, p. 12.
28. Badman, *The Beatles Off the Record*, p. 368.
29. Alistair Taylor, *With the Beatles*, p. 207.
30. Evans, "Diaries," July 13, 1968.
31. Author interview with Julie Evans Rossow, January 20, 2022.
32. Martin, interview with Lily Evans, 2004.
33. Martin, interview with Lily Evans, 2004; Evans, "LTBL," pp. 162–63.
34. Francie Schwartz, *Body Count* (New York: Straight Arrow, 1972), p. 81.
35. Author interview with Gary Evans, December 4, 2020.

36. Evans, "Diaries," July 29, 1968.
37. Author interview with Ned Ryan, February 12, 2022.

CHAPTER 26: TO RULE IS TO SERVE

1. Evans, "The Eighteenth Single," *The Beatles Book* 62 (September 1968), p. 8.
2. Sandford, *McCartney*, p. 158.
3. Lewisohn, *The Complete Beatles Recording Sessions*, p. 146.
4. Author interview with Mansfield, January 14, 2021.
5. Quoted in Matovina, *Without You*, p. 44.
6. Evans, *Diaries*, September 30, 1968.
7. Quoted in Matovina, *Without You*, p. 44.
8. Author interview with Gary Evans, March 25, 2022.
9. Evans, "Mal's Diary," *The Beatles Book* 63 (October 1968), p. 12.
10. Edmonds, "Here, There, and Everywhere," p. 40.
11. Evans, "Diaries," August 21, 1968.
12. Evans, "Diaries," August 21–22, 1968.
13. Lewisohn, *The Complete Beatles Recording Sessions*, p. 151.
14. Lewisohn, *The Complete Beatles Recording Sessions*, p. 151.
15. Author interview with Harrington, February 3, 2021.
16. Author interview with Harrington, February 3, 2021.
17. See Frederick James [Tony Barrow], "The Fifth Beatle Gets Married," *The Beatles Book* (October 1968), pp. 6–9.
18. Author interview with Lewisohn, January 29, 2022.
19. Author interview with Joel Soroka, August 31, 2022.
20. Author interview with Soroka, August 31, 2022.
21. Author interview with Lindsay-Hogg, December 16, 2021.
22. Evans, "Diaries," September 9, 1968.
23. Evans, "Thirty New Beatle Grooves on Double Disc Album," *The Beatles Book* 64 (November 1968), p. 8.
24. Lewisohn, *The Complete Beatles Recording Sessions*, p. 154.
25. Author interview with Mansfield, January 21, 2021.
26. Evans, "LTBL," p. 175.
27. Author interview with Slaybaugh, December 29, 2021.
28. Author interview with Slaybaugh, May 25, 2021, and December 29, 2021.
29. Author interview with Slaybaugh, December 29, 2021, and July 26, 2022.
30. Evans, "LTBL," p. 177.
31. Evans, "Diaries," November 10, 1968.
32. Mal Evans, letter to Lily Evans, November 17, 1968.
33. Evans, "Diaries," November 19, 1968.
34. Evans, "Diaries," November 26, 1968.
35. Mal Evans, letter to Lily Evans, late November 1968.
36. Evans, "LTBL," pp. 182–83.
37. Evans, "LTBL," p. 206.
38. Evans, "LTBL," p. 206.
39. Evans, "Diaries," December 1, 1968.
40. Martin, interview with Lily Evans, 2004.
41. Connolly, "Destroyed by the Beatles," p. 34.

CHAPTER 27: SEE YOU 'ROUND THE CLUBS

1. Tony Barrell, *The Beatles on the Roof* (London: Omnibus, 2017), p. 5.
2. Evans, "LTBL," p. 188.
3. Unless otherwise specified, all quotations from the January 1969 sessions are drawn from *The Beatles: Get Back*, directed by Peter Jackson (Apple Corps, 2021).
4. Sulpy and Ray Schweighardt, *Get Back: The Unauthorized Chronicle of the Beatles' Let It Be Disaster* (New York: Griffin, 1997), p. 127.
5. Evans, "Diaries," January 10, 1969.
6. Evans, "LTBL," p. 189.
7. Evans, "LTBL," p. 189.
8. Peter Doggett, *You Never Give Me Your Money: The Beatles After the Breakup* (New York: HarperCollins, 2011), p. 61.
9. Author interview with Friedland, June 20, 2021.
10. Evans, letter to Brute Force [Stephen Friedland], February 10, 1969.
11. Author interview with Richard Keith Wolff, February 28, 2023.
12. Miles, *Paul McCartney*, p. 567.
13. Evans, "LTBL," p. 188.
14. The Beatles, *The Beatles Anthology*, p. 291.
15. The Beatles, *The Beatles Anthology*, p. 291.
16. The Beatles, *The Beatles Anthology*, p. 318.
17. Sulpy and Schweighardt, p. 232.
18. Evans, "LTBL," p. 191.
19. Barrell, *The Beatles on the Roof*, p. 89.
20. Evans, "Diaries," January 27, 1969.
21. Author interview with Harrington, February 3, 2021.
22. Quoted in Matteo, *Let It Be*, p. 83.
23. Evans, "LTBL," p. 192.
24. Mansfield, *The Roof*, p. 105.
25. O'Dell, *Miss O'Dell*, p. 75.
26. Cavendish, *The Cutting Edge*, p. 151.

CHAPTER 28: PISSPOTS ON A JOURNEY

1. Author interview with Lindsay-Hogg, December 16, 2021.
2. Evans, "LTBL," p. 191.
3. Evans, "LTBL," p. 192
4. Evans, "LTBL," p. 192.
5. Frost, interview with Mal Evans, May 21, 1975.
6. Evans, "Diaries," February 6, 1969.
7. Evans, "Diaries," February 6, 1969.
8. Author interview with Ryan, February 12, 2022.
9. Evans, "LTBL," p. 147.
10. Evans, "Diaries," February 23, 1969.
11. Evans, "Diaries," pp. 147–48.
12. Quoted in Matovina, *Without You*, p. 55.
13. Stefan Granados, *Those Were the Days 2.0: The Beatles and Apple* (London: Cherry Red Books, 2021), p. 57.
14. Author interview with Gary Evans, March 25, 2022.

15. Evans, "LTBL," pp. 193–94.
16. Evans, "LTBL," p. 25.
17. Carol Bedford, *Waiting for the Beatles: An Apple Scruff's Story* (London: Blandford, 1984), p. 58.
18. Author interview with Mike McCartney, January 6, 2022.
19. Evans, "Diaries," March 13, 1969.
20. In September 1973, George was vindicated when Pilcher was convicted and imprisoned for perverting the course of justice, having framed several of his celebrity targets over the years.
21. Author interview with John Kosh, October 30, 2021.
22. Lewisohn, *The Complete Beatles Recording Sessions*, p. 15.
23. Evans, "LTBL," pp. 148–49.
24. Evans, "Diaries," March 26, 1969.
25. Granados, *Those Were the Days 2.0*, p. 10.
26. Evans, "Diaries," April 24, 1969.
27. "Another Beatles Music Boss," *Disc and Music Echo*, May 3, 1969, p. 6.
28. The Beatles, *The Beatles Anthology*, p. 326.
29. The Beatles, *The Beatles Anthology*, p. 326.
30. Lewisohn, "Macca to Me in 1991, Speaking of May 9, 1969," Twitter, May 9, 2019, twitter.com/marklewisohn/status/1126576151072247809?lang=en.
31. Evans, "Diaries," May 9, 1969.

CHAPTER 29: SUN WORSHIPPER

1. Alistair Taylor, *With the Beatles*, pp. 242–43.
2. Fred Goodman, *Allen Klein: The Man Who Bailed Out the Beatles, Made the Stones, and Transformed Rock 'n' Roll* (New York: Houghton Mifflin Harcourt, 2016), p. 187.
3. O'Dell, *Miss O'Dell*, p. 91.
4. Author interview with Lewisohn, December 11, 2021. Lewisohn further noted that not only were Mal and Neil employed directly by the Beatles, but their weekly wages were administered by NEMS and, later, Apple, having been debited directly from Beatles Limited and, since April 1967, Beatles and Company.
5. Bramwell, *Magical Mystery Tours*, p. 325.
6. Author interview with Bramwell, August 6, 2021.
7. Doggett, *You Never Give Me Your Money*, pp. 97–98.
8. Bramwell, *Magical Mystery Tours*, p. 159.
9. Bramwell, *Magical Mystery Tours*, p. 160.
10. See Bedford, *Waiting for the Beatles*, pp. 284–87.
11. Email from the Apple Scruffs [Carole, Chris, and Sue], December 15, 2021.
12. "*Get Back* Postponed," *The Beatles Book* 73 (August 1969), p. 29.
13. Mal Evans, "The Beatles Get Back," *The Beatles Book* 72 (July 1969), pp. 22–25.
14. Evans, "The Beatles Get Back," pp. 22–25.
15. Evans, "The Beatles Get Back," pp. 195–96.
16. Evans, "Diaries," June 12, 1969.
17. Evans, "LTBL," p. 196.
18. Matovina, *Without You*, p. 59.
19. "Iveys Find It Hard to Please the Beatles," *Disc and Music Echo*, July 5, 1969, p. 16.
20. Granados, *Those Were the Days 2.0*, p. 108.

21. Evans, "Diaries," August 2, 1969.
22. Evans, "Diaries," August 1, 1969.
23. Author interview with John Kurlander, November 8, 2017.
24. Author interview with Kurlander, June 23, 2021.
25. Author interview with Kurlander, November 8, 2017.
26. Lewisohn, *The Complete Beatles Recording Sessions*, p. 13.
27. The Beatles, *The Beatles Anthology*, p. 337.
28. Evans, "Diaries," August 5, 1969.
29. Emerick, *Here, There, and Everywhere*, p. 287.
30. Author interview with Kosh, October 30, 2021.
31. See "Unrecognized," *The Beatles Book* 74 (September 1969), p. 31.
32. Lewisohn, *The Complete Beatles Recording Sessions*, p. 190.
33. The Beatles, *The Beatles Anthology*, p. 345.
34. Author interview with Ethan Russell, January 7, 2021.

CHAPTER 30: BADFINGER BOOGIE

1. Author interview with Gary Evans, April 8, 2022.
2. Anthony Fawcett, *John Lennon: One Day at a Time—A Personal Biography of the Seventies* (New York: Grove Press, 1976), pp. 95–97.
3. Fawcett, *John Lennon*, pp. 95–97.
4. Fawcett, *John Lennon*, pp. 95–97.
5. Evans, "Diaries," September 12, 1969.
6. Evans, "LTBL," p. 197.
7. Author interview with Alan White, April 11, 2022.
8. Evans, "LTBL," pp. 197–98.
9. Evans, "LTBL," p. 199.
10. Evans, "LTBL," p. 199.
11. Badman, *The Beatles Off the Record*, p. 466.
12. Badman, *The Beatles Off the Record*, p. 467.
13. The Beatles, *The Beatles Anthology*, p. 348.
14. Author interview with Rod Lynton, August 15, 2021.
15. Quoted in Matovina, *Without You*, p. 66.
16. Quoted in Matovina, *Without You*, p. 67.
17. "Gary Fawkes," *The Beatles Book* 76 (November 1969), p. 31.
18. Mansfield, letter to Mal Evans, November 20, 1969.
19. Evans, "LTBL," p. 201.
20. Evans, "LTBL," p. 203.
21. Evans, "LTBL," pp. 204–5.

CHAPTER 31: DOUBLE AGENT

1. Lewisohn, *The Complete Beatles Recording Sessions*, p. 195.
2. Evans, "Diaries," January 3, 1970.
3. Evans, "Diaries," January 4, 1970.
4. Author interview with Mary McCartney, December 6, 2022.
5. Author interview with Doug Ellis, September 5, 2021.
6. Evans, "Diaries," January 12, 1970.
7. Author interview with Bramwell, August 6, 2021.

8. Evans, "Diaries," January 27, 1970.
9. Author interview with White, April 11, 2022.
10. Evans, "Diaries," February 5, 1970.
11. Evans, "LTBL," p. 205.
12. Evans, "LTBL," p. 205.
13. Evans, "LTBL," p. 205.
14. Evans, "Diaries," February 9, 1970.
15. O'Dell, *Miss O'Dell*, p. 144.
16. Miles, *Paul McCartney*, p. 574.
17. Evans, "LTBL," p. 109.
18. Derek Taylor, *As Time Goes By*, p. 135.
19. Taylor, *As Time Goes By*, pp. 80–81.
20. Taylor, *As Time Goes By*, p. 261.
21. Evans, "LTBL," p. 190.
22. Author interview with Alan Parsons, September 17, 2019.
23. Author interview with Peter Frampton, September 6, 2022.
24. Ken Scott with Bobby Owsinski, *Abbey Road to Ziggy Stardust: Off the Record with the Beatles, Bowie, Elton, and So Much More* (Los Angeles: Alfred Music, 2012), p. 108.
25. Quoted in Matovina, *Without You*, p. 83.
26. Author interview with Joey Molland, April 15, 2023.
27. In this instance, the modification involved amplifying Molland's guitar through a Leslie speaker. Named for its inventor, Donald Leslie, and originally designed for deployment with a Hammond organ, the speaker featured rotating baffles and offered a range of unusual special effects.
28. Quoted in Matovina, *Without You*, p. 90.
29. Quoted in Matovina, *Without You*, p. 90.
30. Evans, "LTBL," p. 148.
31. Emerick, *Here, There, and Everywhere*, p. 325.
32. Quoted in Matovina, *Without You*, p. 91.
33. Quoted in Matovina, *Without You*, p. 91.
34. Quoted in Matovina, *Without You*, p. 92.
35. Author interview with Var Smith, August 29, 2021.
36. Quoted in Matovina, *Without You*, p. 91.
37. Quoted in Matovina, *Without You*, p. 93.
38. Emerick, *Here, There, and Everywhere*, p. 326.
39. Quoted in Matovina, *Without You*, p. 93.
40. Author interview with Marianne Evans, May 14, 2021.
41. Matovina, *Without You*, p. 93.
42. Evans, "LTBL," p. 149.
43. Emerick, *Here, There, and Everywhere*, p. 326.

CHAPTER 32: HITMAKER

1. Author interview with Harrington, February 3, 2021.
2. Author interview with Harrington, February 3, 2021.
3. "It's a Hard Road: 'Beat Instrumental' Looks at the Roadie Scene," *Beat Instrumental and International Recording Studio*, July 1970, p. 41.

4. Cliff Jones, "Apple Scruffs: 'We're Waiting for the Beatles,'" *Mojo* 35 (October 1996), p. 71.
5. Author interview with Steve Brendell, August 17, 2022.
6. Barbara Bennett, "*My Beatle Days*," BlogSpot, June 30, 2019, mybeatledays.blogspot.com/2019/06/apple-people.html.
7. Evans, "Diaries," July 6, 1970.
8. Ruth Ellen Carter, affidavit, July 1972.
9. Quoted in Matovina, *Without You*, p. 101; author interview with Allan Steckler, March 29, 2023.
10. Quoted in Matovina, *Without You*, p. 116.
11. Mansfield, letter to Mal Evans, November 23, 1970.
12. Kane, *Lennon Revealed*, p. 224.
13. Starr, *Postcards from the Boys*, p. 49.
14. Ray Connolly, *The Ray Connolly Beatles Archive* (London: Plumray Books, 2011), p. 88.
15. Evans, "Diaries," July 19, 1970.
16. Evans, "Diaries," October 3, 1970.
17. Evans, "Diaries," November 5–6 and December 1, 1970.
18. Spector, letter to Mal Evans, dated as "Christmas 1970."
19. Evans, "Diaries," January 10, 1971.

CHAPTER 33: HAPPY CRIMBLE!

1. Author interview with Gary Evans, March 31, 2022.
2. Author interview with Gary Evans, March 31, 2022.
3. Author interview with Gary Evans, March 31, 2022.
4. Timothy White, *George Harrison Reconsidered* (London: Larchwood and Weir, 2013), n.p.
5. Connolly, "Destroyed by the Beatles," p. 34.
6. Author interview with Lynton, August 15, 2021.
7. Author interview with Dan Richter, August 22, 2022.
8. Charles Shaar Murray, "Lennon, Lenin, the 'Oz' Schoolkids Issue, and Me," *The Word* (April 2011), www.rocksbackpages.com/Library/Article/lennon-lenin-the-iozi-schoolkids-issue-and-me.
9. Murray, "Lennon, Lenin, the 'Oz' Schoolkids Issue, and Me."
10. Quoted in Matovina, *Without You*, pp. 136–37.
11. Evans, "LTBL," pp. 207–8.
12. Evans, "LTBL," letter to Lily Evans, June 26, 1971.
13. Evans, "LTBL," p. 210.
14. Evans, "LTBL," p. 210.
15. Evans, "LTBL," pp. 210–11.
16. Evans, "LTBL," p. 212.
17. Chip Madinger and Scott Raile, *Lennonology: Strange Days Indeed—A Scrapbook of Madness* (Springfield, Mo.: Open Your Books, 2015), pp. 251, 255.
18. Author interview with Harrington, February 3, 2021.
19. Evans, "LTBL," p. 215.
20. Peter Hicks, interview with Lynda Dearborn, August 6, 2019.
21. Author interview with Mansfield, January 14, 2021.
22. Evans, "Diaries," March 1, 2021.

23. Peter Hicks, interview with Lon Van Eaton, December 27, 2018; author interview with Lon Van Eaton, October 26, 2022.
24. Evans, "LTBL," p. 237.
25. Lily Evans, letter to Mal Evans, October 18, 1971.
26. Evans, "LTBL," p. 216.
27. Author interview with Tony King, February 8, 2023.
28. Peter Hicks, interview with John Mears, March 26, 2018.
29. *Behind the Music: Badfinger* (VH1, 2000).
30. "Harry Nilsson's 10 Best Songs," *Far Out*, June 15, 2021, faroutmagazine.co.uk/harry-nilsson-10-best-songs/.
31. Author interview with Gary Evans, November 27, 2020.
32. Author interview with Gary Evans, April 16, 2022.

CHAPTER 34: MALCONTENTED

1. Evans, "Diaries," January 13, 1972.
2. Evans, "Diaries," January 28, 1972.
3. Evans, Diaries, February 12, 1972.
4. Tony Visconti, *The Autobiography: Bowie, Bolan, and the Brooklyn Boy* (New York: HarperCollins, 2007), p. 191.
5. Evans, "LTBL," p. 235.
6. Peter Hicks, email from Bob Purvis, March 16, 2018.
7. Gross, interview with Mal Evans, November 29, 1975.
8. Author interview with Gary Evans, January 23, 2021.
9. Evans, "Diaries," July 1, 1972.
10. Evans, "Diaries," July 16, 1972.
11. Peter Howard, letter to Mal Evans, April 4, 1972.
12. Elliot J. Huntley, *Mystical One: George Harrison—After the Breakup of the Beatles* (Toronto: Guernica, 2006), pp. 88–89.
13. Evans, "Diaries," November 5, 1972.
14. Author interview with Phil Hilderbrand, August 15, 2022.
15. Evans, "Diaries," February 3, 1973.

CHAPTER 35: PANDORA'S BOX

1. In his diary, Mal compiled the lyrics for "You're Thinking of Me." See *Diaries*, March 4, 1973.
2. Evans, "LTBL," p. 217.
3. Evans, "LTBL," pp. 218–19.
4. Evans, "LTBL," p. 219.
5. Jonathan Cott and Christine Doudna, eds., *The Ballad of John and Yoko* (New York: Dolphin, 1982), p. 223.
6. Lily Evans, letter to Mal Evans, March 17, 1973.
7. Evans, "LTBL," p. 220.
8. Doggett, *You Never Give Me Your Money*, p. 201.
9. Evans, "LTBL," pp. 220–21.
10. Keith Badman, *The Beatles Off the Record 2: The Dream Is Over* (London: Omnibus, 2009), p. 117.
11. Evans, "LTBL," p. 222.

12. Evans, "LTBL," p. 223.
13. Evans, "LTBL," p. 223.
14. Evans, "LTBL," p. 224.
15. Evans, "LTBL," p. 224.
16. Evans, "LTBL," pp. 224–25.
17. Evans, "Diaries," June 2–5, 1973.
18. Evans, "LTBL," p. 228.
19. Evans, "LTBL," p. 228.

CHAPTER 36: FOOLS AND DRUNKS

1. Evans, "Diaries," June 19, 1973.
2. Jimmy Webb, *The Cake and the Rain: A Memoir* (New York: St. Martin's Press, 2018), p. 107.
3. Matovina, *Without You*, p. 243.
4. Author interview with Gary Evans, February 12, 2021.
5. Evans, "Diaries," August 7, 1973.
6. Evans, "Diaries," November 19, 1973; John 15:13 (King James Bible).
7. Evans, "Diaries," November 20, 1973.
8. Author interview with Gary Evans, May 28, 2021.
9. Lennon and Ono, *All We Are Saying*, pp. 22–23.
10. See Connolly, *Being John Lennon: A Restless Life* (New York: Pegasus, 2018), p. 358.
11. May Pang with Henry Edwards, *Loving John: The Untold Story* (New York: Warner, 1983), p. 61.
12. Email from Adrian Sinclair, December 13, 2021.
13. Author interview with Peter Frampton, September 6, 2022.
14. Author interview with Susan Markheim, June 16, 2022.
15. Mansfield, *The White Book*, p. 178.
16. Evans, "LTBL," p. 229.
17. Evans, "LTBL," p. 230.
18. Evans, "LTBL," p. 230.
19. Evans, "LTBL," p. 231.
20. Author interview with Fran Hughes Reynolds, October 15, 2021.
21. Author interview with Reynolds, October 15, 2021; Martin Porter, unpublished manuscript, January 2022.
22. See "Executive Roundtable," *Billboard*, October 25, 1969, p. 6.
23. Martin Porter and David Goggin, "The House That Hendrix Built: Inside the Birth of the Record Plant," *Rolling Stone*, March 19, 2018, www.rollingstone.com/music/music-features/the-house-that-hendrix-built-inside-the-birth-of-the-record-plant-118904/.
24. Author interview with Reynolds, October 15, 2021.
25. Author interview with Reynolds, October 15, 2021.
26. Author interview with Reynolds, October 15, 2021.
27. Badman, *The Beatles Off the Record 2*, pp. 112–13.
28. Evans, "LTBL," p. 232.
29. Lennon, letter to Phil Spector, December 1973.
30. Author interview with Reynolds, October 15, 2021.
31. Evans, "LTBL," p. 233.

32. Evans, "LTBL," pp. 233–34.
33. Evans, "LTBL," p. 234.
34. Evans, "LTBL," p. 234.

CHAPTER 37: SO WHAT?

1. Author interview with Gary Evans, November 19, 2021.
2. Schaffner, *The Beatles Forever*, p. 161.
3. Lennon, *John*, p. 257.
4. Author interview with Reynolds, October 15, 2021.
5. Lennon, *John*, p. 257.
6. Lennon, *John*, p. 257.
7. Martin, interview with Lily Evans, 2004.
8. Author interview with May Pang, February 28, 2019.
9. Cott and Doudna, *The Ballad of John and Yoko*, p. 237.
10. Author interview with Reynolds, October 15, 2021.
11. Author interview with Reynolds, October 15, 2021.
12. Evans, "Notebook, 1975," p. 111.
13. Pang, *Instamatic Karma: Photographs of John Lennon* (New York: St. Martin's Press, 2008), p. 12.
14. The March 28, 1974, session was commemorated with the bootleg release entitled *A Toot and a Snore in '74* (Mistral Music, 1992).
15. Evans, "Diaries," April 6, 1974.
16. Evans, "LTBL," p. 240.
17. Evans, "LTBL," pp. 240–41.
18. Evans, "LTBL," p. 241.
19. Evans, "LTBL," p. 240.
20. Evans, "LTBL," p. 238.

CHAPTER 38: TELL THE TRUTH

1. Author interview with Reynolds, October 15, 2021.
2. Author interview with Reynolds, October 15, 2021.
3. Author interview with Reynolds, October 15, 2021.
4. Evans, "LTBL," p. 91.
5. Mark Lapidos, "Preface," *Fandom and the Beatles: The Act You've Known for All These Years*, ed. Kenneth Womack and Kit O'Toole (Oxford: Oxford University Press, 2021), p. xi.
6. Author interview with Blair Aaronson, April 28, 2022.
7. Author interview with Aaronson, April 28, 2022, November 28, 2021.
8. J. W. Haymer, *Silverspoon: The Greatest Band Nobody Ever Heard*, www.jwhaymer.blogspot.com, 2013.
9. Haymer, *Silverspoon*.
10. Haymer, *Silverspoon*.
11. Haymer, *Silverspoon*.
12. Haymer, *Silverspoon*.
13. Haymer, *Silverspoon*.
14. Author interview with Andrew DiBiccari, September 22, 2021.
15. Doyle, interview with Mal Evans, December 14, 1975.

16. Evans, "LTBL," p. 231.
17. Author interview with DiBiccari, June 21, 2022.
18. Author interview with Var Smith, August 29, 2021.
19. Author interview with Reynolds, October 15, 2021.
20. Author interview with Richard Digby Smith, December 5, 2021.
21. Author interview with Dennis Killeen, September 17, 2021.
22. Author interview with Joanne Lenard, July 13, 2022.
23. Richard Digby Smith, *One Two Three Four: The Life and Times of a Recording Studio Engineer* (Kilworth, U.K.: The Book Guild, 2020), pp. 240–41.
24. Author interview with Var Smith, August 29, 2021.
25. Author interview with Erika Calvert, May 13, 2021.
26. Author interview with Var Smith, August 29, 2021.
27. Author interview with Aaronson, April 28, 2022.
28. Adam Clayson, *Ringo Starr: Straight Man or Joker?* (St. Paul, Minn.: Paragon House, 1992), p. 250.
29. Gross, interview with Mal Evans, November 29, 1975.
30. Haymer, *Silverspoon*.
31. "Interview: Mark Volman," *Music Illuminati* (August 4, 2011), music-illuminati.com /interview-mark-volman/.
32. Haymer, *Silverspoon*.
33. Evans, "LTBL," p. 239.
34. Author interview with Gary Evans, August 29, 2021.
35. Author interview with Laura Gross, March 23, 2021.
36. Gross, interview with Mal Evans, November 29, 1975.

CHAPTER 39: CRYING IN A HOTEL ROOM, NY

1. Author interview with Bramwell, August 6, 2021.
2. John E. Mason Jr., letter to Mal Evans, May 13, 1975.
3. Author interview with Mason, November 16, 2021.
4. Mason, letter to Fran Hughes, October 2, 1974.
5. Author interview with Mason, November 16, 2021.
6. Author interview with Mason, November 16, 2021.
7. Haymer, *Silverspoon*.
8. Author interview with Aaronson, April 28, 2022.
9. Author interview with Aaronson, March 30, 2021.
10. Evans, "Notebook, 1975," p. 6.
11. Harrison, letter to Mal Evans, February 25, 1975.
12. Lennon, letter to Mal Evans, May 1975.
13. McCartney, letter to Mal Evans, 1975.
14. Starr, letter to Mal Evans, April 28, 1975.
15. Frost, interview with Mal Evans, May 21, 1975.
16. Author interview with Gary Evans, March 13, 2021.
17. Martin, interview with Lily Evans, 2004.
18. Matovina, *Without You*, p. 292.
19. Author interview with Alyss Dorese, August 16, 2021.
20. Author interview with Robert Markel, August 16, 2021.
21. Missing page from Evans, "Notebook, 1975," furnished courtesy of Tracks.co.uk.

22. Author interview with Reynolds, October 15, 2021.
23. Evans, letter to David Mook, November 4, 1975.
24. Author interview with Aaronson, November 28, 2021.
25. Author interview with Reynolds, October 15, 2021.

CHAPTER 40: DEAD LETTER OFFICE

1. Author interview with Gross, August 31, 2021.
2. Author interview with Gross, August 31, 2021.
3. Evans, "Notebook, 1975," p. 25.
4. Author interview with Calvert, May 13, 2021.
5. *The John Lennon Letters*, p. 327.
6. Lapidos, letter to Mal Evans, August 8, 1975.
7. Fran Hughes Reynolds, letter to Fred and Joan Evans, February 20, 1976.
8. Author interview with Mark Lapidos, May 10, 2021.
9. Doyle, interview with Mal Evans, December 14, 1975.
10. Gross, interview with Mal Evans, November 29, 1975.
11. Audio from Mal's Grand Ballroom presentation, September 6, 1975, recorded by Tom Carswell and furnished courtesy of Bill Cermak.
12. Audio from Mal's Grand Ballroom presentation, September 6, 1975.
13. Author interview with Teddy Judge, August 19, 2022.
14. Author interview with Shelli Wolis, March 19, 2021.
15. Porter, unpublished manuscript, January 2022.
16. Author interview with Reynolds, October 15, 2021.
17. Author interview with Gross, March 23, 2021.
18. Author interview with Gross, March 23, 2021.
19. Author interview with Gross, March 23, 2021.
20. Author interview with Martin Torgoff, January 24, 2022.
21. Gross, interview with Mal Evans, November 29, 1975.
22. Matovina, *Without You*, pp. 303–4.
23. See Roy Carr, "Apple Corps: They Didn't Have to Be So Nice (We Would Have Liked Them Anyway," *New Musical Express*, May 17, 1975, www.rocksbackpages.com /Library/Article/apple-corps-they-didnt-have-to-be-so-nice-we-would-have-liked -them-anyway.
24. Email from Adrian Sinclair, June 14, 2022.
25. Evans, "LTBL," pp. 205–6. Sandford, *McCartney*, contends that Mal's elation may not merely have been limited to his opportunity to serve as Wings's North American roadie. According to Sandford, Mal had "trumpeted it around town that he confidently expected a 'five-figure cheque [from] the office'" after having "recently been in touch with both McCartney and Lennon to discuss whether he might be due various back wages." See Sandford, *McCartney*, p. 241.
26. Author interview with Rip Rense, December 12, 2021.
27. Doyle, interview with Mal Evans, December 14, 1975.
28. Doyle, interview with Mal Evans, December 14, 1975.
29. Author interview with Mark Clarke, February 27, 2022.
30. Author interview with Lenard, July 13, 2022.
31. Mal Evans, letter to Lily Evans, December 1975.
32. Author interview with Lapidos, May 10, 2021.

33. Martin, interview with Lily Evans, 2004.
34. Elliot Mintz, interview with John Lennon, *Earth News Radio*, January 1, 1976; special thanks are due to Chip Madinger for highlighting this key interaction.
35. Author interview with Gross, March 23, 2021.
36. Author interview with Marianne Evans, May 14, 2021.
37. Author interview with Reynolds, October 15, 2021.
38. Evans, Last Will and Testament, January 3, 1976.
39. Evans, Last Will and Testament, January 3, 1976.
40. Author interview with Reynolds, October 15, 2021.
41. Author interview with Mansfield, January 21, 2021.
42. Reynolds, letter to Fred and Joan Evans, February 20, 1976.
43. Author interview with Calvert, May 13, 2021.
44. Patrick Snyder and Dolores Ziebarth, "'Sixth Beatle' Mal Evans Killed in Los Angeles," *Rolling Stone*, February 12, 1976, p. 10.
45. Author interview with Gross, March 23, 2021.
46. Shooting Review Board Report and Officer-Involved Shooting Report, Los Angeles Police Department, D.R. #76–430 212, July 6, 1976, obtained pursuant to the California Public Records Act.
47. Shooting Review Board Report and Officer-Involved Shooting Report. According to the toxicology analysis conducted on January 5, 1976, Mal had a mild, therapeutic level of Valium in his system (.10 mg of diazepam) and a blood alcohol concentration of .07 percent. This did not constitute legal impairment under existing California statutes. Autopsy Report, Department of Chief Medical Examiner–Coroner, Los Angeles County, D.R. #76–186, January 6, 1976, obtained pursuant to the California Public Records Act.
48. Shooting Review Board Report and Officer-Involved Shooting Report.
49. Shooting Review Board Report and Officer-Involved Shooting Report.
50. Author interview with Reynolds, October 15, 2021.
51. Quoted in Jeff Giles, "The Day Beatles Assistant Mal Evans Was Killed by Police," *Ultimate Classic Rock*, January 5, 2016, ultimateclassicrock.com/mal-evans-killed/.
52. Pang, *Instamatic Karma*, p. 177.

EPILOGUE: A CELLARFUL OF DUST

1. Author interview with Leena Kutti, December 21, 2020.
2. Author interview with Kutti, January 5, 2021.
3. Author interview with Kutti, January 5, 2021.
4. Matthew Martin, letter to Robert P. Mulvey, March 18, 1988.
5. Hughes, affidavit, June 30, 1976.
6. Joanne Lenard and John Hoernle, letter to Lily Evans, January 7, 1976.
7. Author interview with Lenard, July 13, 2022.
8. Mal had left his 1967 diary behind on a shelf in Sunbury. Lipton likely recorded the year in error; also, Mal's 1969 diary was among the items Hoernle returned that February day.
9. Harold Lipton, letter to John Hoernle and Joanne Lenard, February 10, 1976.
10. Author interview with Torgoff, January 24, 2022.
11. Lipton, letter to Ringo Starr, January 13, 1976.
12. Lipton, letter to Lily Evans, June 11, 1976.

13. Lipton, letter to Lily Evans, August 15, 1979.
14. Lily Evans, letter to Joanne Lenard and John Hoernle, April 21, 1976.
15. Author interview with Gary Evans, August 20, 2021.
16. Sakol died in 2014; in a telephone interview conducted on January 23, 2022, Bennett claimed to have no recollection of meeting with Lily and Gary Evans. In 1982, Bennett and Sakol produced the acclaimed documentary *The Compleat Beatles*.
17. Vera Barr, letter to Lily Evans, February 22, 1978.
18. Author interview with June Evans, June 6, 2021.
19. Author interview with Barbara Evans, May 20, 2021.
20. Lennon, letter to Lily Evans, January 1976.
21. Oldfield, "Police to Probe Big Mal Shooting," *Liverpool Echo*, January 14, 1976, p. 5.
22. Author interview with Gary Evans, February 5, 2021.
23. Mal's estate was processed on December 22, 1975, at the Winchester District Probate Registry in the amount of £3,300.
24. Author interview with Barbara Evans, May 20, 2021.
25. Reynolds, letter to Fred and Joan Evans, February 20, 1976.
26. Author interview with Reynolds, October 15, 2021.
27. The Beatles, *The Beatles Anthology*, p. 85.
28. Author interview with Reynolds, October 15, 2021.
29. Shooting Review Board Report and Officer-Involved Shooting Report.
30. Author interview with Julie Evans Rossow, January 20, 2022.
31. Author interview with Gross, August 31, 2021.
32. Martin, interview with Lily Evans, 2004.
33. George Harrison, letter to Lily Evans, October 26, 1982.
34. Author interview with Gary Evans, September 17, 2021.
35. Author interview with Gary Evans, July 16, 2021.
36. Gross, interview with Mal Evans, November 29, 1975.

BIBLIOGRAPHY

Aigmüller, Rudolf [Tony Barrow]. "Filming, Curling, and Playing in Austria." *The Beatles Book* 109 (May 1985): 34–36.

"Alf Bicknell: Gary James's Interview with the Beatles' Chauffeur." *Classic Bands* (1996), www.classicbands.com/AlfBicknellInterview.html.

"Another Beatles Music Boss." *Disc and Music Echo*, May 3, 1969, 6.

Aronowitz, Al. "The Return of the Beatles." *The Saturday Evening Post*, August 8, 1964, 22–28.

Asher, Peter. *The Beatles from A to Zed: An Alphabetical Mystery Tour*. New York: Henry Holt, 2019.

Aspinall, Neil. "The Beatles and Me! [Part 2]." *16 Magazine*, June 1965, 20–26.

———. "Beatles Tour Britain." *Fabulous 208*, August 16, 1966, 11.

———. "The First Official Mal Evans Story." *The Beatles Book* 46 (May 1967): 11–12.

———. "Look What Happened in Just One Year." *Record Mirror*, October 19, 1963, 6.

———. "Neil's Column." *The Beatles Book* 35 (June 1966): 25.

Babiuk, Andy. *Beatles Gear: All the Fab Four's Instruments, from Stage to Studio*. Milwaukee, Wisc.: Backbeat, 2001.

Badman, Keith. *The Beatles Off the Record: Outrageous Opinions and Unrehearsed Interviews*. London: Omnibus, 2001.

———. *The Beatles Off the Record 2: The Dream Is Over*. London: Omnibus, 2009.

Baird, Julia. *Paul Talks: Paul McCartney in Conversation*. Compact disc, 1987.

Baker, Glenn A., with Roger DiLernia. *The Beatles Down Under: The 1964 Australia and New Zealand Tour*. Glebe, Australia: Wild and Woolley, 1982.

Barrell, Tony. *The Beatles on the Roof*. London: Omnibus, 2017.

Barrow, Tony. "Big Mal, the Beatles' Roadie." *The Beatles Book* 180 (April 1991): 4–8.

———. *John, Paul, George, Ringo, and Me: The Real Beatles Story*. London: Carlton, 2005.

———. *The Making of the Beatles' Magical Mystery Tour*. London: Omnibus, 1999.

Beatles, The. *The Beatles Anthology*. San Francisco, Calif.: Chronicle Books, 2000.

"Beatles Firm, Melcher Deal." *Billboard*, December 23, 1967, 4.

Bedford, Carol. *Waiting for the Beatles: An Apple Scruff's Story*. London: Blandford, 1984.

Bennett, Barbara. "My Beatle Days." *BlogSpot*, June 30, 2019. mybeatledays.blogspot.com/2019/06/apple-people.html.

Berkenstadt, Jim. *The Beatle Who Vanished*. Madison, Wisc.: Rock and Roll Detective, 2013.

Bicknell, Al, with Garry Marsh. *Baby, You Can Drive My Car!* Newcastle: Number 9 Books, 1989.

Birkin, Andrew. *POV: A Life in Pictures*. Paris: Albin Michel Beaux Livres, 2022.

Boyer, Richard O. "Profiles: The Hot Bach, Part I." *The New Yorker*, June 24, 1944, 30–44.

Bramwell, Tony, with Rosemary Kingsland. *Magical Mystery Tours: My Life with the Beatles*. London: Robson, 2005.

Braun, Michael. *Love Me Do! The Beatles' Progress*. London: Penguin, 1964.

Carr, Roy. "Apple Corps: They Didn't Have to Be So Nice (We Would Have Liked Them Anyway)." *New Musical Express*, May 17, 1975. www.rocksbackpages.com/Library/Article/apple-corps-they-didnt-have-to-be-so-nice-we-would-have-liked-them-anyway.

"Case Against Beatles' Company Fails: Manager Was Hurt in Road Crash." *Liverpool Echo*, February 24, 1964, 8.

Cavendish, Leslie, with Eduardo Jáuregui and Neil McNaughton. *The Cutting Edge: The Story of the Beatles' Hairdresser Who Defined an Era*. Richmond, U.K.: Alma Books, 2017.

Clayson, Adam. *Ringo Starr: Straight Man or Joker?* St. Paul, Minn.: Paragon House, 1992.

Coleman, Ray. "Inside Showbiz." *Melody Maker*, January 1965, 13, 20.

Connolly, Ray. *Being John Lennon: A Restless Life*. New York: Pegasus, 2018.

———. "Destroyed by the Beatles." *The Daily Mail*, April 20, 2005, 34.

———. *The Ray Connolly Beatles Archive*. London: Plumray Books, 2011.

Cott, Jonathan, and Christine Doudna, eds. *The Ballad of John and Yoko*. New York: Dolphin, 1982.

Craig, James. "The Beatles' Studio Secrets." *Record World*, October 31, 1964, 8–9.

"Daughter for Beatles' Pal." *Liverpool Echo*, April 19, 1966, 4.

Davies, Hunter. *The Beatles: The Authorized Biography*. London: Heinemann, 1968.

———. *The Beatles Book*. London: Ebury, 2016.

———. "The Beatles, Part II." *Life* 65 (September 20, 1968): 60–82.

Davis, Ivor. *The Beatles and Me on Tour*. Los Angeles, Calif.: Cockney Kid, 2014.

Dean, Johnny [Sean O'Mahony]. "The 'Paperback Writer' Session." *The Beatles Book* 35 (June 1966): 6–11.

de Herrera, Nancy Cooke. *All You Need Is Love: An Eyewitness Account of When Spirituality Spread from the East to the West*. San Diego, Calif.: Jodere, 2003.

DiLello, Richard. *The Longest Cocktail Party: An Insider's Diary of the Beatles*. Chicago, Ill.: Playboy, 1972.

Doggett, Peter. *You Never Give Me Your Money: The Beatles After the Breakup*. New York: HarperCollins, 2011.

Drummond, Norrie. "Dinner with the Beatles." *NME*, May 27, 1967, 2–3.

Du Noyer, Paul. "Just Out of Shot: Interview with Neil Aspinall." *Mojo* 35 (October 1996): 74–79.

Edmonds, Mark. "Here, There, and Everywhere." *The Sunday Times Magazine*, March 20, 2005, 30–40.

Emerick, Geoff, with Howard Massey. *Here, There, and Everywhere: My Life Recording the Music of the Beatles*. New York: Gotham, 2006.

Evans, Mal. "The Beatles Get Back." *The Beatles Book* 72 (July 1969): 22–29.

———. "Beatles in India." *The Beatles Book* 58 (May 1968): 7–12.

———. "Beatles—U.S.A." Unpublished manuscript, 1965. Malcolm Frederick Evans Archives.

———. "Diaries." [1963–1974.] 10 vols. Malcolm Frederick Evans Archives.

———. "The Eighteenth Single." *The Beatles Book* 62 (September 1968): 6–11.

———. "Living the Beatles' Legend: Or 200 Miles to Go." Unpublished manuscript, 1976. Malcolm Frederick Evans Archives.

———. "Mal's Diary." *The Beatles Book* 63 (October 1968): 11–12.
———. "Mal's Page." *The Beatles Book* 42 (January 1967): 25.
———. "My Life with the Beatles." *16 Magazine*, May 1965, 10–11.
———. "Notebook, 1966." Unpublished. Malcolm Frederick Evans Archives.
———. "Notebook, 1967–1968." Unpublished. Courtesy of Davinia Taylor.
———. "Notebook, 1975." Unpublished. Malcolm Frederick Evans Archives.
———. "Ringo and George in California." *The Beatles Book* 61 (August 1968): 24–26, 31.
———. "Thirty New Beatle Grooves on Double Disc Album." *The Beatles Book* 64 (November 1968): 6–15.

Evans, Mal, and Neil Aspinall. "Magical Mystery Tour." *The Beatles Book* 53 (December 1967): 6–13.

"Everything Ready." *The Beatles Book* 40 (November 1966): 29.

"Executive Roundtable." *Billboard*, October 25, 1969, 6.

Fabian, Jenny, and Johnny Byrne. *Groupie*. London: New English Library, 1969.

"Fans Clean Van." *The Beatles Book* 36 (July 1966): 29.

Fawcett, Anthony. *John Lennon: One Day at a Time—A Personal Biography of the Seventies*. New York: Grove Press, 1976.

"Frantic Teens Rout Cops and Rush Beatles." *Chicago Tribune*, June 24, 1964, 45.

Frost, David, prod. *A Salute to the Beatles: Once Upon a Time*. ABC-TV, 1975.

"Gary Fawkes." *The Beatles Book* 76 (November 1969): 31.

"'Get Back' Postponed." *The Beatles Book* 73 (August 1969): 29.

Giles, Jeff. "The Day Beatles Assistant Mal Evans Was Killed by Police." *Ultimate Classic Rock*, January 5, 2016. ultimateclassicrock.com/mal-evans-killed.

Gilmore, Mikal. "Beatles' Acid Test: How LSD Opened the Door to 'Revolver.'" *Rolling Stone*, August 25, 2016. www.rollingstone.com/feature/beatles-acid-test-how-lsd-opened-the-door-to-revolver-251417/.

"Girl Slashes Wrists Near Beatles." *Sydney Morning Herald*, June 24, 1964, 1.

Goodman, Fred. *Allen Klein: The Man Who Bailed Out the Beatles, Made the Stones, and Transformed Rock 'n' Roll*. New York: Houghton Mifflin Harcourt, 2016.

Granados, Stefan. *Those Were the Days 2.0: The Beatles and Apple*. London: Cherry Red Books, 2021.

Gunby, George. *Hello Goodbye: The Story of Alistair "Mr. Fixit" Taylor*. Belper, U.K.: Yesterday Once More, 2002.

Gunderson, Chuck. *Some Fun Tonight!: The Backstage Story of How the Beatles Rocked America—The Historic Tours of 1964–1966*. 2 vols. Milwaukee, Wisc.: Backbeat: 2016.

Harrington, Kevin. *Who's the Redhead on the Roof?: My Life with the Beatles*. Forchheim, Germany: Apcor Books, 2015.

Harrison, Louise. *My Kid Brother's Band: A.K.A the Beatles*. Morley, Mo: Acclaim Press, 2014.

"Harry Nilsson's 10 Best Songs." *Far Out*, June 15, 2021. faroutmagazine.co.uk/harry-nilsson-10-best-songs/.

Haymer, J. W. *Silverspoon: The Greatest Band Nobody Ever Heard*. www.jwhaymer.blogspot.com, 2013.

Higham, Brian. "My Story." *Manchester Beat*, 2012. www.manchesterbeat.com/index.php/my-story/brian-higham.

"How John Lennon's Long-Lost $2.4 Million Gibson J-160E Guitar Was Found." *Guitar World*, November 10, 2015. www.guitarworld.com/gear/how-john-lennons-long-lost-24-million.

Hull, Dave. "Visitors to Movie Location Tell of Beatlemania Antics." *KRLA Beat*, March 17, 1965, 1, 4.

Hunter, Nigel. "From the Music Capitals of the World: London." *Billboard*, December 16, 1967, 50–51.

Huntley, Elliot J. *Mystical One: George Harrison—After the Break-Up of the Beatles.* Toronto: Guernica, 2006.

Hutchins, Chris, and Peter Thompson. *Elvis Meets the Beatles: The Untold Story of Their Entangled Lives.* London: John Blake, 2004.

"Interview: Mark Volman." *Music Illuminati*, August 4, 2011. music-illuminati.com/interview-mark-volman/.

"It's a Hard Road: 'Beat Instrumental' Looks at the Roadie Scene." *Beat Instrumental and International Recording Studio*, July 1970, 40–41.

"Iveys Find It Hard to Please the Beatles." *Disc and Music Echo*, July 5, 1969, 16.

Jackson, Peter, dir. *The Beatles: Get Back*. Apple Corps, 2021.

James, Frederick [Tony Barrow]. "Behind the Headlines." *The Beatles Book* 30 (January 1966): 13–14.

———. "The Fifth Beatle Gets Married." *The Beatles Book* (October 1968): 6–9.

Jones, Cliff. "Apple Scruffs: 'We're Waiting for the Beatles.'" *Mojo* 35 (October 1996): 68–72.

Kane, Larry. *Lennon Revealed.* Philadelphia, Pa.: Running Press, 2005.

———. *Ticket to Ride: Inside the Beatles' 1964 Tour that Changed the World.* Philadelphia, Pa.; Running Press, 2003.

———. *When They Were Boys: The True Story of the Beatles' Rise to the Top*. Philadelphia, Pa.: Running Press, 2013.

Keane, Colm. *The Beatles' Irish Concerts*. Bray, Ireland: Capel Island Press, 2008.

Lapidos, Mark. "Preface." *Fandom and the Beatles: The Act You've Known for All These Years.* Ed. Kenneth Womack and Kit O'Toole. Oxford: Oxford University Press, 2021, ix–xi.

Leigh, Spencer. *The Cavern Cave: Rise of the Beatles and Merseybeat.* Carmarthen, Wales: McNidder and Grace, 2015.

Lennon, Cynthia. *John*. London: Hodder and Stoughton, 2005.

Lennon, John. *The John Lennon Letters*. Ed. Hunter Davies. New York: Little, Brown, 2012.

———. *Lennon Remembers*. Interview by Jann Wenner, 1970. New York: Verso, 2000.

Lennon, John, and Yoko Ono. *All We Are Saying: The Last Major Interview with John Lennon and Yoko Ono*. Interview by David Sheff. Ed. G. Barry Golson. New York: Griffin, 2000.

Lewisohn, Mark. *The Beatles Live!* London: Pavilion, 1986.

———. *The Complete Beatles Recording Sessions: The Official Abbey Road Studio Session Notes, 1962–1970*. New York: Harmony, 1988.

———. "Macca to Me in 1991, Speaking of May 9, 1969." *Twitter* (May 9, 2019), twitter.com/marklewisohn/status/1126576151072247809?lang=en.

———. *Tune In: The Beatles—All These Years*. New York: Crown, 2013.

Madinger, Chip, and Scott Raile. *Lennonology: Strange Days Indeed—A Scrapbook of Madness.* Springfield, Mo.: Open Your Books, 2015.

Mansfield, Ken. *The Roof: The Beatles' Final Concert*. New York: Post Hill, 2018.

———. *The White Book: The Beatles, the Bands, the Biz: An Insider's Look at an Era.* New York: Thomas Nelson, 2007.

Martin, George, with Jeremy Hornsby. *All You Need Is Ears*. New York: St. Martin's Press, 1979.

Martin, George, with William Pearson. *With a Little Help from My Friends: The Making of Sgt. Pepper*. Boston: Little, Brown, 1994.

Matovina, Dan. *Without You: The Tragic Story of Badfinger*. San Mateo, Calif.: Frances Glover Books, 2000.
Matteo, Steve. *Let It Be*. New York: Continuum, 2004.
McNab, Ken. *The Beatles in Scotland*. Edinburgh: Birlinn, 2008.
Miles, Barry. *The Beatles Diary*. Volume 1: *The Beatles Years*. London: Omnibus, 2009.
———. *In the Sixties*. London: Pimlico, 2003.
———. *Paul McCartney: Many Years from Now*. New York: Henry Holt, 1997.
Murray, Charles Shaar. "Lennon, Lenin, the 'Oz' Schoolkids Issue, and Me." *The Word*, April 2011. www.rocksbackpages.com/Library/Article/lennon-lenin-the-iozi-schoolkids-issue -and-me.
"Neil's Present." *The Beatles Book* 18 (January 1965): 29.
"New Amps for Beatles." *Beat Instrumental* 31 (November 1965): 25.
Norman, Philip. *Shout!: The Beatles in Their Generation*. New York: Simon and Shuster, 1981.
O'Dell, Chris, with Katherine Ketchum. *Miss O'Dell: My Hard Days and Long Nights with the Beatles, the Stones, Bob Dylan, Eric Clapton, and the Women They Loved*. New York: Touchstone, 2009.
Oldfield, Stephen. "Police to Probe Big Mal Shooting." *Liverpool Echo*, January 14, 1976, 5.
Pang, May. *Instamatic Karma: Photographs of John Lennon*. New York: St. Martin's Press, 2008.
Pang, May, with Henry Edwards. *Loving John: The Untold Story*. New York: Warner, 1983.
Pearce, Vicki. "Charabanc: All Aboard the Sharrabang!" *Warts and All*, July 20, 2019. warts andall.blog/2019/07/20/charabanc-all-aboard-the-sharrabang/.
"People Behind the Stars, No. 4: Road Manager Mal Evans." *Beat Instrumental* 48 (April 1967): 33–34.
Petersen, David, and Dick Denney. *The Vox Story: A Complete History of the Legend*. Westport, Conn.: The Bold Strummer, 1993.
Rayl, A. J. S., and Curt Gunther. *Beatles '64: A Hard Day's Night in America*. New York: Doubleday, 1989.
Roxon, Lillian. "101 Hours with John Lennon and Paul McCartney." *Eye*, September 1968, 32–35, 81–82.
Sandford, Christopher. *McCartney*. New York: Carroll and Graf, 2006.
Schaffner, Nicholas. *The Beatles Forever*. New York: McGraw-Hill, 1977.
Schwartz, Francie. *Body Count*. New York: Straight Arrow, 1972.
Schwensen, Dave. *The Beatles at Shea Stadium: The Story Behind Their Greatest Concert*. Burlington, Vt.: North Shore, 2013.
Scott, Ken, with Bobby Owsinski. *Abbey Road to Ziggy Stardust: Off the Record with the Beatles, Bowie, Elton, and So Much More*. Los Angeles: Alfred Music, 2012.
Shepherd, Billy [Peter Jones]. *The True Story of the Beatles*. New York: Bantam, 1964.
Shotton, Pete, and Nicholas Schaffner. *John Lennon: In My Life*. New York: Stein and Day, 1983.
Smith, Alan. "Alan Smith Goes on Tour with the Beatles!" *NME*, December 10, 1965, 3, 16.
Smith, Richard Digby. *One Two Three Four: The Life and Times of a Recording Studio Engineer*. Kilworth, U.K.: The Book Guild, 2020.
"Sound City to Beatles' Aid." *Beat Instrumental* 33 (January 1966): 25.
Sounes, Howard. *Fab: An Intimate Life of Paul McCartney*. Boston: Da Capo, 2010.
Southall, Brian. *Abbey Road: The Story of the World's Most Famous Studios*. Wellingborough, U.K.: Patrick Stephens, 1982.
Spitz, Bob. *The Beatles: The Biography*. Boston: Little, Brown, 2005.

Starr, Ringo. "I Want to Lead a Normal Life." *Hit Parader*, September 1968, 8–10, 51.
———. *Postcards from the Boys*. San Francisco: Chronicle Books, 2004.
Steele-Waller, Georgiana. *In My Life, So Far . . .* Glendale, Ill.: Georgiana Steele-Waller, 2013.
Sulpy, Doug, and Ray Schweighardt. *Get Back: The Unauthorized Chronicle of the Beatles'* Let It Be *Disaster*. New York: Griffin, 1997.
The Talent Spot. Radio script. January 22, 1963. Malcolm Frederick Evans Archives.
Taylor, Alistair. "Forward." In Tony Barrow, *The Making of the Beatles' Magical Mystery Tour*. London: Omnibus, 1999. 1–5.
———. *With the Beatles*. London: John Blake, 2003.
Taylor, Derek. "Apple 1988: A Year for Nostalgia." *Hit Parader*, March 1969, 36.
———. *As Time Goes By*. London: Faber and Faber, 2018.
———. *Fifty Years Adrift*. Guilford, U.K.: Genesis, 1984.
———. *Gilet de Sauvetage Est Sous la Siege*. Internal newsletter. Apple, November 1968.
———. "Making a Gold Record." *KRLA Beat*, May 5, 1965, 5.
———. *Nadolig Llawen*. Internal newsletter. Apple, December 1968.
———. "Paul McC. Was My House Guest!" *Teen Datebook* 6.4 (September 1967): 30–31.
A Toot and a Snore in '74. LP. Mistral Music, 1992.
Townshend, Pete. *Who I Am: A Memoir*. New York: HarperCollins, 2012.
Tozer, James. "In Paul McCartney's Arms: The Puppy He Loved So Much He Wrote About Her in the Beatles Hit 'Martha My Dear.'" *The Daily Mail*, November 10, 2017. www.dailymail.co.uk/news/article-5071837/In-Paul-McCartney-s-arms-puppy-loved-much.html.
Turner, Steve. *Beatles '66: The Revolutionary Year*. New York: HarperCollins, 2016.
"Unrecognized." *The Beatles Book* 74 (September 1969): 31.
Visconti, Tony. *The Autobiography: Bowie, Bolan, and the Brooklyn Boy*. New York: HarperCollins, 2007.
Webb, Jimmy. *The Cake and the Rain: A Memoir*. New York: St. Martin's Press, 2018.
Weinberg, Max, with Robert Santelli. *The Big Beat: Conversations with Rock's Great Drummers*. Chicago, Ill.: Contemporary Books, 1984.
"Welcome to Mal." *The Beatles Book* 89 (September 1983): 14.
White, Timothy. *George Harrison Reconsidered*. London: Larchwood and Weir, 2013.
Wilson, Brian, with Ben Greenman. *I Am Brian Wilson: A Memoir*. Boston: Da Capo, 2016.

CREDITS

Every effort has been made to contact copyright holders of material reproduced in this book. We would be grateful for the opportunity to rectify any omissions in subsequent editions should they be drawn to our attention.

COVER PHOTO

Paul with Mal, upon their arrival at Maharishi Mahesh Yogi's Transcendental Meditation center in India, February 20, 1968 (Getty)

PROLOGUE

Mal's 1963 diary (Malcolm Frederick Evans Archives [hereafter "MFEA"])
Diary entry, week of January 23, 1963 (MFEA)

CHAPTER 1

Mal with parents in Wales, c. 1936 (MFEA)

CHAPTER 2

Pam, Mal, and Barbara on the Rhyl promenade (MFEA)
1949 Holt High School photo with Mal on the far left (MFEA)
Mal at the GPO with his future best man Gordon Gaskell (right) and boyhood chum Ronnie Gore (MFEA)

CHAPTER 3

Mal in front of his Hillside Road home (MFEA)
Mal and Lily's wedding day (MFEA)
Mal and Lily's wedding departure (MFEA)

CHAPTER 4

Mal's "pros and cons" list (MFEA)

CHAPTER 5

Mal's diary entry from his first day with the Beatles (MFEA)

CHAPTER 6

Mal's 1963 passport (MFEA)
Mal backstage during his early days with the Beatles (MFEA/Mark Lewisohn)

CHAPTER 7

George riding piggyback on Mal (Beatles Book Photo Library [hereafter "BBPL"])

CHAPTER 8

Mal's *Ed Sullivan Show* diary entry (MFEA)
Mal setting up Ringo's drum kit at the Washington Coliseum (Alamy)
George on the set of *A Hard Day's Night* (MFEA)
Paul in a railway car holding a photo of Elvis (MFEA)

CHAPTER 9

Mal with a koala bear in Australia (MFEA)
Mal with a python in Australia (MFEA)
Mal stringing a guitar (BBPL)

CHAPTER 10

Gary with Lady the dog (MFEA)

CHAPTER 11

Mal and the Beatles at Forest Hills (Alamy)
Mal posing with gun and holster (MFEA)
Mal, Neil, and George (BBPL)

CHAPTER 12

John and Paul on the *Help!* set (MFEA)
Mal portraying the Channel Swimmer in *Help!* (BBPL)
Mal on the *Help!* set in the Alps (MFEA)
Mal on the *Help!* set in the Bahamas (MFEA)

CHAPTER 13

Mal and George with a Vox amp (MFEA)

CHAPTER 14

The Colonel presenting Mal with a "Girls! Girls! Girls!" bathrobe (MFEA)

CHAPTER 15

Mal with infant Julie (MFEA)

CHAPTER 16

Brian Epstein in a railway car en route to West Germany (MFEA)
Paul, Mal, and Alf en route to Tokyo (Getty)
Mal protecting Paul from fans rushing the stage at San Francisco's Cow Palace (MFEA)
John, Mal, and Paul backstage at Munich's Circus-Krone-Bau (Robert Whitaker)
Mal with Paul in Tokyo (MFEA)

CHAPTER 17

Mal posing with his shotgun from Kenya and a holstered pistol (MFEA)
Julie with Martha, Paul's beloved sheepdog (MFEA)
John during the making of *Sgt. Pepper's Lonely Hearts Club Band* (MFEA)

CHAPTER 18

Mal's *Sgt. Pepper* logo (Davinia Taylor)

CHAPTER 19

Mal posing on the *Sgt. Pepper* set with, from left to right, Jann Haworth, Mohammed Chtaibi, Peter Blake, Andy Boulton, Trevor Sutton, Nigel Hartnup, unidentified Madame Tussauds employee, and Michael Cooper (Apple Corps Ltd.)
Mal during the *Sgt. Pepper* sessions (BBPL)

CHAPTER 20

Paul jamming with Jefferson Airplane's Jorma Kaukonen and Paul Kantner (MFEA)
Paul relaxing in the Rocky Mountains (MFEA)

Paul and Jane in the Rockies (MFEA)
Mal and Paul return from the United States (Alamy)
Mal and Gary posing with the Starkeys' kitten at Sunny Heights (MFEA)
Mal visiting John at Weybridge (Leslie Samuels Healy)

CHAPTER 21

Mal en route to Brian's wake with, from left to right, Pattie, George, Neil, and Paul (Getty)
Mal posing with the *Magical Mystery Tour* bus (MFEA)
Paul playing drums on the *Magical Mystery Tour* set (MFEA)
Mal in Rome (MFEA)

CHAPTER 22

John during the "Lady Madonna" video shoot (MFEA)
Paul during the "Lady Madonna" video shoot (MFEA)
Mal's various attempts at designing an Apple Corps logo (MFEA)

CHAPTER 23

Mal in Rishikesh (MFEA)
Mal (far right) in a group photo at the ashram (Getty)

CHAPTER 24

Magic Alex, John, Mal, and Paul arriving in New York City to promote Apple (Getty)

CHAPTER 25

Mal, Paul, John, and Lily at the *Yellow Submarine* premiere (BBPL)
Gary posing with Martha and the band at Cavendish Avenue during the Mad Day Out (Don McCullin)

CHAPTER 26

The Evans family at the Apple Christmas party (Tommy Hanley)
Mal with Ken Mansfield (MFEA)

CHAPTER 27

Mal coming to John's rescue during the Canadian TV interview (Richard Keith Wolff)
Mal on the Savile Row rooftop with Metropolitan Police constables (Apple Corps Ltd.)

CHAPTER 28

Mal with Linda, Paul, and Heather after the McCartneys' wedding (Alamy)
Mal's drawing of an infuriated Paul at Olympic Studios (MFEA)

CHAPTER 29

Mal's drawing of the *Abbey Road* cover shoot (MFEA)
Mal and Neil in Portugal (MFEA)

CHAPTER 30

John and Yoko in Toronto (MFEA)

CHAPTER 31

Mal with Badfinger: from left to right, Tom Evans, Pete Ham, Mike Gibbins, and Joey Molland (MFEA)

CHAPTER 32
Mal posing by the gates of EMI Recording Studios (MFEA)

CHAPTER 33
Mal and Ringo astride horses on the set of *Blindman* (MFEA)
Mal on the deck of the SS *France* (MFEA)

CHAPTER 34
Mal with Splinter: Bill Elliott, left, and Bobby Purvis (MFEA)

CHAPTER 35
Mal's 1973 passport (MFEA)
Fran Hughes's photo on the wall of the Record Plant (Francine Hughes Reynolds)

CHAPTER 36
Lily posing in the Evanses' Sunbury garden (MFEA)
Ringo and Mal (MFEA)
Ringo, Mal, and John with Bobby Womack (MFEA)

CHAPTER 37
Julie, Mal, and Gary (MFEA)
Fran and Mal's Fourth Street duplex (Kenneth Womack)
Mal target-shooting with the Winchester rifle (MFEA)

CHAPTER 38
Mal and Fran (MFEA)

CHAPTER 39
Mal with Denny Laine, George, and Olivia Arias on the *Queen Mary* (PIP-Landmark Media)

CHAPTER 40
Laura Gross (Nancy Clendaniel)
Mal with Harry Nilsson (MFEA)
Mal at Beatlefest '75 (Stuart Zolotorow)
Mal and May signing autographs at Beatlefest '75 (Bob Gruen)
"Living the Beatles' Legend" typescript (MFEA)
Joey Molland and Mal at Total Experience Studios (Joey Molland)
Mal's handwritten will (MFEA)

EPILOGUE
Program for Mal's 1976 memorial (MFEA)
Leena Kutti's letter to Yoko (MFEA)
Fred and Joan Evans in later years (MFEA)
Mal in his heyday at EMI Recording Studios (Tracks.co.uk)

INDEX

NOTE: *Italic page numbers* indicate photographs